THIS COUNTRY WAS OURS

THIS

COUNTRY

WAS

OURS

A DOCUMENTARY HISTORY

OF THE AMERICAN INDIAN

By VIRGIL J. VOGEL

HARPER TORCHBOOKS
HARPER & ROW, PUBLISHERS

NEW YORK
EVANSTON
SAN FRANCISCO
LONDON

(*continued on the following page*)

A MARC Corporation Book

This series in Urban and Ethnic Affairs is sponsored by Metropolitan Applied Research Center, Inc., Kenneth B. Clark, President. A hardcover edition is available from Harper & Row, Publishers, Inc.

First HARPER TORCHBOOK edition published 1974.

STANDARD BOOK NUMBER: 06–131735–7

LIBRARY OF CONGRESS CATALOG CARD NUMBER: 77–156556

To Johnny

Contents

II. From the Discovery and Settlement to the Beginning of the Revolutionary War 1492–1775

III. From the Revolutionary War
to the Civil War
1775–1861

IV. From the Civil War
to the Present
1861–1972

Appendixes

Acknowledgments °

I am grateful to the City Colleges of Chicago, which provided financial support for me to begin this work in the summer of 1968 as a fellow of the Curriculum Innovation Center. I especially thank Professor Meyer Weinberg, director of the Center, for his assistance in outlining the scope of the topic to be pursued, for filling my mailbox with clippings about Indians, and for the intellectual stimulation received in sessions with him.

Among others who helped in various ways, such as answering questions at length, providing information and materials, directing me to sources, or giving advice, are the following: Bahe Begay, of the Navajo tribe; Vesper Cook, curator of the Miami County Historical Museum, Peru, Indiana; Albert Dana, legislative representative of the Passamaquoddy tribe of Indian Township, Maine; Mickey Gemmill, chairman (in 1970) of the Pit River tribe of California, and his tribal sisters Hattie Christie and Effie, Geraldine, and Kathy Wilson; Oliver Godfroy and his sister, Mrs. Ava Bossley, of the Miami Tribe of Indiana; Dr. Barbara Graymont, Nyack College, Nyack, New York; Aubrey Grossman, attorney for the Indians of All Tribes, San Francisco; Max Harriger, branch of education, Bureau of Indian Affairs; Angus Horn, Caughnawaga Mohawk Indian; Richard Karnes of the Chicago office, Bureau of Indian Affairs; Rev. Coleman O'Toole, pastor of the Passamaquoddy Indians at Peter Dana Point, Maine; David Risling, Jr., chairman of the Ad Hoc Committee on California Indian Education; Dr. Howard Ryan and Dr. Jaroslaw Petryshyn of the faculty of Mayfair College, City Colleges of Chicago; John Stevens, governor of the Passamaquoddy Indians of Indian Township, Maine; Dr. Stuart Struever, department of anthropology, Northwestern University; and above all others, Dr. Sol Tax, department of anthropology, University of Chicago.

Most of the research work was done at the University of Chicago Libraries, and I am in debt to their personnel for many favors.

My wife, Louise Vogel, provided the kind of environment which makes work possible, and endured without protest the widowhood of one whose husband is working on a book.

VIRGIL J. VOGEL

Chicago
1972

Foreword

An excellent and important book such as this speaks best for itself. To introduce it to a prospective reader with the book already in hand, I should only say: turn at once to the pages ahead; you will find them incredibly rich in fascinating information on American Indians past and present. You will have open to you the files of primary sources—the stuff of history —skillfully selected and arranged by an extraordinary man with the best professional credentials, who is not satisfied to pursue his craft only with the documents he knows so well. Understanding that history is rewritten in every generation and in this generation the characters themselves must help to write their history, Virgil Vogel has used the words of living Indians to guide his work. Thus in the pages ahead you will be introduced to the virtually untold "other side of the story."

After you have at least sampled the book, return to this Foreword to see why I believe the book important to every American. To explain why requires that we step back momentarily to look at a critical aspect of human nature.

The human species is above all moral, which means that we are also immoral. Our culture gives us rights and wrongs to live by; we tend to want to live right; but few of us do. And so arise such universal phenomena as conscience, guilt, and shame with which are associated so many personal problems. Cultures provide means to protect individuals from these consequences. National cultures can do this wholesale, so that a whole population can continue to live. Thus it was and is with the Americans who came from Europe, some as settlers and colonists who first cleared the land and achieved independence and some as later immigrants who built our industrial empire.

Why write of guilt? Great nations, surely empires, are built on the destruction of peoples and cultures. Those who survive often think this natural and inevitable, and indeed the survival of the fittest, and so are able to put aside the unjust and immoral behavior of their forebears even as they enjoy their profits. But the peoples and cultures "left for dead" on the wayside have not died; the descendants of those "fittest" whose guilt seemed safely buried with the ashes find that the ashes are embers which burst into flames because the moral values in the culture have never changed. The fittest of earlier days were only at that time the strongest; and our culture never has accepted that might makes right. So there is no denying the evidence of past wrongs when the victims rise to show themselves.

The Northern Europeans who colonized the American shore of the Atlantic—especially the English—were particularly moral Christians who had much guilt to bury. Indeed, looking backward, they (who are we) seem so to have reveled in guilt as to be driven to collect more and more. Beyond the ongoing task of taking the land from the Indians, we brought Africans to enslave. Then, with the cry of manifest destiny, we took from Mexico what is now our great Southwest and California, a land rich with Indians and those we now call Chicanos, whose lands and liberties we seized. Then, as a last gesture, we liberated Puerto Ricans from their Spanish master. All of these peoples, as well as the Europeans who had settled into a folk life in the Appalachians and the Ozarks, we then disturbed a second time. The march of industrial and urban "progress" and the need for money rendered untenable the rural life of the hills, the deserts, the plains; the villages and towns; and Indian reservations. Peoples were "flushed out" of their ancestral homes and brought to light, to be seen and heard by the children of those who had taken their better lands and their autonomy.

This book tells the whole story of our "Original Sin"—what we have done to the peoples who were living in North America when the Europeans first crossed the Atlantic. Had they followed the "inevitable" path to disappearance (which Europeans convinced themselves was prescribed by history and justified their occupation of the continent), this story would still have been worth the poignant reading. But we must read it not only because the Indians are still here and growing in numbers and in identification with their tribal forebears, but also because it is we—200 million non-Indian Americans in the 1970s—who are behaving still as our forebears did, still taking from them the driblets of land they have left, and living by the same rationalizations. But what may have seemed then to be a necessary evil is now a series of unmitigated unnecessary evils which rise in part from the continued avarice of a few, and in larger part from the psychological need to hide now the enormity of our earlier sin. By no stretch of imagination is it now economically or politically necessary to deny to Indians what they need and ask for:

When Indians speak of the continent they yielded, they are not referring only to the loss of some millions of acres of real estate. They have in mind that the land supported a universe of things they knew, valued, and loved.

With that continent gone, except for the few poor parcels they still retain, the basis of life is precariously held, but they mean to hold those scraps and parcels as earnestly as any small nation or ethnic group was ever determined to hold to identity and survival.

What we ask of America is not charity, not paternalism, even when benevolent. We ask only that the nature of our situation be recognized and made the basis of policy and action.

In short, the Indians ask for assistance, technical and financial, for the time needed, however long that may be, to regain in the America of the space age some measure of the adjustment they enjoyed as the original possessors of their native land.[1]

We have the wealth and the technology, and could garner the wisdom, with the help of the Indians themselves, to do precisely that. With our growing urbanization, we are vacating again almost the whole of the continent. We no longer "need" all that land, and are only misusing it as we once misused the people who treated it as sacred. Yet in November of 1969 when a small group who symbolically represented "Indians of All Tribes" occupied the rocky island of Alcatraz as a symbol of Indian re-possession of what to the white man is barren wasteland (but to the Indian part of a sacred heritage for which he can also find practical use), we could not bring ourselves to give it to them. Over the winter of 1969 the governments in Washington and Sacramento, and the press and the public, enthusiastically applauded the Indian initiative and moved happily to make a priceless (and costless) gesture; but in the end the "higher" need to support law and order prevailed; a single, small, illegal act could not be condoned. From Plymouth Rock, where we had been welcomed, we had moved ruthlessly across the continent; I presume it would have exposed to ourselves our own enormous illegality to have accepted the Indian right to the last rock on the other shore. One newspaper suggested, the day after the first landing, that the federal government simply give the Indians of All Tribes a "permit" to stay on the island. So simple a solution might have changed the course of American thought, making it thereafter unnecessary to oppose restitutive acts.

So much for the hangup of at least the leadership of 200 million non-Indian Americans; and one important effect of this book could be its end. Suppose we now recognize our irrational block and determine not to let it interfere any longer with intelligent policy—what else would be involved?

1. From *Declaration of Indian Purpose*. See pp. 210–12.

The pages to follow amply document that we have assumed, and Indians have been told, that their disappearance is "inevitable." The documents also show what the melting-pot theory happily accepted by European immigrants intent on "becoming Americans" has meant to Indians. To American Indian tribes, this has been far from a promise; it was a *threat,* continually verified as their tribal lands and autonomy were eroded. One must say "American Indian tribes" rather than "Indians" because the identity of an individual member is dependent, in a way difficult for urban people to understand, upon that of his tribe. A person is a Zuni or a Navajo; a Mohawk or a Seneca; a Cherokee or a Choctaw; a Hupa or a Pomo; a Cheyenne or a Crow or an Oglala Sioux; or one of the hundreds of other nations, tribes, and bands. "Non-Indian" is a useful term; but "Indian" is both the classical mistake of Christopher Columbus and a misconception of secular, urbanized non-Indians whose families are parts of large, impersonal populations of classes, religions, and ethnic groups. The family and religion of tribal man are his tribe; his home is the land where in the beginning of the world the tribe was born, where everything important happened, where the spirits dwell and the ancestors are buried. It is purely incidental that the tribe has also a "culture" (the anthropologists' word) different from that of other tribes; the cultures of all the tribes are alike in their overwhelming contrast to the culture of the governing people.

It is understandable that when well-meaning non-Indians propose remedies for poverty and disease based on policies supporting individual freedom, equality, and autonomy, they are surprised and disappointed at the reaction of the Indians they hope to benefit. Pluralism has in recent years become an American value in the context of protecting what have become religious and ethnic voluntary organizations to which individuals may choose to belong. Tribal people are hurt more than helped by policies based on values so deceptively similar, if only because they alienate their well-wishers. Moreover, they have long since tired of trying vainly to explain, much less defend, what is to them life itself.

Our conviction that not the tribe but rather the individual, or the family while children are small, is the building block of society, is the source of the threat that keeps Indian communities from trusting any plans at all that the white man offers. The enemy most feared is not the avarice of white neighbors and their power in government, which exacerbate their impoverishment; these and all injustices—and vain "promises"—they have borne with incredible patience. More difficult to bear is the divisiveness and factionalism which result from the threats and the promises. The highest value in a tribal society is harmony, and life without it causes pain and more destruction.

To one who catches the message of this book, it will be evident that to continue marching in circles in our historic blind alley helps neither us nor the Indian people. It is therefore past time, but never too late, to assume that Indian people will prefer that we expiate our sins by stopping our sinning now, and that they will want far less than we fear. Probably they want and need only genuine autonomy with community security, which will remove the obstacles to their finding their own way in this new environment. As they adapted to the widest variety of environments during the thousands of years before Columbus came; and as late as the eighteenth century autonomous tribes adjusted to the coming of horses, fur traders, and new goods; and as Iroquois tribes have recently discovered that high steel construction crews are not unlike the hunting bands of old, so the people of a secure and autonomous tribe may more readily than we now imagine adapt economic opportunities to tribal ways.

To accomplish tribal autonomy requires that we begin with it and ask them, tribe by tribe, how we should replace some of the assets which once made it possible for tribes to live. From what I have learned from them, the answer of many Indian communities might be, in words they would surely improve:

"To maintain the special relationship that has always existed among our nations and the sovereign government of the United States, and to symbolize and make possible tribal autonomy:

"1. Assign title to unused federal lands, where feasible and where wanted, tax-free and in irrevocable trust, to our individual communities;

"2. Establish for each community a capital trust fund, the nontaxable income from which will provide in perpetuity such services as health, education, and welfare; and

"3. Maintain the Bureau of Indian Affairs as long as our tribes and communities will financially support from the income of the trust fund its banking, management, and service facilities in preference to those of private and nonprofit corporations."

SOL TAX
University of Chicago

Introduction

History is the largely written record of the rise and fall of civilizations, classes, social systems, and contending interests, including nations. The story of these events is written with a viewpoint, expressed or implied, and it is not strange that the viewpoint of the triumphant forces is the prevailing one. Much as historians have labored to create an objective science of history, it is not hard to find the built-in bias of most historical writing. It is seen not only in what is said, but as often in what is left unsaid. Historians are confronted with the necessity of selecting from an overwhelming mass of data that which they believe merits attention, and it is inevitable that their selection will be influenced by their assumptions and prejudices, of which they may frequently be unaware. Historians are, moreover, specialists, and when they undertake to write a textbook dealing with a wide range of topics and periods, it is not surprising that some things are slighted. Moreover, since there is a greater market for specialized knowledge of the winners than of the losers, there is a dearth of experts on the "lost causes" of history, however important they may once have been. American history textbooks are now being justly criticized for their lack of attention to, or distorted treatment of, the role of ethnic minorities, the labor movement, and radical protest movements. We are, of course, past the era when textbooks were exclusively concerned with political and military struggles, with contests for power. We have now a growing attention to social, cultural, economic, and intellectual history. But even this new trend continues to reflect the interests and backgrounds of white, Protestant, and middle-class people who are the great majority of the historical craft.

The extent of changes that have been made in the past, and are continuing now, is governed not so much by a voluntary reappraisal among historians as by the pressure of once forgotten people who have recently attained a new awareness, cohesiveness, and political power which have motivated them to demand these changes. There are admitted dangers in history written simply to please pressure groups, or to supply the ideological needs of ethnic nationalism, regional patriotism, or the sentiments of caste or class. But it would be equally wrong to imagine that historical writing has hitherto been free of such influence. It has been written for the most part to portray the status quo as the best of all possible worlds and to cultivate a kind of nationalism which ignores the ethnic and social diversity in our history. What we are witnessing today is a demand of the dispossessed and overlooked groups that their role in history receive the attention to which it is entitled.

Such a new course can provide to the members of such groups a sense of identity and belonging, a means. of overcoming a collective inferiority complex. It can provide aspiration models to motivate them, and improve scholastic interest and performance. However, the correction of past injustice is not simply a service to the wronged. It is a service to everyone, for we cannot correctly understand the present if we have a distorted interpretation of the past. The arrogance which results from ignorance of the role of minorities in the shaping of America is a burden we can no longer afford. Moreover, it is often forgotten that everyone belongs to one or more minorities in America, and often to one or more majorities as well. History has already been written from a minority viewpoint, but it is the viewpoint of the minority with the power to make itself heard.

A majority of mankind is nonwhite, and much of this majority is to be found in the new nations of Asia and Africa which have only recently assumed a position of political importance. If we have grown up in the belief that nonwhites in America have contributed nothing to our history, how well equipped are we to deal with the evolving nations of brown, yellow, and black people?

The rash of political assassinations in America has brought a belated recognition of the fact that we rank near the top in homicide and violent crimes. Hans Mattick, a University of Chicago sociologist, and some others, have seen this phenomenon as partly rooted in our treatment of the American Indian. Here again is an example of how a better knowledge of neglected aspects of our past can illuminate the present. There is more at stake here than simply knowing what and why for its own sake. This knowledge has a bearing on how we deal with problems. Without any commitment to the doctrine that history should lend itself to practical uses, we can observe that an understanding of the past *can* lead to more rational and workable solutions to present questions. Should the emphasis in alleviating racial upheaval be placed on repression or change? Is the "melting pot" theory, or the recognition of the values in cultural diversity, the soundest basis for dealing with our differences? What are the limits of purely legislative solutions to intergroup problems?

The foregoing comments are the basis for the attempt made here to reorient our teaching about the American Indian in history. Few schools are able to add to an overburdened curriculum special courses in the history of each minority. But all schools can, to a degree, incorporate a new approach into their present history courses. Existing textbooks are not adequate tools for this, and so much depends upon the attitude and enthusiasm of the teacher. He first needs to be convinced of the reality of the problem, and then he needs new tools for attacking it. Supplementary materials of many kinds will need to be used. The material which is gathered in this book could be used as a foundation for a special course in American Indian history, or it could serve as an aid to the incorporation of part of that history into existing courses. It is directed to the particular needs of students in junior colleges and underclassmen in senior colleges, and could be useful as well to accelerated senior history classes in high schools, and to plain citizens who want to know something further about Indians. Specialists of various kinds, however, are not the audience to which it is directed.

Our procedure is to divide the history of the United States into periods, and to provide a brief summary of the role of the Indian during each period, followed by selected documents to illustrate the most significant events or conditions. The chronological boundaries are chosen more for convenience in dividing the work rather than for any special significance in the dates—though it is a fact that important dates in general U.S. history are also important in American Indian history. Documents alone cannot tell everything—and they are necessarily selective, but those dealing with recent and current Indian problems should be especially useful to bring out the links between the past and present. This chronological treatment is followed by a short account of the Indian cultural influence, several lists of informational sources, brief biographies of prominent Indians of the past and present, and a selected bibliography.

Since the Indian, when he is mentioned at all in history, is usually treated as a mere object of the impact of white civilization, and a barrier to expansion, our aim will be to show the Indian's side wherever possible, and in his own words as often as that can be done. The other side has already been amply shown by others.

VIRGIL J. VOGEL

THIS COUNTRY WAS OURS

I have heard that you intend to settle us on a reservation near the mountains. I don't want to settle. I love to roam over the prairies. There I feel free and happy, but when we settle down we grow pale and die. I have laid aside my lance, bow, and shield, and yet I feel safe in your presence. . . . A long time ago *this land belonged to our fathers;* but when I go up to the river I see camps of soldiers on its banks.

> —Satanta, Kiowa chief, quoted in *I Have Spoken,*
> by Virginia I. Armstrong

Those Wasichus [whites] had come to kill our mothers and fathers and us, and *it was our country.*

I can remember when Dull Knife came with what was left of his starving and freezing people. They had almost nothing, and some of them had died on the way. Many little babies died. We could give them clothing, but of food we could not give them much, for we were eating ponies when they died. And afterwhile they left us and started for the Soldiers' Town on White River to surrender to the Wasichus; and so we were all alone there in that *country that was ours* and had been stolen from us.

Wherever we went, the soldiers came to kill us, and it was *all our own country.* It was ours already when the Wasichus made the treaty with Red Cloud, that said it would be ours as long as grass should grow and water flow. That was only eight winters before, and they were chasing us now because we remembered and they forgot.

> —from *Black Elk Speaks,* by John G. Neihardt, ed.

[Italic emphasis added.]

A Note About Parenthetical Inserts

The following system has been used in the documents to indicate the source of parenthetical inserts. If the insertion appears in parentheses, it was supplied by the original author of the text. If the insertion appears in brackets, set roman, it was supplied by the original editor of the quoted source. If the insertion appears in brackets and is set in italics, it was supplied by the present editor of the book.

V.J.V.

1 History of the Indian: Contrasting Views

"Only historical ornaments . . ."

They have left their bones, their flints and pots, their place names and tribal and little else besides except a stain, seldom vivid, on the consciousness of their white successors. . . . There are monuments to them here and there throughout the state, but they are only historical ornaments to the pride of the present.

> SAUL BELLOW, "Illinois Journey," *Holiday* magazine, September 1957, p. 62.

"America has much to learn . . ."

Before we can set out on the road to success, we have to know where we are going, and before we can know that, we must determine where we have been in the past. It seems a basic requirement to study the history of our Indian people. America has much to learn about the heritage of our American Indians. Only through this study can we as a nation do what must be done if our treatment of the American Indians is not to be marked down for all time as a national disgrace.

> PRESIDENT JOHN F. KENNEDY, introduction to Alvin M. Josephy, ed., *The American Heritage Book of Indians* (New York: American Heritage Publishing Co., 1961), p. 7.

2 Distorted History

Again and again when I have visited Indian schools the thoughtful youths and maidens have come to me with complaints about the American history they were compelled to study. In their simple, almost colorless way of expressing themselves, a bystander would never dream of the fierce anger that was raging within, but which I was too experienced in Indian character not to perceive. Listen to what some of them have said: "When we read in the United States history of white men fighting to defend their families, their homes, their corn-fields, their towns, and their hunting-grounds, they are always called 'patriots,' and the children are urged to follow the example of these brave, noble, and gallant men. But when Indians—our ancestors, even our own parents—have fought to defend us and our homes, corn-fields, and hunting-grounds they are called vindictive and merciless savages, bloody murderers, and everything else that is vile. You are the Indians' friend: will you not some time please write for us a United States history that will not teach us such wicked and cruel false-hoods about our forefathers because they loved their homes enough to fight for them—even against such powerful foes as you have been." And I have vowed that if ever I have time and strength and feel competent to do it, I will write such a history.

> GEORGE WHARTON JAMES, *What the White Race May Learn from the Indian* (Chicago: Forbes & Co., 1908), p. 25.

Most American History has been written as if history were a function of white culture—in spite of the fact that well into the nineteenth century the Indians were one of the principal determinants of historical events. . . . American historians have made shockingly little effort to understand the life, the societies, the cultures, the thinking, and the feeling of the Indians, and disastrously little effort to understand how all these affected white men and their societies.

> BERNARD DE VOTO, introduction to Joseph K. Howard, *Strange Empire* (New York: Morrow & Co., 1952), p. 8.

Every student of history knows that his colleagues have been influenced in their selection and ordering of materials by their biases, prejudices, beliefs, affections, general upbringing, and experience, particularly social and economic.

> CHARLES A. BEARD, "Written History as an Act of Faith," presidential address to the American Historical Association, December 28, 1933, *American Historical Review*, XXXIX, No. 2 (January 1934), pp. 219–31.

Berate him as we will, for not reading our books, Mr. Everyman is stronger than we are, and sooner or later we must adapt our knowledge to his necessities. Otherwise he will leave us to our own devices, leave us it may be to cultivate a species of dry professional arrogance growing out of the thin soil of antiquarian research.

CARL L. BECKER, "Everyman His Own Historian," presidential address to the American Historical Association, December 29, 1931, *American Historical Review*, **XXXVII**, No. 2 (January 1932), pp. 221–35.

My parents told me that what the movies and history books said about Indians wasn't necessarily so. This was the greatest gift they could have given me.

BUFFY SAINTE-MARIE, Cree Indian folk singer, *Chicago Sun-Times*, November 17, 1968.

I

BEFORE COLUMBUS CAME:
PREHISTORY

———

Introduction

Much has been written on the prehistory of the American Indians, and the recent discovery of carbon 14 dating has been helpful in establishing chronological sequence. Due to the absence of a fully developed system of writing in America, and the destruction by the Spanish at an early date of nearly the whole of the hieroglyphic records of the Mayas and Aztecs, much detail remains obscure. Archaeology therefore has been an important key to unlock the American aboriginal past.

It is held that the American continents were peopled, from the Arctic coast to Tierra del Fuego, by successive waves of migration of Asiatic peoples commencing at least 20,000 years ago. They were entirely hunters and gatherers, bringing with them no domesticated plant seeds and no domesticated animals except the dog. In this New World which had been unpeopled during the millennia of man's evolution in the Old World, there is no undisputed evidence of any contact with America by other cultures prior to A.D. 1000. Whatever contact occurred from that date until the arrival of Columbus in 1492 was so casual that it produced no evident impact on native development.

During this period of isolation at least three "centers of civilization" arose—in Yucatán-Guatemala, in the valley of Central Mexico, and in the Andean region. The first of these, the Mayan, was in decay when the Spanish arrived, but during the preceding centuries it had devised an embryonic system of writing and made astonishing progress in architecture, astronomy, and mathematics. In the valley or plateau, the Aztecs, the "Romans" of the New World, had an ascending culture which was in full flower when Cortés arrived, having adopted much from earlier civilizations of that region. As in the other centers, intensive maize culture here supported a dense population with a capital city notable for its planning, order, and public facilities.

In the Andean region, stretching from Colombia to Bolivia, a number of civilizations had arisen, but that of the Incas centered in Peru had built a flourishing empire which was a marvel of political organization. Its roads, communications, metallurgy, textiles, and agricultural achievements were most notable. Here the llama and alpaca were domesticated, and potatoes, and peanuts were added to the world's food supply. Their achievements in skull surgery (trephination) and their discovery of the properties of coca leaves (from which comes cocaine) are milestones in medical history.

Given a few more centuries of undisturbed development, it has been theorized, these peoples might have found the means to resist successfully the catastrophe of European invasion. Be that as it may, it is a fact that here in the Americas empires as wondrous as those of Cyrus and Alexander quickly collapsed when confronted by a few hundred Spaniards equipped with horses and firearms. Much has been written to explain this phenomenon, but none of the answers seems to be satisfactory.

To this writer it appears that these "centers of civilization" fell so rapidly precisely because they were so highly organized. Their pyramidal social structure was so arranged, and the masses of the common people so habituated to obedience to the call of priests and rulers, that the invaders had only to capture or annihilate the top layers of the hierarchy in order to assume control of the entire social edifice. In contrast, the wild tribes of the forests, swamps, and plains of both continents, held together not by oligarchy but by the seeming paradox of communal economic life joined with fierce individualism in political matters, were able to maintain their cultural and physical identity for hundreds of years, reaching even to the present time.[1]

So much attention has been given to the achievements of the "civilized" Indians that the so-called primitive tribes have been under-appreciated. Europeans were and are prone to admire most those cultures which more nearly resembled their own, even while they proceeded to dismantle them. Michel de Montaigne, whose "Essays on Cannibals" (p. 256) found more to admire in the personal liberty of the Brazilian natives than in the authoritarian government and piles of masonry commonly equated with "civilization," must be ranked as exceptional.

The so-called wild tribes must be credited with substantial contributions to world civilization. It was these Indians, in South America, who were the first to use rubber, and with it invented the bulbed enema syringe and tube. They invented the hammock and "barbecue." It was they who learned how

1. The tribes of the West Indies might appear to be an exception, but it should be remembered that the small extent of territory in each of their islands made it easy to overwhelm them, not only by arms but with introduced diseases.

to remove the poisonous properties of cassava roots and use them for the food called tapioca, which is now a staple in Africa as well as in the Amazon valley. They discovered the properties of such drugs as ipecac, curare, and cinchona (quinine) which remain vitally important today, and the natural dyes obtainable from Brazil wood and the coccineal insect.

In North America, the whites adopted moccasins and canoes from the "savages," and perhaps most useful of all, snowshoes. His crops, some of them diffused from other centers, including corn, tobacco, beans, squashes, and pumpkins, were adopted by white farmers. The number of North American Indian drugs eventually accepted in white medicine is in excess of a hundred and fifty. The confederate government of the Six Nations provided a model for the English colonies. Our ancestors followed the Indian trails, which took best advantage of the contours of the land, and some of our railways and highways follow them yet. Perhaps most important, these Indians helped the Europeans to recover the long lost arts of survival in the wilderness. Their marks are deeply embedded in our arts, literature, music, language, folklore, and political history. Potentially their greatest endowment, however, has been learned least of all: their notions of liberty. (See p. 255 *et seq.*)

3   The Cakchiquel Creation Myth

The Cakchiquels were a Maya people closely related to the Quiché of Guatemala. Their Annals, *from which the following excerpt was taken, has been compared to the* Popol Vuh *as a mythical-historical epic. The manuscript, written in the Cakchiquel language with European script, was the work of unknown natives, and was discovered in a Guatemalan monastery in 1844. It was soon translated in French and Spanish, but the first English translation was not published until 1885, by Daniel G. Brinton. A new translation was published in 1953 by the University of Oklahoma Press.*

From the west we came to Tulán, from across the sea; and it was at Tulán where we arrived, to be engendered and brought forth by our mothers and fathers. So they told us.

Then the Obsidian Stone[1] was created by the wondrous Xibalbay, by the precious Xibalbay.[2] Then man was made by the Creator and the Maker, and he gave homage to the Obsidian Stone.

1. Worshipped as a symbol of divinity.
2. One of the places endowed with riches and beauty and the cradle of the sacred stone, Chay Abah.

When they made man, they fashioned him of earth, and they fed him with wood, they fed him with leaves. They wished that only earth should enter [into his making].* But he did not talk, he did not walk, he had neither blood nor flesh, so our early fathers and grandfathers told us, oh, my sons! They did not know what should enter [into the man]. But at length they found whereof to make it. Only two animals knew that there was food in *Paxil,* the place where those animals are found which are called the Coyote and the Crow. The Coyote animal was killed, and in his remains, when he was quartered, corn was discovered. And the animal called *Tiuh-tiuh,*[3] searching for the dough of the cc̶ ꞁ, brought from out of the sea the blood of the tapir and the serpent, and with it the maize was kneaded. With this dough the flesh of man was made by the Creator and the Maker. Thus the Creator, the Maker, the Progenitors knew how to make man complete, so they tell. Man having been made, there resulted thirteen males and fourteen females; there was [one woman extra].

Then they talked, they had blood, they had flesh. They married and multiplied. One of them had two wives. Thus they mated, so the old people used to say, oh, our sons! They had daughters, they had sons, those first men. Thus was the creation of man. So the Obsidian Stone was made.

> *The Annals of the Cakchiquels,* translated from the Cakchiquel Maya by Adrián Recinos and Delia Goetz (Norman: University of Oklahoma Press, 1953), pp. 45–47. Footnotes abbreviated and adapted from original notes.

4 The Sacred Book of the Quiché Mayas: *Popol Vuh*

The Popol Vuh, *sacred book of the Quiché Maya of the Guatemalan highlands, was a partly allegorical and partly historical account of that people which has been compared to the Old Testament. One of its translators, Sylvanus Morley, has called it "the most distinguished example of native American literature that has survived the passing centuries." He reported that it was believed to have been first reduced to writing, in the Quiché language, using characters in the Latin script, in the mid-sixteenth century, from oral traditions then current among the Quichés, by some unknown but highly educated native. That original is no longer extant, but a copy found in Guatemala in the middle of the last century was translated into Spanish and published in 1857. No English translation appeared in*

* The following system has been used in the documents to indicate the source of parenthetical inserts. If the insertion appears in parentheses, it was supplied by the original author of the text. If the insertion appears in brackets, set roman, it was supplied by the original editor of the quoted source. If the insertion appears in brackets and is set in italics, it was supplied by the present editor of this book.
3. Sparrow hawk.

*print until 1950. In Morley's view, "the chance preservation of this manu-
script only serves to emphasize the magnitude of the loss which the world
has suffered in the almost total destruction of aboriginal American literature."*

The following selection from the Popol Vuh *tells how the Quichés, living
in peace and harmony, were attacked by a neighboring tribe, the Ilocabs.
The assault was repelled, and the survivors were either sacrificed to the
deity or reduced to slavery. Here are revealed two practices of the "higher
civilizations" of America which have often been cited in expiation of the
excesses of the Spanish conquest. However, the practice of massacring or
enslaving defeated enemies was not unknown in Europe.*

Chi-Izmachí is the name of the site of their town, where they were
afterward and where they settled. There, under the fourth generation of
kings, they developed their power and constructed buildings of mortar and
stone.

And Conaché and Beheleb-Queh, the Galel-Ahau, ruled. Then King
Cotuhá and Iztayul reigned, as they were called the Ahpop and the Ahpop-
Camhá, who reigned there in Izmachí, which was the beautiful city they
had built.

Only three great houses were there in Izmachí. There were not twenty-
four great houses then, only a great house of the Nihaib, and only one of
the people of Ahau-Quiché. Only two had great houses, and two branches
of the family [the Quiché and the Tamub].

And they were in Izmachí with only one thought, without disputes or
difficulties, peaceful was the kingdom, they had no quarrels or disputes, in
their hearts were only peace and happiness. They were not envious or
jealous. Their grandeur was limited, they had not thought of aggrandizing
themselves, nor of expanding. When they tried to do it, they fastened the
shield there in Izmachí but only to give a sign of their empire, as a symbol
of their power and a symbol of their greatness.

Seeing this, the people of Ilocab began the war; they wanted to kill King
Cotuhá, wishing to have a chief of their own. And as for Lord Iztayul, they
wanted to punish him, that he be punished and killed by those of Ilocab.
But their evil plans against King Cotuhá did not succeed, for he fell upon
them before the people of Ilocab were able to kill him.

This, then, was the beginning of the revolution and the dissensions of the
war. First they attacked the town, and the warriors came. And what they
wanted was to ruin the Quiché race; they wanted to reign alone. But they
only came to die; they were captured and fell into captivity, and few among
them succeeded in escaping.

Immediately afterward the sacrifices began; the people of Ilocab were
sacrificed before the god, and this was the punishment for their sins by

order of King Cotuhá. Many also fell into slavery and servitude; they only
went to give themselves up to be overcome because of having arranged the
war against the lords and against the town. The destruction and ruin of the
Quiché race and their king was what they wished, but they did not succeed
in accomplishing it.

In this way the sacrifice of men began before the gods, when the war of
the shields broke out, which was the reason that they began the fortifica-
tions of the city of Izmachí.

> *Popol Vuh, The Sacred Book of the Ancient Quiché Maya,*
> English version by Delia Goetz and Sylvanus G. Morley
> from the translation of Adrián Recinos (Norman: Univer-
> sity of Oklahoma Press, 1965), pp. 212–13. Copyright 1950
> by the University of Oklahoma Press.

5 Lament for the Past in the Land of the Mayas: From the *Chilam Balam*

The following lament is from The Book of Chilam Balam of Chumayel,
*one of several books based on ancient Maya lore which have been de-
scribed by Ralph Roys, the translator, as the most important part of native
Maya literature. Originally written in native pictographs, they were, after
the arrival of the Spanish priests (who burned most of the "heathen"
literature), rewritten by educated natives who had learned to adapt the
Maya language to Spanish script. The book from which the following
quotations are taken is named the "Chilam Balam" for a pre-Columbian
prophet, and "Chumayel" for the village in which it was found. This copy
was compiled in the eighteenth century by one Don Juan Josef Hoil, and
combines ancient lore with knowledge and ideas adopted from the Spanish.
The passage chosen contrasts the serene and healthy life formerly enjoyed
by the natives with the disease and wretchedness brought by the invaders.*

They did not wish to join with the foreigners; they did not desire Christianity. They did not wish to pay tribute, did those whose emblems were
the bird, the precious stone, the flat precious stone and the jaguar, those
with the three magic emblems. Four four-hundreds of years and fifteen
score years was the end of their lives; then came the end of their lives,
because they knew the measure of their days. Complete was the month;
complete, the year; complete, the day; complete, the night; complete, the
breath of life as it passed also; complete, the blood, when they arrived at
their beds, their mats, their thrones. In due measure did they recite the
good prayers; in due measure they sought the lucky days, until they saw the
good stars enter into their reign; then they kept watch while the reign of the
good stars began. Then everything was good.

Then they adhered to the dictates of their reason. There was no sin; in the holy faith their lives were passed. There was then no sickness; they had then no aching bones; they had then no high fever; they had then no small-pox; they had then no burning chest; they had then no abdominal pains; they had then no consumption; they had then no headache. At that time the course of humanity was orderly. The foreigners made it otherwise when they arrived here. They brought shameful things when they came. They lost their innocence in carnal sin; they lost their innocence in the carnal sin of Macxit Xuchit, in the carnal sin of his companions. No lucky days were then displayed to us. This was the origin of the two-day chair [or throne], of the two-day reign; this was the cause of our sickness also. There were no more lucky days for us; we had no sound judgment. At the end of our loss of vision, and of our shame, everything shall be revealed. There was no great teacher, no great speaker, no supreme priest, when the change of rulers occurred at their arrival. Lewd were the priests, when they came to be established here by foreigners. Furthermore they left their descendants here at Tancah [Mayapan]. These then received the misfortunes, after the affliction of these foreigners. These, they say, were the Itzá.[1] Three times it was, they say, that the foreigners arrived. It was because of this that we were relieved from paying tribute at the age of sixty, because of the afflic-tion by these men, the Itzá. It was not we who did it; it is we who pay for it today. However there is at last an agreement so that there may be peace between us and the foreigners. Otherwise there will be great war.

RALPH ROYS, *The Book of Chilam Balam of Chumayel* (Washington: Carnegie Institution of Washington, 1933), pp. 83–84. Translator's footnotes and special textual mark-ings have been omitted. New edition copyright 1967 by the University of Oklahoma Press.

6 An Early Description of Aztec Life

BERNARDINO DE SAHAGÚN

The surviving pre-Columbian literature of Mexico is mainly concerned with religion, legend, war, and dynastic chronicles. For descriptions of the details of native social life, therefore, we must rely on Spanish accounts. One of the most careful recorders of even the most trivial aspects of the life and customs of the people was the Spanish Franciscan priest, Bernardino de Sahagún (1499–1590), from whose writings (said to be the work of Aztec scribes) the following brief sketch of the Nahua (Aztec) people is taken.

1. Roys believed that the confusing mention of the Itzás in this narrative was prob-ably due to the fact that the author really had the Spanish in mind, while ostensibly referring to the Itzás, an earlier conquering people. It could also mean that the Span-ish were considered to be equivalent to the Itzá.

. . . They are the ones who speak the Nahuatl language. They speak a little [like] the Mexicans, although not really perfectly, not really pronounced in the same way; they pronounce it somehow.

These thus mentioned called themselves Chichimeca Mochanecatoca, that is to say, Tolteca. It is said these caused the Tolteca to disperse when they went away, when Topiltzin Quetzalcoatl entered the water, when he went to settle in the place of the red color, the place of the burning.

These [Nahua] were able; they had lords, nobles, rulers. And the nobles, the lords, the rulers governed the inhabitants of the city; they provided song, they set up the ground drum. It is said they enlivened the city; they made it illustrious. There was [food] to eat, provisions. They had drink, food, clothes, necklaces, quetzal feathers, armbands, homes, houses, gardens, maize bins. They had a god; they addressed him, they prayed to him, they worshipped him as a god. They gave him the name of Night [and] Wind. They were devout: they held vigil, held watch, played the two-toned drum, sat singing, bled themselves, mutilated themselves, inserted maguey spines, blew the trumpet shell, entered into the water. Every twenty-day period they proceeded to observe feast days.

In them were all prudence, industry, and craftmanship. [They were] feather workers, painters, masons, gold workers, metal casters, carpenters, stone cutters, lapidaries, grinders, stone polishers, weavers, spinners; they were adroit in speech, distinctive in food preparation, elegant with capes, with clothes. They had gods; they were devout; they were pray-ers, givers of offerings, offerers of incense. They were brave, able in war, takers of captives, conquerors.

This is all which is here to be told. Still, much is omitted concerning the life of the Nahua, of the Nahua people.

FRAY BERNARDINO DE SAHAGÚN, *General History of the Things of New Spain (Florentine Codex)*, Book 10, ed. by Charles Dibble and Arthur J. O. Anderson (Santa Fe: The School of American Research and the University of Utah, 1961), pp. 175–76.

7   The Aztec Land System: Communal Democracy or Feudalism?

ALONSO DE ZORITA

Lewis H. Morgan, the nineteenth-century ethnologist, and his disciples, held that the Spanish misinterpreted or exaggerated the extent of social stratification in Mexico, tending to view Aztec society in familiar European terms. Morgan believed that it was a democratic communal society still based on kinship organization. Later scholars have held that the Aztec clans were not egalitarian and democratic as among the Iroquois with whom Morgan was acquainted. Some have maintained that they were strongly stratified internally and in relation to each other, and that probably there was "one principal clan to which belonged all the chiefs of the whole tribe." (Benjamin Keen, infra, pp. 298–99, citing Arturo Monzón.) In brief, this view holds that "Aztec society combined kinship organization with a strongly aristocratic character," although technical advance and labor productivity had not yet reached the point where the emergence of social classes had dissolved kinship bonds.

A sixteenth-century description of the Aztec agricultural communities, called calpulli *(or* barrio, *in Spanish) is here given from the writings of Alonso de Zorita, a Spanish judge noted for his defense of the Indians, who served ten years in Mexico prior to his retirement in 1566. It does not answer all the questions which concern anthropologists, but it appears to describe a society somewhat more egalitarian than that of the Peruvians, and surely more so than that of Europe.*

A calpulli or chinancalli is a barrio of known people or an ancient lineage which holds its lands and boundaries from a time of great antiquity. These lands belong to the said kindred, barrio, or lineage, and they call such lands calpulli, meaning the lands of that barrio or lineage.

There are many such capullec or lineages or barrios in each province. The barrios assigned for life to lords of the second class also had their heads or calpulli. The lands these barrios possess they obtained in the distribution made when these people first came to this land. At that time each lineage or group obtained its shares or lots of land with their bounds, which were assigned to them and their descendants. These lands, which they call calpulli, they still possess today. They do not hold them individually but communally. Individuals cannot alienate their lots, but can enjoy their use for life and leave them to their sons and heirs.

. . . Some of these calpullec or barrios or lineages are larger than others, depending on the manner in which the ancient conquerors and settlers apportioned the lands among the various lineages. If a certain family dies out, the lands remain in the common ownership of the calpulli, and the head or chief elder assigns them to some other member of the same barrio who has need of them.

Thus the Indians never give these lands to a person who is not a member of the calpulli or barrio, just as the Israelites were not permitted to alienate their tribal lands and possessions. . . .

A barrio or calpulli might rent land to another barrio in order to meet the public and communal needs of the renting calpulli. Only for this reason, and no other, could lands be rented. If it can be helped, the Indians never allow people of one calpulli to work the lands of another, that there may be no mixing of the two groups and that none may leave his lineage.

One reason why the Indians rented these lands, instead of allowing another calpulli to have them for nothing, was that sometimes the land they gave had already been cultivated. The rent was small or simply a part of the harvest, depending on the terms of the agreement. Members of one calpulli would rent from another because the land was better than that which they had or received from their calpulli or because their calpulli had no more land to distribute, or because they could work both their own and the rented fields.

If a member of one calpulli or barrio went to live in another, he lost the lands that had been assigned to him for cultivation. This is a most ancient custom among them, and one that is never broken or contravened in any way. The vacated fields remain the common property of the calpulli; and the chief elder distributes them among the landless members of the barrio.

If some of the land is left vacant or becomes uncultivated in a calpulli, the Indians take great care lest the member of another calpulli encroach upon it. They engage in great litigation over this, each calpulli hotly defending its lands.

If a member of a calpulli has no land, the chief elder, in consultation with the other elders, gives him land in accordance with his needs, condition, and capacity to work it, and he can pass on this land to his heirs. The chief elder does nothing without consulting the other elders of the calpulli or barrio.

If a member of a calpulli held land and cultivated it, no one could intrude on this land, nor could the chief elder take it away and give it to someone else. If the land was not good, he could leave it and look for other land that was better and apply to the chief elder for such land. If this land was vacant and could be given without prejudice to another, it was given to him in the manner aforesaid.

A person who held land from his calpulli and did not work it for two years running through his own fault and negligence, or without some just cause, such as the condition of being a minor, an orphan, very old, or too ill to work, received warning that he must work it the next year or lose it to another. And so it was done.

Inasmuch as this land is the communal property of the calpullec or barrios, there has been much impropriety in allotting it to Spaniards. Let some Spaniard observe or learn that some of this land is not being cultivated, and he will apply to the governor for it. . . .

ALONSO DE ZORITA, "Brief and Summary Relation of the Lords of New Spain," in *Life and Labor in Ancient Mexico*, translated by Benjamin Keen (New Brunswick, N.J.: Rutgers University Press, 1963), pp. 105–8.

8 Quechua (Inca) Civilization

GARCILASO DE LA VEGA

The Spanish found in Peru a highly developed civilization resting upon the achievements of several earlier ones which had declined or been conquered. From the title of its ruler, the Inca, the people were so named by Europeans. Though less "advanced" in some respects than the civilizations of Central America, the Peruvian natives had made enormous progress in scientific agriculture, making wide use of irrigation, terraces, and natural fertilizers. They cultivated at least twenty-two plants for fiber, medicine, or food, of which the potato became ultimately of chief economic importance in our world. They grew cotton and corn, and contributed lima and kidney beans, peanuts, and sweet potatoes to the world food supply.[1] They domesticated the llama and the alpaca, using them both for wool and as beasts of burden. They were skillful in the weaving of cotton and woolen textiles, and in metal work, especially gold. They were able engineers, constructing roads and bridges rivaling those of Rome, and stone buildings which withstood earthquakes, although no mortar was used. They were noted for their medicinal herbs and drugs, among which coca (from which cocaine is derived) is the outstanding contribution,[2] and for surgery, especially trephination of the skull. Although they had no writing, they developed a system of accounts and records, using knotted cords called quipu. A system of relay runners, a "pony express" without ponies, carried oral or quipu messages throughout the empire. Among our many borrowings from them is the currently popular article of clothing called a "poncho."

The Inca social system was a combination of feudalism and bureaucratic collectivism, rather rigidly organized and stratified, but at the same time communal. (Authors have labeled it both a "Socialist Empire" and a "benevolent despotism.") Poverty and want were unknown, as the needs of all were provided for. The political system was a pyramidal structure reaching up from the lowest officials, the decurions, all the way to the top, with each official being in command of a number beneath him, and responsible to one above him. Lower officials were chosen for merit, but the ruler was a hereditary monarch. Allied to him was a class of priests who, like the ruler, received a third of the agricultural produce and led the inhabitants in worship of the sun and moon.

1. Margaret A. Towle, *The Ethnobotany of Pre-Columbian Peru* (Chicago: Aldine Publishing Co., 1961), pp. 142–43.
2. Victor W. Von Hagen, *Realm of the Incas* (New York: New American Library, 1957), p. 104.

A chief source on the history and traditions of the Incas is the Royal Commentaries *of Garcilaso de la Vega (1539–1616), the son of an Inca princess and a Spanish officer. He observed some of the bloody fighting of the post-conquest period and was educated in Spanish schools at Cuzco. About 1560 he went to Spain to plead unsuccessfully at court for a share of his late father's estate, and remained to serve in the army. Eventually he became a priest, and began to write. He published the first part of his* Royal Commentaries *in 1609, and the last parts shortly before his death at Cordova in 1616. His work was a main source for William H. Prescott's* History of the Conquest of Peru. *The edition from which the following excerpts are taken is that edited by Alain Gheerbrant (New York: Orion Press, 1961).*

Instructions to His People by the First Inca, Manco Capac

In order that peace and concord might reign, and that neither anger nor passion should come between them, he succeeded in convincing them that each one should do unto others as he would have others do unto him, so true it is that the law must be the same for all. He particularly inculcated them with respect for women and young girls, since, until then, the lack of it had been a feature of their triumphant barbarism. Adultery, homicide, and theft were punished with death. Marriage was allowed with only one woman, who was chosen in the husband's family, in order not to alter his lineage. A married couple being required, from the moment of their union, to supply their own needs and govern their own household, it was against the law to take a wife who had not attained to her twentieth year. In the same way that the queen, Mama Occlo, had taught the Indian women to spin and weave, the king had all the animals that were wandering freely over the mountains rounded up, so that their wool could be used to clothe men and women. At the head of every village he established a *curaca,* or lord, chosen for his merits, and the others had to obey this leader, in the same way that a son obeys his father.

In all the villages the harvest was reaped in common, after which it was divided equally among all the inhabitants, pending the time when there would be sufficient arable land to permit each one to have his own plot. Divine worship was also prescribed and regulated, and temples were erected on sites chosen by the Inca, in order to make sacrifices to the Sun and thank him for his blessings. At the same time they worshipped the Moon, as being the mother of the royal couple without whom humanity would have remained in its primitive state of barbarism. Lastly, when there were enough girls of royal blood, the Inca founded a home for the brides of the Sun, that is, a convent for dedicated virgins.

Agricultural Methods and Land Distribution

When the Inca had conquered a new province he immediately sent engineers there, who were specialized in building canals for irrigation, in order to increase the corn acreage, which otherwise could not flourish in these torrid lands. In the same way, he irrigated the prairie lands, as may be seen today from the evidences of canals that still subsist all over Peru. On the mountain sides, on the peaks and on all rocky surfaces, they built terraces, sustained by stone walls, which they filled with light soil brought from elsewhere. These terraces grew wider from the top to the bottom of the slope, where they occasionally attained to as much as two hundred and forty acres in size. These were arduous undertakings, but they made it possible to give the maximum development to the tiniest plots of barren land. Indeed, it often happened that they would build canalizations fifteen to twenty leagues long, to irrigate only a few acres of land.

Community records of landholdings were carefully kept up to date in all the provinces and villages, and arable land was divided into three parts: that belonging to the Sun, that of the Inca, and that of his vassals. This latter part was calculated to permit each village to provide for its own needs and, in case there was an increase in population, the Inca reduced the surface of his own holdings. Thus it may be said that he kept for himself only that part that, without him, would have remained uncultivated. The major part of the terrace crops belonged to the king and to the Sun, which was only normal, inasmuch as it was the Inca who had had the terraces built. Other cereals and vegetables were raised, such as potatoes, *oca,* and *anius,* on the other land which, not being irrigated and fertilized the way the corn lands were, did not yield an annual crop. *Quinoa,* which is a sort of rice, was also cultivated in the cold climates.

Distribution of Food and Clothing from the Stores of the Incas

The Inca's reserves did not serve to clothe only the soldiers, but the entire population of the empire as well. Indeed, every two years, under supervision of the decurions,[1] the wool from the royal herds was distributed in every village in order that each person should be decently clothed during his entire life. It should be recalled that the Indians of the people, and even the curacas, possessed only very few cattle [*llamas?*], whereas the Inca's and the Sun's herds were so numerous that, according to some, they no longer knew where to send them to graze by the time the Spaniards

---

1. Decurion (not a native word), "leader of ten," with functions similar to those of an ombudsman, justice of the peace, coroner, and birth registrar. —V.J.V.

arrived in Peru. In hot climates, cotton from the royal plantations replaced wool. Thus, everyone was always provided with clothing, shoes, food, and all that is necessary in life, and it may be said that there was not a single poor man or beggar throughout the Empire. But while there were no poor, there were no rich either, since everyone had what was necessary without ever living in superfluous luxury. . . .

Nor had the Incas forgotten, in their republic, to look out for the needs of travelers, for whom there existed, all along the royal roads, inns called *corpahuaci*, in which they could obtain a meal as well as provisions to take with them, and receive treatment, should they have met with an accident or fallen sick. . . .

Philosophic Maxims of the Inca Pachacutec [*ruled 1438–1471*]

Envy is a worm that gnaws and consumes the entrails of ambitious men.

To envy or to be envied is a source of twofold torment.

If others envy you, it is because you are good; if you envy others, it is because you are bad.

He who envies the happiness of others derives from it only evil, like the spider which, from a flower, derives poison.

Drunkenness, anger, and madness go together; but the first two are a matter of will and may therefore be changed; whereas the last is for all time.

He who attacks the life of another, without authority or just cause, condemns himself to death.

A noble, courageous man is recognizable by the patience he shows in adversity.

Impatience is the sign of a mean, low heart that is underbred and full of bad habits.

Judges who allow a plaintiff to visit them in secret must be considered as thieves and punished with death.

Governors must never forget that he who is unable to run his own house and family is still less competent to be entrusted with public matters.

He who pretends to be counting the stores, when he doesn't know how to count the knots of a quipu,[2] deserves to be jeered at.

The Royal Commentaries of the Inca Garcilaso de la Vega, 1539–1616, ed. by Alain Gheerbrant (New York: The Orion Press, 1961), pp. 11–12, 115–16, 125, 204–205.

2. Quipu: knotted cords which served as accounts and records. —V.J.V.

9 The Beginning of Many Things: An Arapaho Legend

The so-called uncivilized[1] tribes of North America had no hieroglyphic writing like some of the Central American Indians, nor did they leave behind large stone monuments. Aside from archaeology, our knowledge of their prehistory depends upon a few pictographic records and upon oral tradition, popularly called legends. This oral "literature" cannot be relied upon as accounts of how things actually happened, any more than the Romulus and Remus legend of the origin of Rome can be accepted as a historic document. Legends are useful, however, for the light they shed on the culture and values of the people. The following legend is from the Arapaho, an Algonquian-speaking tribe of the Western Plains whose descendants live in Wyoming and Oklahoma.

A man tried to think how the Arapahos might kill buffalo. He was a hard thinker who would go off for several days to fast and think. At last he dreamed that a voice spoke to him and told him what to do.

Going back to his people, he made an enclosure of trees set in the ground with willows wound between them. At one side of the enclosure there was only a cliff with rocks at the bottom. Then four runners who never tired were sent out to the windward of the herd of buffalo, two of them on each side of the herd. They drove the animals toward the enclosure and into it. Then the people drove the buffalo around inside until a heavy cloud of dust rose. Unable to see in the dust, the animals ran over the cliff and were killed.

This man also secured horses for his people. There were many wild horses.[2] The man made another enclosure, complete except for an opening. Into this enclosure horses were driven, just as the buffalo had been, and then the opening was closed. After the horses had run around until they were tired, they were lassoed. At first it took a long time to break them, and only one horse was caught for each family. But this was not enough, so more were caught. After a few years, the horses had had so many colts that every Arapaho man had a herd. No longer did the dogs have to drag the meat and baggage, nor did the women have to carry heavy packs on their backs.

At that time the people had nothing to cut their meat with. Another man

1. The terms "civilized" and "uncivilized," while still used by many historians, have been abandoned by most anthropologists because of the ethnocentric values on which they are based, and the absence of a common definition of such terms.
2. Perhaps these Indians were unaware that the horse was brought to North America by white men. This passage about the horse may have been recently grafted on to an older legend. —V.J.V.

took a buffalo shoulder blade and cut out a narrow piece of it with flint. This he sharpened until it was a good knife. He also made a knife from flint by flaking it into shape. All the people learned how to make knives.

This man made the first bow and arrows also. He made the first arrow point from the short rib of a buffalo. With his bow and four arrows, he went off alone and waited in the woods at a buffalo path. When a buffalo came along the path, he shot; the arrow disappeared in the body and the animal fell dead. Then he killed three others. He went back to camp and told his people: "Harness the dogs; there are four dead buffalo in the woods." Thereafter the Arapahos were able to get meat without driving the buffalo into an enclosure.

In the early days, people used the fire drill. A man, another hard thinker, went off alone to think. He learned that certain stones, when struck, would give a spark and that this spark would light tinder. He gathered stones and filled a small horn with dry, soft wood. Then he went home.

His wife said to him, "Please make a fire." So he took out his horn and his flint stones, struck a spark, blew it, put grass on it, and soon, to the surprise of all who saw it, he had a fire. Making a fire in this way was so much easier than using a fire drill that soon all the people did it.

These three men—the one who made the first enclosure for buffalo and for horses, the one who made the first knife and the first bow and arrows, and the one who showed people how to make fire easily—they were the men who brought our people to the condition in which they live now.

ELLA E. CLARK, *Indian Legends from the Northern Rockies* (Norman: University of Oklahoma Press, 1966), pp. 231–32. Copyright 1966 by the University of Oklahoma Press.

II

FROM THE DISCOVERY
AND SETTLEMENT TO THE BEGINNING
OF THE REVOLUTIONARY WAR
1492–1775

Introduction

When Columbus waded ashore in the Bahamas in 1492 he remarked on the gentle character of the natives, who "exhibit great love towards all others in preference to themselves." The Spanish were not encumbered with like virtue, for they seized whatever Indians they chose to use as slaves, or to take back to Spain as exhibits, along with other specimens of the flora and fauna of the Indies. This pattern was set from the beginning, and was followed by unprovoked massacres wherever the conquistadores went. The frightful toll of introduced diseases, added to the deliberate killing, so rapidly depopulated the Caribbean islands that black slaves from Africa soon had to replace the natives, and descendants of these forced migrants today form the vast majority of the population in that region.

Occasionally, indeed, the Church raised objections to the mistreatment of the natives, as when Pope Paul III wrote in 1537:

By our apostolic authority we define and proclaim that the Indians, or any other peoples who may hereafter be discovered by Catholics, although they be not Christian, must in no way be deprived of their liberty or their possessions.

Such proclamations had no effect, for throughout Spanish America the native peoples were set to work in the gold and silver mines, in forests and fields, extracting wealth for their overlords. Their temples were demolished, their writings burned, their leaders killed. On the mainland, however, the Indians continued to outnumber the whites, and eventually there was enough racial intermixture so that an Amerind-European type, generally called mestizos, became the dominant one in most of Central and South America.[1] This does not mean that the Spanish gentlemen accepted

1. "No part of the world has ever witnessed such a gigantic mixing of races as the one that has been taking place in Latin America and the Caribbean since 1492." Magnus Mörner, *Race Mixture in the History of Latin America* (Boston: Little, Brown

the Indians as equals, for political and economic power was always held by the Europeans, even after the revolts of the nineteenth century, except where it could be torn from them occasionally, as in Mexico. Most racial mixture took place outside formal marriage.

Spanish, English, and French penetration of the territory now occupied by the United States and Canada began almost simultaneously. Despite numerous prior exploratory expeditions and abortive settlements attempted by all three powers, no lasting settlements, except for St. Augustine, were made until the first decade of the seventeenth century. Jamestown was begun in 1607, Quebec in 1608, and Santa Fe in 1609.

The period of time which elapsed from the arrival of the first settlers in North America to the beginning of the Revolutionary War is almost as great as the time that has elapsed since that event. The Indian for a large part of this period held the key to success or failure of the new colonies. In nearly every instance the first arrivals were received with kindness and hospitality. They were offered food and shelter and shown how to survive in the wilderness. Massasoit and Powhatan, principal chiefs in Massachusetts and Virginia, respectively, maintained peace with the whites to the end of their lives.

There was, however, a spirit of arrogance and superiority in the colonists which eventually brought them into conflict with the native tribes. There is a saying that the Pilgrims upon landing fell first upon their knees and then upon the aborigines. They came indeed with no notion that the natives were entitled to any more respectful consideration than prudence might require. It was maintained by William Bradford in 1620 that America was an *unpeopled* country, "being devoyd of all civil inhabitants, where there are only savage and brutish men, which range up and downe, litle otherwise than the wild beasts of the same."[2]

The hospitality shown by Virginia Indians toward the small colony of Englishmen, which they could easily have destroyed, is described by John Smith in the accompanying documents. Without Indian foodstuffs supplied in the nick of time, and without the benevolent attitude of the providers, Jamestown would have been another Roanoke. In those days of weakness,

---

& Co., 1967), p. 1. Professor J. Fred Rippy declared that in 1929 "the pure whites of European descent were in the minority in Latin America as a whole, constituting less than thirty-five per cent of the population. They formed the majority only in Argentina, Uruguay, Chile, and possibly Cuba, Costa Rica, and Brazil. The primitive and mixed races were far in the majority in such countries as Mexico, Paraguay, Bolivia, Peru, Ecuador, Nicaragua, Guatemala, Venezuela, Honduras, and Panama . . ." Rippy, *Historical Evolution of Hispanic America* (New York: F. S. Crofts & Co., 1942), p. 314.

2. Bradford, *History of Plymouth Plantation* (New York: Capricorn Books, 1962), p. 40.

the English found it convenient to arrange the equivalent of a dynastic marriage between John Rolfe and Pocahontas, from which union eminent families were later to claim descent. Though backwoods adventures with dusky maidens could be discreetly accepted, a formal marriage was so unique that Rolfe felt it necessary to explain why he married "one whose education hath bin rude, her manners barbarous, her generation, accursed, and so discrepant in all nurtriture from my selfe." It was, he said, from no "unbridled desire of carnall affection, but for the good of this plantation," that the union was made.

No other such marriage followed, and to ensure the increase of the colony, the London company sent several shipments of "uncorrupted virgins" to Virginia, where they were "very lovingly" received and quickly married off. While there were among the English a few partisans of amalgamation, intermarriage with the Indians was never officially encouraged, and was in fact eventually forbidden in many of the colonies.[3] In New France, on the other hand, intermarriage with the natives was encouraged by both civil and religious authorities, and mixture of the races took place there on a wide scale. While the differences in the circumstances of the two colonies, *i.e.,* a small white population based on the fur trade, contrasted to a relatively large white population based on farming, might explain the difference in the extent of intermarriage, there can be no explanation for the restrictive legislation of the English colonies except the presence of attitudes of racial superiority.

Most of the admixture between the English and the Indians was the result either of illicit and transitory unions with Indian slaves, servants, or captives, or of marriage according to the Indian custom between free Indians and white captives, traders, or soldiers. The fact that the English population was much larger than the French, and that they lived in more thickly settled communities, insulated from direct contact with the Indians, no doubt operated to check intermarriage. The fact that most English settlers were farmers, requiring the aid of the technical skills of European women, may also have been a factor. But the laws against miscegenation reveal certain attitudes not held by the majority of the French inhabitants. It is also notable that the French possessions were never torn by the Indian wars which made life periodically hazardous in the English settlements. Only the excursions of the Iroquois allies of the English acquainted the French with the kind of terror which racked the English colonies, with few exceptions, from Maine to Carolina.

3. Laws prohibiting marriage between whites and Negroes or Indians were enacted by Maryland in 1662, Virginia in 1691, Massachusetts in 1692 and 1705, North Carolina in 1715, South Carolina in 1717, Delaware in 1721, Pennsylvania in 1725, and Georgia in 1754.

The French were in need of a firm alliance with the Indians as a barrier against the more populous English colonies, and intermarriage was apparently considered as one means of accomplishing this. When one M. Gand remarked that "we would like to see only one People in this land,"[4] he meant a mixed race, while the English, in thinking, if not saying, the same thing, meant that the Indians must be exterminated.

The Jesuits looked upon intermarriage as the key to the conversion of the savages and their children, and the traders and *coureurs du bois* found marriage with Indian women the only alternative to a celibate life, as well as an excellent way to advance their trading interests. It also seems evident that the French were relatively free of attitudes of racial superiority. Such attitudes are seldom found in their writings, and certainly not in their practice. The racial admixture of that early period gave rise to a numerous group of mixed-bloods, known as metis, who have been important in Canadian history.

Informal mixture occurred in English America, despite the ban on intermarriage, and the result is seen not only in the fact that most Indian tribes, and particularly Eastern tribes, have a high degree of racial mixture (sometimes with Negroes as well as with whites, giving rise to the term "tri-racial isolates"), but also in the fact that there are in the eastern states several hundred communities of brown-skinned people who are not Negroes or mulattoes, and yet whose early origins are clouded in mystery.[5] Such a group are the Lumbees (formerly called Croatans) of North Carolina, who came to national attention with an armed uprising against the Ku Klux Klan in 1954. They were ignored in the census of 1950 (though numbering 30,000), but after being officially classified as Indians by state and federal laws, they were listed as Indians in 1960. It has been said that if Indians were defined as Negroes are usually defined ("one drop of non-white blood means they are not white"), the number of "Indians" in the United States would number into the millions.

While the charter of Virginia, like later charters in other colonies, declared its purpose to be "propagating of *Christian* Religion to such People, as yet live in Darkness," there was never any serious effort to accomplish that, especially on the part of the Established Church. In New England, villages of "praying Indians" resulted from the labors of John Eliot (whose Algonquian Bible was published in 1663), Roger Williams, and Daniel Gookin, but the bulk of the natives were not converted. In Pennsylvania the Quakers, and to an even greater extent the Moravian Brethren, worked

---

4. Reuben Gold Thwaites, ed., *Jesuit Relations and Allied Documents* (Cleveland: The Burrows Bros. Co., 1896–1901), IX, 103.

5. A fascinating book about these communities is Brewton Berry's *Almost White* (New York: The Macmillan Co., 1960).

among the Indians, the latter with some success among the Delawares. The Catholic missionaries, particularly the Jesuits, were limited to the French possessions for the most part (until they were ejected by Louis XV in 1751), and it is due to them that their faith eventually took hold among tribes of the Great Lakes and Mississippi Valley. The majority of Europeans, however, were far more interested in material gain from their relations with the Indians than they were in their salvation.

The pattern of white relations with the Indians that was established in Virginia was, with few exceptions, characteristic of the relations that were to prevail everywhere for three centuries. In the stage of weakness, friendly relations were to be maintained in the interest of self-preservation: a crown for Powhatan in Virginia; a hundred Indians invited to the first Thanksgiving feast at Plymouth; recognition of the prior right of Indians to the soil, and negotiations between supposed equals. When settlements appeared to be permanent, the numbers of whites had grown, and their stock of arms was adequate, the attitude shifted to one of overbearing arrogance. The English then took the position that they were not guests in the country, but masters, and that the Indians were subjects bound to obey their laws, and to submit to whatever demands the English might make of them. If an accommodation was occasionally necessary, it would last only so long as required to accumulate strength for another blow.

Powhatan having died, violent confrontation followed in Virginia. Opechancanough took up the hatchet in 1622, and very nearly wiped out the English settlements. English arms prevailed, however, and the red men were pushed farther back into the wilderness, north of the York River, from which fastnesses twenty-two years later they made one last frantic assault, led by the same chief, who perished in the effort. The captives were sold as slaves, and the miserable remnants were confined to small reservations to await extinction.

Only sixteen years after the first settlements in New England, the English felt strong enough to exterminate the Pequots, a grisly task made easier because neighboring tribes were either neutral or aided the English. Yet as late as 1638 three Englishmen were executed for the robbery and murder of an Indian, although, as Bradford relates, there were some who "murmured that any English should be put to death for the Indians."

The life of the venerable Massasoit ended in 1662, and his oldest son, Alexander, died in the same year. His second son, Metacomet, called King Philip, then became chief sachem of the Wampanoags, and quietly prepared for a showdown. Provocations were numerous enough. Puritans decreed that Indians must not work or carry burdens on the Sabbath. Disputes arose over land titles. Indians were arrested, punished, and sometimes executed for violating laws they had no part in making. English cattle overran Indian cornfields. In June of 1675 three Indians were hanged for the alleged murder of Sassamon, a Christian Indian who served as an informer for the whites. Within days the Indians struck back by setting homes afire at Swansea, and the greatest Indian outbreak of colonial history was on. Philip had managed to form a confederacy of jealous tribes. Of ninety English towns, his warriors attacked fifty-two and completely destroyed twelve. The fighting lasted a year, but on August 12, 1676, Philip was betrayed and slain, and the "swamp fight" ended in defeat. Philip's head was displayed as a trophy on the palisade at Plymouth; his wife and little son were sold as slaves in the West Indies, along with most other captives. Late in the century sporadic fighting erupted in Maine, but it was too late, and these tribes too sank back into the status of a herd of caged animals.

Prior to the French and Indian War every colony was racked by bloody warfare, with the exception of Pennsylvania and Georgia, in each of which the founding proprietors carefully cultivated friendly relations with the aborigines. The Dutch in New York virtually exterminated the small Algonquian tribes of the Hudson valley and Long Island, but the powerful Iroquois confederacy in the north remained allied to the Dutch, and later, to the English, standing as a powerful wall against French expansion. The only Indian attacks experienced in New York in this period came therefore from Canada, where tribes allied to the French made occasional forays against New York and New England. The Five Nations (Six Nations after 1713) were important as tools for fighting the wars of New York against the French and their Indians, and also in the fur trade, which became the principal enterprise of the colony. The bulk of the Iroquois remained peacefully disposed toward New York until the Revolutionary War.

Maryland was involved in Indian warfare in 1642; South Carolina wiped out the Yamassee and their allies in 1715–1716, while North Carolina forced the Tuscaroras out of the colony in 1711–1712. These Iroquoian-speaking Indians migrated north to join their kinsmen in New York, who were subsequently known as the Six Nations.

In the American phase of what Europe called the Seven Years War (which really began in America), a number of Indian tribes, from the Alleghenies to the Mississippi, and from Kentucky to Canada, were allied to the French. They administered repeated defeats to the English, and for the first time Pennsylvania suffered from the attacks of the Delawares and Shawnees. Even the Senecas, western gatekeepers of the Six Nations, became hostile. Wolfe's victory over Montcalm at Quebec put an end to the fighting between the two European powers, and the peacemakers at Paris redrew the map of North America without regard to the aboriginal inhabitants. The Indians did not lay down their arms for long, however, but soon attacked again under the able Ottawa chief Pontiac. All of the frontier was at their mercy, and the posts recently abandoned by the French fell into their hands, save for Fort Pitt and Detroit. The former was rescued by the timely relief expedition of Colonel Bouquet, who defeated an Indian attack at Bushy Run, and the latter survived an unprecedented five-month siege under the personal direction of Pontiac. The denial of French aid was perhaps as responsible for the ultimate disheartenment of the Indians as any military events. Nevertheless, the conquerors were unable to assume control of the West for two years, and the Lords of Trade, in an effort to avert further trouble with the Indians, induced the Royal edict of October 7, 1763, which forbade white settlement in the region west of the sources of the rivers falling into the sea. This set in motion a chain of events leading toward the separation of the colonies from the mother country. The frontiersmen and land speculators were unwilling to surrender the West to the natives; and His Majesty's government was compelled to station a standing army in the colonies, perhaps to police the Indians, perhaps also to enforce the proclamation against invasion of their domain. When the royal government sought to saddle the colonists with the cost of this venture through a series of taxes, the protests which followed produced a chain reaction which flared into open revolt at Concord Bridge, April 19, 1775.

Only a year before, a struggle took place which did much to guarantee the hostility of many Indians to the "thirteen fires." That was the so-called war of Lord Dunmore, touched off by the murder of the family of the Mingo chief Logan by Indian-hating frontiersmen. (See Logan's speech, p. 58, herein.) A peace was patched up under a legendary elm tree at Circleville, Ohio, but before the document reached the hands of the governor of Virginia, he was already a prisoner of the revolting colonials. The Shawnees, seeing their late tormentors at war with one another, soon disinterred the hatchet just buried, and struck at the Kentucky settlements.

10   The Indians Discover Columbus, 1492–1493

CHRISTOPHER COLUMBUS

Reports of the earliest encounters between white explorers and Indians almost uniformly report astonishment at the friendly reception which the natives accorded to the strange visitors. This account by Columbus is no exception. It is perhaps difficult to understand how the white men could remark so fulsomely on the apparent virtues of the Indians and so soon turn to ruthless exploitation of them. Perhaps the innocence of the Indians was regarded, by persons shaped in a different culture, as a sign of weak-

ness, and an incitation to take advantage of them. The fact that these
peaceable encounters were soon followed by violent conflict can hardly be
attributed to any other causes than the greed and aggression of the so-
called discoverers.

I gave to all I approached whatever articles I had about me, such as
cloth and many other things, taking nothing of theirs in return: but they are
naturally timid and fearful. As soon however as they see that they are safe,
and have laid aside all fear, they are very simple and honest, and exceedingly liberal with all they have; none of them refusing any thing he may
possess when he is asked for it, but on the contrary inviting us to ask them.
They exhibit great love towards all others in preference to themselves: they
also give objects of great value for trifles, and content themselves with very
little or nothing in return. . . .

. . . when they got rid of the fear they at first entertained, [*they*] would
come out in throngs, crowding the roads to see us, some bringing food,
others drink, with astonishing affection and kindness. . . .

. . . these people are so amiable and friendly that even the King took a
pride in calling me his brother. . . .

I could not clearly understand whether the people possess any private
property, for I observed that one man had the charge of distributing
various things to the rest, but especially meat and provisions and the like. I
did not find, as some of us had expected, any cannibals amongst them, but
on the contrary, men of great deference and kindness.

> *The Columbus Letter of March 14th, 1493* (Chicago: The
> Newberry Library, 1953), pp. 6–10.

11   A Public Burning of Indian Chiefs Ordered by Cortés in Front of Montezuma, 1519

There are few incidents in history to match the cruelty and duplicity of
the relations of Hernando Cortés with the Aztecs. Despite the cordiality of
his reception, he soon made Montezuma an abject prisoner and proceeded
to govern the Aztec capital, using the "emperor" as a figurehead. After a
revolt led by some. local chiefs, in which Cortés believed the unhappy
Montezuma to be implicated, he decided to terrify the ruler and his fol-
lowers by a public burning of captured chiefs. The following account is by
a member of Cortés' invading force.

. . . the messengers whom Montezuma sent with his sign and seal to
summon the Captains who had killed our soldiers, brought them before
him as prisoners and what he said to them I do not know, but he sent them

to Cortés, so that he might do justice to them, and their confession was taken when Montezuma was not present and they confessed what I have already stated was true, that their Prince had ordered them to wage war and to exact tribute, and that if any Teules should appear in defence of the towns, they too should be attacked or killed. When Cortés heard this confession he sent to inform Montezuma how it implicated him in the affair, and Montezuma made all the excuses he could, and our Captain sent him his word that he believed the confession himself, but that although Montezuma deserved punishment in conformity with the ordinances of our King . . . yet he was so fond of him and wished him so well, that even if that crime lay at his door, he, Cortés, would pay the penalty with his own life sooner than allow Montezuma's to pass away. With all this that Cortés sent to tell him, Montezuma felt anxious, and without any further discussion Cortés sentenced those Captains [*caciques, or local chiefs*] to death and to be burned in front of Montezuma's palace. This sentence was promptly carried out, and, so that there could be no obstruction while they were being burned, Cortés ordered shackles to be put on Montezuma himself, and when this was done Montezuma roared with rage, and if before this he was scared, he was then much more so.

BERNAL DIAZ DEL CASTILLO, *The Discovery and Conquest of Mexico* (New York: Grove Press, n.d.), pp. 231–32.

12 Aztec Account of the Spanish Massacre of Participants in a Religious Ceremonial

While the Aztec ruler Montezuma was a prisoner of the Spaniards, his people asked him for permission to hold the fiesta of Toxcatl, in honor of the god Huitzpochtli. Cortés approved, and then left with a force to meet Narvaez, who had been sent from Cuba to arrest him. Alvarado, who was left in charge, staged a repeat performance of the massacre committed at Cholula when the Spanish were on the way to Tenochtitlan. Soon after the festival was under way, the Spanish cut off all exits and annihilated most of the participants. The following is an Aztec account of the incident as given later to the priest-historian Bernardino Sahagún.

At this moment in the fiesta, when the dance was loveliest and when song was linked to song, the Spaniards were seized with an urge to kill the celebrants. They all ran forward, armed as if for battle. They closed the entrances and passageways, all the gates of the patio. . . . They posted guards so that no one could escape, and then rushed into the Sacred Patio to slaughter the celebrants. They came on foot, carrying their swords and their wooden or metal shields.

They ran in among the dancers, forcing their way to the place where the drums were played. They attacked the man who was drumming and cut off his arms. Then they cut off his head, and it rolled across the floor.

They attacked all the celebrants, stabbing them, spearing them, striking them with their swords. They attacked some of them from behind, and these fell instantly to the ground with their entrails hanging out. Others they beheaded: they cut off their heads, or split their heads to pieces.

They struck others in the shoulders, and their arms were torn from their bodies. They wounded some in the thigh and some in the calf. They slashed others in the abdomen, and their entrails all spilled to the ground. Some attempted to run away, but their intestines dragged as they ran; they seemed to tangle their feet in their own entrails. No matter how they tried to save themselves, they could find no escape.

Some attempted to force their way out, but the Spaniards murdered them at the gates. Others climbed the walls, but they could not save themselves. Those who ran into the communal houses were safe there for a while; so were those who lay down among the victims and pretended to be dead. But if they stood up again, the Spaniards saw them and killed them.

The blood of the warriors flowed like water and gathered into pools. The pools widened, and the stench of blood and entrails filled the air. The Spaniards ran into the communal houses to kill those who were hiding. They ran everywhere and searched everywhere; they invaded every room, hunting and killing.

MIGUEL LEÓN-PORTILLA, ed., *The Broken Spears, the Aztec Account of the Conquest of Mexico* (Boston: The Beacon Press, 1962), pp. 74–76.

13 Befriending of Cabeza de Vaca by Texas Indians, 1528

CABEZA DE VACA

On November 6, 1528, the exploring party of Cabeza de Vaca, consisting of about eighty men drifting in makeshift boats, were blown ashore on an island off the coast of Texas. In the course of an odyssey of more than sixteen months since leaving Cuba, they had survived shipwreck, thirst, and hunger, but many of their companions had been lost. In this previously unknown wilderness the rest of them might have perished were it not for the aid of friendly Indians. The touching account here given of the great efforts made by the natives to alleviate the hardships of the Spaniards stands in sharp contrast to the treatment later accorded the Indians in return.

At sunrise the next day, the time the Indians appointed, they came according to their promise, and brought us a large quantity of fish with certain roots, some a little larger than walnuts, others a trifle smaller, the greater part got from under the water and with much labor. In the evening they returned and brought us more fish and roots. They sent their women and children to look at us, who went back rich with the hawk-bells and beads given them, and they came afterwards on other days, returning as before. Finding that we had provision, fish, roots, water, and other things we asked for, we determined to embark again and pursue our course. [*Meanwhile their boat capsized and three were drowned; the Indians returned to find the survivors on the beach.*] I gave them to understand by signs that our boat had sunk and three of our number had been drowned. . . . The Indians, at sight of what had befallen us, and our state of suffering and melancholy destitution, sat down among us, and from the sorrow and pity they felt, they all began to lament so earnestly that they might have been heard at a distance, and continued so doing more than half an hour. It was strange to see these men, wild and untaught, howling like brutes over our misfortunes. It caused in me as well as in others, an increase of feeling and a livelier sense of our calamity.

The cries having ceased, I talked with the Christians, and said that if it appeared well to them, I would beg these Indians to take us to their houses. Some, who had been in New Spain, replied that we ought not to think of it; for if they should do so, they would sacrifice us to their idols. But seeing no better course, and that any other led to a nearer and more certain death, I disregarded what was said, and besought the Indians to take us to their dwellings. They signified that it would give them delight, and that we should tarry a little, that they might do what we asked. Presently thirty men loaded themselves with wood and started for their houses, which were far off, and we remained with the others until near night; when, holding us up, they carried us with all haste. Because of the extreme coldness of the weather, lest any one should die or fail by the way, they caused four or five very large fires to be placed at intervals, and at each they warmed us; and when they saw that we had regained some heat and strength, they took us to the next so swiftly that they hardly let us touch our feet to the ground. In this manner we went as far as their habitations, where we found that they had made a house for us with many fires in it. An hour after our arrival, they began to dance and hold great rejoicing, which lasted all night, although for us there was no joy, festivity nor sleep, awaiting the hour they should make us victims. In the morning they again gave us fish and roots, showing us such hospitality that we were reassured, and lost somewhat the fear of sacrifice.

> "The Narrative of Alvar Nuñez Cabeça de Vaca," in Frederick W. Hodge, ed., *Spanish Explorers in the Southern United States* (New York: Barnes & Noble, 1959), pp. 45–48.

14   Indians Cure Cartier's Men of Scurvy, 1535

Near the site of Montreal in the year 1535 occurred the first reported cure performed by Indians in this continent north of Mexico. In the journal of Cartier's second voyage up the St. Lawrence, it is reported that his ships were frozen in the ice from mid-November until mid-March, during which time scurvy caused the death of "five and twentie of our best and chiefest men, and all the rest were so sicke, that wee thought they should never recover againe, only three or foure excepted. Then it pleased God to cast his pitiful eye upon us, and sent us the knowledge of remedie of our healthes and recoverie . . ."

The messengers which it "pleased God" to send with the remedy were the natives of the country. While Cartier was walking upon the ice, he saw a group of Indians,

among whom was Domagaia, who not passing ten or twelve days afore, had bene very sicke with that disease, and had his knee swolne as bigge as a childe of two yeres old, all his sinews shrunke together, his teeth spoyled, his gummes rotten, and stinking. Our Captaine seeking him whole and sound, was thereat marvelous glad, hoping to understand and know of him how he had healed himselfe, to the end that he might ease and help his men. So soone as they were come neere him, he asked Domagaia how he had done to heale himselfe: he answered, that he had taken the juice and sappe of the leaves of a certain Tree, and therewith had healed himselfe: For it is a singular remedy against that disease.

Cartier asked to be shown the healing tree, pretending that he wished to cure a servant, "because he would not shew the number of the sicke men."

Domagaia sent two women to gather branches of it, and showed the French how to use it, boiling the bark and leaves for a decoction, and placing the dregs upon the legs. The Indians declared "that the vertue of this tree was, to heale any other disease: the tree is in their language called Ameda or Hanneda, this is thought to be the Sassafras tree." [*Sassafras does not grow in that climate; present writers conclude that it was white pine, hemlock, or spruce.*]

The French at first hesitated to accept the strange medicine, but once having done so, they were soon cured. The account concluded that if all the physicians of Montpelier and Louvain had been there with all the drugs of Alexandria, "they would not have done so much in one yere, as that tree did in sixe days, for it did so prevaile, that as many as used of it, by the grace of God recovered their health."

HENRY S. BURRAGE, ed., *Early English and French Voyages* (*Hakluyt*) (New York: Charles Scribner's Sons, 1906), pp. 75–77.

15   Powhatan's Indians' Feeding of the Virginia Settlers, 1607, and Later Dispossession, 1622

JOHN SMITH

The first English settlers in Virginia expected the Indians to destroy them, which could easily have been done. Instead, the Indians saved them from starvation, and ensured their own future dispossession. The following account is by John Smith.

. . . and shortly after it pleased God (in our extremity) to move the Indians to bring us Corne, ere it was halfe ripe, to refresh us, when we rather expected when they would destroy us: about the tenth of September there was about 46. of our men dead. . . .

Our provision being now within twentie dayes spent, the Indians brought us great store bothe of Corne and bread already made: and also there came such aboundance of Fowles into the Rivers, as greatly refreshed our weake estates . . . [*Again in want, Smith sought out the Indians to trade.*] With fish, oysters, bread, and deere, they kindly traded with me and my men, beeing no lesse in doubt of my intent, then I of theirs; for well I might with twenty men have fraighted a Shippe with Corne. [*Meeting a hunting party upon his return*] who, having but their hunting provision requested me to return to their Towne, where I should load my boat with corne; and with near thirtie bushels I returned to the fort, the very name whereof gave great comfort to our despairing company. [*Later, discovering four Indian towns, Smith reported that he was*] at each place kindly used; especially at the last, being the hart of the Country; where were assembled 200 people with such aboundance of corne, as having laded our barge, as also I might have laded a ship.

[*Fifteen years of peace ended shortly after the death of Powhatan, when his brother and successor, Opechancanough, launched war against the settlements in 1622. Smith then described the Indians as "beasts," a "viperous brood," "hell-hounds," and "miscreants" who "put on a more unnaturall brutishness than beasts, as by these instances must appear." However, the war had its advantages:]*

. . . where before we were troubled in clearing the ground of great Timber, which was to them of small use; now we may take their own plaine fields and Habitations, which are the pleasantest places in the Countrey. Besides, the Deere, Turkies, and other Beasts and Fowles will exceedingly increase if we beat the Salvages out of the Countrey.

[*Smith then proposed enslaving the Indians, so that Virginia might prosper as the Spanish:*] . . . it is more easy to civilize them by conquest than by faire meanes; for the one may be made at once, but their civilizing will require a long time and much industry. The manner how to suppresse them is so often related and approved, I omit it here: and you have twenty examples of the Spaniards how they got the West Indies, and forced the treacherous and rebellious infidels to doe all manner of drudgery worke and slavery for them, themselves living like Souldiers upon the fruits of their labours. . . . What growing state was there ever in the world which had not the like? Rome grew by oppression, and rose upon the backs of her enemies: and the Spaniards have had many of those counterbuffes, more than we.

L. G. TYLER, ed., *Narratives of Early Virginia* (New York: Barnes & Noble, 1959), pp. 37–41, 359–60, 364–65.

16   The Pilgrims at Plymouth, 1620

WILLIAM BRADFORD

Prior to their landing in America, the Pilgrims were filled with apprehension about their reception by the natives, whom they had been taught to believe were fierce and aggressive.

The place they had thoughts on was some of those vast & unpeopled countries of America, which are frutfull & fitt for habitation, being devoyd of all civill inhabitants, wher ther are only salvage & brutish men, which range up and downe, litle otherwise then the wild beasts of the same. [*Here follows a description of other anticipated difficulties.*] And also those which should escape or overcome these difficulties, should yett be in continuall danger of the salvage people, who are cruell, barbarous, & most trecherous, being most furious in their rage, and merciles wher they overcome; not being contente only to kill, & take away life, but delight to tormente men in the most bloodie maner that may be; fleaing some alive with the shells of fishes, cutting of the members & joynts of others by pees-meale, and broiling on the coles, eate the collops of their flesh in their sight whilst they live; with other cruelties horrible to be related. And surely it could not be thought but the very hearing of these things could not but move the very bowels of men to grate within them, and make the weake to quake & tremble. [*Upon their arrival, Bradford wrote:*] Besids, what could they see but a hidious & desolate wilderness, full of wild beasts & willd men? [*However, the first Indians they saw fled like frightened rabbits:*] . . . they espied 5. or 6. persons with a dogg coming towards them, who were salvages; but they fled from them, & rane up into the woods, and the English followed them, partly to see if they could speake with them, and partly to discover if ther might not be more of them lying in ambush. But the Indeans seeing them selves thus followed, they againe forsooke the woods, & rane away on the sands as hard as they could . . . [*The Pilgrims spent the winter at Plymouth unmolested by Indians.*] But about the 16. of *March* a certaine Indian came bouldly amongst them, and spoke to them in broken English, which they could well understand, but marvelled at it. At length they understood by discourse with him, that he was not of these parts, but belonged to the eastrene parts, wher some English-ships came to fhish, with whom he was aquainted, & could name sundrie of them by their names, amongst whom he had gott his language. He became profitable to them in aquainting them with many things concerning the state of the cuntry in the east-parts wher he lived, which was afterwards profit-able unto them; as also of the people hear, of their names, number, & strength; of their situation & distance from his place, and who was cheefe amongst them. His name was *Samaset;* he tould them also of another Indian whos name was *Squanto,* a native of this place, who had been in England & could speake better English than him selfe. Being, after some time of entertainmente & gifts, dismist, a while after he came againe, & 5. more with him, & they brought againe all the tooles that were stolen away before, and made way for the coming of their great sachem, called *Massasoyt;* who, about 4. or 5. *days after,* came with the cheefe of his freinds & other attendance, with the aforesaid *Squanto.* With whom, after frendly entertainment, & some gifts given him, they made a peace with him (which hath now continued this 24. years). . . .

After these things he returned to his place caled *Sowams,* some 40. mile from this place, but *Squanto* continued with them, and was their inter-preter, and was a spetiall instrument sent of God for their good beyond their expectation. He directed them how to set their corne, wher to take fish, and to procure other comodities, and was also their pilott to bring them to unknowne places for their profitt, and never left them till he dyed. . . .

Afterwards they (as many as were able) began to plant ther corne, in which servise Squanto stood them in great stead, showing them both the manner how to set it, and after how to dress & tend it. Also he tould them excepte they gott fish & set with it (in these old grounds) it would come to nothing, and he showed them that in the midle of Aprill they should have store enough come up the brooke, by which they begane to build, and taught them how to take it, and wher to get other provissions necessary for them; all which they found true by triall & experience.

> WILLIAM BRADFORD, *Of Plymouth Plantation,* ed. by Harvey Wish (New York: Capricorn Books, 1962), pp. 40–41, 60, 62–63, 72–73, 76.

17   Destruction of the Pequots, 1636

WILLIAM   BRADFORD

In 1636 a military force composed of several hundred allied Indians and about a hundred whites from Massachusetts, commanded by John Mason, nearly exterminated the Pequots of Connecticut,[1] after Indians had attacked the crew of a disabled boat. The principal Pequot village was surrounded in midwinter, and set afire. Governor Bradford of Plymouth gave this description, somewhat reminiscent of Joshua's campaign against the Canaanites.

Those that scaped the fire were slaine with the sword; some hewed to peeces, others rune throw with their rapiers, so as they were quickly dispatchte, and very few escaped. It was conceived they thus destroyed about 400, at this time. It was a fearful sight to see them thus frying in the fyer, and the streams of blood quenching the same, and horrible was the stinck and sente there of; but the victory seemed a sweete sacrifice, and they gave the prayers thereof to God, who had wrought so wonderfully for them, thus to inclose their enemise in their hands, and give them so speedy a victory over so proud and insulting an enimie.

> WILLIAM BRADFORD, *History of Plymouth Plantation,* ed. by William T. Davis (New York: Charles Scribner's, 1908), pp. 339–50.

1. The official figure on the number of Pequots now in Connecticut is twenty-one persons. Klein and Icolari, *Reference Encyclopedia of the American Indian,* p. 106.

◈

18   Maryland Indian Reproval of the English for Attempting to Impose Their Customs on the Indians, 1635

ANDREW WHITE

The governor had demanded of the Indians that if any of them should kill or murder an Englishman, the guilty one should be delivered up for punishment according to the English law. The Indian reply is here described.

The *Wicomesse* [*chief*] after a little pause, replyed; It is the manner amongst us *Indians,* that if any such like accident happen, wee doe redeeme the life of a man that is so slaine, with a 100. armes length of *Roanoke* (which is a sort of Beades that they make, and use for money) and since that you are heere strangers, and come into our Countrey, you should rather conform yourselves to the Customes of our Countrey, then impose yours upon us. . . .

[ANDREW WHITE], *A Relation of Maryland* (Ann Arbor: University Microfilms, 1966), pp. 35–36.

19   Customs of the Noble Savage, 1709

JOHN LAWSON

Wilcomb E. Washburn has charged that "historians have failed in the job of interpreting the Indian as he was." Detailed accounts of Indian life and customs by early observers are so abundant that it is difficult to understand why this should be so. One who reads the accounts which most historians have ignored cannot help finding much to admire in Indian life, as Rousseau and Montaigne did. Those who believe that their vision was blurred by one-sided accounts have coined the phrase "the noble savage," and used it as a derogatory label for favorable images of Indians. The slur has been questioned by Washburn, who asks:

Does the fact that early American Indians engaged at times in warfare, thievery, or deception disprove the idea that their societies may have been noble in character? Is the Christian character of a nation proved a "myth" because of the unchristian actions of many of its citizens? Surely "noble savagery" cannot be ridiculed as a myth by citing particular examples of ignoble savagery unrelated to a general study of the behavior of the society as a whole. Did not early observers of the North American Indians generally agree on their generosity, *stoic bearing of pain, dignity, loftiness of speech in council, etc.? If so, are these not "noble" traits? Are they any less noble because they occur among American Indians rather than among Greeks, Romans, Chinese, or Japanese? Is not a tribe which holds such behavior as a norm and attempts to live up to the norm, a tribe of "noble savages"?*[1]

One observer who left detailed descriptions of early Indian customs, and contrasted the serenity of their life with the contentiousness of European existence, was John Lawson. He was an English-born gentleman-surveyor who came to North Carolina in 1701 and made several expeditions into the Indian country. His notes on the Indians with whom he became acquainted on these trips formed a large part of his History of North Carolina, *published at London in 1709 (from which the following selection is taken). On his last surveying trip into the interior, in 1711–1712, Lawson encountered the Tuscaroras, who were enraged at white incursions on their territory. His surveying instruments were recognized by them as the very symbol of their dispossession, and he was put to death.*
See pp. 99, 255–57.

The Victuals is common throughout the whole Kindred Relations, and often the whole Town; especially when they are in Hunting-Quarters, then they all fare alike, whichsoever of them kills the Game. They are very kind and charitable to one another, but more especially to those of their own Nation; for if any one of them has suffered any Loss by Fire, or otherwise, they order the grieved person to make a Feast, and invite them all thereto, which, on the day appointed, they come to, and after every Man's Mess of Victuals is dealt to him, one of their Speakers, or grave old Men, makes an Harrangue, and acquaints the Company, That the Man's House has been burnt, wherein all his Goods were destroyed; That he and his Family very narrowly escaped; That he is every Man's Friend in that Company; and, That it is all their Duties to help him, as he would do to any of them had the like Misfortune befallen them. After this Oration is over, every Man, according to his Quality, throws him down upon the Ground some Present, which is commonly Beads, Ronoak, Peak, Skins, or Furs, and which very often amounts to treble the Loss he has suffered. The same Assistance they give to any Man that wants to build a Cabin, or make a Canoe. They say it is our Duty thus to do; for there are several Works that one Man cannot effect, therefore we must give him our Help, otherwise our Society will fall, and we shall be deprived of those urgent Necessities which Life requires. They have no Fence to part one anothers Lots in their Corn-Fields, but

1. Wilcomb E. Washburn, "A Moral History of Indian-White Relations: Needs and Opportunities for Study," *Ethnohistory*, IV (Winter 1957), pp. 53–55.

every Man knows his own, and it scarce ever happens that they rob one another of so much as an Ear of Corn, which, if any is found to do, he is sentenced by the Elders to work and plant for him that was robbed, till he is recompensed for all the Damage he has suffered in his Corn-Field; and this is punctually performed, and the Thief held in Disgrace that steals from any of his Country-Folks. It often happens that a Woman is destitute of her Husband, and has a great many Children to maintain; such a Person they always help, and make their young men plant, reap, and do every thing that she is not capable of doing herself; yet they do not allow any one to be idle, but to employ themselves in some Work or other.

They never fight with one another unless drunk, nor do you ever hear any Scolding amongst them. They say the Europeans are always rangling and uneasy, and wonder they do not go out of this World, since they are so uneasy and discontented in it. All their Misfortunes and Losses end in Laughter; for if their Cabins take Fire, and all their Goods are burnt therein . . . yet such a Misfortune always ends in a hearty Fitt of Laughter, unless some of their Kinsfolks and Friends have lost their Lives. . . .

. . . there is one Vice very common everywhere, which I never found amongst them, which is, Envying other Men's happiness, because their station is not equal to, or above their Neighbors. Of this Sin I cannot say I ever saw an Example, though they are a People that set as great a Value upon themselves, as any sort of Men, in the World, upon which Account they find something Valuable in themselves above Riches. . . .

> JOHN LAWSON, *History of North Carolina* (Richmond: Garrett and Massie, 1951), pp. 188–89, 208.

20   Colonial Charters: 1606–1732

It was customary in charters granted by the king to companies and proprietors for the establishment of colonies in America, for the aims of such ventures to be stated in idealistic terms. Foremost among the high-minded objectives mentioned was the conversion and civilization of the natives. In the case of Georgia, however, the aim was to erect a barrier for the protection of South Carolina from Indian raids originating in Spanish Florida.

First Charter of Virginia, April 20, 1606

III. We, greatly commending, and graciously accepting of, their desires for the Furtherance of so noble a work, which may, by the Providence of

Almighty God, hereafter tend to the Glory of his Divine Majesty, in propagating the Christian Religion to such People, as yet live in Darkness and
miserable Ignorance of the true Knowledge and Worship of God, and may
in time bring the Infidels and Savages, living in those Parts, to human
Civility, and to a settled and quiet Government; DO, by these our Letters
Patents, graciously accept of, and agree to, their humble and well-inten-
tioned desires. . . .[1]

First Charter of Massachusetts Bay, March 14, 1629

. . . and for the directing, ruling, and disposeing of all other matters
and thinges whereby our said people, inhabitants there, maie be so reli-
giously, peaceablie, and civilly governed, as their good life and orderlie
conversation maie win and incite the natives of that country to the knowledge and obedience of the onlie true God and Savior of mankinde, and the
Christian fayth, which, in our royall intention and the adventurers of free
profession, is the principall ende of this plantation. . . .

Charter of Rhode Island and Providence Plantations, July 18, 1663

WHEREAS WEE have been informed . . . that they, pursueing, with
peaceable and loyall mindes, their sober, serious and religious intentions,
of godlie edifieing themselves, and one another, in the holie Christian ffaith
and worshipp as they were perswaded: together with the gaineing over and
conversions of the poor ignorant Indian natives, in those partes of
America, to the sincere professione and obedienc of the same faith and
worship, did . . . transplant themselves into the middest of the Indian
natives, who, as wee are infformed, are the most potent princes and people
of that country; where . . . they have . . . possessed, by purchase and
consent of the said natives, to their full content, of said lands, islands,
rivers, harbours and roades, as are verie convenient . . . and may much
advance the trade of this our realme, and greatlie enlarge the territories
thereof; they haveinge, by neare neighborhoode to and friendlie societie
with the greate bodie of the Narragansett Indians, given them encouragement, of theire owne accorde, to subject themselves, theire people and
landes, unto us; whereby, as is hoped, there may, in due tym, by the
blessing of God upon theire endeavors, bee layd a sure ffoundation of
happiness to all America. . . . And itt is hereby declared, that itt shall
not bee lawfull to or ffor the rest of the Collonies to invade or molest the
native Indians, or any other inhabitants, inhabiting within the bounds and

---

1. Dates are given here according to the Gregorian calendar, although the Julian
calendar in use in England until 1752 would set these dates ten days earlier.

lymitts hereafter mentioned (they having subjected themselves unto us, and being by us taken into our speciall protection), without the knowledge and consent of the Governour and Company of our Collony of Rhode-Island and Providence Plantations. . . .

Charter of Georgia, June 20, 1732

. . . And whereas our provinces in North America, have been frequently ravaged by Indian enemies; more especially that of South-Carolina, which in the war, by the neighboring savages, was laid waste by fire and sword, and great numbers of English inhabitants, miserably massacred, and our loving subjects who now inhabit them, by reason of the smallness of their numbers, will in case of a new war, be exposed to the late [*like?*] calamities; inasmuch as their whole southern frontier continueth unsettled, and lieth open to the said savages— . . . Know ye therefore, that we . . . by these presents . . . do . . . ordain . . . that our right trusty and well beloved [*here follow the names of the trustees*] be, and shall be one body politic and corporate, in deed and in name, by the name of the Trustees for establishing the Colony of Georgia in America . . .

WILLIAM MCDONALD, ed., *Documentary Source Book of American History* (3d ed.; New York: The Macmillan Co., 1929), pp. 2, 26, 67–68, 71, 96.

21   Indians as a Spur to Colonial Union, 1643–1754

The first efforts to unite the colonies, or a portion of them, were motivated by the need for common action on Indian problems, rather than by any foreign threats. The need to establish a common relationship, or a common defense, in their intercourse with the Indians, whether pacific or belligerent, helped give the colonials that experience in united action which made eventual confederation possible. Moreover the Iroquois example of confederated government impressed Benjamin Franklin, who borrowed from it in his Albany Plan of Union, and later, in the Articles of Confederation.

New England Confederation, May 29, 1643

. . . and whereas we live encompassed with people of severall Nations, and strange languages, which hereafter may prove injurious to us, and our posterity: And forasmuch as the Natives have formerly committed sundry insolencies and outrages upon severall Plantations of the English, and have of late combined against us. And seeing by reason of the said distractions in *England,* which they have heard of, and by which they know we are hindered both from that humble way of seeking advice, and reaping those comfortable fruits of protection which, at other times, we might well expect; we therefore doe conceive it our bounden duty, without delay to enter into a present Consotiation amongst our selves, for mutuall help and strength in all our future concernments, that, as in Nation, and Religion, so, in other respects, we be, and continue, One, according to the tenour and true meaning of the ensuing Articles.

> WILLIAM MCDONALD, *Documentary Source Book of American History 1606–1926,* p. 46.

Iroquois Influence on the Albany Plan of Union, 1754

Lewis Henry Morgan, the first scientific student of the Iroquois, declared that "the Iroquois commended to our forefathers a union of the colonies similar to their own as early as 1755. They saw in the common interests and common speech of the several colonies the elements for a confederation . . ."[1] Later writers have suggested that the Articles of Confederation, modeled after the earlier Albany Plan, were more influenced by the Iroquois model than by any other.[2] Benjamin Franklin, the author of both documents, wrote to a friend in 1751:

It would be a very strange thing if Six Nations of ignorant savages should be capable of forming a scheme for such a union, and be able to execute it in such a manner, as that it has subsisted for ages, and appears indissoluble; and yet that a like union should be impracticable for ten or a dozen English colonies, to whom it is more necessary and must be more advantageous, and whom cannot be supposed to want an equal understanding of their interests.[3]

Excerpt from the Albany Plan

The following excerpt from the Albany Plan contains only those provisions relating to Indian affairs. The bracketed sections are Franklin's comments.

1. Morgan, *Houses and House-Life of the American Aborigines* (Chicago: Phoenix Books, 1965), p. 32. For the most complete description of the Iroquois league, see Morgan, *League of the Ho-de-no sau-nee or Iroquois* (2 vols.; New Haven: Human Relations Area Files, 1954), I.

2. Matthew W. Stirling, "America's First Settlers, the Indians," *National Geographic Magazine,* LXXII, No. 5 (November 1937), p. 575; Felix Cohen, "Americanizing the White Man," *The American Scholar,* XXI, No. 2 (Spring 1952), pp. 179–80.

3. John Bigelow, ed., *The Complete Works of Benjamin Franklin* (New York: G. P. Putnam's Sons, 1887), II, 210.

10. That the President-General, with the advice of the Grand Council, hold or direct all Indian treaties, in which the general interest of the Colonies may be concerned; and make peace or declare war with Indian nations. [". . . it was thought better to have all treaties of a general nature under a general direction, that so the good of the whole may be consulted and provided for."]

11. That they make such laws as they judge necessary for regulating all Indian trade. ["Many quarrels and wars have arisen between the colonies and Indian nations through the bad conduct of traders, who cheat the Indians after making them drunk, &c., to the great expense of the colonies, both in blood and treasure. Particular colonies are so interested in the trade, as not to be willing to admit such a regulation as might be best for the whole; and therefore it was thought best under a general direction."]

13. That they make all purchases, from Indians for the crown, of lands not now within the bounds of particular colonies, or that shall not be within their bounds when some of them are reduced to more convenient dimensions. ["Purchases from the Indians, made by private persons, have been attended with many inconveniences. They have frequently interfered and occasioned uncertainty of titles, many disputes and expensive law-suits, and hindered the settlement of the land so disputed. Then the Indians have been cheated by such private purchases, and discontent and wars have been the consequence. These would be prevented by public, fair purchase."]

> Text of articles, and numeration, from Henry S. Commager, ed., *Documents of American History* (6th ed.; New York: Appleton-Century-Crofts, 1958), p. 44; bracketed explanations are from Franklin's *Works*, II, 365–66.

22   Indians as Pawns of European Powers at War

> I will let loose the dogs of hell,
> Ten thousand Indians who shall yell
> And foam and tear, and grin and roar,
> And drench their moccasins with gore:
> To those I'll give full scope and play
> From Ticonderoga to Florida. . . .

> Quoted in *Orderly Book of Lieut. Gen. John Burgoyne* [1777], ed. by E. B. O'Callaghan (Albany: J. Munsell, 1860), xxii.

Indian intertribal warfare was greatly aggravated by the coming of the white man. The increasing demands for furs by European traders caused

*strife between tribes over hunting grounds, and to this fact a recent writer
has attributed the aggressions of the Iroquois against their neighbors.*[1] *Still
more important were the incessant wars between European powers, during
which European nations encouraged tribes allied with them to attack tribes
allied with other powers, as well as settlements of the white enemy.
Commenting on the War of the Austrian Succession (1742), the English
historian Macaulay wrote:*

*On the head of Frederick is all the blood which was shed in a war which raged
during many years and in every quarter of the globe. . . . The evils produced
by his wickedness were felt in lands where the name of Prussia was unknown;
and in order that he might rob a neighbour whom he had promised to defend,
black men fought on the Coast of Coromandel, and red men scalped each other
by the Great Lakes of North America.*[2]

*Aside from the patriotic bias which led him to exempt his own govern-
ment from blame, Macaulay's remark aptly summarized the role of Indian
warriors as pawns of European intrigue. Indians were solicited as allies by
European powers, and by the United States, down to and through the War
of 1812. (See the Pinckney Treaty, Jay Treaty, and Treaty of Ghent,
herein.)*

*Whites also encouraged the spread of scalping by offering bounties for
the scalps of enemies, red or white. In 1764 the governor of Pennsylvania
offered as reward "for the scalp of every male Indian enemy above the age
of ten years, produced as evidence of their being killed, the sum of one
hundred and thirty-four pieces of eight. And for the scalp of every female
Indian enemy above the age of ten years, produced as evidence of their
being killed, the sum of fifty pieces of eight."*[3] *During the Revolutionary
War, Colonel Henry Hamilton, British commandant at Detroit, was known
as the "hair buyer," because he was charged with paying bounties for
American scalps.*[4]

*Lieutenant Governor Colden of New York related how Indians could be
more humane than whites in warfare. When the French and their Indian
allies attacked some Mohawk villages in the winter of 1693, wrote Colden,*

1. "The European trade was the major circumstance of all intertribal relations in
the Great Lakes area, and the Iroquois and all their works were phenomena of that
contact." George T. Hunt, *The Wars of the Iroquois* (Madison: University of Wisconsin Press, 1960), p. 161.

2. Quoted in Sir Charles Petrie, *Diplomatic History 1713–1933* (London: Hollis
& Carter Ltd., 1947), p. 36.

3. Francis Parkman, *The Conspiracy of Pontiac* (2 vols.; Boston: Little, Brown &
Co., 1922), II, 214–15.

4. James Alton James, "Indian Diplomacy and the Opening of the Revolution in
the West," *Proceedings of the State Historical Society of Wisconsin, 1909* (Madison:
1910), p. 141.

"the French designed to have put them all to the Sword, but their own Indians would not suffer it, and gave Quarter."[5]

In another instance, the Iroquois resisted English pleas that they attack their friendly Indian neighbors who were pro-French. At a treaty council in Albany in 1689, the Iroquois rejected this demand, asserting that *"we cannot declare War against the Eastern Indians, for they have done us no Harm; Nevertheless, our Brethren of New England may be assured, that we will live and die in friendship with them."*[6]

See also pp. 96–98.

Cash Rewards Offered for Indian Scalps

While scalping was not entirely unknown in aboriginal America, it was greatly extended by the whites' introduction of steel knives and their offer of bounties not only for the scalps of hostile Indians, but of European enemies.[1] *Scalping was unknown in New England until after the colonists offered rewards for the heads of enemies. It was soon found more convenient to bring in only the scalp rather than the entire head.*

Below is the text of a scalp bounty poster published in Massachusetts Bay, June 12, 1755. At that time, England and France were at war, with the tribes divided into allies of one or the other. The rewards offered here are for the scalps of Indians allied to the French.

By His Excellency
William Shirley, Esq.

Captain-General and Governor in Chief, in and over His Majesty's Province of *Massachusetts-Bay,* in *New-England,* and Vice-Admiral of the same, and Major-General in His Majesty's Army.

A PROCLAMATION

Whereas the Indians of *Norridgewock, Arresaguntacook, Weweenock* and *St. John's* Tribes, and the Indians of the other Tribes inhabiting in the Eastern and Northern Parts of His Majesty's Territories of *New-England,* the *Penobscot* Tribe only excepted, have, contrary to their solemn Submission unto His Majesty long since made and frequently renewed, been guilty of the most perfidious, barbarous and inhuman Murders of divers of his Majesty's *English* Subjects; and have abstained from all Commerce and Correspondence with His Majesty's said Subjects for many Months past;

5. Colden, *History of the Five Indian Nations* (2 vols.; New York: New Amsterdam Book Co., 1902), I, 182.
6. *Ibid.,* 124.

---

1. Georg Friederici, "The Business of Scalping," in Alain Locke and Bernhard Stern, *When Peoples Meet* (New York: Progressive Education Association, 1942), 165–70.

and the said *Indians* have fully discovered an inimical, traiterious and rebellious intention and Disposition; I have therefore thought fit to issue this Proclamation, and to Declare the Indians of the *Norridgewock, Arresaguntacook, Weweenock* and *St. John's* Tribes, and the Indians of the other Tribes now of late inhabiting in the Eastern and Northern Parts of His Majesty's Territories of *New-England,* and in Alliance and Confederacy with the above-recited Tribes, the *Penobscots* only excepted, to be Enemies, Rebels and Traitors to His Most Sacred Majesty: And I do hereby require His Majesty's subjects of this Province to embrace all Opportunities of pursuing, captivating, killing and destroying all and any of the aforesaid Indians, the *Penobscots* excepted.

And whereas the General Court of this Province have voted, That a Bounty or Encouragement be granted and allowed to be paid out of the Publick-Treasury to the marching Army that shall be employed for the Defence of the Eastern and Western Frontiers from the Twenty-fifth of this Month of *June* until the Twenty-fifth of *November* next;

I have thought fit to publish the same; and I do hereby promise, That there shall be paid out of the Province-Treasury to all and any of the said forces, over and above their Bounty upon Enlistment, their Wages and Subsistence, the Premiums or Bounties following, viz.

For every Male Indian Prisoner above the Age of Twelve Years, that shall be taken and brought to *Boston, Fifty Pounds.*

For every Male Indian Scalp, brought in as Evidence of their being killed, *Forty Pounds.*

For every Female Indian Prisoner, taken and brought in as aforesaid, and for every Male Indian Prisoner under the Age of Twelve Years, taken and brought in as aforesaid, *Twenty-five Pounds.*

For every Scalp of such Female Indian or Male Indian under Twelve Years of Age, brought as Evidence of their being killed, as aforesaid, Twenty Pounds.

Given under my Hand at *Boston,* in the Province aforesaid, this Twelfth Day of June, 1755 [*etc.*]

By His Excellency's Command

J. Willard, Secr'y.

W. Shirley

GOD SAVE THE KING

From a facsimile reproduction of the Pioneer Historical Society.

◈

23   Indian Captivities: 1696–1764

Indian captivity stories form an important part of our early national literature, and generations were brought up on tales of savage cruelty to white captives. These stories were not all myth, yet there is another side to it. For example, the torture of Colonel William Crawford in 1782 was in retaliation for the massacre of nearly a hundred Christian Delaware Indians at the Moravian mission of Gnadenhütten (Ohio) by Kentucky militia. However, many captives were adopted into Indian tribes and grew so attached to the Indian way of life that they could not be persuaded to leave it when the opportunity was offered. The following documents tell of such cases.

Iroquois and Canadian Tribes: 1696

Following the Peace of Ryswick in 1696, which brought an end to King William's War, an exchange of prisoners was agreed upon. Cadwallader Colden, a physician, writer, botanist, and public official, here relates the difficulty in repatriating French prisoners held by the Indians.

. . . Notwithstanding the French Commissioners took all the Pains possible to carry Home the French, that were Prisoners of the Five Nations, and they had full Liberty from the Indians, few of them could be persuaded to return. It may be thought that this was occasioned from the Hardships they had endured in their own Country, under a tyrannical Government and a barren Soil: But this certainly was not the only Reason; for the English had as much difficulty to persuade the People, that had been taken Prisoners by the French Indians, to leave the Indian Manner of living, though no People enjoy more Liberty, and live in greater Plenty, than the common Inhabitants of New-York do. No Arguments, no Intreaties, nor Tears of their Friends and Relations, could persuade many of them to leave their new Indian Friends and Acquaintances; several of them that were by the Caressings of their Relations persuaded to come Home, in a little Time grew tired of our Manner of living, and run away again to the Indians, and ended their Days with them. On the other Hand, Indian Children have been carefully educated among the English, cloathed and taught, yet, I think, there is not one Instance, that any of these, after they had Liberty to go among their own People, and were come to Age, would remain with the English, but returned to their own Nations, and became as fond of the Indian Manner of Life as those that knew nothing of a civilized manner of living. What I now tell of Christian Prisoners among Indians, relates not only to what happened at the Conclusions of this War, but has been found true on many other Occasions.

CADWALLADER COLDEN, *The History of the Five Indian Nations of Canada* (2 vols.; New York: New Amsterdam Book Co., 1902), I, 263–64.

Ohio Tribes: 1764

The following document illustrates how Indians became attached to their white captives. After Bouquet's expedition against the Ohio Indians during Pontiac's rebellion, the Indians were reluctant to give up their white captives, and the captives were unwilling to leave them.

. . . They delivered up their beloved captives with the utmost reluctance; shed torrents of tears over them, recommending them to the care and protection of the commanding officer. Their regard to them continued all the time they remained in camp. They visited them from day to day; and brought them what corn, skins, horses and other matters, they had bestowed on them, while in their families; accompanied with other presents, and all the marks of the most sincere and tender affection. Nay, they did not stop there, but, when the army marched, some of the Indians sollicited [*sic*] and obtained leave to accompany their former captives all the way to Fort-Pitt, and employed themselves in hunting and bringing provisions for them on the road. A young Mingo carried this still further, and gave an instance of love which would make a figure even in romance. A young woman of Virginia was among the captives, to whom he had form'd so strong an attachment, as to call her his wife. Against all remonstrances of the imminent danger to which he exposed himself by approaching the frontiers, he persisted in following her, at the risk of being killed by the surviving relations of many unfortunate persons, who had been captivated or scalped by those of his nation. . . .

Among the children who had been carried off young, and had long lived with the Indians, it is not to be expected that any marks of joy would appear on being restored to their parents or relatives. Having been accustomed to look upon the Indians as the only connexions they had, having been tenderly treated by them, and speaking their language, it is no wonder that they considered their new state in the light of captivity, and parted from the savages with tears.

But it must not be denied that there were even some grown persons who shewed an unwillingness to return. The Shawanese were obliged to bind several of their prisoners and force them along to the camp; and some women, who had been delivered up, afterwards found means to escape and run back to the Indian towns. Some, who could not make their escape, clung to their savage acquaintance at parting, and continued many days in bitter lamentations, even refusing sustenance.

> WILLIAM SMITH, *An Historical Account of an Expedition Against the Ohio Indians, in the Year 1764, Under the Command of Henry Bouquet, Esq.* . . . (Ann Arbor: University Microfilms, 1966), pp. 27–29.

24 Royal Proclamation of King George Closing the West to White Settlement, 1763

Following the end of fighting in the French and Indian War, the Indians who had been allied with the French grew increasingly restive under British rule. The British apparently incensed the Indians with their less liberal credit policies in the Indian trade, their reluctance to issue ammunition, and their parsimony in distributing gifts. However, these grievances may have been only the surface manifestations of deeper discontent caused by the British assumption that they were entitled to occupy the land without the consent of the Indians.[1] In May 1763, a confederation of tribes headed by the Ottawa chief Pontiac launched a coordinated attack on all British-manned frontier forts, and captured eight of them in a few days. Only Fort Pitt and Detroit eluded capture, though the last named was besieged for five months. It was during this war that General Jeffrey Amherst proposed to spread smallpox among the Indians via disease-laden blankets. The Indians continued to prevent occupation of the Mississippi forts, still in French possession, until 1765. Not until July 24, 1766, was a final peace concluded with the Indians.

On October 7, 1763, the king, at the behest of the Lords of Trade, issued a royal proclamation, an excerpt of which follows, closing to settlement all lands beyond the sources of the streams which flowed into the sea. It seems evident that the object of this move was to placate the Indians by removing fears of white intrusion. The enforcement of the proclamation was one of the functions of the standing army which was henceforth stationed in America. Colonial resentment against the closure of the frontier, the permanent military force, and the taxes levied for its support were among the grievances which led to the Revolutionary War.

See also p. 57.

1. On the war and its causes, see Francis Parkman, *The Conspiracy of Pontiac* (2 vols.; Boston: Little, Brown & Co., 1922), and Howard Peckham, *Pontiac and the Indian Uprising* (Princeton: Princeton University Press, 1961).

Royal Proclamation Concerning America, October 7, 1763

. . . And whereas it is just and reasonable, and essential to our interest, and the security of our colonies, that the several nations or tribes of Indians, with whom we are connected, and who live under our protection, should not be molested or disturbed in the possession of such parts of our dominions and territories as, not having been ceded to, or purchased by us, are reserved to them, or any of them, as their hunting grounds; we do . . . declare it to be our royal will and pleasure, that no governor, or commander in chief, in any of our colonies of Quebec, East Florida, or West Florida, do presume, under any pretence whatever, to grant warrants of survey, or pass any patents for lands beyond the bounds of their respective governments, as described in their commissions; as also that no governor or commander in chief of our other colonies or plantations in America, do presume for the present, and until our further pleasure be known, to grant warrant of survey, or pass patents for any lands beyond the heads or sources of any of the rivers which fall into the Atlantic Ocean from the west or north-west; or upon any lands whatever, which not having been ceded to, or purchased by us, as aforesaid, are reserved to the said Indians, or any of them.

And we do further declare it to be our royal will and pleasure, for the present, as aforesaid, to reserve under our sovereignty, protection, and dominion, for the use of the said Indians, all the land and territories not included within the limits of our said three new governments, or within the limits of the territory granted to the Hudson's Bay Company; as also all the land and territories lying to the westward of the sources of the rivers which fall into the sea from the west and north-west as aforesaid. . . .

[*Summary of remainder: Persons who have inadvertently settled upon such reserved lands to remove. No sale of Indian lands to be allowed, except to the crown. The Indian trade to be free to English subjects, under license from the governor or commander in chief of some colony. Fugitives from justice, taking refuge in this reserved territory, to be apprehended and returned.*]

HENRY S. COMMAGER, *Documents of American History* (New York: Appleton-Century-Crofts, 1968), pp. 47–50.

Comment on Royal Proclamation of 1763

The Proclamation of 1763 was a document of importance in Indian history because it added a king's stature to the Indian assertion of sovereignty. It was even more important as a validation of a long forming tradition—of paying for what was coveted or taken.

D'ARCY MCNICKLE, *They Came Here First* (Philadelphia: J. B. Lippincott Co., 1949), p. 299.

25   George Washington's Search for Indian Lands, 1767

As president, Washington in several messages attacked the illegal intrusions on Indian lands as a source of much trouble and expense to the government in putting down Indian uprisings caused by such usurpations.[1] Earlier, however, he was not above obtaining for himself some lands reserved to the Indians by the Royal Proclamation of 1763. The following letter instructs his friend William Crawford (who was later to be tortured to death by Indians during the Revolution) to survey and file claims in Washington's behalf at the Carlisle land office, to two thousand acres of "good rich land" in western Pennsylvania, and other tracts along the Ohio.

Sept. 21, 1767

. . . Could such a piece of land as this be found, you would do me a singular favor in falling upon some method to secure it immediately from the attempts of any other, as nothing is more certain that the lands cannot remain long ungranted, when once it is known that rights are to be had for them. . . .

The other matter, just now hinted at and which I proposed in my last to join you, in attempting to secure some of the most valuable lands in the King's part, which I think may be accomplished after a while, notwithstanding the proclamation that restrains it at present, and prohibits the settling of them at all; for I can never look upon that proclamation in any other light (but this I say between ourselves), than as a temporary expedient to quiet the minds of the Indians, and must fall, of course, in a few years, especially when those Indians are consenting to our occupying the lands. Any person, therefore, who neglects the present opportunity of hunting out good lands, and in some measure marking and distinguishing them for his own (in order to keep others from settling them), will never regain it. . . . For my own part, I should have no objection to a grant of land upon the Ohio, a good way below Pittsburg, but would willingly secure some good tracts nearer hand first.

WORTHINGTON C. FORD, ed., *The Writings of George Washington* (14 vols.; New York: G. P. Putnam's Sons, 1889), II, 218–24.

1. See pp. 74–77.

26   Indian Oratory: The Speech of Chief Logan, 1774

THOMAS JEFFERSON

There is a popular image of the Indian as a taciturn creature capable only of emitting an occasional "ugh!" There is also a false notion that Indian languages are devoid of terms for anything other than the most ordinary material objects. Historical literature, however, is filled with allusions to the eloquence of Indian orators, and preserved transcriptions of their speeches reveal not only a capacity for abstraction, but also a penchant for metaphor and poetic imagery.[1] Much of this oratory is preserved in the journals of treaty councils,[2] and one writer who stumbled onto it exulted:

I wish that some teacher of history had poured for me this strong wine instead of the tea from Boston Harbor with which the genuine thirst of my youth was unsufficiently slaked, or that some teacher of literature had given me to read these vivid, picturesque records instead of saying that the colonial period had nothing to show of literary production except dull sermons, political tracts, prosy essays, and poems of invincible mediocrity.[3]

One of the notable speeches of the eighteenth century is that of the Mingo chief Logan, whose entire family was murdered by whites, triggering Lord Dunmore's war in 1774. The speech was published both in America and abroad, where it was recorded by the French encyclopedist Diderot and, later, was mistakenly attributed to him.[4] The speech was also reprinted in several editions of McGuffey's Reader during the nineteenth century, but the greatest impetus to its fame was its publication by Thomas Jefferson in his Notes on Virginia. *Jefferson defended its authenticity against the challenge of those who questioned the intellectual capacity of Indians. In his own addresses to Indians as president, Jefferson seems to have imitated their oratorical flourishes.[5]*

1. See Louis Thomas Jones, *Aboriginal American Oratory: The Tradition of Eloquence Among the Indians of the United States* (Los Angeles: Southwest Museum, 1965).

2. *E.g.*, see Cadwallader Colden, *The History of the Five Indian Nations* (Ithaca: Cornell University Press, 1964), and Richard M. Dorson, ed., *America Begins* (New York: Pantheon, 1950), pp. 309–30.

3. Lawrence C. Wroth, "The Indian Treaty as Literature," *Yale Review*, XVII (July 1928), p. 766.

4. E. D. Seeber, "Diderot and Chief Logan's Speech," *Modern Language Notes*, LX (March 1945), pp. 176–78.

5. Anthony Hillbruner, "Word and Deed: Jefferson's Addresses to the Indians," *Speech Monographs*, XXX (November 1963), pp. 328–34.

Of their eminence in oratory we have fewer examples, because it is displayed chiefly in their own councils. Some, however, we have of very superior lustre. I may challenge the whole orations of Demosthenes and Cicero, and of any more eminent orator, if Europe has furnished more eminent, to produce a single passage, superior to the speech of Logan, a Mingo chief, to Lord Dunmore, when governor of this state. And, as testimony of their talents in this line, I beg leave to introduce it, first stating the incidents necessary for understanding it. In the spring of the year 1774, a robbery was committed by some Indians on certain land-adventurers on the river Ohio. The whites in that quarter, according to their custom, undertook to punish this outrage in a summary way. Captain Michael Cresap, and a certain Daniel Great-house, leading on these parties, sur-prized, at different times, travelling and hunting parties of the Indians, having their women and children with them, and murdered many. Among these were unfortunately the family of Logan, a chief celebrated in peace and war, and long distinguished as the friend of the whites. This unworthy return provoked his vengeance. He accordingly signalized himself in the war which ensued. In the autumn of the same year a decisive battle was fought at the mouth of the Great Kanhaway [*Kanawha*], between the collected forces of the Shawanese, Mingoes, and Delawares, and a detach-ment of the Virginia militia. The Indians were defeated, and sued for peace. Logan however disdained to be seen among the suppliants. But, lest the sincerity of the treaty should be distrusted, from which so distinguished a chief absented himself, he sent by a messenger the following speech to be delivered to Lord Dunmore.

"I appeal to any white man to say, if ever he entered Logan's cabin hungry, and he gave him not meat; if ever he came cold and naked, and he clothed him not. During the course of the last long and bloody war, Logan remained idle in his cabin, an advocate for peace. Such was my love for the whites, that my countrymen pointed as they passed, and said, 'Logan is the friend of the white men.' I had even thought to have lived with you, but for the injuries of one man. Col. Cresap, the last spring, in cold blood, and unprovoked, murdered all the relations of Logan, not sparing even my women and children. There runs not a drop of my blood in the veins of any living creature. This called on me for revenge. I have sought it: I have killed many: I have fully glutted my vengeance. For my country, I rejoice at the beams of peace. But do not harbour a thought that mine is the joy of fear. Logan never felt fear. He will not turn on his heel to save his life. Who is there to mourn for Logan?—Not one."

THOMAS JEFFERSON, *Notes on the State of Virginia,* ed. by William Peden (Chapel Hill: University of North Carolina Press, 1955), pp. 62–63.

III

FROM THE REVOLUTIONARY WAR
TO THE CIVIL WAR
1775–1861

Introduction

The outbreak of the Revolutionary War in 1775 left the colonies without the protection of the mother country against the Indians. Moreover, the recent protector turned to the task of inciting the Indians to war against the colonists. The Indians rightly supposed that they had more to fear from the land-hungry colonists than from a distant power.

While the Indians were aligned mainly on the side of the British, the first efforts to ally them to either side were probably made by the provincial Congress of Massachusetts. Early in April 1775, this body sent an address to the Stockbridge Indians, a Mohican remnant. They also sent a letter to Reverend Samuel Kirkland, a missionary to the Oneidas, instructing him to attach the Six Nations to the American cause, and if this proved impossible, to persuade them to remain neutral. Overtures were also made to the Penobscot and St. Francis (Abenaki) Indians. The British appointed an Indian superintendent for Nova Scotia to offset the influence of Massachusetts among these tribes.[1]

Massachusetts had well-laid plans to win the Six Nations from the influence of Guy Johnson, nephew and successor to Sir William Johnson, the crown's Indian agent for the northern colonies, who died the previous year. A delegation of Stockbridges, already attached to the colonial cause, was sent to the Mohawks. The Oneidas and Onondagas, it was hoped, would be won over by the missionaries, Kirkland and Crosby. Joseph Brant, noted Mohawk warrior, was to be approached by Dr. Eleazar Wheelock, whose Indian school (now Dartmouth College) he had attended, and for whom he had considerable respect. All of these overtures, however, save that to the Oneidas, were failures. One writer concludes that

1. Walter H. Mohr, *Federal Indian Relations 1774–1788* (Philadelphia: the author, 1933), p. 29.

"here, as elsewhere, encroachments were a prominent factor in making the Indians decide in favor of Great Britain."[2]

The provincial Congress of New York on June 7, 1775, wrote to the delegates of that colony to the Continental Congress:

The importance and the necessity of attention to Indian affairs is more endangered by the situation of the barbarians to the westward of us, than it can be by any inroads made upon the seacoast. Britain will spare the last for her own sake, and policy will teach her ministers to light upon an Indian war upon our frontier, that we may be drawn for protection to embrace the terms of slavery.

The following year, on May 1, the Virginia convention passed a resolution to enlist Indians up to two hundred for the assistance of the regular army. The neighboring Indians were assured that if any persons were encroaching upon their lands such individuals would be removed by the state.

On July 12, 1775, Congress resolved to establish three Indian departments, northern, middle, and southern. The commissioners for each were directed to obtain the assistance of men of influence among the Indians, seek alliances with the Indians if the British should use Indians against the colonies, arrest British agents who stirred up the Indians, and report to Congress on their financial affairs and Indian affairs in general. The northern department was to support Canadian Indian students at Eleazar Wheelock's school since these were mainly loyal to the American cause.[3]

Franklin's plan for the articles of confederation on July 17 proposed a defensive and offensive alliance with the Six Nations, and also forbade any colony to engage in offensive warfare against any nation of Indians without the consent of Congress.[4]

Washington was authorized to employ in Canada Indians up to two thousand in number, and Indian commissioners were directed to find ways to carry out the plan. Later Washington was directed to employ Indians wherever he found it necessary. That summer he enlisted some Stockbridge and St. John (Malecite) Indians, against the advice of General Schuyler. The latter, however, reversed himself and employed several hundred Oneidas and Tuscaroras against Burgoyne.

The general policy of the Congress at the outset was to endeavor to secure Indian neutrality, as that was the most that could generally be hoped for. In an address prepared for the Six Nations on July 13, 1775, Congress

2. Mohr, *op. cit.*, p. 29.
3. *Journals of the American Congress, from 1774 to 1788* (4 vols.; Washington: Way & Gideon, 1823), I, 112–14.
4. *Secret Journals of the Acts and Proceedings of Congress* (Boston: Thomas B. Wait, 1821), I, 281. The articles in final form eliminated these provisions.

tried to explain the causes of the quarrel with the king, and closed with an appeal for the Indians to stand aloof:

This is a family quarrel between us and Old England. You Indians are not concerned in it. We don't wish you to take up the hatchet against the king's troops. We desire you to remain at home, and not join on either side, but keep the hatchet buried deep.[5]

Later, however, on May 25, 1776, Congress resolved that "it is highly expedient to engage the Indians in the service of the United Colonies."[6] On March 7, 1778, Colonel Nathaniel Gist was authorized to engage two hundred Indians on the frontier of Virginia and the Carolinas, and to supply them with goods.

However, during the entire period of the war, the United States succeeded in arranging only one treaty of alliance with an Indian tribe, that with the Delawares at Fort Pitt, September 17, 1778. In this document the two parties mutually forgave each other for past wrongs, promised perpetual peace and friendship, "each party to aid the other in just and necessary wars," and free passage through Delaware territory for American troops, with the Indians agreeing to furnish supplies and warriors to reduce the British posts. The United States was permitted to erect a fort "for the protection of the Indians." Neither side was to inflict punishment for offenses without trial, or to protect criminal fugitives. Trading agents were to be appointed by the United States. Lastly, the Indians were offered eventual statehood with representation in Congress, should they desire it.[7]

The treaty lasted only a year, however. Unable to furnish the Indians with sufficient goods, and powerless to prevent frontier settlers from murdering Indians, or to offset British threats, Congress lost this potential ally. Certain tribes and bands, however, particularly the Oneidas, gave assistance to the United States. Some treaties were also arranged with Indians by state governments.

The details of the military engagements in which Indians were involved are well treated elsewhere. (See Mohr, *op. cit.*) Indians and Loyalists in 1777 carried out the Wyoming (Pa.) "massacre," which was punished in the next year by Sullivan's expedition which destroyed many Iroquois villages. Senecas in St. Leger's British army in the Mohawk valley deserted at a critical time, thus causing his eventual defeat. Hundreds of Indians were

5. *Journals of Congress*, I, 114–17. It was ordered that a similar talk be prepared for the other Indian nations.

6. *Secret Journals*, I, 44.

7. Charles J. Kappler, ed., *Indian Affairs, Laws and Treaties* (5 vols.; Washington: Government Printing Office, 1903–1941), II, 3–5.

in Burgoyne's army which was captured at Saratoga, as well as in the colonial army which defeated him. The Shawnees raided the Kentucky settlements, but Clark's invasion of the Northwest brought neutralization of many tribes in that region, some of whom participated in Hamilton's march to Vincennes, where Clark massacred a group of Indians who were not involved. The Southern tribes, especially Creeks and Cherokees, were active for the British in a number of engagements, but the Catawbas aided the Americans.

The causes of the American failure with the Indians at this time were (1) the Indians' conviction that the Americans represented the greatest threat to their lands, and (2) inability of the Americans to win their allegiance by supplying them with goods to match those of the British. In the West, *i.e.,* the Ohio valley, which was the focal point of the advancing frontier, a third cause was the atrocities committed against the Indians.

While some British officers, such as Burgoyne, discounted the effectiveness of Indians in warfare, Governor Hamilton wrote in his journal:

The Indians support the fatigues of rapid marches and will go a round trot of between four and five miles an hour for a long summers day without halting for refreshment which gives them a vast advantage over the whites, even the best Woodmen.[8]

The Indians in the active service of the American armies were too few to be of any great military importance. They served principally as scouts and guides. The Indian methods of fighting, however, such as ambuscade, camouflage, fighting from cover, and guerrilla tactics, were adopted by the Americans and proved superior to European field methods.

The effect of the Indians as a diversionary factor was very great. Washington in 1780 was compelled to detach some regiments of his army to reinforce Fort Pitt and later was "compelled to postpone all major operations in the east" so that a detachment of his army could join Sullivan's punitive expedition against the Six Nations.[9]

The fact that Indian troubles continued in many places after the Revolution indicates that their attitude was shaped by real grievances rather than by British machinations, and that their role in the war was really only one chapter in a long war for survival and possession of their country.

The measure of British defeat is seen in the fact that no provision for her Indian allies was made in the peace treaty, in contrast to what was done in the Treaty of Ghent thirty-one years later. The Six Nations, however, were

8. John D. Barnhart, ed., *Henry Hamilton and George Rogers Clark in the American Revolution, with the Unpublished Journal of Lieut. Gov. Henry Hamilton* (Crawfordsville, Ind.: R. E. Banta, 1951), p. 123.

9. Mohr, *op. cit.,* p. 89.

given a reservation on Grand River, Upper Canada (Ontario), to which some of the New York Indians, particularly Mohawks, migrated.

The British continued for some years to remain in possession of frontier posts around the Great Lakes, from which they exchanged English goods, including firearms, for Indian furs. The Spanish on the Gulf carried on a similar trade with the Southern Indians, and with the trade in both instances, there is evidence that some political maneuvering was involved. But while these powers sought to maintain their economic and political influence with the Indians, there is no convincing proof that they sought to induce the red men to war on the new republic.[10]

The wars in the Ohio country near the end of the century were the direct result of white intrusion on Indian lands. When Marietta was established at the mouth of the Muskingum in 1788, Fort Harmar was built nearby for the ostensible purpose of restraining the further advance of settlement. But this was only a temporary measure, and it was soon resolved to push the Indians back. The Shawnees of Ohio allied with the Miamis, Wyandots, Potawatomis, Ottawas, and other tribes to keep settlements below and east of the Ohio. After a series of unsuccessful expeditions culminating in the disastrous rout of General Arthur St. Clair by Little Turtle, a Miami chief, Washington at last found Anthony Wayne, who was able, with some Indian allies, to subdue the Indians, now led by the Shawnee warrior, Blue Jacket, at Fallen Timbers, near Toledo. The British at Fort Mims denied refuge to the fleeing Indians. The following year, in 1795, the Indians signed the Treaty of Greenville, which pushed them north of a line crossing north-central Ohio, and secured sites for posts and forts in widely scattered places, including Chicago, with the right of access thereto.

Successive white advances and additional Indian land cessions which followed convinced the indomitable Shawnee, Tecumseh, and his brother, the prophet Tenskitawa, that a confederation of all the tribes was a prime necessity for their preservation. With great skill Tecumseh forged such an alliance, reaching most tribes between the Appalachians and the Mississippi, but its aim was peace, not war. Tecumseh hoped to hold his own by adopting agriculture and raising livestock. But the aggressive governor of Indiana Territory, William H. Harrison, in the fall of 1811 marched on the village of Prophetstown near the junction of the Tippecanoe and Wabash rivers. The Indians first asked for a parley, then attacked early on the morning of November 7. There was no decisive victory for either side, but the Indians withdrew in the face of superior numbers, and their village, grain, and livestock were destroyed. Tecumseh had been absent in the

10. Annie Heloise Abel, "The History of Events Resulting in Indian Consolidation West of the Mississippi River," *Annual Report of the American Historical Association for the Year 1906* (Washington: 1908), I, 260–61.

south at the time, but upon his return he endeavored to restore peace. Within a few months, however, the American war-hawks, with their lurid tales of British-inspired savage attacks, had induced Congress to declare war upon Great Britain.

The sympathies of all the northern tribes were with Britain, a fact in no small way related to the aggressive behavior of the Americans toward the Indians in the preceding period. Tecumseh took a leading role in the war, and legend holds that the British gave him a brigadier general's uniform and commission. Black Hawk of the Sauks came east from Rock Island to join the struggle. The great Shawnee leader was killed at the battle of the Thames in 1813, and Colonel Richard M. Johnson of Kentucky boasted of firing the fatal shot when he bid for the vice-presidency in 1836. The Potawatomi forced the abandonment of Fort Dearborn at the mouth of the Onion (Chicago) River and engaged the retreating soldiers and settlers in battle. Jackson campaigned against the Creeks in Alabama, and slaughtered hundreds of them at Horseshoe Bend. When he fought the battle of New Orleans, however, hundreds of friendly Choctaws aligned themselves with LaFitte's pirates and other strange components of Jackson's motley army.

At the peace conference in Ghent, Belgium, Britain sought to reward its red allies and also to save the fur trade and protect Canada from future invasion by demanding that the Americans evacuate the territory north of the Ohio, which was to be erected as an Indian buffer state. Determined resistance to this demand by the delegation headed by John Q. Adams secured a treaty with no land cessions. Great Britain did insist, however, upon a clause requiring the United States to sign a separate treaty with each of the hostile Indian tribes, and that the Indians should not be punished for their participation in the war. To this the Americans yielded.

The nation was again free to deal with the Indians. Jefferson had early envisaged plans for their voluntary removal to the unsettled portions of the Louisiana Territory, but little was done about Indian removal until Jackson came to power. This was largely due to the fact that Presidents Monroe and Adams were unwilling to use military force to remove tribes which stubbornly clung to their homelands.

The most insistent pressure for removal of the Creeks and Cherokees in the South came from Georgia, which had surrendered her western land claims to the nation in 1802 in return for a compact by which the general government promised to extinguish the Indian land title "peaceably and on reasonable conditions." This could not legitimately be done without persuading the Cherokee to surrender their rights under the Hopewell Treaty of 1785. Before the disaster of Jackson's removal policy, a series of treaties involving land cessions were made with all tribes, north and south, but nearly all the tribes continued to occupy reduced portions of their ancestral lands until Old Hickory took office in 1829.

Jackson took the position that if the state of Georgia chose to extend her laws over the Indians residing within her borders, to dissolve the Indian governments established there, and to expel the Indians, this was a legitimate exercise of state sovereignty with which the general government could not legally interfere. The president, in all of his addresses on the subject, took no cognizance of the government's treaties with the Indian tribes which ran counter to these claims, nor paid any heed to the constitutional dictum that treaties ranked as part of the supreme law of the land, taking precedence over federal and state law. Strangely, and in a contradictory manner, he threatened to use all of the power of the federal government to compel the state of South Carolina to obey the federal tariff laws. It is clear from the writings and actions of President Jackson that his arguments were threadbare and that his Indian policy was an exercise in naked power motivated by no defensible principle.

In the removal bill he sponsored in 1830, the first step was made in appropriating funds for removal of the Indians west of the Mississippi River. A series of forced and fraudulent treaties followed, to give a fig leaf of legality to forcible exile, and in the next decade about 125,000 Indians were driven from the forest to the plains under military escort, and their progress toward "civilization" was abruptly set back. The grim work was accomplished peaceably, for the most part, since only a portion of the Sauks, Creeks, and Seminoles engaged in armed resistance; the war against the last-named raged in the Florida swamps for more than seven years. The Supreme Court under the aging John Marshall had handed down some decisions favorable to the highly civilized Cherokees, but Jackson was in no mood to permit his plans to be set at naught by legal formulas. Neither were the states, and the southern legislatures passed laws depriving Indians of civil rights in court.

With the exception of a few tribes and bands, most Indians from east of the Mississippi were located in Nebraska, Kansas, and Oklahoma by 1840. Left behind in isolated pockets were the Ojibwas and Ottawas of the far north, a few Cherokees in the Smoky Mountains, part of the New York Iroquois, a few Sauks and Foxes in Iowa, soon to be moved again. A small band of Miamis stayed in Indiana, a fragment of Seminoles still eluded the net in Florida, and a handful of Choctaws were left in Mississippi, without any legally recognized tribal organization.

In 1851 the government established its first official relations with the nomadic hunters of the Basin and Great Plains in the Laramie Treaty Council. The forty-niners had been traversing Indian soil, and the government wished to secure the unmolested passage of travelers. It also persuaded the tribes to renounce war upon one another, procured recognition of the guardianship of the Great White Father in Washington, and called for the appointment of a common chief for each tribe in order to facilitate dealing with the Father.

Meanwhile Indian affairs were taken from the War Department and placed in the hands of the Indian office of the newly created Department of the Interior. The army was still much involved with the Indians, however, for they manned the military posts astride the routes of travel. The rash arrogance of white soldiers on the plains and of settlers in the far West soon brought the first of a chain of outbreaks which were not to end until the last shot was fired in the Wounded Knee massacre of December 1890. But before the final struggle for the Plains could take place, another and different catastrophe was to intervene: the Civil War.

In the fifties the political stage was monopolized by the so-called irrepressible conflict between the slave-owning, agricultural South, and the populous, industrially mighty North. Nevertheless, behind all the dust and smoke of the impending conflict the Indian tragedy continued. The Oregon Treaty with Great Britain (1846) and the peace with Mexico (1848) added one and a quarter million square miles to the American territory. During the fifties the brutal repression of the Indians of the Pacific Northwest was practically completed. The California Indians were nearly exterminated; many miners shot them on sight.

Douglas's Kansas-Nebraska bill, which he had actually introduced ten years before its final passage in 1854, has been viewed by many as a victory for slave interests. Without passing judgment on that question, one can say that there is no doubt that it was a defeat for the Indians in that area, for it meant their dispossession in regions which had been solemnly guaranteed to them. Recent scholarship indicates that this was its principal purpose. Oklahoma, already the home of the Five Civilized Tribes of the Southeast, was soon to become a vast concentration camp into which Indians from tribes as far apart as the New York Senecas and the West Coast Modocs were to be squeezed.

When hostilities began at Charleston in April of 1861, the Five Civilized Tribes of Oklahoma (then Indian Territory) were split asunder, many of them being enlisted in the cause of the Confederacy. Some of the Sioux bands and other Plains Indians took advantage of the preoccupation of their masters to attempt a rollback of the frontier. This brought bloody punitive expeditions, the unholy massacre of peaceful Cheyennes at Sand Creek, and the mass hanging of Sioux in Minnesota.

A Seneca Indian, Grant's aide, Brigadier General Ely S. Parker, wrote the surrender terms at Appomattox. Eventually he was to become the first red man to head the Indian Bureau. No bright New Era was in store for the

Indians, however, for Manifest Destiny was in the air. The next quarter century saw the great agony of the Western Indians.

27   George Washington's Request for Assistance from the Passamaquoddy Indians, 1776

Although the Declaration of Independence charged that the king "has endeavored to bring on the inhabitants of our frontiers the merciless Indian savages," the first steps to enlist Indians in the fighting were taken by Massachusetts and by Congress in the early summer of 1775. They were unsuccessful in enlisting cooperation from most of the Six Nations, but did employ some Oneidas and Tuscaroras from the confederation, as well as some Stockbridges, Penobscots, and Catawbas. The British General Thomas Gage declared on June 12, 1775, that "we need not be tender of calling on the savages, as the rebels have shown us the example, by bringing as many Indians down against us here as they could collect."

In the following document General Washington urges the Passamaquoddy Indians of Maine to send him warriors, and warns them to beware of British agents, lest they be punished as the Cherokees were for taking up arms against the colonists.

Brothers of Passamaquodai

I am glad to hear by Major Shaw that you accepted the Chain of Friendship which I sent you last February from Cambridge. & that you are determined to keep it bright & unbroken. When I first heard that you Refused to send any of your Warriors to my Assistance when called upon by our Brother of St. Johns[1] I did not know what to think. I was afraid some enemy had turned your hearts against me. But I am since informed that all your young men were employed in Hunting which was the Reason of their not coming. This has made my mind easy. And I hope you will always in future join with your Brothers of St. Johns & Penobscott when Required———

I have desired my Brother the Governor of Massachusetts Bay to pay you the money which Capt Smith promised you for sending my Letters to the Micmack Indians—

Brothers

I have a piece of news to tell you which I hope you will attend to———

Our Enemy the King of Great Britain endeavoured to stirr up all the Indians from Canada to South Carolina Against Us. But our Brethren of

1. A messenger of the Malecite tribe, called St. John's Indians.

the Six nations and their Allies the Shawanese & Delawares would not hearken to the advice of the Messengers sent among them, but kept fast hold of our Covenant Chain; The Cherokees and the Southern Tribes were foolish enough to listen to them and to take up the hatchet against us. Upon this our Warriors went into their Country [&] burnt their Houses. destroyed their Corn and obliged them to sue for peace and give Hostages for their future good behaivour [*sic*].

Now Brothers never let the kings Wicked Councellor turn your Hearts against me and your Brethren of this country but bear in mind what I told you last February and what I told you now.———

In token of my Friendship I send you this from my Army on the Banks of the great River Delaware this 24th Day of December, 1776.

George Washington
A True Copy
Attest John Avery, Secty to John
Hancock

From a photocopy in Illinois State Historical Library, Springfield.

28 Patrick Henry's Condemnation of Backwoodsmen for inciting the Indians, 1778

Indian troubles in early times were more often caused by outrages committed by unruly frontiersmen than by any action or policy of government. When the authority of government in the thinly settled regions was weak, backwoodsmen were inclined to follow their own judgment in dealing with Indians, and frequently committed unprovoked murders. In the following letter Governor Patrick Henry of Virginia, having learned of the murder of the friendly chief Cornstalk and four other Shawnees by white men, deplores the turmoil created by their undisciplined behavior.

Having now done everything which I can foresee to be necessary for protecting the Frontiers, I must tell you Sir that I really blush for the occasion of this War with the Shawanese. I doubt not but you detest the vile assassins who have brought it on us at this critical Time when our whole Force was wanted in another Quarter. But why are they not brought to Justice? Shall this Precedent establish the Right of involving Virginia in War whenever any one in the back Country shall please? . . .

I desire it may be remembered, that if the frontier people will not submit to the Laws, but thus set them at Defiance, they will not be considered as entitled to the protection of the Government, and were it not for the miserable Condition of many with you, I should demand the Offenders previous to every other Step. For where is this wretched business to end? The Cherokees, the Delawares and every other Tribe may be set on us in this manner this Spring for what I know. Is not this the work of Tories? No Man but an Enemy of American Independence will do it, and thus oblige our People to be hunting after Indians in the Woods, instead of facing Genl Howe in the field, search into the Matter and depend upon it the Murderers are Tories. . . .

But they are Traytors I suspect and Agents for the Enemy, who have taken this method to find employment for the brave Back Woodsmen at home, and prevent their joining Genl Washington to strike a decisive stroke for Independence at this critical time.

> Letter to Colonel William Fleming, February 19, 1778, in Reuben G. Thwaites and Louise P. Kellogg, eds., *Frontier Defense on the Upper Ohio, 1777–1778* (Madison: State Historical Society of Wisconsin, 1912), pp. 207–8.

29   Documents of the Young Republic, 1775–1787

In these times when most Americans have seen Indians, if at all, only as participants in a circus or rodeo (which is where this writer saw his first Indians), it is easy to forget the important role that Indians once played in our national history. When this nation was in its infancy, however, the Indians could still constitute an enormous peril or a welcome asset. That the founding fathers were aware of this is attested in the following excerpts from notable public documents.

Declaration of the Causes and Necessity of Taking up Arms, July 6, 1775 (by the Congress)

We have received certain intelligence, that general Carelton [*Carleton*], the governor of Canada, is instigating the people of that province and the Indians to fall upon us; and we have but too much reason to apprehend, that schemes have been formed to excite domestic enemies against us.

Declaration of Independence, July 4, 1776

He [*the king*] has excited domestic insurrection amongst us, and has endeavoured to bring on the inhabitants of our frontiers, the merciless Indian Savages, whose known rule of warfare, is an undistinguished destruction of all ages, sexes and conditions.

Articles of Confederation, November 15, 1777

THE United States in Congress assembled shall also have the sole and exclusive right and power of . . . regulating the trade and managing all affairs with the Indians, not members of any of the States, providing that the legislative right of any State within its own limits be not infringed or violated . . .

Northwest Ordinance, July 13, 1787

Article III. . . . The utmost good faith shall always be observed towards the Indians; their lands and property shall never be taken from them without their consent; and in their property, rights, and liberty they never shall be invaded or disturbed, unless in just and lawful wars authorized by Congress; but laws founded in justice and humanity shall, from time to time, be made, for preventing wrongs being done to them, and for preserving peace and friendship with them.

Constitution of the United States, September 17, 1787

Article I, Section 8. The Congress shall have Power to . . . regulate Commerce with foreign Nations, and among the several States, and with the Indian Tribes . . .

30   Washington's Views on the Indian Problem

Washington's presidency was marked by violent struggles with the Indians in the Ohio country, while diplomacy and bribery were used to pacify the Indians in the Southeast. Though most general history texts ignore it, the greatest defeat ever inflicted on an American force by Indians occurred on November 3, 1791, when more than six hundred men in the command of General Arthur St. Clair were killed by Indians in western Ohio. All of Washington's eight annual messages contained reports and recommendations on the Indian problem. Some of his correspondence, however, is more revealing of his attitudes than are his formal state papers. He maintained that Indians were like wolves, "both being beasts of prey, tho' they differ in shape." For reasons of expediency, however, and the protection of the public treasury from the drain of costly wars, he held that it was wiser to secure Indian lands by purchase than by force. Despite his earlier activity as a land speculator,[1] he excoriated "land jobbers" whose activities incited

1. See p. 57.

the Indians to take up the hatchet. He was particularly concerned to avoid antagonizing the Six Nations of New York, and the Cherokees and Creeks of the South, which were relatively powerful and also subject to some influence from foreign powers. He was less patient with the Northwest tribes which he believed to be less civilized and less powerful.

Letter to James Duane, September 7, 1783

. . . To suffer a wide-extended Country to be overrun with Land Jobbers, speculators, and monopolizers, or even with scattered settlers, is in my opinion inconsistent with that wisdom and policy, which our true interest dictates, or that an enlightened people ought to adopt; and, be-sides, is pregnant with disputes both with the Savages and among ourselves, the evils of which are easier to be conceived than described. And for what, but to aggrandize a few avaricious men, to the prejudice of many and the embarrassment of Government? For the People engaged in these pursuits, without contributing in the smallest degree to the support of Government, or considering themselves as amenable to its Laws, will involve it, by their unrestrained conduct, in inextricable perplexities, and more than probably in a great deal of bloodshed. . . .

. . . it is my opinion, that, if the legislature of the State of New York should insist upon expelling the Six Nations from all the Country they Inhabited previous to the war, within their Territory, (as General Schuyler seems to be apprehensive of,) it will end in another Indian war, I have every reason to believe from my inquiries, and the information I have received, that they will not suffer their Country (if it were our policy to take it before we could settle it) to be wrested from them without another struggle. That they would compromise for a part of it, I have very little doubt; and that it would be the cheapest way of coming at it, I have no doubt at all. The same observations, I am persuaded, will hold good with respect to Virginia, or any other State, which has powerful tribes of Indians on their Frontiers; and the reason of my mentioning New York is because General Schuyler has expressed his opinion of the temper of its Legislature, and because I have been more in the way of learning the sentiments of the Six Nations than of any other Tribes of Indians on this Subject. . . .

. . . I am clear in my opinion, that policy and oeconomy point very strongly to the expediency of being upon good terms with the Indians, and the propriety of purchasing their lands in preference to attempting to drive them by force of arms out of their Country; which, as we have already experienced, is like driving the wild Beasts of ye forest, which will return as soon as the pursuit is at an end, and fall perhaps upon those that are left there; when the gradual extension of our settlements will as certainly cause the savage, as the wolf, to retire; both being beasts of prey, tho' they differ in shape. In a word, there is nothing to be obtained by an Indian war, but the soil they live on, and this can be had by purchase at less expense, and without that bloodshed and those distresses, which helpless women and children are made partakers of in all kinds of disputes with them. . . .

> Letter to James Duane, in Saul K. Padover, ed., *The Washington Papers* (New York: Harper & Bros., 1955), pp. 350, 352, 355.

Report of St. Clair's Defeat

United States, December 12, 1791

Gentlemen of the Senate and of the House of Representatives:

It is with great concern that I communicate to you the information received from Major-General St. Clair of the misfortune which has befallen the troops under his command.

Although the national loss is considerable according to the scale of the event, yet it may be repaired without great difficulty, excepting as to the brave men who have fallen on the occasion, and who are a subject of public as well as private regret.

A further communication will shortly be made of all such matters as shall be necessary to enable the Legislature to judge of the future measures which it may be proper to pursue.

G°. WASHINGTON

> JAMES D. RICHARDSON, ed., *A Compilation of the Messages and Papers of the Presidents* (10 vols.; Washington: Government Printing Office, 1896), I, 113.

In his fourth annual message Washington first proposed the appointment of Indian agents to live with the tribes, and a regulated trading system. From the latter idea emerged the government "factory" (trading house) system, which existed in competition with private traders from 1795 until 1822.

Excerpt from Fourth Annual Message, November 6, 1792

I can not dismiss the subject of Indian affairs without again recommending to your consideration the expediency of more adequate provision for giving energy to the laws throughout our interior frontier and for restraining the commission of outrages upon the Indians, without which all pacific plans must prove nugatory. To enable, by competent rewards, the employment of qualified and trusty persons to reside among them as agents would also contribute to the preservation of peace and good neighborhood. If in addition to these expedients an eligible plan could be devised for promoting civilization among the friendly tribes and for carrying on trade with them upon a scale equal to their wants and under regulations calculated to protect them from imposition and extortion, its influence in cementing their interest with ours could not but be considerable.

RICHARDSON, op. cit., p. 127.

31   Indians in Early American Diplomacy

From the first settlement until the end of the War of 1812, eastern Indians were a factor in the international relations of the United States. From 1848 until late in the nineteenth century, Southwest Indians figured in several treaties with Mexico.

The Jay Treaty with England, November 19, 1794, was arranged to settle several outstanding differences with Great Britain, and in return for such concessions as abandonment of the frontier forts which British troops continued to occupy in violation of the Peace of Paris, the British exacted some concessions. Two of these involved the Indians. First, it was agreed that Indians on both sides of the border were free to pass back and forth across the U.S.–Canadian border without impediment; the other was that no duty should be levied by either side on normal goods, including peltry, transported across the border by Indians.[1] The reason for these provisions was that Canada wanted U.S. Indians to continue to bring furs to Canadian posts, and to purchase goods there.

The Pinckney Treaty with Spain, October 27, 1795, had a different purpose. Indians in the Spanish Floridas made raids north of the border, and the location of the border itself was in dispute. Moreover, Spanish agents were engaged in intrigues to maintain commercial and political influence with tribes, particularly the Creeks, which lived in territory acknowledged to belong to the United States. The treaty pledged both sides to restrain warfare by their Indians in the territory of the other, and forbade treaties of alliance or any other treaty by either nation with Indians living in the territory of the other. The provisions were entirely to the benefit of the United States, despite the diplomatic pretense of equality in the terms.

Jay's Treaty with Great Britain, November 19, 1794

ARTICLE III. It is agreed that it shall at all times be free to his Majesty's subjects, and to the citizens of the United States, and also to the Indians dwelling on either side of the said boundary line, freely to pass and

1. See pp. 226–27.

repass by land or inland navigation, into the respective territories and countries of the two parties, on the continent of America. . . .

No duty of entry shall ever be levied by either party on peltries brought by land, or inland navigation into the said territories respectively, nor shall the Indians passing or repassing with their own proper goods and effects of whatever nature, pay for the same any impost or duty whatever. But goods in bales, or other large packages, unusual among Indians, shall not be considered as goods belonging bona fide to Indians.

A Recent Controversy Involving the Jay Treaty

INDIAN CHIEFS FIGHT CANADIAN DUTY ON GOODS

Montreal, Sept. 23 [1954] (AP) Eighty Canadian Indian chiefs have decided they will beat a warpath to Canada's Supreme Court to fight a ruling that they must pay duty on goods brought in from the United States.

They said the ruling violated an old United States–British treaty [*Jay Treaty*] permitting the Indians to transport and trade goods freely across the border.

The Canadian government argues that the treaty was terminated by the War of 1812.[1] (*Chicago Tribune,* September 24, 1954)

Indians and the Pinckney Treaty with Spain, October 27, 1795

Article V. The two high contracting parties shall, by all the means in their power, maintain peace and harmony among the several Indian nations who inhabit the country adjacent to the lines and rivers, which, by the preceding articles, form the boundaries of the two Floridas. And the bet-[t]er to obtain this effect, both parties oblige themselves expressly to restrain by force all hostilities on the part of the Indian nations living within their boundaries: so that Spain will not suffer her Indians to attack the citizens of the United States, nor the Indians inhabiting their territory; nor will the United States permit these last mentioned Indians to commence hostilities against the subjects of His Catholic Majesty or his Indians, in any manner whatever.

And whereas several treaties of friendship exist between the two contracting parties and the said nations of Indians, it is hereby agreed that in future no treaty of alliance, or other whatever, (except treaties of peace,) shall be made by either party with the Indians living within the boundary of the other, but both parties will endeavour to make the advantages of the

1. Article IX of the Treaty of Ghent (see herein) restored the *status quo ante bellum* so far as Indians were concerned. Both parties agreed to restore to their Indian tribes "all the possessions, rights and privileges which they may have enjoyed or been entitled to" previous to the beginning of hostilities.

Indian trade commonly and mutual[l]y beneficial to their respective subjects and citizens, observing in all things the most complete reciprocity; so that both parties may obtain the advantages arising from a good understanding with the said nations, without being subject to the expence which they have hitherto occasioned.

> "Treaty of Friendship, Boundaries, Commerce, and Navigation," Ocober 27, 1795, proclaimed August 2, 1796; signed by Thomas Pinckney for the United States, and El Principe de la Paz for Spain. William Malloy, compiler, *Treaties, Conventions* [etc.] (2 vols.; Washington: Government Printing Office, 1910), II, 1642.

Indians and the Peace Negotiations at Ghent, 1814

JOHN QUINCY ADAMS

The British negotiators at Ghent looked out for their Indian allies of the War of 1812 in a way that they had been unable to do after the Revolution. While self-interest was the motive, it was nevertheless a unique experience for the Indians to have a great power demanding that a huge buffer state be set up for their occupancy, reaching from the Great Lakes to the Ohio River. The American position was that the Indians were mere subjects of the United States, and their status was not negotiable with foreign powers. The British maintained that the United States had acknowledged the sovereign status of Indian tribes by making treaties with them. The stubborn resistance of the American negotiators, headed by John Quincy Adams, stalled the negotiations for months, and the British finally yielded the point. They did succeed, however, in placing in the treaty a proviso that the United States must sign separate treaties with each Indian tribe allied with Great Britain, and that the terms of these treaties should restore the status quo as of 1811, i.e., no land cessions. The following letter describing the buffer state controversy was written by Adams to Secretary of State James Monroe on September 5, 1814. It is not only important for the light it sheds on the treaty negotiations, but for the exposition of the American attitude on Indian occupancy rights.

The great argument to which he [*Mr. Goulborn*] continually recurred in support of the Indian boundary and the exclusive military possession of the Lakes by the British, was the necessity of them for the security of Canada. The American government, he said, had manifested the intention and the determination of conquering Canada. . . . In order, however, to guard against the same thing in future it is necessary to make a barrier against the American settlements, upon which neither party shall be permitted to encroach. The Indians are but a secondary object. As the allies of Great

Britain she must include them in the peace, as in making peace with other powers she included Portugal as her ally. But when the boundary is once defined it is immaterial whether the Indians are upon it or not. Let it be a desert. But we shall know that you cannot come upon us to attack us, without crossing it. . . .

I answered that the conquest of Canada had never been an object of the war on the part of the United States. It had been invaded by us in consequence of the war. . . .

With respect to the Indian allies, I remarked that there was no analogy between them and the case of Portugal. The peace would of itself include all the Indians included within the British limits; but the stipulation which might be necessary for the protection of Indians situated within the boundaries of the United States who had taken the British side in the war, was rather in the nature of an amnesty than of a provision for allies. It resembled more the case of subjects who in case of invasion took part with the invader, as had sometimes happened to Great Britain in Ireland. He insisted that the Indians must be considered as independent nations, for that we ourselves made treaties with them and acknowledged boundaries of their territories. I said that wherever they *would* form settlements and cultivate lands, their possessions were undoubtedly to be respected, and always were respected by the United States. That some of them had become civilized in a considerable degree; the Cherokees, for example, who had permanent habitations and a state of property like our own. But the greater part of the Indians never could be prevailed upon to adopt this mode of life. Their habits, and attachments, and prejudices were so averse to any settlement that they could not reconcile themselves to any other condition than that of wandering hunters. It was impossible for such people ever to be said to have possessions. Their only right upon land was a right to use it as hunting grounds;[1] and when those lands where they hunted became necessary or convenient for the purposes of settlement, the system adopted by the United States was by amicable arrangement with them to compensate them for renouncing the right of hunting upon them, and for removing to remoter regions better suited to their purposes and mode of life. This system of the United States was an improvement upon the former practice of all European nations, including the British. The original settlers of New England had set the first example of this liberality towards the Indians, which was afterwards followed by the founder of Pennsylvania. Between it and taking the lands for nothing, or exterminating the Indians who had used them, there was no alternative. To condemn vast regions of territory to perpetual barrenness and solitude, that a few

---

1. *Cf.* p. 103, *et seq.*

hundred savages might find wild beasts to hunt upon it, was a species of game law that a nation descended from Britons would never endure. It was as incompatible with the moral as with the physical nature of things. If Great Britain meant to preclude forever the people of the United States from settling and cultivating those territories, she must not think of doing it by a treaty. She must formally undertake to accomplish their utter extermination. If the government of the United States should ever submit to such a stipulation, which I hoped they would not, all its force, and all that of Britain combined with it, would not suffice to carry it long into execution. . . .

. . . He said that Great Britain had no intention to carry on a war either of extermination or conquest, but recurred again to our superior force, and to the necessity of providing against it. He added that in Canada they never took any of the Indian lands, and even the government (meaning the provincial government) was prohibited from granting them. That there were among the Indians very civilized people; there was particularly one man whom he knew, Norton, who commanded some of the Indians engaged on the British side in the war, and who was a very intelligent and well informed man. But the removing the Indians from their lands to others was one of the very things of which Great Britain complained. That it drove them over into their provinces, and made them annoy and encroach upon the Indians within their limits. . . .

The strangest feature in the general complexion of his discourse was the inflexible adherence to the proposed Indian boundary line. But the pretext upon which this proposition had in the first instance been placed, the pacification with the Indians and their future security, was almost abandoned—avowed to be a secondary and very subordinate object. The security of Canada was now substituted as the prominent motive. . . .

WORTHINGTON CHAUNCEY FORD, ed., *Writings of John Quincy Adams* (12 vols.; New York: The Macmillan Co., 1915), V, 110–21.

Article Nine, Treaty of Ghent, December 24, 1814

ARTICLE THE NINTH. The United States of America engage to put an end, immediately after the ratification of the present treaty, to hostilities with all the tribes or nations of Indians with whom they may be at war at the time of such ratification; and forthwith to restore to such tribes or nations, respectively, all the possessions, rights, and privileges, which they may have enjoyed or been entitled to in . . . [*1811*] previous to such hostilities: *Provided always* That such tribes or nations shall agree to desist from all hostilities against the United States of America, their citizens and subjects, upon the ratification of the present treaty being notified to such tribes or nations, and shall so desist accordingly. And his Britannic Majesty engages, on his part, to put an end immediately after the ratification of the present treaty, to hostilities with all the tribes or nations of Indians with whom he may be at war at the time of such ratification, and forthwith to restore to such tribes or nations, respectively, all the possessions, rights and privileges which they may have enjoyed or been entitled to in . . . [1811] previous to such hostilities: *Provided always,* that such tribes of nations shall agree to desist from all hostilities against his Britannic Majesty, and his subjects, upon the ratification of the present treaty being notified to such tribes or nations, and shall so desist accordingly.

32 From Hunters to Farmers: Thomas Jefferson's Indian Policy

While Thomas Jefferson voiced admiration for the liberty in Indian society (see pp. 260–61), this attitude did not dissuade him from getting hold of whatever Indian land he could for white settlement. He first proposed to the Indians that they might find advantages in removing to the Louisiana Territory recently acquired from France.[1] He also proposed to Congress two ways of easing their grip on lands they occupied. First, they should be encouraged to become farmers and stock raisers so that they could live on a smaller area than hunting required, and secondly, they should be induced to accumulate debts at the government trading houses, with a view to asking them later to cede lands in settlement of their debts. He reiterated the first of these objectives in several addresses to the Indians.

Address to the Miami, Potawatomi, and Wea Indians, January 7, 1802

. . . We shall, with great pleasure, see your people become disposed to cultivate the earth, to raise herds of the useful animals, and to spin and weave, for their food and clothing. These resources are certain; they will never disappoint you: while those of hunting may fail, and expose your women and children to the miseries of hunger and cold. We will with pleasure furnish you with implements for the most necessary arts, and with persons who may instruct you how to make and use them.

ADRIENNE KOCH AND WILLIAM PEDEN, *Selected Writings of Thomas Jefferson* (New York: Modern Library, 1944), p. 33.

1. Annie H. Abel, "Indian Consolidation West of the Mississippi," *Annual Report of the American Historical Association,* 1906, I, 250–60.

Message to the Senate and House of Representatives, January 18, 1803

. . . The Indian tribes residing within the limits of the United States have for a considerable time been growing more and more uneasy at the constant diminution of the territory they occupy, although effected by their own voluntary sales, and the policy had long been gaining strength with them of refusing absolutely all further sale on any conditions, insomuch as this time it hazards their friendship and excites dangerous jealousies and perturbations in their minds to make any overture for the purchase of the smallest portions of their land. A few tribes only are not yet obstinately in these dispositions. In order peaceable to counteract this policy of theirs and to provide an extension of territory which the rapid increase of our numbers will call for, two measures are deemed expedient. First. to encourage them to abandon hunting, to apply to the raising [of] stock, to agriculture, and domestic manufacture, and thereby prove to themselves that less land and labor will maintain them in this better than in their former mode of living. The extensive forests necessary to the hunting life will then become useless, and they will see advantage in exchanging them for the means of improving their farms and of increasing their domestic efforts. Secondly. To multiply trading houses among them, and place within their reach those things which will contribute more to their domestic comfort than the possession of extensive but uncultivated wilds. Experience and reflection will develop to them the wisdom of exchanging what they can spare and we want for what we can spare and they want. In leading them thus to agriculture, to manufactures, and civilization; in bringing together their and our sentiments, and in preparing them ultimately to participate in the benefits of our Government, I trust and believe we are acting for their greatest good.

> JAMES D. RICHARDSON, ed., *A Compilation of the Messages and Papers of the Presidents* (10 vols.; Washington: Government Printing Office, 1898), I, 352.

To the Chiefs of the Cherokee Nation, Washington, January 10, 1806

. . . You are becoming farmers, learning the use of the plough and the hoe, enclosing your grounds and employing that labor in their cultivation which you formerly employed in hunting and in war; and I see handsome specimens of cotton cloth raised, spun and wove by yourselves. You are also raising cattle and hogs for your food, and horses to assist your labors. Go on, my children, in the same way and be assured the further you advance in it the happier and more respectable you will be. . . .

. . . You will find your next want to be mills to grind your corn, which by relieving your women from the loss of time in beating it into meal, will enable them to spin and weave more. When a man has enclosed and improved his farm, builds a good house on it and raised plentiful stocks of animals, he will wish when he dies that these things shall go to his wife and children . . .

KOCH AND PEDEN, op. cit., p. 578.

33 The Shoshonis' Impression of Lewis and Clark and Lewis's Impression of the Shoshonis, 1805

The following two documents present an unusual opportunity to compare reactions of both Indians and whites to the same event: the appearance of the expedition of Meriwether Lewis and William Clark among the Shoshoni Indians of the Northern Rockies in 1805. These Indians had apparently never seen white men before. It is interesting that both documents reveal the care taken by the Indians to respect the property of the visitors.

Lewis and Clark Among the Shoshonis

The following account was given by an Indian to the American Fur Company agent, Warren A. Ferris, in 1831. Although the Indians are described as Flatheads, who were friends of the Shoshonis, this was believed to be erroneous by Paul Phillips, Ferris's editor, and by Ella E. Clark.[1] Neither Flathead traditions nor the journals of the expedition support this identification. Miss Clark identifies them as Shoshonis, which seems to be verified by the Lewis account, while Phillips believes they were Bannocks, a Shoshoni-speaking tribe.

[*The Shoshonis had encamped in the mountains, because of fears of the Blackfeet, who possessed firearms.*] After several moons, however, this state of tranquil happiness was interrupted by the unexpected arrival of two strangers. They were unlike any people we had hitherto seen, fairer than ourselves, and clothed with *skins* unknown to us. They seemed to be descended from the regions of the great "Edle-a-ma-hum." They gave us things like solid water, which were sometimes brilliant as the sun, and which sometimes showed us our own faces. Nothing could equal our wonder and delight. We thought them the children of the Great Spirit. But

1. Clark, *Indian Legends from the Northern Rockies* (Norman: University of Oklahoma Press, 1966), pp. 26–27.

we were destined to be again overwhelmed with fear, for we soon discovered that they were in possession of the identical thunder and lightning that had proved in the hands of our foes so fatal to our happiness. We also understood that they had come by the way of Beaver-head River, and that a party of beings like themselves were but a day's march behind them.

Many of our people were now exceedingly terrified, making no doubt but that they were leagued with our enemies the Blackfeet, and coming jointly to destroy us. This opinion was strengthened by a request they made for us to go and meet their friends. At first this was denied, but a speech from our beloved chief, who convinced us that it was best to conciliate if possible the favor of a people so terribly armed, and who might protect us, especially since our retreat was discovered, induced most of our warriors to follow him and accompany the strangers to their camp. As they disappeared over a hill in the neighborhood of our village, the women set up a doleful yell, which was equivalent to bidding them farewell forever, and which did anything but elevate their drooping spirits.

After such dismal forebodings imagine how agreeably they were disappointed, when, upon arriving at the strangers encampment, they found, instead of an overwhelming force of their enemies, a few strangers like the two already with them, who treated them with great kindness, and gave them many things that had not existed before even in their dreams or imaginations. Our eagle-eyed chief discovered from the carelessness of the strangers with regard to their things, that they were unacquainted with theft, which induced him to caution his followers against pilfering any article whatever. His instructions were strictly obeyed, mutual confidence was thus established. The strangers accompanied him back to the village, and there was peace and joy in the lodges of our people. They remained with us several days, and the Flatheads [Shoshonis] have been ever since the friends of the white men.

W. A. FERRIS, *Life in the Rocky Mountains,* ed. by Paul C. Phillips (Denver: The Old West Publishing Co., 1940), pp. 90–93.

Meriwether Lewis Meets the Shoshonis

. . . on a sudden they saw three female Indians, from whom they had been concealed by the deep ravines . . . one of them, a young woman, immediately took to flight; the other two, an elderly woman and a little girl, seeing we were too near for them to escape, sat on the ground, and holding down their heads seemed as if reconciled to the death which they supposed awaited them. . . . Captain Lewis instantly put down his rifle, and advancing towards them, took the woman by the hand, raised her up, and repeated the words tabba bone! [*white man*] at the same time stripping up his shirt sleeve to prove that he was a white man. . . . She appeared immediately relieved from her alarm, and . . . Captain Lewis gave them some beads, a few awls, pewter mirrors, and a little paint, and told Drewyer to request the woman to recall her companion who had escaped to some distance, and by alarming the Indians might cause them to attack him without any time for explanation. She did as she was desired, and the young woman returned, almost out of breath. . . . After they had become composed, he informed them by signs of his wish to go to their camp in order to see their chiefs and warriors; they readily obeyed, and conducted the party along the same road down the river. In this way they marched two miles, when they met a troop of nearly sixty warriors, mounted on excellent horses, riding at full speed towards them. As they advanced Captain Lewis put down his gun, and went with the flag about fifty paces in advance. The chief, who, with two men, were riding in front of the main body, spoke to the women, who now explained that the party was composed of white men, and showed exultingly the presents they had received. The three men immediately leaped from their horses, came up to Captain Lewis and embraced him with great cordiality, putting their left arm over his right shoulder and clasping his back. . . . The whole body of warriors now came forward, and our men received the caresses, and no small share of the grease and paint, of their new friends.

. . . Having now secured the good will of Cameahwait [*the chief*], Captain Lewis informed him of his wish that he would speak to the warriors and endeavour to engage them to accompany him to the forks of the Jefferson river, where by this time another chief [*William Clark*] with a large party of white men were waiting his return. . . . He readily consented to do so, and after collecting the tribe together he made a long harangue, and in about an hour and a half returned, and told Captain Lewis that they would be ready to accompany him in the morning. . . .

[*Next morning*] . . . Captain Lewis now endeavoured to hasten the departure of the Indians, who still hesitated and seemed reluctant to move, although the chief addressed them twice for the purpose of urging them; on inquiring the reason, Cameahwait told him that some foolish person had suggested that he was in league with their enemies the Pahkees, and had come only to draw them into ambuscade, but that he himself did not believe it. [*Lewis now remonstrated with the chief, who made another speech.*] This harangue produced an effect on six or eight only of the warriors, who now joined their chief. With these Captain Lewis smoked a pipe, and then, fearful of some change in their capricious temper, set out immediately. . . . their departure seemed to spread a gloom over the village; those who would not venture to go were sullen and melancholy, and the women were crying and imploring the Great Spirit to protect their warriors as if they were going to certain destruction. . . .

. . . [*Captain Clark, six days later*] resumed his march early, and at the distance of five miles reached an Indian lodge of brush, inhabited by seven families of Shoshonees. They behaved with great civility, gave the whole party as much boiled salmon as they could eat, and added as a present several dried salmon and a considerable quantity of chokecherries. . . .

. . . an Indian brought him a tomahawk which he said he had found in the grass, near the lodge where Captain Lewis had staid on his first visit to the village. This was a tomahawk which had been missed at the time, and supposed to be stolen; it was, however, the only article which had been lost in our intercourse with the nation, and as even that was returned the inference is highly honourable to the integrity of the Shoshonees. . . .

. . . The Indians who visit us behave with the greatest decorum, and the women are busily engaged in making and mending the moccasins of the party. . . .

. . . We have again to admire the perfect decency and propriety of their conduct, for although so numerous, they do not attempt to crowd round our camp or take anything which they see lying about, and whenever they borrow knives or kettles or any other article from the men, they return them with great fidelity.

JAMES K. HOSMER, ed., *History of the Expedition of Captains Lewis and Clark* (2d ed., 2 vols.; Chicago: A. C. McClurg & Co., 1903), II, pp. 387–88, 396–98, 422–23, 432, 437.

34   Frontier Indignities Against the Indians, 1810

FORTESCUE CUMING

The following incident was reported by Fortescue Cuming, an English traveler, while descending the Ohio River in 1810. The conversation with a settler named Wheatly indicates an outrageous contempt for Indians which may help explain why so many Indians took to the warpath in 1812.

He told us that a small tribe of Miami Indians were encamped on Oil creek about two miles distant. On asking if they were troublesome, he replied with much sang froid . . . "We never permit them to be troublesome, for if any of them displease us, we take them out of doors and kick them a little, for they are like dogs, and so will love you the better for it." . . . He informed us, that they frequently get the Indians together, take their guns, knives and tomahawks from them, then treat them with whisky until they are drunk, when they set them by the ears, to have the pleasure of seeing them fight, at which they are so awkward . . . that they scuffle for hours without drawing blood, and when their breath is exhausted they will sit down quietly to recruit, and then "up and at it again."

Cuming's "Tour to the West," in Reuben G. Thwaites, ed., Early Western Travels, 1748–1846 (32 vols.; Cleveland: Arthur H. Clark Co., 1904–6), IV, 263.

35 A Cherokee Plea for Justice, 1813

TO-CHA LEE and CHU LI-OA

While the desperate struggles of America's second war with Great Britain were going on, prudence should have dictated a policy of accommodation toward those Indians who had not already joined with the enemy. Nevertheless, undisciplined frontiersmen continued to inflict outrages upon the Cherokees, who were by that time one of the most peaceful and civilized of tribes. Unauthorized intrusions continued, and murders of Indians by whites went unpunished. The following is one of many in a long train of memorials issued by leading men of the tribe in the hope of touching the conscience of Americans and their government and of bringing redress. Its publication was arranged by Return J. Meigs, United States Indian agent to the Cherokees.

Cherokee Indians' Appeal

To the Editors of the National Intelligencer

Highwasse Garrison, March 6, 1813

Gentlemen:

The enclosed address of the Cherokees to the citizens of the United States, is transmitted to you with a request that you will give it a place in the National Intelligencer. The object of the address is to remove prejudices, if any exist, and to smooth the path of peace, which they are determined to keep white and clean between them and their white brothers.

I am, gentlemen, very respectfully, your obedient servant.

RETURN J. MEIGS

To the Citizens of the United States—particularly to the good people living in the states of Tennessee, North Carolina, South Carolina, Georgia, and Mississippi territory.

Neighbors, Friends and Brothers,—By the rapid progress of settlements in the western part of the United States, our country is now nearly surrounded by our white brothers; our intercourse with you keeps pace with your and our population. It is for the interest of all that harmony and good neighborhood should be preserved between us—and when from misunderstanding, or the disorderly conduct of individuals on either side, our harmony may have been temporarily interrupted, it gives you and us concern and uneasiness, because we cannot control the passions of men; but as it has been, so it will be our constant care, to remove as far as it shall be in our power, the causes of complaint, and to make remuneration for injustice suffered, and we have no doubt that the good people on your part will do the same. The present circumstances of the United States contending honorably for their just rights, against an overbearing, haughty and powerful enemy, has awakened and aroused the spirit of the citizens to a degree of vigilance, in some perhaps bordering on severity. Our local situation and close connection with our white brothers, has necessarily made the contest interesting to us. Our interest and yours are the same and cannot be separated.

In former years we were of *necessity* under the influence of your enemies. We spilled our blood in their cause; they were finally compelled by your arms to leave us; they made no stipulation for our security. When those years of distress had passed away, we found ourselves in the power of a generous nation; past transactions were consigned to oblivion; our boundaries were established by compact, and liberal provision was made for our future security and improvement, for which we placed ourselves under the protection of the United States. Under these provisions our nation has prospered, our population has increased.—The knowledge and practice of agriculture and some of the useful arts, have kept pace with time. Our stocks of cattle and other domestic animals fill the forests, while the wild animals have disappeared. Our spinning wheels and looms now in use by the ingenious hands of our wives and our daughters, enable us to clothe ourselves principally in decent habits, from the production of materials the growth of our soil. In addition to these important acquisitions, many of our youth of both sexes have acquired such knowledge of letters and figures as to shew to the most incredulous that our mental powers are not by nature inferior to yours—and we look forward to a period of time, when it may be said, this artist, this mathematician, this astronomer, is a Cherokee; but in order to the attainment of these things, there must be tranquility. There may be individuals on both sides, whose ignorance and illiberal prejudices may occasionally lead us into difficulties; this has already been experienced by the imprudence of some of our people, and by the fabrication of reports, some of which have found their way into the newspapers, having been so ingeniously constructed as to induce a belief that they were true, and having a tendency to produce acts of violence. The recent transactions near Battle Creek have deprived us of the lives of two of our people. The previous bad conduct of some of our people, it is said, led to the commission of these murders, alluding to the cruel treatment of John Tally, a citizen of Franklin county. This shall be strictly enquired into, and justice shall be done as far as the nature of the case will admit, and we sincerely regret that any of our people should so far deviate from what we flatter ourselves is our national character. And here we beg leave to appeal to you whether we are not kind to strangers, whether we let a white man leave our houses hungry. We confidently believe that hospitality is a trait in our character; this has been handed down to us from our ancestors and we will not spoil it. We detest as much as you do the treatment of John Tally, but the punishment we have received bears no proportion to the crime committed—we do not meditate revenge, we appeal to the treaties and to the laws for redress. If these cannot afford satisfaction, we have only to regret it, knowing that the best institution cannot in every case reach the real aggressor. The intrusions on our lands are serious causes of complaint, they are deliberate acts of fraudulent calculation, not induced by sudden impulse of passion; they are meditated on the pillow, and to aggravate the nature of these breaches of law and justice, every intruder has his rifle and all the apparatus of a warrior—for what? to defend his just rights? No, but to keep forcible possession, to keep the rightful owner out of his patrimony, descended to him from his ancestors from time immemorial.

Brothers, we are sensible that it is not possible for you or for us to restrain the licentious conduct of all our people at all times; but when we find the facts fully substantiated, we are willing to make such indemnity to the sufferers as the nature of the cases require, and we believe this to be the case on your part. One of the citizens of Tennessee has lately been grossly abused in our nation by a white man, amenable to our laws—the white man has fled from our country—we have with much care examined the case, and have resolved to make a present of a small sum to the injured citizen— not as full compensation for his sufferings—this cannot be done by pecuniary means; but as an expression of our regret for what has been done within the limits of our country, and we hope it will be received in the same spirit of conciliation, as we present it *as a peace offering,* for we wish it to be believed that we detest the conduct of bad men, more especially where the laws of hospitality are infringed. Since our connection with the United States we have been taught to lay aside the barbarous practice of retaliation, especially not to punish the innocent where the guilty cannot be found; but we find that there are bad men in the best governments. Some unprincipled men have killed two of our people for injuries alleged to have been received—not for the life of any man, but for property, as they say, stolen. They took the legislative, the judicial, and the executive power into their own hands, and the result is as might have been expected. Brothers, we do not mention these things in a spirit of recrimination, or resentment, for we really respect and esteem the great body of the citizens, and we admire the wise institutions of your government, and only remark, that the wisest provisions and institutions cannot at all times restrain the passions of men. Brothers, we find that you are honorably contending for your just rights with a nation who feeling power is forgetful of right. When the whole receives a shock, all the parts feel it, and although we have not the honor to share an active part with you, we wish for you, that you may be carried through the contest with that success which a good cause entitles you with confidence to expect, and beg leave to subscribe ourselves your friends and brothers.

In behalf of the Cherokee Nation.
    [Signed]

TO-CHA LEE, X *Head Chief*
CHU LI-OA, X *A Principal Chief*

CHARLES HICKS, Sec'y.
    Alexander M'Coy, Clerk
In full Council at Highwassee, March 6th, 1813.

From *Niles Weekly Register,* April 10, 1813, pp. 96–97.

36   A Plea for Humane Consideration of the Indians, 1820

JEDIDIAH MORSE

In 1820 the Reverend Jedidiah Morse, a geographer, was commissioned by President Monroe to tour among the Indian tribes of the upper Mississippi valley and Great Lakes region, and to make a report to the Secretary of War, "for the purpose of ascertaining, for the use of the government, the actual state of the Indian tribes in our country."

In the Report to the Secretary of War on Indian Affairs, *published in 1822 and excerpted below, Morse advocated the establishment of government-operated trading posts in the Indian country, in order to take the trade away from the British who still worked in the area, to end the liquor trade, and to end the practice of extending credit to the Indians, which he believed was harmful to them. While he favored the assignment of reduced land areas to the Indians as they were converted to agriculture, he was opposed to their removal, and also to treating them as an inferior people.*

. . . they are certainly an intelligent and noble part of our race, and capable of high moral and intellectual improvement. . . . They are a race, who on every correct principle ought to be saved from extinction, if it be possible to save them. . . .

. . . They, as well as ourselves, are made to be immortal. To look down upon them, therefore, as an inferior race, as untameable, and to profit from their ignorance and weakness; to take their property from them for a small part of its real value, and in other ways to oppress them; is undoubtedly wrong, and highly displeasing to our common Creator. . . .

To remove these Indians far away from their present homes . . . into a wilderness, among strangers, possibly hostile, to live as their new neighbors live, by hunting, a state to which they have not lately been accustomed, and which is incompatible with civilization, can hardly be reconciled with the professed views and objects of the Government in civilizing them.

> JEDIDIAH MORSE, *Report to the Secretary of War on Indian Affairs* (New Haven: S. Converse, 1822), pp. 73, 82–83.

37   Delaware Indians' Rebuke to Missionaries on Slavery, ca. 1820

ADAM HODGSON AND ELIAS BOUDINOT

The Indians were quick to detect moral hypocrisy in white men, and were prone to put missionaries on the defensive by asking them searching questions about injustices of whites toward nonwhites and even toward each other. The following account tells how Delaware Indians put the question of slavery to Dr. Elias Boudinot.

". . . we wrote a letter in the Indian style to the Delaware Nation, then residing on the north-west of the Ohio, informing them, that we had, by the goodness of the Great Spirit, been favoured by a knowledge of his will as to the worship he required of his creatures, and the means he would bless to promote the happiness of men both in this life, and that which is to come. . . . We had therefore sent them two ministers of the Gospel, who would teach them these great things, and earnestly recommended them to their careful attention. . . .

On their arrival, the chiefs of the natives were called together, who answered them, that they would take the subject into consideration; but in the mean time, they might instruct the women, but must not speak to the men. They spent fourteen days in council, and then dismissed them very courteously, with an answer to us. This answer made great acknowledgement for the favour we had done them. They rejoiced exceedingly at our happiness in being thus favoured by the Great Spirit, and felt very grateful that we had condescended to remember our Red Brethren in the wilderness. But they could not help recollecting that we had a people among us, who, because they differed from us in colour, we had made slaves of, and made them suffer great hardships, and lead miserable lives. Now they could not see any reason, if a people's being Black entitled us thus to deal with them, why a Red colour should not equally justify the same treatment. They therefore had determined to wait to see whether all the Black people amongst us were made thus happy and joyful, before they put confidence in our promise; for they thought a people who had suffered so much and so long, by our means, should be entitled to our first attention; that therefore they had sent back the two missionaries, with many thanks—promising, that when they saw the Black people amongst us restored to freedom and happiness, they would gladly receive our missionaries."

Such was the moral lesson which these wild sons of the forest, these uncultivated heathens, read to enlightened Christians. We slighted their lesson, and, as if to silence these untutored monitors, and drown the voice of truth and nature, we overcame their virtues, we corrupted them by our example: and I found slaves held in bondage by the Indians themselves—in the nations of the Creeks, the Choctaws, the Chickasaws, and the Cherokees.

ADAM HODGSON, *Remarks During a Journey Through North America in the Years 1819, 1820, and 1821* (New York: 1823), pp. 218–20, quoting a letter of Dr. Elias Boudinot.

38   The Delawares' Account of Their Own History from the Coming of the White Man Until Their Removal from Indiana, 1820: The *Walam Olum*

The Delaware, or Lenni Lenape Indians, who occupied eastern Pennsylvania when the whites arrived, were pushed steadily westward until by the end of the eighteenth century they were settled on White River in central Indiana. Here, in 1820, a remarkable pictographic record, painted on sticks of wood, known as the Walam Olum, *was obtained from them by a Kentucky physician who passed it on to Constantine S. Rafinesque, a noted botanist on the faculty of Transylvania University at Lexington. It was nothing less than a history of the world since the creation, and ending with the coming of the white man. The story was told in five "songs," divided into 183 verses. A later portion, or annex, which told of events from the arrival of the whites until 1820, was obtained two years later. These pictographs were translated into Delaware in 1822, and later into English by Rafinesque and an inter-*

preter. The first five songs were published by Daniel Brinton in 1885,[1] but the last fragment was published by Jacob Piatt Dunn in 1909.[2] The entire document, with original pictographs, and translations in Delaware and English, with analytical comments, was published in 1954.[3] The sixth song, or fragment, which follows below, is from Dunn's version. All footnotes are by the present author.

1. Alas, alas! We now know who they are, these Wapsinis [East people], who came out of the sea to rob us of our lands. Starving wretches! they came with smiles, but soon became snakes [or enemies].

2. The Walumolum was made by Lekhibit [The Writer] to record our glory. Shall I write another to record our fall? No! Our foes have taken care to do that; but I speak what they know not or conceal.

3. We have had many other chiefs since that unhappy time. There were three before the friendly Mikwon [Miquon or Pen(n)] came. Mattanikum [Not Strong] was chief when the Winakoli [Swedes] came to Winaki [*the good land*]; Nahumen [Raccoon] when the Sinalwi [Dutch] came, and Ikwahon [Fond-of-Women] when the Yankwis [English] came. Miquon [Penn] and his friends came soon after.

4. They were all received and fed with corn; but no land was ever sold to them; we never sold any land.[5] They were allowed to dwell with us, to build houses and plant corn, as friends and allies. Because they were hungry and we thought them children of Gishaki [or sun land], and not serpents and children of serpents.

5. And they were traders, bringing fine new tools, and weapons, and cloth, and beads, for which we gave them skins and shells and corn. And we liked them and the things they brought, for we thought them good and made by the children of Gishaki.

6. But they brought also fire-guns, and fire-waters, which burned and killed, also baubles and trinkets of no use, for we had better ones before.

7. After Mikwon, came the sons of Dolojo-Sakima [King George], who said more land, more land we must have, and no limit could be put on their steps.

1. Daniel G. Brinton, *The Lenape and Their Legends* (Philadelphia: the author, 1885).

2. Jacob Piatt Dunn, *True Indian Stories* (Indianapolis: Sentinel Printing Co., 1909), pp. 188–95.

3. *Walam Olum, or Red Score: The Migration Legend of the Lenni Lenape or Delaware Indians* (Indianapolis: Indiana Historical Society, 1954).

4. *Mikwon* or *Miquon* is an Algonquian term for feather or quill, and since the whites used quill pens, the Delawares applied the term to William Penn.

5. European concepts of land title were not understood by the Indians, and in treaty "cessions," they believed that they were only allowing the privilege of occupancy.

8. But in the north were the children of Lowi-Sakima [King Louis], who were our good friends, friends of our friends, foes of our foes, yet with [*whom*] Dolojo wished always to war.

9. We had three chiefs after Mikwon came—Skalich, who was another Tamenend [*"Tammany"*] and Sasunam-Wikwikhon [Our-uncle-the-builder], and Tutami [Beaver-taker], who was killed by a Yankwako [English snake], and then we vowed revenge.

10. Netatawis [First-new-being] became chief of all the nations of the west. Again at Talligewink [Ohio, or place of Tallegwi] on the River Cuyahoga, near our old friends, the Talamatans [*Wyandots*]. And he called on all them of the east [to go to war].

11. But Tadeskung was chief in the east at Mahoning, and was bribed by Yankwis; then he was burnt in his cabin, and many of our people were killed at Hickory [Lancaster][6] by the land-robber Yankwis.

12. Then we joined Lowi in war against the Yankwis [*French and Indian War, 1756–1763*]; but they were strong, and they took Lowanaki [North-land, Canada][7] from Lowi, and came to us in Talegawink, when peace was made, and we called them Kichikani [Big Knives].

13. Then Alimi [White eyes] and Gelelenund [Buck-killer][8] were chiefs, and all the nations near us were friends, and our grandchildren again.

14. When the Eastern fires [*the thirteen colonies*] began to resist Dolojo, they said we should be another fire with them.[9] But they killed our chief Unamiwi [the Turtle] and our brothers on the Muskingum.[10] Then Hopokan [Strong-pipe][11] of the Wolf tribe [*clan*] was made chief, and

6. Probably a reference to the slaughter of twenty peaceable Conestoga Indians by the "Paxtang boys" on December 14 and 27, 1763. This outrage has been vividly described by Benjamin Franklin (*Works*, 1887–1888, III, 260 ff.), by Francis Parkman (*Conspiracy of Pontiac*, 1922, II, 130–35) and by Helen Hunt Jackson (*A Century of Dishonor* [New York: Harper Torchbooks, 1965], pp. 298 ff.). On the murder of "Tadeskung," April 19, 1763, see Anthony F. C. Wallace, *King of the Delawares: Teedyuscung* (Freeport, N.Y.: Books for Libraries Press, 1970), pp. 258 ff.

7. Lowanaki means "land of Lowi" (Louis, the king of France).

8. More commonly known in historical records, treaties, and place names, as Killbuck.

9. This recalls the first Indian treaty signed by the United States, at Fort Pitt, September 17, 1778, which provided for the eventual formation of an Indian state to be headed by the Delawares, and which would be represented in Congress. See Charles J. Kappler, ed., *Indian Affairs, Laws, and Treaties* (Washington: Government Printing Office, 1904), II, 3–5.

10. A reference to the massacre at Gnadenhütten (Ohio), in March 1782, when ninety-six unarmed Christian Delawares were murdered by Kentucky frontiersmen. See John Heckewelder, *Narrative of the Mission of the United Brethren* (Philadelphia: McCarty and Davis, 1820), p. 321; Helen Hunt Jackson, *A Century of Dishonor*, pp. 317–23.

11. Biography in F. W. Hodge, ed., *Handbook of American Indians*, Bulletin 30, Bureau of American Ethnology (2 vols.; Washington: Government Printing Office, 1907–1910), I, 568–69.

he made war on the Kichikani-Yankwis, and became the friend of Dolojo, who was then very strong.

15. But the Eastern fires [*United States*] were stronger; they did not take Lowinaki [*Canada*], but became free from Dolojo. We went to Wapahani [White River][12] to be farther from them; but they followed us everywhere, and we made war on them, till they sent Makhiakho [Black-snake, General Wayne], who made strong war.[13]

16. We next made peace and settled limits,[14] and our chief was Hackingpouskan [Hard-walker], who was good and peaceful. He would not join our brothers, the Shawanis and Ottawas, and Dolojo in the next war [*War of 1812*].

17. Yet after the last peace, the Kichikani-Yankwis came in swarms all around us, and they desired also our lands of Wapahani. It was useless to resist, because they were getting stronger and stronger by joining fires [*adding states*].

18. Kithtilkand and Lapanibit were the chiefs of our two tribes when we resolved to exchange our lands, and return at last beyond the Masispek [Mississippi River], near to our old country.[15]

19. We shall be near our foes the Wakon [Osages],[16] but they are not worse than the Yankiwakon [English snakes],[17] who want to possess the whole Big-island [*North America*].

20. Shall we be free and happy, then, at the new Wapahani? We want rest and peace, and wisdom.

JACOB PIATT DUNN, *True Indian Stories* (Indianapolis: Sentinel Printing Co., 1909), pp. 188–95.

39 Indian Warfare

Indian methods of warfare, such as fighting from cover, guerrilla actions, etc., were in sharp contrast to the European custom of having armies fire at one another in an open field. Indians saw no merit in foolhardy waste of lives, and were so disinclined to make suicidal attacks that they were sometimes accused of cowardice. The Indian methods of fighting proved

12. In central Indiana. See Lawrence H. Gipson, ed., *The Moravian Indian Mission on White River* (Indianapolis: Indiana Historical Bureau, 1938).

13. Battle of Fallen Timbers (near Toledo), August 20, 1794.

14. Treaty of Greenville, August 3, 1795.

15. This indicates that the Delawares had a tradition of former residence in the West.

16. In Kansas, near the junction of the Kansas and Missouri rivers. In 1867 they were induced to leave this reservation and were assigned to lands in the Cherokee Nation, Indian Territory (Oklahoma).

17. The Americans.

useful to the colonists in the Revolutionary War. George Washington wrote that Colonel Morgan's riflemen were "well acquainted with . . . that mode of fighting, which is necessary to make a good counterpoise to the Indians."[1] The contribution of Indian tactics to the struggle for independence has been described by the poet Robert P. Tristram Coffin in these lines:

> We bent down to the bob-cat's crouch
> Took color from the butternut tree,
> At Saratoga, Lexington,
> We fought like Indians and went free.[2]

To many Indians, war was a kind of game, and even among the Plains tribes, where fighting prowess was most honored, more prestige was won through counting coup (touching the enemy), or stealing his horses, than from killing a man.

The following account by Washington Irving, describing Indian warfare among Indians in Oregon Territory, seems to indicate that war in that region resembled a somewhat over-violent football game.

Feuds are frequent among these tribes, but are not very deadly. They have occasionally pitched battles, fought on appointed days, and at specified places, which are generally the banks of a rivulet. The adverse parties post themselves on the opposite sides of the stream, and at such distances that the battles often last a long time before any blood is shed. The number of killed and wounded seldom exceed half a dozen. Should the damage be equal on each side, the war is considered honorably concluded; should one part lose more than another, it is entitled to compensation in slaves or other property, otherwise hostilities are liable to be renewed at a future day.

> WASHINGTON IRVING, *Astoria* (2 vols.; Philadelphia: Lea & Blanchard, 1841), II, 30.

The following account of a battle on the Plains is by John Tanner, a white captive who lived thirty years among the Ojibwa.

. . . The Mandan village was surrounded by a wall of pickets, and close to these the Sioux fought all day. At length, an intermission took place, and the Mandan chief, calling to the Sioux from the inside, said to them, "Depart from about our village, or we will let out upon you our friends, the Ojibbeways, who have been sitting here all day, and are now fresh and un-

---

1. Washington to Clinton, August 16, 1777, in Saul K. Padover, ed., *The Washington Papers* (New York: Harper & Bros., 1955), pp. 150–51.

2. "We Put the Feathers On," in R. P. Tristram Coffin, *Primer for America* (New York: The Macmillan Co., 1943), pp. 54–55.

wearied." The Sioux answered, "This is a vain boast, made with a design to conceal your weakness. You have no Ojibbeways in your house, and if you had hundreds, we neither fear nor regard them. The Ojibbeways are women, and if your village were full of them, we would, for that reason, the sooner come among you." The Crees and Assinneboins, hearing these taunts, became irritated and ran out to attack the Sioux, which the latter perceiving, fled in all directions. The Ojibbeways, though they had little share in the fight, were allowed to have some of the scalps taken during the day . . .

JOHN TANNER, *A Narrative of the Captivity and Adventures of John Tanner,* ed. by Edwin James (Minneapolis: Ross & Haines, 1956), p. 142.

The prevalence of torture in Indian warfare has been misrepresented, argues George Bird Grinnell, a student of Cheyenne customs, in the following letter written in 1929.

Dear Mr. Campbell:

. . . I suspect that the fear felt and expressed by white men who took part in the wars with the Western Plains Indians were no more than survivals of the old time belief that Indians always tortured captives.

The books tell us that the Indians of the East did this, but in my opinion those of the plains practically never did anything of the kind. I feel confident that they never made a practice of it. Of course, a group of Indians, if they were particularly angry at a man, or a small group of men, might in this way satisfy their feelings of revenge, but in my association with Western Indians I think I never heard of anything of this kind. If acts, such as you allude to, ever took place among the Western Indians they were, in my opinion, the result of some special occurrence, and in revenge for some particular injury thought to have been received by the group. There was practically no torture of captives by the Western Indians. I have been told of many cases where captives were kindly treated and even adopted into the tribe. [See pp. 53–55.]

I have always been somewhat skeptical about many stories of torture reported as practised by the Eastern Indians.

The Western Indians, of course, wished to destroy their enemies, men, women and children, but I think they never practiced torture, except, possibly, in some cases where they were still very angry over some injury they believed they had received.

GEORGE BIRD GRINNELL to W. S. Campbell [Stanley Vestal], May 6, 1929, in Stanley Vestal, *New Sources of Indian History 1850–1891* (Norman: University of Oklahoma Press, 1934), pp. 156–57.

40   James Fenimore Cooper and the Indians, 1828

Earlier generations of youth learned about Indians from James Feni-more Cooper's Last of the Mohicans *and* Leatherstocking Tales, *novels in an eighteenth-century setting. Later writers insist that Cooper created a false, idyllic image of the Indian as a "noble savage," and those who have focused attention upon the virtues or achievements of the Indians have been accused of having their vision distorted by Cooper's influence.*[1] *So strong has been the assault on the supposed Cooper myth that writers who found something to admire in Indian life, or who wished to condemn injustices practiced against them, felt compelled to preface their remarks by dis-claiming any addiction to the alleged Cooper stereotype. A nation which rose to greatness over the bones of a conquered people has frequently found it necessary to protect its own image by denigrating the memory of the slain and dispossessed.*

Cooper has been misjudged, and the truth does not do him credit. The Indians he admired were the obsequious types, such as Uncas, who trusted the white man. He joined in the common contempt for the wild, uncon-verted Indians who rejected white civilization. At no time did he question for a moment the superiority of any part of his own culture over that of the "savages." He spoke of them as a "stunted, dirty, and degraded race." He did not concede any Indian right to the soil, and regarded treaties with them as only "a deference to general principles of justice and humanity." He considered the treaties to be humane, and denied that Indians had ever been wrongfully dispossessed. He argued that "the inroad of the whites of the United States has never been marked by the gross injustice and brutal-ity that have distinguished similar inroads elsewhere."

All of these views were expounded in the form of a series of "letters" written by an imaginary traveler, which he published in 1828 under the title of Notions of the Americans, *from which the following excerpts are taken.*

By far the most numerous, and the most important of the native tribes, which still continue in the immediate vicinity of the whites, are those which occupy reservations in Georgia, the Floridas, Alabama, Mississippi, and Ten[n]essee. The lingering fragments of a hundred tribes are certainly seen scattered over the immense surface of this country, living on greater or less tracts that had been secured to them, or dwelling by sufferance in the woods; but the only people now residing east of the Mississippi who can aspire to the names of nations, are the Creeks, the Choctaws, the Chicka-saws, the Cherokees, and the Seminoles, all of them dwell in the portion of country I have named.

1. *E.g.,* see "Custer's View of Indian Character," pp. 166–67.

As a rule, the red man disappears before the superior moral and physical influence of the white, just as I believe the black man will eventually do the same thing, unless he shall seek shelter in some other region. In nine cases out of ten, the tribes have gradually removed west; and there is now a confused assemblage of nations and languages collected on the immense hunting grounds of the Prairies. . . .

The ordinary manner of the disappearance of the Indian is by a removal deeper into the forest. Still, many linger near the graves of their fathers, to which their superstitions, no less than a fine natural feeling, lend a deep interest. The fate of the latter is inevitable; they become victims to the abuses of civilization, without ever attaining to any of its moral elevation. . . .

Trifling districts of territory have been, in every instance in which they were sufficiently numerous to make such a provision desirable, secured to them, and on these little tracts of land many of them still remain. I have visited one or two of their establishments.

In point of civilization, comforts and character, the Indians, who remain near the coasts, are about on a level with the lowest classes of European peasantry. Perhaps they are somewhat below the English, but I think not below the Irish peasants. They are much below the condition of the mass of the slaves. It is but another proof of the wayward vanity of man that the latter always hold the Indians in contempt, though it is some proof that they feel their own condition to be physically better: morally, in one sense, it certainly is not. . . .

In the more interior parts of the country, I frequently met families of the Indians either traveling, or proceeding to some village, with their wares. They were all alike, a stunted, dirty, and degraded race. Sometimes they encamped in the forests, lighted their fires, and remained for weeks in a place; and at others, they kept roaming daily, until the time arrived when they should return to their reservations.

The reservations in the old states, and with tribes that cannot aspire to the dignity of nations, are managed on a sufficiently humane principle. The laws of the state, or of the United States, have jurisdiction there, in all matters between a white man and an Indian; but the Indians themselves are commonly permitted to control the whole of their own internal policy. Bargains, exceeding certain amounts, are not valid between them and whites, who cannot, for instance, purchase their lands. Schools are generally provided in the more important tribes, by the general government, and in the less, by charity. Religious instruction is also furnished by the latter means.

I saw reservations in which no mean advances had been made in civilization. Farms were imperfectly tilled, and cattle were seen grazing in the fields. Still, civilization advances slowly among a people who consider labour a degradation, in addition to the bodily dislike that all men have to its occupations.

There are many of these tribes, however, who fill a far more important, and altogether a remarkable position. There is certainly no portion of country within the admitted boundaries of the United States, in which their laws are not paramount [*U.S. laws*], if they choose to exert them. Still, savage communities do exist within these limits, with whom they make treaties, against whom they wage open war, and with whom they make solemn peace. As a treaty is, by the constitution, the paramount law of the land, the several states are obliged to respect their legal provisions.[1]

That neither the United States, nor any individual state has ever taken possession of any land that, by usage or construction, might be decreed the property of the Indians, without a treaty and a purchase, is, I believe, certain. How far an equivalent is given, is another question: though I fancy that these bargains are quite as just as any that are ever driven between the weak and the strong, the intelligent and the ignorant. It is not pretended that the value of the territory gained is paid for; but the purchase is rather a deference to general principles of justice and humanity, than a concession to a right in the Indians, which itself might admit of a thousand legal quibbles. The treaties are sufficiently humane, and, although certain borderers, who possess the power of the white man with the disposition of the savage, do sometimes violate their conditions, there is no just reason to distrust the intentions or the conduct of the government. . . .

The annuities are sums paid for grants of land. At the treaties, presents are always made to the tribes, and the agents and sub-agents are men employed to maintain the influence of the government, and at the same time, to see that the rights of the Indian are respected.

There is a bureau of the war department that is called the "office of the Indian affairs." A humane and discreet individual is at its head,[2] and a good deal is endeavored to be done in mitigating the sufferings, and in meliorating the condition of the Indians, though, owing to the peculiar habits and opinions of these people, but little, I fear, is effected. I see by the report of the current year, [1827] that, in nine months, requisitions towards the support of the objects of this bureau, were made to the amount of 759,116 dollars, or at the rate of a little more than a million dollars a year. This, you will remember, is one tenth of the current expenditure of the whole government, and nearly as much as is paid for the support of the whole civil list strictly speaking. . . .

The government, it would appear by the reports, puts the utmost latitude

1. This was written before Georgia successfully violated the Cherokee treaties, in defiance of the Supreme Court, but with the support of President Jackson.
2. Thomas L. McKenney; see pp. 111–13.

on the construction of their constitutional powers, by even paying money for the support of missionaries among the Indians. I believe, however, that the alleged and legal object of this charge, is for general instruction, though in point of fact, the teachers are missionaries. . . .

Where there is much intercourse between the very strong and very weak, there is always a tendency in the human mind to suspect abuses of power. I shall not descend into the secret impulses that give rise to these suspicions: but, in this stage of the world, there is no necessity for suspecting a nation like this of any unprovoked wrongs against a people like the savages. The inroad of the whites of the United States has never been marked by the gross injustice and brutality that have distinguished similar inroads elsewhere. The Indians have never been slain except in battle, unless by lawless individuals; never hunted by blood-hounds, or in any manner aggrieved, except in the general, and, perhaps, in some degree, justifiable invasion of a territory that they did not want, and could not use. If the government of the United States was poor and necessitous, one might suspect them of an unjust propensity; but not only the facts but the premises, would teach us to believe the reverse. . . .

. . . As there is little reluctance to mingle the white and red blood, (for the physical difference is far less than in the case of the blacks, and the Indians have never been menial slaves), I think an amalgamation of the two races would in time occur. Those families of America who are thought to have any of the Indian blood, are rather proud of their descent; and it is a matter of boast among many of the most considerable persons of Virginia, that they are descended from the renowned Pocahontas.

The character of the American Indian has been too often faithfully described to need any repetition here. The majority of them, in or near the settlements, are a humbled and much degraded race. As you recede from the Mississippi, the finer traits of savage life become visible; and, though most of the natives of the Prairies, even there, are far from being the interesting and romantic heroes that poets love to paint, there are specimens of loftiness of spirit, of noble bearing, and of savage heroism to be found among the chiefs, that it might embarrass the fertility of the richest invention to equal.[3]

JAMES FENIMORE COOPER, *Notions of the Americans, Picked up by a Travelling Bachelor* (2 vols.; London: Henry Colburn, 1828), II, 367–83.

3. See also Doc. 19, pp. 43–45.

◈

41   Diverse Views on Indian Land Rights

Father Francis P. Prucha has aptly remarked that "the conflict between the whites and Indians that marked American Indian relations was basically a conflict over land."[1] Expediency alone determined the formula that was used to acquire Indian land, and a variety of arguments have been used at various times to justify expropriation of the Indians. These have included the right of discovery, the right of conquest, purchase, the doctrine of the primacy of civilized over uncivilized man, and the principle that unused or underused land may be appropriated by those who will cultivate it. Usually the Indian right of occupancy only of such land as they required to survive was grudgingly conceded, but even this idea was abandoned by some in favor of a belief in the extermination of the aboriginal inhabitants. The following documents illustrate some of the views that have been advanced on aboriginal land rights during the last three hundred and fifty years.

A Juridical Rationale for Indian Dispossession, 1760

EMMERICH DE VATTEL

Those who felt the necessity of providing some sort of legal or philosophical fig leaf to cover the reality of Indian dispossession were prone to cite scholars such as Vattel. The following passage from the eighteenth-century Swiss jurist embodies principles which were not only used to justify the old-style colonialism, but also Fascist expansion in the twentieth century.

There is another celebrated question, to which the discovery of the new world has principally given rise. It is asked if a nation may lawfully take possession of a part of a vast country, in which there are found none but erratic nations, incapable by the smallness of their numbers, to people the whole? We have already observed in establishing the obligation to cultivate the earth, that these nations cannot exclusively appropriate to themselves more land than they have occasion for, and which they are unable to settle and cultivate. Their removing their habitations through these immense regions, cannot be taken for a true and legal possession, and the people of Europe, too closely pent up, finding land of which these nations are in no particular want, and of which they make no actual and constant use, may lawfully possess it, and establish colonies there. We have already said that the earth belongs to the human race in general, and was designed to furnish

1. Prucha, *American Indian Policy in the Formative Years* (Cambridge: Harvard University Press, 1962), p. 139.

it with subsistence; if each nation had resolved from the beginning to appropriate to itself a vast country, that the people might live only by hunting, fishing, and wild fruits, our globe would not be sufficient to maintain a tenth part of its present inhabitants. People have not then deviated from the laws of nature in confining the Indians within narrow limits.

> EMMERICH DE VATTEL, *The Law of Nations; or Principles of the Law of Nature* . . . (1760, American edition, 1820), cited in Francis P. Prucha, *American Indian Policy in the Formative Years*, p. 241.

Indian Right to the Soil: A Hostile View, 1782

H. H. BRACKENRIDGE

Convenience and self-interest, and not morality or even legal concepts formed the basis of the prevalent views on Indian land rights in the period of national expansion. The following document holds that Indians were no more entitled to the land than the four-footed animals that roamed over it.

Mr. Baily:

With the narrative enclosed, I subjoin some observations with regard to the animals, vulgarly called Indians. . . .

In the United States Magazine in the year 1777, I published a dissertation denying them to have a right in the soil. . . .

On what is their claim founded? —Occupancy. A wild Indian with his skin painted red, and a feather through his nose, has set foot on the broad continent of North and South America; a second wild Indian with his ears cut in ringlets, or his nose slit like a swine or a malefactor, also sets his foot on the same extensive tract of soil. Let the first Indian make a talk to his brother, and bid him take his foot off the continent, for he being first upon it, has occupied the whole, to kill buffaloes, and tall elks with long horns. This claim in the reasoning of some men would be just, and the second savage ought to depart in his canoe, and seek a continent where no prior occupant claimed the soil. . . .

The whole of this earth was given to man, and all descendants of Adam have a right to share it equally. There is no right of primogeniture in the laws of nature and of nations. . . .

I have conversed with some persons and found their mistakes on this subject, to arise from a view of claims by individuals in a state of society, from holding a greater proportion of the soil than others, but this is according to the laws to which they have consented; an individual holding one acre, cannot encroach on him who has a thousand, because he is bound by the law which secures property in this unequal manner. This is the municipal law of the state under which he lives. . . .

The idea of an exclusive right to the soil in the natives had its origin in the policy of the first discoverers, the kings of Europe. Should they deny the right of the natives from their first treading on the continent, they would take away the right of discovery in themselves, by sailing on the coast. As the vestige of the moccasin in one case gave a right, so the cruise in the other was the foundation of a claim.

Those who under these kings, derived grants were led to countenance the idea, for otherwise why should kings grant or they hold extensive tracts of country. Men become enslaved to an opinion that has long been entertained. Hence it is that many wise and good men will talk of the right of savages to immense tracts of soil.

What use do these ring, streaked, spotted and speckled cattle make of the soil? Do they till it? Revelation said to man, "Thou shalt till the ground." . . . I would as soon admit a right in the buffalo to grant lands, as in Killbuck, the Big Cat, the Big Dog, or any of the ragged wretches that are called chiefs and sachems. What would you think of going to a big lick or place where the beasts collect to lick saline nitrous earth and water, and addressing yourself to a great buffalo to grant you land? It is true he could not make the mark of the stone or the mountain reindeer, but he could set his cloven hoof to the instrument like the great Ottomon, the father of the Turks, when he put his signature to an instrument, he put his large hand and spreading fingers in the ink and set his mark to the parchment. To see how far the folly of some would go, I had once a thought of supplicating some of the great elks or buffaloes that run through the woods, to make me a grant of a hundred thousand acres of land and prove he had brushed the weeds with his tail, and run fifty miles.

I wonder if Congress or the different States would recognize the claim? I am so far from thinking the Indians have a right to the soil, that not having made a better use of it for many hundred years, I conceive they have forfeited all pretence to claim, and ought to be driven from it.

With regard to forming treaties or making peace with this race, there are many ideas:

They have the shapes of men and may be of the human species, but certainly in their present state they approach nearer the character of Devils; take an Indian, is there any faith in him? Can you bind him by favors? Can you trust his word or confide in his promise? . . .

The tortures which they exercise on the bodies of their prisoners, justify extermination. . . . If we could have any faith in the promises they make we could suffer them to live, provided they would only make war amongst themselves, and abandon their hiding or lurking on the pathways of our citizens, emigrating unarmed and defenceless inhabitants; and murdering men, women and children in a defenceless situation; and on their ceasing in the meantime to raise arms no more among the American citizens.

> *Indian Atrocities: Narratives of the Perils and Sufferings of Dr. Knight and John Slover Among the Indians* (Cincinnati: U. P. James, 1867), pp. 62–72. (First published 1782.)

Letter on Indian Land Rights, 1817

PRESIDENT JAMES MADISON

The doctrine that underdeveloped land may be taken by people who intend to put it to more intensive use can be a double-edged sword, suggests the fourth president, in a letter to James Monroe.

Dec. 27, 1817

. . . My quere . . . relating to the right to Indian lands was suggested by the principle which has limited the claim of the U.S. to a right of pre-emption. It seemed also that an *unqualified* right of a Civilized people to land used by people in the hunter-state, on the principle that the earth was intended for those who would make it most conducive to the sustenance & increase of the human race, might imply a right in a people cultivating it with the Spade, to say to one using the plow, either adopt our mode, or let us substitute it ourselves. It might also be not easy to repel the claims of those without land in other Countries, if not in our own, to vacant lands within the U.S. likely to remain for a *long* period unproductive of human food. The quere was not meant to contest the doctrine of the Message, under qualifications which were probably entertained without being specified.

> GAILLARD HUNT, ed., *The Writings of James Madison* (9 vols.; New York: G. P. Putnam's Sons, 1908), VIII, 404.

The Cherokee Proclamation of Their Prior Rights, 1823

When President Monroe, under pressure from the state of Georgia, tried to induce Cherokee chiefs in January 1823, to cede their land and remove to Arkansas Territory, they asserted that their original sovereignty, recognized by treaty, antedated the sovereignty claimed by Georgia.

Sir, to these remarks we beg leave to observe and to remind you that the Cherokee are not foreigners but original inhabitants of America, and that they now inhabit and stand on the soil of their own territory and that the limits of this territory are defined by the treaties which they have made with the government of the United States, and that the states by which they are now surrounded have been created out of land which was once theirs, and that they cannot recognize the sovereignty of any state within the limits of their territory.

> Quoted in R. S. COTTERILL, *The Southern Indians* (Norman: University of Oklahoma Press, 1954), p. 218.

Serpents and Savages, 1829

CALEB ATWATER

That such a Beautiful country, was intended by its Author to be forever in the possession and occupancy of serpents, wild fowls, wild beasts and savages, who derive little benefit from it, no reasonable man, can for one moment believe who sees it.

> CALEB ATWATER, *The Indians of the Northwest, Their Manners, Customs &c. . . .* (Columbus: 1850), p. 256. Atwater represented the government in treaty negotiations with several tribes at Prairie du Chien in 1829.

42 Presidential Argument for Indian Removal, 1829

PRESIDENT ANDREW JACKSON

In his first annual message, an excerpt of which appears below, President Andrew Jackson devoted much attention to the conflict between the Cherokee Nation and the state of Georgia, and argued, in effect, that it would be an infringement of the sovereignty of that state for the federal government to stand behind its solemn treaties. He advanced as the only solution to the Indian problem the removal of the Indians to that territory beyond the Mississippi which is now called Oklahoma. (See also pp. 110– 36 inclusive, and pp. 189–93.)

Jackson's arguments are filled with inconsistencies and evasions, if not outright falsehoods. While maintaining that the federal government was obliged to remove the Cherokees by terms of the Georgia compact of 1802,[1] he failed to mention that the government was bound more firmly by the Hopewell Treaty of 1785, and later treaties, which were both prior to and subsequent to the compact and constitutionally superior to it. (See Documents 45–46, infra.) He lamented that the Indians had been "made to retire from river to river and mountain to mountain," yet proposed more

1. On April 24, 1802, Georgia ceded her western land claims to the United States in return for a promise that the government would extinguish Indian titles in the state "as early as the same can be peaceably obtained on reasonable terms."

*of the same as the solution to it. He said that the emigration should be
voluntary, yet instructed his commissioners to use every means to compel
submission, and the emigration of most of the Indians was in fact carried
out by armed force. He repeated the old frontier argument (see Brackenridge, pp. 104–106) that Indians had no claim on "tracts of country on
which they have neither dwelt nor made improvements, merely because
they have seen them from the mountains or passed them in the chase,"
when he was certainly aware, and in one place acknowledged, that the
Southern tribes he was about to remove had made astonishing improvements in the land they occupied.² Finally he asserted that if any Indians
chose to submit to the laws of the states they might remain and receive
the same protection in their persons and property as other citizens, when
in fact the states were already passing laws denying these rights to Indians.³*

The condition and ulterior destiny of the Indian tribes within the limits
of some of our States have become objects of much interest and importance. It has long been the policy of Government to introduce among them
the arts of civilization, in the hope of gradually reclaiming them from a
wandering life. This policy has, however, been coupled with another wholly
incompatible with its success. Professing a desire to civilize and settle
them, we have at the same time lost no opportunity to purchase their lands
and thrust them farther into the wilderness. By this means they have not
only been kept in a wandering state, but been led to look upon us as unjust
and indifferent to their fate. Thus, though lavish in its expenditures upon the
subject, Government has constantly defeated its own policy, and the Indians in general, receding farther and farther to the west, have retained
their savage habits. A portion, however, of the Southern tribes, having
mingled much with the whites and made some progress in the arts of
civilized life, have lately attempted to erect an independent government
within the limits of Georgia and Alabama. These states, claiming to be the

2. A census taken among the Cherokees in 1825 showed that they owned 33 grist
mills, 13 sawmills, 1 powder mill, 69 blacksmith shops, 2 tan yards, 762 looms, 2,486
spinning wheels, 172 wagons, 2,923 plows, 7,683 horses, 22,531 black cattle, 46,732
swine, and 2,566 sheep. (Albert Gallatin, "Synopsis of Indian Tribes," in *Transactions and Collections of the American Antiquarian Society* [Cambridge: 1836], II,
157.) By 1829 also, Sequoyah's alphabet had brought literacy to most Cherokees, and
the national newspaper, the *Cherokee Phoenix,* was being published. They had
schools, a mounted police force, and a government modeled after that of the United
States.

3. For example, on December 19, 1829, the Georgia legislature enacted "that no
Indian or descendant of an Indian residing within the Creek or Cherokee nations of
Indians, shall be deemed a competent witness in any court of this state to which a
white person may be a party." Grant Foreman, *Indian Removal* (Norman: University
of Oklahoma Press, 1953), p. 229.

only sovereigns within their territories, extended their laws over the Indians, which induced the latter to call upon the United States for protection.

Under these circumstances the question presented was whether the General Government had a right to sustain those people in their pretensions. The Constitution declares that "no new State shall be formed or erected within the jurisdiction of any other State" without the consent of its legislature. If the General Government is not permitted to tolerate the erection of a confederate State within the territory of one of the members of this Union against her consent, much less could it allow a foreign and independent government to establish itself there. Georgia became a member of the Confederacy which eventuated in our Federal Union as a sovereign State, always asserting her claim to certain limits, which, having been originally defined in her colonial charter and subsequently recognized in the treaty of peace, she has ever since continued to enjoy, except as they have been circumscribed by her own voluntary transfer of a portion of her territory to the United States in the articles of cession of 1802. . . .

Actuated by this view of the subject, I informed the Indians inhabiting parts of Georgia and Alabama that their attempt to establish an independent government would not be countenanced by the Executive of the United States, and advised them to emigrate beyond the Mississippi or submit to the laws of those States.

Our conduct toward these people is deeply interesting to our national character. Their present condition, contrasted with what they once were, makes a most powerful appeal to our sympathies. Our ancestors found them the uncontrolled possessors of these vast regions. By persuasion and force they have been made to retire from river to river and from mountain to mountain, until some of the tribes have become extinct and others have left but remnants to preserve for awhile their once terrible names. Surrounded by the whites with their arts of civilization, which by destroying the resources of the savage doom him to weakness and decay, the fate of the Mohegan, the Narragansett, and the Delaware is fast overtaking the Choctaw, the Cherokee, and the Creek. That this fate surely awaits them if they remain within the limits of the States does not admit of a doubt. Humanity and national honor demand that every effort should be made to avert so great a calamity. It is too late to inquire whether it was just in the United States to include them and their territory within the bounds of new States, whose limits they could control. That step can not be retraced. A State can not be dismembered by Congress or restricted in the exercise of her constitutional power. But the people of those States and of every State, actuated by feelings of justice and a regard for our national honor, submit to you the interesting question whether something can not be done, consistently with the rights of the States, to preserve this much-injured race.

As a means of effecting this end I suggest for your consideration the propriety of setting apart an ample district west of the Mississippi, and without the limits of any State or Territory now formed, to be guaranteed to the Indian tribes as long as they shall occupy it, each tribe having a distinct control over the portion designated for its use. There they may be secured in the enjoyment of governments of their own choice, subject to no other control from the United States than such as may be necessary to preserve peace on the frontier and between the several tribes. There the benevolent may endeavor to teach them the arts of civilization, and, by promoting union and harmony among them, to raise up an interesting commonwealth, destined to perpetuate the race and to attest the humanity and justice of this Government.

This emigration should be voluntary, for it would be as cruel as unjust to compel the aborigines to abandon the graves of their fathers and seek a home in a distant land. But they should be distinctly informed that if they remain within the limits of the States they must be subject to their laws. In return for their obedience as individuals they will without doubt be protected in the enjoyment of those possessions which they have improved by their industry. But it seems to me visionary to suppose that in this state of things claims can be allowed on tracts of country on which they have neither dwelt nor made improvements, merely because they have seen them from the mountain or passed them in the chase. Submitting to the laws of the States, and receiving, like other citizens, protection in their persons and property, they will ere long become merged in the mass of our population.

> JAMES D. RICHARDSON, ed., *A Compilation of the Messages and Papers of the Presidents* (10 vols.; Washington: National Bureau of Literature and Art, 1908), II, 456–59.

43   Congressional Opposition to Jackson's Removal Bill, 1830

Opinion on the merits of President Jackson's Indian Removal Bill of 1830 was far from unanimous. A fierce debate raged in Congress for nearly two months, and some distinguished legislators were arrayed against the president, among them his fellow Tennessean, Representative David Crockett, of Alamo fame, who spoke against the bill on May 19. Senator Theodore Frelinghuysen of New Jersey spoke for six impassioned hours against the pending injustice, and Representative Edward Everett of Massachusetts contributed his renowned oratorical talents to the losing battle. Brief excerpts from the speeches of the two last-named are reproduced below.

Address of Senator Theodore Frelinghuysen, April 7, 1830

. . . in our public intercourse with the Indians, ever since the first colonies of white men found an abode on these shores, we have distinctly recognized their title; treated with them as the owners; and in all our acquisition of territory, applied ourselves to these ancient proprietors, by purchase and cession alone, to obtain the right of soil. Sir, I challenge the record of any other or different pretension. When or where did the assembly or convention meet, which proclaimed, or even suggested to these tribes, that the right of discovery contained a superior efficacy to all prior titles?

Address of Representative Edward Everett, May 19, 1830

. . . Sir, if Georgia will recede, she will do more for the Union, and more for herself, than if she would add to her domain the lands of all the Indians, though they were paved with gold.

The evil, Sir, is enormous; the inevitable suffering incalculable. Do not stain the fair fame of the country; it has been justly said, it is in the keeping of Congress, on this subject. It is more wrapped up in this policy, in the estimation of the civilized world, than in all your other doings. Its elements are plain, and tangible, and few. Nations of dependent Indians, against their will, under color of law, are driven from their homes into the wilderness. You cannot explain it; you cannot reason it away. The subtleties which satisfy you will not satisfy the severe judgement of enlightened Europe. Our friends will view this measure with sorrow, and our enemies alone with joy. And we ourselves, Sir, when the interests and passions of the day are past, shall look back upon it, I fear, with self-reproach, and a regret as bitter as unavailing.

> JEREMIAH EVARTS, ed., *Speeches on the Passage of the Bill for the Removal of the Indians Delivered in the Congress of the United States, April and May 1830* (Boston: Perkins and Marvin, 1830), pp. 9, 299.

44   Excoriation of Jackson's Indian Policy, 1830

THOMAS L. MCKENNEY

At all times when the Indians have been victimized, there has been a minority voice raised in their defense. Such a voice was that of Colonel Thomas L. McKenney. In 1816 he was appointed by President James Madi-

son to the post of superintendent of United States Indian Trade, which involved the administration of the government "factory" system which was originated by Washington as a means of protecting Indians from the extortions of some private traders, when exchanging their furs for trade goods. This office was abolished by Congress in 1822, under the pressure of the fur trading companies and their political allies. Two years later McKenney was appointed by President Monroe to head the newly created Bureau of Indian Affairs, then a division of the War Department. During his administration he sought to protect the Indians from abuse by settlers and traders and from forcible removal by the government. After he had made known to President Jackson, in a personal audience, his opposition to the dissolution of the Cherokee government in Georgia, he was dismissed from the government service, in August 1830. The following is an abbreviated account, by McKenney, of this incident and events leading up to it.

The fifth article of the treaty of Washington, of the 27th of February, 1819, between John C. Calhoun, on the part of the United States, and a delegation of chiefs and head men of the Cherokee nation, duly authorized and empowered by said nation, contains this provision: "—And all white people who *have* intruded, or may *hereafter* intrude, on the lands reserved for the Cherokees, *shall be removed by the United States,* and proceeded against, according to the provisions of the act passed thirtieth of March, eighteen hundred and two, entitled an act to regulate trade and intercourse with the Indian tribes, and to preserve peace on the frontiers." . . .

But this law was destined, at last, though unrepealed, to become a dead letter! The solemn compacts with the Indians, guaranteeing to them "protection," were treated as things obsolete, or regarded as mockeries. In the face, and in violation of the provisions of the one, and of the enactments of the other, surveyors were permitted to penetrate the Indian territory, roam over it, lay it off into counties, and to proceed, in all things, for its settlement, as though no Indians occupied it, and no laws existed, demanding the interference of the government to prevent it! In vain did the Indians implore the government to protect them; in vain did they call the attention of the Executive to the provisions of treaties, and to the pledges of the law. It was when these outrages first began to show themselves, and thinking President Jackson could not be aware of their existence, that I called on him, and referred to them, and also to the provisions of laws and treaties that guarantied [*sic*] to the Indians a freedom from such trespasses. His answer was, *"Sir, the sovereignty of the States must be preserved,"* concluding with a termination so solemn, and the whole being spoken in a manner so emphatic, as to satisfy me that he had concluded to permit Georgia, and the other States in which the Indians were included, to take their own way in their plans, to harass, persecute, and force out their Indian population. . . .

[*On a visit to Philadelphia shortly thereafter, to confer with the publishers of his* History of the North American Indians, *he received a letter from Dr. Randolph, chief clerk of the War Department and brother-in-law of Secretary Eaton, a Jackson favorite, "informing me that, from and after the first day of October next ensuing, my services in the Indian Department would not be required."*] Returning to Washington, I inquired of him what the grounds of my dismissal were. "Why, sir," was his reply, "everybody knows your qualifications for the place, but General Jackson has been long satisfied that you are not in harmony with him, in his views in regard to the Indians." And thus closed my connexion with the government.

THOMAS L. MCKENNEY, *Sketches of Travels among the Northern & Southern Indians* [etc.] (3d ed.; New York: Daniel Burgess & Co., 1854), I, 256–62.

President Jackson, as indicated above by McKenney, and in many other documents, insisted that he was powerless to restrain Georgia's actions against the Cherokees, because of the doctrine of state sovereignty.

He took exactly an opposite position in his quarrel with South Carolina, when that state passed an ordinance of nullification, designed to void the federal tariff law of 1828 in that state. In a proclamation issued on December 10, 1832, he asserted:

I consider then, the power to annul a law of the United States, assumed by one State, incompatible with the existence of the Union, contradicted expressly by the letter of the Constitution, unauthorized by its spirit, inconsistent with every principle on which it was founded, and destructive of the great object for which it was formed. . . .

The Constitution declares that the judicial powers of the United States extend to cases arising under the laws of the United States, and that such laws, the Constitution, and treaties shall be paramount to the State constitutions and laws.[1]

In that same year, the judicial power of the United States attempted to assert itself, in the case of Worcester v. Georgia *(see pp. 124 ff.), against the drive of the state of Georgia to nullify both federal laws and federal treaties relating to the Cherokees. Jackson declined to support the decision, but on the contrary, exerted all his power in the opposite direction.*

---

1. James D. Richardson, ed., *A Compilation of the Messages and Papers of the Presidents* (Washington: Bureau of National Literature and Art, 1908), II, 643, 647. Original emphasis.

45   Cherokee Nation v. Georgia, 1831

This suit resulted from the passage by the Georgia legislature of two acts calculated to totally destroy the Cherokee nation and deprive its members of any avenue of redress in state courts.

In December 1828, it was enacted that all territory lying within the state of Georgia and occupied by Cherokee Indians was to be divided into parcels, added to five Georgia counties, and opened up for white settlement. Moreover, the laws of Georgia were to be extended over the region. One year later a second act reaffirmed the first, and went on to annul all laws and ordinances made by the Cherokee nation, and further declared that no Cherokee Indian could testify in court against a white man.

The effect and purposes of these laws, according to the complaint of the Cherokees, was:

. . . to parcel out the territory of the Cherokees, to extend all the laws of Georgia over the same; to abolish the Cherokee laws, to prevent them, as individuals, from enrolling for emigration, under the penalty of indictment before the state courts of Georgia; to make it murder in the officers of the Cherokee government to inflict the sentence of death in conformity with the Cherokee laws, subjecting them to indictment therefor, and death by hanging; extending the jurisdiction of the justices of the peace of Georgia into the Cherokee territory, and authorizing the calling out of the militia of Georgia to enforce the process; and finally, declaring that no Indian, or descendant of any Indian, residing within the Cherokee nation of Indians, shall be deemed a competent witness in any Court in the state of Georgia, in which a white person may be a party, except such white person resides within the said nation.

The Cherokees argued that all these laws were null and void because they were repugnant to the Constitution of the United States, to the Indian Trade and Intercourse Act of March 30, 1802, to the Treaty of Hopewell, signed November 28, 1785, and eleven other treaties up to the year 1819, which recognized the right of the Cherokee nation to an existence outside the jurisdiction of state laws.

The Cherokees argued that treaties, according to the Constitution, were part of the supreme law of the land, that the Supreme Court had original jurisdiction over cases involving treaties, and over controversies between a state of the union and a foreign nation.

Chief Justice John Marshall, speaking for the majority, avoided dealing with the merits of the case by denying that the court had jurisdiction. His argument was based on the allegation that the Indian tribes were not foreign nations but "domestic dependent nations," and that the framers of the Constitution "had not the Indian tribes in view, when they opened the

Courts of the union to controversies between a state or the citizens thereof, and foreign states."

Marshall did not deal at all with the point that the judicial power of the United States extended to all cases involving treaties. This point was instead made the main basis of a dissenting opinion by Justice Thompson, supported by Justice Story.

Marshall further maintained that "If it be true that the Cherokee nation have rights, this is not the tribunal in which those rights are to be asserted." This meant that there was in fact no place, short of the battlefield, to which the Indians could turn for relief, since all other channels of redress were effectively closed to them.

Justice Johnson, who, along with Justice Baldwin, supported Marshall, held that Indian treaties were really little more than contracts. If this reasoning should be accepted, it would still be necessary to confront the constitutional proviso that "No state shall . . . pass any Bill . . . or Law impairing the Obligation of Contracts" (Art. I, Sec. 10). Instead, Johnson fell back on the "might makes right" argument, maintaining that the situation in Georgia was in effect a state of war, in which Georgia could enforce its will as a conqueror.

In the case of Worcester v. Georgia, *one year later (pp. 124 ff.) it was again alleged that the laws of Georgia were invalid in Cherokee Territory, and this time the allegation was sustained, the majority opinion again being written by John Marshall. The only real difference in the case was that the appeal was brought by a private American citizen instead of by an Indian tribe asserting itself to be a foreign nation.*

Opinion of Chief Justice Marshall in *Cherokee Nation* v. *Georgia*

This bill is brought by the Cherokee nation, praying an injunction to restrain the state of Georgia from the execution of certain laws of that state, which, as is alleged, go directly to annihilate the Cherokees as a political society, and to seize, for the use of Georgia, the lands of the nation which have been assured to them by the United States in solemn treaties repeatedly made and still in force. . . .

Before we can look into the merits of the case, a preliminary inquiry presents itself. Has this Court jurisdiction of the cause?

The third article of the constitution describes the extent of the judicial power. The second section closes an enumeration of the cases to which it is extended, with "controversies" "between a state or the citizens thereof, and foreign states, citizens, or subjects." A subsequent clause of the same section gives the Supreme Court original jurisdiction in all cases in which a state shall be a party. The party defendant may then unquestionably be sued in this Court. May the plaintiff sue in it? Is the Cherokee nation a foreign state in the sense in which that term is used in the constitution?

The counsel for the plaintiffs have maintained the affirmative of this proposition with great earnestness and ability. So much of the argument as was intended to prove the character of the Cherokees as a state, as a distinct political society, separated from others, capable of managing its own affairs and governing itself, has, in the opinion of a majority of the judges, been completely successful. They have been uniformly treated as a state from the settlement of our country. The numerous treaties made with them by the United States recognise them as a people capable of maintaining the relations of peace and war, of being responsible in their political character for any violation of their engagements, or for any aggression committed on the citizens of the United States by any individual of their community. Laws have been enacted in the spirit of these treaties. The acts of our government plainly recognise the Cherokee nation as a state, and the Courts are bound by those acts.

A question of much more difficulty remains. Do the Cherokees constitute a foreign state in the sense of the constitution?

The counsel have shown conclusively that they are not a state of the union, and have insisted that individually they are aliens, not owing allegiance to the United States. An aggregate of aliens composing a state must, they say, be a foreign state. Each individual being foreign, the whole must be foreign.

This argument is imposing, but we must examine it more closely before we yield to it. The condition of the Indians in relation to the United States is perhaps unlike that of any other two people in existence. In the general, nations not owing a common allegiance are foreign to each other. The term foreign nation is, with strict propriety, applicable by either to the other. But the relation of the Indians to the United States is marked by peculiar and cardinal distinctions which exist no where else.

The Indian territory is admitted to compose a part of the United States. In all our maps, geographical treatises, histories, and laws, it is so considered. In all our intercourse with foreign nations, in our commercial regulations, in any attempt at intercourse between Indians and foreign nations, they are considered as within the jurisdictional limits of the United States, subject to many of those restraints which are imposed upon our own citizens. They acknowledge themselves in their treaties to be under the protection of the United States; they admit that the United States shall have the sole and exclusive right of regulating the trade with them, and managing all their affairs as they think proper; and the Cherokees in particular were allowed by the treaty of Hopewell, which preceded the constitution, "to send a deputy of their choice, whenever they think fit, to Congress."

Treaties were made with some tribes by the state of New York, under a then unsettled construction of the confederation, by which they ceded all their lands to that state, taking back a limited grant to themselves, in which they admit their dependence.

Though the Indians are acknowledged to have an unquestionable, and, heretofore, unquestioned right to the lands they occupy, until that right shall be extinguished by a voluntary cession to our government; yet it may well be doubted whether those tribes which reside within the acknowledged boundaries of the United States can, with strict accuracy, be denominated foreign nations. They may, more correctly, perhaps, be denominated domestic dependent nations. They occupy a territory to which we assert a title independent of their will, which must take effect in point of possession when their right of possession ceases. Meanwhile they are in a state of pupilage. Their relation to the United States resembles that of a ward to his guardian.

They look to our government for protection; rely upon its kindness and its power; appeal to it for relief to their wants; and address the president as their great father. They and their country are considered by foreign nations, as well as by ourselves, as being so completely under the sovereignty and dominion of the United States, that any attempt to acquire their lands, or to form a political connexion with them, would be considered by all as an invasion of our territory, and an act of hostility.

These considerations go far to support the opinion, that the framers of our constitution had not the Indian tribes in view, when they opened the Courts of the union to controversies between a state or the citizens thereof, and foreign states.

. . . the peculiar relations between the United States and the Indians occupying our territory are such, that we should feel much difficulty in considering them as designated by the term foreign state, were there no other part of the constitution which might shed light on the meaning of these words. But we think that in construing them, considerable aid is furnished by that clause in the eighth section of the third article, which empowers Congress to "regulate commerce with foreign nations, and among the several states, and with the Indian tribes."

In this clause they are as clearly contradistinguished by a name appropriate to themselves, from foreign nations, as from the several states composing the union. They are designated by a distinct appellation; and as this appellation can be applied to neither of the others, neither can the appellation distinguishing either of the others be in fair construction applied to them. The objects, to which the power of regulating commerce might be directed, are divided into three distinct classes—foreign nations, the several states, and Indian tribes. When forming this article, the convention considered them as entirely distinct. We cannot assume that the distinction was lost in framing a subsequent article, unless there be something in its language to authorize the assumption. . . .

The Court has bestowed its best attention on this question, and, after mature deliberation, the majority is of opinion that an Indian tribe or nation within the United States is not a foreign state in the sense of the constitution, and cannot maintain an action in the Courts of the United States.

A serious additional objection exists to the jurisdiction of the Court. Is the matter of the bill the proper subject for judicial inquiry and decision? It seeks to restrain a state from the forcible exercise of legislative power over a neighbouring people, asserting their independence; their right to which the state denies. On several of the matters alleged in the bill, for example on the laws making it criminal to exercise the usual powers of self government in their own country by the Cherokee nation, this Court cannot interpose; at least in the form in which those matters are presented.

The part of the bill which respects the land occupied by the Indians, and prays the aid of the Court to protect their possession, may be more doubtful. The mere question of right might perhaps be decided by this Court in a proper case with proper parties. But the Court is asked to do more than decide on the title. The bill requires us to control the legislature of Georgia, and to restrain the exertion of its physical force. The propriety of such an interposition by the Court may be well questioned. It savours too much of the exercise of political power to be within the proper province of the judicial department. But the opinion on the point respecting parties makes it unnecessary to decide this question.

If it be true that the Cherokee nation have rights, this is not the tribunal in which those rights are to be asserted. If it is true that wrongs have been inflicted, and that still greater are to be apprehended, this is not the tribunal which can redress the past or prevent the future.

The motion for an injunction is denied.

Excerpts from Concurring Opinion of Justice Johnson

. . . I cannot but think that there are strong reasons for doubting the applicability of the epithet state, to a people so low in the grade of organized society as our Indian tribes most generally are. . . .

What does this series of allegations exhibit but a state of war, and the fact of invasion? They allege themselves to be a sovereign independent state, and set out that another sovereign state has, by its laws, its functionaries, and its armed force, invaded their state and put down their authority. This is war in fact; though not being declared with the usual solemnities, it may perhaps be called war in disguise. And the contest is distinctly a contest for empire. It is not a case of meum and tuum in the judicial but in the political sense. Not an appeal to laws but to force. A case in which a sovereign undertakes to assert his right upon his sovereign responsibility; to right himself, and not to appeal to any arbiter but the sword, for the justice of his cause. If the state of Maine were to extend its laws over the province of New Brunswick, and send its magistrates to carry them into effect, it would be a parallel case.[1] . . . In the exercise of sovereign right, the sovereign is sole arbiter of his own justice. The penalty of wrong is war and subjugation. . . .

Excerpts from Dissenting Opinion of Justice Thompson

. . . In the opinion pronounced by the Court, the merits of the controversy between the state of Georgia and the Cherokee Indians have not been taken into consideration. The denial of the application for an injunction has been placed solely on the ground of want of jurisdiction in this Court to grant the relief prayed for. It became, therefore, unnecessary to inquire into the merits of the case. But thinking as I do, that the Court has jurisdiction of the case, and may grant relief, at least in part; it may become necessary for me, in the course of my opinion, to glance at the merits of the controversy; which I shall, however, do very briefly, as it is important so far as relates to the present application. . . .

. . . If they are entitled to other than judicial relief, it cannot be admitted that in a government like ours, redress is not to be had in some of its departments; and the responsibility for its denial must rest upon those who have the power to grant it. But believing as I do, that relief to some extent falls properly under judicial cognizance, I shall proceed to the examination of the case under the following heads.

1. Is the Cherokee nation of Indians a competent party to sue in this Court?

2. Is a sufficient case made out in the bill, to warrant this court in granting any relief?

3. Is an injunction the fit and appropriate relief?

1. By the constitution of the United States it is declared, (Art. 3, § 2) that the judicial power shall extend to all cases in law and equity, arising under this constitution, the laws of the United States, and treaties made, or which shall be made under their authority, &c.; to controversies between two

---

1. "No State shall, without the Consent of Congress . . . engage in War, unless actually invaded, or in such imminent Danger as will not admit of delay." (Constitution, Art. I, Sec. 10, p. 3.)—V.J.V.

or more states, &c. and between a state and the citizens thereof, and foreign states, citizens or subjects. . . .

Whether the Cherokee Indians are to be considered a foreign state or not, is a point on which we cannot expect to discover much light from the law of nations. We must derive this knowledge chiefly from the practice of our own government, and the light in which the nation has been viewed and treated by it.

That numerous tribes of Indians, and among others the Cherokee nation, occupied many parts of this country long before the discovery by Europeans, is abundantly established by history; and it is not denied but that the Cherokee nation occupied the territory now claimed by them long before that period. . . .

That they are entitled to such occupancy, so long as they choose quietly and peaceably to remain upon the land, cannot be questioned. The circumstance of their original occupancy is here referred to, merely for the purpose of showing, that if these Indian communities were then, as they certainly were, nations, they must have been foreign nations, to all the world; not having any connexion, or alliance of any description, with any other power on earth. And if the Cherokees were then a foreign nation; when or how have they lost that character, and ceased to be a distinct people, and become incorporated with any other community? . . . It is the political relation in which one government or country stands to another, which constitutes it foreign to the other. The Cherokee territory being within the chartered limits of Georgia, does not affect the question. . . .

It is manifest . . . that a foreign state, judicially considered, consists in its being under a different jurisdiction or government, without any reference to its territorial position. . . .

And what possible objection can lie to the right of the complainants to sustain an action? The treaties made with this nation purport to secure to it certain rights. These are not gratuitous obligations assumed on the part of the United States. They are obligations founded upon a consideration paid by the Indians by cession of part of their territory. And if they as a nation, are competent to make a treaty or contract, it would seem to me to be a strange inconsistency to deny to them the right and the power to enforce such a contract. And where the right secured by such a treaty forms a proper subject for judicial cognizance, I can perceive no reason why this Court has not jurisdiction of the case. The constitution expressly gives to the Court jurisdiction in all cases of law and equity arising under treaties made with the United States. . . .

If we look to the whole course of treatment by this country of the Indians, from the year 1775, to the present day, when dealing with them in their aggregate capacity as nations or tribes, and regarding the mode and manner in which all negotiations have been carried on and concluded with them; the conclusion appears to me irresistible, that they have been regarded, by the executive and legislative branches of the government, not only as sovereign and independent, but as foreign nations or tribes, not within the jurisdiction nor under the government of the states within which they were located. . . . . All negotiations carried on with the Cherokees and other Indian nations have been by way of treaty with all the formality attending the making of treaties with any foreign power. The journals of Congress, from the year 1775 down to the adoption of the present constitution, abundantly establish this fact. And since that period such negotiations have been carried on by the treaty-making power, and uniformly under the denomination of treaties.

What is a treaty as understood in the law of nations? It is an agreement or contract between two or more nations or sovereigns, entered into by agents appointed for that purpose, and duly sanctioned by the supreme power of the respective parties. And where is the authority, either in the constitution or in the practice of the government, for making any distinction between treaties made with the Indian nations and any other foreign power? They relate to peace and war; the surrender of prisoners; the cession of territory; and the various subjects which are usually embraced in such contracts between sovereign nations. . . .

. . . If exercising exclusive jurisdiction over a country is sufficient to constitute the state or power exercising it as a foreign state, the Cherokee nation may assuredly with the greatest propriety be so considered.

The phraseology of the clause in the constitution, giving to Congress the power to regulate commerce, is supposed to afford an argument against considering the Cherokees a foreign nation. The clause reads thus, "to regulate commerce with foreign nations, and among the several states, and with the Indian tribes." . . . The argument is, that if the Indian tribes are foreign nations, they would have been included without being specially named, and being so named imports something different from the previous term "foreign nations."

This appears to me to partake too much of a mere verbal criticism, to draw after it the important conclusion, the Indian tribes are not foreign nations. But the clause affords, irresistibly, the conclusion, that the Indian tribes are not there understood as included within the description of, the "several states;" or there could have been no fitness in immediately thereafter particularizing "the Indian tribes." . . .

Cases may arise where the trade with a particular tribe may require to be regulated, and which might not have been embraced under the general description of the term nation, or it might at least have left the case somewhat doubtful; as the clause was intended to invest in Congress the power to regulate all commercial intercourse, this phraseology was probably adopted to meet all possible cases; and the provision would have been imperfect, if the term Indian tribes had been omitted. . . .

The twelfth article of the treaty of Hopewell contains a full recognition of the sovereign and independent character of the Cherokee nation. To impress upon them full confidence in the justice of the United States respecting their interest, they have a right to send a deputy of their choice to Congress. No one can suppose that such deputy was to take his seat as a member of Congress; but that he would be received as the agent of that nation. It is immaterial what such agent is called, whether minister, commissioner or deputy; he is to represent his principal.

There could have been no fitness or propriety in any such stipulation, if the Cherokee nation had been considered in any way incorporated with the state of Georgia, or as citizens of that state. The idea of the Cherokees being considered citizens is entirely inconsistent with several of our treaties with them. . . .

It may be necessary here briefly to notice some of the provisions of this [the Indian Trade and Intercourse] act of 1802, so far as it goes to protect the rights of property in the Indians; for the purpose of seeing whether there has been any violation of those rights by the state of Georgia, which falls properly under judicial cognizance. By this act it is made an offence punishable by fine and imprisonment, for any citizen or other person resident in the United States, or either of the territorial districts, to cross over or go within the boundary line, to hunt or destroy the game, or drive stock to range or feed on the Indian lands, or to go into any country allotted to the Indians, without a passport, or to commit therein any robbery, larceny, trespass, or other crime, against the person or property of any friendly Indian, which would be punishable, if committed within the jurisdiction of any state against a citizen of the United States; thereby necessarily implying that the Indian territory secured by treaty was not within the jurisdiction of any state. . . . And by the fifth section it is declared, that if any citizen of the United States, or other person, shall make a settlement on any lands belonging or secured, or guarantied, by treaty with the United States to any Indian tribe; or shall survey or attempt to survey, such lands, or designate any of the boundaries, by marking trees or otherwise; such offender shall forfeit a sum not exceeding one thousand dollars, and suffer imprisonment not exceeding twelve months.

This act contains various other provisions for the purpose of protecting the Indians in the free and uninterrupted enjoyment of their lands: and authority is given (§ 16) to employ the military force of the United States to apprehend all persons who shall be found in the Indian country, in violation of any of the provisions of the act, and deliver them up to the civil authority, to be proceeded against in due course of law. . . .

The laws of Georgia set out in the bill, if carried fully into operation, go the length of abrogating all the laws of the Cherokees, abolishing their government, and entirely subverting their national character. Although the whole of these laws may be in violation of the treaties made with this nation, it is probable this Court cannot grant relief to the full extent of the complaint. Some of them, however, are so directly at variance with these treaties and the laws of the United States touching the rights of property secured to them, that I can perceive no objection to the application of judicial relief. The state of Georgia certainly could not have intended these laws as declarations of hostility, or wish their execution of them to be viewed in any manner whatever as acts of war; but merely as an assertion of what is claimed as a legal right, and in this light ought they to be considered by this Court.

The act of the 2d of December, 1830, is entitled "an act to authorize the governor to take possession of gold and silver and other mines lying and being in that section of the chartered limits of Georgia, commonly called the Cherokee country, and those upon all other unappropriated lands of the state, and for punishing persons who may be found trespassing on the mines." The preamble to this act asserts the title to these mines to belong to the state of Georgia; and by its provisions twenty thousand dollars are appropriated, and placed at the disposal of the governor to enable him to take possession of those mines; and it is made a crime, punishable by imprisonment in the penitentiary of Georgia at hard labour, for the Cherokee Indians to work these mines. And the bill alleges that under the laws of the state in relation to the mines, the governor has stationed at the mines an armed force who are employed in restraining the complainants in their rights and liberties in regard to their own mines, and in enforcing the laws of Georgia upon them. These can be considered in no other light than as acts of trespass; and may be treated as acts of the state; and not of the individuals employed as agents. . . . It is not perceived on what ground the state can claim a right to the possession and use of these mines. The right of occupancy is secured to the Cherokees by treaty, and the state has not even a reversionary interest in the soil. It is true, that by the compact with Georgia in 1802, the United States have stipulated, to extinguish, for the use of the state, the Indian title to the lands within her remaining limits, "as soon as it can be done peaceably and upon reasonable terms." But until this is done, the state can have no claim to the lands. . . .

The doctrine of this Court in the case of Osborne *vs.* The United States Bank, 9 Wheat. 338, fully sustains the present application for an injunction. The bill in that case was filed to obtain an injunction against the auditor of the state of Ohio, to restrain him from executing a law of that state, which was alleged to be to the great injury of the bank, and to the destruction of rights conferred by their charter. . . .

The laws of the state of Georgia in this case go as fully to the total destruction of the complainants' rights as did the law of Ohio to the destruction of the rights of the bank in that state; and an injunction is as fit and proper in this case to prevent the injury, as it was in that. . . .

Upon the whole, I am of opinion,

1. That the Cherokees compose a foreign state within the sense and meaning of the constitution, and constitute a competent party to maintain a suit against the state of Georgia.

2. That the bill presents a case for judicial consideration, arising under the laws of the United States, and treaties made under their authority with the Cherokee nation, and which laws and treaties have been, and are threatened to be still further violated by the laws of the state of Georgia referred to in this opinion.

3. That an injunction is a fit and proper writ to be issued, to prevent the further execution of such laws, and ought therefore to be awarded.

And I am authorized by my brother Story to say, that he concurs with me in this opinion.

> RICHARD PETERS, *Reports of Cases Argued and Adjudged in the Supreme Court of the United States, January Term,* 1831 [Peters, V], (Philadelphia: Thomas, Cowperthwait & Co., 1851), 9–69 [1–79].

46 A Judicial Determination of the Rights of Indian Nations: Worcester v. Georgia, 1832

JOHN MARSHALL

On September 16, 1831, a Georgia court convicted Samuel A. Worcester, a missionary to the Cherokee Indians, and ten other men, of violating a newly enacted state law forbidding whites to reside in the Cherokee nation without permission of the state. All were sentenced to four years at hard labor. The law was not intended to protect the Indians from encroaching settlers, but to keep out missionaries and white friends who were suspected of encouraging the Indians to oppose state jurisdiction over their lands.

Suit was brought before the Supreme Court, arguing that Georgia laws were invalid in Cherokee Territory, due to special treaty relations between the tribe and the federal government. The court ruled in favor of the appellants, and ordered them freed, but the state of Georgia refused to obey. President Jackson, who vigorously supported Georgia's plans to expel the Indians, reportedly remarked: "John Marshall has made his decision, now let him enforce it." At the same time that the president backed Georgia's defiance of the federal judiciary and federal treaties, he was upholding the supremacy of federal tariff legislation in the famous "nullification" quarrel with South Carolina.

The eleven imprisoned men sought relief once more from the Supreme Court, but the governor of Georgia, not wishing to see the president's contradictory policies further exacerbated during his quarrel with South Carolina, promised to release them if the new suit was withdrawn. Consequently they were released in January 1833.[1]

The importance of the case of Worcester v. Georgia *is that it established the quasi-sovereignty of Indian tribes, and upheld the supremacy of Indian treaties over state laws.*

Worcester v. Georgia: Majority Opinion of Chief Justice John Marshall (Official Summary)

. . . The plaintiff in error was indicted in the Supreme Court for the County of Gwinnett in the state of Georgia, "For residing, on the 15th of July, 1831, in that part of the Cherokee nation attached by the laws of the state of Georgia to that county, without a license or permit from the governor of the state, or from any one authorized to grant it, and without having taken the oath to support and defend the constitution and laws of the state of Georgia, and uprightly to demean himself as a citizen thereof, contrary to the laws of the said state." To this indictment he pleaded that he was, on the 15th July, 1831, in the Cherokee nation, out of the jurisdiction of the Court of Gwinnett county; that he was a citizen of Vermont, and entered the Cherokee nation as a missionary under the authority of the President of the United States, and has not been required by him to leave it, and that with the permission and approval of the Cherokee nation he was engaged in preaching the gospel; that the state of Georgia ought not to maintain the prosecution, as several treaties had been entered into by the United States with the Cherokee nation, by which that nation was acknowledged to be a sovereign nation, and by which the territory occupied by them was guarantied to them by the United States, and that the laws of Georgia, under which the plaintiff in error was indicted, are repugnant to the treaties, and unconstitutional and void, and also that they are repugnant to the act of Congress of March, 1802, entitled, "An act to regulate trade and intercourse with the Indian tribes." The Superior Court of Gwinnet[t] overruled the plea, and the plaintiff in error was tried and convicted, and sentenced, "to hard labour in the penitentiary for four years." Held, that this was a case in which the Supreme Court of the

---

1. For a detailed account, see Althea Bass, *Cherokee Messenger* (Norman: University of Oklahoma Press, 1968).

United States had jurisdiction by writ of error, under the twenty-fifth section of the "Act to establish the Judicial Courts of the United States," passed in 1789.

The indictment and plea in this case draw in question the validity of the treaties made by the United States with the Cherokee Indians; if not so, their construction is certainly drawn in question; and the decision has been, if not against their validity, "against the right, privilege, or exemption specially set up and claimed under them." They also draw into question the validity of a statute of the state of Georgia, "on the ground of its being repugnant to the Constitution, treaties, and the laws of the United States, and the decision is in favour of its validity." . . .

The act of the legislature of Georgia, passed 22d December, 1830, entitled, "An act to prevent the exercise of assumed and arbitrary power by all persons, under pretext of authority from the Cherokee Indians," &c., enacts that, "All white persons, residing within the limits of the Cherokee nation on the 1st day of March next, or at any time thereafter, without a license or permit from his excellency the governor . . . shall be guilty of a high misdemeanor, and upon conviction thereof, shall be punished by confinement to the penitentiary at hard labour, for a term not less than four years." . . . The extra-territorial power of every legislature being limited in its action to its own citizens or subjects, the very passage of this act is an assertion of jurisdiction over the Cherokee nation, and of the rights and powers consequent thereto.

The principle, "that discovery of parts of the continent of America gave title to the government by whose subjects, or by whose authority it was made, against all other European governments, which title might be consummated by possession," acknowledged by all Europeans, because it was the interest of all to acknowledge it; gave to the nation making the discovery, as its invariable consequence, the sole right of acquiring the soil and making settlements on it. It was an exclusive principle, which shut out the right of competition among those who had agreed to it; not one of which could annul the previous rights of those who had not agreed to it. It regulated the right given by discovery among the European discoverers, but could not affect the rights of those already in possession, either as aboriginal occupants, or as occupants by virtue of a discovery made before the memory of man. It gave the exclusive right to purchase, but did not found that right on a denial of the right of the possessor to sell.

The relation between the Europeans and the natives was determined in each case by the particular government which asserted and could maintain this pre-emptive privilege in the particular place. The United States succeeded to all the claims of Great Britain, both territorial and political, but no attempt, so far as it is known, has been made to enlarge them. So far as they existed merely in theory, or were in their nature only exclusive of the claims of other European nations, they still retain their original character, and remain dormant. So far as they have been practically exerted, they exist in fact, are understood by both parties, are asserted by the one, and admitted by the other.

Soon after Great Britain determined on planting colonies in America, the king granted charters to companies of his subjects, who associated for the purpose of carrying the views of the crown into effect, and of enriching themselves. The first of these charters was made before possession was taken of any part of the country. They purport generally to convey the soil, from the Atlantic to the South Sea. This soil was occupied by numerous and warlike nations, equally willing and able to defend their possessions. The extravagant and absurd idea, that the feeble settlements made on the sea coast, or the companies under whom they were made, acquired legitimate power by them to govern the people, or occupy the lands from sea to sea, did not enter the mind of any man. They were well understood to convey the title which, according to the common law of European sovereigns respecting America, they might rightfully convey, and no more. This was the exclusive right of purchasing such lands as the natives were willing to sell. The crown could not be understood to grant what the crown did not affect to claim, nor was it so understood.

Certain it is, that our history furnishes no example, from the first settlement of our country, of any attempt, on the part of the crown, to interfere with the internal affairs of the Indians, farther than to keep out the agents of foreign powers, who, as traders or otherwise, might seduce them into foreign alliances. The king purchased their lands when they were willing to sell, at a price they were willing to take; but never coerced a surrender of them. He also purchased their alliance and dependence by subsidies; but never intruded into the interior of their affairs, or interfered with their self-government, so far as respected themselves only.

The third article of the treaty of Hopewell acknowledges the Cherokees to be under the protection of the United States of America, and of no other power.

This stipulation is found in Indian treaties, generally. It was introduced into their treaties with Great Britain; and may probably be found in those with other European powers. Its origin may be traced to the nature of their connexion with those powers; and its true meaning is discerned in their relative situation.

The general law of European sovereigns respecting their claims in America, limited the intercourse of Indians, in a great degree, to the particular potentate whose ultimate right of domain was acknowledged by others. This was the general state of things in time of peace. It was sometimes changed in war. The consequence was, that their supplies were derived chiefly from that nation, and their trade confined to it. Goods, indispensable for their comfort, in the shape of presents, were received from the same hand. What was of still more importance, the strong hand of government was interposed to restrain the disorderly and licentious from intrusions into their country, from encroachments on their lands, and from those acts of violence which were often attended by reciprocal murder. The Indians perceived in this protection, only what was beneficial to themselves—an engagement to punish aggressions on them. It involved practically no claim to their lands, no dominion over their persons. It merely bound the nation to the British crown, as a dependant [*sic*] ally, claiming the protection of a powerful friend and neighbour, and receiving the advantages of that protection, without involving a surrender of their national character.

This is the true meaning of the stipulation, and is undoubtedly the sense in which it was made. Neither the British government, nor the Cherokees, ever understood it otherwise.

The same stipulation entered into with the United States, is undoubtedly to be construed in the same manner. They receive the Cherokee nation into their favour and protection. The Cherokees acknowledge themselves to be under the protection of the United States, and of no other power. Protection does not imply the destruction of the protected. The manner in which this stipulation was understood by the American government is explained by the language and acts of our first president.

So with respect to the words "hunting grounds." Hunting was at that time the principal occupation of the Indians, and their land was more used for that purpose than for any other. It could not, however, be supposed, that any intention existed of restricting the full use of the lands they reserved.

To the United States, it could be a matter of no concern, whether their whole territory was devoted to hunting grounds, or whether an occasional village and an occasional cornfield interrupted, and gave some variety to the scene.

These terms had been used in their treaties with Great Britain, and had never been misunderstood. They had never been supposed to imply a right in the British government to take their lands, or to interfere with their internal government.

The sixth and seventh articles stipulate for the punishment of the citizens of either country, who may commit offences on or against the citizens of the other. The only inference to be drawn from them is, that the United States considered the Cherokees as a nation.

The ninth article is in these words: "for the benefit and comfort of the

Indians, and for the prevention of injuries or oppressions on the part of the citizens or Indians, the United States, in Congress assembled, shall have the sole and exclusive right of regulating the trade with the Indians, and managing all their affairs, as they think proper." To construe the expression "managing all their affairs," into a surrender of self-government would be a perversion of their necessary meaning, and a departure from the construction which has been uniformly put on them. The great subject of the article is the Indian trade. The influence it gave made it desirable that Congress should possess it. The commissioners brought forward the claim, with the profession that their motive was, "the benefit and comfort of the Indians, and the prevention of injuries or oppressions." This may be true, as respects the regulation of their trade, and as respects the regulation of all affairs connected with their trade; but cannot be true, as respects the management of all their affairs. The most important of these, is the cession of their lands, and security against intruders on them. Is it credible, that they could have considered themselves as surrendering to the United States the right to dictate their future cessions, and the terms on which they should be made; or to compel their submission to the violence of disorderly and licentious intruders? It is equally inconceivable that they could have supposed themselves, by a phrase thus slipped into an article, on another and mere[1] interesting subject, to have divested themselves of the right of self-government on subjects not connected with trade. Such a measure could not be "for their benefit and comfort," or for "the prevention of injuries and oppression." Such a construction would be inconsistent with the spirit of this and of all subsequent treaties; especially of those articles which recognise the right of the Cherokees to declare hostilities, and to make war. It would convert a treaty of peace covertly into an act annihilating the political existence of one of the parties. Had such a result been intended, it would have been openly avowed.

This treaty contains a few terms capable of being used in a sense which could not have been intended at the time, and which is inconsistent with the practical construction which has always been put on them; but its essential articles treat the Cherokees as a nation capable of maintaining the relations of peace and war; and ascertain the boundaries between them and the United States.

The treaty of Holston, negotiated with the Cherokees in July, 1791, explicitly recognising the national character of the Cherokees, and their right of self-government; thus guarantying their lands; assuming the duty of protection; and of course pledging the faith of the United States for that protection; has been frequently renewed, and is now in full force.

---

1. So in text.

To the general pledge of protection have been added several specific pledges, deemed valuable by the Indians. Some of these restrain the citizens of the United States from encroachments on the Cherokee country, and provide for the punishment of intruders.

The treaties and laws of the United States contemplate the Indian territory as completely separated from that of the states; and provide that all intercourse with them shall be carried on exclusively by the government of the Union.

The Indian nations had always been considered as distinct, independent, political communities, retaining their original natural rights, as the undisputed possessors of the soil, from time immemorial; with the single exception of that imposed by irresistible power, which excluded them from intercourse with any other European potentate than the first discoverer of the coast of the particular region claimed; and this was a restriction which those European potentates imposed on themselves as well as on the Indians. The very term "nation," so generally applied to them, means "a people distinct from others." The constitution, by declaring treaties already made, as well as those to be made, to be the supreme law of the land, has adopted and sanctioned the previous treaties with the Indian nations, and, consequently, admits their rank among those powers who are capable of making treaties. The words "treaty" and "nation" are words of our own language, selected in our diplomatic and legislative proceedings, by ourselves, having each a definite and well understood meaning. We have applied them to Indians as we have applied them to the other nations of the earth. They are applied to all in the same sense.

Georgia herself has furnished conclusive evidence that her former opinions on this subject concurred with those entertained by her sister states, and by the government of the United States. Various acts of her legislature have been cited in the argument, including the contract of cession made in the year 1802, all tending to prove her acquiescence in the universal conviction that the Indian nations possessed a full right to the lands they occupied, until that right should be extinguished by the United States with their consent; that their territory was separated from that of any state within whose chartered limits they might reside, by a boundary line, established by treaties; that, within their boundary, they possessed rights with which no state could interfere; and that the whole power of regulating the intercourse with them was vested in the United States. . . .

The Cherokee nation, then, is a distinct community, occupying its own territory, with boundaries accurately described, in which the laws of Georgia can have no force, and which the citizens of Georgia have no right to enter, but with the assent of the Cherokees themselves, or in conformity with treaties, and with the acts of Congress. The whole intercourse between the United States and this nation, is, by our Constitution and laws, vested in the government of the United States.

The act of the state of Georgia, under which the plaintiff in error was prosecuted, is consequently void, and the judgment a nullity.

The acts of the legislature of Georgia interfere forcibly with the relations established between the United States and the Cherokee nation, the regulation of which, according to the settled principles of our Constitution, is committed exclusively to the government of the Union.

They are in direct hostility with treaties, repeated in a succession of years, which mark out the boundary that separates the Cherokee country from Georgia; guaranty to them all the land within their boundary; solemnly pledge the faith of the United States to restrain their citizens from trespassing on it; and recognise the pre-existing power of the nation to govern itself.

They are in equal hostility with the acts of Congress for regulating this intercourse and giving effect to the treaties.

The forcible seizure and abduction of the plaintiff in error, who was residing in the nation, with its permission, and by authority of the president of the United States, is also a violation of the acts which authorize the chief magistrate to exercise this authority.

Will these powerful considerations avail the plaintiff in error? We think they will. He was seized and forcibly carried away, while under guardianship of treaties guarantying the country in which he resided, and taking it under the protection of the United States. He was seized while performing, under the sanction of the chief magistrate of the Union, those duties which the humane policy adopted by Congress had recommended. He was apprehended, tried, and condemned, under colour of a law which has been shown to be repugnant to the Constitution, laws, and treaties of the United States. Had a judgment, liable to the same objections, been rendered for property, none would question the jurisdiction of this Court. It cannot be less clear when the judgment affects personal liberty, and inflicts disgraceful punishment—if punishment could disgrace when inflicted on innocence. The plaintiff in error is not less interested in the operation of this unconstitutional law than if it affected his property. He is not less entitled to the protection of the Constitution, laws, and treaties of his country.

[*A concurring opinion was written by Justice McLean. One important phrase in it has been often cited by Indians: "How the words of the treaty were understood by this unlettered people, rather than their critical meaning, should form the rule of construction." The court record goes on to say:*]

Mr. Justice Baldwin dissented: stating that in his opinion, the record was not properly returned upon the writ of error; and ought to have been returned by the state Court, and not by the clerk of that Court. As to the merits he said his opinion remained the same as was expressed by him in the case of the Cherokee Nation *v.* The State of Georgia, at the last term.

The opinion of Mr. Justice Baldwin was not delivered to the reporter.

> RICHARD PETERS, *Report of Cases Argued and Adjudged in the Supreme Court of the United States. January Term, 1832.* [Peters, VI.] (Philadelphia: Thomas, Cowperthwait & Co., 1851), pp. 405–66 [515–96].

47   Black Hawk as a Prisoner of War, 1832

Black Hawk, the Sauk chief who had been expelled with the last of his people from his village at Rock Island in 1831, spent the winter in Iowa but recrossed the Mississippi with nearly a thousand of his people—men, women, and children, on April 5, 1832. Their motives were peaceful, but they were pursued and attacked, and followed for hundreds of miles until the remnants were cornered near the mouth of the Bad Axe River, in Wisconsin, on August 1st, between pursuing regulars on land and an armed steamboat in the river. Despite the Indians' flag of truce, they were relentlessly fired upon; women and children perished as well as warriors. Black Hawk escaped, but surrendered to Zachary Taylor at Prairie du Chien the following month. From there he was sent by steamboat to Jefferson Barracks, Missouri. The following memoir indicates the emotional agony he suffered at this time.

On our way down, I surveyed the country that had cost us so much trouble, anxiety and blood, and that now caused me to be a prisoner of war. I reflected upon the ingratitude of the whites, when I saw their fine houses, rich harvests, and every thing desirable around them; and recollected that all this land had been ours, for which me and my people had never received a dollar, and that the whites were not satisfied until they took our village and our grave-yards from us, and removed us across the Mississippi. . . .

We were now confined to the barracks, and forced to wear the *ball and chain!* This was extremely mortifying, and altogether useless. Was the White Beaver [*General Henry Atkinson*] afraid that I would break out of his barracks, and run away? Or was he ordered to inflict this punishment upon me? If I had taken him prisoner on the field of battle, I would not have wounded his feelings so much, by such treatment—knowing that a

brave war chief would prefer *death* to *dishonor!* But I do not blame the
White Beaver for the course he pursued—it is the custom among white
soldiers, and, I suppose, was a part of his duty.

> *Autobiography of Black Hawk,* ed. by Donald Jackson
> (Urbana: University of Illinois Press, 1955), pp. 164–65.

48   Second Presidential Message on Indian Removal, 1835

PRESIDENT ANDREW JACKSON

*A contemporary historian, Father Francis Paul Prucha, has recently
undertaken the hard task of demolishing the image of Andrew Jackson as an
Indian hater. While some historians, such as Arthur M. Schlesinger, Jr.* (The
Age of Jackson), *have for inexplicable reasons chosen to say nothing at all
about Jackson's Indian policy, others have cast the seventh president's Indian
policy in a dim light. Those so mentioned by Professor Prucha are Oscar
Handlin, T. Harry Williams, Richard N. Current, Frank Freidel, Thomas
A. Bailey, Dale Van Every, and R. S. Cotterill. They have, he charges,
depicted Old Hickory as a diabolical Indian hater. In considering Jackson's
Indian policy, he warns, "historians must not listen too eagerly to Jackson's political opponents or to less-than-disinterested missionaries. Jackson's contemporary critics and the historians who have accepted their
arguments have certainly been too harsh, if not, indeed, quite wrong."[1]*

*In his effort to rehabilitate Jackson, Professor Prucha has relied almost
exclusively upon the president's own letters and public addresses. In this
book we have given as ample space to Jackson's own remarks as to those
of his critics, but we cannot agree with Father Prucha's views because: (1)
We cannot accept Jackson's protestations of moral concern for the Indians
at face value; even though a president, he was not a saint, and his writings
are, as shown so far, filled with contradictions and misrepresentations of
fact; (2) It is necessary to compare the man's words with his deeds.
Jackson was no different from contemporary political leaders in his use of
self-serving rhetoric.*

*In his seventh annual message, December 7, 1835, a section of which
follows, Jackson comments on the provisions that had been made for the
Indians being compelled to migrate, and says nothing of the property and
improvements they had to abandon. He reiterates the liberality, generosity,
and kindness of his government toward the Indians, and beclouds, ignores,
or misrepresents fact after fact. For example, the bribery, liquor, threats,*

---

1. Francis Paul Prucha, "Andrew Jackson's Indian Policy: A Reassessment,"
Journal of American History, LVI, No. 3 (December 1969), 527–39.

intimidation, and force used to secure some kind of assent to removal treaties, most of which were never agreed to by the duly constituted chiefs, warriors, or tribal officials, but by unrepresentative persons only; the entirely false remark that the territory being assigned to them in Indian Territory was greater in extent than the land being relinquished; the exaggeration of the fertility and productiveness of the land, which he had never seen; the tiresome and oft-repeated promise that the Indians in their new homes were guaranteed protection forever against further white pressure; the pretense that most of the Indians being removed were mere hunters, all combined to present a distorted picture. Moreover, there was no mention of the frightful loss of life on the migrations, already begun, partly due to inadequate provision being made for them. There is also a hollow reavowal that the expulsion of the Indians is being carried out for their own best interest. The fact that the most competent scholars of the period seem to agree that the overwhelming majority of the Indians did not agree with Jackson on what their own best interest was, should warn all but the most naïve that Andrew Jackson's efforts to portray himself as a friend of the Indian was either prevarication or self-deception.

The plan of removing the aboriginal people who yet remain within the settled portions of the United States to the country west of the Mississippi River approaches its consummation. It was adopted on the most mature consideration of the condition of this race, and ought to be persisted in till the object is accomplished, and prosecuted with as much vigor as a just regard to their circumstances will permit, and as fast as their consent can be obtained. All preceding experiments for the improvement of the Indians have failed. It seems now to be an established fact that they can not live in contact with a civilized community and prosper. Ages of fruitless endeavors have at length brought us to a knowledge of this principle of intercommunication with them. The past we can not recall, but the future we can provide for. Independently of the treaty stipulations into which we have entered with the various tribes for the usufructuary rights they have ceded to us, no one can doubt the moral duty of the Government of the United States to protect and if possible to preserve and perpetuate the scattered remnants of this race which are left within our borders. In the discharge of this duty an extensive region in the West has been assigned for their permanent residence. It has been divided into districts and allotted among them. Many have already removed and others are preparing to go, and with the exception of two small bands living in Ohio and Indiana, not exceeding 1,500 persons, and of the Cherokees, all the tribes on the east side of the Mississippi, and extending from Lake Michigan to Florida, have entered into engagements which will lead to their transplantation.

The plan for their removal and reestablishment is founded upon the knowledge we have gained of their character and habits, and has been dictated by a spirit of enlarged liberality. A territory exceeding in extent that relinquished has been granted to each tribe. Of its climate, fertility, and capacity to support an Indian population the representation is highly favorable. To these districts the Indians are removed at the expense of the United States, and with certain supplies of clothing, arms, ammunition, and other indispensable articles; they are also furnished gratuitously with provisions for the period of a year after their arrival at their new homes. In that time, from the nature of the country and of the products raised by them, they can subsist themselves by agricultural labor, if they choose to resort to that mode of life; if they do not they are upon the skirts of the great prairies, where countless herds of buffalo roam, and a short time suffices to adapt their own habits to the changes which a change of the animals destined for their food may require. Ample arrangements have also been made for the support of schools; in some instances council houses and churches are to be erected, dwellings constructed for the chiefs, and mills for the common use. Funds have been set apart for the maintenance of the poor; the most necessary mechanical arts have been introduced, and blacksmiths, gunsmiths, wheelwrights, millwrights, etc., are supported among them. Steel and iron, and sometimes salt, are purchased for them, and plows and other farming utensils, domestic animals, looms, spinning wheels, cards, etc., are presented to them. And besides these beneficial arrangements, annuities are in all cases paid, amounting in some instances to more than $30 for each individual of the tribe, and in all cases sufficiently great, if justly divided and prudently expended, to enable them, in addition to their own exertions, to live comfortably. And as a stimulus for exertion, it is now provided by law that "in all cases of the appointment of interpreters or other persons employed for the benefit of the Indians a preference shall be given to persons of Indian descent, if such can be found who are properly qualified for the discharge of the duties."

Such are the arrangements for the physical comfort and for the moral improvement of the Indians. The necessary measures for their political advancement and for their separation from our citizens have not been neglected. The pledge of the United States has been given by Congress that the country destined for the residence of this people shall be forever "secured and guaranteed to them." A country west of Missouri and Arkansas has been assigned to them, into which the white settlements are not to be pushed. No political communities can be formed in that extensive region, except those which are established by the Indians themselves or by the United States for them and with their concurrence. A barrier has thus been raised for their protection against the encroachment of our citizens, and guarding the Indians as far as possible from those evils which have brought them to their present condition. Summary authority has been given by law to destroy all ardent spirits found in their country, without waiting the doubtful result and slow process of a legal seizure. I consider the absolute and unconditional interdiction of this article among these people as the first and great step in their melioration. Halfway measures will answer no purpose. These can not successfully contend against the cupidity of the seller and the overpowering appetite of the buyer. And the destructive effects of the traffic are marked in every page of the history of our Indian intercourse. . . .

[See also pp. 189–93.]

JAMES D. RICHARDSON, ed. *A Compilation of the Messages and Papers of the Presidents* (Washington: 1908), III, 171–73.

49   Forecasting the Extinction of the Indians

Throughout the nineteenth century it was commonly held that the Indians were doomed to extinction. Frequently their extermination was openly advocated as a means of clearing the way for "civilization." However, even the friends of the Indians believed that they were doomed by the spread of disease, war, alcoholism, the disappearance of game, and their inability to adjust to the white man's ways. The general acceptance of the inevitability of the demise of the Indians helped to take the edge from humanitarian indignation and similar responses which the outrages against them might be expected to arouse. Consequently, the literature of that time fails to reveal any deep current of genuine empathy for the Indians such as was developing for the blacks held in slavery.

Indian Population

GEORGE CATLIN

The famous painter of Indians estimated that the aboriginal population of North America before Anglo-American settlement had been fourteen million, and that it had been reduced to under two million at the time he wrote, the late 1830s. With sadness, he predicted their ultimate extinction. (See also pp. 250–55.)

The present condition of these once numerous people, contrasted with what it was, and what it is soon to be, is a subject of curious interest, as well as some importance, to the civilized world—a subject well entitled to the attention, and very justly commanding the sympathies of enlightened communities. There are abundant proofs recorded in the history of this country . . . to show that this very numerous and respectable part of the human family, which occupied the different parts of North America, at the time of its first settlement by the Anglo-Americans, contained more than fourteen millions, who have been reduced since that time, and undoubtedly in consequence of that settlement, to something less than two millions!

This is a startling fact, and one which carries with it, if it be the truth, other facts and their results, which are equally startling, and such as every inquiring mind should look into. The first deduction that the mind draws from such premises, is the rapid declension of these people, which must at that rate be going on at this day; and sooner or later, lead to the most melancholy result of their final extinction.

Of this sad termination of their existence, there need not be a doubt in the minds of any man who will read the history of their former destruction; contemplating them swept already from two-thirds of the Continent; and who will then travel as I have done, over the vast extent of Frontier, and witness the modes by which the poor fellows are falling, whilst contending for their rights with acquisitive white men. Such a reader, and such a traveller I venture to say, if he has not the heart of a brute, will shed tears for them; and be ready to admit that their character and customs, are at *this time,* a subject of interest and importance.

GEORGE CATLIN, *Letters and Notes on the Manners, Customs, and Condition of the North American Indians* (2 vols.; Philadelphia: 1857), II, 751.

"Indians' Bones Must Enrich the Soil," 1839

THOMAS FARNHAM

Thomas Farnham, a Vermont lawyer, traveled westward to Oregon in 1839, and commented in detail throughout his account of his travels on the Indian tribes. The following remarks were occasioned by the condition of the Sauks and Foxes, who had been driven out of Illinois in 1832, and were then resident in Iowa. Later they were removed first to Kansas and then to Oklahoma, but some of the Foxes returned to Iowa and bought land which is still occupied by several hundred of them.

. . . many is the honest old settler on the borders of their old dominion, who mentions with the warmest feelings, the respectful treatment he has received from them, while he cut the logs for his cabin, and ploughed his "potato patch" on that lonely and unprotected frontier.

Like all the tribes, however, this also dwindles away at the approach of the whites. A melancholy fact. The Indians' bones must enrich the soil, before the plough of civilized man can open it. The noble heart, educated by the tempest to endure the last pang of departing life without a cringe of muscle; that heart educated by his condition to love with all the powers of being, and to hate with the exasperated malignity of a demon; that heart, educated by the voice of its own existence—the sweet whisperings of the streams—the holy flowers of spring—to trust in, and adore the Great producing and sustaining Cause of itself, and the broad world and the lights of the upper skies, must fatten the corn hills of a more civilized race! The sturdy plant of the wilderness droops under the enervating culture of the garden. The Indian is buried with his arrows and bow.

> Farnham's Travels in REUBEN GOLD THWAITES, ed., *Early Western Travels* (32 vols., Cleveland: Arthur H. Clark Co., 1904–1907), XXVIII, 142–43.

50 Views of the Indians

Civilization's Pretensions Examined: A Sioux Chief's Reply to George Catlin, 1830s

Even whites who were sympathetic to the Indians tended to judge their customs by the alien standards of their own society, and to be blind to the manifestations in the white world of the same evils they deplored in "savage" communities. This bias, now called ethnocentrism, was displayed at times by the most enlightened defenders of the Indians. Spokesmen for a civilization that had invented such refined tortures as the rack and the wheel were inclined to lecture the Indians on the subject of cruelty. George Catlin, the painter of Indians, was an eloquent advocate of justice for the Indians, yet he seldom doubted that white civilization was more humane than "savage" society. The following passage from Catlin describes the "perfect squelch" that he received from a Sioux chief to whom he had exposed his opinions.

On an occasion when I had interrogated a Sioux chief, on the upper Missouri, about their Government—their punishments and tortures of prisoners,[1] for which I had freely condemned them for the cruelty of the practice, he took occasion, when I had got through, to ask *me* some questions relative to modes in the *civilized world*, which, with his comments upon them, were nearly as follows: and struck me, as I think they must every one, with great force.

1. See p. 98.

"Among white people, nobody ever take your wife—take your children—take your mother, cut off nose—cut eyes out—burn to death?" No! "Then *you* no cut off nose—*you* no cut out eyes—*you* no burn to death—very good."

He also told me he had often heard that white people hung their criminals by the neck, and choked them to death like dogs, and those their own people; to which I answered, "yes." He then told me he had learned that they shut each other up in prisons, where they keep them a great part of their lives *because they can't pay money!* I replied in the affirmative to this, which occasioned great surprise and excessive laughter, even among the women. He told me that he had been to our Fort, at Council Bluffs, where we had a great many warriors and braves, and he saw three of them taken out on the prairies and tied to a post and whipped almost to death, and he had been told that they submit to all this in order to get a little money, "yes." He said he had been told that when all the white people were born, their white *medicine-man* had to stand by and look on—that in the Indian country the women would not allow that—they would be ashamed—that he had been along the Frontier, and a good deal amongst the white people, and he had seen them whip their little children—a thing that is very cruel—he had heard also, from several white *medicine-men,* that the Great Spirit of the white people was the child of a white woman, and that he was at last put to death by the white people! This seemed to be a thing that he had not been able to comprehend, and he concluded by saying, "the Indians' Great Spirit got no mother—the Indians no kill him, he never die." He put me a chapter of other questions as to the trespasses of the white people on their lands—their continual corruption of the morals of their women—and digging open the Indians' graves to get their bones, &c. To all of which I was compelled to reply in the affirmative, and quite glad to close my note-book, and quietly to escape from the throng that had collected around me, and saying (though to myself and silently), that these and an hundred other vices belong to the civilized world, and are practiced upon (but certainly, in no instance, reciprocated by) the "cruel and relentless savage."

GEORGE CATLIN, Letters and Notes on the Manners, Customs,
and Condition of the North American Indians, II, 756–57.

Among the Flatheads, 1841

FATHER DE SMET

In 1838 the Belgian-born Jesuit priest, Father Pierre-Jean De Smet (1801–1873), was sent by his superior from St. Louis to found a mission among the Potawatomi who were then living in western Iowa. From that time until his death thirty-five years later he was to spend the greater part of his time in missionary work among Western Indians. Because of the influence he acquired among the Indians, he was frequently called upon by the government to induce the Indians to make treaties.

In 1841, in response to the earlier request of two Flathead Indians who came to St. Louis to request a missionary, he was sent to the homeland of that tribe in Idaho, where he established a mission. His letters of that time show that he acquired great respect and admiration for these Indians, although he was scornful of many other tribes, especially those living near the whites.

The government of the nation is confided to chiefs, who have merited this title by their experience and exploits, and who possess more or less influence, according to the degree of wisdom and courage they have displayed in council or battle. The chief does not command, but seeks to persuade; no tribute is paid to him, but, on the contrary, it is one of the appendages of his dignity to contribute more than any other to the public expense. He is generally one of the poorest in the village, in consequence of giving away his goods for the relief of his indigent brethren, or for the general interests of his tribe. Although his power has nothing imperious in it, his authority is not the less absolute; and it may, without exaggeration, be asserted, that his wishes are complied with as soon as known. Should any mutinous individual be deaf to his personal command, the public voice would soon call him to account for his obstinacy. I know not of any government where so much personal liberty is united with greater subordination and devotedness. . . .

As I before mentioned, the only prevailing vice that I found amongst the Flat Heads was a passion for games of chance—it has since been unanimously abolished. On the other hand, they are scrupulously honest in buying and selling. They have never been accused of stealing. Whenever any lost article is found, it is immediately given to the chief, who informs the tribe of the fact, and restores it to the lawful owner. Detraction is a vice unknown even amongst the women; and falsehood is particularly odious to them. A forked-tongue (a liar) they say, is the scourge of a people. Quarrels and violent anger are severely punished. Whenever any one happens to fall into trouble, his neighbors hasten to his aid. The gaiety of their disposition adds a charm to their union. Even the stranger is received as a friend; every tent is open to him, and that which he prefers is considered the most honored. In the Rocky Mountains they know not the use of locks or bolts.

In looking at this picture, which is in nowise overdrawn, you will perhaps ask, are these the people whom civilized men call barbarians? We have been too long erroneously accustomed to judge of all the savages by the Indians on the frontiers, who have learned the vices of the whites. And even with respect to the latter, instead of treating them with disdain, it would perhaps be more just not to reproach them with a degradation, of which the example has been given them, and which has been promoted by selfish and deplorable cupidity. . . .

I have spoken of the simplicity and the courage of the Flat Heads; I shall make some other remarks concerning their character. They little resemble the majority of the Indians, who are, generally speaking, uncouth, importunate, improvident, insolent, stubborn and cruel.—The Flat Heads are disinterested, generous, devoted to their brethren and friends; irreproachable, and even exemplary, as regards probity and morality. Among them, dissensions, quarrels, injuries and enmities are unknown. During my stay in the tribe last year, I have never remarked any thing that was contrary to modesty and decorum in the manners and conversation of the men and women. It is true that the children, whilst very young, are entirely without covering, but this is a general custom among the Indians, and seems to have had no bad effect upon them; we are determined, however, to abolish this custom as soon as we shall be able to do it. . . .

When I speak of the Indian character, I do not mean to include the Indians that live in the neighborhood of civilized man, and have intercourse with him. It is acknowledged in the United States, that the whites who trade with those Indians, not only demoralize them by the sale of spirituous liquors, but communicate to them their own vices, of which some are shocking and revolting to nature. The Indian left to himself, is circumspect and discreet in his words and actions. He seldom gives way to passion; except against the hereditary enemies of his nation. When there is question of them, his words breathe hatred and vengeance. He seeks revenge, because he firmly believes that it is the only means by which he can retrieve his honor when he has been insulted or defeated; because he thinks that only low and vulgar minds can forget an injury, and he fosters rancor because he deems it a virtue. With respect to others, the Indian is cool and dispassionate, checking the least violent emotion of his heart. . . .

The Indian is endowed with extraordinary sagacity, and easily learns whatever demands attention. Experience and observation render him conversant with things that are unknown to the civilized man. Thus, he will traverse a plain or forest one or two hundred miles in extent, and will arrive at a particular place with as much precision as the mariner by the aid of the compass. Unless prevented by obstacles, he, without any material deviation, always travels in a straight line, regardless of path or road. . . . Generally speaking, he has an excellent memory.—He recollects all the articles that have been concluded upon in their councils and treaties, and the exact time when such councils were held or such treaties ratified.

> PIERRE-JEAN DE SMET, S.J., "Letters and Sketches, with a Narrative of a Year's Residence among the Indian Tribes of the Rocky Mountains," in Reuben Gold Thwaites, ed., *Early Western Travels* (32 vols.; Cleveland: Arthur H. Clark Co., 1904–1907), XXVII, 172–74, 287–88, 302–4.

51   The Drive for Indian Dispossession as a Spur to the Kansas-Nebraska Act, 1854

STEPHEN A. DOUGLAS

Historians have tended to treat the Kansas-Nebraska Act, authored by Senator Stephen A. Douglas and passed in 1854, as a mere phase in the slavery controversy and the spark which led to the formation of the Republican Party in an effort to bar slavery from the territories.

Professor James C. Malin of the University of Kansas argued, a few years ago, that the aims of Douglas and his supporters were to get rid of the "Indian barrier" to westward expansion, to open the way for railroads and settlements by halting the placement of expatriated Eastern Indians in this region, and to organize governments to protect settlers. In support of his thesis, Professor Malin presented a little-known letter by Senator Douglas, addressed to a pro-Nebraska convention being held at St. Joseph, Missouri, early in 1854. An excerpt follows.

Stephen A. Douglas: Text of a Letter to the St. Joseph Convention of January 9, 1854, Dated, Washington, December 17, 1853, and Published in the St. Joseph *Gazette,* March 15, 1854.

It seemed to have been the settled policy of the government for many years, to collect the various tribes in the different States and organized Territories, and to plant them permanently on the western borders of Arkansas, Missouri and Iowa under treaties guaranteeing to them perpetual occupancy, *with an express condition that they should never be incorporated within the limits of territory or state[s] of the Union.*[1] This policy evidently contemplated the creation of a perpetual and savage barrier to the further progress of emigration, settlement and civilization in that direction. Texas not having been annexed, and being, at that time a foreign country, this barbarian wall against the extension of our institu-

1. Original emphasis.

tions, and the admission of new states, could not start from the Gulf of Mexico, and consequently the work was commenced at Red River, and carried northward with the obvious purpose of continuing it to the British Possessions. It had already penetrated into the Nebraska country, and the war department in pursuance of what was then considered a settled policy, was making its arrangements to locate immediately several other Indian Tribes on the Western borders of Missouri and Iowa with similar guarantees of perpetuity. It was obvious to the plainest understanding that if this policy should be carried out and the treaty stipulations observed in good faith it was worse than folly to wrangle with Great Britain about our right to the whole or any part of Oregon—much less to cherish the vain hope of ever making this an Ocean-bound Republic. This Indian Barrier was to have been a colossal monument to the God terminus saying to christianity, civilization and Democracy "thus far mayest thou go, and *no* farther." It was under these circumstances, and with a direct view of arresting the further progress of this savage barrier to the extension of our institutions, and to authorize and encourage a continuous line of settlements to the Pacific Ocean, that I introduced the first Bill to create the Territory of Nebraska at the session of 1853–4 [1843–4?].[2] The mere introduction of the Bill with a request to the Secretary of War to suspend further steps for the location of Indians within the limits of the proposed Territory until Congress should act upon the measure had the desired effect, so far as to prevent the permanent location of any more Indians on the frontier during the pendancy of the Bill before Congress, and from that day to this I have taken care always to have a Bill pending when Indians were about to be located in that quarter. Thus the policy of a perpetual Indian barrier has been suspended, if not entirely abandoned, for the last ten years, and since the acquisition of California, and the establishment of Territorial governments for Oregon and Washington the Idea of arresting our progress in that direction, has become so ludicrous that we are amazed, that wise and patriotic statesmen ever cherished the thought.

But, while the mischief has been prevented by prescribing limits to the onward march of an unwise policy, yet there are great national interests involved in the question which demand prompt patience, and affirmative action. To the States of Missouri and Iowa, the organization of the Territory of Nebraska is an important and desirable local measure; to the interests of the Republic it is a national necessity. How are we to develope [*sic*], cherish and protect our immense interests and possessions in the Pacific, with a vast wilderness fifteen hundred miles in breadth, filled with hostile

2. Malin's brackets. Douglas said in the same letter that he had introduced his first Nebraska bill ten years earlier.

savages, and cutting off all direct communication. The Indian barrier must be removed. The tide of emigration and civilization must be permitted to roll onward until it rushes through the passes of the mountains, and spreads over the plains, and mingles with the waters of the Pacific. Continuous lines of settlements with civil, political and religious institutions all under the protection of law, are imperiously demanded by the highest national considerations. These are essential, but they are not sufficient. No man can keep up with the spirit of this age who travels on anything slower than the locomotive, and fails to receive intelligence by lightning [telegraph]. We must therefore have Rail Roads and Telegraphs from the Atlantic to the Pacific, through our own territory. Not one line only, but many lines, for the valley of the Mississippi will require as many Rail Roads to the Pacific as to the Atlantic, and will not venture to limit the number. The removal of the Indian barrier and the extension of the laws of the United States in the form of Territorial governments are the first steps toward the accomplishment of each and all of those objects. . . .

JAMES C. MALIN, "The Motives of Stephen A. Douglas in the Organization of Nebraska Territory: A Letter Dated December 17, 1853," *The Kansas Historical Quarterly*, XIX, No. 4 (November 1951), pp. 321–53. This article was called to my attention by Professor Avery Craven when I was a student in his class at the University of Chicago in 1956.

52 The Metaphysics of Indian-Hating, 1857

HERMAN MELVILLE

Indian-hating was not only handed down to the children in frontier homes, it was taught in the schools, and was a permissible exception to the moral maxim: "Love your neighbor." Thus the attitude that the Indian was a subhuman creature who was not entitled to the same consideration as ordinary people was firmly ingrained in the national character at an early da·e.[1]

Herman Melville, in his novel The Confidence Man, *devotes two chapters to a conversation which outlines the manner of this indoctrination and the reasons for it.*

1. One writer holds that Indian-hating represented a turn from an earlier idealization of the Indian, and was rooted in the doctrines associated with Manifest Destiny. He also links it with "the general moral confusion of the 19th-century American culture." (Roy Harvey Pearce, "The Metaphysics of Indian-Hating," *Ethnohistory*, IV, [Winter 1957], pp. 27–40.) In truth, both attitudes can be found in all periods.

"The judge always began in these words: 'The backwoodsman's hatred of the Indian has been a topic for some remark. In the earlier times of the frontier the passion was thought to be readily accounted for. But Indian rapine having mostly ceased through regions where it once prevailed, the philanthropist is surprised that Indian-hating has not in like degree ceased with it. He wonders why the backwoodsman still regards the red man in much the same spirit that a jury does a murderer, or a trapper a wild cat—a creature, in whose behalf mercy were not wisdom; truce is vain; he must be executed.' "

.   .   .   .   .

" 'As the child born to a backwoodsman must in turn lead his father's life—a life which, as related to humanity, is related mainly to Indians—it is thought best not to mince matters, out of delicacy, but to tell the boy pretty plainly what an Indian is, and what he must expect from him. For however charitable it may be to view Indians as members of the Society of Friends, yet to affirm them such to one ignorant of Indians, whose lonely path lies a long way through their lands, this, in the event, might prove not only injudicious but cruel. At least something of this kind would seem the maxim upon which backwoods' education is based. Accordingly, if in youth the backwoodsman incline to knowledge, as is generally the case, he hears little from his schoolmasters, the old chroniclers of the forest, but histories of Indian lying, Indian theft, Indian double-dealing, Indian fraud and perfidy, Indian want of conscience, Indian blood-thirstiness, Indian diabolism—histories which, though of wild woods, are almost as full of things unangelic as the Newgate Calendar of the Annals of Europe. In these Indian narratives and traditions the lad is thoroughly grounded. "As the twig is bent the tree's inclined." The instinct of antipathy against an Indian grows in the backwoodsman with the sense of good and bad, right and wrong. In one breath he learns that a brother is to be loved, and an Indian to be hated.' "

HERMAN MELVILLE, *The Confidence Man* (New York: Hendricks House, 1954), Chap. XXVI, pp. 163, 165.

IV

FROM THE CIVIL WAR TO THE PRESENT

1861-1972

Introduction

The Civil War was disastrous for many Indians. The Five Civilized Tribes of Oklahoma were torn by a little civil war of their own, as tribes and factions of tribes took sides with either the Federal or Confederate cause. The pro-Southern faction was stronger, and Indian units under the Cherokee Brigadier General Stand Watie won distinction at the battle of Pea Ridge, Arkansas. Watie's force was the last to surrender, on June 23, 1865. Elsewhere, Indian-white warfare broke out. A Sioux uprising in Minnesota, partly caused by the failure of the government to deliver promised goods, ended in the mass hanging of thirty-eight Indians at Mankato, December 26, 1862. Kit Carson rounded up 8,500 Navajos in 1863 and held them in captivity at Bosque Redondo, New Mexico, for five years. Episodic guerrilla warfare on the Plains was followed by the massacre of Black Kettle's band of peaceful Cheyennes on Sand Creek, Colorado, on November 29, 1864. The chief result of the Civil War for the Indians was that it settled the sectional questions dividing the whites, and prepared the way for the settlement of the West and the final defeat of the Indians.

The Homestead Act of 1862 was a stimulus to the settlement of the West, as was also the construction of the first transcontinental railroad, completed in 1869. The three decades following the beginning of the Civil War saw the final triumph of white expansion over the aboriginal population of the United States. In this period the Plains Indian made his last stand. The aim of the government was total submission of the Indians and their confinement to reservations, or total extermination.

Directly in the path of the advancing tide stood the tribes of Plains Indians, the Sioux, Arapaho, Cheyenne, Blackfoot, Kiowa, and Comanche, to name the strongest. Soldiers released from Civil War service now manned the growing number of frontier forts and sallied forth periodically on "Indian campaigns" which resulted in the massacre of women and children as well as warriors. The white invaders proceeded to wipe out the Indian staff of life, the buffalo, and to occupy their lands. There was no inclination to understand the Indian, or to forge any consistent policy for assisting his adaptation to change. General Philip Henry Sheridan's reputed remark that "the only good Indian is a dead Indian" fairly represented the common sentiment on the frontier. When the Indian food supply was gone, the tribesmen were herded into reservations and placed on a dole to languish and die.

It was a time of bloody massacre on both sides, of which the massacres of whites by Indians received the greater publicity. It was a time of rampant graft and corruption in the Indian Bureau, of confusion from divided responsibility or inconsistent policies, of betrayals and broken promises, and growing despair for the Indian. By act of Congress, treaty-making with Indian tribes was ended in 1871. Henceforth there was little pretense that they enjoyed a fragment of sovereignty; they were treated as subjects.

There were also fumbling efforts of a few Indian well-wishers to win reforms based on a gross misunderstanding of Indian needs, ways, and culture. Such a blunder was the Dawes Act, or Land Allotment Act of February 8, 1887. Intended to make the Indian an independent farmer, and at the same time cut him loose from tribal society, this act only succeeded in depriving the Indians of two thirds of their remaining "surplus" lands, which were sold to whites, eventually leaving a hundred thousand Indians landless.[1]

With the frantic efforts of the government to stamp out the Ghost Dance religion, culminating in the murder of Sitting Bull and the slaughter of Wounded Knee in 1890, the plains warfare came to a close, although there were sporadic local outbreaks elsewhere into the twentieth century. By 1900 the red men, scattered by war and disease, were reduced to a quarter million persons. A generation raised on stories of Indian barbarism was slow to see any need for further concern with Indians now that they were defeated and marked for slow death. Grover Cleveland was the last president to mention them in an inaugural address, and not until 1928 did any political party platform devote any attention to their needs.

The Indian was called the Vanishing American, but he did not vanish. Even a core of his culture survived, to trouble the conscience of a new generation. In the land he once owned, he was not a citizen and could not vote. The Fourteenth Amendment was not considered applicable to Indians. The individual land allotments proved to be too small for economic operation in the semi-arid plains, and the problem of fractionated heirship

1. Oliver LaFarge, *As Long as the Grass Shall Grow* (New York: Alliance Book Co., 1940), pp. 26 *ff.*

arose to further complicate the problem. Alienation of Indian land into white ownership proceeded rapidly until some brakes were applied in 1934. Indian boarding schools operated by the government and religious denominations were used to extinguish Indian language and culture, and make Indian children ashamed of their inheritance.

The Indian Citizenship Act of 1924 was intended to make Indians voters, but court action was required two and even three decades later to make this right a reality in some states. The first extensive study of Indian problems appeared in 1928: the Meriam Report, prepared by the Institute for Government Research under the direction of Lewis Meriam, at the request of Secretary of the Interior Hubert Work.[2] Charles Rhoads, a Quaker who was Indian commissioner for President Hoover, launched some reforms, which were carried further by Roosevelt's commissioner, ethnologist John Collier, who gave the Bureau of Indian Affairs nearly a dozen years of relatively enlightened leadership from 1933 to 1945. The Indian Reorganization Act (Wheeler-Howard Act) of 1934 gave Indian tribes an official status and power of self-rule they had not recently enjoyed. The Dawes Act was suspended and some lost lands were even recovered. The act excluded from its provisions, however, all Oklahoma tribes, and some others, and it was criticized for placing too much power in the hands of the secretary of the interior. One of its better features was the establishment of a revolving loan fund to provide money for economic development through tribal corporations, but the sum involved was only ten million dollars.

The Arts and Crafts Board was created to restore Indian arts. In 1946 the Indian Claims Commission was created to hear and adjudicate claims for compensation for land losses during the treaty period. Indian health advanced under the care of Indian hospitals, first under bureau management, but now under the U.S. Public Health Service. Indian life expectancy, however, still lags behind that of whites and even of Negroes, and their infant death rate remains high. Many of the old boarding schools are gone, though they still exist in some western states where thinly scattered population allegedly makes them necessary. Even the schools of the Bureau of Indian Affairs are under pressure to teach respect for the old culture. English and the tribal language are used in some of the elementary reading books in Indian schools. Integration of Indian pupils into public schools is now the government policy, wherever possible, but it should be understood that many Indian tribes resist the trend toward "integrated education" because they feel, with cause, that it is another white device for forcible assimilation and destruction of Indian identity. The Fox tribe at

2. *The Problem of Indian Administration* (Baltimore: Johns Hopkins Press, 1928).

Tama, Iowa, recently won a reprieve from the death sentence pronounced on their elementary school, and the Navajos in Arizona have attracted national attention to their experiment in a community-controlled school adapted to Indian needs, at Rough Rock.

In the late forties Indians suffered new setbacks from Indian policies of the government. A campaign of pressuring Indians to accept termination of federal protection and federal services was begun, and the Klamaths and Menominees, among others, are now outside that umbrella which, for all its faults, provided much-needed shelter. The government until recently was pressing the states to take over the task of social and welfare services for Indians, together with law enforcement on reservations. Another policy which has been received with mixed feelings is the program of relocating Indians to urban areas, with an initial government subsidy, to be set adrift in an alien way of life. The number of Indians who are unable to make the adaptation and who return to the reservation is admittedly large, though accurate figures are hard to come by.

Still another recent policy of the government, in the sixties, sometimes carried out with tribal cooperation, has been the effort to attract industry to Indian reservations, and to develop tourist attractions and facilities. While these measures are calculated to alleviate poverty on reservations, there are some indications that low-wage employers are attracted by the chance to take advantage of an underpaid work force with no experience in labor organization.[3] These plans for economic development have built-in threats to the survival of Indian culture (for instance, better paid jobs have reduced Indian craft activity), but they are perhaps preferable to the old alternatives of dire poverty on the reservation or submersion in the urban jungle.

The Indian is still victimized by white power. In New York the Senecas and Tuscaroras, and in North Dakota the Mandans, Hidatsas, and Arikaras, had large portions of their lands flooded by dams, in violation of solemn treaties. In Washington state, Indian fishing rights guaranteed by treaty have been violated by the state. Assaults and murders of Indians go unpunished in Maine. Hunting rights have been challenged in Oklahoma and Nevada by the arrest of Indian hunters. Even piñon nut gatherers are forced to pay a federal tax. The water rights of the Pimas and Paiutes have been violated, the mineral rights of the Papagos have been denied them, and the Indians of Taos Pueblo only recently saved their sacred Blue Lake from being turned into a tourist attraction. Pit River Indians of northern

3. At an Indian Industrial Development Exposition held in Chicago, September 29–30, 1971, Navajo tribal chairman Peter MacDonald announced that employers locating on Indian reservations would find "a stable labor force to work at starting rates of $1.60 an hour," and "no union problems." *Chicago Daily News*, October 1, 1971.

California have been beaten and arrested while engaged in symbolic reoccupation of land taken from them without their consent and without payment. Indians are still treated as second-class citizens in towns adjoining reservations, and are exploited by employers and merchants.

The outlines of a reasonably decent Indian policy were laid before Congress in a special message from President Johnson on "Goals and Programs for the American Indian," on March 6, 1968. In it was proposed a large dose of federal aid to Indians in overcoming problems of poverty, health, education, and bad housing, but more important than the promise of aid was the affirmation that "we must pledge to respect fully the dignity and the uniqueness of the Indian citizen. . . . We must affirm the right of the first Americans to remain Indians while exercising their rights as Americans. We must affirm their right to freedom of choice and self-determination." Unfortunately, such noble sentiments have been expressed before by people in high places, and have too frequently foundered on the rocks of congressional indifference, political log-rolling, and resistance by vested interests. In June of 1970 President Richard Nixon announced his Indian policy, which likewise focused on self-determination for the Indians, and the right of Indians to preserve their communities and culture without paternalistic interference. Unfortunately, at least one proposal in the president's message could prove dangerous: namely, the legalization of ninety-nine-year leases of Indian land, in contrast to the present five-year, but renewable, limits. It is said that long-term leases would encourage investment and industrial development by outside capital. Such long-term leases are, however, equivalent to permanent surrender of Indian land, which would be Indian in name only, like the city of Salamanca, N.Y. Theoretically the property of the Senecas, it was leased for ninety-nine years at an absurdly low rental, which cannot now be changed, and the Indians exercise no control over it.

It should not be surprising, in the light of the past record, that Indians are skeptical of promises. The climate of the times with its note of protest and resistance to wrongs has begun to affect Indians. There is a "red power" movement afoot among them, in which the young are joining with the old to protect their heritage.[4] Although the National Congress of American Indians, formed in 1944, has constituted the most important lobby and educational campaign for Indian interests, there has appeared in recent years an eruption of new organizations with militant programs,

4. Stan Steiner, *The New Indians* (New York: Harper & Row, 1968); Vine Deloria, *Custer Died for Your Sins* (New York: Collier-Macmillan, 1969); Edgar Cahn, ed., *Our Brother's Keeper* (New York: World Publishing Co., 1969); and Virgil J. Vogel, "After 80 Years: The Indians Rise Again," *New Politics*, VIII, No. 2 (Spring, 1970), 62–72.

youthful leadership, and a commitment to direct action. Such is the Indians of All Tribes movement which occupied Alcatraz Island from November of 1969 to June of 1971, and its offshoots which have tried to seize several other federal properties. The American Indian Movement, Chicago Indian Village, the National Indian Youth Council, and many other groups, largely but not entirely organized in cities, are signs of a burgeoning new spirit of Indian pride. There is a large and growing body of white sympathy and support for the Indian cause, but it is often confused by conflicting ideas of what is "best for the Indian." In the end, this must be decided by the Indians, and it would be best to pay them heed.

53   Massacre of Cheyennes and Blackfeet

Massacre at Sand Creek, 1864

JOINT COMMITTEE ON THE CONDUCT OF THE WAR

While the Civil War was still raging, there occurred one of the most indefensible outrages in the history of this country's relations with the Indians: the massacre of a band of peaceful Cheyenne Indians encamped on Sand Creek, Colorado, on November 29, 1864. The attack was unprovoked and made without warning by a group of 700 mounted militia led by Colonel J. M. Chivington, a former preacher, assisted by Major Scott J. Anthony with 125 federal troops and two cannon from Fort Lyon.

The principal chief of this band of Indians, Black Kettle, was among those who escaped, only to be killed four years later in a similar attack on the Washita River, Indian Territory, led by Colonel George A. Custer.

The Joint Committee on the Conduct of the War, consisting of members of both houses of Congress, and headed by Senator Benjamin F. Wade of Ohio, held hearings on the Sand Creek massacre, and issued a stinging report calling for the punishment of the persons responsible. No one, however, was punished in any way, except in the judgment of history.

The document reproduced below is the entire report of the committee, signed by Chairman Wade, minus the testimony, and with the excision of a single paragraph excoriating Colonel Chivington which adds nothing to the statement of facts as ably presented in the report.

For further information on the Sand Creek affair, see Stan Hoig, The Sand Creek Massacre *(Norman: University of Oklahoma Press, 1961). For a defense of the incident, written by a participant, see Irving Howbert,* The Indians of the Pikes Peak Region *(New York: Knickerbocker Press, 1914).*

Massacre of Cheyenne Indians
Thirty-Eighth Congress, Second Session

The Joint Committee on the Conduct of the War submit the following report:

In the summer of 1864 Governor Evans, of Colorado Territory, as acting superintendent of Indian affairs, sent notice to the various bands and tribes of Indians within his jurisdiction that such as desired to be considered friendly to the whites should at once repair to the nearest military post in order to be protected from the soldiers who were to take the field against the hostile Indians.

About the close of the summer, some Cheyenne Indians, in the neighborhood of the Smoke Hills, sent word to Major Wynkoop, the commandant of the post of Fort Lyon, that they had in their possession, and were willing to deliver up, some white captives they had purchased of other Indians. Major Wynkoop, with a force of over 100 men, visited those Indians and received the white captives. On his return he was accompanied by a number of the chiefs and leading men of the Indians, whom he had invited to visit Denver for the purpose of conferring with the authorities there in regard to keeping peace. Among them were Black Kettle and White Antelope of the Cheyennes, and some chiefs of the Arapahoes. The council was held, and these chiefs stated that they were very friendly to the whites, and always had been, and that they desired peace. Governor Evans and Colonel Chivington, the commander of that military district, advised them to repair to Fort Lyon and submit to whatever terms the military commander there should impose. This was done by the Indians, who were treated somewhat as prisoners of war, receiving rations, and being obliged to remain within certain bounds.

All the testimony goes to show that the Indians, under the immediate control of Black Kettle and White Antelope of the Cheyennes, and Left Hand of the Arapahoes, were and had been friendly to the whites, and had not been guilty of any acts of hostility or depredation. The Indian agents, the Indian interpreter and others examined by your committee, all testify to the good character of those Indians. Even Governor Evans and Major Anthony, though evidently willing to convey to your committee a false impression of the character of those Indians, were forced, in spite of their prevarication, to admit that they knew of nothing they had done which rendered them deserving of punishment.

A northern band of the Cheyennes, known as the Dog Soldiers, had been guilty of acts of hostility; but all the testimony goes to prove that they had no connexion with Black Kettle's band, but acted in despite of his authority and influence. Black Kettle and his band denied all connexion with or responsibility for the Dog Soldiers, and Left Hand and his band of Arapahoes were equally friendly.

These Indians, at the suggestion of Governor Evans and Colonel Chivington, repaired to Fort Lyon and placed themselves under the protection of Major Wynkoop. They were led to believe that they were regarded in the light of friendly Indians, and would be treated as such so long as they conducted themselves quietly.

The treatment extended to those Indians by Major Wynkoop does not seem to have satisfied those in authority there, and for some cause, which does not appear, he was removed, and Major Scott J. Anthony was assigned to the command of Fort Lyon; but even Major Anthony seems to have found it difficult at first to pursue any different course toward the Indians he found there. They were entirely within the power of the military. Major Anthony having demanded their arms, which they surrendered to him, they conducted themselves quietly, and in every way manifested a disposition to remain at peace with the whites. For a time even he continued issuing rations to them as Major Wynkoop had done; but it was determined by Major Anthony (whether upon his own motion or at the suggestion of others does not appear) to pursue a different course toward these friendly Indians. They were called together and told that rations could no longer be issued to them, and they had better go where they could obtain subsistence by hunting. At the suggestion of Major Anthony (and from one in his position a suggestion was equivalent to a command) these Indians went to a place on Sand creek, about thirty-five miles from Fort Lyon, and there established their camp, their arms being restored to them. He told them that he then had no authority to make peace with them; but in case he received such authority he would inform them of it. In his testimony he says:

"I told them they might go back on Sand creek, or between there and the headwaters of the Smoky Hill, and remain there until I received instructions from the department headquarters, from General Curtis; and that in case I did receive any authority to make peace with them I would go right over and let them know it. *I did not state to them that I would give them notice in case we intended to attack them.* They went away with that understanding, that in case I received instructions from department headquarters I was to let them know it."

And in order, as it were, to render these Indians less apprehensive of any danger, One Eye, a Cheyenne chief, was allowed to remain with them to obtain information for the use of the military authorities. He was employed at $125 a month, and several times brought to Major Anthony, at Fort Lyon, information of proposed movements of other and hostile bands. Jack Smith, a half-breed son of John S. Smith, an Indian interpreter, employed by the government, was also there for the same purpose. A United States soldier was allowed to remain there, and two days before the massacre Mr. Smith, the interpreter, was permitted to go there with goods to trade with the Indians. Everything seems to have been done to remove from the minds of these Indians any fear of approaching danger; and when Colonel Chivington commenced his movement he took all the precautions in his power to prevent these Indians learning of his approach. For some days all travel on that route was forcibly stopped by him, not even the mail being allowed to pass. On the morning of the 28th of November he appeared at Fort Lyon with over 700 mounted men and two pieces of artillery. One of his first acts was to throw a guard around the post to prevent any one leaving it. At this place Major Anthony joined him with 125 men and two pieces of artillery.

On the night of the 28th the entire party started from Fort Lyon, and, by a forced march, arrived at the Indian camp, on Sand creek, shortly after daybreak. This Indian camp consisted of about 100 lodges of Cheyennes, under Black Kettle, and from 8 to 10 lodges of Arapahoes under Left Hand. It is estimated that each lodge contained five or more persons, and that more than one-half were women and children.

Upon observing the approach of the soldiers, Black Kettle, the head chief, ran up to the top of his lodge an American flag, which had been presented to him some years before by Commissioner Greenwood, with a small white flag under it, as he had been advised to do in case he met with any troops on the prairies. Mr. Smith, the interpreter, supposing that they might be strange troops, unaware of the character of the Indians encamped there, advanced from his lodge to meet them, but was fired upon, and returned to his lodge.

And then the scene of murder and barbarity began—men, women, and children were indiscriminately slaughtered. In a few minutes all the Indians were flying over the plain in terror and confusion. A few who endeavored to hide themselves under the bank of the creek were surrounded and shot down in cold blood, offering but feeble resistance. From the sucking babe to the old warrior, all who were overtaken were deliberately murdered. Not content with killing women and children, who were incapable of offering any resistance, the soldiers indulged in acts of barbarity of the most revolting character; such, it is to be hoped, as never before disgraced the acts of men claiming to be civilized. No attempt was made by the officers to restrain the savage cruelty of the men under their command, but they stood by and witnessed these acts without one word of reproof, if they did not incite their commission. For more than two hours the work of murder and barbarity was continued, until more than one hundred dead bodies, three fourths of them women and children, lay on the plain as evidences of the fiendish malignity and cruelty of the officers who had so sedulously and carefully plotted the massacre, and of the soldiers who had so faithfully acted out the spirit of their officers.

It is difficult to believe that beings in the form of men, and disgracing the uniform of United States soldiers and officers, could commit or countenance the commission of such acts of cruelty and barbarity as are detailed in the testimony, but which your committee will not specify in their report. It is true that there seems to have existed among the people inhabiting that region of country a hostile feeling towards the Indians. Some of the Indians had committed acts of hostility towards the whites; but no effort seems to have been made by the authorities there to prevent these hostilities, other than by the commission of even worse acts. The hatred of the whites to the Indians would seem to have been inflamed and excited to the utmost; the bodies of persons killed at a great distance—whether by Indians or not, is not certain—were brought to the capital of the Territory and exposed to the public gaze for the purpose of inflaming still more the already excited feeling of the people. Their cupidity was appealed to, for the governor in a proclamation calls upon all, "either individually or in such parties as they may organize," "to kill and destroy as enemies of the country, wherever they may be found, all such hostile Indians," authorizing them to "hold to their own private use and benefit all the property of said hostile Indians that they may capture." What Indians he would ever term friendly it is impossible to tell. His testimony before your committee was characterized by such prevarication and shuffling as has been shown by no witness they have examined during the four years they have been engaged in their investigations; and for the evident purpose of avoiding the admission that he was fully aware that the Indians massacred so brutally at Sand creek, were then, and had been, actuated by the most friendly feelings towards the whites, and had done all in their power to restrain those less friendly disposed.

The testimony of Major Anthony, who succeeded an officer disposed to treat these Indians with justice and humanity, is sufficient of itself to show how unprovoked and unwarranted was this massacre. He testifies that he found these Indians in the neighborhood of Fort Lyon when he assumed command of that post; that they professed their friendliness to the whites, and their willingness to do whatever he demanded of them; that they delivered their arms up to him; that they went to and encamped upon the place designated by him; that they gave him information from time to time of acts of hostility which were meditated by other and hostile bands, and in every way conducted themselves properly and peaceably, and yet he says it was fear and not principle which prevented his killing them while they were completely in his power. And when Colonel Chivington appeared at Fort

Lyon, on his mission of murder and barbarity, Major Anthony made haste to accompany him with men and artillery, although Colonel Chivington had no authority whatever over him. . . .

There were *hostile* Indians not far distant, against which Colonel Chivington could have led the force under his command. Major Anthony testifies that but three or four days' march from his post were several hundreds of Indians, generally believed to be engaged in acts of hostility towards the whites. And he deliberately testifies that only the fear of them prevented him from killing those who were friendly and entirely within his reach and control. It is true that to reach them required some days of hard marching. It was not to be expected that they could be surprised as easily as those on Sand creek; and the warriors among them were almost, if not quite, as numerous as the soldiers under the control of Colonel Chivington. Whatever influence this may have had upon Colonel Chivington, the truth is that he surprised and murdered, in cold blood, the unsuspecting men, women, and children on Sand creek, who had every reason to believe they were under the protection of the United States authorities, and then returned to Denver and boasted of the brave deeds he and the men under his command had performed.

The Congress of the United States, at its last session, authorized the appointment of a commission to investigate all matters relating to the administration of Indian affairs within the limits of the United States. Your committee most sincerely trust that the result of their inquiry will be the adoption of measures which will render impossible the employment of officers, civil and military, such as have heretofore made the administration of Indian affairs in this country a byword and reproach.

In conclusion, your committee are of the opinion that for the purpose of vindicating the cause of justice and upholding the honor of the nation, prompt and energetic measures should be at once taken to remove from office those who have thus disgraced the government by whom they are employed, and to punish, as their crimes deserve, those who have been guilty of these brutal and cowardly acts.

Respectfully submitted.

B. F. WADE, *Chairman.*

Report of the Joint Committee on the Conduct of the War, at the Second Session Thirty-Eighth Congress. (Washington: Government Printing Office, 1865), post pp. 120, i–vi; emphasis in original.

A Military View of the Piegan Massacre, 1870

MICHAEL SHERIDAN

One of the more deplorable incidents in the Indian warfare of the West was the massacre of 174 Piegan Indians, including many women and children, by troops commanded by Colonel E. M. Baker, on January 23, 1870. The one-sided nature of the surprise attack is shown by the fact that only one soldier was killed. One of the consequences of public indignation over the event was that a pending bill to transfer the Indian Bureau back to the War Department was defeated.

Baker acted under the direction of General Philip M. Sheridan, whose orders were to "strike hard." The following defense of the action was written by General Sheridan's brother, Brigadier General Michael Sheridan, and published in the memoirs of Philip Sheridan. The account falsely maintains that the Piegan village attacked was "under control of one of its most prominent warriors and noted thieves, 'Mountain Chief.'" Actually, the camp was headed by a friendly chief, Heavy Runner, and Mountain Chief was in Canada at the time. The account also minimizes the number of women and children killed.

John C. Ewers, historian of the Blackfeet, of which the Piegans were a sub-tribe, says that the village attacked by Baker was suffering from smallpox. Moreover:

Army and Indian accounts of what happened in this brief but disastrous action are irreconcilable. Baker's reports profess that he did not know he was attacking the camp of the friendly Heavy Runner. The Indians have claimed that as soon as Heavy Runner learned troops were approaching, he walked out alone to meet them, and that he was holding up his hands and waving his identification paper when a soldier shot him dead. A later apologist for the army claimed that the Indians fired first and that casualties to their noncombatant women and children resulted from the fact that the red-skinned warriors fought from inside their tipis, forcing the soldiers to shoot into the tipis until all resistance ceased. Not until two months after the action did Baker submit a report, which stated that in the judgment of the officers of his command, all of the Indians killed were able men except for fifty-three women and children who were killed accidentally. He admitted the reports were estimates. Baker's estimate was submitted at the request of his superiors, after the Indian agent, W. A. Pease, himself an army lieutenant, had reported that only fifteen of the dead Indians had been fighting men between the ages of twelve and thirty-seven, while ninety were women and fifty were children under twelve years of age. Of the soldiers' losses, there was no question. One man was killed. Another suffered a broken leg when he fell from his horse.[1]

1. John C. Ewers, *The Blackfeet* (Norman: University of Oklahoma Press, 1958), pp. 250–51.

Although in 1869 a solemn treaty had been made with the Blackfeet, including, of course, the Piegans, as early as August of that year Colonel Alfred Sully, the superintendent of Indian affairs in Montana, began to report to the Interior Department a renewal of depredations by the Piegans —the murder of men, women, and children, the burning of their homes, and the stealing of cattle. Later in the fall these reports increased in frequency, and in due time, at the request of the Indian Bureau, were referred by the War Department to General Sheridan, with instructions to take the most effective steps to put an end to these marauding raids by the use of military force. Remembering the success that had attended his winter campaign against the Cheyennes, Arapahoes, Kiowas, and Comanches in the preceding year, he decided, notwithstanding the rigorous winter climate of Montana, to strike the Piegans in midwinter. He therefore directed a column of troops to be "fitted out" under the command of Colonel E. M. Baker, Second U.S. Cavalry, and ordered it to move about the middle of January, being convinced, from past experiences, that at that season Baker could strike a more telling blow at the Piegan village, then in its winter camp at the big bend of the Marias River, under control of one of its most prominent warriors and noted thieves, "Mountain Chief."

Colonel Baker, with five troops of cavalry and a small detachment of mounted infantry, moved at the appointed time, and, although the mercury was from twenty to thirty degrees below zero during his entire march, drew near the Indians in the evening of January 22d. After resting his men and animals, he, by a rapid night march, reached the village early next morning. Leaving his mounted infantry in charge of the packs, he rode his troopers at a gallop into the midst of the village. The impetuous rush was over in a few minutes, the Indians being completely surprised and panic-stricken. Relying for security on the extreme cold, they had no pickets out, and consequently their first warning came from the fire of Baker's carbines. They defended themselves, however, after their usual manner, but, the surprise being complete, resistance was futile. One hundred and seventy-four Indians were killed and twenty wounded, and one hundred and forty women and children made prisoners. These were afterward turned loose to join the Blackfeet. A large number of horses were captured, many of which had just been stolen from the settlements, while much other property was recovered. Colonel Baker lost one man killed and one wounded.

During the fight, which occurred just at dawn, fifty-three women and children were shot, and this unfortunate incident of the combat gave rise to great clamor among certain professional philanthropists in the East, who invariably see the Indian from a sentimental standpoint, notwithstanding the cruel barbarism of his nature. They denounced the fight as a "massacre," demanded the immediate punishment of Colonel Baker, and through the press hurled at General Sheridan, who loyally defended his subordinate, all the venom of their wrath, without even waiting for a statement of facts from the scene of the fight. On this occasion some "fool friend" in Montana attributed to General Sheridan the expression that "a dead Indian is the only good Indian," and, though he immediately disavowed the inhuman epigram, his assailants continued to ring the changes on it for months.[1]

In time, however, the true story of the fight and the causes leading to it—the numerous murders of white men, women, and children and their unspeakable mutilation—became known. Then it was seen that, while in the attack fifty-three of the Piegan women and children had met a sad and much-to-be-deplored fate at the hands of Colonel Baker's troopers, no account had been taken of the fact that he had made prisoners of one hundred and forty more, who were unharmed.[2] It also transpired that about one hundred had escaped during the fight to a neighboring village, whence they had fled to the camps of their relatives and friends, the Blackfeet. Moreover, considering the conditions of close quarters and the similarity of appearance between buck and squaw, it was found that the number of killed women and children was not in undue proportion to the number of Indians in the field. It developed also that the "Indian ring," a gang of conspirators who thrived on Indian wars, with headquarters in Washington and branches throughout the Indian country, were at the bottom of much of the abuse heaped on General Sheridan and Colonel Baker . . .

> *Personal Memoirs of Philip M. Sheridan* (2 vols.; New York: D. Appleton Co., 1902), II, 462–65.

54   The End of Indian Treaty-Making

During the ninety-three years from 1778 to 1871, the United States Senate had ratified 372 treaties with Indian tribes, which were handled in the same way as treaties with foreign powers. Congress formally ended the practice of treaty-making with Indian tribes by means of a rider attached to the Indian Appropriation Act of March 3, 1871. Despite this provision, however, the government found it expedient to continue the practice, and

1. This famous quote, or variants of it, has also been attributed to General William T. Sherman. *Bartlett's Quotations*, however, says that in January 1869, at Fort Cobb, Indian Territory, a Comanche chief named Toch-o-way (Turtle Dove) was introduced to General Philip M. Sheridan as "a good Indian." The general is said to have retorted: "The only good Indians I ever saw were dead."

2. These prisoners were released in the wilderness in sub-zero weather after their lodges and property had all been burned. Usually in such cases, many died from exposure. —V.J.V.

did continue it, in one guise or another, into the present century. While these documents were sometimes designated as treaties (e.g., the Southern Ute Treaty of June 15, 1880), more often they were called "agreements," which were submitted to both houses of Congress for ratification, instead of the Senate only, as heretofore. Seventy-four such agreements were made up to 1902.[1] *An anomalous legal situation was created by the Act of 1871. What provision existed in the Constitution for ratification of "agreements" made with groups of people hitherto recognized as "dependent nations" sovereign in all matters except relations with foreign powers (Worcester v. Georgia), and who did not yet possess United States citizenship? To what extent could Congress legislate for such groups of people, who were excluded from the protection of the Fourteenth and Fifteenth Amendments? (By 1948, five thousand Indian laws were passed by Congress.)*[2] *To what extent were they subject to state legislation? The Indian was consigned to a legal no-man's-land, where things were often done to him without his consent, though he had no part in choosing the government which was doing it, where his status and rights were always in doubt, where bureaucratic expediency was the chief guide for those who controlled his destiny, and where a host of questions had later to be decided in the courts.*[3] *(See also pp. 181–82.)*

Act of March 3, 1871

Sec. 2079. No Indian nation or tribe within the territory of the United States shall be acknowledged or recognized as an independent nation, tribe, or power with whom the United States may contract by treaty; but no obligation of any treaty lawfully made and ratified with any such Indian nation or tribe prior to March third, eighteen hundred and seventy-one, shall be hereby invalidated or impaired.

CHARLES J. KAPPLER, ed., *Indian Affairs, Laws and Treaties,*
(Washington: Government Printing Office, 1904), I, 8.

A Legal Opinion on the Significance of the Act of March 3, 1871

When Congress in 1871 enacted a law prohibiting further treaty making with the Indian tribes, the form of governmental dealing with the Indians was changed, but the essential character of those dealings was not modi-

---

1. Cyrus Thomas, "Treaties," in F. W. Hodge, ed., *Handbook of American Indians,* II, 803–14.

2. D'Arcy McNickle, *They Came Here First* (Philadelphia: J. B. Lippincott, 1949), p. 259.

3. Felix S. Cohen, *Handbook of Federal Indian Law* (Washington: Government Printing Office, 1942), *passim.*

fied. Congress continued to deal with the Indian tribes, in large measure, through "agreements," ratified by both Houses of Congress, which do not differ from treaties in legal effect. The only substantial change accomplished by the law of 1871 was that whereas Indian treaties were submitted for the ratification of the Senate alone, as the Constitution of the United States provides, agreements are ratified by the action of both Houses, and thus the House of Representatives, which had long been excluded from equal participation in Indian affairs, has achieved an equal status with the Senate in that field. Apart from treaties and agreements with particular tribes, the dealings of the Federal Government with the Indians have been predominantly by way of special statutes applying to named tribes, and, most recently, by way of tribal constitutions and tribal charters, all varying very considerably among the different tribes. Until the last years of the nineteenth century there was very little general legislation applying a uniform pattern to all tribes, and what little there was usually turns out, on analysis, to be in the nature of generalization from provisions that had appeared in several treaties.

> NATHAN R. MARGOLD, Solicitor for the Department of Interior, in introduction to Felix Cohen, *Handbook of Federal Indian Law* (Washington: U.S. Government Printing Office, 1942), viii.

The Legal Force of Indian Treaties: A Lawyer's View, 1942

FELIX S. COHEN

One who attempts to survey the legal problems raised by Indian treaties must at the outset dispose of the objection that such treaties are somehow of inferior validity or are of purely antiquarian interest. These objections apparently spring from the belief that when the treaty method of dealing with the natives was abandoned in the Indian Appropriation Act of 1871 the force of treaties in existence at that time also disappeared.

Such an assumption is unfounded. Although treaty making itself is a thing of the past, treaty enforcement continues. As a matter of fact, the act in question expressly provides that there shall be no lessening of obligations already incurred.

The reciprocal obligations assumed by the Federal Government and by the Indian tribes during the period of almost a hundred years constitute a chief source of present-day Indian law. As one legal commentator has pointed out:

. . . The chief foundation [of federal power over Indian affairs] appears to have been the treaty-making power of the President and Senate with its corollary of Congressional power to implement by legislation the treaties made. . . .

. . . And by a broad reading of these treaties the national government obtained from the Indians themselves authority to legislate for them to carry out the purpose of the treaties.

That treaties with Indian tribes are of the same dignity as treaties with foreign nations is a view which has been repeatedly confirmed by the federal courts and never successfully challenged.

> FELIX S. COHEN, *Handbook of Federal Indian Law* (Washington: 1942), pp. 33–34.

55   On the Indian Problem, 1872

GENERAL ELY S. PARKER

Brigadier General Ely S. Parker (1828–1895) was a Seneca Indian and aide to General U.S. Grant who wrote the surrender terms handed to Lee at Appomattox. During Grant's first term, he was appointed U.S. Indian commissioner, the first Indian to hold that post. During his tenure the "peace policy," to which Grant had been converted by church leaders, was initiated. The Indian reservations were parceled out among various religious denominations, whose members were then appointed as agents for those Indians under their supervision. The military authorities were supposedly subject to their control in Indian matters, though this did not prevent the Baker massacre in 1870 (see pp. 160–62).

Parker was loyal to the traditions and culture of his own tribe, and held a rather critical view of the influence of missionaries. He was not familiar, from personal experience, with the Plains Indians with whom he had to deal. He took the view that "civilization" must triumph, and advocated, without success, the transfer of the Indian Bureau from civilian control in the Interior Department back to the War Department, where it had been until 1849. He held that this would eliminate the crooked Indian agents who enriched themselves by withholding treaty goods and cash. He also favored abolition of the private traders, and their replacement by a government monopoly of Indian trade, a policy initiated by Washington and supported by Jefferson, which was terminated in 1822.

Parker was unable to eliminate corruption in the Indian Bureau, and was blamed to the extent of being tried by the House in 1871. He was acquitted of any wrongdoing, but resigned six months later.

. . . Treaties have been made with a very large number of the tribes, and generally reservations have been provided as homes for them. Agents appointed from civil life, have generally been provided to protect their lives and property, and to attend to the prompt and faithful observance of treaty stipulations. But as the hardy pioneer and adventurous miner advanced into the inhospitable regions occupied by the Indians in search of the precious metals, they found no rights possessed by Indians that they were bound to respect. The faith of treaties solemnly entered into was totally disregarded, and Indian territory wantonly violated. If any tribe remonstrated against the violation of their natural and treaty rights, members of the tribe were inhumanly shot down, and the whole treated as mere dogs. Retaliation generally followed, and bloody Indian wars have been the consequence, costing many lives and much treasure. . . .

. . . I would provide for the complete abolishment of the system of Indian traders, which, in my opinion, is a great evil to Indian communities. I would make government the purchaser of all articles usually brought in by Indians, giving them a fair equivalent for the same in money, or goods at cost prices. In this way it would be an easy matter to regulate the sale or issue of arms and ammunition to Indians, a question which of late has agitated the minds of the civil and military authorities. . . .

. . . Indian trading licenses are very much sought after, and when once obtained, although it may be for a limited period, the lucky possessor is considered as having already made his fortune. The eagerness also with which Indian agencies are sought after, and large fortunes made by the agents in a few years, notwithstanding the inadequate salary given, is presumptive evidence of frauds against the Indians and the government. Many other reasons might be suggested why the Indian department should altogether be under military control, but a familiar knowledge of the practical working of the present system would seem to be the most convincing proof of the propriety of the measure. It is pretty generally advocated by those most familiar with our Indian relations, and, so far as I know, the Indians themselves desire it.

> Quoted by General George A. Custer in *My Life on the Plains* (Norman: University of Oklahoma Press, 1962), pp. 178–79.

56   A View of Indian Character, 1872

GENERAL GEORGE ARMSTRONG CUSTER

General George Armstrong Custer, who perished with his entire command at the Little Big Horn (Crow Agency, Mont.), on June 25, 1876, has by that fact assured himself of an eternal place in American folklore. Whether he was an authentic hero, however, is a matter of considerable dispute. He certainly was never able to bring himself to view the Indians as people. In his language, the Indians did not inhabit the plains, but infested them, like coyotes. While temporarily withdrawn from active service in the spring of 1868, he regretted that while his friends "were attempting to kill Indians, I was studying the problem of how to kill time." Late that same year, he became noted or notorious, depending on one's viewpoint, for his attack on Black Kettle's peaceful band of Cheyennes on the Washita River (Oklahoma).

Like many others before and since, Custer believed that a sympathetic disposition toward the Indians could only be founded on ignorance and fictional images of the Indian derived from such writers as James Fenimore Cooper.

It is to be regretted that the character of the Indian as described in Cooper's interesting novels is not the true one. But as, in emerging from childhood into the years of a maturer age, we are often compelled to cast aside many of our earlier illusions and replace them by beliefs less inviting but more real, so we, as a people, with opportunities enlarged and facilities for obtaining knowledge increased, have been forced by a multiplicity of causes to study and endeavor to comprehend thoroughly the character of the red man. So intimately has he become associated with the government as ward of the nation, and so prominent a place among the questions of national policy does the much mooted "Indian question" occupy, that it behooves us no longer to study this problem from works of fiction, but to deal with it as it exists in reality. Stripped of the beautiful romance with which we have been so long willing to envelope him, transferred from the inviting pages of the novelist to the localities where we are compelled to meet with him, in his native village, on the war path, and when raiding our frontier settlements and lines of travel, the Indian forfeits his claim to the appellation of the *"noble* red man." We see him as he is, and, so far as all knowledge goes, as he ever has been, a savage in every sense of the word; not worse, perhaps, than his white brother would be similarly born and bred, but one whose cruel and ferocious nature far exceeds that of any wild beast of the desert. That this is true no one who had been brought into intimate contact with the wild tribes will deny.

GEORGE ARMSTRONG CUSTER, *My Life on the Plains* (Norman: University of Oklahoma Press, 1962), p. 13.

57   The Surrender of Chief Joseph, 1877

Few Indian wars attracted as much sympathy for the Indian cause as the Nez Perce war of 1877. The origin of the war lay in the treaty of 1863 which supposedly surrendered the Nez Perce lands in the Wallowa valley of

Oregon, and consolidated scattered Nez Perce bands on the Lapwai reservation in Idaho. Only a minority of head men signed the treaty, and none from the Wallowa valley did so. A government commission upheld the right of the Wallowa band to remain in their ancient home, but under white pressure the decision was reversed in 1875. Agent John B. Monteith and General O. O. Howard were determined to force the Wallowa band to give up their land.

In a conference at Lapwai in the spring of 1877, Chief Joseph and other leading men steadfastly refused to consent to removal. When Toohoolhoolzote demanded to know by what right General Howard sought to force the Indians from their homes, he was ordered seized and thrown in the guard house, where he was held five days, his release being accomplished only by Joseph's reluctant decision to give in. The Indians were told to round up all their livestock and come to Lapwai within thirty days. The season for such a journey was unfavorable, but Monteith would permit no delay. Many horses and cattle were lost while crossing swollen streams. When the Indians reached the borders of Lapwai, they halted, and three young men stole away and killed four white men in retaliation for earlier murders of Indians. The band now decided to flee eastward to the Montana buffalo country, and Joseph, after some hesitation, joined them.

During the next four months they were pursued by General Howard over more than 1,200 miles of rugged country, and on several occasions beat off attacks by both their pursuers and other forces. They raided no settlements, and at one town in Montana, they purchased supplies and paid for them with gold dust and cash.

At the end of September they were besieged in the Bear Paw Mountains, only thirty miles from the Canadian border which they now hoped to cross, by Colonel Nelson Miles with troops from Fort Keogh. While the Indians were digging in to resist, advance units of Howard's force arrived, and Joseph decided to surrender. During a parley with his own people, his loyal follower, Looking Glass, was killed by a Cheyenne scout. About a third of the Indians were still unwilling to surrender, and during the night they stole away. Some of these were later rounded up, while others reached Canada.

Miles and Howard assured Joseph and his followers that they could return to "their own country" but they were overruled from Washington, and the Indians, after spending the winter at Fort Keogh, were removed to Indian Territory (Oklahoma). In 1885 a small number of them were allowed to go to Lapwai, and the remainder were placed on the Colville reservation in Washington Territory, where Joseph died in 1909.

The following account of the surrender to Chief Joseph was given by General Howard.

General O. O. Howard's Account, 1877

. . . I had with me two aides, Lieutenant C. E. S. Wood and Lieutenant Guy Howard. I had also the two Nez Perce scouts, Captains John and George, and several American scouts. We promptly took up the Indian trail, plain enough now for anybody to follow, and on we went, meeting now and then messengers who apprised us of the situation.

Miles had had a battle, but it had not been altogether decisive. It was near what was called "The Little Rockies," a part of the upper portion of the Bear Paw Mountain.

. . . During the day we met some scouts, who reported that Indians were between us and Miles' bivouac. They said that they could not go on and had turned back, but we found the supposed Indians to be friendly hunters and so pursued our way.

It was early in the evening when we came upon the crest of a hill and saw the campfires of our troops. We heard firing, and some of the bullets whistled over our heads, and as I thought that our party had been mistaken for savages I cried out: "What are you firing at us for?"

Just then Miles himself with a small escort met and took me to his headquarters. That night we consulted together; he showed me how the Indians had dug deep holes instead of ordinary entrenchments; that part of the herd of Indian ponies had been captured and a part was still in the possession of the Indians; that he was very anxious for a speedy surrender. He had sent in a brave and capable officer, who had been for a while detained by Joseph, but at last had returned, having been unable to bring matters to a decision. I proposed to send in my two Nez Perce scouts, Captains John and George, bearing a white flag. I believed that they could secure a prompt surrender of Joseph and all his people who were with him.

The next day this was done. Miles and myself sat side by side upon the slope of a hill in plain view of both contestants, when "Captain John," accompanied by George, moved off on foot swinging his white flag.

We did not have very long to wait. The scouts returned and bore Joseph's message to the effect that he had done all he could and that he left his people and himself in our hands. Some of the Indians violated the promise they had made to Joseph, creeping out of camp in the night and escaping. One of them was Chief White Bird.

It was rather a forlorn procession that came up out of that Indian bivouac. They were covered with dirt, their clothing was torn, and their ponies, such as they were, were thin and lame. A few of the Indians preserved their dignified bearing and had attired themselves as best they could for the occasion. When Joseph appeared he extended his rifle to me and I waived it over to Colonel Miles, who had planned and made a swift diagonal march, and so bravely fought the last battle.

That night Miles and I slept again in his tent. He made his report to his department commander, and a little later I made mine. I had been instructed by McDowell[1] to send the Indians back to the Department of the Columbia, and I so gave Joseph to understand, but I was overruled from Washington, and Miles was ordered to keep them for the time being and finally send them to the Indian Territory.

> MAJOR GENERAL OLIVER OTIS HOWARD, *My Life and Experiences among Our Hostile Indians* (Hartford: A. D. Worthington & Co., 1907), pp. 299–300.

Chief Joseph's Remarks upon Surrendering, October 5, 1877

Chief Joseph's surrender speech has perhaps been quoted more widely, as an example of Indian oratory, than the speech given by Chief Logan in 1774 (pp. 58–59). It is filled with pathos and seems to sum up in a few words the tragedy of Indian suffering and defeat. There are slightly different versions of this speech, and also different reports of the circumstances. Francis Haines took his version from the Report of the Secretary of War *for 1877 (actually, General Howard's report therein), and said it was given by Joseph in a parley with his own headmen and two Nez Perce scouts sent to them by Howard.[2] Alvin Josephy, relying upon an account by Lieutenant C. E. S. Wood, Howard's aide, published in Charles A. Fee's* Chief Joseph *(1936), said the speech was given by Chief Joseph to General Howard just after he surrendered his rifle to Miles.[3] He reports that it was translated by Arthur Chapman and recorded by Lieutenant Wood, and first published in* Harper's Weekly, *November 17, 1877 (page 906). The unsigned account in* Harper's, *which Josephy believes was obtained, along with a copy of the speech, from Wood, agrees as to facts with the account in Haines and in Howard's report to the Secretary of War, and contradicts Wood's report in Fee. It appears, therefore, that no white man heard the speech as first given by Joseph, but only as it was rendered by Captain John.*

Oddly enough, there is no mention of this sad speech in the personal

1. Major General Irwin McDowell, commander of the Military Division of the Pacific and Department of California. —V.J.V.

2. Francis Haines, *The Nez Perces* (Norman: University of Oklahoma Press, 1955), pp. 279–80.

3. Alvin Josephy, *The Nez Perce Indians and the Opening of the Northwest* (New Haven: Yale University Press, 1965), pp. 630–31.

memoirs of either Howard or Miles. The following text of the speech and the account of the circumstances are taken from General Howard's report to the Secretary of War.

. . . Colonel Miles told me of his interview with Joseph and his failure to bring about a surrender.

I mentioned my two friendly Nez Perces, members of Joseph's band, old men, with daughters in the hostile camps, and as I had brought these men from Idaho for this very purpose, I suggested that we try them and see what we could do with Joseph. Accordingly, on the following morning at about eleven o'clock these Indians, Captain "John" and "George," were sent with a flag of truce to the enemy. After much parleying and running to and fro between the camps, Joseph being promised good treatment, sent the following reply, and White Bird concurred, saying: "What Joseph does is all right; I have nothing to say."

This reply of Joseph's was taken verbatim on the spot by Lieutenant Wood, Twenty-first Infantry, my acting aide-de-camp and acting adjutant-general, and is the only report that was ever made of Joseph's reply:

Tell General Howard I know his heart. What he told me before I have in my heart. I am tired of fighting. Our chiefs are killed. Looking Glass is dead. Too-hul-hul-sote is dead. The old men are all dead. It is the young men who say yes or no. He who led on the young men is dead.[3] It is cold and we have no blankets. The little children are freezing to death. My people, some of them, have run away to the hills, and have no blankets, no food; no one knows where they are —perhaps freezing to death. I want to have time to look for my children and see how many of them I can find. Maybe I shall find them among the dead. Hear me, my chiefs. I am tired; my heart is sick and sad. From where the sun now stands I will fight no more forever.

In accordance with this pledge, Joseph himself, accompanied by four or five of his warriors, came inside our lines, and Joseph set the example by offering me his rifle; but as the surrender was being made to Colonel Miles, I so instructed Joseph, and then they all delivered up their weapons to that officer. From this time, about 4 p.m., until after dark, a straggling stream of captives flowed into Miles's camp.

> Report of Brigadier-General O. O. Howard, in *Annual Report of the Secretary of War . . . for the Fiscal Year Ending June 30, 1877* (Washington: Government Printing Office, 1877), pp. 630–31.

3. According to Josephy (*loc. cit.*), this is a reference to Joseph's brother Ollokot, or Ollicut, who was killed, along with Too-hul-hul-sote, in the first encounter with Miles a few days earlier.

58   The Indian Problem, 1877

PRESIDENT RUTHERFORD B. HAYES

All presidents of the United States from George Washington to Theodore Roosevelt had something to say about Indian affairs either in their inaugural addresses or in their annual messages to Congress.[1] Most of these papers, even those of Jackson, are couched in terms of benevolence and paternal concern for the welfare of Indians. All endorsed measures to "civilize" the Indians and several proposed their assimilation into American society. None envisaged separate, entirely self-governing, culturally different Indian communities as a permanent part of America. President Hayes stayed in that tradition, but his first annual message has been widely quoted for its honest assignment of blame for frontier violence: "Many, if not most, of our Indian wars have had their origin in broken promises and acts of injustice upon our part." This address also contains the first endorsement by a chief executive of a plan to allot individual homesteads to Indians "who are willing to detach themselves from their tribal relations." This proposal was again endorsed by President Arthur in 1881 (see pp. 175–76), and enacted into law in 1887 (see pp. 177 ff.).

After a series of most deplorable conflicts—the successful termination of which, while reflecting honor upon the brave soldiers who accomplished it, can not lessen our regret at their occurrence—we are now at peace with all the Indian tribes within our borders. To preserve that peace by a just and humane policy will be the object of my earnest endeavors. Whatever may be said of their character and savage propensities, of the difficulties of introducing among them the habits of civilized life, and of the obstacles they have offered to the progress of settlement and enterprise in certain parts of the country, the Indians are certainly entitled to our sympathy and to a conscientious respect on our part for their claims upon our sense of justice. They were the original occupants of the land we now possess. They have been driven from place to place. The purchase money paid to them in some cases for what they called their own has still left them poor. In many instances, when they had settled down upon land assigned to them by compact and begun to support themselves by their own labor, they were rudely jostled off and thrust into the wilderness again. Many, if not most, of our Indian wars have had their origin in broken promises and acts of injustice upon our part, and the advance of the Indians in civilization has been slow because the treatment they received did not permit it to be faster

1. Excepting Garfield, who was mortally wounded less than four months after his inaugural.

and more general. We can not expect them to improve and to follow our guidance unless we keep faith with them in respecting the rights they possess, and unless, instead of depriving them of their opportunities, we lend them a helping hand.

. . . The faithful performance of our promises is the first condition of a good understanding with the Indians. I can not too urgently recommend to Congress that prompt and liberal provision be made for the conscientious fulfillment of all engagements entered into by the Government with the Indian tribes. To withhold the means necessary for the performance of a promise is always false economy, and is apt to prove disastrous in its consequences. Especial care is recommended to provide for Indians settled on their reservations cattle and agricultural implements, to aid them in whatever efforts they may make to support themselves, and by the establishment and maintenance of schools to bring them under the control of civilized influences. I see no reason why Indians who can give satisfactory proof of having by their own labor supported their families for a number of years, and who are willing to detach themselves from their tribal relations, should not be admitted to the benefit of the homestead act and the privileges of citizenship, and I recommend the passage of a law to that effect. It will be an act of justice as well as a measure of encouragement. Earnest efforts are being made to purify the Indian service, so that every dollar appropriated by Congress shall redound to the benefit of the Indians, as intended. Those efforts will have my firm support. With an improved service and every possible encouragement held out to the Indians to better their condition and to elevate themselves in the scale of civilization, we may hope to accomplish at the same time a good work for them and for ourselves.

JAMES D. RICHARDSON, ed., *A Compilation of the Messages and Papers of the Presidents* (10 vols.; Washington: Government Printing Office, 1898), VII, 475–76.

59   The Indian Homestead Acts

The first Indian Homestead Act, passed as an amendment to the deficiency appropriation bill of March 3, 1875, has generally been forgotten because it was seldom used and was superseded by the Dawes Act of 1887 and its amendments. The act of 1875 extended the benefits of the homestead act of 1862 to Indian heads of families who abandoned their tribal relations. They could lay claim to 160 acres from the public domain, which would be inalienable for a period of five years after the patent was issued.

The Dawes Act (see pp. 177 ff.) differed from the above in that it pro-

vided for the allotment of reservation lands, instead of the public domain, provided for smaller tracts for single Indians and minors, and protected the land from alienation for twenty-five years. The amendment of 1891 provided for reduced allotments.

Act of March 3, 1875

Sec. 15. That any Indian born in the United States, who is the head of a family, or who has arrived at the age of twenty-one years, and who has abandoned, or may hereafter abandon, his tribal relations, shall, on making satisfactory proof of such abandonment, under rules prescribed by the Secretary of the Interior, be entitled to the benefits of the act entitled "An act to secure homesteads to actual settlers on the public domain," approved May twentieth, eighteen hundred and sixty-two, and the acts amendatory thereof, except that the provisions of the eighth section of the said act shall not be held to apply to entries made under this act:

Provided however, That the title to lands acquired by any Indian by virtue hereof shall not be subject to alienation or incumbrance, either by voluntary conveyance or the judgment decree, or order of any court, and shall be and remain inalienable for a period of five years from the date of the patent issued therefor:

Provided, That any such Indian shall be entitled to his distributive share of all annuities, tribal funds, lands, and other property, the same as though he had maintained his tribal relations; and any transfer, alienation, or incumbrance of any interest he may hold or claim by reason of his former tribal relations shall be void.

Sec. 16. [*Summary: Wherever Indians have already entered public lands under the homestead law, and have complied with pertinent laws and regulations, their entries shall be confirmed and patents issued.*]

CHARLES J. KAPPLER, *Indian Affairs, Laws and Treaties*
(Washington: Government Printing Office, 1904), I, 23.

The Indian Homestead Act (Dawes Act)

Some of the worst despoliation of the American Indians has occurred in the guise of benevolent reform, and due to the Janus-like character of most such legislation, the most disparate persons and groups have found common ground in supporting it. The motivating force behind the Indian removals of the 1830s was a lust for land, yet the underlying greed was masked with arguments that nothing but removal would preserve the Indians and save them from extinction. Consequently the most selfless idealists were found on both sides of the debate which Jackson's policies aroused. This situation was repeated in the late nineteenth century, when proposals were advanced to divide Indian lands in severalty, and make every Indian family head a private farmer. Such a program was proposed by President Arthur in his annual message of 1881, and was enacted into law as the Dawes Act in 1887. This alleged beneficence enjoyed the support of our oldest Indian welfare group, the Indian Rights Association. Thus was revealed the terrible consequences of appalling ignorance of the Indian spirit and the meaning of his culture, and the astonishing ease with which greed has been able to enlist the backing of philanthropy.

The object of the reform was to dissolve Indian tribes, end communal land holding, and make every Indian ultimately a citizen. After each Indian had been compelled to take his holding, the remaining lands were often declared surplus and opened for sale to whites by the government. No lands were to be kept in reserve for future generations of Indians, because of the assumption that their population would continue to decline. No allowance was made for the lack of farming skills among Plains Indians, or for the fact that 160-acre parcels were not economically viable units in semi-arid regions. Few foresaw that Indians once vested with full title would be soon divested of their ownership by clever white men. Neither was any consideration paid to the importance of communal existence to the integrity of the Indian character. In short, the white man arrogated to himself the paternalistic right to decide unilaterally what was best for the Indians.

The Dawes Act was responsible for the alienation from Indian occupancy of a hundred million acres of land, and the creation of a hundred thousand landless Indians, not to mention the tangled legal and economic problems later to arise from "fractionated heirship." In Oklahoma alone, of thirty million acres of land allotted to individual Indians when tribal governments were dissolved in 1906, only five per cent remains in Indian hands today.[1] Not until 1928 was the Dawes Act subjected to a searching criticism, in the Meriam Report (see pp. 195–96). In 1934 the Dawes Act was superseded by the passage of the Wheeler-Howard Act, which forbade further allotments in severalty. (The full text of this act is reproduced herein on pp. 196–203.)

"Their Hunting Days Are Over"

PRESIDENT CHESTER A. ARTHUR

As the white settlements have crowded the borders of the reservations, the Indians sometimes contentedly and sometimes against their will, have

1. See pp. 189–90.

been transferred to other hunting grounds, from which they have again been dislodged whenever their newfound homes have been desired by the adventurous settlers.

These removals and the frontier collisions by which they have often been preceded have led to frequent and disastrous conflicts between the races. . . .

We have to deal with the appalling fact that though thousands of lives have been sacrificed and hundreds of millions of dollars expended in the attempt to solve the Indian problem, it has until within the past few years seemed scarcely nearer a solution than it was half a century ago. . . .

For the success of the efforts now making to introduce among the Indians the customs and pursuits of civilized life and gradually to absorb them into the mass of our citizens, sharing their rights and holden to their responsibilities, there is imperative need for legislative action. . . .

First. I recommend the passage of an act making the laws of the various States and Territories applicable to the Indian reservations within their borders and extending the laws of the State of Arkansas to the portion of the Indian Territory not occupied by the Five Civilized Tribes.

The Indian should receive the protection of the law. He should be allowed to maintain in court his rights of person and property. He has repeatedly begged for this privilege. Its exercise would be very valuable to him in his progress toward civilization.

Second. . . . The enactment of a general law permitting the allotment in severalty, to such Indians, at least, as desire it, of a reasonable quantity of land secured to them by patent, and for their own protection made inalienable for twenty or twenty-five years, is demanded for their present welfare and permanent advancement.

In return for such considerate action on the part of the Government, there is reason to believe that the Indians in large numbers would be persuaded to sever their tribal relations and to engage at once in agricultural pursuits. Many of them realize the fact that their hunting days are over and that it is now for their best interests to conform their manner of life to the new order of things. By no greater inducement than the assurance of permanent title to the soil can they be led to engage in the occupation of tilling it.

The well-attested reports of their increasing interest in husbandry justify the hope and belief that the enactment of such a statute as I recommend would be at once attended with gratifying results. A resort to the allotment system would have a direct and powerful influence in dissolving the tribal bond, which is so prominent a feature of savage life, and which tends so strongly to perpetuate it.

Third, I advise a liberal appropriation for the support of Indian schools, because of my confident belief that such a course is consistent with the wisest economy.

JAMES D. RICHARDSON, ed., *A Compilation of the Messages and Papers of the Presidents* (1908), VIII, 55–56.

The Dawes Act, February 8, 1887

Also called the General Allotment Act and the Indian Homestead Act, the Dawes Act provided for the allotment of reservation lands in severalty, as urged by President Arthur in his message of December 6, 1881. While President Arthur had proposed allotments, however, "to such Indians . . . as desire it," the law provided (sec. 2) for compulsory allotments. Important amendments to the act were made in 1889, 1891 (see p. 180), 1906, and 1910. Special acts created variant provisions for particular tribes. For a criticism of the act, see the excerpt from the Meriam Report of 1928 pp. 195–96).

Be it enacted &c. That in all cases where any tribe or band of Indians has been, or shall hereafter be, located upon any reservation created for their use, either by treaty stipulation or by virtue of an act of Congress or executive order setting apart the same for their use, the President of the United States be, and he hereby is, authorized, whenever in his opinion any reservation or any part thereof of such Indians is advantageous for agriculture and grazing purposes to cause said reservation, or any part thereof, to be surveyed, or resurveyed if necessary, and to allot the lands in said reservation in severalty to any Indian located thereon in quantities as follows:

To each head of a family, one-quarter of a section;

To each single person over eighteen years of age, one-eighth of a section; and,

To each other single person under eighteen years now living, or who may be born prior to the date of the order of the President directing an allotment of the lands embraced in any reservation, one-sixteenth of a section. . . .

Sec. 2. That all allotments set apart under the provisions of this act shall be selected by the Indians, heads of families selecting for their minor children, and the agents shall select for each orphan child, and in such manner as to embrace the improvements of the Indians making the selection. . . .

Provided, That if any one entitled to an allotment shall fail to make a selection within four years after the President shall direct that allotments may be made on a particular reservation, the Secretary of the Interior may direct the agent of such tribe or band, if such there be, and if there be no agent, then a special agent appointed for that purpose, to make a selection for such Indian, which selection shall be allotted as in cases where selections are made by the Indians, and patents shall issue in like manner.

Sec. 3. [*Procedural details.*]

Sec. 4. That where any Indian not residing upon a reservation, or for whose tribe no reservation has been provided by treaty, act of Congress or executive order, shall make settlement upon any surveyed or unsurveyed lands of the United States not otherwise appropriated, he or she shall be entitled, upon application to the local land-office for the district in which the lands are located, to have the same allotted to him or her, and to his or her children, in quantities and manner as provided in this act for Indians residing upon reservations; and when such settlement is made upon unsurveyed lands, the grant to such Indians shall be adjusted upon the survey of the lands so as to conform thereto; and patents shall be issued to them for such lands in the manner and with the restrictions as herein provided. . . .

Sec. 5. That upon the approval of the allotments provided for in this act by the Secretary of the Interior, he shall cause patents to issue therefor in the name of the allottees, which patents shall be of the legal effect, and declare that the United States does and will hold the land thus allotted for the period of twenty-five years, in trust for the sole use and benefit of the Indian to whom such allotment shall have been made, or, in case of his decease, of his heirs according to the laws of the State or Territory where such land is located, and that at the expiration of said period the United States will convey the same by patent to said Indian, or his heirs as aforesaid, in fee, discharged of said trust and free of all charge or incumbrance whatsoever; *Provided,* That the President of the United States may in any case in his discretion extend the period.

And if any conveyance shall be made of the lands set apart and allotted as herein provided, or any contract made touching the same before the expiration of the time above mentioned, such conveyance or contract shall be absolutely null and void. . . .

And provided further, That at any time after lands have been allotted to all the Indians of any tribe as herein provided, or sooner if in the opinion of the President it shall be for the best interests of said tribe, it shall be lawful for the Secretary of the Interior to negotiate with such Indian tribe for the purchase and release by said tribe in conformity with the treaty or statute under which such reservation is held, of such portions of its reservation not allotted as such tribe shall, from time to time, consent to sell, on such terms and conditions as shall be considered just and equitable between the United States and said tribe of Indians, which purchase shall not be complete until ratified by Congress, and the form and manner of executing such release shall also be prescribed by Congress. . . .

And the sums agreed to be paid by the United States as purchase money for any portion of any such reservation shall be held in the Treasury of the United States for the sole use of the tribe or tribes of Indians to whom such reservations belonged; and the same, with interest thereon at three per cent per annum, shall be at all times subject to appropriation by Congress for the education and civilization of such tribe or tribes of Indians or the members thereof. . . .

And if any religious society or other organization is now occupying any of the public lands to which this act is applicable, for religious or educational work among the Indians, the Secretary of the Interior is hereby authorized to confirm such occupation to such society or organization, in quantity not exceeding one hundred and sixty acres in any one tract. . . .

And hereafter in the employment of Indian police, or any other employes in the public service among any of the Indian tribes or bands affected by this act, and where Indians can perform the duties required, those Indians who have availed themselves of the provisions of this act and become citizens of the United States shall be preferred.

Sec. 6. That upon the completion of said allotments and the patenting of the lands to said allottees, each and every member of the respective bands or tribes of Indians to whom allotments have been made shall have the benefit of and be subject to the laws, both civil and criminal, of the State or Territory in which they may reside; and no Territory shall pass or enforce any law denying any such Indian within its jurisdiction the equal protection of the law.

And every Indian born within the territorial limits of the United States to whom allotments shall have been made under the provisions of this act, or under any law or treaty, and every Indian born within the territorial limits of the United States who has voluntarily taken up, within said limits, his residence separate and apart from any tribe of Indians therein, and has adopted the habits of civilized life, is hereby declared to be a citizen of the United States, and is entitled to all the rights, privileges, and immunities of such citizens, whether said Indian has been or not, by birth or otherwise, a member of any tribe of Indians within the territorial limits of the United States without in any manner impairing or otherwise affecting the right of any such Indian to tribal or other property.

Sec. 7. [*Irrigation provisions.*]

Sec. 8. [*Exclusion of most tribes in Indian Territory, the New York Senecas, and a strip of Sioux land in Nebraska.*]

Sec. 9. [*Appropriation for surveys.*]

Sec. 10. [*Congress reserves right to grant rights of way for railroads, etc.*]

Sec. 11. [*Act may not be construed to prevent removal of the Colorado Utes.*]

Amendment to the Dawes Act, February 28, 1891

Be it enacted, &c. [*Section 1 of the Dawes Act is amended "to allot each Indian located thereon one-eighth of a section of land."*]

Provided, That in case there is not sufficient land in any of said reservations to allot lands to each individual in quantity as above provided the land . . . shall be allotted to each individual pro rata, as near as may be, according to legal subdivisions:

Provided further [*Allotments larger than provided herein may be allowed where required by treaties, agreements, or laws.*]

And provided further, That when the lands allotted, or any legal subdivision thereof, are only valuable for grazing purposes, such lands shall be allotted in double quantities.

Sec. 2. That where allotments have been made in whole or in part upon any reservation under the provisions of said act of February eighth, eighteen hundred and eighty-seven, and the quantity of land in such reservation is sufficient to give each member of the tribe eighty acres, such allotment shall be revised and equalized under the provisions of this act:

Provided, That no allotment heretofore approved by the Secretary of the Interior shall be reduced in quantity.

Sec. 3. [*Allotments of aged or disabled persons may be leased up to three years for farming or grazing, and ten years for mining.*]

Provided, That where lands are occupied by Indians who have bought and paid for the same, and which lands are not needed for farming or agricultural purposes, and are not desired for individual allotments, the same may be leased by authority of the Council speaking for such Indians, for a period not to exceed five years for grazing purposes, or ten years for mining purposes in such quantities and upon such terms and conditions as the agent in charge of such reservation may recommend, subject to the approval of the Secretary of the Interior.

Sec. 4. [*Provision for Indians to take allotments on public lands.*]

Sec. 5. That for the purpose of determining the descent of land to the heirs of any deceased Indian under the provisions of the fifth section of said act, whenever any male or female Indian shall have co-habited together as husband and wife, according to the custom and manner of Indian life the issue of such co-habitation shall be, for the purpose aforesaid, taken and deemed to be the legitimate issue of the Indians so living together, and every Indian child, otherwise illegitimate, shall for such purpose be taken and deemed to be the legitimate issue of the father of such child:

Provided, [Lands in the Cherokee Outlet, and certain Sac and Fox Indians, excluded from provisions of the act.]

Kappler, *Indian Affairs, Laws and Treaties,* I, 33–36, 56–58.

60   Sitting Bull, Dakota Chief

Sitting Bull's Opinion of Treaties, 1889

STANLEY VESTAL

The Indians did not always understand what they were doing when they signed a treaty. "The commissioners bring a paper containing what they wish already written out. It is not what the Indians want, but what the commissioners want. All they have to do is to get the signatures of the Indians. Sometimes the commissioners *say* they compromise, but they never change the document." Sitting Bull said this to the Silent Eaters,[1] in 1888.

At the council of the Silent Eaters, in 1889, upon the request of the members, Sitting Bull delivered the following speech.

"Friends and Relatives: Our minds are again disturbed by the Great Father's representatives, the Indian Agent, the squaw-men, the mixed-bloods, the interpreters and the favorite ration-chiefs. What is it they want of us at this time? They want us to give up another chunk of our tribal land. This is not the first time or the last time. They will try to gain possession of the last piece of ground we possess. They are again telling us what they intend to do if we agree to their wishes. Have we ever set a price on our land and received such a value? No, we never did. What we got under the former treaties were promises of all sorts. They promised how we are going to live peaceably on the land we still own and how they are going to show us the new ways of living—even told us how we can go to heaven when we die, but all that we realized out of the agreements with the Great Father was, we are dying off in expectation of getting things promised us.

"One thing I wish to state at this time is, something tells me that the Great Father's representatives have again brought with them a well-worded paper, containing just what they want but ignoring our wishes in the matter. It is this that they are attempting to drive us to. Our people are

1. Silent Eaters: a sort of dinner club of Hunkpapa Sioux warriors, of which Sitting Bull was a leading member. —V.J.V.

blindly deceived. Some are in favor of the proposition, but we who realize that our children and grandchildren may live a little longer, must necessarily look ahead and flatly reject the proposition. I, for one, am bitterly opposed to it. The Great Father has proven himself an *unktomi* [trickster] in our past dealings.

"When the White People invaded our Black Hills country our treaty agreements were still in force but the Great Father has ignored it—pretending to keep out the intruders through military force, and at last failing to keep them out they had to let them come in and take possession of our best part of our tribal possession. Yet the Great Father maintains a very large standing army that can stop anything.

"Therefore I do not wish to consider any proposition to cede any portion of our tribal holdings to the Great Father. If I agree to dispose of any part of our land to the white people I would feel guilty of taking food away from our children's mouths, and I do not wish to be that mean. There are things they tell us sound good to hear, but when they have accomplished their purpose they will go home and will not try to fulfill our agreements with them.

"My friends and relatives, let us stand as one family, as we did before the white people led us astray."

[*See also pp. 162–65.*]

STANLEY VESTAL, *New Sources of Indian History 1850–91*
(Norman: University of Oklahoma Press, 1934), pp. 303–4.
Copyright 1934 by the University of Oklahoma Press.

Grasping Eagle's Report of Sitting Bull's Words on Being Told That He Was to Be Arrested, 1890

Major James McLaughlin, believing that Sitting Bull was responsible for the spread of the Ghost Dance religion, which prophesied that the Indians would recover their country, ordered the arrest of the aging chief at Grand River, South Dakota, in 1890. Indian police appeared at his cabin on the early morning of December 15, and when the chief refused to accompany them, he was shot to death by Bullhead, and a few minutes later, his seventeen-year-old son, Crow Foot, was also murdered. The following remarks were made when he received advance information of his impending arrest.

For a time he was silent, then broke out: "Why should the Indian police come against me? We are of the same blood, we are all Sioux, we are relatives. It will disgrace the nation, it will be murder, it will defile our race. If the white men want me to die, they ought not to put up the Indians to kill me. I don't want confusion among my own people. Let the soldiers come and take me away and kill me, wherever they like. I am not afraid. I was born a warrior. I have followed the warpath ever since I was able to draw a bow."

Indignantly, he went on, venting his suspicions: "White Hair [McLaughlin] wanted me to travel all around [with Buffalo Bill] and across the sea, so that he could make a lot of money. Once was enough; I would not go. Then I would not join his church, and ever since he has had it in for me." Sitting Bull smiled scornfully, "Long ago I had two women in my lodge. One of them was jealous. White Hair reminds me of that jealous woman."

Still the chief poured out his grievances: "Why does he keep trying to humble me? Can I be any lower than I am? Once I was a man, but now I am a pitiful wretch—no country, no fast horses, no guns worth having. Once I was rich, now I am poor. What more does he want to do to me? I was a fool ever to come down here. I should have stayed with the Red Coats in the Grandmother's country. [*Queen Victoria's Canada*]

"I did not start this Ghost Dance; Kicking Bear came here of his own accord. I told my people to go slow, but they were swept into this thing so strong nothing could stop them. I have not joined the sacred dance since I was told to stop, away back."

The pent-up indignation of years had spent itself. Thereafter, Sitting Bull believed that his days were numbered. He went no more to the agency, but asked others to bring his rations. It was no surprise, this news; as early as the summer of '89 he had told his nephew, Chief Joseph White Bull, "Great men are generally destroyed by those who are jealous of them." Bear Ribs, Spotted Tail, Crazy Horse, plenty of examples rose up from the past to give warning. For Sitting Bull was a soldier, and had many people jealous of him.

STANLEY VESTAL, *New Sources of Indian History 1850–91*, pp. 309–11.

61   Last Agony of the Indians: Wounded Knee Massacre, December 29, 1890

> You may bury my body in Sussex grass,
> You may bury my tongue at Champmedy.
> I shall not be there. I shall rise and pass.
> Bury my heart at Wounded Knee.
>
> STEPHEN VINCENT BENÉT, "American Names."

The Ghost Dance religion, a messianic movement initiated by Wovoka, of the Paiutes, prophesied that the white man would be driven back and the Indians would recover their country. It was a spiritual movement rather than a military one, and its main activity was the Ghost Dance, performed in a white "ghost shirt" which was decorated with figures of birds and animals, and was believed to be bulletproof. The movement attracted followers in many tribes, and was spread among the Sioux by Kicking Bear in 1890. Major James McLaughlin, the Indian agent at Standing Rock, North Dakota, tried to suppress the dancing, and believing that Sitting Bull was responsible for it, ordered his arrest. Indian police were sent to bring in the chief who, after some hesitation, declared his refusal to accompany them, whereupon he was shot to death. A few minutes later his teen-aged son, Crow Foot, was dragged from his cabin and killed.

Frightened Indians fled toward the Badlands, where many gathered under the ailing chief Big Foot. Severe weather and hunger forced them to return, however, and they surrendered to soldiers near Wounded Knee Creek, in South Dakota, agreeing to give up their weapons. After many of the Indians had been disarmed, a struggle ensued when one Indian resisted, and an officer was accidentally shot. Big Foot, suffering from pneumonia, was then shot, and the Indians, four fifths of them women and children, fled toward a gulch, but were slaughtered by pursuing troops, many using Gatling guns. Approximately three hundred Indians perished that day, and they are buried in a common grave behind a Catholic mission overlooking the battleground.

The following account of what proved to be the last major clash between Indians and whites is by a Sioux named Black Elk, who was twenty-seven years old at the time. He had not been with Big Foot's band, but upon hearing the shooting from Pine Ridge, he mounted his pony and raced for the scene in the company of twenty Indians. His story was dictated in the Sioux language, through interpreters, to John G. Neihardt, poet laureate of Nebraska, in 1931.

> For further information see: Stanley Vestal, *Sitting Bull: Champion of the Sioux* (Norman: University of Oklahoma Press, 1957), and *New Sources of Indian History, 1850–91* (Norman: University of Oklahoma Press, 1934); James Mooney, *The Ghost Dance Religion and the Sioux Outbreak of 1890* (Chicago: University of Chicago Press, 1965); Robert M. Utley, *The Last Days of the Sioux Nation* (New Haven: Yale University Press, 1963), and John G. Neihardt, *Black Elk Speaks* (Lincoln: University of Nebraska Press, 1961).

Account of the Wounded Knee Massacre, 1890

BLACK ELK

It was about this time that bad news came to us from the north. We heard that some policemen from Standing Rock had gone to arrest Sitting

Bull on Grand River, and that he would not let them take him; so there was a fight, and they killed him.

It was now near the end of the Moon of Popping Trees, and I was twenty-seven years old [December, 1890]. We heard that Big Foot was coming down from the Badlands with nearly four hundred people. Some of these were from Sitting Bull's band. They had run away when Sitting Bull was killed, and joined Big Foot on Good River. There were only about a hundred warriors in this band, and all the others were women and children and some old men. They were all starving and freezing, and Big Foot was so sick that they had to bring him along in a pony drag. They had all run away to hide in the Badlands, and they were coming in now because they were starving and freezing. When they crossed Smoky Earth River, they followed up Medicine Root Creek to its head. Soldiers were over there looking for them. The soldiers had everything and were not freezing and starving. Near Porcupine Butte the soldiers came up to the Big Foots, and they surrendered and went along with the soldiers to Wounded Knee Creek where the Brenan store is now.

It was in the evening when we heard that the Big Foots were camped over there with the soldiers, about fifteen miles by the old road from where we were. It was the next morning [December 29, 1890] that something terrible happened.

That evening before it happened, I went in to Pine Ridge and heard these things, and while I was there, soldiers started for where the Big Foots were. These made about five hundred soldiers that were there next morning. When I saw them starting I felt that something terrible was going to happen. That night I could hardly sleep at all. I walked around most of the night.

In the morning I went out after my horses, and while I was out I heard shooting off toward the east, and I knew from the sound that it must be wagon-guns [cannon] going off. The sounds went right through my body, and I felt that something terrible would happen. [*He donned his ghost shirt, and armed only with a bow, mounted his pony and rode in the direction of the shooting, and was joined on the way by others.*]

In a little while we had come to the top of the ridge where, looking to the east, you can see for the first time the monument and the burying ground on the little hill where the church is. That is where the terrible thing started. Just south of the burying ground on the little hill a deep dry gulch runs about east and west, very crooked, and it rises westward to nearly the top of the ridge where we were. It had no name, but the Wasichus [*white men*] sometimes call it Battle Creek now. We stopped on the ridge not far from the head of the dry gulch. Wagon guns were still going off over there on the little hill, and they were going off again where they hit along the gulch. There was much shooting down yonder, and there were many cries, and we could see cavalrymen scattered over the hills ahead of us. Cavalrymen were riding along the gulch and shooting into it, where the women and children were running away and trying to hide in the gullies and the stunted pines.

A little way ahead of us, just below the head of the dry gulch, there were some women and children who were huddled under a clay bank, and some cavalrymen were there pointing guns at them. . . .

By now many other Lakotas [*Dakotas, Sioux*], who had heard the shooting, were coming up from Pine Ridge, and we all charged on the soldiers. They ran eastward toward where the trouble began. We followed down along the dry gulch, and what we saw was terrible. Dead and wounded women and children and little babies were scattered all along there where they had been trying to run away. The soldiers had followed along the gulch, as they ran, and murdered them in there. Sometimes they were in heaps because they had huddled together, and some were scattered all along. Sometimes bunches of them had been killed and torn to pieces where the wagon guns hit them. I saw a little baby trying to suck its mother, but she was bloody and dead.

There were two little boys at one place in this gulch. They had guns and they had been killing soldiers all by themselves. We could see the soldiers they had killed. The boys were all alone there, and they were not hurt. These were very brave little boys.

When we drove the soldiers back, they dug themselves in, and we were not enough people to drive them out from there. In the evening they marched off up Wounded Knee Creek, and then we saw all that they had done there.

Men and women and children were heaped and scattered all over the flat at the bottom of the little hill where the soldiers had their wagon-guns, and westward up the dry gulch all the way to the high ridge, the dead women and children and babies were scattered.

When I saw this I wished that I had died too, but I was not sorry for the women and children. It was better for them to be happy in the other world, and I wanted to be there too. But before I went there I wanted to have revenge. I thought there might be a day, and we should have revenge.

After the soldiers marched away, I heard from my friend, Dog Chief, how the trouble started, and he was right there by Yellow Bird when it happened. This is the way it was:

In the morning the soldiers began to take all the guns away from the Big Foots, who were camped in the flat below the little hill where the monument and burying ground are now. The people had stacked most of their guns, and even their knives, by the tepee where Big Foot was lying sick. Soldiers were on the little hill and all around, and there were soldiers across the dry gulch to the south and over east along Wounded Knee Creek too. The people were nearly surrounded, and the wagon-guns were pointing at them.

Some had not yet given up their guns, and so the soldiers were searching all the tepees, throwing things around and poking into everything. There was a man called Yellow Bird, and he and another man were standing in front of the tepee where Big Foot was lying sick. They had white sheets around and over them, with eyeholes to look through, and they had guns under these. An officer came to search them. He took the other man's gun, and then started to take Yellow Bird's. But Yellow Bird would not let go. He wrestled with the officer, and while they were wrestling, the gun went off and killed the officer. Wasichus and some others have said he meant to do this, but Dog Chief was standing right there, and he told me it was not so. As soon as the gun went off, Dog Chief told me, an officer shot and killed Big Foot who was lying sick inside the tepee.

Then suddenly nobody knew what was happening, except that the soldiers were all shooting and the wagon-guns began going off right in among the people.

Many were shot down right there. The women and children ran into the gulch and up west, dropping all the time, for the soldiers shot them as they ran. There were only about a hundred warriors and there were nearly five hundred soldiers. The warriors rushed to where they had piled their guns and knives. They fought soldiers with only their hands until they got their guns.

Dog Chief saw Yellow Bird run into a tepee with his gun, and from there he killed soldiers until the tepee caught fire. Then he died full of bullets.

It was a good winter day when all this happened. The sun was shining. But after the soldiers marched away from their dirty work, a heavy snow began to fall. The wind came up in the night. There was a big blizzard, and it grew very cold. The snow drifted deep in the crooked gulch, and it was one long grave of butchered women and children and babies, who had never done any harm and were only trying to run away.

Black Elk Speaks, Being the Life Story of a Holy Man of the Oglala Sioux, as told through John G. Neihardt (Lincoln: University of Nebraska Press, 1961), pp. 257–68.

Report on Wounded Knee Massacre and the Decrease in Indian Land Acreage, 1891

PRESIDENT BENJAMIN HARRISON

The first was necessary to protect the settlers; the second is progressing well, the president announced in his third annual message, December 9, 1891, excerpted below.

The outbreak among the Sioux which occurred in December last is as to its causes and incidents fully reported upon by the War Department and the Department of the Interior. That these Indians had some just complaints, especially in the matter of-the reduction of the appropriation for rations and in the delays attending the enactment of laws to enable the Department to perform the engagements entered into with them, is probably true; but the Sioux tribes are naturally warlike and turbulent, and their warriors were excited by their medicine men and chiefs, who preached the coming of an Indian messiah who was to give them power to destroy their enemies. In view of the alarm that prevailed among the white settlers near the reservation and of the fatal consequences that would have resulted from an Indian incursion, I placed at the disposal of General Miles, commanding the Division of the Missouri, all such forces as were thought by him to be required. He is entitled to the credit of having given thorough protection to the settlers and of bringing the hostiles into subjection with the least possible loss of life. . . .

Since March 4, 1889, about 23,000,000 acres have been separated from Indian reservations and added to the public domain for the use of those who desired to secure free homes under our beneficent laws. It is difficult to estimate the increase of wealth which will result from the conversion of these waste lands into farms, but it is more difficult to estimate the betterment which will result to the families that have found renewed hope and courage in the ownership of a home and the assurance of a comfortable subsistence under free and healthful conditions. It is also gratifying to be able to feel, as we may, that this work has proceeded upon lines of justice toward the Indian, and that he may now, if he will, secure to himself the good influences of a settled habitation, the fruits of industry, and the security of citizenship.

JAMES D. RICHARDSON, ed., *Messages and Papers* (Washington: 1898), IX, 201–3.

❖

62   Dissolution of Indian Territory into the State of Oklahoma, 1884–1907

When the Five Civilized Tribes, and for that matter, dozens of other tribes, were forced to remove from their eastern homes to the "Indian Territory" west of Arkansas, they were given solemn promises that they would never again be disturbed or asked to cede more land. In less than half a century the waves of white settlement were again lapping around the edges of their last refuge. During that time they had reestablished tribal governments patterned on the white model, built roads and towns, started newspapers, created thriving farms and ranches, and established a school system more advanced than in many parts of the Old South.

The first assault came in the western part of Indian Territory, where a number of tribes from other parts of the West had been placed on reservations. This district was opened to white settlement in 1884, and in 1890 it became the Territory of Oklahoma. A year earlier some Cherokee lands and two million acres of Creek lands were opened to white settlement. In 1891 the lands of the Sauk, Fox, and Potawatomi tribes were made available. Next, in 1892, the Cheyenne-Arapaho lands were occupied, and in 1893 the "Cherokee Outlet" succumbed to the Sooners. Other tracts were opened from year to year.

In 1893 Congress created the Dawes Commission, which was directed to secure agreements with the Five Civilized Tribes to the extinguishment of title to all their remaining lands in Indian Territory. It was also instructed to prepare tribal rolls for the purpose of allotting homesteads to individual Indians, prior to sale of the remaining land to whites. There was stubborn resistance to cooperating with the Dawes Commission, on the part of the tribes, but they were warned that Congress could and would accomplish its aims by legislation if they did not negotiate. One by one they were forced to submit.[1]

Although President McKinley reported in 1897 that the population of the Five Civilized Tribes was only 45,494, no less than a quarter million persons now applied for a share of the tribal property. When the Dawes Commission completed its rolls, the recognized tribal members numbered 77,942. All of those who applied (some did not) were given allotments in accordance with the Dawes Act: 160 acres for family heads, 80 acres for single persons, with full title to be vested in the individual after twenty-five years. The last proviso was eliminated in 1906, so that any Indian declared

1. Muriel H. Wright, *A Guide to the Indian Tribes of Oklahoma* (Norman: University of Oklahoma Press, 1965), pp. 19–21.

"competent" could secure title at once. In that same year, the tribal governments were declared dissolved, and the two territories of Oklahoma and Indian Territory were merged into the State of Oklahoma, admitted to the Union as the forty-sixth state in 1907.

Swarms of scheming white men, reminiscent of post-Civil War carpetbaggers, descended upon the Indian allottees with the aim of getting possession of their allotments by fraud and sharp dealing.[1] Of thirty million acres allotted to these Indians, only five per cent remains in Indian ownership today.[2] Although well over a hundred thousand Indians live in the state, most of them are landless, and there are no Indian reservations remaining. Thus ended the homeland which was solemnly promised to them forever, with only its name (Oklahoma: "red people"—Choctaw) to remind us that it was once theirs.

In his first annual message to Congress, an excerpt of which follows below, President McKinley presented arguments for the dissolution of the Indian governments, and outlined the resistance the Dawes Commission met in securing agreement by the Indians. The president greatly understated the number of Indians residing in the territory, and presented a one-sided case, filled with contradictions. He maintained that white settlers, who outnumbered the Indians, were there by Indian consent, yet in another paragraph he held that "it has been found impossible for the United States to keep its citizens out of Indian Territory." He complained that white settlers were denied the same privileges as tribal citizens, when neither the United States nor any other nation places aliens on the same footing as their own people. He argued that leading Indians had absorbed great tracts of land, while simultaneously denouncing the prevalence of communal ownership and demanding individual allotment in its place. Moreover, it was a strange complaint from the head of a government which had allowed a large part of the public domain to fall into the hands of large holders. The president also insisted that certain provisions of the treaties with these tribes had become "impossible of execution," when really the will was lacking; but if the argument was valid, the government itself had created the circumstances which made the treaties hard to enforce. Lastly, he made the negotiations with the tribal governments a farce, a mere fig leaf for determined rapacity, by declaring that Congress would legislate its will unilaterally upon the Indians if they refused to comply with the demands of the government.

1. For a touching account of the dispossession of the Creeks, see Angie Debo, *The Road to Disappearance* (Norman: University of Oklahoma Press, 1951).
2. *The Amerindian*, March–April, 1966, p. 6.

First Annual Message, December 6, 1897

PRESIDENT WILLIAM MCKINLEY

For a number of years past it has been apparent that the conditions under which the Five Civilized Tribes were established in the Indian Territory under treaty provisions with the United States, with the right of self-government and the exclusion of all white persons from within their borders, have undergone so complete a change as to render the continuance of the system thus inaugurated practically impossible. The total number of the Five Civilized Tribes, as shown by the last census, is 45,494, and this number has not materially increased; while the white population is estimated at from 200,000 to 250,000 which, by permission of the Indian Government has settled in the Territory. The present area of the Indian Territory contains 25,694,564 acres, much of which is very fertile land. The United States citizens residing in the territory, most of whom have gone there by invitation or with the consent of the tribal authorities, have made permanent homes for themselves. Numerous towns have been built in which from 500 to 5,000 white people now reside. Valuable residences and business houses have been erected in many of them. Large business enterprises are carried on in which vast sums of money are employed, and yet these people, who have invested their capital in the development of the productive resources of the country, are without title to the land they occupy, and have no voice whatever in the government either of the Nations or Tribes. Thousands of their children who were born in the Territory are of school age, but the doors of the schools of the [*Indian*] Nations are shut against them, and what education they get is by private contribution. No provision for the protection of the life or property of these white citizens is made by the Tribal Governments and Courts.

The Secretary of the Interior reports that leading Indians have absorbed great tracts of land to the exclusion of the common people, and government by an Indian aristocracy has been practically established, to the detriment of the people. It has been found impossible for the United States to keep its citizens out of the Territory, and the executory conditions contained in the treaties with these Nations have for the most part become impossible of execution. Nor has it been possible for the Tribal Governments to secure to each individual Indian his full enjoyment in common with other Indians of the common property of the Nations. Friends of the Indians have long believed that the best interests of the Indians of the Five Civilized Tribes would be found in American citizenship, with all the rights and privileges which belong to that condition.

By section 16, of the act of March 3, 1893, the President was authorized to appoint three commissioners to enter into negotiations with the Cherokee, Choctaw, Chickasaw, Muscogee (or Creek), and Seminole Nations, commonly known as the Five Civilized Tribes in the Indian Territory. Briefly, the purposes of the negotiations were to be: The extinguishment of the Tribal titles to any lands within that Territory now held by any and all such Nations or Tribes, either by cession of the same or some part thereof to the United States, or by allotment and division of the same in severalty among the Indians of such Nations or Tribes respectively as may be entitled to the same, or by such other method as may be agreed upon between the several Nations and Tribes aforesaid, or each of them, with the United States, with a view to such an adjustment upon the basis of justice and equity as may be necessary, be requisite and suitable to enable the ultimate creation of a State or States of the Union which shall embrace the lands within said Indian Territory.

The Commission met much opposition from the beginning. The Indians were very slow to act, and those in control manifested a decided disinclination to meet with favor the propositions submitted to them. A little more than three years after this organization the Commission effected an agreement with the Choctaw Nation alone. The Chickasaws, however, refused to agree to its terms, and as they have a common interest with the Choctaws in the lands of said Nations, the agreement with the latter Nation could have no effect without the consent of the former. On April 23, 1897, the Commission effected an agreement with both tribes—the Choctaws and Chickasaws. This agreement, it is understood, has been ratified by the constituted authorities of the respective Tribes or Nations parties thereto, and only requires ratification by Congress to make it binding.

On the 27th of September, 1897, an agreement was effected with the Creek Nation, but it is understood that the National Council of said Nation has refused to ratify the same. Negotiations are yet to be had with the Cherokees, the most populous of the Five Civilized Tribes, and with the Seminoles, the smallest in point of numbers and territory.

The provision in the Indian Appropriation Act, approved June 10, 1896, makes it the duty of the Commission to investigate and determine the rights of applicants for citizenship in the Five Civilized Tribes, and to make complete census rolls of the citizens of said Tribes. The Commission is at present engaged in this work among the Creeks, and has made appointments for taking the census of these people up to and including the 30th of the present month.

Should the agreement between the Choctaws and Chickasaws be ratified by Congress and should the other Tribes fail to make an agreement with the Commission, then it will be necessary that some legislation shall be had by Congress, which, while just and honorable to the Indians, shall be equitable to the white people who have settled upon these lands by invitation of the Tribal Nations.

Hon. Henry L. Dawes, Chairman of the Commission, in a letter to the Secretary of the Interior, under date of October 11, 1897, says: "Individual ownership is, in their [the Commission's] opinion, absolutely essential to any permanent improvement in present conditions, and the lack of it is the root of nearly all the evils which so grievously afflict these people. Allotment by agreement is the only possible method, unless the United States Courts are clothed with the authority to apportion the lands among the citizen Indians for whose use it was originally granted."

I concur with the Secretary of the Interior that there can be no cure for the evils engendered by the perversion of these great trusts, except by their resumption by the Government which created them.

JAMES D. RICHARDSON, ed., *A Compilation of the Messages and Papers of the Presidents* (10 vols.; Washington: National Bureau of Literature and Art, 1908), X, 45–47.

63 "Break Up the Tribal Mass": First Annual Message, December 3, 1901

PRESIDENT THEODORE ROOSEVELT

President Theodore Roosevelt viewed the Dawes land allotment act as "a mighty pulverizing engine to break up the tribal mass." He favored efforts to deprive Indians of group identity, and to break up their tribal funds. Their marriage laws, he declared, should conform to white custom, and the men should be compelled to earn their living in the same way as whites. Indian education should be vocational only, as the Indian need for anything more was "very limited." These are the ideas expressed in his first annual message, an excerpt of which follows.

In my judgement the time has arrived when we should definitely make up our minds to recognize the Indian as an individual and not as a member of a tribe. The General Allotment Act is a mighty pulverizing engine to break up the tribal mass. It acts directly upon the family and the individual. Under its provisions some sixty thousand Indians have already become citizens of the United States. We should now break up the tribal funds, doing for them what allotment does for the tribal lands; that is, they should be divided into individual holdings. There will be a transition period during which the funds will in many cases have to be held in trust. This is the case also with the lands. A stop should be put upon the indiscriminate permission to Indians to lease their allotments. The effort should be steadily to make the Indian work like any other man on his own ground. The marriage laws of the Indians should be made the same as those of the whites.

In the schools the education should be elementary and largely industrial. The need of higher education among the Indians is very, very limited. On the reservations care should be taken to try to suit the teaching to the needs of the particular Indian. There is no use in attempting to induce agriculture in a country suited only for cattle raising, where the Indian should be made a stock grower. The ration system, which is merely the corral and the reservation system, is highly detrimental to the Indians. It promotes beggary, perpetuates pauperism, and stifles industry. It is an effectual barrier to progress. It must continue to a greater or less degree as long as tribes are herded on reservations and have everything in common. The Indian should be treated as an individual—like the white man. During the change of treatment inevitable hardships will occur; every effort should be made to minimize these hardships; but we should not because of them hesitate to make the change. There should be a continuous reduction in the number of agencies.

ARTHUR M. SCHLESINGER and FRED L. ISRAEL, eds., *The State of the Union Messages of the Presidents* (3 vols.; New York: Chelsea House, 1966), II, 2047.

64   Indian Citizenship Act, June 2, 1924

Persons unversed in the interpretation of legal verbiage might easily suppose that Indians were covered by the Fourteenth Amendment, which says that "All persons born or naturalized in the United States, and subject to the jurisdiction thereof, are citizens of the United States, and of the State wherein they reside." Although Indians had long been deprived of their nationhood, they were still considered "wards of the government" and were not accorded the usual citizenship and voting rights, except for those who had received land title under the Dawes Act. It was expected that the Citizenship Act of 1924 would obtain these rights for all Indians, but due to resistance in several states, court action had to be resorted to in order to make these rights a reality.

Senator Charles Curtis of Kansas, later vice-president (1929–1933), who was partly of Kaw and Osage descent, is credited with the authorship of this act.

CHAP. 233.—An Act to authorize the Secretary of the Interior to issue certificates of citizenship to Indians.

Be it enacted by the Senate and House of Representatives of the United States of America in Congress assembled, That all non-citizen Indians born within the territorial limits of the United States be, and they are hereby, declared to be citizens of the United States; Provided, That the granting of such citizenship shall not in any manner impair or otherwise affect the right of any Indian to tribal or other property.

Approved, June 2, 1924.

H.R. 6355, 43 Stat., 253.

CHARLES J. KAPPLER, ed., *Indian Affairs, Laws and Treaties* (Washington: Government Printing Office, 1903–29), IV, 420.

65 Criticism of the Indian Land Allotment Policy (Dawes Act)

FROM THE MERIAM REPORT, 1928

When the government adopted the policy of individual ownership of land on the reservations, the expectation was that the Indians would become farmers. Part of the plan was to instruct and aid them in agriculture, but this vital part was not pressed with vigor and intelligence. It almost seems as if the government assumed that some magic in individual ownership of property would in itself prove an educational civilizing factor, but unfortunately this policy has for the most part operated in the opposite direction. Individual ownership has in many instances permitted Indians to sell their allotments and to live for a time on the unearned income resulting from the sale. Individual ownership brought promptly all the details of inheritance, and frequently the sale of property of the deceased Indians to whites so that the estate could be divided among the heirs. To the heirs the sale brought further unearned income, thereby lessening the necessity for self-support. Many Indians were not ready to make effective use of their individual allotments. Some of the allotments were of such a character that they could not be effectively used by anyone in small units. The solution was to permit the Indians through the government to lease their lands to the whites. In some instances government officers encouraged leasing, as the whites were anxious for the use of the land and it was far easier to administer property leased to whites than to educate and stimulate Indians to use their own property. The lease money, though generally small in amount, gave the Indians further unearned income to permit the continuance of a life of idleness.

Surplus land remaining after allotments were made was often sold and the proceeds placed in a tribal fund. Natural resources, such as timber and oil, were sold and the money paid either into tribal funds or to individual

Indians if the land had been allotted. From time to time per capita payments were made to the individual Indians from tribal funds. These policies all added to the unearned income of the Indian and postponed the day when it would be necessary for him to go to work to support himself.

LEWIS MERIAM, *The Problem of Indian Administration,* a report by the Institute for Government Research (Baltimore: Johns Hopkins University Press, 1928), pp. 7–8.

66 Partial Restoration of Indian Self-Government, 1934–1936

Most Indians, and friends of the Indian, have regarded the Indian Reorganization Act of 1934, despite serious shortcomings, as an improvement over previous policy. The allotment of Indian lands in severalty (individual ownership), and the sale to whites of unallotted lands, as provided by the Dawes Act of 1887, was terminated, and provision was made for adding to reservation lands. A limited degree of Indian self-government was restored, and tribes, at their own option, could incorporate under the provisions of the act and elect tribal governments invested with certain legal powers. A revolving loan fund was created, in the amount of $10,000,000, for the purpose of aiding tribal councils in promoting economic development. Scholarship aid, not exceeding $250,000 a year, was provided for Indians attending vocational and trade schools. Indians were to be given preference for civil service jobs in the Indian Bureau. These provisions were hailed as positive accomplishments by all except those who desired the total dispersal of Indian communities.

Other parts of the bill, however, were a severe blow to many Indians. Most importantly, the Papago tribe was deprived of control of its mineral resources, and the reservation was made available for mining operations at a rental of five cents per acre annually. All the tribes of Oklahoma, listed by name, and composing the largest Indian population of any state at the time, were excluded from all significant portions of the act.[1] Several sections were made inapplicable to the Indians of Alaska. The enlargement of the Navajo reservation, with its fast-growing population, was expressly prohibited. Indian land could still be taken for irrigation projects, and the Klamath reservation was excluded from the provisions of Section 4.

Extraordinary power was vested in the person of the secretary of the interior. He was to prescribe rules under which tribal elections were to be held. He must approve the constitutions adopted before they became effec-

1. Some provisions were made for Oklahoma Indians two years later in the Oklahoma Indian Welfare Act. See pp. 203–205.

tive. He was given veto power over the choice of tribal attorneys. He was to make rules for the management of forests and grazing lands, and his power in the latter instance resulted in the notorious Navajo stock reduction program which was carried out in a most dictatorial manner. The secretary, in short, was made a supreme potentate, exercising power for good or evil as he saw fit.

The sums allowed for land acquisition, for scholarships, and for development loans were grossly inadequate, and of the paltry vocational education fund, not more than one fifth ($50,000) was to be used for attendance in high schools or colleges.

Perhaps these shortcomings were the result of that kind of political horse-trading and log-rolling which often requires submission to emasculating amendments as the only alternative to the total defeat of constructive legislation. This act fell far short of meeting Indian needs, and left whole areas of crying neglect in such fields as health, education, water and mineral rights, and redress for past expropriations. Some of these, especially the last, were partially met by later enactments (e.g., the Indian Claims Commission Act), but other laws have turned the clock back (e.g., Public Law #280, the Relocation Act, various termination acts, and the revocation of treaty rights in acquisition of dam sites).

Indian Reorganization Act, June 18, 1934

AN ACT to conserve and develop Indian lands and resources; to extend to Indians the right to form business and other organizations; to establish a credit system for Indians; to grant certain rights of home rule to Indians; to provide for vocational education for Indians; and for other purposes.

Be it enacted by the Senate and House of Representatives of the United States of America in Congress assembled, That hereafter no land of any Indian reservation, created or set apart by treaty or agreement with the Indians, Act of Congress, Executive order, purchase, or otherwise, shall be allotted in severalty to any Indian.

SEC. 2. The existing periods of trust placed upon any Indian lands and any restriction on alienation thereof are hereby extended and continued until otherwise directed by Congress.

SEC. 3. The Secretary of the Interior, if he shall find it to be in the public interest, is hereby authorized to restore to tribal ownership the remaining surplus lands of any Indian reservation heretofore opened, or authorized to be opened, to sale, or any other form of disposal by Presidential proclamation, or by any of the public-land laws of the United States: *Provided, however,* That valid rights or claims of any persons to any lands so withdrawn existing on the date of the withdrawal shall not be affected by this Act: *Provided further,* That this section shall not apply to lands within any reclamation project heretofore authorized in any Indian reservation: *Provided further,* That the order of the Department of the Interior signed, dated, and approved by the Honorable Ray Lyman Wilbur, as Secretary of the Interior, on October 28, 1932, temporarily withdrawing lands of the Papago Indian Reservation in Arizona from all forms of mineral entry or claim under the public land mining laws, is hereby revoked and rescinded, and the lands of the said Papago Indian Reservation are hereby restored to exploration and location, under the existing mining laws of the United States, in accordance with the express terms and provisions declared and set forth in the Executive orders establishing said Papago Indian Reservation: *Provided further,* That damages shall be paid to the Papago Tribe for loss of any improvements on any land located for mining in such a sum as may be determined by the Secretary of the Interior but not to exceed the cost of said improvements: *Provided further,* That a yearly rental not to exceed five cents per acre shall be paid to the Papago Tribe for loss of the use or occupancy of any land withdrawn by the requirements of mining operations, and payments derived from damages or rentals shall be deposited in the Treasury of the United States to the credit of the Papago Tribe: *Provided further,* That in the event any person or persons, partnership, corporation, or association, desires a mineral patent, according to the mining laws of the United States, he or they shall first deposit in the Treasury of the United States to the credit of the Papago Tribe the sum of $1.00 per acre in lieu of annual rental, as hereinbefore provided, to compensate for the loss or occupancy of the lands withdrawn by the requirements of mining operations: *Provided further,* That patentee shall also pay into the Treasury of the United States to the credit of the Papago Tribe damages for the loss of improvements not heretofore paid in such a sum as may be determined by the Secretary of the Interior, but not to exceed the cost thereof; the payment of $1.00 per acre for surface use to be refunded to patentee in the event that patent is not acquired.

Nothing herein contained shall restrict the granting or use of permits for easements or rights-of-way; or ingress or egress over the lands for all proper and lawful purposes; and nothing contained herein, except as expressly provided, shall be construed as authority for the Secretary of the Interior, or any other person, to issue or promulgate a rule or regulation in conflict with the Executive order of February 1, 1917, creating the Papago Indian Reservation in Arizona or the Act of February 21, 1931 (46 Stat. 1202).

SEC. 4. Except as herein provided, no sale, devise, gift, exchange or other transfer of restricted Indian lands or of shares in the assets of any

Indian tribe or corporation organized hereunder, shall be made or approved: *Provided, however,* That such lands or interests may, with the approval of the Secretary of the Interior, be sold, devised, or otherwise transferred to the Indian tribe in which the lands or shares are located or from which the shares were derived or to a successor corporation; and in all instances such lands or interests shall descend or be devised, in accordance with the then existing laws of the State, or Federal laws where applicable, in which said lands are located or in which the subject matter of the corporation is located, to any member of such tribe or of such corporation or any heirs of such member: *Provided further,* That the Secretary of the Interior may authorize voluntary exchanges of lands of equal value and the voluntary exchange of shares of equal value whenever such exchange, in his judgement, is expedient and beneficial for or compatible with the proper consolidation of Indian lands and for the benefit of cooperative organizations.

SEC. 5. The Secretary of the Interior is hereby authorized, in his discretion, to acquire through purchase, relinquishment, gift, exchange, or assignment, any interest in lands, water rights or surface rights to lands, within or without existing reservations, including trust or otherwise restricted allotments whether the allottee be living or deceased, for the purpose of providing land for Indians.

For the acquisition of such lands, interests in lands, water rights, and surface rights, and for expenses incident to such acquisition, there is hereby authorized to be appropriated, out of any funds in the Treasury not otherwise appropriated, a sum not to exceed $2,000,000 in any one fiscal year: *Provided,* That no part of such funds shall be used to acquire additional land outside of the exterior boundaries of Navajo Indian Reservation for the Navajo Indians in Arizona and New Mexico, in the event that the proposed Navajo boundary extension measures now pending in Congress and embodied in the bills (S. 2499 and H.R. 8927) to define the exterior boundaries of the Navajo Indian Reservation in Arizona, and for other purposes, and the bills (S. 2531 and H.R. 8982) to define the exterior boundaries of the Navajo Indian Reservation in New Mexico and for other purposes, or similar legislation, becomes law.

The unexpended balances of any appropriations made pursuant to this section shall remain available until expended.

Title to and lands or rights acquired pursuant to this Act shall be taken in the name of the United States in trust for the Indian tribe or individual Indian for which the land is acquired, and such lands or rights shall be exempt from State and local taxation.

SEC. 6. The Secretary of the Interior is directed to make rules and regulations for the operation and management of Indian forestry units on the principle of sustained yield management, to restrict the number of livestock grazed on Indian range units to the estimated carrying capacity of such ranges, and to promulgate such other rules and regulations as may be necessary to protect the range from deterioration, to prevent soil erosion, to assure full utilization of the range, and like purposes.

SEC. 7. The Secretary of the Interior is hereby authorized to proclaim new Indian reservations on lands acquired pursuant to any authority conferred by this Act, or to add such lands to existing reservations: *Provided,* That lands added to existing reservations shall be designated for the exclusive use of Indians entitled by enrollment or by tribal membership to residence at such reservations.

SEC. 8. Nothing contained in this Act shall be construed to relate to Indian holdings of allotments or homesteads upon the public domain outside of the geographic boundaries of any Indian reservation now existing or established hereafter.

SEC. 9. There is hereby authorized to be appropriated, out of any funds in the Treasury not otherwise appropriated, such sums as may be necessary, but not to exceed $250,000 in any fiscal year to be expended at the order of the Secretary of the Interior, in defraying the expenses of organizing Indian chartered corporations or other organizations created under this Act.

SEC. 10. There is hereby authorized to be appropriated, out of any funds in the Treasury not otherwise appropriated, the sum of $10,000,000 to be established as a revolving fund from which the Secretary of the Interior, under such rules and regulations as he may prescribe, may make loans to Indian chartered corporations for the purpose of promoting the economic development of such tribes and of their members, and may defray the expenses of administering such loans. Repayment of amounts loaned under this authorization shall be credited to the revolving funds and shall be available for the purposes for which the funds are established. A report shall be made annually to Congress of transactions under this authorization.

SEC. 11. There is hereby authorized to be appropriated, out of any funds in the United States Treasury not otherwise appropriated, a sum not to exceed $250,000 annually, together with any unexpended balances of previous appropriations made pursuant to this section, for loans to Indians for the payment of tuition and other expenses in recognized vocational and trade schools: *Provided,* That not more than $50,000 of such sum shall be available for loans to Indian students in high schools and colleges. Such loans shall be reimbursable under rules established by the Commissioner of Indian Affairs.

SEC. 12. The Secretary of the Interior is directed to establish standards of health, age, character, experience, knowledge, and ability for Indians who may be appointed, without regard to civil-service laws, to the various positions maintained, now or hereafter, by the Indian Office, in the administration of functions or services affecting any Indian tribe. Such qualified Indians shall hereafter have the preference to appointment to vacancies in any such positions.

SEC. 13. The provisions of this Act shall not apply to any of the Territories, colonies, or insular possessions of the United States, except that sections 9, 10, 11, 12, and 16, shall apply to the Territory of Alaska: *Provided:* That Sections 2, 4, 7, 16, 17, and 18 of this Act shall not apply to the following-named Indian tribes, the members of such Indian tribes, together with members of other tribes affiliated with such named tribes located in the State of Oklahoma, as follows: Cheyenne, Arapaho, Apache, Comanche, Kiowa, Caddo, Delaware, Wichita, Ottawa, Quapaw, Seneca, Wyandotte, Iowa, Sac and Fox, Kickapoo, Pottawatomi, Cherokee, Chickasaw, Choctaw, Creek, and Seminole. Section 4 of this Act shall not apply to the Indians of the Klamath Reservation in Oregon.

SEC. 14. The Secretary of the Interior is hereby directed to continue the allowance of the articles enumerated in section 17 of the Act of March 2, 1889 (23 Stat. L. 894), or their commuted cash value under the Act of June 10, 1896 (29 Stat. L. 334), to all Sioux Indians who would be eligible but for the provisions of this Act, to receive allotments of lands in severalty under section 19 of the Act of May 29, 1908 (25 Stat. L. 451), or under any prior Act, and who have the prescribed status of head of a family or single person over the age of eighteen years, and his approval shall be final and conclusive, claims therefor to be paid as formerly from the permanent appropriation made by said section 17 and carried on the books of the Treasury for this purpose. No person shall receive in his own right more than one allowance of the benefits, and application must be made and approved during the lifetime of the allottee or the right shall lapse. Such benefits shall continue to be paid upon such reservation until such time as the lands available therein for allotment at the time of the passage of this Act would have been exhausted by the award to each person receiving such benefits of any allotment of eighty acres of such land.

SEC. 15. Nothing in this Act shall be construed to impair or prejudice any claim or suit of any Indian tribe against the United States. It is hereby declared to be the intent of Congress that no expenditures for the benefit of Indians made out of appropriations authorized by this Act shall be considered as offsets in any suit brought to recover upon any claim of such Indians against the United States.

SEC. 16. Any Indian tribe, or tribes, residing on the same reservation shall have the right to organize for its common welfare, and may adopt an appropriate constitution and bylaws, which shall become effective when ratified by a majority vote of the adult members of the tribe, or of the adult Indians residing on such reservation, as the case may be, at a special election authorized and called by the Secretary of the Interior under such rules and regulations as he may prescribe. Such constitution and bylaws when ratified as aforesaid and approved by the Secretary of the Interior shall be revocable by an election open to the same voters and conducted in the same manner as hereinabove provided. Amendments to the constitution and bylaws may be ratified and approved by the Secretary in the same manner as the original constitution and bylaws.

In addition to all powers vested in any Indian tribe or tribal council by existing law, the constitution adopted by said tribe shall also vest in such tribe or its tribal council the following rights and powers: To employ legal counsel, the choice of counsel and fixing of fees to be subject to the approval of the Secretary of the Interior; to prevent the sale, disposition, lease, or encumbrance of tribal lands, interests in lands, or other tribal assets without the consent of the tribe; and to negotiate with the Federal, State, and local Governments. The Secretary of the Interior shall advise such tribe or its tribal counsel of all appropriation estimates or Federal projects for the benefit of the tribe prior to the submission of such estimates to the Bureau of the Budget and the Congress.

SEC. 17. The Secretary of the Interior may, upon petition by at least one-third of the adult Indians, issue a charter of incorporation to such tribe: *Provided,* That such charter shall not become operative until ratified at a special election by a majority vote of the adult Indians living on the reservation. Such charter may convey to the incorporated tribe the power to purchase, take by gift, or bequest, or otherwise, own, hold, manage, operate, and dispose of property of every description, real and personal, including the power to purchase restricted Indian lands and to issue in exchange therefor interests in corporate property, and such further powers as may be incidental to the conduct of corporate business, not inconsistent with law, but no authority shall be granted to sell, mortgage, or lease for a period exceeding ten years any of the land included in the limits of the reservation. Any charter so issued shall not be revoked or surrendered except by Act of Congress.

SEC. 18. This Act shall not apply to any reservation wherein a majority of the adult Indians, voting at a special election duly called by the Secretary of the Interior, shall vote against its application. It shall be the duty of the Secretary of the Interior, within one year after the passage and approval of this Act, to call such an election, which election shall be held by secret ballot upon thirty days' notice.

SEC. 19. The term "Indian" as used in this Act shall include all persons of Indian descent who are members of any recognized Indian tribe now under Federal jurisdiction, and all persons who are descendants of such members who were, on June 1, 1934, residing within the present boundaries of any Indian reservation, and shall further include all other persons of one-half or more Indian blood. For the purposes of this Act, Eskimos and other aboriginal peoples of Alaska shall be considered Indians. The term "tribe" wherever used in this Act shall be construed to refer to any Indian tribe, organized band, pueblo, or the Indians residing on one reservation. The words "adult Indians" wherever used in this Act shall be construed to refer to Indians who have attained the age of twenty-one years.

Approved, June 18, 1934.

> From *Report with Respect to the House Resolution Authoriz-
> ing the Committee on Interior and Insular Affairs to Con-
> duct an Investigation of the Bureau of Indian Affairs*, pur-
> suant to H. Res. 698 (82d Cong.), December 15, 1952
> (Washington: G.P.O., 1953), pp. 1035–39.

Oklahoma Indian Welfare Act, June 26, 1936

The Indians of Oklahoma were excluded from the provisions of the Indian Reorganization Act of 1934. The governments of the Five Civilized Tribes had been dissolved in 1906, and many Oklahoma tribes retained no organization. Formal reservations, as well, were no longer in existence, and acculturation was far advanced. Many charged that any revival of orga-nized Indian communities and tribes in Oklahoma would be "going back to the blanket." It was a view held by certain Oklahoma Indian representa-tives in the Congress, as well as by whites. Among rank-and-file Indians, however, it was ascertained by Commissioner John Collier and his aides, there was considerable sentiment for some provisions to be made for them. After consultations and meetings with Indians in the state, the Oklahoma Indian Welfare Act was written and enacted. As a result, many Oklahoma tribes were reorganized and gained a legal identity once more.

AN ACT to promote the general welfare of the Indians of the State of Oklahoma, and for other purposes.

Be it enacted by the Senate and House of Representatives . . . That the Secretary of the Interior is hereby authorized, in his discretion, to acquire by purchase, relinquishment, gift, exchange, or assignment, any interest in lands, water rights, or surface rights to lands, within or without existing Indian reservations; including trust, or otherwise restricted lands now in Indian ownership: *Provided.* That such lands shall be agricultural and grazing lands of good character and quality in proportion to the respective needs of the particular Indian or Indians for whom such purchases are made. Title to all lands so acquired shall be taken in the name of the United States, in trust for the tribe, band, group, or individual Indian for whose benefit such land is so acquired, and while the title thereto is held by the United States such lands shall be free from any and all taxes, save that the State of Oklahoma is authorized to levy and collect a gross-production tax, not in excess of the rate applied to production from lands in private ownership, upon all oil and gas produced from said lands, which said tax the Secretary of the Interior is hereby authorized and directed to cause to be paid.

SEC. 2. [*The Secretary of the Interior given a preference right to purchase certain lands in behalf of Indians.*]

SEC. 3. Any recognized tribe or band of Indians residing in Oklahoma shall have the right to organize for its common welfare and to adopt a constitution and bylaws, under such rules and regulations as the Secretary of the Interior may prescribe. The Secretary of the Interior may issue to any such organized group a charter of incorporation, which shall become operative when ratified by a majority vote of the adult members of the organization voting: *Provided, however,* That such election shall be void unless the total vote cast be at least 30 percentum of those entitled to vote. Such charter may convey to the incorporated group, in addition to any powers which may properly be vested in a body corporate under the laws of the State of Oklahoma, the right to participate in the revolving credit fund and to enjoy any other rights or privileges secured to an organized Indian tribe under the Act of June 18, 1934 (48 Stat. 984): *Provided,* That the corporate funds of any such charter group may be deposited in any national bank within the State of Oklahoma or otherwise invested, utilized, or disbursed in accordance with the terms of the corporate charter.

SEC. 4. [*Any ten or more Indians may organize cooperative associations for purposes of credit administration, production, marketing, consumers' protection, or land management.*]

SEC. 5. [*Provisions concerning legal status of Indian cooperatives; authority to transfer suits against them from state to federal courts.*]

SEC. 6. [*Provisions for loans.*]

SEC. 7. [*Oklahoma Indians entitled to a share of appropriations made under the Indian Reorganization Act; mineral revenues from lands purchased under this act to be held in the treasury for land acquisition and loans.*]

SEC. 8. [*Osage County excluded.*]

SEC. 9. The Secretary of the Interior is hereby authorized to prescribe such rules and regulations as may be necessary to carry out the provisions of this Act. All Acts or parts of Acts inconsistent herewith are hereby repealed.

Report . . . Pursuant to H. Res. 698 (82d Cong.), December 15, pp. 1051–53.

Federal Indian Law and Tribal Self-Government

FELIX S. COHEN

The Wheeler-Howard Act and the Oklahoma Indian Welfare Act once more gave legal recognition to tribal rights that former policy-makers had sought to extinguish. It was discovered that the legal status of Indian tribes was an unfamiliar subject to many members of Congress, the bar, and the bench, and particularly to administrative officials. The size of the problem may be seen in the fact that the United States had accumulated 372 ratified Indian treaties by 1871, in addition to some dozens of "agreements" since that date, and by 1940, there were about 5,000 laws dealing with Indians on the federal statute books. Moreover, there were hundreds of court decisions having an important effect on the status of Indians. To systematize and interpret this extensive body of legal information, Felix S. Cohen and his staff in the Department of the Interior prepared the Handbook of Federal Indian Law, *first published in 1941, and reissued the following year with an index and reference tables. A revision of this work, entitled* Federal Indian Law, *was released in 1958. Cohen's work is an indispensable sourcebook for anyone searching for understanding in this area. It has been quoted on pp. 163–65. Below is another selection from it, briefly but clearly summarizing the basis of Indian self-government.*

The Scope of Tribal Self-Government: Introduction

The Indian's right of self-government is a right which has been consistently protected by the courts, frequently recognized and intermittently ignored by treaty-makers and legislators, and very widely disregarded by administrative officials. That such rights have been disregarded is perhaps due more to lack of acquaintance with the law of the subject than to any drive for increased power on the part of administrative officials.

The most basic of all Indian rights, the right of self-government, is the Indian's last defense against administrative oppression, for in a realm where the states are powerless to govern and where Congress, occupied with more pressing national affairs, cannot govern wisely and well, there remains a large no-man's-land in which government can emanate only from officials of the Interior Department or from the Indians themselves.

Self-government is thus the Indians' only alternative to rule by a government department.

Indian self-government, the decided cases hold, includes the power of an Indian tribe to adopt and operate under a form of government of the Indians' choosing, to define conditions of tribal membership, to regulate domestic relations of members, to prescribe rules of inheritance, to levy taxes, to regulate property within the jurisdiction of the tribe, to control the conduct of members by municipal legislation, and to administer justice.

Perhaps the most basic principle of all Indian law, supported by a host of decisions hereinafter analyzed, is the principle that *those powers which are lawfully vested in an Indian tribe are not, in general, delegated powers granted by express acts of Congress, but rather inherent powers of a limited sovereignty which has never been extinguished*. Each Indian tribe begins its relationship with the Federal Government as a sovereign power, recognized as such in treaty and legislation. The powers of sovereignty have been limited from time to time by special treaties and laws designed to take from the Indian tribes control of matters which, in the judgment of Congress, these tribes could no longer be safely permitted to handle. The statutes of Congress, then, must be examined to determine the limitations of tribal sovereignty rather than to determine its sources or its positive content. What is not expressly limited remains within the domain of tribal sovereignty.

The acts of Congress which appear to limit the powers of an Indian tribe are not to be unduly extended by doubtful inference.

> FELIX S. COHEN, *Handbook of Federal Indian Law* (Washington: Government Printing Office, 1942), p. 122; emphasis in original.

67 Urban Indians

Since the early 1950s a government-sponsored relocation program has been in operation, by which selected reservation Indians are given financial assistance in moving to designated cities. For a brief period, they are helped to find housing and employment, after which the government terminates all responsibility for them. Many other Indians come to the cities on their own initiative, hoping for a better life. Los Angeles, Denver, Minneapolis, Milwaukee, and Chicago are among the cities that have attained notable Indian populations in recent years.

The sudden change in environment and life-styles is often too much for them, with the consequence that many return to the reservation, despite the poverty there. The impersonality of the large city, the loneliness in the midst of the crowd, the gulf which separates them from other ethnic groups, the separation from friends, relatives, and familiar surroundings, the lock-step of fixed working hours and days, and the complex of stresses which some people call the "rat race" are among the problems which Indians, like other people of rural origin, find it difficult to deal with. The following two documents illustrate the feelings of Indians who are facing this transition.

A New Arrival, 1968

BELLE JEAN FRANCIS

Here I am in a big city, right in the middle of Chicago. I don't know anybody. I am so lonesome and I have that urge to go home. I don't know which direction to go—south, north, east or west. I can't just take any direction because I don't know my way around yet.

I see strange faces around me and I keep wondering how I will survive in this strange environment. I keep wondering how I can get over this loneliness, and start adjusting to this environment. I know I have to start somewhere along the line and get involved in social activities and overcome the fear I am holding inside me and replace it with courage, dignity, self-confidence and the ambition to reach my goal.

Before I can adjust myself to this strange environment and get involved in things, I need friends who will help me overcome this urge to go home so I can accomplish my goal here in this unknown world which I entered.

> BELLE JEAN FRANCIS (Athabascan), *Program Book of American Indian Festival* (Field Museum, September 23–October 13, 1968), p. 8.

Getting Urbanized: A Winnebago Indian in Chicago

BENNY BEARSKIN

Getting urbanized. I like this term. It means you have to learn the ropes, just like a person moving out from the prairie country into the woods. You know, there are certain dangers in such a transition, and it's the same way in a city. Yes, you have to learn the ropes. And once you become urbanized, this means to me that you're gonna settle down, and you have to have a goal to look forward to. Otherwise, I think it would drive you crazy.

I came to Chicago in 1947, after I had been married, and later on I sent for my wife and my one child and since that time we've lived here in the city. The most important reason was that I could at least feel confident that perhaps fifty paychecks a year here . . . and you can't always get that way. Even though it might be more pleasant to be back home, for instance, Nebraska.

What do you call home: Do you call Nebraska home?

Yes, I think this is one feature most Indians have in common. They have a deep attachment for the land. This has been so for a long, long time. Many different tribes of Indians are now residing in Chicago, but most of them maintain ties with the people back home. Even in cases where the older members of their families have passed away, they still make a point to go home. Many of them make the trip twice a year to go back to the place where they were born and raised. . . .

You put down on the application: INDIAN?

Yes, always. I think that's a source of pride. I think a lot of fellas think this is a source of pride, because we enjoy the distinction that no other person has. We are at home, while everyone else came here from somewhere else.

And I believe that, as time goes on, that society becomes more and more complex, there is that need for a basic pride in order to have something on which to build character. If you don't have that pride, well, then you have no identity. We understand that all the states have these mental institutions that are bulging at the seams. This is evidence of social and psychological maladjustment. So we have to have some values, I believe. . . .

There are some areas where the transition from Indian culture to white culture is going on, and some of the children are born into a situation where the old values are already lost. There being no basic economies in these areas, there's much poverty. And nothing of the white culture is available to them. So they're lost in between.

And it is this type of young Indian who is ashamed he is an Indian. Because he doesn't realize, there's nobody ever told him: his ancestors were a noble race of men who developed over many centuries a way of life, primitive though it was; it existed without prisons, hospitals, jails, courts or anything, or insane asylums or currency or anything. Yet an Indian back in those days was able to live from babyhood till all the hair on his head became white, and he lived a life of complete fulfillment. With no regrets at the end. You rarely see that in this day and age.

Four of our children were born here in this city, and yet, I think, they're oriented as American Indians. I make it a point to take them on my vacation trips in the summer, always to a different reservation to get acquainted with the people of the tribe. We take photographs, we record the songs that are sung, we participate in dancing and compete for prizes. . . .

I think those Indians who retain the greatest amount of their cultural heritage are really very fortunate, because they feel that it's more important to retain one's dignity and integrity and go through life in this manner, than spending all their energy on an accumulation of material wealth. They find this a frustrating situation. I think the Indian is the only nationality under the system who has resisted this melting-pot concept. Everybody else want to jump in, they view this idea, jumping in and becoming American or losing identity.

I don't think the flame has ever went out. Of course, we do have exceptions. We have many Indians who have been orphaned at an early age, who have become completely acculturated and know nothing of their heritage.

It's so impersonal. I think this makes itself felt in many situations. For instance, when you become urbanized, you learn how to think in abstract terms. Now when you get here on Broadway, to catch a CTA bus going south, you subconsciously know there's a driver, but you take no interest in him at all as a person, he's more like an object. And it's the same way in schools. The teacher is there to do a certain function. And I think the teacher also feels that these pupils are like a bunch of bumps on a log. You know, this can be a difficult thing, especially for an Indian child, who, in his family life, learns to establish relationships on a person-to-person basis. And he finds that this is absent in the classroom. And frequently parents go to talk to the principal, to talk to the teacher; it's just like going over there talking to a brick wall. They feel you just aren't hip. Something wrong with you, and if you don't conform, it's just too bad. . . .

Poverty is not merely the lack of wealth, a lack of money. It goes much deeper than that. There's poverty in reservations and where there are no reservations, and where there are no Indians. What we try to do here, at the Center [*American Indian Center*] is to some way, somehow, get people *involved*. Most of these people are coping with their problems on a day-to-day basis. The future is something rarely enters their minds.

I think that perhaps my early training in the home impressed me with the philosophy of our forebears. It was taught to us that if one could be of service to his people, this is one of the greatest honors there is. I think this has been a strong influence on my life. I'll never know all the answers. I'm still learning the answers.

I think there will be some radical changes taking place. We have a younger generation, in the age bracket of my oldest daughter. I think in the future Indians will make a bigger contribution. It's been pointed out that Indians should feel that if it was not for the land which they owned, this would not be the greatest nation on earth. . . .

STUDS TERKEL, *Division Street: America* (New York: Avon Books, 1967), pp. 134–42.

68   What Indians Want: Statements of American Indian Chicago Conference, 1961

Indians have seldom been asked what they want, nor have programs allegedly designed for their benefit often been developed through their participation. Indian initiative was so long repressed that it is only recently that they have rediscovered their own voice. The first effective national organization of Indians was the National Congress of American Indians, organized in 1944. Many large tribes, however, such as the Navajo, do not participate in it. The Indian cause has also been supported by white initiated organizations such as the Indian Rights Association (organized by Quakers in 1882), and the Association on American Indian Affairs (since 1923).

Independently of these organizations, a nationwide Indian conference was convened at the University of Chicago in June 1961. Technical arrangements were handled by a committee headed by Sol Tax, but the conference itself was restricted to Indians, whites being permitted as silent observers at some of the open sessions. Seven hundred Indians from sixty-four tribes took part, and produced a "Declaration of Indian Purpose" which strongly attacked the termination bills by which the government sought to withdraw from its responsibilities to Indian tribes (as it did in the case of the Klamaths and Menominees), and called for the right to maintain and develop their own communities with government assistance. The following document, "What Indians Want," is taken from their report.

Statement of Purpose:
. . . in order to give recognition to certain basic philosophies by which the Indian People live, We, the Indian People, must be governed by principles in a democratic manner with a right to choose our way of life. Since our Indian culture is threatened by presumption of being absorbed by the American society, we believe we have the responsibility of preserving our precious heritage. We believe that the Indians must provide the adjustment and thus freely advance with dignity to a better life. . . .
Creed:
WE BELIEVE in the inherent right of all people to retain spiritual and cultural values, and that the free exercise of these values is necessary to the normal development of any people. Indians exercised this inherent right to live their own lives for thousands of years before the white man came and took their lands. It is a more complex world in which Indians live today, but the Indian people who first settled the New World and built the great civilizations which only now are being dug out of the past, long ago demonstrated that they could master complexity.

WE BELIEVE that the history and development of America show that the Indian has been subjected to duress, undue influence, unwarranted pressures, and policies which have produced uncertainty, frustration, and despair. Only when the public understands these conditions and is moved to take action toward the formulation and adoption of sound and consistent policies and programs will these destroying factors be removed and the Indian resume his normal growth and make his maximum contribution to modern society.

WE BELIEVE in the future of a greater America, an America which we were first to love, where life, liberty, and the pursuit of happiness will be a reality. In such a future, with Indians and all other Americans cooperating, a cultural climate will be created in which the Indian people will grow and develop as members of a free society.

Concluding Statement:

To complete our Declaration, we point out that in the beginning the people of the New World, called Indians by accident of geography, were possessed of a continent and a way of life. In the course of many lifetimes, our people had adjusted to every climate and condition from the Arctic to the torrid zones. In their livelihood and family relationships, their ceremonial observances, they reflected the diversity of the physical world they occupied.

The conditions in which Indians live today reflect a world in which every basic aspect of life has been transformed. Even the physical world is no longer the controlling factor in determining where and under what conditions men may live. In region after region, Indian groups found their means of existence either totally destroyed or materially modified. Newly introduced diseases swept away or reduced regional populations. These changes were followed by major shifts in the internal life of tribe and family.

The time came when the Indian people were no longer the masters of their situation. Their life ways survived subject to the will of a dominant sovereign power. This is said, not in a spirit of complaint; we understand that in the lives of all nations of people, there are times of plenty and times of famine. But we do speak out in a plea for understanding.

When we go before the American people, as we do in this Declaration, and ask for material assistance in developing our resources and developing our opportunities, we pose a moral problem which cannot be left unanswered. For the problem we raise affects the standing which our nation sustains before world opinion.

Our situation cannot be relieved by appropriated funds alone, though it is equally obvious that without capital investment and funded services, solutions will be delayed. Nor will the passage of time lessen the complexities which beset a people moving toward new meaning and purpose.

The answers we seek are not commodities to be purchased, neither are they evolved automatically through the passing of time.

The effort to place social adjustment on a money-time interval scale which has characterized Indian administration, has resulted in unwanted pressure and frustration.

When Indians speak of the continent they yielded, they are not referring only to the loss of some millions of acres in real estate. They have in mind that the land supported a universe of things they knew, valued, and loved.

With that continent gone, except for the few poor parcels they still retain, the basis of life is precariously held, but they mean to hold the scraps and parcels as earnestly as any small nation or ethnic group was ever determined to hold to identity and survival.

What we ask of America is not charity, not paternalism, even when benevolent. We ask only that the nature of our situation be recognized and made the basis of policy and action.

In short, the Indians ask for assistance, technical and financial, for the time needed, however long that may be, to regain in the America of the space age some measure of the adjustment they enjoyed as the original possessors of their native land.

> *Declaration of Indian Purpose* (American Indian Chicago Conference, University of Chicago, June 13–20, 1961), pp. 4, 5, 19–20.

69 A White Endorsement of the Right to Be Indian, 1961

There is a growing body of informed white opinion which holds that forced assimilation is not the only answer to Indian problems, and that Indians should have a free choice of alternatives, without duress. It recognizes that "no program imposed from above can serve as a substitute for one willed by Indians themselves." The following document represents this trend.

To encourage pride in Indianness is not to turn back the clock. On the contrary, it is to recognize that the United States policy has hitherto failed to use this vital factor effectively as a force for assimilation and for enriching American culture. As a result, Indians who have already entered the dominant society have generally disdained their historic background, drawing away from it as though ashamed. Instead of serving as a bridge to enable others to move freely between the two worlds, they have too often interpreted their heritage imperfectly to the majority race and have proved useless in explaining their adopted culture to their own people. Only men who have a foot in each way of life and an appreciation of both can effectively lessen the gap which divides the two and thus cross-fertilize both.

No program imposed from above can serve as a substitute for one willed by Indians themselves. Nor is their mere consent to a plan to be taken as sufficient. Such "consent" may be wholly passive, representing a submission to the inevitable, or it may be obtained without their full understanding or before they are either able or willing to shoulder unfamiliar responsibilities. What is essential is to elicit their own initiative and intelligent cooperation.

An objective which should undergird all Indian policy is that the Indian individual, the Indian family, and the Indian community be motivated to participate in solving their own problems. The Indian must be given responsibility, must be afforded an opportunity he can utilize, and must develop faith in himself.

Indian-made plans should receive preferential treatment and, when workable, should be adopted.

Government programs would be more effective if plans for education, health and economic development drew on those parts of the Indian heritage which are important not only to the Indians but also to the cultural enrichment of modern America.

> *A Program for Indian Citizens,* summary report by the
> Commission on the Rights, Liberties, and Responsibilities of
> the American Indian, established by the Fund for the Republic, January 1961, pp. 1, 4.

70   Indians as a Tourist Attraction: A Few Representative News Quotations, 1964

Ask any child in Europe, or any adult for that matter, what he would most like to see in the United States and the answer is likely to be "Cowboys and Indians."

> LUCIA LEWIS, *Chicago Daily News,* June 13, 1964.

Indians have always been important in Michigan history and we have recently started to help establish their communities as tourist attractions. We have nearly 7,000 Indians in Michigan, mostly Chippewas, and that is one of the larger concentrations in the nation.

The Gitchie Gumee of Longfellow's Hiawatha is Lake Superior, and Indian legend locates Hiawatha's home as the Tahquamenon Falls district.

> GOVERNOR GEORGE ROMNEY, *Chicago Tribune Magazine,* July 19, 1964.

INDIAN AREAS NOW WELCOME U.S. TOURISTS

Washington, June 15—Vacationers can enjoy camping facilities and excellent hunting and fishing, while witnessing the pageant of a colorful and ancient pattern of life on Indian reservations.

Today, many tribes include recreational facilities in their plans for the economic development of their lands. Tourists are warmly welcomed to such areas, and, each year, the tribes play host to increasing numbers of visitors of all ages.

To whet the traveler's appetite for Indian life, two publications will soon be issued by the bureau of Indian affairs of the department of the interior.[1] Both will be available from the superintendent of documents.

Chicago Tribune, June 16, 1965.

71   The White Man's Continuing Theft of Indian Land

Indian lands are still being eaten away by white encroachments. In 1948, the three tribes of the Fort Berthold, N.D., reservation (Mandan, Gros Ventre, and Arikara) had to sacrifice 155,000 acres for the Garrison dam, with very moderate compensation. During the 1950s, Mohawks of the United States and Canada lost land on both sides of the St. Lawrence River when the Seaway was constructed. In the late fifties, the Tuscaroras, one of the six Iroquois tribes, struggled to prevent the New York State Power Authority from building a dam which would flood part of their lands. By passive resistance, they tried to interfere with the surveys. They also went to court, maintaining that they were protected by the Pickering Treaty of 1794. After some victories in the lower courts, which were appealed by the state, the Tuscarora claims were rejected by the U.S. Supreme Court on March 7, 1960, in a 6 to 3 decision. Justice Hugo Black declared, in a dissenting opinion supported by Earl Warren and William O. Douglas: "I regret that this court is the agency that breaks faith with this dependent people. Great nations, like great men, should keep their word."

Before the Tuscarora case was settled, the federal government, through the Army Corps of Engineers, was simultaneously moving in on the Senecas, another Iroquois tribe in western New York, whose land was also guaranteed by the Pickering Treaty. Plans were made to build a dam, for purposes of flood control, at Kinzua, Pa., which would back up water on

1. *American Indian Calendar,* issued annually, which lists Indian dances, powwows, rodeos, etc., and *Vacationing with Indians: A Guide to Campgrounds and Tourist Attractions on Indian Reservations.*

the Allegheny River for thirty miles, flooding virtually all of the Corn-
planter reservation in Pennsylvania, and one third of the Seneca reserva-
tion southwest of Salamanca, New York. The ten thousand acres to be
flooded included the best land, occupied by about half the reservation's
population of fifteen hundred. Dr. Arthur Morgan, a former director of the
TVA, testified that a better alternative site was available, but the govern-
ment insisted on the original plan. On November 25, 1958, the U. S. Court
of Appeals in Washington rejected the tribe's plea for an injunction.
Though admitting that the Indians' treaty rights were infringed, the court
held that Congress had the right to abrogate (break) treaties. On June 16,
1959, the U.S. Supreme Court refused to hear an appeal from this deci-
sion, and plans went ahead.

Still more grief was in store for the Senecas. A two-lane road through the
reservation was converted to a limited access freeway, cutting communica-
tions between the Indians (they called it "the Berlin Wall"). On March 29,
1965, the Supreme Court refused to hear an appeal against this new
invasion, thus letting stand a lower court decision that treaty-protected
land was subject to eminent domain just as any other land. As a crowning
insult, Congress delayed action on compensation for the Indians' land for
five years, before the two houses finally agreed on the sum of 15 million
dollars. Then, in a move which has been repeated frequently when bills for
Indian claims are passed, a rider was added to the compensation act direct-
ing the secretary of the interior to submit within three years a plan for
termination of all federal services and protections to the Senecas, despite
the perpetual annuity provisions of the Pickering Treaty.

The losing battles of the Tuscarora and Seneca tribes have become
widely known through Edmund Wilson's book, Apologies to the Iroquois
(New York: Farrar, Straus, & Cudahy, 1960).

The following two documents, the Six Nations Treaty of 1794 (Picker-
ing Treaty) and Seneca tribal president Heron's testimony on the Kinzua
dam, illustrate the issues involved. It is especially important to note Heron's
point that the spiritual and emotional attachment of Indians to their land
is so deep that money can never compensate for the loss of it.

Treaty with the Six Nations, November 11, 1794

The President of the United States having determined to hold a conference with the Six Nations of Indians, for the purpose of removing from
their minds all causes of complaint, and establishing a firm and permanent
friendship with them; and Timothy Pickering being appointed sole agent
for that purpose; and the agent having met and conferred with the
Sachems, Chiefs and Warriors of the Six Nations, in a general council:

Now in order to accomplish the good design of this conference, the parties have agreed on the following articles, which, when ratified by the President, with the advice and consent of the Senate of the United States, shall be binding on them and the Six Nations.

ARTICLE I
Peace and friendship are hereby firmly established, and shall be perpetual, between the United States and the Six Nations.

ARTICLE II
The United States acknowledge the lands reserved to the Oneida, Onondaga and Cayuga Nations, in their respective treaties with the state of New York, and called their reservations, to be their property; and the United States will never claim the same, nor disturb them or either of the Six Nations, nor their Indian friends residing thereon and united with them, in the free use of enjoyment thereof: but the said reservations shall remain theirs, until they choose to sell the same to the people of the United States who have right to purchase.

ARTICLE III
The land of the Seneka nation is bounded as follows: [*description follows*]. Now, the United States acknowledge all the land within the aforementioned boundaries, to be the property of the Seneka nation; and the United States will never claim the same, nor disturb the Seneka nation, nor any of the Six Nations, or their Indian friends residing thereon and united with them, in the free use and enjoyment thereof: but it shall remain theirs, until they choose to sell the same to the people of the United States, who have the right to purchase.

ARTICLE IV
The United States having thus described and acknowledged what lands belong to the Oneidas, Onondagas, Cayugas, and Senekas, and engaged never to claim the same, nor to disturb them, or any of the Six Nations, or their Indian friends residing thereon and united with them, in the free use and enjoyment thereof: Now the Six Nations, and each of them, hereby engage that they will never claim any other lands within the boundaries of the United States; nor ever disturb the people of the United States in the free use and enjoyment thereof.

ARTICLE V
[*Provides for a wagon road through Seneca land, and free passage through Six Nations land by road and water.*]

ARTICLE VI

[*United States will deliver ten thousand dollars worth of goods to the Indians, and United States will also pay a perpetual annuity in goods, tools, animals, and services, to the value of forty-five hundred dollars annually.*]

ARTICLE VII

Lest the firm peace and friendship now established should be interrupted by the misconduct of individuals, the United States and Six Nations agree, that for injuries done by individuals on either side, no private revenge or retaliation shall take place; but, instead thereof, complaint shall be made by the party injured, to the other: By the Six Nations or any of them, to the President of the United States, or the Superintendent by him appointed: and by the Superintendent, or other person appointed by the President, to the principal chiefs of the Six Nations, or of the nation to which the offender belongs: and such prudent measures shall then be pursued as shall be necessary to preserve our peace and friendship unbroken; until the legislature (or great council) of the United States shall make the equitable provision for the purpose.

[*Note (annexed): Annuities to be paid only to Indians living within the United States.*]

> *American Historical Documents*, The Harvard Classics, Vol. 43 (New York: P. F. Collier & Son, 1963), pp. 229–32; Charles J. Kappler, ed., *Indian Affairs, Laws and Treaties* (Washington: Government Printing Office, 1904), II, 34–37.

"To Lose Their Homes on the Reservation Is Really to Lose a Part of Their Life": Statement of George Heron, President of the Seneca Nation of Indians, to the House Subcommittee on Indian Affairs, 1960

My name is George D. Heron. I live on the Allegany Reservation in New York, and I am president of the Seneca Nation of Indians. I appear before this Subcommittee today as an official representative of my people to express once again their unaltered opposition to construction of the Kinzua Dam. As you know, this project will flood the heart of our reservation homeland, which we Senecas have peacefully occupied since the Treaty of November 11, 1794, under the protection of the United States, and will force the relocation of more than 700 members of the Nation.

Before starting the main part of my remarks this morning, I would like to clear up several misstatements which were made to this Subcommittee during the hearings yesterday. My friends from Pennsylvania seem to believe that some Senecas are willing to sell their lands. I do not know where these witnesses got their information, though I suppose every group, even an Indian nation, contains a few unhappy people who will sell out their birthright. I do know that the overwhelming majority of my people, including every councilman and other tribal leader, both in and out of office, is trying desperately to save our reservation. The thought that we would freely give up the lands of our ancestors, which we are pledged to hold for our children yet unborn, is so contrary to the Seneca way of life that it is not even considered seriously.

Next my friends from Pennsylvania have said that the Treaty of November 11, 1794, was abrogated when all Indians became citizens in 1924. I would like to point out that the 1794 Treaty was signed by the *Seneca Nation,* not by individual Seneca Indians, and the Nation has not yet become a citizen. It remains today exactly what it was 165 years ago—in the words of the courts as reported to us by our attorney, Mr. Lazarus, a "quasi-sovereign dependent nation." More important, our tribal lawyer tells me that the Supreme Court of the United States has held not once, but at least a dozen times, that the grant of citizenship does not affect any Indian treaty rights or in any other way change the special relationship of Indians and their property to the Federal Government. I am not an educated man, but it seems very strange to me that these lawyers from Pennsylvania are willing to say that the Supreme Court ruled against the Senecas, when it did not even hear the case, while at the same time they are ignoring a whole series of actual Supreme Court decisions which go against their arguments.

I am proud to be an American citizen, and have four years in the United States Navy to prove it. I am just as proud to be a Seneca Indian. And I do not see any reason why I cannot be both.

Now let me tell you a little bit about what the Kinzua Dam will do to my people. Our own census shows that over 700 members of the Nation or more than half the population of the Allegany Reservation will be forced to move by the reservoir. On paper, this does not seem like very many people: other lands, substitute houses can be found, say the supporters of the project. It you knew these Senecas the way I do, though, if you knew how much they love that land— the last remnant of the original Seneca country—you would learn a different story. To lose their homes on the reservation is really to lose a part of their life.

The Corps of Engineers will tell you that Kinzua Dam will flood only 9,000 out of the 29,000 acres within the Allegany Reservation. What the Corps does not say is that this 9,000 acres includes almost all of the flat lowlands and fertile riverbanks, while the remainder of the reservation is inaccessible and thus virtually uninhabitable mountainside. What the Corps also does not say is that during the dry season these 9,000 acres will not be a lake but rather muck and mud flats. What a pleasant yearly reminder, what an annual memorial to the breaking of the 1794 Treaty that will be!

Lastly, I know it will sound simple and perhaps silly, but the truth of the matter is that my people really believe that George Washington read the 1794 Treaty before he signed it, and that he meant exactly what he wrote. For more than 165 years we Senecas have lived by that document. To us it is more than a contract, more than a symbol; to us, the 1794 Treaty is a way of life.

Times have not always been easy for the Seneca people. We have known and we still know poverty and discrimination. But through it all we have been sustained by a pledge of faith, unbroken by the Federal Government. Take that pledge away, break our Treaty, and I fear that you will destroy the Senecas as an Indian community.

The Seneca Nation always has taken the position that we will abandon our opposition to the Kinzua Dam if and when it is shown by competent evidence that the existing plans of the Corps of Engineers are better than any alternative plans. The facts are that Dr. Morgan's study has revealed an alternative, the Conewango-Cattaraugus plan, which appears superior to the authorized project. For this reason, we urge that the Committee pass H.J. Res. 703, which would provide an independent investigation of the merits of the two proposals.

On behalf of the Seneca Nation, may I thank you for granting us this hearing.

The Kinzua Dam Controversy, Kinzua Project of the Indian Committee, Philadelphia Yearly Meeting of Friends [1961], pp. 8–10.

72   The Battle for Indian Fishing Rights in Washington State

When Indian tribes in Washington Territory ceded most of their land by treaty in 1855, they reserved the right to fish "in their usual and accustomed places." Some of these traditional fishing places have since been destroyed by the white man's "improvements." Years ago this writer recalls seeing a Saturday Evening Post *cover portraying Indians net-fishing for salmon from wooden platforms beside the Celillo Falls on the Columbia River. Upon visiting this spot in the summer of 1967, he discovered to his dismay that the falls were no longer there, having been "drowned" ten years earlier by a dam which created a large lake. Only a bronze marker recalled the former use of this spot by the Indians. Many other hydroelec-*

tric dams on the Columbia and its tributaries have destroyed choice fishing spots.

Beginning in 1964, several Washington tribes, including the Nisqually, Yakima, Muckleshoot, Tulalip and Puyallup, became involved in conflict with state conservation officers when fishing with nets outside their small reservations. Many were arrested, some were assaulted, and their expensive fishing gear and boats were confiscated. Widespread sympathy was attracted to their plight. While the sport fishermen fish for pleasure and the commercial fisheries for profit, the Indians must fish to live. Among famous persons who came to join their fight were Marlon Brando, the movie actor, and Dick Gregory, comedian and civil rights activist. Gregory and his wife were arrested in a "fish-in" in 1966, and while Mrs. Gregory was let off with a one-month suspended sentence, her husband was sentenced to serve six months, with three months suspended. After losing an appeal, he began serving the sentence in May of 1968, but immediately began a hunger strike which undermined his health. He was released after serving forty days. Shortly before his release, the Supreme Court upheld the restrictions of Washington state laws on Indian fishing rights, but the controversy continues.

In the following document, written before his arrest, Dick Gregory discusses the fish-in and its relationship to the whole problem of Indian and minority rights in America. A statement by the Nisqually tribe follows next, giving the historic background of the issue, and closing with a defiant challenge.

The Fish-In, Justice, and Red Power, 1968

DICK GREGORY

All my life I have had a passionate sympathy for the Indian in America, because I knew that Wrong America slanted her history books. When the Indians won a battle, the history books called it a "massacre." When the cavalry won a battle, on the other hand, it was called "a great victory." The Indians' real problems have never been given a fair hearing. One day, while I was playing a nightclub date in Seattle, Washington, I finally had the opportunity to see and hear the Indians' problems firsthand and to join with them in their struggle against injustice.

I received an invitation from Janet and Donald McCloud, Pauline Matheson and William Frank to attend a powwow sponsored by an organization called the Survival of the American Indians. The organization was formed as a response to existing governmental policy to help the Indian and protect him. Whenever there is a complaint to the government concerning Indian problems, it is sent to the Bureau of Indian Affairs. From what I have seen, this is about equal to the Ku Klux Klan running the enforcement arm of civil rights legislation.

I went to the powwow to ask what I could do to help. After talking about some of the Indian problems in the state of Washington, we developed the idea of a "fish-in." The basic injustice we sought to correct was this. The Nisqually Indians have had a treaty with the government for 112 years which gives them the right to fish in any water, using any means.

The state of Washington decided it is bigger than the treaty. But it is unfair to point a finger at the state of Washington without also putting the blame on Washington, D.C. America has gone all over the world dropping bombs and upholding treaties. We are in Vietnam today and we are one of the few countries that did not sign the treaty.[1] Now we turn our backs on the Indian in America, who is the oldest resident American, and say, "*Your* treaty was no good."

The state of Washington has three types of fisherman: the commercial fisherman, the sports fisherman, and the Indian. Of these three, the sports fisherman is the most important from the state's point of view. The fish involved in our dispute, steelhead, is one of the most difficult fish to catch. Sportsmen spend a great deal of money trying to catch it, which helps the economy (not of the fish, but of the state). Only the sports and commercial fishermen are given any real consideration by the state. In addition, Russian and Japanese fishermen fish in the international waters three miles offshore. There is continual furor over the activities of these foreign fishermen, but nothing has been done. So out of all the steelheads being caught in the whole state of Washington, Indians catch less than 2 per cent.

Why? The state of Washington tells the Indian he cannot fish with a net. He must use a fishhook. But such a ruling does not take into consideration the peculiar nature of the fish. Wherever a fish is born, it will return to that same area at spawning time. Even though the fish has been halfway around the world, it will buck the stream and come back home to lay its eggs and die. At this time, the fish doesn't have an appetite. If the Indian is forced to fish with a hook, obviously the steelhead is not going to eat it.

So it is like a game the state of Washington is playing with the Indian. It is the same as the South's attitude about voting rights. The South has always said, "We don't mind Negroes voting, we just don't want them coming in crowds." Yet the Negro knows he will be beaten and lynched if he comes to the polls by himself. The state of Washington said, "We don't mind the Indian fishing, but he must use a hook." When the Indians started fishing with nets, the state brought out an injunction against them.

1. Geneva agreement of 1954. —V.J.V.

Justice or "Just Us"?

After experiencing such unfair legal maneuvers, you can imagine the image the Indian has of the courthouse. An Indian woman said to me, "You might say that the courthouse represents justice, but what that word means to the Indian is 'just us.' " When you see firsthand the many injustices against the Indian, you begin to realize what "just us" means. An Indian will be arrested and claim his treaty rights. The court will insist that he prove he is an Indian. I couldn't prove legally that I am a Negro. The Indian is forced to spend a fortune, using up all of his legal funds, proving to the court that he is an Indian.

We must realize that America *was* the Indian's country. Either America should admit that the Indian is an American and say she is sorry for what she has done—this would involve reviewing existing treaties and, wherever they have been violated, paying reparation—or America should say openly that the Indian is not an American. Then it becomes the Indian's duty to throw off colonialism, as people all over the world are doing. They are reclaiming their land, which is the Indian's only alternative, if America is not going to share equally with him and admit that he is a part owner of this country.

The Indian is a partial owner of America as is every other minority group in this country. Every minority has had a struggle to realize this ownership. It has always bothered me to hear people pride themselves on their victory against a nation full of bigotry. People say the Irish had a fight and won. So did the Jews, the Catholics, the Italians, and other minorities. But it is a pity that the Irish, Jews, Italians, and others did not fight for the Constitution instead of themselves. We will probably look back one day and be forced to say the same thing about Negroes. Somebody has to fight for the Constitution and do away with all bigotry once and for all.

If we continue to make the mistake of turning our backs, we will find one day that the biggest problem in America's history is the Indian. The only way for the Indian to be recognized as an American is for America to lose a war with Russia or China. The conqueror, in taking over the country, would recognize the Indian as an American and give him the same kind of dirty treatment other Americans would receive. This should make a nation full of savages ashamed, but America sleeps with this truth every night.

The issues involved in the injustice to the Indian must be heard and dealt with before it is too late. If the Communists were up on the reservations organizing the Indians, or if the Indians were armed and shooting people on the highways, the whole country would be immediately concerned. We only seem to get concerned about a problem when the Communists are concerned. If we had been concerned about Vietnam before the Communists, we might not have lost one American life. We never seem to be able to handle an issue in this country *before* it becomes an open problem. I hope this will not be the same pattern with the Indian problem.

Red Power

There are some encouraging rays of light in the dark night of America's injustice to the Indian. The Indian is voting now for the first time in many parts of the country, as a result of the deaths in Alabama and the voting rights legislation. There have been laws giving the Indian the right to vote, but the literacy tests have always stood in his way. There are thousands of Indians who speak only their tribal tongue. With the lifting of the requirement regarding the English language, these Indians can now vote.

In the little town of St. John's, Arizona, Indians marched for voter registration. There are ten thousand Indians in that area. The reaction was the same as we saw in Mississippi. People said, "These Indians are not responsible; they don't know what the politicians are talking about. They don't even understand the English language." That only means the politicians are not responsible. If the Indian is ignorant of the language—due to America's failure to educate him—he should not have to suffer the penalty of not voting. If anyone should suffer it should be the politician. He must learn the Indian's language to discuss political issues, if he wants the Indian vote. Otherwise, the Indian has every right to vote him out of office.

Our "fish-in" demonstration produced encouraging reactions. By publicizing this particular issue of treaty violation, we were able to begin to open the eyes of America to her tragic disregard of the Indian. When my wife and I were placed in jail for fishing, there was worldwide reaction. I received telegrams from Bertrand Russell, Dr. Martin Luther King, James Farmer, and the unions representing teachers and college professors.

When we first started demonstrating, the reaction within the state of Washington was mixed. But in a short period of time, college students in the state began holding demonstrations on behalf of the Indian. Radio and television talk shows began to see that the Indian has a just demand. They saw the issue in concrete terms which they could easily understand. They knew there was a fish involved and a very powerful fish economically. Such a personal reaction was something totally new for the state of Washington and a beginning of an honest confrontation with the Indian problem.

An aroused citizenry should now take the problem of the Indian directly to the White House. A group of Indians should hold a vigil on the White House lawn until LBJ decides that the Indians count too. The Justice Department should be made to protect the Indian treaties. Such a vigil would let the whole world see that, if America will break her treaty with the Indian, she might not uphold her treaty with anyone.

I do not believe this about America. I think Americans would die defending their treaties. The day must come when America shows the same concern for her treaties with the Indians as she does for treaties with other countries. Other Indian treaties are being broken; treaties concerning timber rights, for example. We may be having some "Timber Wiggles" in the future. This will be the maximum expression of nonviolent demonstration. The demonstrator will climb a tree and when he hears "Timber!" he will ride down with it nonviolently.

The day these problems with the Indian are solved will be the day America can breathe her first clean breath of fresh air. Moral pollution is more destructive than air pollution. But if we clean up every other problem and leave the Indian in his misery, the shadow of shame will destroy us.

DICK GREGORY, *The Shadow That Scares Me* (New York: Pocket Books, 1968), pp. 146–52.

Proclamation or Declaration of Facts, January 1, 1965

NISQUALLY NATION

WHEREAS the Treaty of Medicine Creek (10 Stat. 1132) and all other treaties with the Indian people as one party and the United States as the other party was a grant of rights and land from the Indians, to the United States Government. The Supreme law of the land is the right to govern and tax all citizens of the United States by the United States Government except the Indian people. The self governing rights were reserved by the Indian People.

WHEREAS the Bureau of Indian Affairs was created to protect the rights and interests of the American Citizens, not the Indian People.

WHEREAS the citizens of the United States has consistently and persistently with force and coersion denied the existing reserved rights and powers of the Indian people.

WHEREAS the United States Government has never, past or present, honored or protected in any way or manner the rights of the Indian people.

Be it therefore resolved that we the undersigned Indians declare:

That as much as the citizens of the United States have denied the power and effects of said treaty they no longer have a legal right to reside, tax or hunt or fish upon said lands or waters, within the ceded areas of the treaties made with the Indian people.

Be it also known that as we are without power to enforce or expel said citizens from this land we never the less declare that said citizens have denied their own right to be here legally.

Be it also resolved that we will resist to the best of our abilities the continued attacks upon the Indian people.

We also declare that we are weary of being forced into pauperism upon our own land.

This flag is raised today[1] as a distress signal to any or all nations, kindreds, our tongues, who believes that the Indian people also have God given rights, upon this land. We say to these nations, kindreds, our tongues, that if the policies inacted by the United States Government concerning the Indian people were examined under close scrutiny the similarities between them and Hitler's policies concerning the Jewish people would be self evident.

We declare that this declaration is just and true with only God as our witness.

(Signed and subscribed to by 150 people).

> From broadside furnished by Survival of American Indians Association, Inc., P.O. Box 719, Tacoma, Washington, 98402. Grammar and spelling in the original.

For further information:

Uncommon Controversy: Fishing Rights of the Muckleshoot, Puyallup, and Nisqually Indians, a Report Prepared for the American Friends Service Committee. Seattle: University of Washington Press, 1970.

Peter Collier, "Salmon Fishing in America: The Indians vs. the State of Washington," *Ramparts,* April 1971, pp. 29 ff.

73   Protests: East and West

The following news items reveal a stiffening attitude among Indians in defense of what they believe to be their just and legal rights.

Red Man's Fight on Draft, Taxes, 1968

NEVADA SHOSHONES

The medicine man of the Shoshones, whose historic hunting grounds stretch from the skyscrapers of Los Angeles to the mountains of Nevada, declared solemnly yesterday:

"We're standing up for our rights for the first time in a hundred years. The white man is not going to push us any further."

1. At Frank's Landing, favorite Indian fishing spot on the Nisqually River, and site of confrontations with state officers. —V.J.V.

John "Rolling Thunder" Pope, most of whose people still depend on wild deer and pine nuts for their food, was in San Francisco to testify today for an Indian objecting to being drafted into the army.

Rolling Thunder is also legal adviser to his tribe and maintains it is a violation of Indian treaties for his people to be drafted.

"Why should we go fight over there when we've got things to fight for here?" he asked.

Rolling Thunder's legal warpath was prompted by two recent incidents:

°The Federal government has ordered a tax of 5 cents a pound on all pine nuts over 25 pounds harvested by Indian families.

°The levying of a $100 fine on a Shoshone brave who shot a deer out of season to get food for his wife and nine children.

The Indians are in court over these—they claim their treaty gives them unfettered hunting rights over their extensive tribal lands—and they also took the law into their own hands over a third case.

That time they mounted a war party which surrounded a troup of 25 white hunters camped on one of their seven reservations and drove them off the land.

Rolling Thunder would not say how many Shoshones there are: "We will not allow a census. Then they know who to draft and who to tax. But there's a lot more than they think there are and they're increasing fast. Our people are going to take back our original hereditary rights as handed down by the Great Spirit. We're going to fight in every legal way we can. This gives the white man every chance he can to correct himself. If he has justice in his courts . . ."

The final appeal, Rolling Thunder said, would be to the United Nations. Failing there, he said, the Great Spirit would take reprisal through an atomic holocaust.

"The great spirit put the deer there for people to eat . . . not to hunt for sport. We hunt only to feed our families. We're not an aggressive people. We believe in peace. We never sent riding parties into other territories but only fought if attacked. We would much rather live in peace and friendship with all people; that's what the Great Spirit intended."

San Francisco Chronicle, Tuesday, November 12, 1968, p. 9.

Another Indian Rebellion, 1968: Mohawk Invocation of the Jay Treaty

The Mohawks who demonstrated on an international bridge at Cornwall, Ontario, the other day had more on their minds than taxes. At the moment they were protesting duties that Canada imposes on commodities they take in from the United States, but fundamentally they were rebelling against history.

Most of the demonstrators live on the St. Regis reserve, which straddles the border. It is home for about 6,000 members of the Iroquois nation— the Mohawks, Onondagas, Oneidas, Tuscaroras, Cayugas and Senecas. These are famous names that the white man has appropriated for mountains, rivers, valleys, cities, counties and commercial products. The white man appropriated much more—he took all the real estate too.

For the white man knew how to turn treaties into scraps of paper long before a European tyrant said that was what they were. The Mohawks say that the Canadians are breaking the terms of a 1794 treaty that gave them the right of free movement across the border.[1] Technically they may be right or wrong, but history bears out the Mohawks' plight. The white man took an entire continent from the Indians, and has repaid them with injustice and callous disregard ever since.

Editorial, *Chicago Daily News,* December 30, 1968.

The Occupation of Alcatraz, 1969

On the cold, foggy morning of November 14, 1969, an invading force of fourteen American Indian college students occupied Alcatraz Island, the notorious "Rock" in San Francisco Bay. Since its abandonment as a maximum-security federal prison six years earlier, these sixteen waterless acres had been inhabited only by seagulls and a caretaker, who offered no resistance. The Coast Guard soon arrived in force, however, and persuaded the students to evacuate their conquest. Less than a week later the Rock was reoccupied by eighty-nine Indians, claiming the right of possession under a Sioux treaty of 1868 which said unused federal land would revert to the Indians. Calling themselves "Indians of All Tribes," they announced that they were there to stay, and the government chose to avoid a confrontation. Recalling how the white man acquired Manhattan in 1626, the Indians offered $24 worth of beads and red cloth for title to Alcatraz, announcing that "our offer of $1.24 an acre is greater than the 47¢ per acre the white men are now paying the California Indians" for land stolen more than a hundred years ago. They even offered the "white inhabitants" a reservation, to be run by a Bureau of Caucasian Affairs, where these unfortunate people might be gradually brought up to the level of Indian civilization.

The Indians acknowledged the government's claim that the island was a grim and inhospitable place to be inhabited by anyone, but added that in this respect it only resembled most Indian reservations. They announced their intention to establish there several institutions where urban Indians might assemble and carry on tribal life. They were motivated by the conviction that "we must hold on to the old ways." In a manifesto to their

1. The Jay Treaty; see pp. 77–78.

Indian brethren, the Indians of All Tribes declared that "the only reason Indian people have been able to hold on and survive through decades of persecution and cultural deprivation is that the Indian way of life is and has been strong enough to hold the people together."

In the spring of 1970 the government cut off the supply of electricity and water to the island, and as a consequence the Indians were unable to extinguish a fire on June 2 which destroyed the lighthouse, the warden's home, and the infirmary. On June 11, 1971, federal agents evicted the Indians from the island.

During the spring of 1970 groups of Indians also attempted unsuccessfully to seize Fort Lawton, near Seattle, Ellis Island, in New York Harbor, and Lassen Volcanic National Park.

The following documents were issued late in 1969 by the Indians who seized Alcatraz.

Proclamation to the Great White Father and to All *His* People, 1969

We, the native Americans, re-claim the land known as Alcatraz Island in the name of all American Indians by right of discovery.

We wish to be fair and honorable in our dealings with the Caucasian inhabitants of this land, and hereby offer the following treaty:

We will purchase said Alcatraz Island for twenty-four dollars (24) in glass beads and red cloth, a precedent set by the white man's purchase of a similar island about 300 years ago. We know that $24 in trade goods for these 16 acres is more than was paid when Manhattan Island was sold, but we know that land values have risen over the years. Our offer of $1.24 per acre is greater than the 47¢ per acre the white men are now paying the California Indians for their land.

We will give to the inhabitants of this island a portion of the land for their own to be held in trust by the American Indian Affairs and by the bureau of Caucasian Affairs to hold in perpetuity—for as long as the sun shall rise and the rivers go down to the sea. We will further guide the inhabitants in the proper way of living. We will offer them our religion, our education, our life-ways, in order to help them achieve our level of civilization and thus raise them and all their white brothers up from their savage and unhappy state. We offer this treaty in good faith and wish to be fair and honorable in our dealings with all white men.

We feel that this so-called Alcatraz Island is more than suitable for an Indian Reservation, as determined by the white man's own standards. By this we mean that this place resembles most Indian reservations in that:

1. It is isolated from modern facilities, and without adequate means of transportation.

2. It has no fresh running water.
3. It has inadequate sanitation facilities.
4. There are no oil or mineral rights.
5. There is no industry and so unemployment is very great.
6. There are no health care facilities.
7. The soil is rocky and non-productive; and the land does not support game.
8. There are no educational facilities.
9. The population has always exceeded the land base.
10. The population has always been held as prisoners and kept dependent upon others.

Further, it would be fitting and symbolic that ships from all over the world, entering the Golden Gate, would first see Indian land, and thus be reminded of the true history of this nation. This tiny island would be a symbol of the great lands once ruled by free and noble Indians.

American Indian Center

Proposals for the Use of Alcatraz Island, 1970

INDIANS OF ALL TRIBES

Since the San Francisco Indian Center burned down, there is no place for Indians to assemble and carry on our tribal life here in the white man's city. Therefore, we plan to develop on this island several Indian institutions:

1. A Center for Native American Studies will be developed which will train our young people in the best of our native arts and works, as well as educate them to the skills and knowledge relevant to improve the lives and spirits of all Indian peoples. Attached to this center will be travelling universities, managed by Indians, which will go to the Indian Reservations, learning those necessary and relevant materials now absent.

2. An American Indian Spiritual Center which will practice our ancient tribal religious and sacred healing ceremonies. Our cultural arts will be featured and our young people trained in music, dancing, and healing rituals.

3. An Indian center of ecology which will train and support our young people in scientific research and practice to restore our lands and waters to their true and natural state. We will seek to de-pollute the air and the Bay Area. We will seek to restore fish and animal life to the area and to revitalize sea life which has been threatened by the white man's way. We will set up facilities to desalt sea water for human benefit.

4. A great Indian Training School will be developed to teach our

peoples how to make a living in the world, improve our standards of living, and to end hunger and unemployment among all our peoples. This training school will include a center for Indian arts and crafts, and an Indian Restaurant serving native foods, which will restore Indian culinary arts. This center will display Indian arts and offer Indian foods to the public, so that all may know of the beauty and spirit of the traditional *Indian* ways.

5. Some of the present buildings will be taken over to develop an Indian Museum, which will depict our native foods and other cultural contributions we have given to the world. Another part of the Museum will present some of the things the white man has given to the Indians, in return for the land and life he took: disease, alcohol, poverty, and cultural decimation (as symbolized by old tin cans, barbed wire, rubber tires, plastic containers, etc.). Part of the Museum will remain a dungeon, to symbolize both those Indian captives who were incarcerated for challenging white authority, and those who were imprisoned on reservations.[1] The Museum will show the noble and the tragic events of Indian history, including the broken treaties, the documentary of the Trail of Tears, the Massacre of Wounded Knee, as well as the victory over Yellow-Hair Custer and his army.

In the name of all Indians, therefore, we re-claim this island for our Indian nations, for all these reasons. We feel this claim is just and proper, and that this land should rightfully be granted to us for as long as the rivers shall run and the sun shall shine.

Signed,

Indians of All Tribes
November, 1969
San Francisco, California

From copies of original material furnished by Mr. Aubrey Grossman of the Alcatraz Lawyers Committee.

Pit River Indians Fight for Recovery of Lost Land, 1970

The Pit River Indians of northern California include remnants of several small tribes[2] having in 1970 an enrolled membership of 529. Their ancestral lands lie between Mt. Lassen and Mt. Shasta, just north of the region oc-

1. Passage slightly garbled in original; corrected version taken from *Indians of All Tribes Newsletter*, January 1970, p. 3.

2. For an ethnohistorical account of these people, see Roland Dixon, "Notes on the Achomawi and Atsugewi Indians of Northern California," *American Anthropologist*, new series, Vol. X (1908), pp. 208–20.

cupied by the now extinct Yahi made famous by Theodora Kroeber's book Ishi *(1961). Like many California tribes victimized by the gold rushers and their successors, these Indians were stripped of their land without benefit of any payment and without the sanction of a ratified treaty. In the land their people had occupied for thousands of years, they were left as homeless squatters.*

Today the Pit Rivers claim 3,368,000 acres of land as rightfully theirs. In 1963 they refused a government offer of 47 cents an acre in settlement for land which is today valued at $250 an acre. They demand instead the return of the land, much of which is still under federal control, and in 1970 began a campaign to reoccupy it. Rebuffed in an attempt to occupy Lassen Volcanic National Park, they occupied resort property claimed by the Pacific Gas and Electric Company, and thirty-eight people were arrested. The following complaint, filed in the United States District Court for Northern California, by attorney Aubrey Grossman of San Francisco, was a response to that incident. It asked for injunctive relief and monetary damages.

On October 27, 1970, about one hundred Pit River Indians who had erected a quonset hut in national forest land near Burney, California, were attacked by a large force of federal and local law officers. The Indians defended themselves with tree branches. There were several injuries and 23 arrests, but no convictions resulted. (See biographical sketch of Mickey Gemmill, p. 316.) For further information on these events and others in this continuing struggle see various issues of Akwesasne Notes *beginning with July–August 1970. A brief account of the historical background of the California Indians' struggle for survival is contained in the pamphlet* One of the Last Human Hunts of Civilization . . . , *by Roxanne Bailin and Aubrey Grossman. For a copy send 50 cents to Justice for the Pit River Tribe, 275 Capp Street, San Francisco, California 94110.*

In the United States District Court for the Northern District of California.

First Amended Complaint for Violation of Civil Rights Act

    . . . From the time of its formation the State of California, its legislature, governor, various of its state officials, the various subdivisions of the state and their officials carried out a program to deprive Pitt[2] River Indians of California, and all other California Indians, of the land to which they

    2. The name is properly *Pit* River, according to Dixon (*op. cit.*), a name arising from their former custom of digging pits to trap deer. —V.J.V.

held Indian Title—which comprised at least 90 per cent of the State of California. This program continued at least until 1900.

The purpose of this program was to deprive California Indians of their land so that it could be given, sold or conveyed to whites. This program was so successful that, by 1900, the land holdings of California Indians had declined to a few hundred thousand acres, almost all of which were worthless and valueless.

. . . After the Indians were driven off their land, and in some cases even before, the land was made part of the public domain of the United States and homesteaded or patented to white men, Indians being legally ineligible to participate until long after all the worthwhile land was passed out. The only exceptions were national forest land and national park land which the government has retained for its own use and profit.

. . . On September 30, 1850, Congress set in motion the machinery to negotiate treaties with the California Indians (9 Stat. 544). In 1851 and 1852 eighteen different treaties were negotiated with a number of Indian tribes and other Indian groups. The total effect of such treaties was that the Indians were to give up approximately 75 million acres of land, including all on which substantial amounts of gold were known or suspected to exist, in exchange for approximately eight and a half million acres of the poorest land in California. These treaties were forwarded by the President to the Senate with a request for their ratification. While this was going on the California legislature . . . called for the Senate to reject the treaties in their existing or any other form, and further requested the federal government to remove all Indians from the State of California. As a result of this Resolution the Senate refused to ratify the treaties and caused them to be hidden away until they were discovered by clerks of the Senate in 1905.

Before and after the adoption of the Resolution by the state legislature, the white homesteaders and miners proceeded to use violence, murder and massacre to either take land away from Indians, or to take life away from Indians who were on the land. All observers agree that, as a result of murder, massacres, starvation and disease, the Indian population was reduced by 1900 to approximately 17,000. . . . Meanwhile a number of laws were passed which discriminated against Indians in the courts and made it impossible for them to use the legal machinery. . . .

After the Pitt River Indians were driven off their land, it was incorporated by the United States government into the public domain and either sold to whites or retained as national forest land or national park land. No compensation was ever paid to Pitt River Indians of California, or any of them for this land. It is now proposed to pay the individual members of the Tribe for the land at the rate of about 20 cents an acre, as a result of the Indian Claims Act decision (Docket #347). The Pitt River Indians will not accept this money, proposing instead the return of their land.

In June 1970, after a thorough discussion, extending over many months, among the membership and within the Tribal Council of Pitt River Indians of California, it was resolved that the tribe should and would, as a tribe, use self-help and reoccupy the Tribe's ancestral lands.

. . . On or just before June 6, 1970, a large number of Pitt River Indians, and Indians from other tribes, together with a small number of white sympathizers, attempted to reoccupy that portion of their land which is now known as Lassen National Park. Faced with a concentration of government force and violence which threatened to injure if not kill the Indians, the Tribe decided to abandon, for the moment, re-occupation of Lassen National Park. Therefore the same grouping re-occupied a different portion of the tribe's ancestral land; a location which is claimed by Pacific Gas and Electric Company to be owned by it.

. . . The individual plaintiffs were arrested . . . by deputy sheriffs and police officers. Neither prior to the arrest, nor later, were the public officials furnished any proof by P.G.&E. that it owned the land in question. However, prior to the arrests these public officials had been notified by Pitt River Indians of California that they owned the land and P.G.&E. did not. After this notification the public officials made no effort to verify or refute the notification that had been given to them.

. . . Plaintiffs request the issuance of an injunction enjoining trespass prosecution against anyone for participating with the Pitt River Indians of California in re-occupation of any land described in Exhibit A. Such an injunction is necessary because a judgment in damages will not return their ancestral land to the Pitt River Indians of California, and to the Indian land is of vital importance, from the standpoint of religion, spirituality, customs and economics. . . .

AUBREY GROSSMAN, September 23, 1970.

74   American Indian Education Under Fire

From late 1967 until late 1969, American Indian education was investigated by a special subcommittee of the Senate Committee on Labor and Public Welfare. Headed first by Senator Robert F. Kennedy, and after his tragic death by his brother, Senator Edward M. Kennedy, the committee held hearings in various parts of the country, and visited many schools attended by Indian children, federal, local public, and private. Much of the testimony was published, along with a report containing sixty recommenda-

tions for change. The committee's criticism focused largely on under-achievement and a heavy dropout rate among Indian children, the absence of any effort to teach Indians about their own history and culture, and the lack of Indian participation in the control of their own schools. A selection from the summary of the committee's report is reproduced below. For a critical reply to it, see Madison Coombs, "The Indian Student Is Not Low Man on the Totem Pole," Journal of American Indian Education, *IX (May 1970), 1–9.*

Indian Education: A National Tragedy—A National Challenge, 1969

SPECIAL SUBCOMMITTEE ON INDIAN EDUCATION

For more than 2 years the members of this subcommittee have been ga[u]ging how well American Indians are educated. We have travelled to all parts of the country; we have visited Indians in their homes and in their schools; we have listened to Indians, to Government officials, and to experts; and we have looked closely into every aspect of the educational opportunities this Nation offers its Indian citizens. . . .

We are shocked at what we discovered.

Others before us were shocked. They recommended and made changes. Others after us will likely be shocked, too—despite our recommendations and efforts at reform. For there is so much to do—wrongs to right, omissions to fill, untruths to correct—that our own recommendations, concerned as they are with education alone, need supplementation across the whole board of Indian life.

We have developed page after page of statistics. These cold figures mark a stain on our national conscience, a stain which has spread slowly for hundreds of years. They tell a story, to be sure. But they cannot tell the whole story. They cannot, for example, tell of the despair, the frustration, the hopelessness, the poignancy, of children who want to learn but are not taught; of adults who try to read but have no one to teach them; of families which want to stay together but are forced apart; or of 9-year-old children who want neighborhood schools but are sent thousands of miles away to remote and alien boarding schools.

We have seen what these conditions do to Indian children and Indian families. The sights are not pleasant.

We have concluded that our national policies for educating American Indians are a failure of major proportions. They have not offered Indian children—either in years past or today—an educational opportunity anywhere near equal to that offered the great bulk of American children. Past generations of lawmakers and administrators have failed the American Indian. Our own generation thus faces a challenge—we can continue the unacceptable policies and programs of the past or we can recognize our own failures, renew our commitments, and reinvest our efforts with new energy.

It is this latter course that the subcommittee chooses. We have made 60 separate recommendations. If they are all carried into force and effect, then we believe that all American Indians, children and adults, will have the unfettered opportunity to grow to their full potential. Decent education has been denied Indians in the past, and they have fallen far short of matching their promise with performance. But this need not always be so. Creative, imaginative, and above all, relevant educational experiences can blot the stain on our national conscience. This is the challenge the subcommittee believes faces our own generation. . . .

In its investigation of "any and all matters pertaining to the education of Indian children" . . . the subcommittee thus was compelled to examine not only the Federal schools, but the State and local public schools and the mission schools as well.

What concerned us most deeply, as we carried out our mandate, was the low quality of virtually every aspect of the schooling available to Indian children. The school buildings themselves; the course materials and books; the attitude of teachers and administrative personnel; the accessibility of school buildings—all these are of shocking quality.

A few of the statistics we developed:

Forty thousand Navajo Indians, nearly a third of the entire tribe, are functional illiterates in English;

The average educational level for all Indians under Federal supervision is 5 school years;

More than one out of every five Indian men have less than 5 years of schooling;

Dropout rates for Indians are twice the national average;

In New Mexico, some Indian high school students walk 2 miles to the bus every day and then ride 50 miles to school;

The average age of top level BIA education administrators is 58 years;

In 1953 the BIA began a crash program to improve education for Navajo children. Between then and 1967, supervisory positions in BIA headquarters increased 113 percent; supervisory positions in BIA schools increased 144 percent; administrative and clerical positions in BIA schools increased 94 percent. Yet, teaching positions increased only 20 percent;

In one school in Oklahoma the student body is 100-percent Indian; yet it is controlled by a three-man, non-Indian school board.

Only 18 percent of the students in Federal Indian schools go on to college; the national average is 50 percent;

Only 3 percent of Indian students who enroll in college graduate; the national average is 32 percent;

The BIA spends only $18 per year per child on textbooks and supplies, compared to a national average of $40;

Only one of every 100 Indian college graduates will receive a master's degree; and

Despite a Presidential directive 2 years ago, only one of the 226 BIA schools is governed by an elective school board. . . .

We have recommended that the Nation adopt as national policy a commitment to achieving educational excellence for American Indians. We have recommended that the Nation adopt as national goals a series of specific objectives relating to educational opportunities for American Indians. Taken together, this policy and these goals are a framework for a program of action. Clearly, this action program needs legislative and executive support if it is to meet its promise. Most of all, however, it needs dedicated and imaginative management by those Federal officials, and State and local officials as well, who have the principal responsibilities for educating American Indians. . . .

One theme running through all our recommendations is increased Indian participation and control of their own education programs. For far too long, the Nation has paid only token heed to the notion that Indians should have a strong voice in their own destiny. We have made a number of recommendations to correct this historic, anomalous paternalism. We have, for example, recommended that the Commissioner of the BIA be raised to the level of Assistant Secretary of the Department of Interior; that there be established a National Indian Board of Indian Education with authority to set standards and criteria for the Federal Indian schools; that local Indian boards of education be established for Indian school districts; and that Indian parental and community involvement be increased. These reforms, taken together, can—at last—make education of American Indians relevant to the lives of American Indians.

We have recommended programs to meet special, unmet needs in the Indian education field. Culturally-sensitive curriculum materials, for example, are seriously lacking; so are bi-lingual education efforts. Little educational material is available to Indians concerning nutrition and alcoholism. We have developed proposals in all these fields, and made strong recommendations to rectify their presently unacceptable status. . . .

The scope of this subcommittee's work was limited by its authorizing resolution to education. But as we travelled, and listened, and saw, we learned that education cannot be isolated from the other aspects of Indian life. These aspects, too, have much room for improvement. This lies in part behind the recommendation for a Senate Select Committee on Human Needs of American Indians. Economic development, job training, legal representation in water rights and oil lease matters—these are only a few of the correlative problems sorely in need of attention.

In conclusion, it is sufficient to restate our basic finding: that our Nation's policies and programs for educating American Indians are a national tragedy. They present us with a national challenge of no small proportions. We believe that this report recommends the proper steps to meet this challenge. But we know that it will not be met without strong leadership and dedicated work. We believe that with this leadership for the Congress and the executive branch of the Government, the Nation can and will meet this challenge.

> *Indian Education: A National Tragedy—A National Challenge.* 1969 Report of the . . . Special Subcommittee on Indian Education. (Washington: U.S. Government Printing Office, 1969), pp. xi–xiv.

Teach the Indian Heritage, 1970

THE COMMITTEE ON CALIFORNIA INDIAN EDUCATION

The following is a brief extract from recommendations of a conference on Indian education held at North Fork, California, October 20–22, 1970. The overwhelming majority of the participants were Indians.

Recommendations on the Indian Heritage

The conference participants believe very strongly that the Indian heritage should be an integral part of the programs of the school and the Indian community, that the use of the Indian heritage in the school is especially important for helping Indian pupils develop a sense of identity and personal worth (but that it is also important as a part of the common heritage of all pupils), and that local Indian people must be actively involved in any programs developed by a school that touch upon the Indian heritage. More specifically,

1. The Indian people must unify and emphasize their Indian culture, and learn how to retain it and teach it to the younger generation;
2. Indian people should be brought into the school to help professional staff develop materials for the curriculum and to teach arts and crafts, dancing, singing, et cetera;
3. The school and Indian adults and children together should develop projects to record local Indian history, protect historical and cemetery sites, construct exhibits, preserve Indian place-names, and put on pageants; and

4. Non-Indians must recognize that the Indian heritage is a living, evolving legacy which has not been static in the past and is not static today and that the "core" of being Indian is being a member of an Indian community and not a particular style of dress or ornamentation. Teachers must avoid the idea that a "real" Indian needs to dress and act as Indian people did a century ago.

Recommendations on Textbooks and Mass Media

Indian people are not pleased with most of the textbooks utilized in the schools. It is recommended that textbooks used in California be changed so as to deal accurately with the history and culture of California Indians, that new supplementary materials dealing specifically with California Indian history and culture be prepared, that all texts include pictures of children of different racial backgrounds and that the "mass media" (television, et cetera) deal accurately and adequately with minority groups. For example, in documentary materials Indian actors should be utilized for Indian roles and the use of stereotypes should be discarded.

> *California Indian Education* (Modesto, Calif.: Ad Hoc Committee on California Indian Education [1968]), pp. 14–15.

75 Our Last Chance to Change: Alaska

It is popular to say that the American frontier disappeared in 1890, and with it the Indian land problem. But another frontier still exists in Alaska, the sleeping giant. Though still last among the states in population, it has begun to grow since World War II, and was admitted to statehood in 1959. Until the 1940 census, Indians were a majority of the population of our largest territory (state), and even today they compose over 20 per cent of the population. Spacious though Alaska is, its Indians, Aleuts, and Eskimos are beginning to feel the hot breath of land greed upon their necks, both from the state government and from private interests. As the exploitation of oil and gas on the northern slope is about to begin, both the land rights of the native people and the natural ecology upon which their livelihood depends are threatened. A controversy is shaping up over the settlement of native land claims in Alaska, in which the American people have one last chance either to write a new page in justice and fairness toward the original possessors of the soil, or to repeat the wrongs of the last century.

As this is being written, Congress has been deadlocked for more than a year over a bill to settle the native land question in Alaska.[1] *Even the best compromise worked out so far provides less than half the amount of land for native use that the Alaska Federation of Natives deems to be reasonable. The following summary of the Alaska land question is by the Association on American Indian Affairs.*

Alaska: Deadline for Justice, 1969

THE ASSOCIATION ON AMERICAN INDIAN AFFAIRS

The United States and its people are offered a priceless opportunity to do justice to its aboriginal people whose treatment in the past has reflected little glory on our Nation.

A hundred years ago on the Western frontier, Indians and whites were killing each other for possession of land. Today in Alaska, sixty thousand Indians, Eskimos and Aleuts are fighting to preserve their ancient rights and heritage, and to save a fair portion of their lands from expropriation by the State. They are waging a peaceful war for a decent share of America's future. Congress is now deciding their fate. The Alaska Native people urgently appeal to the conscience of every American for help in their search for justice.

Alaska's Indian, Eskimo, and Aleut citizens have conclusive legal (original Indian title) and moral rights to 340 million acres of land—90 per cent of the Alaska landmass. They are asking Congress to grant them formal legal title to 40 million acres essential to their present livelihood and future well-being, and for just compensation for the remaining 300 million acres they feel are beyond the possibility of saving. Their hopes are expressed in legislation submitted to Congress by the Alaska Federation of Natives— the "AFN Alaska Native Claims Settlement Bill."

The decision Congress makes will profoundly affect the lives of Alaska Natives for generations and will reflect on the honor of our Nation for centuries.

To the Alaska Natives, the land is their life; to the State of Alaska, it is a commodity to be bought and sold. Alaska Native families depend on the land and its waters for the food they eat. They exist by hunting and fishing as they have done for thousands of years. . . .

The land is today's certainty and tomorrow's promise. Industrious and adaptive, the Natives look forward to the day when they can profit, if they choose, from rational commercial development of their resources and can

1. The Alaska Native Claims bill was passed by Congress on December 14, 1971, and signed by President Nixon on December 18. It provides a cash payment of $962.5 million to eligible enrolled Indians, Aleuts, and Eskimos of one quarter or more native blood and reserves 40 million acres of land for their use.

create local employment opportunities through their own initiatives. In short, only if the Natives obtain title to a reasonable amount of their land will they possess the secure economic base upon which to build a better life in a changing world.

The present dispute between the State and the Natives has its origins in a century of inaction by Congress. The State claims the right to select 103 million acres from the public domain under a provision of the 1958 Statehood Act. The Natives rely on a pledge by Congress in 1884 to respect their aboriginal claim, buttressed by a provision included by Congress in the Statehood Act that subjects the State's selection to their prior aboriginal claim.

In 1867, when the United States acquired Alaska from Russia, it purchased not the land itself but only the right to tax and govern. The United States Government recognized at that time, in accordance with longstanding Federal policy and Supreme Court precedent, that the land belonged to the original occupants—the Native people of the villages.

Congress, in the Organic Act of 1884 establishing a territorial government in Alaska, acknowledged the Natives' *right* to the land, stating: "The Indians . . . shall not be disturbed in the possession of any lands actually in their use or occupancy or now claimed by them." However, it postponed for future legislation the matter of conveying *title* to the Natives. Congress has yet to act.

Until the Statehood Act in 1958 there was no massive threat to Native land rights or their way of life. Indeed, prior to 1939 the Natives were a majority in Alaska, and even today non-Natives use only a minute fraction of the land. To protect land rights against the new State, Congress provided that the "State and its people do agree and declare that they forever disclaim all right and title . . . to any lands or other property (including fishing rights) the right or title to which may be held by any Indians, Eskimos, or Aleuts."

Nonetheless the State subsequently moved to take over lands clearly used and occupied by Native villages and to claim, under the Statehood Act, royalties from Federal oil and gas leases on Native lands. The Department of Interior's U.S. Bureau of Land Management, without informing the villages affected and ignoring the claims they had on file, began to process the State's selections. The lands of the Indians of Minto Village, where the lakes provide one of the best duck-breeding grounds in the world, were slated to be taken over by the State for the use of sports hunters and vacationers. The Indians of Tanacross Village were to discover that their lands on beautiful Lake George were being offered for sale at the New York World's Fair as "Wilderness Estates." The multi-billion dollar

North Slope oil strike by Atlantic Richfield Company at Prudhoe Bay is on land the State has claimed from the Eskimos at Barrow.

As word of the State's actions spread from village to village, the Natives began to organize regional associations for their common defense, and in 1962 the *Tundra Times,* a Native weekly, was founded to provide a voice for Native aspirations. In 1964, Indian and Eskimo leaders from across the State met in Fairbanks to mobilize their joint forces; and two years later the statewide Alaska Federation of Natives was formed to champion Native rights. . . .

Ten years ago few Alaskans in positions of power recognized the validity and urgency of Alaska Native land rights. Today the Natives are united and their newly discovered political strength and adroit defense have gained respect for their cause.

The legal validity of Native land rights in Alaska, based on aboriginal use and occupancy, is not subject to serious challenge at this late date in history. A long series of Federal statutes and Supreme Court decisions establishes the rule that aboriginal occupancy creates a property right which the United States alone has the power to extinguish and that Native land rights carry with them the right of the tribe or Native group to enjoy the protection of the United States against interference from all others, including State Governments. . . .

The Alaska Federation of Natives, on behalf of the sixty thousand people it represents, offers in the "AFN Alaska Native Claims Settlement Bill" a solution with these major provisions:

1. Conveyance to the villages of fee-simple title to 40 million acres of land, with mineral rights to be held by Native regional development corporations;

2. Cash compensation in the amount of $500 million dollars (roughly $1.50 per acre) payable over a nine-year period with interest at 4 per cent; and a 2 per cent residual royalty on gross revenues from Federal lands to which Native title is extinguished.

Given the vast amount of land in Alaska and the extent of Native land rights and needs, 40 million acres is a reasonable request. It represents 10 per cent of the land for 20 per cent of the people who have valid claims to nearly 100 per cent of the land. The State still would find ample land from which to make its selection of 103 million acres, and a balance of about 230 million acres would be retained by the federal Government.

Justice further dictates that the Natives enjoy fee-simple title to the lands that are to remain theirs. This is consistent with repeated Supreme Court decisions that aboriginal land rights include all mineral rights. Without such title, a village not only would be denied its rightful benefits, but also would be at the mercy of the conservation practices of the oil and mining companies for protection of the subsistence value of the surface of the land.

Considering the fact that the lands to which the Natives have legal rights have a value conservatively estimated in the tens of billions of dollars, the cash settlement proposed by the Natives based on $1.50 per acre is a modest one. The State of Alaska expects to receive in 1969 alone $1 billion from bonus bids offered in September by oil companies for exploration rights to 431,000 acres of oil land it has taken from the Eskimos of the Arctic Slope. . . .

In view of the Natives' legal rights and our moral obligations, their social and economic needs, and the value of the land to which they have rightful claim, the settlement the Alaska Federation of Natives seeks is just, reasonable, and humane. It will afford a wise and courageous Native people a meaningful opportunity for self-determination and the base for a better life for themselves and their children.

> *Indian Affairs,* Newsletter of the Association on American Indian Affairs, New York, No. 75 (July–September 1969).

The Voice of the Natives, 1969

THOMAS RICHARDS, JR.

The following editorial on the need for political unity of Alaska natives, and a careful distinction between friends and foes, for the protection of native interests, is from the Tundra Times, *of Fairbanks, Alaska, a paper owned and controlled by Eskimos, Indians, and Aleuts.*

A Plea and a Reminder to the Eskimos, Indians, and Aleuts

We deceive ourselves. Our native peoples of Alaska too often believe that we are no longer being exploited—that we no longer receive glass trinkets for furs. We too often believe that no one will use our native peoples to the personal advantage of that individual: as did the Russians when they thirsted for our furs, as did the first White settlers when they made their fortunes from the wealth of our lands.

It would be shameful to say that all or even most, of the non-native population of Alaska has no sympathy for our cause. Yet now, in the time of our greatest need, we must begin to count our friends.

We deceive ourselves. During each and every election year, we listen to both those who have promise, and those who have promises.

Our greatest shame would come if, in-between elections, we hesitate to evaluate the performance of politicians on those issues which concern us.

We have tried to bring these issues to light through the *Tundra Times* and, because of the interest of native individuals and their organizations, our paper is reviewed by virtually every native in the state.

Our native land claims settlement is the single, most important issue. It will directly affect our lives, and the lives of our children, and the descendants of our race for all time. Now is the time to evaluate our elected officials. We must not allow them to make promises during one election year, and ignore our interests during the following three, or one. . . .

Regardless of our political affiliation, we must certainly realize that our primary loyalty is with that stuff which flows in our veins—the blood of our birthright.

We must all awaken to that reality more quickly than the icy water puts an end to our sleep. It would be sinful to accept the idea that we are part-time citizens for only the moment that we mark our ballots. Let us bury the thought and leave it to the worms.

We must be full time, first class citizens with a full time responsibility to elect officials who will represent our interests. We must watch them closely to see that they will not be so stupid as to ignore our needs.

Let us guard our heritage. Let us exercise our rights, and our responsibilities. Let us not forget what we are made of. Let us not allow the politicians to forget who we are, and what we want, and what will happen if we are ignored. To do otherwise would be fatal.

Please do not consider this plea as an insult to your intelligence. Think of it as a reminder of your responsibilities. Let us no longer deceive ourselves.

Brotherhood among all our peoples.

THOMAS RICHARDS, JR. [*Vice-president, Eskimo, Indian, Aleut Publishing Co.*] *Tundra Times*, September 12, 1969, p. 2.

76   A Plea for Indian Cultural Survival

Once the period of violent struggle with the Indians had ended, and the goal of genocide could no longer be defended, a tutelary attitude toward the Indian became prevalent. It holds that Indians are quite incapable of ordering their own affairs, and that if such a luxury is insisted upon, it must be at the sacrifice of all assistance from the white community. In the excerpt that follows, Professor Sol Tax, of the anthropology department of the University of Chicago, maintains that the Indians can well manage their own communities, and that they are entitled to assistance, but not

domination, in doing so. He further argues that there are important values
that the white man can learn from the Indian.

The Importance of Indian Culture in Modern America

SOL TAX

From the beginning of our history on this continent we have made it
difficult for Indians to continue to live as Indians. We took away their
means of making a living as Indians, offering them this difficult choice:
"Maintain your communities and live in terms of Indian values," we told
them. "If you can't feed yourselves that way in our competitive, utilitarian,
impersonal society, then change into white men. Leave your communities
and your values; stop living in ways you think proper; and you can eat and
have the things you need." It was an act of will of which they should feel
proud. They chose the way of our fathers who left Europe in small ships to
face unknown hazards and hardships rather than submit to tyranny or
violation of conscience.

What is no less important is that we still offer them only the impossible
choice—live like white men, or not at all—and that they still refuse. To
resolve the problem—which is our problem—we say, "Keep your culture if
you will, but not at our expense"—and impatiently we throw them into the
water to sink or swim, as we say. But the Indians stubbornly neither sink
nor swim; they float. They retreat into themselves, unable to explain that
they cannot and will not be like us—that would be discourteous and
aggressive and not good Indian behavior. They plead silently for understanding, patience, and help. And the help that we give them is offered as
charity, in paternal spirit, forcing them in order to live to lose the independence which is their traditional heritage and the birthright of every
community. Outsiders manage their affairs; because they cannot pay for
their community schools and hospitals, they are not allowed to manage
them. And then we complain that they do not know how.

Indian tribes have from time immemorial managed the most difficult
community decisions, and have done so with consummate skill. Otherwise
they would not have survived. They could do it now if we let them do it in
their own way. What needs to be done to protect Indian communities is to
help them to protect their small remaining land base—which *is* their
tribe—and to help them to provide means to earn a living and to maintain
health and education; help them to do what needs to be done—help them
with money and skills—but let them do it for themselves. We shall prove
ourselves wise enough to run their lives only when we find ways to let them
run their own. But we have to provide some replacement for the continent
which we took from them, until they, as communities, can freely invent

means to adjust to this new environment of the white man as once they adjusted to changes in nature.

If indeed we dedicate ourselves to helping Indian communities to independence and to creation, by whatever means is necessary, we will give life again to the oldest and most valuable flower in our American garden of different cultural flowers. It will contribute, in ways that we cannot now even imagine, to the beauty and integrity of the lives of all of us in North America. We may find that if American Indian cultures are preserved in this genuine creative way, they will show us how our technical civilization can preserve also our own humanity.

> Address given at First Annual meeting of the Foundation of North American Indian Culture, Bismarck, North Dakota, December 6, 1963.

"Cultural Differences Are Not a National Burden," 1968

SENATOR ROBERT F. KENNEDY

. . . cultural differences are not a national burden, they are a national resource—the American vision of itself is of a nation of citizens determining their own destiny; of cultural differences flourishing in an atmosphere of mutual respect; of diverse peoples shaping their own lives and destiny in their own fashion. . . . That is what we understand as the United States of America.

> Remarks as Chairman of the Senate Subcommittee on Indian Education, during hearings at Twin Oaks, Oklahoma, February 19, 1968. Quoted in *Indian Truth,* Spring–Summer 1968, pp. 6, 13.

V

THE INDIAN IN PERSPECTIVE

Introduction

After this journey through dozens of documents on the Indian in American history, a summing up seems in order. What do we make out of it all? One recent writer asserted that "the Indian is no great personal issue to us."[1] However that may be, we cannot escape the enormous influence he has had on our past, and equally important, on our present. The following documents attempt to gauge some of that influence, and to answer some questions which keep bobbing up, such as:

How many Indians were there, and how many remain?

How do Indians live?

Why don't Indians like to work?

Why don't they all want to assimilate?

What remains of the old culture?

Why are there so many Indian names on the map?

We started to write a guide to American Indian history, not an encyclopedia of the Indian. The following fragments of information, therefore, cannot serve as a complete survey of things Indian, nor even to answer all of the most common questions. They can, however, serve to illuminate a few fascinating aspects of the Indian's role in America, and may, it is hoped, arouse sufficient interest in the subject to lead to further study.

1. Roy H. Pearce, *The Savages of America* (rev. ed.; Baltimore: Johns Hopkins Press, 1965), p. 105.

77 How Many Indians Were There When the White Man Came, and How Many Remain?

Most historians give low estimates of the former Indian population on this continent. The late John Spencer Bassett claimed that "in 1500 there were about half a million Indians in North America."[1] Since such a figure is close to recent estimates of surviving Indian population, the implication is that white contact has not been too destructive of Indians.

The first serious study of North American aboriginal population was published by anthropologist James Mooney in 1928.[2] Mooney tried to ascertain from early reports the probable numbers of the various tribes at the date of first white disturbance, or contact, and their surviving numbers at a late date, which was 1907 in most instances. The date of first white contact for the various tribes ranged from about 1600 to 1780. On this basis, Mooney presented the following estimates:

Indian population in:	Early date	Late date
United States proper	849,000	266,000
British America [*Canada*]	221,000	101,000
Alaska	73,000	28,000
Greenland	10,000	11,000
Totals	1,153,000	406,000

Mooney commented that the figures of the first column applied to different dates but that they agreed in that they were intended to represent the population just before it suffered the first disturbance from Europeans.

Anyone who has examined early sources will suspect that Mooney's figures are conservative. His estimate for the Five Nations before the accession of the Tuscaroras was only slightly above 5,000 persons. Some early observers estimated that the Iroquois could muster 2,000 warriors, which would indicate a larger population than Mooney assigned them. If there were only one wife and two children for each warrior, the population would be 8,000. The old people would add more to the total.

Mooney failed to consider the effects of early epidemics from introduced diseases. Many tribes had already been decimated by white-introduced contagion before the first literate white man with pen in hand had come

1. Bassett, *A Short History of the United States* (rev. ed.; New York: The Macmillan Co., 1933), p. 21.
2. Mooney, *The Aboriginal Population of America North of Mexico* (Washington: Smithsonian Institution, Pub. No. 2955, 1928).

amongst them.[3] *Such, for example, was the fate of the coastal tribes of Massachusetts, who were swept away by ills brought to them by coastal adventurers four years before the pilgrims landed. John Lawson believed (1708) that only one sixth as many Carolina Indians survived within two hundred miles of the white settlements as had lived in the area a half century earlier. Since there were no wars in that period, the loss was due to the spread of diseases previously unknown in the country. Smallpox, which remained for centuries the greatest killer of Indians, was introduced to the Cherokees by a runaway slave. Other leading causes of death, previously unknown in North America, were measles, diphtheria, venereal disease, and alcoholism.*

Very recently a new study has been made of aboriginal American population of the entire hemisphere, by Professor Henry F. Dobyns, an anthropologist at the University of Kentucky.[4] *His studies in epidemiology led him to the conclusion that the aboriginal population was about twenty times as great before contact as it was at its nadir. Therefore the aboriginal population of North America alone was estimated to have been 9,800,000, and for the entire hemisphere, a figure of 90,000,000 was postulated. His conclusions follow.*

Estimated Aboriginal Population, 1966

HENRY F. DOBYNS

Assuming a "standard" hemispheric depopulation ratio of 20 to 1 between initial contact and the beginning of population recovery should permit estimating aboriginal American population if sound figures on the size of the various Indian groups when they reached their respective nadirs can be found. If a population did not recover and the group became extinct, a depopulation ratio has little utility for calculating its original precontact scale. It may be possible to use a ratio to approximate the aboriginal magnitude of such extinct groups based on the number of survivors about 130 years after initial contact. There is some evidence that this was frequently the time native American populations required to reach nadir and begin to recover—at least it was so among the central Mexicans and California Indians.

As an antidote to previous overly low estimates of aboriginal American population, and as a working hypothesis to stimulate research into this

3. Magnus Mörner asserts that "if there were 50 million or more Indians in the New World, the demographic disaster that took place after 1492 is probably without counterpart in the history of mankind." *Race Mixture in the History of Latin America* (Boston: Little Brown & Co., 1967), p. 12.

4. Now at Prescott College, Prescott, Arizona.

question, a summary of the calculations performed in this paper is offered in Table 2.

Abstract

Social scientists often consider population size as an independent variable of major importance. The author analyzes, therefore, methodological reasons why most prior estimates of aboriginal American population imply small-scale preconquest societies and concludes that the population was far larger than has been thought. The range of previous estimation is so great as to indicate that some methods or data must have been faulty. Skeptical anthropologists and historians have regarded historic population figures reported by contemporary observers as larger than reality. Ethnohistorical estimations based on careful cross-checking of direct and indirect sources of population data demonstrate that contemporary observers underreported the true magnitude of native American populations.

Estimates obtained by projecting backward through time population data from modern Indian census counts are seriously defective, as are past applications of the dead reckoning mode of estimation. Ethnohistorical methods are less deficient. Cross-checking sources serves to increase the accuracy of estimation, and informant knowledge is evaluated in terms of opportunities for accurate observation and especially for accurate memory, since it is more difficult to retain quantitative than qualitative data.

Additive reconstruction of Indian population from historical records is handicapped because the geographic spread of literate Europeans lagged behind the diffusion of new disease agents which decimated aboriginal populations. Direct observation of Indian population trends by anthropologists suffers the same limitation, even though several have recorded extremely rapid depopulation of Amazon basin peoples within the century.

Calculation of aboriginal population from preconquest social structure is possible only in 1 area governed by an imperial ideal of administrative units consistent in population.

Approximately accurate estimates of aboriginal American population may be achieved by comparing the population of a given area at two or more times in order to establish population trends expressed as ratios of the size of the population at 1 time to its size at another. Early historic depopulation was great in the Americas: a well-documented instance of recovery following depopulation from 50 to 1 over one century indicates limits to such a trend. Greater population loss probably results in extinction. A hemisphere-wide historic depopulation ratio of 20 to 1 is postulated. Applying it to more or less well-established historic Indian nadir populations suggests that the New World was inhabited by approximately 90,000,000 persons immediately prior to discovery.

TABLE 2

Estimated Aboriginal Population

Area	Nadir population	Date of nadir	Projections × 20	× 25
North America	490,000	1930+	9,800,000	12,250,000
Mexican Civilization	1,500,000	1650	30,000,000	37,500,000
Central America	540,000	1650	10,800,000	13,500,000
Caribbean Islands	22,150	1570	443,000	553,750
Andean Civilization	1,500,000	1650+	30,000,000	37,500,000
Marginal South America	450,000	?	9,000,000	11,250,000
Western Hemisphere			90,043,000	112,553,750

[*Author's footnotes omitted.*]

HENRY F. DOBYNS, "Estimating Aboriginal American Population, an Appraisal of Techniques with a New Hemispheric Estimate," *Current Anthropology,* Vol. VII, No. 4 (October 1966), pp. 395–416.

Counting Indians, 1950

BUREAU OF INDIAN AFFAIRS

Figures of Indian population issued by the Bureau of the Census, the Bureau of Indian Affairs, and Indian organizations are never in agreement. Part of the difficulty lies in the lack of an agreed-upon definition of an Indian, partly it is due to faulty methods, and to some extent it is caused by the characteristics of the Indian population. The following two documents discuss these problems.

Defining "Indians"

Because there is no "standard" or universally accepted definition of the term "Indian" in United States law or usage, estimates of the total Indian population of the country for 1950 or any other specific year necessarily will vary in accordance with the definition being used. Since the earliest colonial admixture of the white and Indian races, about the time of the marriage of Pocahontas and John Rolfe, the population has included "mixed blood" people who might be considered either Indian or non-Indian depending upon the point of view. Today the number of such people in the United States is large enough to make possible an extremely wide range of estimates of the "Indian population."

The theoretical definition of an Indian used by the United States Bureau of the Census includes the following categories: (1) full-blood Indians, (2) persons of any degree of mixed blood enrolled at an Indian agency or reservation, (3) persons of one-fourth or more Indian blood, and (4) persons regarded as "Indians" in the community of their residence. In practice, however, this definition has little significance since the Census enumerators are instructed not to ask specifically the question of race but to make their own determinations.[1] The probabilities are that enumerations are reasonably accurate race-wise in the vicinity of Indian reservations, where the enumerator usually knows which persons meet the Census definition of an Indian, but are highly unreliable in other localities.

Even though no completely accurate computation is possible, the Bureau of Indian Affairs believes that the total number of persons actually meeting the Census definition of an "Indian" is probably well over 400,000 and there can be no doubt that the number is steadily increasing. Included in this total, however, are a number of tribal groups and a substantial number of individuals having no specific relations with the Federal government under terms of laws or treaties. It would include, for example, the Indians of Maine, the Croatans of North Carolina, and other groups whose relations are with the State governments under treaties dating back to colonial days. It would also include some Indians of Canadian or Mexican origin who have never had any special relations with either Federal or State government. Finally, it would include a large number of individuals no longer maintaining residence on reservations for whom tribal relation, and perhaps even Indian identity, have lost all practical significance.

> Department of the Interior, Bureau of Indian Affairs, *Resident Population on Indian Reservations*, 1950, pp. 3–4.

Indian Population Statistics, 1968

STAN STEINER

The more questions asked about race, and the more freely Indians answered them, the larger the population. When in 1930 and 1940 no such questions were asked, the population accordingly declined.

Population statistics therefore reflected the methods and attitudes of the census takers, as much as the numbers of Indians. Nowhere was this more obvious than in the counts of the city Indians, who were an increasingly large proportion of the total Indian population.

And there is the additional problem that faces the census taker on the rural reservation. The isolated and scattered back-country settlements, where family relations do not fit the census forms, and people are frequently moving within the extended kinship family, make an educated

---

1. In 1960 census takers were permitted to ask about race, and the number of Indians tallied rose from 343,410 to 523,591, exclusive of Alaska.

guess difficult. Estimates by the various tribes, in such cases, invariably are greater than the seemingly precise statistics of the Census Bureau.

For instance: the Navajo tribe's population was listed as 84,302 in the 1960 Census. Yet the tribal estimates ranged from 105,000 to 115,000. On the more than sixteen-million-acre reservation an accurate count of the constantly shifting nomadic population is quite impossible. Tribal officials have said the *only* accurate count ever made of Navajos occurred during World War II when sugar rations were issued, and every Navajo voluntarily registered to receive his ration.

These problems have led to some widely varied estimates of the Indian population. As can be seen by the following:

Bureau of Indian Affairs, 1962	367,179
U.S. Census Bureau, 1960	552,220[a]
Robert Thomas and Samuel Stanley, University of Chicago, 1950	571,824
Vine Deloria, Jr., director, National Congress of American Indians	1,000,000 [at least]
Mel Thom, chairman, National Indian Youth Council	1,500,000

a. Preliminary census figures for 1970 set the American Indian population of the United States at 792,000, an increase of more than 50 per cent since 1960. About 500,000 of these are said to live on or near reservations.—V.J.V.

STAN STEINER, *The New Indians* (New York: Harper & Row, 1968), p. 323.

78   Liberty and Authority Among the Indians

In an age of authoritarianism and oligarchy, political philosophers who dreamed of a society in which men might be free were invariably impressed by the libertarianism of Indian societies. There are even those who believe that the Indian example is the root of a certain contempt for command which they see in American society. Rousseau saw in savage society the state which the ancestors of all men enjoyed before power was usurped from them by malefactors. Jefferson was a keen student of Indian ways of life, and was doubtless influenced in his thinking by what he knew of their social structure.

We introduce the subject with some opinions of Montaigne and Rousseau, who lived more than two hundred years apart, and whose opinions have been questioned because they had no direct contact with the Indians. Following this we introduce documents by observers from 1540 to 1830, all of whom, except Jefferson, had direct personal contact with primitive Indians. The uniformity of views from such a variety of witnesses cannot easily be refuted.

On Cannibals, 1540

MICHEL EYQUEM DE MONTAIGNE

The following was inspired by accounts of the Brazilian natives.

These nations, then, seem to me barbarous in this sense, that they have been fashioned very little by the human mind, and are still very close to their original naturalness. The laws of nature still rule them, very little corrupted by ours; and they are in such a state of purity that I am sometimes vexed that they were unknown earlier, in the days when there were men able to judge them better than we. I am sorry that Lycurgus and Plato did not know of them, for it seems to me that what we actually see in these nations surpasses not only all the pictures in which poets have idealized the golden age and all their inventions in imagining a happy state of man, but also the conceptions and the very desire of philosophy. They could not imagine a naturalness so pure and simple as we see by experience; nor could they believe that our society could be maintained with so little artifice and human solder. This is a nation, I should say to Plato, in which there is no sort of traffic, no knowledge of letters, no science of numbers, no name for a magistrate or for political superiority, no custom of servitude, no riches or poverty, no contracts, no successions, no partitions, no occupations but leisure ones, no care for any but common kindred, no clothes, no agriculture, no metal, no use of wine or wheat. The very words that signify lying, treachery, dissimulation, avarice, envy, belittling, pardon —unheard of.

> "Essay on Cannibals," in Donald Frame, ed., *Complete Works of Montaigne* (Stanford, Calif.: Stanford University Press, 1958), p. 153.

On the Origin of Inequality

JEAN JACQUES ROUSSEAU

Jean Jacques Rousseau, French philosopher (1712–1778), expounded generalizations which were not based on observation, but on reading and thought. Some of his conclusions were wide of the mark, as for example his belief that joint labor brought an end to primeval equality. American Indians north of Mexico did very little as individuals—even hunting was an

organized community venture. So also, in many places, was house building,
sugar making, gardening, and other activities.

. . . nothing is more gentle than man in his primitive state, as he is
placed by nature at an equal distance from the stupidity of brutes, and the
fatal ingenuity of civilized man. Equally confined by instinct and reason to
the sole care of guarding himself against the mischiefs which threaten him,
he is restrained by natural compassion from doing any injury to others, and
is not led to do such a thing even in return for injuries received. For,
according to the axiom of the wise Locke, "There can be no injury, where
there is no property."

. . . so long as they undertook only what a single person could accomplish, and confined themselves to such arts as did not require the joint
labour of several hands, they lived free, healthy, honest, and happy lives,
so long as their nature allowed, and as they continued to enjoy the pleas-
ures of mutual and independent intercourse. But from the moment one
man began to stand in need of the help of another; from the moment it
appeared advantageous to any one man to have enough provisions for two,
equality disappeared, property was introduced, work became indispensable, and vast forests became smiling fields, which man had to water with
the sweat of his brow, and where slavery and misery were soon seen to
germinate and grow up with the crops.

Metallurgy and agriculture were the two arts which produced this great
revolution. The poets tell us it was gold and silver, but, for the philosophers, it was iron and corn [*grain*], which first civilized men, and ruined
humanity. Thus both were unknown to the savages of America [*sic*] who for
that reason are still savage: the other nations also seem to have continued
in a state of barbarism while they practiced only one of these arts. One of
the best reasons, perhaps, why Europe has been, if not longer, at least
more constantly and highly civilized than the rest of the world, is that it is
at once the most abundant in iron and the most fertile in corn.

JEAN JACQUES ROUSSEAU, "A Discourse on the Origin of In-
equality," in *The Social Contract and Discourses,* translated
by G. D. H. Cole (New York: E. P. Dutton & Co., 1950),
pp. 242–44.

Pueblo of Acoma, 1540

FRANCISCO DE CORONADO

[*After the inhabitants had fled, following the capture of the city*] I
found a few of them there, whom I told that they ought not to feel any fear,
and I asked them to summon their lord to me. By what I can find out or

observe, however, none of these towns have any, since I have not seen any principal house by which any superiority over others could be shown.

Afterward, an old man, who said he was their lord, came with a mantle made of many pieces, with whom I argued as long as he stayed with me. He said that he would come to see me with the rest of the chiefs of the country, three days later, in order to arrange the relations which should exist between us.

> FRANCISCO DE CORONADO, letter to Mendoza, August 4, 1540, in *Fourteenth Annual Report of the Bureau of American Ethnology,* p. 1, 1892–1893, p. 561.

Canadian Algonquians, 1612

PIERRE BIARD

They love justice and hate violence and robbery, a thing really remarkable in men who have neither laws nor magistrates; for among them each man is his own master and his own protector. They have Sagamores, that is, leaders in war; but their authority is most precarious, if, indeed, that may be called authority to which obedience is in no wise obligatory. The Indians follow them through the persuasion of example or custom, or of ties of kindred and alliance . . .

> PIERRE BIARD, in Reuben G. Thwaites, ed., *The Jesuit Relations and Allied Documents* (75 vols., Cleveland: The Burrows Bros. Co., 1896–1901), II, 73.

Indians of New Netherland, 1624

NICOLAES VAN WASSENAER

There is little authority known among these nations. They live almost equally free. In each village, indeed, is found a person who is somewhat above the others and commands absolutely when there is war and when they are gathered from all the villages to go to war. But the fight once ended, his authority ceases.

> NICOLAES VAN WASSENAER's *Historisch Verhael,* in J. Franklin Jameson, ed., *Narratives of New Netherland 1609–1664* (New York: Charles Scribner's Sons, 1909), pp. 69–70.

The Hurons, 1648

JEROME LALEMANT

From the beginning of the world to the coming of the French, the Savages have never known what it was so solemnly to forbid anything to their people, under any penalty, however slight. They are free people, each of whom considers himself of as much consequence as the others; and they submit to their chiefs only in so far as it pleases them.

> JEROME LALEMANT, April 16, 1648, in Reuben G. Thwaites,
> ed., *The Jesuit Relations,* XXXIII, p. 51.

The Iroquois Confederacy, 1727

CADWALLADER COLDEN

Their great Men, both Sachems and Captains, are generally poorer than the common People for they affect to give away and distribute all the Presents or Plunder they get in their Treaties or in War, so as to leave nothing for themselves. There is not a Man in the Ministry of the Five Nations, who has gain'd his Office, otherwise than by Merit; there is not the least Salary, or any Sort of Profit, annexed to any Office, to tempt the Covetous or Sordid; but, on the contrary, every unworthy Action is unavoidably attended with the Forfeiture of their Commission; for their Authority is only the Esteem of the People, and ceases the Moment that Esteem is lost. Here we see the natural Origin of all Power and Authority among a free People, and whatever artificial Power of Sovereignty any Man may have acquired, by the Laws and Constitution of a Country, his real Power will be ever much greater or less, in Proportion to the Esteem People have of him.

The Five Nations have such absolute Notions of Liberty, that they allow of no Kind of Superiority of one over another, and banish all Servitude from their Territories. They never make any Prisoner a Slave; but it is customary among them to make a Compliment of Naturalization into the Five Nations; and, considering how highly they value themselves above all others, this must be no small compliment. . . .

> LT. GOV. CADWALLADER COLDEN [1688–1776], *History of the*
> *Five Indian Nations, Which are Dependent on the Province*
> *of New York* . . . (2 vols.; New York: New Amsterdam
> Book Co., 1902), I, xvii–xix.

The Illiniwek, 1750

LOUIS VIVIER

As there is neither rank nor dignity among them, all men seem equal to them. An Illinois would speak as boldly to the King of France as to the lowest of his subjects. Most of them are capable of sustaining a conversation with any person, provided no question be treated of that is beyond their sphere of knowledge . . .

They all live in great peace, which is due, in a great measure, to the fact that each one is allowed to do what he pleases.

LOUIS VIVIER, June 8, 1750, Reuben G. Thwaites, ed., Jesuit Relations, LXIX, p. 146.

Ohio Valley, 1764–1780

WILLIAM SMITH, ROBERT ROGERS, and THOMAS FILSON

The love of liberty is innate in the savage; and seems the ruling passion of the state of nature.[1]

Nor is a servile regard paid to the distinction of high and low, rich and poor, noble and ignoble.[2]

Among the Indians, all men are equal, personal qualities being most esteemed. No distinction of birth, no rank, renders any man capable of doing prejudice to the rights of private persons; and there is no pre-eminence from merit, which begets pride, and which makes others too sensible of their own inferiority.

Their King has no power to put any one to death by his own authority; but the murderer is generally delivered up to the friends of the deceased, to do as they please. . . . Their kings are hereditary, but their authority extremely limited. No people are a more striking evidence of the miseries of mankind in the want of government than they. Every chief, when offended, breaks off with a party, settles at some distance, and then commences hostilities against his own people.[3]

Aborigines of Virginia, 1787

THOMAS JEFFERSON

. . . Very possibly there may have been antiently three different stocks, each of which multiplying in a long course of time, had separated into so many little societies. This practice results from the circumstance of their having never submitted themselves to any laws, any coercive power, any shadow of government. Their only controls are their manners, and the moral sense of right and wrong, which, like the sense of tasting and feeling,

1. William Smith, *Expedition Against the Ohio Indians* [1765], (Ann Arbor: University Microfilms, 1966), p. 38.

2. Robert Rogers, *Concise Account of North America* (London: 1765), p. 219.

3. Thomas Filson, *The Discovery, Settlement, and Present State of Kentucky* [1784], (Ann Arbor: University Microfilms, 1966), pp. 101, 106.

in every man makes a part of his nature. An offense against these is punished by contempt, by exclusion from society, or, where the case is serious, as that of murder, by the individuals whom it concerns. Imperfect as this species of coercion may seem, crimes are very rare among them: insomuch that were it made a question, whether no law, as among the savage Americans, or too much law, as among the civilized Europeans, submits man to the greatest evil, one who has seen both conditions of existence would pronounce it to be the last: and that the sheep are happier of themselves, than under care of the wolves. It will be said, that great societies cannot exist without government. The Savages therefore break them up into small ones.

> WM. PEDEN, ed., *Notes on the State of Virginia* (Chapel Hill: University of North Carolina Press, 1955), pp. 92–93.

Letter to Carrington, 1787

THOMAS JEFFERSON

I am convinced that those societies (as the Indians) which live without government, enjoy in their general mass an infinitely greater degree of happiness than those who live under the European governments. Among the former, public opinion is in the place of law, and restrains morals as powerfully as laws ever did anywhere. Among the latter, under the pretence of governing, they have divided their nations into two classes, wolves and sheep.

> Letter to Col. Edward Carrington, in ADRIENNE KOCH AND WILLIAM PEDEN, eds., *The Life and Selected Writings of Thomas Jefferson* (New York: The Modern Library, 1944), p. 411.

The Shoshonis, 1805

MERIWETHER LEWIS

This manliness of character may cause or it may be formed by the nature of their government, which is perfectly free from any restraint. Each individual is his own master, and the only control to which his conduct is subjected, is the advice of a chief supported by his influence over the rest of the tribe. The chief himself is in fact no more than the most confidential person among the warriors, a rank neither distinguished by external honor, nor invested by any ceremony, but gradually acquired from the good wishes of his companions and by superior merit. Such an officer has therefore strictly no power; he may recommend or advise or influence, but his commands have no effect on those who incline to disobey, and who may at any time withdraw from their voluntary allegiance. His shadowy authority which cannot survive the confidence which supports it, often decays with the personal vigour of the chief. . . .

> MERIWETHER LEWIS, *History of the Expedition Under the Command of Captains Lewis and Clark,* ed. by John B. McMaster (2 vols.; New York: Allerton Book Co., 1922), II, p. 118.

Plains Tribes, Early 1800s

JOHN D. HUNTER

The chiefs and candidates for public preferment render themselves popular by their disinterestedness and poverty. Whenever any extraordinary success attends them in the acquisition of property, it is only for the benefit of their most meritorious adherents; for they distribute it with a profuse liberality, and pride themselves in being estimated the poorest men in the community. Valour, intrepidity, and liberality, are the passports to popular favour; while the contrasts are the damning sins of Indian politicians. In general, each family elects a chief to overlook and attend to its interests; he is its orator, attends the councils, and is, whenever occasion requires, an aid to the principal chief. . . .

These heads of the nation receive no emolument for their services; the honour attached to the situation being considered a most enviable and satisfactory reward. . . .

They live under an implied social compact; have chiefs and other superior officers, and traditionary laws for their government; but, nevertheless, they surrender comparatively no portion of their personal liberty: they chastise offences, and revenge insults, regardless of all considerations, and neither yield obedience nor acknowledge fealty to any one.

> JOHN D. HUNTER, *Memoirs of a Captivity among the Indians of North America* (London: Longman, Hurst, *et al.,* 1823), pp. 317–18, 365.

Plains Tribes, 1830s

GEORGE CATLIN

The chief has no control over the life or limbs, or liberty of his subjects, nor other power whatever, excepting that of *influence* which he gains by his virtues, and his exploits in war, and which induces his warriors and braves to follow him, as he leads them to battle—or to listen to him when he speaks in council. In fact, he is no more than a *leader,* whom every young warrior may follow, or turn about and go back from, as he pleases, if he is willing to meet the disgrace that awaits him, who deserts his chief in the hour of danger.

> GEORGE CATLIN, *Letters and Notes on the Manners, Customs and Conditions of the North American Indians*, 2 vols. (Philadelphia: Willis P. Hazard, 1857), II, 753. Original emphasis.

Ojibwa, 1830

JOHN TANNER

It is rare that oppression or injustice in affairs of private right between men and man, take place among the Indians.

> *Narrative of the Captivity and Adventures of John Tanner*, ed. by Edwin James (Mineapolis: Ross & Haines, 1956), p. 75.

79   The Indian Concept of Time: A Cultural Trait

CARL SWEEZY

Some years ago this writer, with a friend, visited the Court Oreilles Ojibwa reservation near Hayward, Wisconsin. My friend wanted to see "some Indian culture." He saw unpainted wooden houses, and Indians dressed like white people, from which he quickly concluded that "there is no such thing as Indian culture nowadays." This mistaken judgment is easily made, since much of the Indian culture cannot be seen, because it is inside the Indian. That is why anthropologists try to live among Indians in order to learn about them.

The nonmaterial or intangible part of Indian culture, which is the most persistent, includes what we call a value system. One of the ways in which the culture of Indians and other pre-industrial peoples differs from ours is in the concept of time. We who live in an urban industrial society have become so inured to the tyranny of clocks and calendars that we seldom reflect on the extent to which our lives are circumscribed by these inventions. George Woodcock, an English writer, once pointed out that "in no characteristic is existing society in the West so sharply distinguished from the earlier societies . . . than in its conception of time." The Industrial Revolution led us to measure lengths of time like yards of calico, and the clock became "an element of mechanical tyranny in the lives of modern men more potent than any individual exploiter or than any other machine." Consequently, "men actually became like clocks, acting with a repetitive regularity which had no resemblance to the rhythmic life of a natural being."[1]

More recently, Professor Sebastian de Grazia of Rutgers University declared that modern technology (which depends so heavily on the clock) has not increased our leisure. On the contrary, he argued, we spend more time traveling to jobs through urban congestion, and our leisure is further reduced by do-it-yourself chores and the tasks of maintenance of our proliferating possessions. He held that "any primitive tribe enjoys more free time than the United States today. It is doubtful that any civilization ever had as little free time as we do. We have transformed civilization to win time and find leisure, but we have failed."[2]

Because many Indians are unaccustomed to the rigid routines of urban man, problems arise when they are relocated to cities. When this writer was preparing a paper on urban Indians a few years ago, an Indian Bureau official in Chicago reported that one of the difficulties of recently arrived Indians was learning to live by the clock, and getting to work at the same time every day. They were also apt to return temporarily to the reservation for some social purpose, without notice to their employers. While many eventually adjusted to the required mold, others chose to return to the rural poverty which was the price of a larger measure of freedom.

Similar problems arise when industries are established on or near reservations, a development which the Indian Bureau is encouraging. In these establishments, usually white-owned, Indians are compelled to conform to white standards of punctuality and regular attendance. In a fishhook factory employing Sioux Indians at Pine Ridge, South Dakota, "all must punch a time clock, and if late, wages are docked. Absenteeism without excuse means dismissal. TIME is now becoming a reality on the reservation where once it was only a word without meaning."[3] A uniquely contrary practice is followed at the Yankton Sioux reservation in the same state, where a small tribal-owned electronic component factory operates successfully without violating traditional ways. There, the Indians come to work when they want to, work as long as they wish, and are paid accordingly. No one is penalized because of irregular hours or days.[4]

1. George Woodcock, "The Tyranny of the Clock," *Politics*, Vol. I: 9 (October 1944), pp. 265–67.
2. "Leisure Time Is a Myth for Most People," *Chicago Tribune*, January 14, 1968. Dr. Meyer Friedman, a San Francisco heart specialist, maintains that the clock is modern man's worst enemy—far worse than cholesterol. "The Navajo Indian," he declares, "eats as much cholesterol as we do, but he doesn't worry about time, and he doesn't have coronaries." *Chicago Sun-Times*, Dec. 5, 1971.
3. *The Amerindian*, March-April 1967, p. 6. This factory closed during the summer of 1968.
4. Stan Steiner, *The New Indians* (New York: Harper & Row, 1968), pp. 124 ff.

The Indian lived in harmony with his environment, and his attitude toward time was shaped by that relationship. The following testimony on the contrast between Indian and white concepts of time was given by an Arapaho Indian who was born on an Oklahoma reservation about 1881.

Every white man seemed to have a great concern about time. We had our own names for the seasons and for the months that made up the year, but they were not the same as those the white man used. And we did not know how he counted time, by minutes and hours and days of the week, or why he divided the day into such small parts. And we found that there were two ways of counting it, for the Quakers spoke of First-day, Second-day, and Third-day, and of First-month, Second-month, and Third-month, while others spoke of Sunday and Monday and Tuesday, and of January and February and March. . . . It was a long time before we knew what the figures on the face of a clock meant, or why people looked at them before they ate their meals or started off to church. We had to learn that clocks had something to do with the hours and minutes that the white people mentioned so often. Hours, minutes, and seconds were such small divisions of time that we had never thought of them. When the sun rose, when it was high in the sky, and when it set were all the divisions of the day we had ever found necessary when we followed the old Arapaho road. When we went on a hunting trip or to a sun dance, we counted time by sleeps.

White people who did not try so hard to understand the ways of the Cheyenne and the Arapaho as we did to understand their ways, thought we were all lazy. That was because we took a different attitude toward time than theirs. We enjoyed time, they measured it. Our women did not say, on Monday . . . we wash our clothes; on Tuesday we iron them; on Saturday we bake and clean; on Sunday we do not work and we go to church. Our men did not say, after breakfast, at eight o'clock I go to my schoolroom, or to my office, or to the commissary; at twelve I go home to my dinner; at one I go back to work all afternoon. They did not say, this week we break sod and plough, next week we plant our corn or our potatoes and melons and cabbage.

For hundreds of years we had gone on a long hunt twice a year, whenever our scouts had come in to report that buffalo were plenty out on the Plains; we had held our buffalo dance before we left, and had set out with our best bows and arrows, our shields and lances for protection from our enemies if we should meet with any of them, and pemmican for food to eat until we killed meat. We had taken our women and children along because they too loved to move over the prairies, making camp where grass was green and water fresh, and because our women must skin the animals and dress the hides and dry the meat where we killed it. No Sundays could be set aside for church or rest, or Mondays for washing, when we followed the buffalo road. And we had no set date for coming back, for that depended on the buffalo and the weather. When we had meat enough and the skins were dry enough to pack, we started back to the home camp.

But we were not an idle nation of people. If we had been idlers, we would have been wiped out by our enemies, or by bad weather and starvation long ago. Before our Reservation days, we had hunted and traded over the land that makes up many states now. . . . Those were brave, free days. We had no time, and no need, to plant crops or raise corn and hogs and chickens, or build houses and barns like the white man's then. But when we followed the buffalo road we worked hard, just as white people who followed the corn road worked hard. No people who get their living from Mother-Earth as she provides it for them, and who fight off other tribes wanting to hunt and graze their horses over the same land, can be lazy.

> CARL SWEEZY, as told to Althea Bass, in *The Arapaho Way: A Memoir of an Indian Boyhood* (New York: Clarkson N. Potter, 1966), pp. 5–6, 17–18.

80 Indian Influence on Frontier Life: A Check on the Turner Thesis

That at first the frontiersmen had to live like the Indians in order to survive is one of the points made by historian Frederick Jackson Turner, in his seminal book on the frontier, which grew out of an essay he wrote after reading a passage in the census report of 1890 which announced the end of the frontier. The key remarks of Turner on this subject are given below, followed by testimony from early observations which appears to support this part of his conclusions.

The wilderness masters the colonist. It finds him a European in dress, industries, tools, modes of travel, and thought. It takes him from the railroad car and puts him in the birch canoe. It strips off the garments of civilization and arrays him in the hunting shirt and the moccasin. It puts him in the log cabin of the Cherokee and Iroquois and runs an Indian palisade around him. Before long he has gone to planting Indian corn and plowing with a sharp stick; he shouts the war cry and takes the scalp in orthodox Indian fashion. In short, at the frontier the environment is at first too strong for the man. He must accept the conditions which it furnishes, or perish, and so he fits himself into the Indian clearings and follows the

Indian trails. Little by little he transforms the wilderness, but the outcome is not the old Europe. . . . The fact is, that here is a new product that is American.

FREDERICK JACKSON TURNER, *The Frontier in American History* (New York: Henry Holt & Co., 1958), p. 4.

Indian Medicine: Maryland, 1635

ANDREW WHITE

This Countrey affords naturally many excellent things for Physicke and Surgery, the perfect use of which, the *English* cannot yet learne from the Natives: They have a roote which is an excellent preservative against Poyson, called by the English, the *Snake roote*. Other herbes and rootes they have, wherewith they cure all manner of woundes; also *Saxafras, Gummes,* and *Balsum.* An *Indian* seeing one of the *English,* much troubled with the tooth-ake, fetched of the roote of a tree, and gave the party some of it to hold in his mouth, and it eased the pain presently. They have other rootes fit for dyes, wherewith they make colours to paint themselves.

[ANDREW WHITE] *A Relation of Maryland* (Ann Arbor: University Microfilms, 1966), p. 17.

Indian Corn Used as Money, Massachusetts Bay, 1630s

JOHN WINTHROP

. . . so now as all our money was drained from us, and cattle and all commodities grew very cheap, which enforced us at the next general court, in the 8th month, to make an order, that corn should pass in payment of new debts; Indian at 4s. the bushel . . .

Winthrop's Journal: History of New England 1630–1649, ed. by J. K. Hosmer (2 vols.; New York: Barnes & Noble, 1953), II, 6.

Indian Wampum Used as Money, 1700s

JOHN LAWSON

Their money is of different sorts, but all made of Shells, which are found on the Coast of Carolina, which are very large and hard, so that they are very difficult to cut. Some English Smiths have tried to drill this sort of Shell-Money, and there by thought to get an Advantage; but it proved so hard, that nothing could be gained. . . . the general and current Species [*Specie?*] of all the Indians in Carolina, and, I believe, all over the Continent, as far as the Bay of Mexico, is that which we call Peak and Ronoak;

but Peak more especially. This is that which at New York, they call Wampum, and have used it as current Money amongst the Inhabitants for a great many Years.

JOHN LAWSON, *History of North Carolina* [1708] (Richmond: Garrett & Massie, 1951), pp. 204–5.

Imitation of Indian Customs, Canada, 1750

PETER KALM

Though many nations imitate the French customs, I observed, on the contrary, that the French in Canada in many respects follow the customs of the Indians, with whom they have constant relations. They use the tobacco pipes, shoes, garters, and girdles of the Indians. They follow the Indian way of waging war exactly; they mix the same things with their tobacco; they make use of the Indian bark boats and row them in the Indian way; they wrap a square piece of cloth around their feet, instead of stockings, and have adopted many other Indian fashions.

Peter Kalm's Travels in North America, ed. by Adolph Benson (2 vols.; New York: Wilson-Erickson, Inc., 1937), II, 511.

Europeans Become Like Indians

PETER KALM

The Swedes themselves were accused of being already half Indians when the English arrived in the year 1682. And we still see that the French, English, Germans, Dutch, and other Europeans, who have lived for several years in distant provinces, near and among the Indians, grow so like them in their behavior and thought that they can only be distinguished by the difference of their color.

Ibid., I, 226.

Indian Hominy and Maple Sugar as Food: Northern Lakes, 1763

ALEXANDER HENRY

The village of L'Arbre Croche [*Ottawa Indian settlement near present Petoskey, Mich.*] supplied, as I have said, the maize, or Indian corn, with which the canoes are victualled. This species of grain is prepared for use, by boiling it in a strong lie, after which the husk may be easily removed; and it is next mashed and dried. In this state, it is soft and friable, like rice. The allowance, for each man, on the voyage, is a quart a day; and a bushel with two pounds of prepared fat, is reckoned to be a month's subsistence.

No other allowance is made, of any kind; not even of salt; and bread is never thought of. The men, nevertheless, are healthy and capable of performing their heavy labour.

[*Michipicoten Island, L. Superior*] Sugar-making continued till the twelfth of May. On the mountain, we eat nothing but our sugar, during the whole period. Each man consumed a pound a day, desired no other food, and was visibly nourished by it.

> ALEXANDER HENRY, *Travels and Adventures in Canada* (Ann Arbor: University Microfilms, 1966), pp. 52, 218.

Indian Trails, Southern Michigan, 1830

CATHERINE STEWART

Riding through this section of country, one is led to admire the power of intuition, or rather the close observation of the Indian, when viewing the trail along side of the road, which served as a guide to the commissioners when laying it off, a distance of 300 miles from Detroit to Chicago. These trails were made by the Sauk and Fox Indians, on their journeyings to Malden, where they were lured for many years, by annual presents or bribes from the English.

> CATHERINE STEWART, *New Homes in the West* (Ann Arbor: University Microfilms, 1966), p. 7.

The Indian Look Among Lead Miners, Southwest Wisconsin, 1831

MRS. JOHN H. KINZIE

. . . They were the roughest-looking set of men I ever beheld, and their language was as uncouth as their persons. They wore hunting-shirts, trowsers, and moccasins of deer-skin, the former being ornamented at the seams with a fringe of the same, while a colored belt around the Waist, in which was stuck a large hunting-knife, gave each the appearance of a brigand.

> MRS. JOHN H. KINZIE, *Wau-Bun, the Early Day in the Northwest* (Chicago: Rand McNally & Co., 1901), p. 118.

Imitation of Indian Architecture, New Mexico, 1830s

JOSIAH GREGG

In architecture, the people do not seem to have arrived at any great perfection, but rather to have conformed themselves to the clumsy style which prevailed among the aborigines, than to waste their time in studying modern masonry and the use of lime. The materials generally used for building are of the crudest possible description; consisting of unburnt bricks . . . laid in mortar of mere clay and sand. These bricks are called *adobes*, and every edifice, from the church to the *palacio*, is constructed of the same stuff.

> Gregg's "Commerce of the Prairies," in Reuben G. Thwaites, ed., *Early Western Travels* (32 vols.; Cleveland: Arthur H. Clark Co., 1904), XIX, 334.

81 Political Party Platform Planks Relating to Indians

It is almost trite to say that there is a wide gap between the promises of party platforms and the performance of the parties when they are in power. This is especially true when there is no powerful pressure being applied to ensure compliance with pledges made. The Indians in the nineteenth century were still a military adversary, and when the conquest was completed, they remained isolated, demoralized, few in numbers, and devoid of powerful white support. They were therefore ignored in party platforms until recently, when, in consequence of their now growing numbers and increased use of the suffrage, they have captured some attention. Indian planks in party platforms, however, are rarely to be viewed as forecasts of changing policies, but rather as pitches for votes. This may soon change, as Indians are beginning to develop some political muscle. Indians hold a potential balance of power in Alaska, Arizona, and some other states. Several Indians are now members of state legislatures, one was until recently a member of Congress, and prominent white politicians are often seen touring Indian communities and championing Indian causes.

No party platforms were adopted before 1840. Indians were not mentioned in any platform until 1872, when the Republican party claimed that it had "initiated a wise and humane policy toward the Indians." Incredibly, fifty-four years elapsed before Indians were again mentioned in any major party platform. Indians were likewise ignored by all minor parties until 1948, save for a brief mention in the American Prohibition platform of 1884.

In contrast to the long blackout of Indian Americans by our political parties, there was frequently expressed concern for other oppressed minorities at home and abroad—but particularly abroad, where the government was incapable of acting. In 1892 both the Republican and Democratic platforms expressed sympathy for the Irish home rule movement and for the Jews being persecuted in Russia, but were silent concerning outrages against the Indians, even though the massacre at Wounded Knee, South

Dakota, was a fresh memory. Four years later both parties extended their sympathy to the Cuban independence movement, and the nation soon went to war ostensibly to aid it, among other reasons. The Republicans went further and condemned the massacre of Armenians (in Turkey) and lynchings in the United States—often committed in states governed by the opposite party. The Fusion Faction of the Populists declared moral support for the Boers of South Africa in 1900. The Republican party in 1908 devoted a paragraph to the rights of American Negroes, who had been virtually forgotten since the bargain of 1876. Lynching was denounced by the Republican party in 1920. All parties were silent about all minorities in 1924 (the Progressives were no exception), but in 1928 the Democrats again sympathized with the Armenians, while the Republicans again denounced lynching, and for the first time included a paragraph on Indian rights, which was the precursor of reforms to come, in itself an unusual fact, since platforms are so often forgotten. In 1932 the Republican concern for Indians was reduced to one sentence, while the Negroes got a paragraph. The Democrats said nothing about any minority in 1932 or 1936, while the Republicans briefly mentioned Negroes and Indians each time.

In 1940, the Democrats for the first time in their history devoted some attention to Indians and Negroes, allotting a paragraph in the platform to each group. Both minorities were again briefly mentioned by the Republicans. In 1944 only the Republicans mentioned Indians, but the Democrats confined themselves to a few words about Jewish rights—in Palestine. In 1948 the Indians were omitted from the platform of both major parties, but were included in the minority rights plank of the Progressives, the first minor party platform to mention Indians since 1884. The Democrats, however, in response to the Henry Wallace threat and the growing civil rights movement, adopted a strong civil rights program, and from that day until now, civil rights planks have proliferated and expanded at each quadrennial convention of the parties. The Indians have been included as well: from 1952 to 1968 both major parties have included an Indian plank in every platform, except for the year 1964, when the Republican party, aiming for Southern support, omitted mention of all ethnic minorities. Some of the civil rights planks which have become common in party platforms since 1948, though mainly directed to the black constituency, may be construed to apply to Indians and other minorities as well.

This brief summary of the material which follows seems to bear out the often heard claim that parties do not take a stand on any issue until that issue has become of burning importance to a significant voting bloc, and a stand does not often lead to action. Even the record of minor parties, often credited with initiating issues before they are popular, is not creditable where Indians are concerned, although those of the left preceded the major parties in their concern for Negro rights, and the Socialist party was the only one to condemn the wartime evacuation of the West Coast Japanese.

One generalization about American political parties which may perhaps be underscored by all this is that our parties do not lead, they react.

[Regular] Republican Platform, 1872

It [*the party*] has steadily decreased with firm hand the resultant disorders of a great war, and initiated a wise and humane policy toward the Indians.

American Prohibition National Platform, 1884 [a splinter from the regular Prohibition Party]

We hold that the civil equality secured to all American citizens by Arts. 13, 14, and 15 of our amended National Constitution should be preserved inviolate, and the same equality should be extended to Indians and Chinamen.

[There was no further mention of Indians in any party platform, major or minor, until:]

Republican Platform, 1928

Our Indian Citizens

National citizenship was conferred on all native-born Indians in the United States by the General Indian Enfranchisement Act of 1924. We favor the creation of a Commission to be appointed by the President including one or more Indian citizens to investigate and report to Congress upon the existing system of the administration of Indian affairs and to report any inconsistencies that may be found to exist between that system and the rights of the Indian citizens of the United States. We also favor the repeal of any law and the termination of any administrative practice which may be inconsistent with Indian citizenship, to the end that the Federal guardianship existing over the persons and properties of Indian tribal communities may not work a prejudice to the personal and property rights of Indian citizens of the United States. The treaty and property rights of the Indians of the United States must be guaranteed to them.

◈

Republican Platform, 1932

We favor the fullest protection of the property rights of the American Indians and the provision for them of adequate educational facilities.

Republican Platform, 1936

To our Indian population we pledge every effort on the part of the national government to ameliorate living conditions for them.

Democratic Platform, 1940

We favor and pledge the enactment of legislation creating an Indian Claims Commission for the special purpose of entertaining and investigating claims presented by Indian groups, bands, and tribes, in order that our Indian citizens may have their claims against the Government considered, adjusted, and finally settled at the earliest possible date.

Republican Platform, 1940

We pledge an immediate and final settlement of all Indian claims between the government and the Indian citizenship of the nation.

Republican Platform, 1944

We pledge an immediate, just and final settlement of all Indian claims between the Government and the Indian citizenship of the Nation. We will take politics out of the administration of Indian affairs.

Progressive (Henry Wallace) Platform, 1948

We demand that Indians, the earliest Americans, be given full citizenship rights without loss of reservation rights and be permitted to administer their own affairs.

We will develop special programs to raise the low standards of health, housing, and educational facilities for Negroes, Indians, and nationality groups, and will deny Federal funds to any state or local authority which withholds opportunities or benefits for reasons of race, creed, color, sex, or national origin.

Democratic Platform, 1952

We shall continue to use the powers of the Federal government to advance the health, education and economic well-being of our American Indian citizens, without impairing their cultural traditions. We pledge our support to the cause of fair and equitable treatment in all matters essential to and desirable for their individual and tribal welfare.

The American Indian should be completely integrated into the social, economic and political life of the nation. To that end we shall move to secure the prompt final settlement of Indian claims and to remove restrictions on the rights of Indians individually and through their tribal councils to handle their own fiscal affairs.

We favor the repeal of all acts or regulations that deny to Indians rights or privileges held by citizens generally.

Progressive Platform, 1952

Full citizenship for the American Indians and the right to administer their own affairs without loss of Reservation rights. Adequate compensation for loss of tribal land rights.

Republican Platform, 1952

All Indians are citizens of the United States and no longer should be denied full enjoyment of their rights of citizenship.

We shall eliminate the existing shameful waste by the Bureau of Indian Affairs which has obstructed the accomplishment of our national responsibility for improving the condition of our Indian friends. We pledge to undertake programs to provide the Indians with equal opportunities for education, health protection and economic development.

The next Republican Administration will welcome the advice and counsel of Indian leaders in selecting the Indian Commissioner.

Democratic Platform, 1956

Recognizing that all American Indians are citizens of the United States and of the States in which they reside, and acknowledging that the Federal Government has a unique legal and moral responsibility for Indians which is imposed by the Constitution and spelled out in treaties, statutes and court decisions, we pledge:

Prompt adoption of a Federal program to assist Indian tribes in the full development of their human and natural resources, and to advance the health, education and economic well-being of Indian citizens, preserving their traditions without impairing their cultural heritage.

No alteration of any treaty or other Federal-Indian contractual relationships without the free consent of the Indian tribes concerned; reversal of the present policies which are tending toward erosion of Indian rights, reduction of their economic base through alienation of their lands, and repudiation of Federal responsibility;

Prompt and expeditious settlement of Indian claims against the United States, with full recognition of the rights of both parties; and

Elimination of all impediments to full citizenship for American Indians.

Republican Platform, 1956

We shall continue to pursue our enlightened policies which are now producing exceptional advances in the long struggle to help the American Indian gain the material and social advantages of his birthright and citizenship, while maintaining to the fullest extent the cultural integrity of the various tribal groups.

We commend the present administration for its progressive programs which have achieved such striking progress in preparing our Indian citizens for participation in normal community life. Health, educational and employment opportunities for Indians have been greatly expanded beyond any previous level, and we favor still further extensions of these programs.

We favor most sympathetic and constructive execution of the Federal trusteeship over Indian affairs, always in full consultation with Indians in the management of their interests and the expansion of their rights of self-government in local and tribal affairs.

We urge the prompt adjudication or settlement of pending Indian claims.

Democratic Platform, 1960

We recognize the unique legal and moral responsibility of the Federal Government for Indians in restitution for the injustice that has sometimes been done them. We therefore pledge prompt adoption of a program to assist Indian tribes in the full development of their human and natural resources and to advance the health, education, and economic well-being of Indian citizens while preserving their cultural heritage.

Free consent of the Indian tribes concerned shall be required before the Federal Government makes any change in any Federal-Indian treaty or other contractual relationship.

The New Democratic Administration will bring competent, sympathetic, and dedicated leadership to the administration of Indian affairs which will end practices that have eroded Indian rights and resources, reduced the Indians' land base and repudiated Federal responsibility. Indian claims against the United States can and will be settled promptly, whether by negotiation or other means, in the best interests of both parties.

Republican Platform, 1960

As recently as 1953, thirty per cent of Indian school-age children were unable to obtain an education. Through Republican efforts, this fall, for the first time in history, every eligible Indian child will be able to attend an elementary school. Having accomplished this, we will now accelerate our efforts to open up both secondary and higher education opportunities for every qualified Indian youth.

As a result of a stepped-up health program there has been a marked decrease in death rates from tuberculosis and in the infant mortality rate. Also substantial progress has been made in the modernization of health facilities. We pledge continued progress in this area.

We are opposed to precipitous termination of the federal Indian trusteeship responsibility, and pledge not to support any termination plan for any tribe which has not approved such action.

Socialist Platform, 1960

We are opposed to the current effort to deprive American Indians of their remaining community lands and resources. Premature and enforced assimilation of Indians into the dominant culture is no answer to their special problems. No major programs affecting Indians should be launched without the free consent of the tribes or bands involved. As a first step to alleviate sufferings and amend ancient wrongs, we endorse the proposal of the National Congress of American Indians, for a "Point Four" program for Indians.

Democratic Platform, 1964

We will: . . . Assist our Indian people to improve their standard of living and attain self-sufficiency, the privileges of equal citizenship, and full participation in American life.

In 1960, we pledged—

"Prompt adoption of a program to assist Indian tribes in the full development of their human and natural resources and to advance the health, education and economic well-being of Indian citizens while preserving their cultural heritage."

In these 3½ years:

New classrooms have been provided for more than 7,000 Indian children; summer educational programs have been expanded tenfold so they now serve more than 20,000 students; and a special institute to train artistically gifted Indian youth has been established.

Indian enrollment in vocational training programs has been doubled.

For the first time in history, Federal low-rent housing programs have been launched on Indian reservations, and more than 3,100 new housing units have now been authorized.

Industrial plants offering employment opportunities for thousands of Indians are being opened on Indian reservations.

Accelerated Public Works projects on 89 reservations in 21 states have provided nearly 30,000 man-months of employment.

The Vocational Education Act and the Adult Indian Vocational Training Act have been amended to provide improved training for Indians.

[*The Republican platform of 1964 did not mention Indians.*]

Republican Platform, 1968

The plight of American Indians and Eskimos is a national disgrace. Contradictory Government policies have led to intolerable deprivation for these citizens. We dedicate ourselves to the promotion of policies responsive to their needs and desires and will seek the full participation of these people and their leaders in the formulation of such policies.

Democratic Platform, 1968

The American Indian has the oldest claim on our national conscience. We must continue and increase Federal help in the Indian's battle against poverty, unemployment, illiteracy, ill health and poor housing. To this end, we pledge a new and equal Federal-Indian partnership that will enable Indian communities to provide for themselves many services now furnished by the Federal Government and Federal sponsorship of industrial development programs, owned, managed and run by Indians. We support a quick and fair settlement of the land claims of Indians, Eskimo and Aleut citizens of Alaska.

From Kirk H. Porter and Donald B. Johnson, *National Party Platforms 1840–1964* (Urbana: University of Illinois Press, 1964). Platforms of 1968 taken from *The New York Times*.

82 Representation of Contemporary Indians in the Legislature of the State of Maine

[Maine is the only state which provides for Indian representation.]

DEPARTMENT OF STATE
State of Maine
Augusta

December 17, 1964

Mr. Virgil J. Vogel

Dear Mr. Vogel:
This will acknowledge receipt of your recent letter with reference to the Indians of Maine.

Election of the two Indian representatives to the State Legislature is provided for in the Revised Statutes in Chapter 25.

Section 370 provides: "Biennially on the even-numbered years, on the 1st Tuesday of September, the Penobscot Indians shall hold their election for the choice of Governor and Lieutenant Governor of said tribe, and a representative of the legislature of this state . . . "

Section 371 provides: "Biennially on the even-numbered years, on the 1st Tuesday of November, the Passamaquoddy tribe of Indians shall hold their election for the choice of governor and lieutenant governor of each reservation of said tribe, a representative at the legislature of this state . . . The representative at the legislature of this state shall be chosen alternately between the 2 reservations. . . ."

We trust this information may be of assistance to you in writing your book on the influence of the Indians on the American life.

Very truly yours,
[signature]

Joseph T. Edgar
Deputy Secretary of State

83 "We Put the Feathers On"

ROBERT P. TRISTRAM COFFIN

The ash bow broke, the tepee fell,
And the Indian was gone.
In history books they tell such lies,
The Red Man lives—we put him on!

We slipped his eyes like diamond stones
Into our tired Old World eyes,
Crept through a continent of woods
Wise as the panther-cat is wise.

We took over the eye that flew
Along the arrow to the deer,
We put on the hunter's foot,
We put on the hunter's ear.

On our pale skins we slipped the skin
Brown and bare, alive to the breath
Of every wind that blows, to run
The narrow path between life and death.

We bent down to the bob-cat's crouch,
Took color from the butternut tree,
At Saratoga, Lexington,
We fought like Indians and went free.

We put our lips to maple boles
And drink the sweet strong woodland milk,
We feed our Indian muscles and bones
On golden food that stands in silk.

We eat the smoke the Red Men ate,
Softer than the clouds' light fleece,
The food that buries care and hate
Coming from the pipe of peace.

We even put the pow-wow on,
We dance the night before we fight,
Republicans, Democrats, football teams
With red-hot songs build up their might.

When little boys fill up with Spring
So full their seams are fit to rip,
They throw their voice high in their throat,
The old warwhoop springs from their lip.

We put on white thunderclouds,
We put on the eagle's feather,

The brotherhood with the buffalo,
The brotherhood with wind and weather.

We are brothers of the sun,
Moon and stars, the beaver, snake.
We shall need the eagle's feathers
The high long journey that we take.

From *Primer for America* by Robert P. Tristram Coffin
(New York: The Macmillan Co., 1943), pp. 54–55.

84 "Indian Names"

LYDIA HUNTLEY SIGOURNEY

Ye say they all have passed away
    That noble race and brave
That their light canoes have vanished
    From off the crested wave;
That 'mid the forests where they roamed,
    There rings no hunter's shout;
But their name is on your waters
    Ye may not wash it out.

'Tis where Ontario's billow
    Like ocean's surge is curled
Where strong Niagara's thunders wake
    The echo of the world;
Where red Missouri bringeth
    Rich tribute from the West,
And Rappahannock sweetly sleeps
    On green Virginia's breast.

Ye say their conelike cabins,
    That clustered o'er the vale,
Have fled away like withered leaves
    Before the autumn's gale;
But their memory liveth on your hills,
    Their baptism on your shore;
Your everlasting rivers speak
    Their dialect of yore.

Old Massachusetts wears it
　　Within her lordly crown
And broad Ohio bears it
　　'Mid all her young reknown;
Connecticut has wreathed it
　　Where her quiet foliage waves,
And bold Kentucky breathes it hoarse,
　　Through all her ancient caves.

Wachusett hides its lingering voice
　　Within his rocky heart,
And Allegheny graves its tone
　　Throughout his lofty chart;
Monadnock on his forehead hoar
　　Doth seal the sacred trust;
Your mountains build their monument,
　　Though ye destroy their dust.

LYDIA HUNTLEY SIGOURNEY (1791–1865), in *America History in Verse,* ed. by Burton Stevenson (Boston: Houghton-Mifflin Co., 1932), pp. 345–47.

85　"I Love a People . . . ," 1867

GEORGE CATLIN

George Catlin, noted painter of Western Indians, attacked the fur-trading companies which, with the cooperation of Indian agents, illegally brought whiskey into the Indian country, using it as a principal currency in buying buffalo hides. He predicted that the extinction of the buffalo was approaching, and with it, the end of the Indians who depended on it for a livelihood. Denounced in some quarters as an "Indian lover," Catlin responded, in his last book, with the remarks which follow. Sometimes called Catlin's "Indian creed," they have been widely reprinted, but often in abridged form.

For the above prophecy and *"unjust attack upon the Fur Company,"* I have had some unfriendly denunciations by the press, and by those critics I have been reproachfully designated the *"Indian-loving Catlin."* What of this? What have I to answer? Have I any apology to make for loving the Indians? The Indians have always loved me, and why should I not love the Indians?

I love the people who have always made me welcome to the best they had.

I love a people who are honest without laws, who have no jails and no poor-houses.

I love a people who keep the commandments without ever having read them or heard them preached from the pulpit.

I love a people who never swear, who never take the name of God in vain.

I love a people who "love their neighbours as they love themselves."

I love a people who worship God without a Bible, for I believe that God loves them also.

I love the people whose religion is all the same, and who are free from religious animosities.

I love the people who never have raised a hand against me, or stolen my property, where there was no law to punish for either.

I love the people who never have fought a battle with white man,[1] except on their own ground.

I love and don't fear mankind where God has made and left them, for there they are children.

I love a people who live and keep what is their own without locks and keys.

I love all people who do the best they can. And oh, how I love a people who don't live for the love of money!

It has been sneeringly said that I have "spoken too well of the Indians," (better to speak too well of them than not to speak well enough)—"that I have flattered them"—(better to *flatter* them than to *caricature* them; there have been enough to do this). If I have overdone their character, they have had in *me one friend,* at least; and I will not shrink from the sin and responsibility of it.

GEORGE CATLIN, *Last Rambles Amongst the Indians of the Rocky Mountains and the Andes* (New York: D. Appleton & Co., 1867), pp. 354–55.

86 Why They Remain Indians, 1967

DEAN A. CRAWFORD, DAVID L. PETERSON, AND VIRGIL WURR

Casual visitors to an Indian community are apt to be so impressed by the external signs of poverty that they frequently wonder why so many Indians choose to remain there. It is not that they enjoy the poverty, but

1. men?

that they are attached to certain intangible values of their community life that are lost in the urban environment. They feel that we pay too high a price for our comforts. The following document tries to explain this feeling.

We are frequently asked about life on, or near, a Minnesota Indian reservation, in ways that suggest that the person asking the question is baffled that anyone might prefer such a life. Yet many Indian people are equally baffled about the supposed attractiveness of living in a high-density populated area. Let us consider, for a moment, the way in which a "reservation Indian" might view the life of the middle-class urban dweller. He might ask *you* many questions about your life.

Why are you so materialistic? Must you always judge other human beings on the basis of their acquisition of worldly goods? Why do you measure success in terms of dollars? We don't have that kind of status-seeking or "keeping up with the Joneses" on the reservation.

Aren't you a lot busier than you need to be? It seems you are caught up in so many unimportant little tasks, running errands, hurrying from one meeting to the next, continually watching the clock. Don't you belong to too many organizations? In fact, isn't your whole life over-organized? We avoid getting caught in the "rat race" by living as we do.

Haven't you gotten to the point of being *too* competitive? Don't lots of folks get hurt in your struggle for success at someone else's expense? Isn't there a lot of pressure to excel, to do better than "the next guy" in business, in education, in your social relations, even in recreation? We don't play that kind of oneupsmanship very much where I live.

Why can't you seem to relax? Why do even little frustrations and setbacks upset you so seriously? Can't you learn to accept the facets of life that you're incapable of changing? And what about your complaints of boredom? Your housewife is bored, your teenagers are bored, even your exalted steady wage-earner complains about wanting to "get out of the rut."

What about the impersonality of the big city? Wouldn't you feel better if you knew your neighbors better? How can you possibly stand to live in a crowded set of houses with little privacy; or, worse yet, in an apartment development, like a bee in a hive? And speaking of bees, don't you show a longing to get back in closer touch with nature? We chuckle at the man who works himself to a frazzle in order to afford a quiet spot in the country for his vacations or for a retirement home.

Whatever happened to your individuality? It seems as if the middle-class city dwellers all dress alike, talk alike and punish anyone who doesn't conform. Isn't that the meaning of the complaints about "the organization man" or "the man in the grey flannel suit"? Can't you keep from interfering in the lives of other people? Why don't you "let your hair down" and just be yourself? We'd let you live like that on the reservation.

And so, many Indian people look at the city and wonder, "Why would anyone want to live like that?" And many non-Indians look at the reservation and ask the same question. Of course, most people feel a certain nostalgia for the neighborhood [of] their youth. They would like either to live there as adults or to visit there from time to time. Even though people are highly mobile today, travel is costly and many Indian people cannot afford the weekly or monthly trip to "the cabin" or "the old home town" or "to visit the folks." It is both convenient and reassuring to live close to relatives and close to familiar scenes.

One Indian man of our acquaintance describes his feelings about this eloquently. He has saleable skills that have enabled him successfully to live and work in several non-Indian communities in past years. As a serviceman he traveled abroad and extensively in this country. Yet, he says, no matter how interesting or happy his life away from the reservation, he "always felt homesick" for the woods and lakes of northern Minnesota. Surely anyone can understand how he feels about *home,* regardless of one's own attitude toward the North Woods.

DEAN A. CRAWFORD, DAVID L. PETERSON, and VIRGIL WURR,
Minnesota Chippewa Indians, A Handbook for Teachers
(St. Paul: Upper Midwest Regional Educational Laboratory,
1967), pp. 14–15.

87 The Indian in American History, 1968

VIRGIL J. VOGEL

There is a growing interest in the maltreatment of Indians in American history books, and especially in textbooks. It is hardly necessary to expand here on the consequences of such deformed history: the creation or reinforcement of feelings of racial arrogance, and the disgorgement from our schools of students with a warped understanding of their cultural heritage, with no comprehension of the revolutionary changes taking place in the world, and no intellectual equipment for dealing with the problems of race relations here and abroad.

Historians have used four principal methods to create or perpetuate false impressions of aboriginal Americans, namely: *obliteration, defamation, disembodiment,* and *disparagement.* Often the four methods overlap and interlace with one another. Their use does not necessarily flow from conscious malice. More probably, they result from confinement within the narrow limits of the discipline, unfamiliarity with the other social sciences, and the mindsets and assumptions imposed by the historian's own cultural background. The following remarks are based on an examination of more than a hundred books, mainly, but not entirely, designed for use as history texts. Space will permit citing only a few which typify the attitudes we seek to illustrate.

Obliteration

Perhaps the chief problem in the historical treatment of American Indians and other minorities is not the biased presentation, but the blackout. We remember that in George Orwell's novel, *1984,* the names of politically disgraced persons were eradicated from the history books. In the language of *newspeak,* they became *unpersons.* To some historians, the American Indian is an unperson, or nearly so. Incredible as it may seem, there are American history books in which the aborigines are nearly or even totally consigned to oblivion. Much of our history has been written by the scribes of the conquerors in the interest of glorification of the winners, and there is little that is glorious in the way they won.

During the nineteenth century the early extermination of the Indian was freely predicted, and even advocated. It is a persistent theme in commentaries of the period, of which Francis Parkman serves as a typical example:

Their intractable, unchanging character leaves no alternative than their gradual extinction, or the abandonment of the western world to eternal barbarism; and of this and similar plans . . . it may alike be said that sentimental philanthropy will find it easier to cavil at than to amend them.[1]

Although these genocidal aims fell short of accomplishment, the historical obliteration of the Indian was more nearly successful. The treatment of the Jackson era is a revealing case study. One of the cruelest ordeals of the American Indian occurred during the administration of Andrew Jackson and his immediate successor, Martin Van Buren, when more than 125,000 of them were dragged from their homes and deported west of the Mississippi by military force. The "treaties" which preceded these expulsions (ninety-four of them in Jackson's time) were masterpieces of intimidation, bribery, threats, misrepresentation, force, and fraud. Following these efforts to produce a fig leaf of legality for the operation, Indians were hunted down like animals, bound as prisoners, and confined in stockades to await removal. The conditions of the deportation were so barbarous that about one third of the émigrés died on the journey. In the few cases where

1. Parkman, *The Conspiracy of Pontiac* (New York: E. P. Dutton, 1908), II, p. 101.

open resistance was encountered, as with Black Hawk's Sauks, the defiant Indians were massacred.

Jackson also made a farce of the separation of powers in the federal scheme when it did not suit his ends, by encouraging Georgia to violate solemn treaties and to defy the decisions of the Supreme Court in the Cherokee cases. He denied the support of the executive arm to carry out the decisions, while simultaneously threatening to use force against the tariff nullifiers in South Carolina.

Surely such episodes in Old Hickory's administration deserve as much attention as his Maysville veto or his Specie Circular. Yet, in the most widely touted book on the period, *The Age of Jackson,* by Arthur M. Schlesinger, Jr., there is not one word about the "Trail of Tears" and the "Trail of Death."

To draw the curtain over unpleasant happenings in history is not less to be deplored than conscious falsification. The selectivity of the historian is revealing. If omitted events are of a sort which would dampen the impression the writer seeks to create, we are getting historical fiction, for only novelists can take such liberties. Silence cannot save us from the stain of our Indian policies. Mr. Carleton Beals believed that our acquiescence in Indian dispossession has molded the American character:

Has not this perhaps led us into demanding no proper accounting from public servants so long as they feed us righteous pap . . . ? Perfect training for later financial plundering . . . the whole ethic of later corporation growth and monopoly—here in the Indian struggle is to be observed the whole American psychology of getting something for nothing, or at most for a little trickery.[2]

Schlesinger has not been exceptional in shutting his eyes to the tragedy of Indian removal. Edward Channing in the nineteenth century praised the Christian concern of the colonists for the Indians' welfare, but his *History of the United States* says nothing about Jackson's Indian policy.[3] Charles and Mary Beard, although seemingly free of racial bias, ignored it in three separate works.[4] W. E. Woodward was blind to Indian removal for, like the Beards, he did not mention Indians in any event later than the year of 1818.[5] Francis Butler Simkins, in his history of the South,[6] also remained silent. Like others, he managed to discuss South Carolina's quarrel with Jackson over nullification without linking it with the Indian nullification

2. Beals, *American Earth* (Philadelphia: J. B. Lippincott, 1939), pp. 63–64.

3. New York: Macmillan, 1928.

4. *The Making of American Civilization* (New York: Macmillan, 1938); *Basic History of the United States* (Philadelphia: Blakiston, 1944); and *The Rise of American Civilization* (New York: Macmillan, 1956).

5. Woodward, *A New American History* (New York: Garden City Publishing Co., 1938).

6. Simkins, *The South, Old and New* (New York: Alfred A. Knopf, 1947).

policy of Georgia, with which it was not only contemporaneous, but in the opinion of Commager, Dodd, and others, entirely comparable.[7] Harold Syrett's Jacksonian documents include none of the Tennessean's messages on Indian removal.[8] Carl Becker failed altogether to mention Indians in his book, *The United States, Experiment in Democracy.*[9]

The Indians of the Old Northwest, who were somewhat less acculturated than their southern brethren, put up a stiffer fight against despoliation. In the 1790s an alliance of these tribes, led by Little Turtle, soundly whipped two armies under Josiah Harmar and Arthur St. Clair before they finally succumbed to Anthony Wayne at Fallen Timbers, and signed the Treaty of Greenville in 1795. A random sampling of ten textbooks (one elementary, one junior high, six senior high, and two college) revealed that these struggles were entirely ignored in half of them, and two others mentioned only Wayne's victory but not the Indian victories preceding it. For some reason Tecumseh, whose efforts to create Indian solidarity were destroyed by Harrison in 1811, has captured the interest of several historians, but almost none of them mention the fate of the Indians in this region after the War of 1812.

Disembodiment

This school acknowledged the existence of the Indian, but only as a subhuman nomad, a part of the fauna belonging to the wilderness yet to be conquered; in short, a troublesome *obstacle* to be overcome. "We may guess," wrote the Puritan preacher Cotton Mather, "that probably the devil decoyed those miserable savages hither, in hopes that the gospel of the Lord Jesus Christ would never come here to destroy or disturb his *absolute empire* over them."[10] No moral restraint was required in dealing with them. As late as 1872, this attitude found voice in remarks of U.S. Indian Commissioner Francis Walker:

With wild men, as with wild beasts, the question of whether in a given situation one shall fight, coax, or run, is a question merely of what is easiest and safest.[11]

7. Samuel E. Morison and Henry S. Commager, *The Growth of the American Republic* (2 vols.; New York: Oxford University Press, 1962), I, 489; William E. Dodd, *Expansion and Conflict* (Boston: Houghton Mifflin Co., 1915), pp. 87–89. See also Woodrow Wilson, *Division and Reunion* (New York: Longmans Green & Co., 1932), pp. 37–40.
8. Syrett, *Andrew Jackson, His Contribution to the American Tradition* (Indianapolis: Bobbs Merrill, 1953).
9. New York: Harper & Brothers, 1920.
10. Mather in *Magnalia Christi Americana,* quoted in Alden T. Vaughan, *New England Frontier* (Boston: Little, Brown & Co., 1965), p. 20.
11. Quoted in Jack D. Forbes, ed., *The Indian in America's Past* (Englewood Cliffs, N.J.: Prentice-Hall, 1964), p. 113.

Accepting the definition of the Indian as less than human, William Bradford in 1620 considered New England to be uninhabited:

. . . the vast and unpeopled countries of America, which are fruitfull & fitt for habitation, being devoyd of all civil inhabitants, where there are only savage & brutish men, which range up and downe, litle otherwise than the wild beasts of the same.[12]

John Smith urged the enslavement of the "viperous brood," which had earlier, he admitted, saved Jamestown from starvation.[13] Benjamin Trumbull held that "as Connecticut abounded in wild animals, so it did also with wild and savage men."[14] If Indians were defined as a kind of animal, it was proper to hunt them as such, and bounties were offered for their scalps, just as for those of wolves.[15] On the far western frontier in the nineteenth century, Indian flesh was eaten, like game.[16]

The view of the Indian as a wild beast in the path of civilization has never died. It was a dominant theme in the treatment of Indians by historians until quite recently. It still lurks in history books in phrases like "Indian menace," "Indian peril," "savage barrier," and "obstacle to settlement." Harold U. Faulkner, in his otherwise commendable book, *American Political and Social History,*[17] listed some cultural contributions of the Indian, but kept old stereotypes alive by calling the Virginia frontier "a constant source of trouble." Indians and loyalists carried on "cruel border warfare" during the Revolutionary War, and the frontier generally was "a red line of cruelty." One of the persistent faults in many historians is the inability to see that the whites were also a constant source of trouble to the Indians, and that the Indians, too, were often innocent victims of "cruel

12. Bradford, *Of Plymouth Plantation* (New York: Capricorn Books, 1962), p. 40.

13. L. G. Tyler, ed., *Narratives of Early Virginia* (New York: Scribner's, 1907), pp. 37–41, 360, 364 ff. "Our provision being now within twentie dayes spent, the Indians brought us great store both of Corne and bread ready made," is one of several tributes Smith earlier paid to Indian generosity.

14. Trumbull, *A Complete History of Connecticut, 1630–1764* (New London: H. D. Utley, 1898), p. 21.

15. On scalp bounties, see Emerson Hough, *The Passing of the Frontier* (New Haven: Yale University Press, 1893), p. 134; Bancroft, *History,* I, 128–29; M. W. Stirling, *National Geographic Magazine,* November, 1937, p. 582: Beals, *American Earth,* p. 46; Daniel Boorstin, *The Americans, the National Experience* (New York: Random House, 1966), p. 127. Edward Channing relates that Leonard Calvert and his agent, Giles Brent, advised Maryland colonists to shoot all Indians on sight (*History,* I, 259). On biological warfare, see Woodward, *A New American History,* p. 106.

16. Everett Dick, *Vanguards of the Frontier* (New York: D. Appleton Century, 1944), p. 511; Raymond W. Thorp and Robert Bunker, *Crow Killer* (New York: Signet, n.d.), p. 9.

17. 7th ed.; New York: Appleton-Century-Crofts, 1965, pp. 33, 126.

border warfare." Not only are massacres of Indians generally overlooked, but also the fact that thousands of Indians were enslaved, some even being shipped to the Barbary States and the West Indies.[18] The "cruelty" stereotype of the Indian needs an examination it seldom gets. Cruelty there sometimes was, but in retaliation for cruelty inflicted, and then hardly worse than the tortures in vogue among whites of that time. The many cases of white captives who were unwilling to return to "civilization" is an eloquent commentary on old images of the Indian.

Indian removal, or slaughter, is customarily presented as the inexorable march of civilization displacing savage hunters. Glyndon G. Van Deusen finds that the white invasion "was deeply resented by the red men, who saw their hunting grounds disappearing before these waves of intruders."[19] The "primitive hunter" myth is the usual expiation for the triumph of brute force. It appears repeatedly in the refrain that "the natives did not develop the land." We deplored the same logic when it was used by Mussolini in Ethiopia. If the right of ownership depended on land use, some wealthy white land owners would today be in jeopardy.

The myth of the Indian as a mere hunter, like many other myths, arises from ignorance concerning the variety of Indian cultures which flourished in America. Most Indians were farmers, and the southeastern Indians had so far embraced "civilization" by the 1830s that they were known as the "Five Civilized Tribes." The Cherokees had adopted a constitution patterned after that of the United States, and published books and a newspaper in their own language, with Sequoyah's alphabet. A census taken among them in 1825 showed that they owned 33 grist mills, 13 saw mills, 1 powder mill, 69 blacksmith shops, 2 tan yards, 762 looms, 2,486 spinning wheels, 172 wagons, 2,923 plows, 7,683 horses, 22,531 black cattle, 46,732 swine, and 2,566 sheep.[20] This adaptation to white concepts of progress, urged upon them by Jefferson, did not save them, but rather accelerated demands for their expulsion.

The inconsistency of Indian removal with alleged civilizing aims was pointed out by Jedidiah Morse, who was commissioned by President Monroe in 1820 to report to Secretary of War Calhoun on the state of the Indians. Morse warned:

To remove these Indians far away from their present homes . . . into a wilderness among strangers, possibly hostile, to live as their new neighbours live,

18. Almon W. Lauber, *Indian Slavery in Colonial Times* (New York: Columbia University Press, 1913).
19. Van Deusen, *The Jacksonian Era* (New York: Harper & Brothers, 1959), p. 48.
20. Albert Gallatin, "Synopsis of Indian Tribes," in *Transactions and Collections of the American Antiquarian Society* (Cambridge, 1836), II, 157.

by hunting, a state to which they have not lately been accustomed, and which is incompatible with civilization, can hardly be reconciled with the professed views and objects of the Government in civilizing them.[21]

But the argument persisted that their removal was not only inevitable, but (as a salve for troubled consciences), necessary for their own good. Jackson's claim that "they cannot live in contact with a civilized community, and prosper,"[22] was echoed by historians Louis Hacker and Benjamin Kendrick, who held that "the westward progress of the white man could not be stayed and by the end of the century the Indians were all safely confined on reservations."[23] The notion that "progress" required the nearly complete expropriation of the Indians does not stand up. Indians could have been persuaded, and in fact, before their final expulsion, were persuaded, to live on reduced acreage in their old habitat. Yet, in state after state, in the 1830s and 1840s, the last scraps of land were torn from tribes east of the Mississippi. If greed had been kept within bounds, as it was in Canada, the traumatic effects of forced emigration could have been avoided.

Defamation

This school denigrates the Indian, calls attention to all of his faults and none of his virtues, and condemns him to a status of inferiority in intelligence and adaptability. To this group belongs John Bach McMaster, who may be taken as representative of the late-nineteenth-century historians. To him the Indian "was never so happy as when, in the dead of night, he roused his sleeping enemies with an unearthly yell, and massacred them by the light of their burning homes." The Indian was, moreover, only an "idle, shiftless savage." When not hunting or warring, he yielded himself to debauchery, and enslaved his women. His mental attainments,

were quite of a piece with his character. His imagination was singularly strong, his reason singularly weak. He was as superstitious as a Hottentot negro and as unreasonable as a child.[24]

His contemporary, George Bancroft, blamed the Indians themselves for bringing destruction upon their heads. His judgment was that they would

21. Morse, *Report to the Secretary of War on Indian Affairs* (New Haven: S. Converse, 1822), p. 82.
22. Message on Indian removal, December 7, 1835, in Commager, ed., *Documents*, pp. 259–61.
23. Hacker and Kendrick, *The United States Since 1865* (New York: F. S. Crofts Co., 1934), pp. 136–38.
24. McMaster, *History of the People of the United States from the Revolution to the Civil War* (New York: Farrar, Straus & Co., 1964), p. 15.

have been treated generously if they had behaved better. Because of their "hasty cruelty" and "inconsiderate revenge" they vanished, "leaving no enduring memorials but the names of rivers and mountains."[25]

To the same school and generation belonged John Fiske, who falsely claimed that New England Indians had been paid for every foot of their land, and, defending the incineration of the Pequots in 1636, maintained that it was wrong "to suppose that savages, whose business is to torture and slay, can always be dealt with according to the methods in use between civilized peoples . . ."[26]

These historians are gone, but their influence is not. Their crude racism has gone out of fashion, but derogation of Indian character continues. In his Pulitzer prize-winning history, R. Carlyle Buley proclaims that "the Potawatomi and the Menominee were . . . a fairly dirty, lazy, and harmless lot."[27] The late David Saville Muzzey, whose books are widely used in high schools, promotes the myth of the nomadic warrior: [the Indians] "were constantly on the warpath, and shifting their hunting grounds."[28] The nomad myth is often used to deny the validity of Indian land claims. Most Indians were in fact less mobile than the current white population. (How many of us were born where we now live?) The Mohawk village of Caughnawaga, Que., is 300 years old. Tuscaloosa, Ala., was an Indian village when DeSoto came by in 1540. Oraibi, a Hopi village in Arizona, is the oldest continuously inhabited place in the United States. Tree ring evidence dates it back to A.D. 1100. Therefore, it is older than Berlin or Moscow.

The charge that all Indians were perpetual warriors arises from ascribing Plains Indian customs to all Indians. It is entirely inapplicable to the sedentary Pueblo tribes, and to some Pacific coast and eastern woodland Indians as well. The role of Indians as peacemakers has been so hidden that a book has been written to rescue this aspect of their history from obscurity, but, like so many of the better books on Indians, it was the work of an "amateur."[29]

25. Bancroft, *History of the United States of America* (New York: D. Appleton & Co., 1893), I, pp. 128–29, 165.

26. Fiske, *The Beginnings of New England* (Boston: Houghton Mifflin Co., 1889), p. 184.

27. Buley, *The Old Northwest* (2 vols.; Bloomington: University of Indiana Press, 1964), II, p. 127. Cf. the view of the Potawatomi by Pierre-Jean De Smet, who reported in 1838 that he "had not seen so imposing a sight nor such fine-looking Indians in America." *Life, Letters and Travels of Father Pierre-Jean De Smet, S.J.* (New York: Francis P. Harper, 1905), I, p. 157.

28. Muzzey, *A History of Our Country* (Boston: Ginn & Co., 1957), p. 24.

29. Mabel Powers, *The Indian as Peacemaker* (New York: Fleming H. Revell Co., 1932).

Disparagement

The fourth way the Indian is scalped by historians is by *disparagement* of, or denial of his extensive contributions to our culture. Richard N. Current and his collaborators declare that "American civilization . . . owed very little to the aborigines of the New World." They further allege that "even the most brilliant of the native cultures were stunted in comparison with the growing civilization of Europe. None of the Indians had an alphabet and . . . none had any conception of the wheel."[30]

The last statement is false; the Aztecs used wheels on children's toys, but had no beasts of burden to enable them to put the principle to better use. But the comparisons made above are perniciously unfair. Barbaric Europe borrowed its wheel and its alphabet, not to mention its numerals and many domesticated plants and animals, from Semitic peoples of Asia. Its gunpowder, compass, and printing press were inventions of Oriental people. Moreover, the argument ignores the instances in which American achievements exceeded those of the Old World: the Mayas had a superior calendar and understood the zero before Europe did. Indians domesticated more than forty plants, of which corn is the outstanding example, because it does not and cannot grow wild. In some respects, they excelled in medicine and surgery, e.g., trephination, and knew the properties of drugs like coca (from whence cocaine), cinchona (whence quinine), curare, cascara sagrada, and many more. They alone discovered rubber, and with it invented the bulbed syringe. Middle American hieroglyphics, in time, would have evolved into an alphabet.

The remarks of Prof. Current also illustrate the selective criteria which are used to rank cultures into false categories called "higher" and "lower." To measure social advance in *our* terms reveals an ethnocentric bias. This is ABC to an anthropologist, but not to all historians. We are reminded of a tale, perhaps apocryphal but yet pertinent, that Sitting Bull declared the whites to be "inhuman," because they beat their children, whereas Indians did not. If we measure a society by its nonmaterial culture, which admittedly involves value judgments (as does the material criterion), the Indians might come out ahead. This is the meaning of the opening remarks in John Collier's eloquent book, *The Indians of the Americas:*

They had what the world has lost. They have it now. What the world has lost, the world must have again, lest it die. . . . It is the ancient, lost reverence and

30. Richard N. Current, T. Harry Williams, and Frank Freidel, *American History, A Survey* (2d ed.; New York: Alfred A. Knopf, 1966), p. 4.

passion for human personality, joined with the ancient, lost reverence for the earth and its web of life.

W. E. Woodward held that the Indians "were singularly lacking in inventive ability, and in the sense of adaptation." He even berated them for not learning how to make whiskey from corn![31] However, Clark Wissler has listed twenty-four Indian inventions not known in the Old World in 1492, and sixteen others known in the Old World which were independently discovered in the New World.[32] There are also many examples of adaptation, such as use of the horse, which transformed the culture of the Plains tribes. Indians were also prompt to adopt guns, metal tools, and a wide range of white trade goods. In fact, their dependence on these commodities was a factor in their downfall.

Entirely forgetting the services of Squanto and other Indians to the Mayflower passengers, Henry Bamford Parkes declared that the Pilgrims discovered how to survive "entirely by their own labors."[33] Even in areas where the Indian has made spectacular contributions, they are denied. Alden T. Vaughan alleges that "the Indians had no bona fide medicine to speak of."[34] In fact, the Indians of North America (north of Mexico) used about 150 medicines which were later included in the *U.S. Pharmacopeia* and *National Formulary,* and the Indians of Latin America contributed about fifty more. Accounts of explorers, from Cartier on, are filled with tributes to Indian medical skill which, although frequently mixed with magic, was considered by many to excel that of Europe at the time.

"Nor have the Indians made any substantial contribution to the civilization that we now have in the United States," comments Oliver Perry Chitwood.[35] To be sure, he admits that the Indians aided the colonists at first. They taught colonists how to clear the land and grow corn and tobacco, acted as guides, procured furs for trade, taught the colonials how to make maple sugar, to hunt and trap, and dress their skins. They showed the white man how to make a bark canoe, and endowed our map with

31. Woodward, *A New American History*, pp. 103–4.
32. Wissler, *Indians of the United States* (Garden City, N.Y.: Doubleday, 1949), p. 295. See also E. Nordenskjoeld, "The American Indian as an Inventor," in A. L. Kroeber and T. T. Waterman, eds., *Sourcebook in Anthropology* (rev. ed.; New York: Harcourt Brace & Co., 1931), pp. 489–505.
33. Parkes, *The American Experience* (New York: Alfred A. Knopf, 1947), p. 30. Cf. Charles and Mary Beard: "From red Indians 'the paleface' recovered some of the primitive arts of survival which had been lost by the English since their own primitive times." *Basic History*, p. 25.
34. Vaughan, *New England Frontier*, p. 34.
35. Chitwood, *A History of Colonial America* (New York: Harper & Bros., 1931), p. 19.

euphonious place names. Yet, he concludes, "aside from these contributions, American life has not been modified by Indian influence."

Unlike earlier writers, Chitwood did not ascribe the retardation of the Indians to racial inferiority. "The race is not lacking in mental vigor," he conceded. Instead, he held that they were handicapped by the lack of beasts of burden and milk cattle, and were cut off from Old World centers of culture from which they could have learned. Nevertheless, he continued, "the fact remains that the aboriginal inhabitants of our part of this continent failed to appreciate and exploit the richest gifts that nature has ever bestowed on any land."

A third of a century has passed since that was written, yet few later historians have advanced beyond the tunnel vision it exhibits. The really comprehensive account of the Indian contributions remains to be written. What we have is mainly the work of anthropologists, and it is not always easily available.

Let us take a closer look at the argument. Chitwood confines his attention to the aborigines of *our part* of this continent. Thus, not a nod or a footnote is accorded to the mighty attainments of the Middle American and Andean civilizations: the Mayan astronomy, mathematics, and architecture, the skillful metal work and other arts of the Aztecs and Incas, the domestication of the turkey, Muscovy duck, honeybee, alpaca, llama, and guinea pig; the roads, communications, scientific land use and political organization of the Incas; the invention of paper and the weaving of cotton cloth in Mexico, and other achievements previously mentioned. To judge Indian attainments by the more limited material progress of those living north of the Rio Grande is as one-sided as if we should measure European civilization by the achievements of the Lapps, or the primitive Germans described by Tacitus, or if we should subtract from Europe's culture all that was borrowed from Asia.

Our Indians, it is said, failed to appreciate and exploit the resources at their disposal. This view fails to consider that the demographic facts caused no pressure for extensive development. Moreover, the Indian use of resources was different from ours. For example, the rivers and lakes were canoe routes and sources of food. We have turned them into foul sewers. The Plains were a hunting ground. There we overcultivated and turned the region into a dustbowl scarred by wind and rain. Recognizing no value in forests except as lumber, we cut them down and unleashed floods in our river valleys. We were so committed to the idea that all of nature's bounty should yield financial gain, that for a long time we failed to appreciate the recreational, ecological, and aesthetic value of unspoiled wilderness. The concept of nature as an enemy to be slain lives on in the dogmas of Eric

Hoffer. Belatedly we are returning some lands to their wild state, a retreat which would astonish our practical forefathers.

But North American Indians were not averse to resource development. They mined and worked copper, lead, mica, and coal. (Latin American Indians mined gold, silver, tin, platinum, and jade.) They discovered oil and made salt by evaporation. Southwestern Indians built irrigation canals, raised cotton, and farmed the land to a near optimum level. Where conditions permitted, North American Indians planted corn, squash, beans, pumpkins, tobacco, sunflowers, and drug plants. They discovered natural dyes which were used by the pioneers, and used hundreds of wild plants for food and medicine.

As Rome hid its debt to the Etruscans, we have obscured our inheritance from the red men. Anthropologists know that acculturation proceeds in both directions when two societies are in any kind of contact, and that even a conquered people helps to shape the destiny of their overlords. "North Americans have maintained the European level with the strictest possible puritanism," wrote psychiatrist Carl Jung, "yet they could not prevent the souls of their Indian enemies from becoming theirs."[36] For our own benefit, let us resurrect some lost truth.

Indians picked the sites now occupied by many of our great cities, and plotted the trails and canoe portages which are followed to this day by our highways, railroads, and canals. We copied their dress, and not only in the fringed buckskin of Daniel Boone. From them we learned to substitute long pants for knee breeches; our women borrowed their feathers and paint, and we wear their moccasins, their parkas, and ponchos. Their beads and bells are popular with our hippies. We smoke their tobacco and eat their foods: the tapioca of the Amazon, the beans, avocados, pineapples, chocolate, peppers, and vanilla of Mexico, the tomatoes, potatoes, and peanuts of Peru, the cranberries, squashes, and pecans of North America. The pemmican of the Plains Indian has served as food for Antarctic explorers. From the Mexican Indians we borrowed chewing gum, tamales, chili, and tortillas; from our own, hominy, succotash, corn pone, and popcorn.

They have influenced our literature far beyond Cooper's *Mohicans,* and Longfellow's *Hiawatha,* which is our truest national epic. Edna Ferber, Hamlin Garland, Helen Hunt Jackson, and Oliver LaFarge are a few among many who have portrayed the Indian in novels. Thomas Wolfe and Ernest Hemingway used Indian themes in short stories, while Philip Freneau, John Neihardt, Lew Sarett, and Walt Whitman glorified them in poetry. Indian mythology constitutes our most authentic American folk-

36. Jung, *Contributions to Analytical Psychology* (New York: Harcourt Brace & Co., 1928), p. 139.

lore. Appropriately, the first Bible printed in this country was in an Algonquian language, John Eliot's *Indian Bible* (1663).

Indians have influenced composers of music; among those indebted to them are Charles Wakefield Cadman, Anton Dvořák, Anton P. Heinrich, Victor Herbert, Thurlow Lieurance, Harvey W. Loomis, Edward A. McDowell, and Charles S. Skilton.

Their arts and designs have influenced our arts, jewelry, home decoration, and even our architecture. Not only did early settlers imitate the Indian wigwam and palisade, but the army modified the Plains tepee into the Sibley tent. Today, a prefabricated vacation home in the shape of a tepee, called *Wigwam 70,* has been marketed by the National Design Center in Chicago. The Quonset hut, which is widely used where simplicity is demanded, has both an Indian name and an Indian design. Buckminster Fuller's "geodesic dome" is an aboriginal wigwam covered with metal or glass instead of bark. Our modern skyscrapers copy the terraced setback of the Mayas. Pueblo adobe bricks became the white man's building material in the Southwest. The cube style of the Pueblos appears in the LaFonda hotel in Santa Fe, and Moshe Safdie's *Habitat* in Montreal. Willard Carl Kruger's New Mexico state house is in the shape of the Zia sun symbol. Frank Lloyd Wright acknowledged his debt to the Mayas and incorporated their themes in some of his buildings. Of their temples he wrote: "A grandeur arose in the scale of total building never since excelled, seldom equalled by man either in truth of plan or simple integrity of form."[37]

Not only was the Indian a sculptor, but he has inspired our sculptors as well. Leonard Crunelle, Malvina Hoffman, Ivan Meštrović, and Lorado Taft are among those who have portrayed the Indian in stone and bronze. And let us not forget that authentic American creation, the cigar store wooden Indian. Among painters who made their reputation with Indian subjects are Carl Bodmer, George Catlin, Frederick Remington, and Alfred Miller.

We borrowed Indian inventions, and even used their names for many of them: canoe, kayak, pirogue, cigar, hammock, and toboggan. We use his snowshoes, cradleboard, rubber, pipe, and cigarettes. Some of our youth play lacrosse and other games evolved from Indian sports. Indian lore enlivens the program of youth organizations. Indian dance clubs and craft groups composed of white adults are flourishing in the United States and Europe. Indian themes are in children's toys and juvenile literature. Indians have long been important in the movies, as they were earlier on the stage, but it has only been recently that they have been portrayed on the screen with sympathy and dignity, in films like *Broken Arrow, Devil's Doorway,* and *Cheyenne Autumn.*

37. Wright, *Writings and Buildings* (New York: Meridian Books, 1960), p. 22.

They have enriched our language. We use their names for the animals: caribou, chipmunk, cougar, coyote, jaguar, manatee, moose, opossum, raccoon, skunk, and woodchuck. The trees carry their names: catalpa, chinquapin, hickory, papaw, pecan, persimmon, sequoia, tamarack, and tupelo. Some sixty plants have Indian names, including cohosh, puccoon, pipsissewa, and poke. Because of fancy or Indian usage, other plants have names like Indian paintbrush, Indian pipe, Indian turnip, moccasin flower, papoose root, and squaw vine. We use their names for topographic features such as muskegs, bayous, and savannas, and speak of hurricanes and Chinook winds. Red men taught us to say hooch, okay, punk, and pewee. From them we borrowed caucus, Tammany, powwow, mugwump, podunk, and tuxedo. We have come to use words and phrases like "buck," "bury the hatchet," "go on the warpath," "Indian summer," "Indian giver," "Indian file," "great white father," and "war paint."

We plant Cherokee roses, Catawba grapes, Pima cotton, and Black Hawk raspberries. We drive Pontiac cars and ride in trains called *The Chief* and *Hiawatha*. We call our athletic teams Black Hawks, Braves, Illini, Redskins, and Warriors. We have Cayuse and Appaloosa ponies and Malemute dogs.

From the dispossessed we took the names of twenty-seven states, four of our great lakes, and many of our mountains and rivers, to give, as Mencken said, "a barbaric brilliancy to the American map."[38] Canada and four of its provinces and two of its territories have Indian names, as do ten nations in Latin America. We took Indian names for cities like Chattanooga, Chicago, Kalamazoo, Kenosha, Keokuk, Kokomo, Mankato, Miami, Milwaukee, Muncie, Muskegon, Omaha, Oshkosh, Paducah, Pawtucket, Peoria, Sandusky, Schenectady, Seattle, Sheboygan, Spokane, Tacoma, Tallahassee, Tucson, Tulsa, Waco, and Wichita. Some of their names we translated into colorful English and French equivalents like Bad Axe, Battle Creek, Broken Bow, Medicine Hat, Moose Jaw, Painted Post, and Red Wing; Baton Rouge, Des Plaines, and Fond du Lac.

The Indian brightens our advertising. His totem poles invite us to Alaska, his calendar stone calls us to Mexico. Indians are featured in the advertising of the Santa Fe and Great Northern railroads, and in the tourist advertising of many states. We put an Indian on a baking soda can, on a box of corn starch, on chewing tobacco, patent medicines, and other products. We use their names as trade marks: Black Hawk meats, Cherokee garments, Pequot sheets, Sioux tools, and Wyandotte chemicals. We put the Indian on coins and postage stamps. An Aztec legend is pictured on the

38. H. L. Mencken, *The American Language* (New York: Alfred A. Knopf, 1947), p. 528.

Mexican flag, and Indian symbols decorate the state flags of New Mexico and Oklahoma.

The Indian is an important ingredient of our political history. The colonial charters speak of trade and conversion as objects of the colonizers. The Indian presence was a spur to efforts at colonial union, from the New England confederation to the Albany congress. The Iroquois alliance helped to defeat the French, and Indians were significant participants in all colonial wars, and later ones, both as friends and foes. Their rebellion under Pontiac in 1763 won the royal proclamation closing the West to settlement, and launched a chain of events leading to our independence. Indians are mentioned in the Declaration of Independence, the Articles of Confederation, the Northwest Ordinance, the U.S. Constitution, the constitution of the Confederacy, and in numerous presidential messages and party platforms. They figure in at least five treaties with foreign powers.[39] We have made 372 treaties with them and passed over four thousand laws affecting them. Several government agencies are involved with them.

Montaigne, Rousseau, and Jefferson paid tribute to the Indian capacity to organize human affairs in a libertarian manner. The Iroquois developed a system of confederated government which, according to Benjamin Franklin, served as an example for his Albany Plan of Union, and eventually for the Articles of Confederation. Felix Cohen has lashed the assumption that our democracy was born in Greece:

. . . it is out of a rich Indian democratic tradition that the distinctive political ideals of American life emerged. Universal suffrage for women as for men, the pattern of states within a state that we call federalism, the habit of treating chiefs as servants of the people instead of their masters, the insistence that the community must respect the diversity of men and the diversity of their dreams—all these things were part of the American way of life before Columbus landed.[40]

The followers of Sam Adams masqueraded as Indians at the Boston Tea Party, and we borrowed Indian military tactics in the Revolution, as the poet Robert P. Tristram Coffin has written:

We bent down to the bob-cat's crouch,
Took color from the butternut tree,
At Saratoga, Lexington,
We fought like Indians and went free.

39. Jay's treaty with Great Britain, 1794; Pinckney's treaty with Spain, 1795; Treaty of Ghent, 1814; Treaty of Guadalupe Hidalgo, 1848; Alaska Purchase Treaty, 1867.
40. Cohen, "Americanizing the White Man," *The American Scholar*, XXI, No. 2 (Spring, 1952), 179–80.

Even customs and folkways: frontier hospitality, and neighborly co-operation, such as barn-raising, were copies of Indian manners. We learned his weather and plant lore. His war whoop was the "rebel yell" in the Civil War, and Coffin says:

> We even put the powwow on,
> We dance the night before we fight,
> Republicans, Democrats, football teams
> With red hot songs built up their might.[41]

The predominant ethnic strain in all but four of the nations of Central and South America is Indian. Indians have shaped the study of anthropology, linguistics, and archaeology, particularly in America, and have contributed to thought in psychology, sociology, law, political theory, and education. They taught us progressive, non-authoritarian ways of rearing and teaching children.

It is a trap to measure the worth of any people by the degree to which they have successfully participated as individuals in a rival culture. Because Indians are few in number and have lived a largely separate life, they cannot point to a large number of such persons. In athletics, however, fame came to Jim Thorpe, Louis Tewanima, Don Eagle, and Charles Albert Bender. In military service, there are Brigadier General Ely S. Parker (who wrote the surrender terms at Appomattox), Major General Clarence Tinker, and Rear Admiral Joseph Clark. Indians can point with pride to artists Brummet Echohawk and Beatien Yazz, ballerinas Maria and Marjorie Tallchief, humorist Will Rogers, actor Jay Silverheels (Tonto of the Lone Ranger), William Keeler, executive vice-president of the Phillips Petroleum Corporation, Indian commissioners Robert Bennett and Louis Bruce, and former Congressman Ben Reifel. Vice-President Charles Curtis boasted of his Indian inheritance.

41. Both verses from "We Put the Feathers On," in R. P. Tristram Coffin, *Primer for America* (New York: Macmillan Co., 1943), pp. 54–55.

APPENDIXES

1 Significant Dates in American Indian History

Dates are of limited value in the study of history, and particularly in Indian history. Only the Mayas, Aztecs, and Incas had a calendar which enables us to establish precise dates for happenings before white contact. For other tribes, dates record only the highlights of the interaction of aboriginal culture with that of the invading Europeans. Such dating results in distortion, for those events which do not involve whites are often left unrecorded and considered of no consequence. Moreover, dates have a built-in bias in favor of sudden and dramatic occurrences, and ignore deeper currents of history which are not easily measured by white time concepts, which are, by the way, strange to Indian culture. Dates have a certain value, however, to establish the sequence of events, which is necessary to fit the chronological pattern in which history is usually taught, and to measure off the duration of periods which may have a certain deeper significance. For example, Turner used the date 1890 to mark the end of the American frontier; it also marks the practical end of Indian resistance to white conquest, for 1890 is also the date of Wounded Knee, the last important act of violence in the red and white struggle.

1535	September 7	Jacques Cartier lands at Quebec.
1539–1543		DeSoto expedition in Southeast establishes first contact with Muskhogean tribes and Cherokees.
1540–1542		Coronado's explorations in the Southwest bring the Pueblo and other tribes into European contact.
1585	July 27	Raleigh's colonists land at Roanoke Island.
1607	May 24	105 English settlers disembark at the site of Jamestown, Virginia.
1608	July 8	Champlain founds Quebec.
1609		Spanish settle Santa Fe.
1614	April 14	John Rolfe marries Pocahontas.
1620	December 20	Pilgrims leave the Mayflower and land at Plymouth.
1622	March 22	First Indian rebellion in Virginia, led by Opechancanough.
1636–1637		Pequot Indians of Connecticut exterminated by Underhill's expedition, aided by Mohegans.
1644		Second Indian rebellion in Virginia.
1663		Publication of John Eliot's "Indian Bible."
1675–1676		King Philip's war in New England; most destructive Indian war in colonial history.
1680	August 10	Great Pueblo revolt in the Southwest.
1682		William Penn's treaty with the Delawares.

1711–1712	Tuscarora war in North Carolina.
1715–1716	Yamasee war in South Carolina and Georgia.
1754	Albany conference for purpose of establishing alliance with the Six Nations.
1754	Establishment of Eleazar Wheelock's Indian school, forerunner of Dartmouth College.
1754–1763	French and Indian War.
1763 May–November	Pontiac's rebellion: Indians destroy every British post West of Niagara, except Fort Pitt and Detroit.
1763 October 7	Royal Proclamation reserving territory between crest of the Appalachians and the Mississippi for the Indians.
1774	Lord Dunmore's war, caused by the wanton murder of the family of chief Logan by frontiersmen.
1775–1783	Revolutionary War; many Indians aid British; some aid U.S.
1778 September 17	First U.S. Indian treaty signed, with the Delaware.
1790	Alliance of tribes northwest of Ohio River defeats Josiah Harmar's army in Ohio.
1791 November 4	Indians led by Little Turtle defeat Arthur St. Clair's army in Ohio.
1794 August 20	Battle of Fallen Timbers, near Maumee River, SW of present city of Toledo, won by General Anthony Wayne over northwest tribes.
1794 November 19	Jay's Treaty, certain Indian rights protected.
1795 August 3	Treaty of Greenville (Ohio) signed by twelve Indian tribes, sets up definite boundary in Northwest Territory between Indian lands and those open to settlement.
1795 October 27	Pinckney's Treaty; clauses concerning southern Indians.
1802 April 24	Georgia compact; U.S. promises to extinguish Indian titles in Georgia, with Indian consent.
1803 June 7	Treaty of Vincennes, signed by nine Indian tribes of the Old Northwest, gave U.S. title to disputed lands along Wabash River beyond Greenville line.
1804–1806	Lewis and Clark expedition brings many western tribes into first contact with U.S. government.
1811 November 7	Battle of Tippecanoe (Indiana). Destruction of Tecumseh's village on the Wabash by 1,000 militia commanded by W. H. Harrison.
1812–1814	War with Great Britain. Many Indian tribes, particularly in Old Northwest, and some of the Creeks, take up arms against U.S.
1814 March 27	Defeat of Creeks in battle of Horseshoe Bend (Ala.) by Tennessee militia led by Andrew Jackson; followed by large land cessions.

1814	December 24	Treaty of Ghent protects Indians against retribution.
1816–1818		First Seminole War, Jackson invades Florida.
1824		Creation of Bureau of Indian Affairs in the War Department.
1827	July 26	Cherokee constitution adopted.
1829	July 29	Treaty of Prairie du Chien (Wis.). Large land cessions.
1830	May 28	Jackson's Indian removal bill passed.
1832	March 3	*Worcester* v. *Georgia* decision of Supreme Court upholds Cherokee rights.
1832	May–August	Black Hawk War; troops sent against retreating Sauks in Illinois and Wisconsin.
1832–1833		Treaties of Payne's Landing and Fort Gibson authorizing removal of Seminoles from Florida, leading to Second Seminole War.
1833	September 26	Treaty at Chicago with Potawatomi; most of tribe to remove within two years.
1835		Assembly of the bulk of Potawatomi at Chicago for removal to the West.
1835	March 29	Treaty of New Echota (Ga.), ceded to U.S. all Cherokee lands and provided for transfer of Indians to Oklahoma.
1835–1842		Second Seminole War.
1838		Cherokee Trail of Tears.
		Trail of Death for Indiana Potawatomi.
1846		Expulsion of the Miami from Indiana.
1848	February 2	Treaty of Guadalupe Hidalgo with Mexico, brings many new tribes under U.S. jurisdiction.
1849		Bureau of Indian Affairs transferred to Interior Department.
1851	September 17	Laramie Treaty Council with Plains and Mountain tribes.
1855		Treaties with Indians of Oregon and Washington territories.
1862		Santee Sioux revolt in Minnesota.
1863–1867		Babylonian captivity of the Navajo at Bosque Redondo, New Mexico.
1864	November 29	Massacre of peaceful Cheyennes by Colonel Chivington's troops, Sand Creek, Colo.
1867	October 21	Treaty of Medicine Lodge (Kan.); Southern Plains tribes agree to go on reservations.
1868	November 27	Battle of the Washita, Indian Territory, Custer's 7th Cavalry slaughter Black Kettle and his Cheyennes.
1869		Ely S. Parker, Seneca Indian, appointed head of Bureau of Indian Affairs.
1871	March 3	Congress formally abandons treaty-making with Indian tribes.

1872–1873		Modoc War, northern California.
1876	June 25	Defeat and total extermination of Custer's force by Sioux and Cheyennes at the Little Big Horn, Crow Agency, Mont.
1877	June–October	Nez Perce war, Idaho-Montana, surrender of Chief Joseph.
1878	September 9 to	
1879	January	Flight of the Cheyennes to the north from Indian Territory.
1879		Ute war.
1879		Establishment of Bureau of American Ethnology under direction of John Wesley Powell.
1879		Carlisle (Pa.) Indian School established.
1881		Publication of Helen Hunt Jackson's *A Century of Dishonor.*
1882		Indian Rights Association founded under auspices of Society of Friends (Quakers).
1886	September 4	Geronimo's band of Apaches surrenders to General Nelson Miles.
1887	February 8	Dawes Act passed, for allotment of Indian lands in severalty.
1890	December 15	Murder of Sitting Bull on Standing Rock Reservation, South Dakota.
1890	December 29	Massacre of Sioux of Big Foot's band at Wounded Knee Creek, South Dakota, marking the end of significant Indian fighting.
1901	October	Citizenship act for Five Civilized Tribes.
1906		Most reservations and tribal government liquidated in Indian Territory and Oklahoma Territory preparatory to organization of state of Oklahoma (1907).
1923		Establishment of Association on American Indian Affairs.
1924	June 2	Indian Citizenship Act.
1926		Drive of Indian Bureau to suppress Pueblo religious rites.
1928		Publication of Meriam report, *The Problem of Indian Administration,* by Brookings Institution.
1933		Appointment of John Collier as head of the Bureau of Indian Affairs.
1934	June 18	Indian Reorganization Act (Wheeler-Howard Act) reverses the long drive to liquidate Indian societies.
1936	June 26	Oklahoma Indian Welfare Act passed.
1944		Founding of National Congress of American Indians.
1946	April 13	Congress creates Indian Claims Commission.
1949		Renewal of liquidation drive; Indian relocation program.

1953–1954		Termination bills enacted for several tribes by Congress.
1958	January 18	Armed Lumbee Indians disperse Klan meeting, Robeson County, North Carolina.
1958	April–May	Tuscaroras of New York resist surveys for dam.
1958–1959		Termination of Klamaths of Oregon, and liquidation of tribal assets.
1960	March 7	Supreme Court rules against Tuscaroras in dam fight.
1960	December 31	Menominee tribe terminated; reservation becomes a county.
1961	June 13–20	American Indian Chicago Conference.
1964		Beginning of fight for fishing rights, tribes of Washington State.
1966	May	Robert L. Bennett, Oneida Indian, appointed Commissioner of Indian Affairs.
1968		Navajo tribe celebrates centennial of its treaty with the U.S. government.
1969	July 9	Passamaquoddy road block, Princeton, Maine.
1969	August	Louis R. Bruce, Mohawk-Sioux, appointed Commissioner of Indian Affairs.
1969	November 20	Indian occupation of Alcatraz Island, San Francisco Bay.
1970		Indian sit-ins in several BIA offices; attempted occupation of Fort Lawton, Wash., and other federal property. Active mood of militancy spreads.
1970	October 27	Pit River Indians occupying Lassen National Forest, Burney, California, assaulted by 100 local and federal law officers.
1971	June 11	Indians expelled from Alcatraz Island.
	June 14	Chicago Indian Village occupies Nike site.
	December 18	President Nixon signs Alaska Native Claims Act.
1972	March 7	One thousand Indians march on Gordon, Nebraska, to protest murder of Raymond Little Thunder.
1972	November 4–8	Two hundred Indians in Trail of Broken Treaties march to occupy Bureau of Indian Affairs Building in Washington, D.C. Much property damage, many files removed. Commissioner Bruce and others ousted from office.
1973	February 6	Militant Indians in Custer, S.D., protesting failure of law enforcement agencies to place murder charge against killer of an Indian, burn Chamber of Commerce and set fire to court house.
1973	February 27 –May 8	Occupation of Wounded Knee, S.D., on Pine Ridge Reservation, by two hundred Indians led by AIM.
1973	April 10	Center for the History of the American Indian dedicated with Indian ceremonies at Chicago's Newberry Library.

2 United States Indian Wars, Campaigns, and Disturbances

1782–1787	Wyoming Valley war in Pennsylvania.
1790–1795	War with the Northwest Indians; Mingo, Miami, Wyandot, Delaware, Potawatomi, Shawnee, Chippewa, and Ottawa, September 19, 1790, to August 3, 1795.
1811	War with the Indians in Indiana, September 21 to November 18.
1812	Florida or Seminole war, August 15 to October.
1813	Peoria Indian war in Illinois, September 19 to October 21.
1813–1814	Creek Indian war in Alabama, Georgia, Mississippi, and Tennessee, July 27, 1813, to August 9, 1814.
1817–1818	Seminole Indian war in Georgia and Florida, November 20, 1817, to October 31, 1818.
1823	Campaign against Arickaree Indians, upper Missouri river.
1827	Fever River expedition against the Indians in Illinois.
1827	Winnebago expedition, Wisconsin, June 28 to September 27.
1832	Black Hawk war, April 26 to September 30.
1834	Pawnee expedition in Indian Territory, June to September.
1835–1842	Florida or Seminole Indian war, December 8, 1835, to August 14, 1842.
1836–1837	Sabine or southwestern Indian disturbance in Louisiana, April 1836 to April 1837.
1836–1837	Creek disturbance in Alabama, May 5, 1836, to September 30, 1837.
1836–1838	Cherokee disturbances and removal to Indian Territory.
1837	Osage Indian war in Missouri.
1847–1848	Cayuse Indian war in Oregon, December 1847 to July 1848.
1849–1855	Texas and New Mexico Indian war.
1849–1855	Apache, Navajo, and Utah war.
1849–1861	Navajo troubles in New Mexico.
1849–1861	Continuous disturbances with Comanche, Cheyenne, Lipan, and Kickapoo Indians in Texas.
1850	Pit River expedition, California, April 28 to September 13.
1850–1853	Utah Indian disturbances.
1851–1852	California Indian disturbances.
1851–1856	Rogue River Indian war in Oregon, June 17 to July 3, 1851; August 8 to September 1853; March to June 1856.
1854	Oregon Indian war in Oregon, August and September 1854.
1855	Yakima expedition, Washington Territory, October 11 to November 24.
1855	Klamath and Salmon River Indian war in Oregon and Idaho, January to March.
1855	Expedition against Snake Indians, Oregon, May 24 to September 8.
1855–1856	Sioux expedition, Nebraska Territory, April 3, 1855, to July 27, 1856.

1855–1856   Cheyenne and Arapaho troubles.

1855–1858   Florida Indian war, December 15, 1855, to May 8, 1858.

1857   Sioux Indian troubles in Minnesota and Iowa, March and April 1857.

1858   Expedition against northern Indians, Washington Territory, July 17 to October 17.

1858   Spokane, Coeur d'Alene, and Palouse Indian troubles.

1858   Navajo expedition, New Mexico, September 9 to December 25.

1858–1859   Wichita expedition, Indian Territory, September 11, 1858, to December 1859.

1859   Colorado River expedition, California, February 11 to April 28.

1859   Pecos expedition, Texas, April 16 to August 17.

1860   Kiowa and Comanche expedition, Indian territory, May 8 to October 11.

1860–1861   Navajo expedition, New Mexico, September 12, 1860, to February 24, 1861.

1860–1864   Campaign against the Cheyenne Indians.

1862–1863   Sioux Indian war in Minnesota and Dakota. In 1863 most of the Minnesota Sioux were removed to Dakota.

1863–1869   War against the Cheyenne, Arapaho, Kiowa, and Comanche Indians in Kansas, Nebraska, Colorado, and Indian Territory.

1865–1868   Campaign against Indians in southern Oregon, Idaho, and northern California.

1867–1869   Campaign against Indians in Kansas, Colorado, and Indian Territory.

1867–1881   Campaign against Lipan, Kiowa, Kickapoo, and Comanche Indians, and Mexican border disturbances.

1872–1873   Modoc Indian war in Oregon and California, November 22, 1872, to October 3, 1873.

1873   Campaign against Apache Indians in Arizona and New Mexico.

1874   Sioux expedition, Wyoming and Nebraska, February 13 to August.

1874–1875   Campaign against Kiowa, Cheyenne, and Comanche Indians in Indian Territory, August 1, 1874, to February 16, 1875.

1875   Expedition against Indians in eastern Nevada, September 7 to 27.

1876–1877   Big Horn and Yellowstone expeditions, Wyoming and Montana, February 17, 1876, to June 13, 1877.

1876–1879   War with northern Cheyenne Indians in Indian Territory, Kansas, Wyoming, Dakota, Nebraska, and Montana.

1877   Nez Perce Indian war, May 14 to October 1.

1878   Bannock Indian war in Idaho, Washington Territory, and Wyoming Territory.

1878–1879   Campaign against Cheyenne Indians in Dakota and Montana.

1879   Ute expedition, Colorado, April 3 to September 9.

1879   Snake or Sheepeater Indian troubles, Idaho, August to October.

1879   White River campaign against Ute Indians in Utah and Colorado, September 29 to October 5.

1881–1887	Apache campaigns, Arizona and northern Mexico.
1890	Sioux Indian disturbances in South Dakota, December.
1898	Chippewa Indian disturbances, Leech Lake, October.
1915	Ute troubles in Utah.

> Adapted with omissions, corrections, and additions, from "Wars and Local Disturbances," leaflet of the Bureau of Indian Affairs, October 1963.

3   Famous Americans of Indian Descent

The shortcomings of most lists of this sort is that they spotlight chiefly those Indians who have "made it" in the rival culture, and this has meant, for many of them, the abandonment of their "Indian-ness." Despite that cultural bias, such a list can serve a constructive purpose in providing evidence that Indians have the intelligence and potential ability to accomplish as much in the world as anybody else.

It was distressing to discover that in a list of three hundred famous Americans chosen for biographical sketches in Richard Morris's *Encyclopedia of American History*, there are no Indians, living or dead, and only two nonwhites. Contemporary biographical reference books also appear, to this writer, to omit the names of many Indians whose achievements appear to justify their inclusion. It is hard to avoid the conclusion that WASP arrogance is powerful in the field of scholarship still, despite rumblings from minorities.

Miss Marion Gridley's *Indians of Today* (3d ed., Chicago: Indian Council Fire, 1960; 4th ed., 1971) is the only current available sourcebook on distinguished living Indians. It has some deficiencies in standards of selection, and a technical shortcoming in the omission of dates of birth in every instance. Many Indians are listed in the Who's Who section of Klein and Icolari's *Reference Encyclopedia of the American Indian* (1967), but the list also includes many white scholars and writers in the Indian field, and the text does not always indicate which biographies are of Indians. The Bureau of Indian Affairs has a five-page leaflet entitled "Indians of National Prominence," listing both living and deceased Indians. A. H. Verrill, *The Real Americans* (1954), contains short biographical sketches of 106 Indians, mainly from the past. We have used these sources, but have had to go beyond them.

All the lists, except Verrill's, focus largely on Indians who have been successful in politics, business, or the professions, and largely exclude those who are activist leaders in the militant promotion of Indian causes. The first list which follows is aimed at partial correction of this imbalance by including notable figures of the current "Indian power" movement, as well as those who have become notable for other pursuits. We have tried to restrict the list to persons of at least one-quarter Indian blood, as far as this can be determined. A short separate list of persons of lesser degree of Indian blood is appended in Parts I and II.

In Part II we have compiled a separate list of distinguished Indians who are no longer living, from earliest times to the recent past. There is no comprehensive list of such Indians available anywhere today that this writer has been able to discover. Compilation of the list raised the problem of whether to include the old-time warriors and chiefs along with those whose claims to fame often rest on achievements in white society rather than in their own.

It would seem to be a cultural bias of the worst sort to exclude the chiefs and warriors and to denigrate their importance. They are the heroes and patriots of a conquered people, and are the source of much sentimental, romantic, and scholarly interest to white Americans as well. They are therefore included in a list of their own, Part III.

Miss Gridley, in her third edition of *Indians of Today* (1960), listed 153 distinguished Indians then living. A breakdown of their chief occupations provides a rough estimate of the areas in which Indians have become successful. Since the selection, however, is determined by the subjective evaluations of the author, it may be out of balance.[1] The breakdown follows:

FAMOUS AMERICANS OF INDIAN DESCENT

Clergymen	22
Painters	20
Indian Bureau officials	16
Tribal officers	12
Teachers and principals (below college level)	9
Indian arts and crafts	8
Theatrical (inc. acting, ballet, singing)	7
Physicians	7
Lawyers and judges	7
Government service (not BIA)	5
Career military	5
Lecturer-entertainers	4
Businessmen	4
Elected legislators (state, federal)	4
Officers of Indian organizations (not tribes)	4
Athletes, including coaches	4

1. Since the above was written, the fourth edition of Miss Gridley's *Indians of Today* has appeared, bearing the imprint of "ICFP" (Indian Council Fire Press), and dated 1971. Although the book is considerably expanded and improved over earlier editions, the virtual total exclusion from its pages of dozens of prominent Indians who have risen to prominence as "activist" or "militant" leaders in recent years, compels the conclusion that a strong bias against such individuals on the part of Miss Gridley has caused their exclusion. Consequently, the value of this book as an introduction to the leading "Indians of Today" is seriously weakened.

Famous Americans of Indian Descent (cont.)

Anthropologists	3
College teachers (not anthropology)	3
Musicians (except singers)	2
Dentists	2
Writers	2
Officers of non-Indian service organizations	2
Journalist	1
Radio-TV announcer	1
Nonteaching historian	1
Civil engineer	1
Farmer	1
	Total: 153

Prominent Living American Indians: United States and Canada, 1972

(Explanation of abbreviations is given at the end of this section.)

Hank Adams (Assiniboin-Sioux), 1944–   Director of the Survival of American Indians Association, which was formed to fight for fishing rights guaranteed by treaty to Indian tribes in Washington State. He was born on the Fort Peck reservation in Montana, but was brought to Washington while an infant, and spent most of his youth on the Quinault reservation. At Moclips High School he was an outstanding scholar and athlete as well as president of the student body, but he dropped out of the University of Washington. He was involved in the march on Olympia led by Marlon Brando in 1964 and joined the Poor People's March on Washington in 1968. Between those dates he served in the army (after declaring he would not serve because of Indian treaty violations) and worked for a variety of Indian organizations and causes. Late in 1968 he led forbidden "fish-ins" at Frank's Landing, Washington. On January 12, 1971, while net fishing in the Puyallup River, he was shot in the stomach by an unknown white man armed with a rifle. He recovered, but was sentenced to a six-month jail term for his part in a march on Olympia in 1968. A few days before going to jail he was given the Abraham Lincoln Award of the National Education Association "for courageous actions in pursuit of equal opportunities." He is married to Allison Bridges, daughter of Al and Maiselle Bridges (Puyallup-Nisqually). (*The Renegade,* June, 1971.)

Dolly Smith Akers (Assiniboin). Elected to Montana legislature in 1932, the only woman legislator, and the first Indian woman so elected. Chairman of her tribal council, 1960. (IOT, 1960: 53.)

Wallace Mad Bear Anderson (Tuscarora), 1926–   Merchant seaman, arrested for passive resistance to state power project on Tuscarora land

(1958). He has led many struggles. On March 29, 1959, he attempted a citizen's arrest of Indian Commissioner Glenn Emmons. He has led a fight against imposition of state sales taxes on Indians, and was active in the leadership of the Indian unity conferences held on various Six Nations reserves in August 1969. (CT Apr. 18 '58:1; TGM Aug. 30 '69:4.)

John Artichoker, Jr. (Sioux) 1930–   . Holder of a master's degree from the University of South Dakota, he was in 1959 director of Indian education for the state of South Dakota, and was in that year elected to a second term as president of the Governors' Interstate Indian Council. He was chosen by the U.S. Junior Chamber of Commerce as one of the ten outstanding young men of 1964. His most recent post was superintendent of the Northern Cheyenne agency, Lame Deer, Mont. (Amer Nov.–Dec. '59: 1; Sep.–Oct. '65: 1; IOT, 1960: 114–15; Look Jan. 26, '65: 34; KI, 346.)

James D. Atcitty (Navajo). With another Navajo, Monroe Jymm (*q. v.*), he was one of the first two Indians elected to the House of Representatives of the state of New Mexico (Dem.), November 3, 1964. (CT Nov. 5 '64; IV Feb. '65: 3.)

Louis Wayne Ballard (Quapaw-Cherokee), 1931–   . Ballet music composer. His principal work is *Koshare,* an American Indian ballet based on a Hopi creation myth (Harkness Ballet Co., 1966). He is chairman of the Music and Living Arts Department, Institute of American Indian Art, Santa Fe, N.M. (AIP, 12–13.)

Dennis Banks (Ojibwa, Leech Lake), 1938–   . Co-founder and chairman of the American Indian Movement (*q. v.*), in Minneapolis. (CST Jun. 11 '70: 72.)

Beatien Yazz [Jimmy Toddy] (Navajo), 1928–   . Considered "the greatest living primitive painter," Beatien Yazz specializes in scenes from Indian life, and of animals. His fame was increased by Alberta Hannum's two books, *Spin a Silver Dollar* (1945) and *Paint the Wind* (1958). Some of his work is reproduced in color in *Arizona Highways,* July 1956. He is the illustrator of Stan Steiner's book, *The Last Horse* (1961). As a marine in World War II, the artist was a member of the famous Navajo code unit. (ICT, 1960: 210–12; Amer May–Jun. '61: 3–4; AIP, 14–15.)

Harrison Begay (Navajo), 1917–   . One of the best known of the Navajo painters. "Begay's paintings have exerted greater influence on Navajo artists than any others. His work is internationally known." [Snodgrass] (AIP, 17–18.)

Wilbert C. Begay (Navajo), 1939–   . Elected to the House of Representatives, state of New Mexico, in 1966. He attended Fort Lewis College and Utah State University for a total of three years, and spent two years in the army. (IT May '67: WWAP, 77.)

Johnny Belindo (Navajo-Kiowa). Elected executive director, National Congress of American Indians, in 1967. (IT Aut. '67: 5.)

Clyde Bellecourt (Ojibwa, White Earth), 1936–   . Director of the American Indian Movement (Minneapolis), "the most sophisticated radical Indian organization in the country." [William Granger.] (CST Jun. 11 '70: 72.)

Harry Belvin (Choctaw), 1901– . Principal chief, Choctaw Nation, 1948–1965; member Oklahoma House of Representatives, three terms, 1954–1960; state senator, 1960–1964. (IOT, 81–82; IV Apr. '64: 8; KI, 352.)

Robert L. Bennett (Oneida), 1912– . Commissioner of the U.S. Bureau of Indian Affairs, 1966–1969, the second Indian to hold that post. His administration was popular with most tribes. Recipient of Indian Council Fire achievement medal, 1962, he now directs the American Indian Law center at the University of New Mexico. (IOT, '60: 89–90; Amer Sep.–Oct. '62: 1; May–Jun. '66: 1; Nov.–Dec. '63: 3; KI, 353.)

Brantley Blue (Lumbee), 1925– . Attorney, born and educated in Pembroke, N.C., later a judge in Kingsport, Tenn., Mr. Blue was appointed chairman of the Indian Claims Commission by President Nixon in 1969. (Amer Sep.–Oct. '69: 4; WWAP, 106.)

Ruth Muskrat Bronson (Cherokee). Author, public health educator, United States Public Health Service; formerly executive secretary, National Congress of American Indians. Recipient of the achievement medal, Indian Council Fire, 1937, and the Oveta Culp Hobby award, 1962. Author of *Indians Are People Too* (1944). (IT Jan.–Apr. '60: 1–5; IOT, 1960: 75; Amer May–Jun. '62: 5.)

Louis R. Bruce, Jr. (Mohawk-Sioux), 1907– . Former public relations and advertising executive, dairy farmer, and executive secretary of the National Congress of American Indians. He was appointed commissioner of the Bureau of Indian Affairs in August 1969, the third Indian to hold that post. (IOT, 1960: 36–37; Amer Sep.–Oct. '69: 1; CST Jun. 12 '70: 42.)

Frank Calder (Nishga, British Columbia). Elected to the provincial legislative assembly in 1949, with the support of labor and the Cooperative Commonwealth Federation (now the New Democratic party). He was twice reelected. His views are assimilationist. (Amer Mar.–Apr. '56: 2; IOT, 1960: 91; Hum Org, Win. '61–62: 225.)

Harold Cardinal (Cree), 1945– . President and executive director of the Indian Association of Alberta; author of *The Unjust Society: The Tragedy of Canada's Indians* (1969). He is an advocate of Indian cultural survival. (NYT Jul. 6 '70; AN Nov. '69: 18.)

Hote Casella (Cherokee). Mezzo-soprano, folk-singer, promoter of American Indian music. (CHA Nov. 24 '63.)

Jake C. Chee (Navajo). Elected to the New Mexico House of Representatives, 1966. (IT May '67: 5.)

Wendell Chino (Mescalero Apache). President of the Mescalero Apache tribe and of the National Congress of American Indians, 1969. (AN Nov. '69: 15.)

Michael Chosa (Ojibwa, Lac du Flambeau), 1936– . Leader of Chicago's "Indian village," established along the railroad tracks north of Wrigley Field, in May 1970, to protest the eviction of a Menominee mother and her six children, and to publicize conditions affecting Indians. In the summer of 1971 he led an occupation of an abandoned Nike missile site in Chicago, and subsequently the Argonne National Laboratory grounds outside the city, in protest against the lack of suitable housing for Indians. He has been in the air force, attended Haskell, worked for the BIA, and has been an agricultural and factory laborer. (CST Jun. 7 '70: sec. 2, p. 1; Jun. 8: 5–6.)

Raymond C. Christiansen (Eskimo). Elected to the Alaska State Senate in 1966; chairman of the Alaska Democratic party, 1968. (Amer Jan.–Feb. '67: 1; IT May '67: 6; WWAP, 210.)

Dr. Henry Roe Cloud (Winnebago). Coauthor of the Meriam report (1928); former superintendent of Haskell Institute and supervisor of Indian education, BIA (1936); winner of achievement award, Indian Council Fire, 1935. (IOT: 1947: 24.)

Rupert Costo (Cahuila). Founder and president of the American Indian Historical Society (est. 1964), and member of the editorial board of *The Indian Historian*. Promoter of and participant in the first Convocation of Indian Scholars, Princeton, N.J., March 1970; author: *Redmen of the Golden West* (1970). (AIA, 15; IH Nov. '67: 20; and AIHS brochures.)

John O. Crow (Cherokee), 1912–   . Deputy Commissioner of the Bureau of Indian Affairs since July 1971. He was a professional football player in his youth, but later spent thirty years in the employ of the BIA. Just prior to his latest appointment, he was Associate Director of the Bureau of Land Management in the Interior Department. In Indian affairs he is considered an assimilationist, and promoted the termination of the Utah Utes in the 1950s. Upon his return to the BIA, some Indians accused him of seeking to reverse reforms begun by Commissioner Louis Bruce, and demonstrated against him at the BIA offices. Others, such as Leon Cook (who resigned from the BIA in the fall of 1971, and was then elected president of the National Congress of American Indians), charge that Bruce and Crow have a common anti-Indian policy. Both were ousted after the destructive occupation of the BIA building by militant Indians in November 1972. (CB 1969: 16–18; News Service of American Indian Press Association.)

Albert Dana (Passamaquoddy). Representative of the Indians of Indian Township in the Maine legislature, 1968–1970, by tribal vote. This seat alternates biennially with the other Passamaquoddy community, at Pleasant Point. Maine is the only state with representation of tribes, as such, in the legislature. The Penobscots of Old Town also have a seat. Mr. Dana has fought to maintain and extend Indian rights, and was a participant in the roadblock protest of July 1969. His wife, Philomene, is a member of the tribal council. (Interview, Aug. 26, 1969; letter from Joseph T. Edgar, deputy secretary of state, Augusta, Dec. 17, 1964.)

Vine Deloria, Jr. (Sioux), 1933–   . The son of Vine Deloria, Sr., a well-known Sioux clergyman, and a nephew of Ella Deloria, Vine Jr. has made a name in his own right, attaining national fame with his books *Custer Died for Your Sins* (1969) and *We Talk, You Listen* (1970). He is also a former executive secretary of the National Congress of American Indians. (IOT, 1960: 60; Amer Jan.–Feb. '65: 2; SR Oct. 4 '69: 39.)

Percy DeWolf (Blackfoot). Elected to the Montana State Senate, 1966. (IT May '67: 5.)

Dr. Frederick Dockstader (Oneida), 1919–   . Anthropologist, director of the Museum of the American Indian, New York; specialist in American Indian arts; author of five books, including *Indian Art in South America* (1967). (AIA, 17; KI, 382–83.)

Brummet Echohawk (Pawnee), 1922–   . Artist, cartoonist, illustrator; creator of comic strip "Little Chief" in the *Tulsa World*. (IOT, 1960: 22–23; KI, 387; AIP, 52.)

Steven Fastwolf (Oglala Sioux), 1949–   . Director of the Native American Committee, a militant organization in Chicago. He is a student at Roosevelt University. In 1973 he launched the *Native American Publication*, a monthly. (CST Jun. 7 '70: sec. 2, p. 6.)

W. E. S. Folsom-Dickerson (Choctaw). 1898–   . Teacher, author. Phi Beta Kappa graduate of the University of Texas; author of *The Handbook of Texas* (2 vols., 1952), and *The White Path* (1965), a book about the Alabama and Koasati Indians of Texas. (IOT, 1947: 99; KI, 397.)

David Fox (Ottawa), 1934–   . Born on the Canadian Ottawa reserve at Wikwemikong, on Manitoulin Island, Georgian Bay. Educated in a mission school, he later worked in sawmills and lumber camps, on road construction and in structural steel. He now lives in Griffith, Indiana, and commutes to Chicago where he is head of Great Lakes Indian Craftsmen, a company that markets Indian arts. He is also on the board of American Indian Development and Education (AIDE). (CDN Jan. 12 '71: Sec. 3 p. 17.)

Joseph R. Garry (Coeur d'Alene). First Indian elected to the Idaho legislature (Senate, 1956). He has held the seat continuously since then. He is president of his tribal council, has served eight terms as president of the Affiliated Tribes of Northwest Indians, and was five times the president of the National Congress of American Indians. (Amer Mar.–Apr. '60: 3; May–Jun. '68: 4; IOT, 1960: 71; IV Oct. '65: 6; IA Jan.–Feb. '67; IT May '67; 5.)

Mickey Gemmill (Pit River), 1944–   . Former chairman of the tribal council, Pit River Indians of northern California. Under his leadership, these Indians of the southern Cascades demanded the recovery of most of the land between Mt. Lassen and Mt. Shasta, which was taken from them without payment 115 years ago, when the Senate neither ratified the treaties made with them nor made other provision for most California tribes. Gemmill and his followers have participated in several attempts to occupy parts of the lost lands, and he has been arrested several times in these attempts. In June 1970, he led a band that entered a campground of the Pacific Gas and Electric Co., which resulted in the arrest of thirty-eight people. In October 1970, Gemmill and about a hundred Indians, including women and children, occupied a corner of Lassen National Forest near Burney, California, and erected a metal Quonset hut. On October 27, the Indians were assaulted by more than ninety men, including sheriff's deputies, federal marshals, park rangers, and forest service employees. Mace and clubs were used against the Indians, who defended themselves with tree branches. Twenty-six Indians were arrested. The Indians have rejected a cash offer of 47 cents an acre for their land, saying they want the land, not money. (AN, Dec. '70: 12–16; personal visit, Aug. '70.)

Chief Dan George (Squamish), 1899–   . Winner of the New York Film Critics Award for 1970 as best supporting actor for his role as Old Lodge Skins, a Cheyenne chief and Dustin Hoffman's adopted grandfather in *Little Big Man.* He lives in Vancouver, B.C., and worked as a longshoreman until he began playing bit parts for TV and movies about 1960. (AN Mar. '71: 29.)

La Donna C. Harris (Comanche), 1931–   . Granddaughter of a Comanche medicine man, Mrs. Harris is the wife of Senator Fred Harris of Oklahoma, former chairman of the Democratic National Committee. She is founder and president of Oklahomans for Indian Opportunity, and a board member of numerous other welfare groups, especially those concerned with Indians and with mental health. (CST Dec. 17 '64: 96; Amer May–Jun. '65: 7; Jul.–Aug. '65: 4; IV Dec.–Jan. '66–'67: 4; CDN Oct. 22 '68; WWAW, 525.)

Martinez Heath (Warm Springs). Heath is the only full-blooded American Indian riding on the American turf. In 1968 he led the jockeys with 28 winners, which collected $134,739 in purses. (Amer Sep.–Oct. '67: 4; CDN Oct. 22 '68.)

Jeanette Henry (Cherokee). Editor of *The Indian Historian* and coauthor with her husband, Rupert Costo, of *Textbooks and the American Indian,* published by the American Indian Historical Society, 1970. (Source: above publications.)

William L. Hensley (Eskimo), 1941–   . Alaska state representative since 1967 (Dem.), and Democratic Convention delegate, 1968. He is a graduate of the University of Washington and did graduate work at the University of Alaska. He is vice-chairman of the Alaska Federation of Native Associations and executive director of the Northwest Alaska Native Association. (Amer Jan.–Feb. '67: 1; IT May '67: 6; WWAP, 512.)

Eben Hopson (Eskimo). Member of the Alaska legislature since statehood (1959), and mayor of Barrow, on the Arctic coast. (Amer Mar.–Apr. '66: 1; Sep.–Oct. '66: 2.)

Kahn-Tineta Horn (Mohawk, Caughnawaga, Que.) 1943–   . Former model, beauty contest winner, and TV actress, Miss Horn has proven her ability to "make it" in the white world, but has not forsaken her people. She has chosen to be a militant leader of Indian protests, and was among 47 arrested in a demonstration against tolls and duties for Indians on the Massena-Cornwall international bridge, in December 1968. The Indians hold that the charges violate the Jay Treaty of 1794. An ardent defender of Indian land-holdings, she maintains that Indians should depend upon themselves, and turn to young leadership. (IV Jun. '64: 12; CT Jun. 15 '69; NFG Sep. 5 '69: 1.)

Lloyd House (Navajo), 1931–   . Arizona State Representative since 1967, and first Indian elected to the State Assembly. He has a bachelor of education degree from Northern Arizona University, is a Korean veteran, has worked for the Bureau of Indian Affairs, the Social Security Administration, and the Navajo Tribe, for which he has been Social Security Director since 1963. (IT May '67: 5; Amer May.–Jun. '68: 6; WWAP, 544.)

Oscar Howe (Sioux), 1915–   . Artist and teacher, winner of numerous awards from the Philbrook Art Center and other institutions. He has illustrated several books and teaches at the University of South Dakota. (KI, 422–23.)

Axel Johnson (Eskimo). Elected to the Alaska Legislature in 1966. (Amer Mar.–Apr. '66: 1.)

Napoleon B. Johnson (Cherokee), 1892–   . First president of the National Congress of American Indians (1944); chief justice of the Supreme Court of Oklahoma, 1955–65; awarded the achievement medal of the Indian Council Fire, 1966. (Amer Jan.–Feb. '55: 3; Sep.–Oct. '55: 1; May–Jun. '64: 2; IOT, 1960: 136–37; CT Mar. 23 & May 12 '65.)

Arthur S. Junaluska (Cherokee), 1918–   . Executive and artistic director, American Indian Society for Creative Arts, writer of plays for radio, TV, and stage. (IOT, 1960: 141–42; KI, 431.)

Monroe Jymm (Navajo), 1933–   . While still a student at the University of New Mexico, he was elected to the House of Representatives of New Mexico on November 3, 1964, as a Democrat. He and James Atcitty (*q.v.*), elected at the same time, were the first Indians so elected. (CT Nov. 5 '64; IV Feb. '65: 3; WWAP, 600.)

Fred Kabotie (Hopi), 1900–   . The list of this talented painter's works and exhibits is long. The mural in the Grand Canyon's Desert View Tower is one of his creations. He was the recipient of a Guggenheim fellowship, 1945–1946, and the Indian Council Fire medal, 1949. He is listed in *Who's Who in American Art.* (IOT, 1960: 217–18; AIP, 89–90.)

William Wayne Keeler (Cherokee), 1908–   . It may come as a surprise to many that the titular head of the American industrial establishment is an Indian chief. Mr. Keeler began his professional career as an assistant chemist with the Phillips Petroleum Corporation in 1929, and rose to executive vice-president in 1956, chairman of the executive committee in 1962, and president and chief executive officer in 1967. In 1969 he was elected chairman of the board of the National Association of Manufacturers. In 1949, by appointment of President Truman, he became principal chief of the Cherokee Nation, although he is a quarter-blood. In 1971, in the first tribal election since Oklahoma statehood, he was elected to the same post. He has held and now holds a number of posts of responsibility in government, business, and welfare organizations. He was a founder and is a trustee of the Cherokee Foundation, and was a member of the Commission on the Rights, Liberties, and Responsibilities of the American Indian, of the Fund for the Republic. Writer Peter Collier charges that Keeler's policies are detrimental to and opposed by most of the fullbloods ["Theft of a Nation," *Ramparts,* Sep. 1970, pp. 35–45]. (IOT, 1960: 31–33; Amer Sep.–Oct. '63: 1; Sep.–Oct. '67: 6; Jan.–Feb. '70: 1–2; KI, 432; WWA v35: 1178.)

Yeffe Kimball (Osage), 1914–   . Painter, illustrator, textile designer, consultant on native arts, author of articles on Indian art; coauthor, with Jean Anderson, of *The Art of American Indian Cooking* (1965). (AIP, 94; AIA, 24.)

Tom Lee (Navajo), 1920–   . New Mexico state senator since 1966 (Rep.), and the first Indian to be elected to that office in New Mexico. Tom Lee was educated in an Indian boarding school at Tohatchi for eight years. During World War II he was captured by the Japanese and was on the Bataan march; upon his release he was the recipient of many decorations. He operates a trading post at Twin Lakes, N.M., served on the board of a BIA school for six years, and is a community leader for the Navajo Tribe. (Amer Jan.–Feb. '67: 2; IT May '67: 5; WWAP, 671.)

Janet McCloud (Nisqually). Active leader in the Washington State fish-ins, the Fort Lawton movement, and the Indian peace movement. She led the camp-in on the state capitol grounds at Olympia, June 22–30, 1968, to protest the enforcement of fishing restrictions against Indians in violation of treaties. (*The Renegade,* May '68: 1; CST Jun. 10 '70.)

Solomon McCombs (Creek), 1913–   . Artist, lecturer, architectural draftsman, cartographer; winner of sixteen awards at the Philbrook Art Center, Tulsa; he has exhibited at several leading museums. One of his paintings was purchased by the late Robert Kennedy, and another hangs in the American embassy in Madrid. (IOT, 1960: 220; CNJ, 1967; AIP, 114–15.)

Peter MacDonald (Navajo), 1928–   . Tribal chairman of the Navajo, America's largest Indian tribe, inaugurated in January 1971. Left fatherless at two, he left school after seventh grade, herded sheep and worked in a sawmill and on railway construction. Fibbing about his age, he entered the marines at fifteen and saw action in the Pacific. He later finished high school in a few months, attended Bacone college, and received a degree in electrical engineering from the University of Oklahoma. He became an executive with Hughes Aircraft Corporation at Los Angeles, but left it to take a federal job at less pay on the Navajo reservation. Eight years later he was elected tribal chairman. His aims include more businesses owned by Navajos and employing Navajos, more education, and government aid for economic development. (CT Feb. 14 '71.)

D'Arcy McNickle (Flathead [Salish]-Kootenai), 1904–   . Author and organization executive; director of the Center for the History of the American Indian at Newberry Library in Chicago. He was educated at the University of Montana and at Oxford, worked as a writer, spent sixteen years in the Bureau of Indian Affairs, and since 1952 has been director of American Indian Development, Inc., Boulder, Colo. He was a co-founder of the National Congress of American Indians, and is the author of several books. His writings include *The Surrounded,* a novel (1936), *They Came Here First,* a history of Indian-white relations (1949), *Indians and Other Americans,* coauthored with Harold E. Fey (1949), *Runner in the Sun,* a novel (1954), *IndianTribes of the U.S.: Ethnic and Cultural Survival* (1962), and "North American Indians" in the *Encyclopedia Britannica.* (IOT, 1960: 106; KI, 451; CA v9–10: 333; AIA, 27.)

Clem Rogers McSpadden (Cherokee), 1925–   . An Oklahoma state senator since 1954 (Dem.), he was assistant floor leader for two years and was president pro-tempore, 1965–1967. He has a degree in animal husbandry from Oklahoma State University, owns a cattle ranch, and has been engaged in rodeo management, announcing, and sportscasting. (IT May '67: 6; WWAP, 741.)

Leonard S. Marchand (Okanagan), 1933–   . Mr. Marchand in 1968 became the first Indian to be elected to the Canadian federal parliament (House of Commons). Prior to that time he served for three years as special assistant to the federal minister of citizenship and immigration. He is a resident of Kamloops, B.C., and was educated at the University of British Columbia and the University of Idaho, where he received the degree of MS in forestry. (IV Jun. '65: 9; Amer May–Jun. '65: 2; May–Jun. '66: 3; Jan.–Feb. '69: 5; CT Jun. 15 '69.)

Maria Martinez (San Ildefonso Pueblo), 1904–   . Made famous by her pottery and by Alice Marriott's book, *Maria: the Potter of San Ildefonso* (1963), she is the one who rediscovered the ancient method of making a unique style of highly polished black pottery with decorative design in a dull-black etched effect. (IOT, 1960: 13–14.)

John Massey (Choctaw), 1936–   . Oklahoma state senator since 1967; he was also a state representative, 1960–1964. He graduated from Southeast State College, Ada, in 1960. (Amer Jan.–Feb. '67: 2; IT May '67: 6; WWAP, 765.)

John Joseph Mathews (Osage), 1895–   . A graduate of the University of Oklahoma and of Oxford, where he was a Rhodes scholar, Mathews's first book, *Wahkontah* (1932, reissued 1968), a story of Osage history, was the first in the Civilization of the American Indian series of the University of Oklahoma Press. His other books are *Sundown*, a novel (1934), *Talking to the Moon* (1945), *Life and Death of an Oilman* (1952), and *The Osages: Children of the Middle Waters* (1961). (AIA, 27–28; book jackets.)

Russell Means (Sioux), 1940–   . Director of the American Indian Movement of Cleveland. (CST Jun. 7 '70: sec. 2 p. 2.)

Billy Mills (Oglala Sioux, Pine Ridge), 1938–   . Champion distance runner in the 1964 Olympic Games at Tokyo; winner of the first-place gold medal in the 10,000 meter race, he was the first American to win this event. The next year at an AAU meet in New York he made the second fastest three-mile run ever registered, and set a record for an American, in 13 minutes, 25.4 seconds. An ex-marine lieutenant, Mills was appointed information officer at the Bureau of Indian Affairs in 1970. (CT Oct. 15 '64; CDN Oct. 17 '64; IV Dec. '64: 7; Feb. '65: 7; Jun. '65: 10; CSM Feb. 27 '65; Amer Nov.–Dec. '64: 1; May–Jun. '70: 1; IT Jun. '70: 7.)

Sid Mills (Yakima-Cherokee), 1948–   , and *Suzette Mills* (Nisqually-Puyallup-Duwamish), 1948–   . Active leaders in the Washington State fish-ins. Sid Mills served two years and four months in Vietnam, where he won a Purple Heart for serious wounds, but upon returning to the U.S., deserted, saying "I have given enough to the U.S. army—I choose now to serve my people." His wife Suzette is the daughter of Al Bridges, arrested twelve times for "illegal fishing," and Maiselle Bridges, secretary of the Survival of American Indians Association. In 1968 Suzette, a graduate of Haskell Institute, and her husband were both arrested for fishing in the Nisqually river at Frank's Landing, in accordance with treaty guarantees. Sid was turned over to the military and eventually discharged. (*The Renegade*, May 1969.)

Navarre Scott Momaday (Kiowa), 1934–   . Educator and prize-winning novelist. Momaday was born at Lawton, Okla., the only son of two well-known Indian artists, Alfred M., a Kiowa, and Natachee (Scott) Momaday, a Cherokee-Choctaw. He graduated from the University of New Mexico, and received M.A. and Ph.D. degrees from Stanford, the latter in 1963. His only novel so far, *House Made of Dawn* (Harper & Row, 1968), won the 1969 Pulitzer prize for fiction. It deals with the adjustment problems of an urbanized Indian ex-soldier. His account of Kiowa traditions, *The Way to Rainy Mountain* (1969), was illustrated by his father. Earlier, he published *The Complete Poems of Frederick Goddard Tuckerman* (1965). Dr. Momaday first taught at the University of California, Santa Barbara, 1962–1969, and has been professor of English and comparative literature, University of California, Berkeley, since 1969. (IOT, 1960: 153–54; KI, 461; CDN Pan May 17 '69; NYT Jul. 26 '69; AIA, 28–29; WWA v36: 1593.)

Dr. Gilbert C. Monture (Mohawk). Mineralogist; among many posts he has held is his latest, chief of the Mineral Resources Division of Canada. He received the achievement award of the Indian Council Fire in 1957. (IOT 1960: 101–102; IT Win '57–'58: 4; CT Jun. 15 '69.)

Carl Eugene Moses (Aleut), 1929–   . Alaska State Representative since 1965. He is a veteran and a merchant in Unalaska. (Amer Mar.–Apr. '66: 1; WWAP, 817.)

Robert M. Murphy (Cherokee). Oklahoma State Senator, 1967–   . (Amer Jan.–Feb. '67: 2; IT May '67: 6.)

Raymond Nakai (Navajo), 1918–   . Chairman of the Navajo Tribal Council from 1963 to 1971, when he was succeeded by Peter MacDonald (*q.v.*). His policies favored modernization and industrial development. He has broadcast a disc jockey program in the Navajo language. (Amer Mar.–Apr. '63: 5; IV Jan. '66: 7; Nov. '66: 7–8.)

Richard Oakes (Mohawk, St. Regis), 1942–1972. A leader of the Alcatraz island occupation in 1969–1970, and also of the land reoccupation movement of the Pit River Indians of California. Tragedy has followed him. His twelve-year-old daughter died January 8, 1970, from injuries received when she fell three stories in a building in which she was playing on Alcatraz island. On June 12, 1970, he was hospitalized with critical injuries after being beaten in San Francisco by three men. The incident ocurred only a few hours after he had managed a citizen's arrest of the president of Pacific Gas and Electric Co., holder of lands claimed by the Pit River Indians. He was shot to death, while unarmed, in a quarrel with a private camp guard, near the Pomo reservation in northern California, September 20, 1972. (AN Nov. '69: 45; Jul.–Aug. '70: 4; CST Jan. 11 '70: 12, 23.)

Abraham Okpik (Eskimo), 1929–   . Trapper's son who is the first Canadian Eskimo elected to the Northwest Territory Legislative Council. He lives in Yellowknife, N.W.T., Canada. (Amer Mar.–Apr. '66: 5.)

Earl Old Person (Blackfoot). Chairman of the Blackfeet Tribe of Montana, elected president of the National Congress of American Indians at the 1969 convention. (NCAI Sent Win '70: 8; IT Jun. '70: 1–3.)

Dr. Alfonso Ortiz (Tewa, San Juan Pueblo). Assistant professor of anthropology, Princeton University; author of *The Tewa World* (1969). (IH Sum '69: 8.)

Frank Peratrovich (Tlingit). Unanimously elected president of the Alaska Senate in 1961, and served in that post longer than any other senator. In 1963 he was chairman of the Alaska Democratic party. (Amer Mar.–Apr. '66: 1.)

Helen Peterson (Oglala Sioux). A former executive secretary of the National Congress of American Indians, she has also worked with Spanish-speaking people and in 1948 was appointed director of the Mayor's Commission on Human Relations, Denver. In 1970 she was appointed assistant to the commissioner of Indian Affairs. (IOT, 1960: 93–94; IT Jun. '70: 7.)

George Pierre (Colville), 1926–   . Washington state representative (Dem.), from the 34th district (Seattle), 1964–1966. In 1963 he was installed as chief of the Colville Confederated Tribes. He has attended several colleges and universities, and is a professional writer. His publications include *Autumn's Bounty* (1959), and *Indian Country* (1964), by the Amerindic Lore Press. (Amer Nov.–Dec. '64: 2; WWAP, 907.)

Pop Chalee (Taos Pueblo), 1908–   . Mural painter who "long ago developed a unique style of painting which combines Oriental and Amerindian motifs" [Snodgrass]. Color reproductions of her work appeared in *Arizona Highways,* February 1950. (IOT, 1947: 74; AIP, 148–49.)

Benjamin Reifel (Sioux), 1906–   . U.S. congressman from South Dakota (Rep.) 1960–1971; member of the Appropriations Committee. He was appointed chairman of the National capitol planning commission in 1971. He was born in a log cabin on a Sioux reservation, of a Sioux mother and a German-American father who worked as a cowhand. Mr. Reifel received a Ph.D. degree in public administration from Harvard University in 1952, and has held several posts in the Bureau of Indian Affairs, the last of which was area director at Aberdeen, S.D. He was named Outstanding American Indian at Sheridan, Wyo., in 1956, and received the Indian Council Fire Award in 1960. He is president of Arrow, Inc., and an officer in other organizations. A brother, Alexander, is a civil engineer, and another, Albert, is a physician. (IOT, 1960: 228–32; IT Sep. '60: 4; Amer Nov.–Dec. '60: 4; IV Apr. '65: 8; KI, 485; CD '70: 165.)

Allie Reynolds (Creek), 1919–   . Professional baseball player, starting with the Cleveland Indians in 1942, and with the New York Yankees, 1947–1954. He was for seven years a member of the American League Allstars, and led the American League in strikeouts in 1942 and 1952. In 1952 he had the best earned run average in his league, and also pitched the most shutouts in 1945 and 1952. Upon his retirement from baseball in 1954 he was given the first achievement award of the Creek Nation. He is now in business in Oklahoma City. (CB, 1952: 494–96; IOT, 1960: 148–49; CNJ 1967.)

Howard Rock (Eskimo). Editor of the *Tundra Times,* a flourishing native weekly newspaper published at Fairbanks, Alaska. (IT Jun. '64: 11.)

John Sackett (Athapascan), 1949–   . Honor student at the University of Alaska, elected to the Alaska House of Representatives (Rep.) in 1966. (Amer Jan.–Feb. '67: 1; IT May '67: 6.)

Buffy Sainte-Marie (Cree), 1941–   . Popular folk-singer, poet, and recording artist. She was born on the Piapot reserve in Saskatchewan, Canada, and became the adopted daughter of Albert and Winifred Sainte-Marie. She graduated from the University of Massachusetts in 1962. Besides appearances at nightclubs and coffee houses, she has had concerts at Carnegie Hall, Royal Albert Hall in London, and the New York Philharmonic. Several of her recordings are her own compositions. She is a champion of Indian rights, and several of her songs and poems are related to past and present conditions of the Indians; among these are "My Country 'Tis of Thy People You're Dying," and "Now That the Buffalo's Gone." (CT Aug. 2 '68; Aug. 3 '68: sec. 10, p. 2; CST Nov. 17 '68: sec. 3, p. 5; May 4 '69: sec. 3 p. 5; NYT Nov. 30 '68; KI, 493; WWA v36: 1979.)

Frank See (Tlingit). Elected to the Alaska House of Representatives in 1966. (IT May '67: 6.)

Jay Silverheels [Harry Smith] (Mohawk). Film and TV actor, played Tonto in "The Lone Ranger" beginning in 1949. On the screen he played in *Broken Arrow* and *Brave Warrior.* He has also been a champion athlete, distinguishing himself in boxing, wrestling, lacrosse, hockey, football, and track. (Amer Nov.–Dec. '57: 2; IOT, 1960: 131; TV mag in CDN Mar. 6 '60: 53.)

Jess Sixkiller (Cherokee), 1937–   . Oklahoma-born Cherokee, a Chicago detective who was a founder and full-time director of American Indians United during its first year (1969). (Amer. Mar.–Apr. '67: 8; CT Jan. 26 '69; CDN Feb. 1 '69: 17; CST Jun. 8 '70: 5–6.)

Keely Smith (Cherokee), 1935–   . Singer, TV and film actress, recording artist. She has appeared on television shows with Dinah Shore, Frank Sinatra, and Dean Martin. She co-starred with Robert Mitchum in the film *Thunder Road* (1957). In 1958 she received four awards: the Disc Jockeys' Favorite Female award, the Most Promising TV Performer award of the National Academy of Musical Arts, and the Grammy award of the National Academy of Recording Arts and Sciences. She received the Number One Female Vocalist award of *Billboard* and *Variety* magazines in both 1958 and 1959. In 1959 she also won the Playboy Jazz award and the Top Variety Entertainer award of the Diners Club, and in 1960 the Joey award for the number-one variety act. She is a member of her union, the ASCAP, and the American Indian Center of Los Angeles. (CT Mar. 27 '60; BIA, 4; WWAW, 1147–48.)

Jacob Stalker (Eskimo). Member of the Alaska legislature in 1966. He is a river barge mechanic. (Amer Mar.–Apr. '66: 1.)

Kay Starr (Cherokee). Singer, entertainer, television and recording artist. (BIA, 4.)

Orange Walter Starr (Cherokee). Physician, member of the Oklahoma legislature, 1942–1946. (IOT, 1960: 214.)

John W. Stevens (Passamaquoddy), 1933–   Governor (chief) of the Passamaquoddies of Indian Township, Maine, since 1955. He is an active fighter for Indian rights, and participated in the roadblock protest, July 1969. (IT Oct. '66: 1; KI, 505; interview, Aug. 27, '69.)

Yma Sumac [Emperatriz Chavarri] (Quechua [Inca]), 1928–   . Singer and actress; born in the Peruvian mountain village of Ichocan, of a full-blooded Indian mother and a mixed Indian and Spanish father. She was brought up as a Quechuan, participating from childhood in Indian festivities, some descended from pre-Conquest times. While singing in one of these, her talent was brought to the attention of the Ministry of Education, which brought the family to Lima, where Yma was enrolled in school and presented in concert. There she eventually joined the Compañia Peruana de Arte, composed of forty-six Indian dancers, singers, and musicians, with whom she toured Latin American cities. She married the troupe's director, Moiser Vivanco, in 1942. The couple moved to New York in 1946, together with Yma's cousin, Cholito Rivero, and sought engagements as the Inca Taky Trio, with small success. Eventually Miss Sumac made a hit record, *Songs of Xtabay*, composed of ancient Peruvian melodies. Her repertoire for this and other songs was composed by her husband, and derived from ancient Andean folk themes, influenced by Inca traditions. Subsequent to her recording success, she sang at the Hollywood Bowl and Carnegie Hall, in a Broadway musical, *Flahooley*, on radio and television, and in concerts at home and abroad. In 1954 she played in the Paramount motion picture, *Secret of the Incas*. She became an American citizen in 1955, and now lives in Los Angeles with her husband. (CB '55: 587–89; WWA v36: 2225.)

Maria Tallchief [Paschen] (Osage), 1925–   . Solo ballerina, the daughter of Alexander Joseph Tallchief, an Osage Indian, and Ruth Mary Porter, of Scotch-Irish descent. Her great-grandfather was Chief Peter Bigheart. She says "My grandmother wore a blanket and my father was born in a tepee and rode horseback." When she was eight, her family moved to Los Angeles; she had been practicing ballet since she was three. She made her dancing debut in Canada in 1942 with the Ballet Russe de Monte Carlo, with which she remained five years. For the remainder of her career she was prima ballerina with the New York City Ballet Company, though she toured Russia with the American Ballet Theatre in 1960. She was a favorite performer in *Firebird*, but has also been acclaimed for her performance in *Swan Lake* and *The Nutcracker*. She received the Indian Council Fire medal in 1967. She retired from the stage in 1966 and lives with her husband, Henry Paschen Jr., and an eleven-year-old daughter, in Chicago. (CB '51:

618–20; CND Roto Apr. 27 '57; IOT, 1960: 190–92; Time Oct. 31 '60: 61; CST Sep. 6 '67: 24; CDN Sep. 22 '67: 16; Amer Sep.–Oct. '67: 1; WWA v36: 2243.)

Marjorie Tallchief (Osage). Ballerina, and sister of Maria Tallchief. She starred in the premiere of Louis Ballard's *Koshare* in Barcelona. She now lives in Paris, where she has danced for the Paris Opera Ballet. (IOT, 1960; 191–92; IV Nov. '65: 9; Apr.–May '66: 16.)

Melvin Thom (Paiute), 1939–   . Civil engineer, a founder of the National Indian Youth Council, and a leader of the Coalition of American Indian Citizens. He has been chairman of the Walker River Tribal Council (Nevada). (Amer Jul.–Aug. '62: 2; IV Jan. '66: 8; WSJ Apr. 30 '69: 24.)

Robert K. Thomas (Cherokee). Professor of anthropology, Wayne State University, Detroit; a founder and editor of *Indian Voices* (Chicago, 1963–1968). (IV Apr. '63: 1; WSJ Apr. 30 '69: 1.)

Joe Thornton (Cherokee). World's champion Olympic archer, Oslo, 1961. Self-taught, he made his first bow and arrows at Chilocco Indian School (Oklahoma), and learned to shoot Indian style. (IV Oct. '63: 1.)

Jean A. Turnage (Flathead). Elected to the State Senate of Montana in 1966. (Amer Jan.–Feb. '67: 2; IT May '67: 5.)

Tillie Walker (Mandan). Born on the reservation of the three associated tribes of Fort Berthold, N.D., Miss Walker has worked for the Indian Rights Association, the American Friends Service Committee, and the United Scholarship Service. (IOT, 1960: 142; IT Jul. '63: 2.)

Annie Dodge Wauneka (Navajo). First woman elected to the 74-member Navajo Tribal Council (1951), of which she is still a member. Always seen in traditional dress, she is perhaps most noted for promoting the acceptance of modern medicine and sanitation in the Navajo Nation. She received the Indian Council Fire medal in 1959 and the Presidential award in 1963. (IOT, 1960: 49–50; Amer Sep.–Oct. '59: 1–2; Jul.–Aug. '63: 1; BIA, 4.)

Bernie Whitebear (Colville), 1928–   . Coordinator of the United Indians of All Tribes, Seattle, which has been active in seeking to take possession of Fort Lawton for the benefit of the Indian people. (CSM May 19 '70.)

Harry Whitehorse (Sauk-Winnebago), 1928–   . Sculptor, whose favorite medium is metals. Among his clients have been the Aluminum Company of America, the 1968 Olympic Committee, and the Credit Union National Association. (*Family Horizons,* CUNA quarterly, Sum. '70.)

Jules Wright (Athapascan), 1933–   . Alaska state representative (Rep.), 1967–1969. He is president of the Fairbanks Native Association, and is a contractor. (Amer Jan.–Feb. '67: 1; IT May '67: 6; WWAP, 1260.)

Muriel Wright (Choctaw), 1889–   . Daughter of Allen Wright, a Choctaw chief who named the state of Oklahoma, Miss Wright has been for many years the editor of *Chronicles of Oklahoma,* quarterly magazine of the state historical society. She is the author of some two hundred articles and four books, including *Guide to the Indian Tribes of Oklahoma* (1951). (IOT, 1960: 193–94; CO, Aut. '61: 335–37.)

Evelyn Yellow Robe (Brule Sioux). Speech pathologist. She has taught at Vassar and at Northwestern University, but now lives in Germany with her husband, a native of that country. She received the Indian Council Fire achievement award in 1947. (Amer May–Jun. '54: 3; IOT, 1960: 164–65; BIA, 4.)

Persons of Less Than One Quarter Indian Blood, or of Uncertain or Unknown Degree of Indian Blood

Burnu Acquanetta (Iroquois). Screen actress who played Indian roles in several films. (CT Mar. 25 '53.)

Linda Darnell (Cherokee). Screen actress. While in Chicago in 1959 to raise money for the Kidney Disease Foundation, she told the press: "I'm a Cherokee, and if you like you can call this an Indian uprising against an enemy that kills little children." (Tony Weitzel, CDN Oct. 17 '59.)

Johnston Murray (Chickasaw), 1902–   . Fourteenth governor of Oklahoma (Dem.), 1951–1955. He was a son of the colorful William H. (Alfalfa Bill) Murray (1869–1956), a former Congressman who was governor of Oklahoma, 1931–1935. When most of the future state was Indian Territory, the senior Murray was legal adviser to the governor of the Chickasaw Nation, Douglas Johnston, and married his niece, thereby acquiring Chickasaw citizenship. Their second son, born July 21, 1902, near Tishomingo, was named for his mother's uncle, and his father lived to see him installed as governor nearly fifty years later. For all his illustrious ancestry, he is apparently only 1/16 Indian. (Gordon Hines, *Alfalfa Bill* [1932], *passim;* A. H. Verrill, *The Real Americans* [1954], 287; USNWR Mar. 26 '54: 18; BDAC, 1376.)

Patti Page (Cherokee), 1927–   . Singer, screen and TV actress. Best known for her popular records of the early fifties, "Tennessee Waltz," which sold seven million copies, and "How Much Is That Doggie in the Window?" By 1965 her record sales totaled forty million. She also played in three movies, including *Elmer Gantry* (1960). Her home town, Claremore, Okla., was also the birthplace of Will Rogers, Sr. (CB '65: 309–11; WWA v35: 1669.)

Will Rogers, Jr. (Cherokee), 1911–   . Former film actor and former U.S. congressman, son of the famous humorist. Elected to the House as a Democrat from California in 1942, he served from January 3, 1943, until May 23, 1944, when he resigned his seat to return to the army. He was wounded in Germany, April 9, 1945, and awarded the Purple Heart. In 1946 he ran unsuccessfully for the U.S. Senate against William F. Knowland. For eighteen years following his graduation from Stanford (1935) he was editor and publisher of the weekly *Beverly Hills Citizen,* which he sold when he turned to acting. In his first film role, he played his famous father (*q.v.*) in *The Story of Will Rogers* (1951). After another film, *The Boy from Oklahoma* (1953), he turned to radio and TV acting. He and his wife have adopted three Navajo Indian children; he is a member of the National

Congress of American Indians and in 1949 was president of Arrow, Inc. (CB 1953: 540–42; BDAC, 1538; KI, 490.)

John Tebbel (Ojibwa), 1902–   . Professor of journalism, New York University; author of seventeen books, including *The American Indian Wars* (coauthored with Keith Jennison, 1960), and *The Battle for North America* (1948), an edited compilation of selections from works of Francis Parkman. He was descended on his mother's side from Henry R. Schoolcraft (1793–1864), whose wife, Jane Johnston, was the granddaughter of an Ojibwa chief. (CB '53: 618–19; KI, 510.)

Prominent Deceased American Indians: United States and Canada

(Most of the persons on this list, as on the previous list of living Indians, were at least partly assimilated or acculturated. The distinguished chiefs, warriors, statesmen, medicine men, and other accomplished men and women of the Indian nations, who functioned mainly in tribal society, will be named in Part III.)

Crispus Attucks, d. 1770. A leader of the famous Boston Massacre of March 5, 1770, when he and four others died as British troops fired upon them. A monument to his memory was erected on Boston Common in 1888. A native of Framingham, a giant in stature and a professional sailor, he was the son of a black father and an Indian mother. His family name was that of his mother, Ahtuk, meaning "a small deer." (A. H. Verrill, *The Real Americans* [1954], 250.)

William E. Beltz (Eskimo), 1912–1960. Elected to the Alaska House of Representatives in 1948, he served one two-year term, and was then elected to the Territorial Senate. He retained the seat for the remainder of his life. He was elected president of the Senate, January 26, 1959, the year Alaska became a state. In 1955 he was also elected president of the Alaska Council of Carpenters. (Amer Mar.–Apr. '59: 1; Mar.–Apr. '66: 1; CT Nov. 23 '60.)

Charles Albert Bender (Ojibwa), 1883–1954. Major league baseball player, who began his career with the Philadelphia Athletics, where he was called "Connie Mack's meal ticket for more than a decade." He was the leading American League pitcher in 1910, 1911, and 1914. Later he was a coach for the U.S. Naval Academy and the Chicago White Sox. A story is told that a female autograph hunter, upon learning that he was an Indian, gushed in astonishment: "But Mr. Bender, I always thought Indians wore feathers." The Chief, as he was called, retorted: "We do, madam, but this happens to be the molting season." [Merman L. Masin, *Curve Ball Laughs,* New York: Pyramid Books, 1958, p. 25.] (IOT 1947: 9; Amer Jul.–Aug. '54: 3.)

Acee Blue Eagle (Creek-Pawnee), 1907–1959. Artist, craftsman, and lecturer. (Amer Jul.–Aug. '59: 1; CNJ, 1957; AIP, 23–24.)

Charles D. Carter (Chickasaw), 1868–1929. In territorial days in the Chickasaw Nation, Indian Territory, he began his career as a cowhand, and in

1897 became superintendent of schools for the Chickasaws. When the state of Oklahoma was created in 1907, he was elected as a Democrat to the House of Representatives and held the seat for twenty years. For the last two years of his life, he was a member of the State Highway Commission. (BDAC, 667.)

Ella Deloria (Sioux), d. 1971. Anthropologist and linguist, appointed to the faculty of Columbia University, 1929. She is the author of *Dakota Texts* (1932) and many other works for specialists, as well as the popular book, *Speaking of Indians* (1944). (IOT, 1960: 60.)

Dr. Edward P. Dozier (Tewa, Santa Clara), 1916–1971. Anthropologist, chairman of the Department of Indian Studies, University of Minnesota, 1970. He was the author of more than twenty articles, and two books: *Hano: A Pueblo Community in Arizona* (1966), and *Pueblo Indians of the Southwest* (1970). (IOT, 1960: 17–18; Amer Jan.–Feb. '70: 9; AIA, 18.)

William A. Durant (Choctaw), d. 1948. A former Speaker of the Oklahoma House of Representatives. At the reorganization of the Choctaw Nation in 1934, he was chosen as principal chief. The city of Durant, Okla., is named for him. (Angie Debo, *And Still the Waters Run* [1940], pp. 270, 377; IOT, 1947: 34; NYT obit Aug. 2 '48: 21.)

Don Eagle (Mohawk), 1926–1966. Professional wrestler. He also starred in football, track, lacrosse, and boxing. (CT mag Apr. 24 '66.)

Dr. Charles A. Eastman (Ohiyesa), M.D. (Santee Sioux), 1858–1939. Physician and author. Born in the Sioux country in the buffalo-hunting days, he never saw a white man until he was sixteen years old. He graduated from Dartmouth in 1887, and received his M.D. degree from Boston University in 1890. Late in the same year, he was in charge of wounded captives from the Wounded Knee massacre. Later he entered private practice in St. Paul. He briefly held several government positions, including that of Indian Inspector under Calvin Coolidge. He was active in YMCA and Boy Scout work, and was also a busy writer, producing nine books between 1902 and 1918, all of them about Indians. Two of them, *Indian Boyhood* (1902), and *From the Deep Woods to Civilization* (1916), are autobiographical. (IOT, 1947: 110–11; WWW, IV: 275; Amer Jul.–Aug. '69; 5.)

James Gladstone (Blood [Blackfoot] of Alberta), 1887–1971. On February 1, 1958, Mr. Gladstone became the first treaty Indian appointed to the Canadian Senate, and gave part of his maiden speech in his native tongue. He was co-chairman of the Joint Committee of the Senate and Commons on Indian Affairs, 1959–1960. He was president of the Indian Association of Alberta, 1948–1954, and 1956. Frequently he was called to Ottawa to represent the Indians in negotiations with the government. He was a rancher, and in his youth (1911) was a scout and interpreter for the Royal Northwest Mounted Police. On the reserve, he was a member of the Crazy Dog Society. (Amer Mar.–Apr. '58: 1; Nov.–Dec. '58: 2; IOT, 1960: 120–21; WWC, 338.)

José Gonzales (Taos Pueblo), fl. 1837. After the revolt of 1837, against Mexican rule, he was elected governor of New Mexico. (Warren A. Beck, *New Mexico* [1962], 122.)

William W. Hastings (Cherokee), 1866–1938. Served ten terms in Congress as a representative from Oklahoma (Dem.), 1915–1921, and 1923–1935. In territorial days, he was educated in Cherokee tribal schools, and graduated from the Cherokee Male Seminary at Tahlequah in 1884; he taught for a time in Cherokee schools, and graduated from the law department of Vanderbilt University in 1889. He served four years as attorney-general for the Cherokee Nation, and after statehood, was attorney for the tribe for seven years. After taking his seat in Congress in 1915, he remained there for a total of eighteen years, being defeated only once for reelection, in 1920. He retired from politics in 1935, and died in 1938. (BDAC, 1022.)

Ira Hayes (Pima), 1922–1955. As a U.S. marine in the Pacific in World War II, Ira Hayes was with a group of marines photographed raising the flag on Mt. Suribachi, a picture which became the most famous of any to come out of the war, and which has been reproduced in painting and sculpture. Re-adjustment to peacetime life was difficult for him, and he became an alcoholic on the streets of Chicago. He returned to the reservation in Arizona, where he was found dead in the desert, January 24, 1955. A screenplay based on his life, *The Outsider*, was produced soon after. (NYT Jan. '55: 7; Jan. 26 '55: 27; *Newsweek* Feb. 7 '55: 53; *Time* Feb. 7 '55: 16.)

John Napoleon Brinton Hewitt (Tuscarora), 1859–1937. Ethnologist. He became an expert in American Indian linguistics, mythology, and sociology. He was employed many years by the Bureau of American Ethnology, Smithsonian Institution, and contributed numerous articles to its publications, including the famous *Handbook of American Indians,* edited by F. W. Hodge. (WWW, IV: 435.)

E. Pauline Johnson (Mohawk), 1861–1913. Canadian poet. She was a great-granddaughter of Sir William Johnson and Molly Brant, and was honored in the centennial year of her birth by a 5¢ Canadian postage stamp. (Amer Mar.–Apr. 61: 1; Jul.–Aug. '68: 4.)

William Jones (Fox [Mesquakie]), 1871–1909. Ethnologist. Born on the Sauk and Fox reservation in Indian Territory (Oklahoma), he was educated in the Indian school at Newton, Kansas, and the Friends Boarding School, Wabash, Ind. Returning home, he became a cowboy. In 1889 at age eighteen he went to Hampton Institute, thence to Phillips Academy at Andover, Mass., and finally entered Harvard University in 1896. He spent the summer of 1897 gathering data in the Sauk-Fox community at Tama, Iowa, to which he had ready access because of his Fox origin. He became editor of the *Harvard Monthly,* and graduated with an A.B. degree in 1900. He undertook graduate study at Columbia under the auspices of the Bureau of American Ethnology and the American Museum of Natural History, and pursued further field work among the Sauks and Foxes. Receiving his Ph.D. degree in 1904 he began investigations among northern Algonquian tribes. In 1906 the Field Columbian Museum in Chicago sent him to investigate native tribes in the interior of the Philippines, and he was killed by some of these tribesmen in 1909. During his short career he contributed an astonishing amount of work to research in Algonquian languages and folklore. He contributed several articles to the *Handbook of American Indians,* then in preparation under the direction of F. W. Hodge, and to several learned publications, as well as to popular magazines. His most notable publication, *Fox Texts* (Publications American Ethnological Society, I, 1907), was highly praised by Franz Boas, the linguist and anthropologist. Mr. Jones's Indian background coupled with his attainment of a quality education rare among Indians, especially for his time, particularly qualified him to make unusual contributions in Indian studies. It is tragic that through a shortage of wisdom in the learned community his talents were not further used in that area, instead of allowing his life to be thrown away in an assignment alien to his special talents. (DAB, V: 205–206; lecture by Charles F. Hockett, 1955.)

Joseph Juneau (Menominee), fl. 1880. Co-founder of the capital of Alaska, which bears his name. He was an early gold prospector at the site in 1880, and was a son of the French-Canadian, Solomon Juneau (1793–1856), founder and first mayor of the city of Milwaukee, and his mixed-blood Menominee wife. (Louise Houghton, *Our Debt to the Red Man* [1918]: 112; DAB V: 247–48.)

Francis La Flesche (Omaha), ca. 1860–1932. Ethnologist, author. Born on the Omaha reservation in Nebraska, son of the former head chief of the Omaha tribe, he was educated in mission schools and received the LL.M. degree from the National University Law School in 1892. He spent most of his career in the service of the Bureau of American Ethnology, and did field studies of the Osage tribe, and among his own people. Among his four books are *The Middle Five,* dealing with Indian education (1900), and *The Omaha Tribe* (coauthor, 1907). (A. H. Verrill, *The Real Americans* [1954]: 277–78; WWW, I: 697.)

Josette La Framboise (Potawatomi). Sister-in-law of President Franklin Pierce. She was the daughter of Alexander La Framboise of Milwaukee, and his wife Madeline, a French-Ojibwa. Her father was a cousin of Joseph and Claude La Framboise, prominent mixed-blood leaders of the Chicago Potawatomi. In 1817 she married Captain Benjamin Pierce, commander of Fort Mackinac, whose father was twice governor of New Hampshire, and whose brother Franklin became the fourteenth president of the United States. (Louise Houghton, *Our Debt to the Red Man,* 107–10; DAB, VII: 575.)

Charles Michel de Langlade (Ottawa), 1729–ca. 1801. Known as the "Father of Wisconsin," being a prominent early settler at Green Bay. His father was a French noble, and his mother was a full-blooded Ottawa, the sister and the daughter of chiefs. (Houghton, *Our Debt to the Red Man,* 60–66; DAB, III: 216–17.)

Frank Little, d. 1917. Half-Indian organizer for the Industrial Workers of the World (IWW). He was lynched at Butte, Mont., for his labor activities,

August 1, 1917. His tribal affiliation is unknown. (Melvin Dubofsky, *We Shall Be All* [1969], 186–87, *et passim*.)

Dan M. Madrano (Caddo), d. 1966. Educated at Carlisle and the National School of Law; twice elected to the Oklahoma House of Representatives, where he was chairman of the Indian Affairs Committee; unsuccessful candidate for the U.S. Senate in 1965. He was a founder of the National Congress of American Indians (1944), and its first national secretary. Author: *Heap Big Laugh* (1955), a book of Indian humor. (Amer May–Jun. '56: 2; Jul.–Aug. '60: 2; IOT, 1960: 26.)

Dr. Carlos Montezuma, M.D. (Apache), ca. 1867–1923. Physician, graduate of Chicago Medical School, admitted to practice in 1889, at age twenty-two. At about age six he was captured by Pima Indians and sold to an itinerant photographer for $30. He spent most of his life in Chicago, and taught medicine in addition to his practice. He was a specialist in stomach and intestinal diseases. He was the author of three books, including *Let My People Go* (1914), and editor of an Indian magazine, *Wassaja*. (CT Nov. 30 '66; WWW, I: 855.)

Samson Occum (Mohegan), 1723–1792. Clergyman; a protégé of Rev. Eleazar Wheelock, the founder of Dartmouth College, he preached in England to raise funds for the school. (Harold Blodgett, *Samson Occum* [1935]; WWW [H]: 384; Amer May–Jun. '58: 2.)

John Milton Oskison (Cherokee), 1874–1947. Author, former staff writer for *Collier's* magazine. He published three books: *A Texas Titan: the Story of Sam Houston* (1929), *Brothers Three*, a novel (1935), and *Tecumseh and His Times* (1938). (Angie Debo, *And Still the Waters Run* [1940], 240; AA, 548; NYT (obit) Feb. 27 '47: 21; AIA, 32–33.)

Robert L. Owen (Cherokee), 1856–1947. United States senator (Dem.) from Oklahoma for three terms, 1907–1925. He received a degree from Washington and Lee University in 1877, studied law, and upon admission to the bar began practice in Tahlequah, Indian Territory, capital of the Cherokee Nation. (WWW, II: 408; BDAC, 1416.)

Arthur C. Parker (Seneca), 1882–1955. Anthropologist, archaeologist. He was the great-nephew of General Ely S. Parker, and was for many years an archaeologist for the New York State Museum. He was also the founder–director of the Rochester Museum of Arts and Sciences, 1925–1946. He was the author of six books, including *The Life of General Ely S. Parker,* (1919), and *Red Jacket: Last of the Senecas* (1952). He received the Indian Council Fire award in 1936. (Amer Nov.–Dec. '52: 2; Jan.–Feb. '55: 1; AIA, 33–34.)

Brigadier General Ely S. Parker (Seneca), 1828–1895. An aide to General U. S. Grant who penned the surrender terms at Appomattox, April 9, 1865. By appointment of President Grant, he became the first Indian to head the U.S. Indian Bureau, 1869–1871, resigning the post six months after he was acquitted by the House of unfounded charges of malfeasance. Parker, whose Indian name was Donehogawa, was installed as a Seneca chief in 1852. He collaborated with Lewis Henry Morgan in gathering information for his *League of the Iroquois* (1851). Parker was denied admission to law school because he was an Indian, so he turned to the study of civil engineering, and while engaged in government work at Galena, Ill., became acquainted with U. S. Grant, and became his close friend. He frequently was called upon to represent his people in negotiations with the state government of New York. (Arthur C. Parker, *The Life of General Ely S. Parker,* [1919]; WWW [H], 394.)

Pocahontas (Powhatan), 1595–1617. Daughter of Chief Powhatan of Virginia, alleged rescuer of John Smith, who was baptized and married John Rolfe in 1614. While on a visit to England, she was presented at court, and died there of smallpox, March 21, 1617. She left a son, Thomas Rolfe, to whom some illustrious Virginia families have traced their ancestry. Among his descendants was the second Mrs. Woodrow Wilson. (Amer Jul.–Aug. '67: 4; Grace Woodward, *Pocahontas* [1969]).

Alexander Lawrence Posey (Creek), 1873–1908. Poet, superintendent of Public Instruction for the Creek Nation, 1897–. His *Poetical Works* was published in 1968 by the Okmulgee Cultural Foundation, Okmulgee, Okla. (CNJ, 1967; brochure, Okmulgee Cultural Foundation.)

Clinton Rickard (Tuscarora), 1882–1971. Chief of his tribe, founder of the Indian Defense League of America, of which he was president, and a leader in the resistance to flooding of Indian land by the New York Power Authority. (IV-LONAI, No. 4; Amer Sep.–Oct. '63: 3.)

William Rickard (Tuscarora), 1918–1964. Active leader of the Indian Defense League of America and the fight against the New York State Power Authority's appropriation of Indian land for a reservoir; a son of Clinton Rickard (*q.v.*). (IV Dec. '64: 7.)

Louis David Riel (1844–1885). Mixed-blood French-Indian (Meti), of Canada, who led the Red River rebellion in 1869–1870 and the Metis' rebellion in Saskatchewan in 1884. He was hanged for "treason" at Regina in 1885, and is regarded as a hero and liberator by most Metis and many Canadian Indians. (Joseph K. Howard, *Strange Empire* [1952]; AN Jun. '70: 17.)

Will Rogers, Sr. (Cherokee), 1879–1935. Humorist, born in Oolagah, Indian Territory, Cherokee Nation. After working as a cowboy several years and touring the world, he became a vaudeville performer, doing rope tricks and expounding homespun philosophy. He became a hit in the Ziegfeld Follies in 1915. Subsequently he conducted a newspaper column, acted in motion pictures, and wrote several books, including *Rogersisms: What We Laugh At* (1920). He was killed with Wiley Post in an air crash in Alaska, August 15, 1935. His posthumous *Autobiography of Will Rogers,* edited by Donald Day, was published in 1944. His son, Will Rogers, Jr. (*q.v.*), played his father in a movie of his life, *The Story of Will Rogers* (1952). (WWW, I: 1053; CE, 1692.)

Thomas Segundo (Papago), d. 1971. Veteran of World War II, first Papago to earn a college degree (University of Chicago), seven times chairman of the Papago Tribal Council, winner of the achievement medal of the Indian

Council Fire, 1952. He was killed in an airplane crash in June 1971. (Amer Sep.–Oct. '52: 1; IOT, 1960: 199–200.)

Dr. Paschal Sherman (Colville [Wenatchee]), d. 1970. A full-blooded Indian, an attorney, who received his LL.B. degree from the Washington (State) College of Law, and a Ph.D. degree from the Catholic University of America. He worked for forty-four years in the Veterans Administration, but always found time to aid Indian causes. (IOT, 1960: 173–74; Amer Jul.–Aug. '61: 2; Mar.–Apr. '63: 5; NCAI Sent Spring '70: 8, 9, 12.)

Simeon Simon (Narragansett). An aide to George Washington during the Revolutionary War, who participated in the crossing of the Delaware, Christmas eve, 1776. (Amer Jan.–Feb. '65: 6.)

William G. Stigler (Choctaw), 1891–1952. Oklahoma state senator (Dem.), 1924–1932, president pro tem in 1931; elected to the U.S. House of Representatives to fill a vacancy, and remained in that office from March 22, 1944, until his death, August 21, 1952. He was an attorney. (IOT, 1960: 80; Amer Sep.–Oct. '52: 2; WWW, III: 821; BDAC, 1658–59.)

Houston B. Teehee (Cherokee). Registrar of the U.S. Treasury, 1915–1919. His predecessor in this post, Gabe E. Parker, was a Choctaw Indian. During the war Mr. Teehee's signature appeared on fifty billion dollars' worth of government securities. Upon retiring from government, he became treasurer for a group of oil companies. Teehee was the son of a Cherokee chief, was mayor of Tahlequah, Okla., from 1904–1910, and a member of the Oklahoma House of Representatives in 1911. Among other posts he held were assistant attorney general of Oklahoma, and justice of the state supreme court. He was considered an influential speaker. (Louis Jones, *Aboriginal American Oratory* [1965], 126–28; IOT, 1947: 84; CT Oct. 28 1919.)

Kateri Tekakwitha (Mohawk), 1656–1680. A candidate for sainthood in the Catholic Church. Her father was a Mohawk chief, her mother an Algonquin captive, both of whom died of smallpox when Kateri was four. Raised by an uncle, she was baptized, against his wishes, at age twenty by the Jesuit priest Jacques de Lamberville. He helped her escape from her home village near the site of Auriesville, N.Y., to the Christian Mohawk village at Caughnawaga, near Montreal, where she died at age twenty-four, and where her bones are now enshrined. Miraculous powers have been ascribed to pieces of her clothing, and she is venerated as "The Lily of the Mohawks." An opera based on her life is being composed by Mrs. Virginia Gordoni, a part Mohawk professional singer. (CT Jan. 18 '56; Evelyn Brown, *Kateri Tekakwitha* [1958]; *Time* Sep. 6 '64: 42; *Kateri* magazine [Caughnawaga, Que.] Spring '69; Amer Nov.–Dec. '69: 7.)

Louis Tewanima (Hopi), ca. 1878–1969. Olympic marathon track star. Long-distance running is an old Hopi custom. While at Carlisle Indian school, Louis Tewanima ran on Coach Glenn (Pop) Warner's team. He finished ninth in the 26-mile run in the 1908 Olympic games at London, and four years later placed second in the 10,000-meter race at Stockholm. No American bettered his time for that event until another Indian, Billy Mills (*q.v.*), did it at the 1964 Olympics in Tokyo. Tewanima went back to herding sheep on the Hopi reservation, and was forgotten until 1954, when he was flown to New York to be feted at a banquet for former Olympic stars. When he was over ninety years old, on January 18, 1969, he attended a Hopi religious ceremony at the kiva in Shungopovi (Ariz.), and while going home in the dark, fell from a cliff and was killed. (*American Observer,* Nov. 1 '54; CST Jan. 21 '69: 84.)

James F. (Big Jim) Thorpe (Sauk-Fox), 1888–1953. Olympic champion, all-around athlete. At Carlisle Indian School he starred in track and football under Coach Glenn L. (Pop) Warner. In 1911, playing against top college teams, he made touchdown runs of 90 yards or more in seven games; he punted for 80 yards or more, and place-kicked field goals from mid-field. In 1912 he scored 25 touchdowns and racked up 198 points, an unequaled record. He was twice named to the All America team by Walter Camp. He was a sensation in track events, and at the Olympic Games in Stockholm in 1912, Thorpe won four of the five events in the pentathlon, and topped all previous records in the decathlon by scoring 8,412 out of a possible 10,000 points. King Gustav of Sweden called him "the greatest athlete in the world," but the next year the AAU stripped him of his trophies because he had played "professional" baseball in North Carolina a short time for $40 a month. He joined major league baseball with the New York Giants in 1913, remaining in the sport for seven years, and also played professional football, 1915–1929, being one of the founders of the National Football League. In 1932 he collaborated with T. F. Collison in writing *Jim Thorpe's History of the Olympics,* and the next year began playing bit parts in motion pictures. In 1937 he became active in Indian affairs, and later went on lecture tours. He lived to see his life portrayed in the film *Jim Thorpe: All American* (1951). In a poll of sportswriters by the Associated Press in 1950 he was voted the greatest football player and the greatest male athlete of the half century. The town of Mauch Chunk, Pa., changed its name to Jim Thorpe in his honor. (IOT, 1947: 85; Amer May–Jun. '53: 1; CB '50: 569–72, 624 [obit]; AO Oct. 13 '54.)

Major General Clarence Tinker, USAF (Osage), 1887–1942. The first Indian general since Ely S. Parker, he was placed in charge of the Air Force in Hawaii in December 1941, after the Pearl Harbor debacle. He was lost in action in the Battle of Midway, June 13, 1942. The Distinguished Service Medal, awarded to him posthumously, was presented to his widow in November 1942. Tinker Air Force Base, Oklahoma City, is named for him. (CB '42: 835–36; WBD, 1473; WWW, II: 534.)

Clyde Warrior (Ponca), d. 1968. A founder of the National Indian Youth Council, and president at the time of his death; co-editor (with Robert Thomas) of *Indian Voices,* 1963–1967. (IV Win '68: 24; Amer Sep.–Oct. '68: 4.)

Brigadier General Stand Watie, CSA (Cherokee), 1806–1871. The only Indian general officer in the Confederate army; he operated mainly with Indian units in Indian Territory (Oklahoma), Arkansas, Kansas, and Texas. He was the southern hero of the battle of Pea Ridge, Ark., March 6–8,

1862, and was the last officer of the Confederate army to surrender to the Union, at Doaksville, Choctaw Nation, Indian Territory, June 23, 1865. (Frank Cunningham, *Confederate Indians* [1959]; Amer Jan.–Feb. '66: 4.)

William D. Wilkerson (Cherokee), d. 1966. Film actor who played in *Juarez*. (Amer Mar.–Apr. '66: 5.)

Scott T. Williams (Chief Thunder Cloud), (Ottawa), 1898–1967. A full-blooded Ottawa who claimed descent from Pontiac, Williams was a screen actor in Western movies in the twenties, and played Geronimo in a film of the same name in 1939. In the radio show, *The Lone Ranger*, he played the role of Tonto from 1936 to 1939. (CT Feb. 1 '67; CST Feb. 1 '67.)

Less Than One Quarter Indian Blood

Joseph J. (Jocko) Clark (Cherokee), 1893–1971. Rear-admiral, later vice-admiral, U.S. Navy. Born in Indian Territory, Admiral Clark's father was listed as one quarter Cherokee on the tribal roll; his mother was white. Said to be the first Annapolis appointee of Indian blood, he was "very proud of his Indian heritage." Active in many parts of the Pacific theater in World War II, when he was rear-admiral, he became commander of the Seventh Fleet during the last year and a half before his retirement at the end of 1953. In 1967 he published his autobiography, *Carrier Admiral*, in collaboration with Clark G. Reynolds. (CB Jan. '54: 180–83; WWA v35: 433.)

Charles Curtis (Osage-Kaw), 1860–1936. Vice-president of the United States (Rep.) under Herbert Hoover, 1929–1933. He was born on the Kaw reservation near Topeka, Kan., a direct descendant of Pawhuska, Osage chief, and White Plume, Kaw chief. He worked as a jockey before he studied law and was admitted to the bar in 1881. He was a member of the House of Representatives for fourteen years (1893–1907) and of the Senate for twenty years (1907–1913, 1915–1929). He was majority leader during his last five years in the Senate, and was the author of the Indian Citizenship Act (1924). In November 1929, he was elected vice-president. Mr. Curtis was one-eighth Indian. (IOT, 1947: 109; WWW, I: 286; Amer Mar.–Apr. '59: 1; BDAC, 766–67.)

Chiefs, Warriors, Statesmen, Medicine Men, and Other Distinguished Men and Women of the Indian Nations

Black Hawk (Sauk), 1767–1838. A Sauk war chief of subordinate rank, born at Saukenuk, at the mouth of Rock River, Illinois, who, after being forced to cross the Mississippi River into Iowa with his people in 1831, returned the following spring with about a thousand men, women, and children. He was pursued by Illinois militia, whom he easily defeated, and later by federal troops commanded by General Henry Atkinson. Black Hawk held them at bay with only fifty warriors at Wisconsin Heights (near Sauk City,

Wis.), on the night of July 21 while his people crossed the Wisconsin River. Troops caught up with them ten days later near the mouth of the Bad Axe, on the Mississippi, and many were slaughtered by troops and by fire from an armed boat on the river. Black Hawk escaped, but surrendered at Prairie du Chien a few weeks later. After several months' confinement in irons, he was set free and returned to Iowa, where he dictated his memoirs to Antoine LeClaire, a trader. (F. W. Hodge, *Handbook of American Indians,* I, 150–52; Donald Jackson, ed., *Autobiography of Black Hawk* [1955, 1965]; WWW [H]: 58.)

Black Kettle (Southern Cheyenne), ca. 1803–1868. Cheyenne chief whose band encamped on Sand Creek, Colorado, was attacked without provocation on November 29, 1864, by a combined force of militia and federal troops from Fort Lyon, causing the death of many women and children amid scenes of "barbarity of the most revolting character," according to an official congressional report. (See "Massacre at Sand Creek" herein, p. 154.) Black Kettle escaped, but was killed four years later, November 27, 1868, when his camp on the Washita River, Indian Territory, was attacked, again without cause, by the Seventh Cavalry under Colonel George A. Custer. (George A. Custer, *My Life on the Plains* [1952]; Stan Hoig, *The Sand Creek Massacre* [1961]; Donald Berthrong, *The Southern Cheyennes* [1963]; WWW [H]: 58.)

Black Partridge (Potawatomi). A friendly chief of the Illinois River Potawatomi, who on August 14, 1812, came to Fort Dearborn at Chicago to warn Captain Nathan Heald of impending danger, at the same time returning a medal he had previously received as a sign of friendship, with the explanation that his warriors could no longer be restrained. During the battle which occurred the next day, Black Partridge is credited with saving the life of Mrs. Margaret Helm. Black Partridge's village on the Illinois River opposite Peoria was destroyed in the fall of 1812 by troops under Governor Ninian Edwards. He signed treaties with the United States in 1815 and 1816. (Mrs. John H. Kinzie, *Wau-Bun* [1901], 177–78; Milo M. Quaife, *Chicago and the Old Northwest* [1913], 415–21; C. Henry Smith, *Metamora* [1947]; Virgil J. Vogel, *Indian Place Names in Illinois* [1963], 15, 104.)

Elias Boudinot (Cherokee) d. 1839. First editor of the *Cherokee Phoenix,* he was murdered by tribesmen in 1839 for having favored emigration from Georgia. (Ralph Gabriel, *Elias Boudinot, Cherokee, and His America* [1941]; Hodge, I: 162–63.)

Joseph Brant (Thayendanegea), (Mohawk), 1742–1807. A sachem of his tribe, whose sister Molly was married to Sir William Johnson, British superintendent of Indian affairs. He attended Eleazar Wheelock's Indian school at Lebanon, Conn., and once visited England. He aided the British in the French and Indian War, in the campaign against Pontiac, and in the American Revolution, when he was commissioned as a colonel. After the war, he was given a tract of land on Grand River, Ontario, where he lived until his death. (Harvey Chalmers and Ethel Monture, *Joseph Brant: Mohawk* [1955]; Albert Britt, *Great Indian Chiefs* [1938, 1969], 67–94; Hodge, II: 741–42.)

Cochise (Chiricahua Apache), ca. 1815–1874. While at war with U.S. forces in

1860, he made a pact with T. J. Jeffords to protect the mail route to Yuma, which he kept despite provocations. In 1872 General O. O. Howard made an arduous journey to his camp to persuade Cochise and his band to accept a reservation. A pact was made which Cochise observed until his death. (O. O. Howard, *My Life and Experiences among Our Hostile Indians* [1907]; David Cooke, *Fighting Indians of the West* [1954], Chap. II.)

Cornplanter (Seneca), 1732–1836. He was noted principally for signing away large tracts of Indian lands, for which he received a pension from the government and a personal reservation in Pennsylvania. In later years, however, he became bitter against the whites. The Cornplanter reservation, where the chief was buried, was flooded by the Kinzua dam in 1960. (Anthony F. C. Wallace, *The Death and Rebirth of the Seneca* [1970]; Hodge, I, 349–50.)

Crazy Horse (Oglala Sioux), d. 1877. A leader of resistance to white occupation of the sacred Black Hills, his camp was attacked by troops under General George Crook in the winter of 1875. In the following months he joined with Sitting Bull and several bands of Sioux and Cheyennes, who were all encamped on the Little Big Horn (Montana), when General George A. Custer attacked them on June 25, 1876. Custer and his entire force of some 250 men, and many of those in detached columns under Captain Benteen and Major Reno, were killed. The following fall and winter, Crazy Horse's band was twice attacked. He surrendered in the spring of 1877 with 2,000 followers, but was arrested on September 7, under the pretext that he was stirring up trouble. Brought to Fort Robinson (Neb.), he began to resist when he saw the barred cells and the chains, and was fatally bayoneted in the back. (Mari Sandoz, *Crazy Horse* [1942].)

Dull Knife (Northern Cheyenne), d. 1883. Dull Knife participated in the battle with Custer, June 25, 1876, and five months later his camp was attacked by Colonel Mackenzie; all the Indian lodges and property were destroyed, and most of their ponies were captured. Despite heavy loss of life, many Indians escaped, but surrendered some months later. Much against their wishes, they were placed on a reservation in Oklahoma. A band of several hundred of them under Dull Knife and Little Wolf fled to the north in September 1878, but during the winter many of them surrendered at Fort Robinson, Neb., and were imprisoned without food or heat when they refused to go back to Oklahoma. In a desperate break for freedom on the night of January 9, 1879, most of them, including Dull Knife, were killed. In a desperate break for freedom on the night of January 9, 1879, most of them were killed, but Dull Knife escaped to Montana, where he died in 1883. (Mari Sandoz, *Cheyenne Autumn* [1953]; Peter Powell, *Sweet Medicine* [1969]; Hodge, I, 406.)

Geronimo (Chiricahua Apache), 1829–1909. Between 1876 and 1886 Geronimo fled several times into Mexico with his band, in protest against reservation conditions. Because of his raids on Mexican settlements, American troops pursued him south of the border, but he repeatedly escaped. In 1886 he was hunted down by General Nelson Miles, with the indispensable aid of Apache scouts, and finally surrendered, with 340 people. After imprisonment for some years in Florida and Alabama, he and his leading men were sent to Fort Sill, Oklahoma, and provided with land. He remained there quietly until his death. (John G. Bourke, *On the Border with Crook* [1891]; S. M. Barrett, *Geronimo's Own Story of His Life* [1906]; Britton Davis, *The Truth about Geronimo* [1929]; Jason Betzinez (with W. S. Nye), *I Fought with Geronimo* [1960]; Odie B. Faulk, *The Geronimo Campaign* [1969].)

Francis Godfroy (Miami), 1788–1840. Last war chief of the Miami tribe. His father, from whom the surname comes, was Jacques Godfroy, a Frenchman of Detroit. Francis grew up in the vicinity of Fort Wayne, Ind., and died near Peru, Ind. Some reports say he was in the Tippecanoe battle, November 7, 1811, but this was denied by his son Gabriel. Generally it is reported that he led the Indians who attacked Colonel Campbell's force on the Mississinewa, December 18, 1812, and forced them to return to Greenville, Ohio. Following the war he opened a trading post, at a place on the Wabash called Mt. Pleasant, and became wealthy for his day. He corresponded with leading citizens, including Vice-President R. M. Johnson; about a hundred letters received by the chief are preserved in the museum at Peru. From 1818 to 1840 he and other half-breed leaders, especially Francis LaFontaine and Jean Richardville, signed treaties which ultimately disposed of all Miami lands, in return for which they received personal grants of land and cash. By the treaty of St. Mary's, October 6, 1818, Godfroy received six sections at Petite Prairie on the Salomonie River. By the treaty of October 26, 1826, he received one section and a house not exceeding $600 in value was to be built for him. By a treaty signed November 6, 1838, he received a total of seven sections, and in the final treaty, which ceded the last remaining tribal lands in Indiana, and prescribed that the Indians must leave the state within five years, $15,000 was directed to be paid to Godfroy's executor (the chief having recently died), "for claims against the tribe," and after the tribe migrated, a "just proportion" of the tribal annuities was to be paid to his heirs. Although the bulk of the Miamis were compelled to migrate to Kansas in 1846, about 300 relatives, friends, and associates of the several holders of individual grants remained in Indiana. Godfroy was a big man, variously reported at from 240 to 350 pounds in weight, and over six feet tall. His portrait was painted in 1839 by George Winter. He had two wives and left numerous progeny. Many of his descendants still live in Indiana. (J. H. Stephens, *History of Miami County, Ind.* [1896], 29–34; Ross Lockridge, "History on the Mississinewa," IMH Mar. '34: 29–56; Kappler, *Treaties;* interview with Oliver Godfroy and Mrs. Ava Bossley, great-grandchildren of Francis Godfroy, Peru, Ind., Aug. 1–2, 1964, and with Vesper Cook, curator of Miami County Historical Museum.)

Handsome Lake (Seneca), 1735–1815. Religious leader who developed an ethical code, the record of which is called the *Gai'wiio'*. It upheld Indian ways as against white, counseled against alcohol and witchcraft, defended marital fidelity and kindness to children and the aged. The code consists of

130 sections, many of them parables. The Handsome Lake religion was embraced by many traditionalists among the Iroquois, and while it replaced the older religion, it also hindered the spread of Christian sects. (Arthur C. Parker, *The Code of Handsome Lake* [1912]; A. F. C. Wallace, *The Death and Rebirth of the Seneca* [1970].)

Hiawatha (Mohawk), fl. 1570. Statesman and reformer who, together with Dekanawida, an Onondaga, ended conflicts between the five Iroquois tribes by forming the League of the Longhouse, or Five Nations, regarded by Benjamin Franklin as a model for the colonists. (Alvin Josephy, *The Patriot Chiefs* [1961], Chap. I; Hodge, I, 546.)

Chief Joseph (Nez Perce), ca. 1840–1904. Chief leader of the Nez Perce war of 1877, precipitated because of the expulsion of the Nez Perces from the Wallowa valley of Oregon. His surrender in Montana is described elsewhere in this book. General O. O. Howard regarded him as a military genius. (Alvin Josephy, *The Nez Perce Indians* [1965].)

Keokuk (Sauk), 1780–1848. William Jones, a Fox Indian who became a noted anthropologist, has described Keokuk as an ambitious Sauk leader who rose to chieftainship by intrigue and cooperation with the U.S. government, which appointed him to the post. He yielded to the pressure to emigrate to Iowa, and opposed Black Hawk's return to Illinois in 1832, which resulted in the Black Hawk war. He died in Kansas, to which the Sauks and Foxes were banished after a few years in Iowa, and now lies buried beneath his statue in Keokuk, Iowa, the city which is named for him. (Josephy, *The Patriot Chiefs*, Chap. VII; Hodge, I, 673–74.)

Kintpuash [Captain Jack], (Modoc), d. 1873. Indian leader in the Modoc war, 1872–1873. The war resulted from the refusal of the government to give the Modocs a reservation in their traditional homeland on the California-Oregon border. It tried instead to force them to live among the Klamaths who, although linguistic relatives, were not congenial to them. An attempt to arrest Captain Jack, November 29, 1872, resulted in the death of eight soldiers and fifteen Indians, following which the Indians fled to the "lava beds" and resisted all attempts to dislodge them. A peace parley was arranged on April 11, 1873, during which Captain Jack shot General E. R. S. Canby to death, and others killed Reverend E. Thomas. The Indians again withdrew to the lava beds; Captain Jack had only 80 warriors opposed to a force of 986 soldiers and 71 allied Indians, but skirmishes continued until Captain Jack and the last hostiles surrendered, June 1, 1873. Captain Jack and three other Indians were sentenced to death and hanged October 3, 1873. The remaining Indians were deported to Oklahoma. (Keith Murray, *The Modocs and their War* [1965]; Hodge, I, 697–98.)

Little Turtle (Miami), 1752–1812. Principal leader of the allied Indian forces that defeated General Josiah Harmar on the Miami River (Ohio), in October 1790, and General Arthur St. Clair at St. Mary's, November 4, 1791 (see pp. 67, 76). These events mark the greatest Indian victory over white armies ever achieved by U.S. Indians, despite the greater fame of Custer's defeat eighty-five years later. The Indian forces, which included Shawnees, Wyandots, and others, were finally defeated by Mad Anthony Wayne's army at Fallen Timbers, near Toledo, August 20, 1794. By the Treaty of Greenville, August 3, 1795, the Indians ceded more than half of Ohio, and several enclaves throughout the Northwest for the construction of forts. Little Turtle visited George Washington in 1797, refused to join Tecumseh's confederacy, and lived quietly at Fort Wayne, Indiana Territory, until his death, July 14, 1812. His adopted son and brother-in-law, Captain William Wells, a former white captive, was killed in the Fort Dearborn massacre a month later. (Norman B. Wood, *Lives of Famous Indian Chiefs* [1906], Chap. IX; Jacob P. Dunn, *True Indian Stories* [1909, 1964], Chap. II; Otho Winger, *The Last of the Miamis and Little Turtle* [1961].)

John Logan (Cayuga [Mingo]), 1720–1780. Though he was known as a friend to the whites, a band of settlers, in a fashion often repeated on the frontier when they were unable to vent their wrath on hostiles, killed his entire family in their cabin on the Ohio River, in 1774. The crime triggered Dunmore's war, which ended just as the American Revolution was beginning. The speech Logan is believed to have made upon surrendering is reproduced on p. 59, herein.

Alexander McGillivray (Creek), 1739–1793. Mixed-blood chief who espoused the British cause in the American Revolution. The confiscation by Georgia authorities of properties left him by his Scottish father further antagonized him. After the Revolution he made a pact with the Spanish at Pensacola, and refused a peace treaty with the Americans until 1790, when he visited George Washington in New York. He nevertheless continued to receive an annuity from Spain. He was engaged in a trade partnership with William Panton, an Englishman, and amassed a considerable fortune. (John W. Caughey, *McGillivray of the Creeks* [1959]; Hodge, I, 779–81.)

Massasoit (Wampanoag), 1580–1661. The chief who befriended the Pilgrims and attended the first Thanksgiving feast. Despite usurpations he remained a friend of the English until his death, forty-one years after the arrival of the *Mayflower*. His eldest son Alexander succeeded him. King Philip (*q.v.*) was his second son. (Wood, Chap. III; Hodge, I, 817; Alvin G. Weeks, *Massasoit of the Wampanoags* [1920].)

Oconostota (Cherokee), d. 1785. In 1759, during the French and Indian War, he was cast into jail by the governor of South Carolina when he came with a delegation to treat for peace in Charleston. He was ransomed by the surrender of an Indian the whites wanted to prosecute for murder. He renewed the war with vigor, but during hostilities, the lower Cherokee towns were destroyed. His awareness of whence the greatest threat to Cherokee lands emanated caused him to support the British during the Revolutionary War, following which he resigned the chieftainship. (Hodge, II, 105; R. S. Cotterill, *The Southern Indians* [1954].)

Opechancanough (Powhatan), ca. 1545–1644. Brother of Powhatan (*q.v.*), Virginia chieftain. When Powhatan died in 1618, Opechancanough succeeded to leadership and prepared to expel the English. The planned uprising began on March 22, 1622, and nearly half the colony was wiped out. The English recovered, however, and drove the Indians back. A new outbreak began April 18, 1644, when Opechancanough was about a hundred years old and so feeble he had to be carried on a litter. After 300 settlers died, Opechancanough was captured and brought to Jamestown, where he was shot to death by a guard. (Hodge, II, 139.)

Osceola (Seminole), ca. 1803–1838. Though not a chief, he was a distinguished warrior while still in his teens. He refused to sign the Treaty of Payne's Landing in 1832, by terms of which the Florida Indians were to be removed to Oklahoma. When General Wiley Thompson called a parley to get the assent of the holdouts, Osceola drove his knife through the treaty, declaring he would never accept it. The general had Osceola seized and placed in irons. To secure his release, Osceola feigned a change of heart, then began a campaign of guerrilla resistance from the swamps. When 100 soldiers under Major Dade set out to capture him on December 24, 1835, all but three were killed within three days. Osceola was wounded soon after in the battle of Withlacoochee River, but escaped. The war continued at great expense to the government. Osceola was only captured by trickery. General T. S. Jesup called a pretended peace parley, to which Osceola came in good faith under a flag of truce. He and several followers were at once seized and imprisoned in a dungeon at Fort Moultrie, S.C., where he died within three months, January 1, 1838. His death did not end the resistance, which continued until 1842, when the government abandoned the war, leaving a few bands of Seminoles still in the Everglades, where they remain. ("The Complete Story of Osceola," FHQ, XXXIII [Jan. + Apr. '55]; Edwin McReynolds, *The Seminoles* [1957].)

Oshkosh (Menominee), 1795–1850. Menominee chief who participated with the British in capturing Fort Mackinac from the Americans in July 1812. He was also in the British-Indian attack on Fort Sandusky, Ohio, in 1813. He signed a treaty at Butte des Morts, Wisconsin, August 11, 1827. The city of Oshkosh, Wis., is named for him. (Hodge, II, 160; Phebe Jewell Nichols, *Oshkosh the Brave* [1954].)

Ouray (Uncompahgre Ute), 1820–1880. Known as a firm friend of the whites, whom he protected during hostilities. In the so-called Ute war which followed the killing of N. C. Meeker and others in 1879, he restrained his band from joining the hostiles. For his services the government gave him an annuity of $1,000. Ouray, Colo., is named for him. (A. H. Verrill, *The Real Americans*, 287–88; Robert Emmitt, *The Last War Trail* [1958].)

Payepot (Canadian Cree), 1816–1908. Left an orphan by smallpox, he was raised by his grandmother. Both were captured by a Sioux war party from the U.S. and spent fourteen years in captivity before being rescued by the Cree. Payepot became known as a warrior and medicine man, and signed a treaty in 1875 to surrender ancestral lands in Qu'appelle valley in exchange for a reservation elsewhere. After a difficult winter there, when 130 died from hunger and disease, Payepot obtained permission to lead his people back to Qu'appelle valley. In 1882 when the Canadian Pacific Railroad was pushing across the country, Payepot and a group of braves tried to block it by camping in the right of way. When the Indians refused RCMP orders to move, the mounties knocked the tepees down and the Indians left. When the Riel rebellion began in 1884, and many young Indians were joining it, Payepot after some hesitation assured a government emissary that his people would remain aloof. In 1901 he was feted by the Manitoba government in Winnipeg. He died aged ninety-two. (Abel Watetch, *Payepot and his People* [Regina: 1959]; *Saskatchewan News* Jul. '63: 4.)

King Philip [Metacomet], (Wampanoag), 1620–1676. Son of Massasoit (*q.v.*), and younger brother of Alexander, who died only a few months after his father, in 1662. Philip became chief, and carefully prepared for war, because of white encroachments and arrogance. The fuse was lit when an Indian informer, Sassamon, was found dead, and the English hanged three Indians as the alleged killers. War began in June 1675, and continued more than a year. Philip and his allies attacked fifty-two of the ninety towns in New England and completely destroyed twelve of them. The English and their Mohegan allies finally trapped Philip and most of his warriors in a swamp in Rhode Island, August 12, 1676, and the great chief was killed by one of the English Indians. His body was beheaded and quartered; his wife and little son, among others, were sold into slavery in the West Indies. His chief lieutenant, Annawan, was betrayed by an informer soon after, captured by Benjamin Church, and beheaded at Plymouth. (Hodge, I, 58–59, 690; Douglas E. Leach, *Flintlock and Tomahawk* [1958].)

Pleasant Porter (Creek), 1840–1907. Last chief of the Creek Nation before its dissolution to become part of the state of Oklahoma. He was a founder of the Creek school system and a diplomat who made frequent trips to Washington in the tribal interest. (Hodge, I, 287–88.)

Plenty Coups (Crow), 1848–1932. Born near Billings, Montana, he became a minor war chief and was mainly distinguished for his work as a scout with U.S. army units pursuing hostiles. He was with General George Crook at the battle of the Rosebud on June 17, 1876, shortly before Custer's defeat. With the destruction of the buffalo, he urged adjustment to white rule, and was praised as "a real statesman" by a railroad official. When he was in his eighties, he told the story of his life to Frank Bird Linderman, who published it in 1930 under the title *American*. (Ruthe M. Edwards, *American Indians of Yesterday*. Naylor '48, 57–58, por.)

Pontiac (Ottawa), 1720–1769. Chief, leader of the great rebellion of 1763, and one of the greatest of the Indian organizers. Though he accepted the transfer of authority in the West from France to Britain at the end of the French and Indian War, he soon became disenchanted with his new masters, being antagonized partly by their lesser generosity and their denial of credit in trade. He merged most of the tribes west of Pittsburgh and north of the Ohio, and even some Senecas and Delawares, into an alliance, and launched a well-planned simultaneous attack throughout the Northwest on May 7, 1763. Of the ten British-held forts west of Niagara, eight fell quickly to the

Indians. Only Detroit, which he besieged for five months, and Fort Pitt, which was relieved by Colonel Bouquet's expedition, failed to fall into the Indians' hands. A message from the French commander at Fort Chartres on the Mississippi, which the British had not yet occupied, mainly due to Indian control of the river, persuaded Pontiac to lay down arms. He made a preliminary peace pact with George Croghan at Ouiatenon on the Wabash in July 1765, and agreed to a treaty at Detroit, August 17, 1765. Four years later he was killed at Cahokia, Ill., by an Illinois Indian, said to have been bribed by an Englishman. The deed was punished by raids on the Illinois from northern tribes. There are towns named for Pontiac in Michigan, Illinois, and Missouri, not to mention an automobile. (Francis Parkman, *The Conspiracy of Pontiac* [1922]; Howard Peckham, *Pontiac and the Indian Uprising* [1947, 1961].)

Popé (Tewa-San Juan Pueblo), d. 1688. A medicine man and leader of the great Pueblo revolt which began August 10, 1680, resulting in the complete expulsion of the Spanish priests, soldiers, and settlers from New Mexico. Four hundred Spanish and nearly 250 Indians died in the uprising. Popé set out to obliterate all elements of Spanish culture from Pueblo life, including Catholicism and plants and animals of foreign origin. Dissension broke out among the Indians and the province was recaptured by the Spanish in 1692. Popé did not live to see the event, for he died in 1688. (Robert Silverberg, *The Pueblo Revolt* [1970].)

Powhatan [Wahunsonacook], (Powhatan), 1547–1618. Powhatan was a place and tribal name applied to this chief by mistake. He was the head of a confederacy of Algonquian-speaking tribes inhabiting Virginia when the colonists came in 1607, and the father of Pocahontas (*q.v.*), who married John Rolfe. He aided the colonists with provisions, and kept the peace until his death. The English gave him a crown as "king" in 1609. (Wood, Chap. II.)

Pushmataha (Choctaw), 1764–1824. Known as a friend of the whites, chief Pushmataha turned down overtures from Tecumseh in 1811. During the War of 1812 he aided Jackson against both the English and the Creeks. He died on a trip to Washington in 1824, where he had come to negotiate a treaty. He was eulogized in the Senate, given a military funeral, and buried in the Congressional Cemetery. (Anna Lewis, *Pushmataha* [1959].)

Quanah Parker (Comanche), ca. 1845–1911. Son of Ann Parker, a white captive, and Nokoni, a Comanche chief. Parker succeeded his father as chief, though the office was not hereditary. He refused to sign the Medicine Lodge Treaty of 1867 and go on a reservation. When white hunters in the early seventies invaded Indian lands in large numbers and killed vast numbers of buffalo for hides, Parker rallied 700 warriors, including Cheyennes and Kiowas, and attacked the post at Adobe Walls, Texas, where thirty buffalo hunters were staying. The assault failed, but Parker remained at large on the Llano Estacado until 1875 before surrendering. From that time on, he encouraged agriculture, education, and home building, while still adhering to traditional beliefs and ceremonies. He joined the Peyote cult, which aided his influence with his own and other tribes. (Wood, Chap. XVI; Ernest Wallace and E. A. Hoebel, *The Comanches* [1952].)

Red Bird (Winnebago), ca. 1788–1828. Leader of the "Red Bird War." In the neighborhood of Prairie du Chien, Wis., he was known as a friend and protector of the whites, until he was erroneously informed, according to Hodge, that two Winnebagoes arrested for murder had been turned over to the Ojibwa and clubbed to death. On June 28, 1827, he killed two men in Prairie du Chien, and with thirty-seven warriors attacked the crew of a keelboat grounded on a sandbar, with the loss of four whites and seven Indians. Pursued by troops, he gave up to protect the women and children. He died in prison at Fort Crawford, February 16, 1828. (Hodge, II, 358).

Red Cloud (Oglala Sioux), ca. 1810–1909. A chief "as full of action as a tiger," according to General George Crook. His determined resistance forced the government to abandon plans to fortify the Bozeman Trail, which led from Nebraska across Wyoming to Montana. Fort Phil Kearney was besieged and when Captain William Fetterman left the fort with eighty men to rescue a woodcutting party nearby, all were ambushed and killed. After two years of incessant warfare by Red Cloud, the government called a parley in November 1868. Red Cloud would accept nothing less than complete abandonment and destruction of all posts and an end to further attempts to open the Bozeman Trail. He refused to negotiate until these demands were met. The government capitulated completely, in one of the few instances where Indians were able to achieve victory both in war and at the peace table. After signing the Fort Laramie Treaty, Red Cloud settled at the agency named for him in Nebraska. His acceptance of reservation life made him unpopular with the still hostile bands who scorned agency Indians. Red Cloud never made war again, though some of his followers joined Sitting Bull. In 1878 he and his people moved to Pine Ridge, South Dakota, where he remained until his death at an age of approximately one hundred. (James C. Olson, *Red Cloud and the Sioux Problem* [1965].)

Red Jacket (Seneca), 1751–1830. Noted Seneca subchief, orator, and warrior. He was the leader of the so-called pagan faction, opposed both to Christianity and to the religion of Handsome Lake. He sought to preserve Iroquois culture from white inroads, and to ban all whites, especially missionaries, from the reservations of the Six Nations. (Wood, Chap. VIII; Wallace. *Death and Rebirth of the Seneca* [1970].)

Red Wing (Sioux), ca. 1750–1825. Chief for whom a Minnesota city is named. He fought on the British side in the War of 1812, as far east as Sandusky, Ohio, but later became known as a friend of the Americans. (WWW [H]: 435.)

Alexander Robinson [Che-Che-Pinqua], (Potawatomi), 1789–1872. Born at Mackinaw of a Scottish trader, whose name he bore, and an Ottawa woman; through marriage to Catherine Chevalier, daughter of a prominent French-Potawatomi half-blood at St. Joseph, Mich., he became one of an illustrious band of mixed-blood statesmen of the Potawatomi. Like others of this group (which included Billy Caldwell, Claude La Framboise, François Bourbonnais, and François Chevalier), his friendship for the whites was often placed ahead of tribal interests. Following the Fort Dearborn massacre (August 15, 1812), during which he was not present, he escorted the Kinzie and Heald families to safety at Mackinac. He signed several treaties surrendering Indian lands to the whites, and in the treaty of Prairie du Chien, July 29, 1829, he was given a private reserve of two square miles on the Des Plaines River, where he lived until his death in 1872, being the only leading man who failed to migrate to Kansas with his people. His granddaughter lived on his reserve, now a forest preserve, until her house burned in 1955. Robinson and his family are buried near where the house stood. (Juliette Kinzie, "Chicago Indian Chiefs," CHSB Aug. '35: 105–16; V. J. Vogel, *Indian Place Names in Illinois* [1963], 21–22, 119.)

John Ross (Cherokee), 1790–1866. Son of a Scotsman and a mixed-blood Cherokee woman, he was the principal chief of the Cherokee Nation from 1828 to 1839, and after the tribe arrived in Indian Territory, he was again chosen chief and remained in that post until his death. Despite his large degree of white blood, he fought to the last against the forced removal of the Cherokee people from Georgia to Indian Territory. (Rachel C. Eaton, *John Ross and the Cherokee Indians* [1914].)

Sacajawea (Shoshoni), 1788–1884? Wife of a Frenchman, and captive among the Hidatsa when Lewis and Clark arrived on the upper Missouri in 1804, she guided the party of thirty-nine men to the Rocky Mountains, where she rejoined her brother, a Shoshoni chief. He provided guides, provisions and horses to continue the journey. It is probable that more statues have been erected in memory of this woman than for any other Indian. (Grace R. Hebard, *Sacajawea* [1957].)

Satanta (Kiowa), 1830–1878. "The orator of the Plains." Though he signed the Treaty of Medicine Lodge in 1867 and agreed to go on a reservation, the band delayed until Custer attacked them and seized Satanta and Lone Wolf as hostages. Because of a prior alleged raid in Texas, Satanta and two others were held for trial in Texas. One of these was killed while resisting a guard; Satanta and Big Tree were sentenced to life imprisonment. They were released after two years, on condition that the Kiowas remain peaceful. When war was resumed in 1874, Satanta was again arrested and returned to prison, where he committed suicide by jumping from a window. (Verrill, 293; Mildred Mayhall, *The Kiowas* [1962].)

Sauganash [The Englishman; Billy Caldwell], (Potawatomi), 1781–1841. Mixed-blood Potawatomi chief, born in Canada of a Potawatomi mother and Captain William Caldwell, an Irish officer in the British army. He was the best educated of the Potawatomis at Chicago, and was a voter and justice of the peace at that place in 1826. He signed several treaties giving up Potawatomi lands, and received from the government in the treaty of 1833 a cash grant of $5,000 (the same amount was given to Alexander Robinson, *q.v.*), and $600 for each of his children. By an earlier treaty, signed at Prairie du Chien in 1829, he was given a private reserve of 2½ square miles on the north branch of the Chicago River. The government also built him a frame house on the site of the present chancery office of the archdiocese of Chicago. When the Potawatomi moved west in accordance with the treaty of 1833, Sauganash went into exile with them. (DAB, VIII: 376–77; Kinzie, CHSB Aug. '35: 105–16; Vogel, *Indian Place Names,* 16–17, 125–26; Kappler, *Treaties,* II.)

Seattle (Dwamish [Suquamish]), d. 1866. As a boy he witnessed the arrival of Vancouver in Puget Sound in 1792. When the region passed to American sovereignty he was the first to sign the treaty of Port Elliott (1855), which placed the Indians of the future state of Washington on reservations. When trouble erupted later among tribes east of the Cascades, he counseled peace. He is reported to have said: "The red man has ever fled the approach of the white man as morning mist flees the rising sun. It matters little where we pass the remnant of our days. They will not be many." Washington's largest city bears his name, while his descendants are fighting for the right to fish in the country their ancestors owned. (Eva G. Anderson, *Chief Seattle* [1950]; BIA, *Famous Indians,* n.d.: 26–27.)

Shabbona (Potawatomi), 1775–1859. Said to be a nephew of Tecumseh and a grandnephew of Pontiac, Shabbona was born of an Ottawa father and a Seneca mother, and married a Potawatomi woman, joining her tribe after the War of 1812. He fought in the battle of Tippecanoe in 1811, and later for the British (until Tecumseh was killed at the Thames), then transferred his allegiance to the United States. He influenced the Potawatomi to remain neutral during the Winnebago scare of 1827, and again during the Black Hawk war of 1832, when he joined his son in a Paul Revere-like night ride to warn settlers of impending attack. Shabbona was given two sections of land at Shabbona Grove, DeKalb Co., Ill., by the treaty of Prairie du Chien in 1829. He migrated west with his tribe in 1836, but later returned to his grove. During a second visit to Kansas his land was declared abandoned and sold to speculators. The new owner forcibly evicted Shabbona from the land when he returned. White friends bought him a small tract of land near Morris, Ill., where he lived on a small pension until his death. He is buried in Evergreen Cemetery at Morris, beneath a plain granite boulder bearing only his name and the dates "1775–1859." (Wayne C. Temple, *Shabbona, Friend of the Whites* [Springfield: 1957]; Vogel, *Indian Place Names,* 132–35.)

Sequoya (Cherokee), ca. 1760–1843. Inventor of the Cherokee syllabary, a unique alphabet by means of which most Cherokees became literate. Newspapers and books were published with it both in Georgia and in Indian Territory. America's largest and oldest trees are named in his memory. (Grant Foreman, *Sequoyah* [1938].)

Sitting Bull (Hunkpapa Sioux), ca. 1834–1890. Close associate of Crazy Horse in 1876, and one of the greatest heroes of the Dakota people. When orders went out in the winter of 1875 that all roaming Indians must be on the reservations by spring, there was no time to comply, even for those Indians so inclined. Expeditions were sent out to attack their camps, and the first clash, on the Rosebud River, pitched General George Crook with 1,000 soldiers and 260 Indian scouts (Crows, Shoshonis, and Rees) against less than a thousand Sioux and Cheyennes, only half of them with guns. Crazy Horse and Sitting Bull acquitted themselves well, forcing Crook to retreat. Ten days later George A. Custer came near the Indian camp on the Little Big Horn, where Sitting Bull and Crazy Horse had now been joined by another 2,000 Indians, mainly Cheyennes. Custer unwisely divided his command and rashly attacked. His own command was wiped out. The story that Sitting Bull was in the mountains making medicine at this time is a fabrication. Following the battle, the Indians broke into smaller groups, and Sitting Bull's band crossed the border into Canada, where he remained until 1881. He returned because of promises of amnesty from American agents, but he was confined two years at Fort Randall before being allowed to settle at Standing Rock, Dakota Territory. He spent a year on tour with Buffalo Bill's Wild West Show, but found it an unsatisfactory experience. In 1888 he opposed further land cessions by the Sioux, and in other ways incurred the antagonism of agent James McLaughlin. In 1890 McLaughlin accused Sitting Bull of spreading the Ghost Dance religion of Wovoka (*q.v.*) among the Dakotas, and issued an order for his arrest. When Indian police in McLaughlin's service arrived at his cabin at dawn, December 15, 1890, Sitting Bull hesitated to obey orders, and was shot to death. His seventeen-year-old son, Crow Foot, was dragged from beneath a bed and murdered. Six others also died. The massacre at Wounded Knee Creek on Pine Ridge two weeks later was a consequence of the outrage at Grand River, for because of it, Big Foot's band had taken to the hills in fear, only to be slaughtered. (See pp. 183–87.)

Like many great heroes of the Indian people, Sitting Bull has been maligned, misrepresented, and lied about, even in scholarly works. The unsigned sketch of him in Hodge, II, 583, is filled with bias and error, and reflects the views of James McLaughlin, whose self-serving book, *My Friend, the Indian,* has often been cited as an authority. We are fortunate that the record has been corrected by Stanley Vestal's excellent biography and other writings. (Stanley Vestal, *Sitting Bull* [1957].)

Spotted Tail (Brule Sioux), ca. 1833–1881. A warrior and chief noted for his fighting qualities. When he learned the great value of the minerals in the Black Hills, he demanded sixty million for the cession, which the government refused. He did not join the hostiles in 1876, however, and the government appointed him chief of the agency Indians, and it was he who negotiated the surrender of his nephew, Crazy Horse, (*q.v.*), in 1877. He was killed at Rosebud, South Dakota, in 1881, by another Sioux, Crow Dog. (George E. Hyde, *Spotted Tail's Folk* [1961].)

Tammany [Tamanend], (Delaware), fl. late 1600s. A chief of the Lenni Lenape (Delawares), about whom little is known. He was born along the Delaware River in Bucks Co., Pa., and in 1683 signed a deed giving lands to William Penn. He attended a council of settlers and Indians in 1694, where he spoke in favor of friendship. The date and place of his death are unknown, but his name was commemorated in Tammany societies which sprang up in several cities in 1786 and thereafter. (James Mooney in Hodge, II: 683–84; WWW [H], 519; DAB, IX: 289.)

Tecumseh (Shawnee), 1768–1813. Organizer of a confederacy of tribes to resist land cessions, he has been called "the most extraordinary Indian character in United States history." His village on Tippecanoe R., Ind., was destroyed by troops led by Gov. William H. Harrison, Nov. 7, 1811. He joined the British at war the next year and was killed in battle near Chatham, Ont., Oct. 5, 1813. See also pp. 67–68, 287 herein. (Glenn Tucker, *Tecumseh* [1956].)

Tedyuskung (Delaware), ca. 1700–1763. A chief who became a member of the Christian Indian settlement established by the Moravians at Gnadenhütten on the Mahoning River; he became chief in 1754 and asserted his independence from the Iroquois. He is credited with being largely responsible for British success at Fort Duquesne, and also for the ultimate failure of French arms in that region during the French and Indian War. (Anthony F. C. Wallace, *Teedyuscung: King of the Delawares* [1970]; DAB, IX: 360–61; Hodge II, 714–17.)

Washakie (Shoshoni), 1804–1900. A chief known principally as a friend and protector of the whites; his scouts rode with Crook against the Sioux on the Rosebud, and pursued the Cheyennes after the Custer battle; Washakie himself scouted against Utes and Arapahoes. His people were given a reservation in central Wyoming, and the town where the agency headquarters is located is called Washakie. (Virginia Trenholm and Maurine Carley, *The Shoshonis* [1966]; Hodge, II, 919–20; DAB, X: 494.)

Waubansee (Potawatomi), d. 1848. A Potawatomi war chief; he participated in the Fort Dearborn battle at Chicago, August 15, 1812, but is reported to have guarded the Kinzie family afterward. He was neutral during the Winnebago troubles in 1827, and campaigned with the Illinois militia in the Black Hawk war of 1832. For his services the treaty of Prairie du Chien (1829) assigned him "five sections of land at the Grand Bois, on Fox River of the Illinois." The treaty of Tippecanoe three years later awarded him five sections "in the Prairie near Rock village." Waubansee migrated to Council Bluffs, Iowa, with his tribe in 1835, after which accounts concerning him are contradictory. According to the best evidence, he died near Council Bluffs in 1848. Places are named for him in Illinois, Iowa, and Kansas. (Thomas McKenney and James Hall, *History of the Indian Tribes* [1855], III: 31–35; Seth Dean, "Waubansee, the Indian Chief (A Fragment)," AI, XVI 3d ser. Jul. '27: 3–24; Vogel, *Indian Place Names*, 160–62.)

White Eyes (Delaware), d. 1778. Chief sachem of the Delaware Indians on the Ohio in the 1770s; he encouraged the Moravian missionaries; maintained the neutrality of his people in Lord Dunmore's war, 1774 (see Logan); in defiance of the Iroquois he embraced the American cause in the Revolutionary War, and signed a treaty of alliance with the United States, September 17, 1778, the first Indian treaty concluded by the new government. It promised the eventual formation of a Delaware state with repre-

sentation in Congress should the Indians desire it. He joined General
Lachlin McIntosh's planned expedition to Sandusky and Detroit, but died
before it left Fort Pitt. (Hodge, II, 944; Kappler, *Treaties,* II: 3–5.)

Sarah Winnemucca (Paiute), 1844–1891. "The Indian Joan of Arc" (Forbes).
Daughter of Chief Winnemucca, of Nevada, she was briefly educated at
San Jose, Calif., and became an interpreter for General O. O. Howard and
various Indian agents. She taught a school for Indian children at Van-
couver, Wash., in 1881, and again at Lovelock, Nev., in the mid-eighties.
She lectured in eastern states on the problems of the Indians, singling out
the Indian agents for particular attack. In 1883 she published a book,
Life among the Piutes: Their Wrongs and Claims. (Hodge, II: 962; Jack
D. Forbes, *Nevada Indians Speak* [1967]: 96–99, 148–52, 155–58.)

Wovoka (Paiute), ca. 1856–1932. The prophet who created the Ghost Dance.
He believed that he was a messenger from heaven to tell the Indians to live
righteously, love all men, live in peace, and pray for the reunion of the
Indians. The government was alarmed at the spread of his philosophy, fear-
ing it augured a new Indian uprising, and attempts to suppress it led to the
Wounded Knee massacre. (Paul Bailey, *Wovoka, the Indian Messiah*
[1957]; James Mooney, *The Ghost Dance Religion* [1965]; Hodge, II, 975;
WWW, IV: 1035.)

Key To Abbreviations Used in Biographical Section

AA	*American Authors,* by W. J. Burke and Will D. Howe. New York: Crown Publishing Co., 1962.
AI	*Annals of Iowa*
AIA	*American Indian Authors,* by Arlene Hirschfelder. New York: Association on American Indian Affairs, 1970.
AIHS	American Indian Historical Society (San Francisco)
AIP	*American Indian Painters,* by Jeanne O. Snodgrass. New York: Museum of the American Indian, 1968.
Amer	*The Amerindian* (Chicago)
AN	*Akwesasne Notes* (Rooseveltown, N.Y.)
AO	*American Observer*
BDAC	*Biographical Directory of the American Congress, 1774–1961.* Washington: Government Printing Office, 1961.
BIA	Bureau of Indian Affairs, "Indians of National Prominence," leaf-let, 3 pp., 1964 (if initials only appear).
BIA	*Bureau of Indian Affairs, Famous Indians, a Collection of Short Biographies.* Washington: n.d. (Appears in text as "BIA, *Famous Indians.*")
CA	*Contemporary Authors,* + vol. no.
CB	*Current Biography*
CD	*Congressional Directory*
CDN	*Chicago Daily News*
CDN-Pan	*Chicago Daily News, Panorama* magazine
CE	*The Columbia Encyclopedia,* 2d ed., 1950

CHA	*Chicago Herald-American*
CHSB	*Chicago Historical Society Bulletin*
CNJ	*Creek Nation Journal, 1967*
CO	*Chronicles of Oklahoma*
CSM	*Christian Science Monitor*
CST	*Chicago Sun-Times*
CT	*Chicago Tribune*
CUNA	*Credit Union National Association*
DAB	*Dictionary of American Biography*
FHQ	*Florida Historical Quarterly*
Hum Org	*Human Organization,* journal of Society for Applied Anthropology, Ithaca, N.Y.
IH	*The Indian Historian* (San Francisco)
IMH	*Indiana Magazine of History*
IOT	*Indians of Today,* by Marion Gridley. Chicago: 1937, 1947, 1960.
IT	*Indian Truth,* Indian Rights Association, Philadelphia
IV	*Indian Voices* (Chicago)
IV-LONAI	*Indian Views,* League of North American Indians
KI	Bernard Klein and Daniel Icolari, *Encyclopedia of the American Indian.* New York: B. Klein & Co., 1967.
NCAI Sent	National Congress of American Indians *Sentinel*
NFG	*Niagara Falls* [N.Y.] *Gazette*
NYT	*New York Times*
SR	*Saturday Review*
TGM	*Toronto Globe and Mail*
USNWR	*U.S. News and World Report*
v	volume
WBD	*Webster's Biographical Dictionary,* 1st ed.
WWA	*Who's Who in America* + vol. no.; v35 = 1968–1969; v36 = 1970–71.
WWAW	*Who's Who of American Women,* 6th ed., 1970–1971.
WWAP	*Who's Who in American Politics,* 2d ed., 1969–1970.
WWC	*Who's Who in Canada,* 1966–1968.
WWW	*Who Was Who in America,* + vol. no.
WWW [H]	*Who Was Who in America,* Historical Volume, 1607–1896.

4 Selected Audio-Visual Aids

Films

Sources of films abbreviated; key and addresses of film sources given at the end. Most descriptions are from catalogs. All are sound films.

American Indians before European Settlement
    1 reel. Rental $1.75. (Minnesota)
American Indians of Today
    1½ reels. Rental $2.25. (Minnesota)

Arts and Crafts of the Southwest Indians
>Free loan to groups. (Santa Fe)

Catlin and the Indians
>Illustrates the contribution made by George Catlin in preserving for future generations the culture and customs of the American Plains Indians.
>24 minutes, color. Sale $300, rental $16. (McGraw-Hill)

Circle of the Sun
>This study of the migration of the Blood Indians from the farms and reservations to the city explains the whys and wherefores of the movement and the advancement and displacement of the Indian. Product of the National Film Board of Canada.
>30 minutes, color. Free loan (3 days) to Chicago groups from CPL.

Cortez and the Legend
>An account of how 500 Spaniards conquered an empire of 14 million people. It was filmed entirely in Mexico, and portrays the epic clash between two extraordinary personalities, Cortés and Montezuma.
>Two reels, total 52 minutes. Color. Sale $550, rental $35. (McGraw-Hill)

Custer: The American Surge Westward
>Special documentary about one of the most significant and famous battles in U.S. history, the factors that made it inevitable, and the man immortalized by it. The film examines the background of the conflict—the nation's expansion; the pressures on the U.S. government to take over the Indian lands; the determination of the Indians, once pacific, to fight for what was theirs.
>33 minutes, color. Sales $360, rental $25. (McGraw-Hill) Free loan (3 days) to Chicago groups from CPL.

Desert People
>How the Papago Indians live a full life in the Sonoran Desert.
>25 minutes, sound & color. Sale $63.06. (BIA)

End of the Trail: The American Plains Indian
>Surveys the westward movement in America during the last century and shows its tragic impact upon the American Indian. Explores the folklore of the American Plains Indian and aids an appreciation of the contributions of the Indian. It is a history of the American Indian in the post-Civil War era.
>2 reels, 53 minutes. Black & white, sound. Sale $275, rental $25. (McGraw-Hill) Free loan (3 days) to Chicago groups from CPL.

George Catlin and Alfred Jacob Miller
>The American West through the works of two American painters. George Catlin concentrated on the lives of the Indians while Miller depicted also the pioneers, traders, hunters, and the lakes, rivers, and mountains. Narrated by Frederic March.
>6 minutes, color, sound. Free loan (3 days) to Chicago groups from CPL.

High Steel
>Mohawk Indian structural steel workers.
>National Film Board of Canada, Ottawa, Ont.

Indian Ceremonials (Southwest)

18 minutes, sound and color. Free loan to groups. (Santa Fe)

Indian Influences in the United States

Surveys contributions of Indians to modern American culture.

1 reel, rental $3. (Minnesota)

The Loon's Necklace

Indian legend of how the loon acquired his white neckband, re-created with authentic ceremonial masks carved by Indians of British Columbia. Striking in color and in their ability to convey personality and emotions, the masks establish the character of each person and lend a dimension of reality to the tale.

11 minutes, color, sound. Rental $3 (Minnesota). Free loan (3 days) to Chicago groups from CPL.

Mahnomen: Harvest of the North

The wild-rice harvest of the Ojibwa.

2 reels, rental $3. (Minnesota)

Modern Chippewa Indians

Produced in a Chippewa reservation.

1 reel, rental $3. (Minnesota)

Navaho: A People between Two Worlds

Navajo country on the borders of Arizona, Utah, and New Mexico is the home of more than 100,000 persons who have lived an isolated life against a background of hogans, poverty, and sheep-herding. This life is changing as the oil, gas, and uranium industries pull the Navajo away, and better schools open up new worlds for the young.

17½ minutes, color, sound. Free loan (3 days) to Chicago groups from CPL.

People of the Pueblos

A film presentation about the Pueblo people of the Southwest which depicts the culture of their past and shows how their culture has survived to become a part of their present-day life.

20 minutes, sound and color. Sale $90.12. (BIA)

The Real West

Re-creates the American West as it was when the pioneers moved westward to fill in the last frontiers (1849–1900). Still-picture animation technique graphically explores the social and economic development of the expanding West. The conquest of the proud Plains Indians in the last of the great Indian wars is vividly brought to life. Has won several prizes.

54 minutes, black and white. Sale $300, rental $25. (McGraw-Hill)

River People

The story of the Pimas exemplifies one of America's Indian problems.

25 minutes, sound and color. Sale $60.48. (BIA)

Sisibakwat: The Ojibwa Maple Harvest

How northern Indians make maple sugar.

2 reels. Rental $6. (Minnesota)

The Song of the Feathered Serpent

Dances, reenactment of rituals, and the archaeological ruins of the Toltec, Mayan, and Aztec cultures, all centered about Quetzalcoatl, god of civilization, reveal the aspirations of past and present-day Mexico. Sponsored by P. Lorillard Co.

22 minutes, color. Free loan to Chicago groups (3 days) from CPL.

Spirit in the Earth

An Indian legend in which the fury of the rejected suitor of an Indian maiden is immortalized in the birth of the famous geyser, Old Faithful.

21 minutes, color. Free loan to Chicago groups (3 days) from CPL.

The Tree Is Dead

Shows the decline of Indian culture. Filmed on Red Lake Ojibwa reservation.

10 minutes, black and white. Rental $1.75. (Minnesota) Free loan (3 days) to Chicago groups from CPL.

War Dance

The Grass Dance of the Sioux, and variations of it, as performed by Reginald Laubin. Colorful, restrained, and dignified, preserving the original spirit of the dance.

13 minutes, color. Free loan (3 days) to Chicago groups from CPL.

Woodland Indians of Early America

The daily life of the Ojibwa family, as it was before the arrival of the white man, is authentically reproduced.

1 reel, rental $1.75. (Minnesota)

KEY TO ABBREVIATIONS OF SOURCES

BIA	U.S. Bureau of Indian Affairs, Division of Education, Washington, D.C. 20242. Films marked BIA are produced by it but sold only through private channels. Write for information.
CPL	Chicago Public Library, Randolph St. and Michigan Ave., Chicago, Ill. 60601. Does not rent or loan films to groups outside the area it is authorized to service. Loans films for three days to city groups only. Check your local library for similar services.
McGraw-Hill	McGraw-Hill Films, a Division of the McGraw-Hill Book Co., 330 West 42nd St., New York, N.Y. 10036.
Minnesota	Audio-Visual Extension Services Department, University of Minnesota, Minneapolis, Minnesota.
Santa Fe	Santa Fe R.R. Film Bureau, 80 East Jackson Blvd., Chicago, Ill. 60604.

Other Lists of Films and Sources of Films for Loan, Rental, or Purchase

A list of 300 educational films on the American Indian is contained in Roger C. Owen, *et al.*, *The American Indians* (New York: The Macmillan Co., 1967), pp. 718–44.

A list of 31 films about Indians, with requisite information, is given in Bernard Klein and Daniel Icolari, eds., *Reference Encyclopedia of the American Indian* (New York: B. Klein & Co., 1967), pp. 163–66.

Various audio-visual aids are listed in Dean Crawford, *et al., Minnesota Chippewa Indians: a Handbook for Teachers* (St. Paul: Upper Midwest Regional Educational Laboratory, 1967), pp. 96–97.

Bureau of Indian Affairs, Washington, D.C., *Films About Indians of the Americas.* Lists 57 films.

"The American Indian in Films," a comprehensive list compiled by Carla M. Blakey, with list of sources. *Film News,* Vol. 27, No. 5, 1970.

Film Strips or Slides

Hohokam slides: illustrates the prehistoric Hohokam culture of the Southwest; packaged in sets of five, at $1 a set, or $6 for the series: pottery, shell, stone, effigies, figurines, general artifacts.
Arizona State Museum, Tucson, Arizona 85721

Indian Arts and Crafts, from museum collections. Color slides.
Museum of the American Indian, 3751 Broadway, New York, N.Y., 10032. Write for information.

The Story of the American Indian, a set of nine strips covering all areas of the United States.
Eye Gate House, Inc., 2716 41st St., Long Island City, N.Y.

Chicago Public Library, film strips dealing with Indians:

A-599	The American Indian
A-841	Heritage of the Maya
A-866	The Navajos
A-323	Southwest Indian Art
A-736	Trail Blazers and Indians
A-155	Highland People of Bolivia

For loan to Chicago organizations.

Recordings

Sources of American Indian Music and Dance Recordings

American Indian Center
1630 W. Wilson Ave.
Chicago, Ill. 60640

American Indian Soundchief
1415 Carlson Drive
Klamath Falls, Ore. 87601

Canyon Records
834 N. 7th Ave.
Phoenix, Ariz.

Children's Music Center Inc.
5373 W. Pico Blvd.
Los Angeles, Calif. 90019

Catalog

Cuca Records Co.
Baraboo, Wis.

Chants from Wisconsin Dells Stand Rock ceremonials; 45 rpm hi-fi, 2 records, $1 each.

Disc Company of America
117 West 46th St.
New York, N.Y. 10019

Folkways Records
165 West 46th St.
New York, N.Y. 10036

Folkways-Scholastic Records
50 West 44th St.
New York, N.Y. 10036

Music of the Sioux and Navajo, #1401, 33 rpm Music of American Indians, Southwest, #1420, 33 rpm

Kroch's Book Store
29 S. Wabash Ave.
Chicago, Ill. 60603

Library of Congress Music Division
Superintendent of Documents
U.S. Government Printing Office
Washington, D.C. 20402

Catalog, *Folk Music,* 40¢. Has extensive Indian listings.

Rio Grande Press
1734 E. 71st Place
Chicago, Ill. 60649

Hopi Kachina songs.

Taylor Museum
Colorado Springs Fine
Arts Center
Colorado Springs, Colo. 80901

Music of the Pueblos, Apaches, and Navajos.

Descriptive list of records and sources of records: Bernard Klein & Daniel Icolari, *Reference Encyclopedia of the American Indian* (New York: B. Klein & Co., 1967), pp. 168–72.

Pictures

A Portfolio of Indian Life reproduced from *The Indian's Secret World,* by Robert Hofsinde (William Morrow & Co.)

Sold by Field Museum of Natural History, Chicago. $1.25

Blackfeet Indians of Glacier National Park—reproductions in color of 24 paintings by Reinold Reiss.

Sold by Great Northern Railway Company, St. Paul, Minnesota. $1.00, with explanatory pamphlet.

Indians in Michigan
Eighteen black and white reproductions on 8½ × 11″ paper, of authentic photos and paintings of Michigan Indians, with descriptive captions, a selective reading list, and a portfolio folder.

Sold by Michigan Historical Commission, Lansing, Mich. 48918. Price, $1.00.

Indians of Minnesota
Packet containing 24 illustrations and a map.

Minnesota Historical Society, 690 Cedar St., St. Paul, Minnesota 55101. Price, 50¢.

Indians in the United States: Select Picture List. National Archives General Information Leaflet No. 21.

National Archives & Records Service, Washington, D.C. 20408.

A Portfolio of Indian Paintings by George Catlin. 12 portraits in color, on heavy stock.

Smithsonian Institution, Washington, D. C. Price, $4.25

A collection of a dozen pictures in full color, of Indian life in various tribes, is available from the Pontiac Division of General Motors Corporation.

Indian Chiefs. "Eight engravings from the renowned McKenney & Hall Folio (1840) reproduced in full color."

Penn Prints, New York.

Full color silk screen reproductions of original paintings by famous American Indian artists.

Tewa Enterprises, 724A Canyon Rd., Santa Fe, New Mexico. $1 to $10. Free list.

"Famous Indian Chiefs," a set of 11 color reproductions of paintings by James L. Vlasaty, 10″ × 12″.

Published by M. A. Donohue Co., 771 S. Dearborn St., Chicago, Ill. 60605. Sold by Field Museum of Natural History, Chicago, Ill. 60605. $1.45 by mail.

Follow the Powwow Drums. Set of four color prints of Indian dancers, painted by S. Stranger, Sac-Fox Indian. 9″ × 12″.

David Fox, Great Lakes Indian Craftsmen, 1327 E. Elm Street, Griffith, Ind. 46319. $1.50 the set.

Four Chiefs, color prints of paintings by Indian artist S. Stranger: Geronimo, Sitting Bull, Quanah Parker, and Wolf Robe. 17″ × 20″.

David Fox, Great Lakes Indian Craftsmen, 1327 E. Elm Street, Griffith, Ind. 46319. $6 the set.

Indians of North America
Informational poster, beautifully illustrated in color. Portraits of members of representative tribes, pictures of Indian crafts, inventions, and designs, house types, masks, costumes, implements, canoes, etc. 24" × 30".

Jo Mora Publications, P.O. Box 990, Monterey, Calif. 93940. $2.35 including postage and insurance.

Indian Symbolic Designs. A chart, illustrating nearly 100 Indian symbols. 16" × 19".

Southwest Museum, Highland Park, Los Angeles, Calif. 90042. 35¢.

Typical Indian Dwellings of the U.S. Chart illustrating 22 different types of aboriginal dwellings. 16" × 19".

Southwest Museum, Highland Park, Los Angeles, Calif. 90042. 35¢.

Large poster photographs of six historic Indian chiefs and warriors: Gall, Red Cloud, Red Shirt, Joseph, Sitting Bull, and Geronimo.

United Native Americans, Inc. P. O. Box 26149, San Francisco, Calif. 94126. $2 each.

Another set of three poster photographs.

Akwesasne Notes, Rooseveltown, N.Y. 13683. $1.00.

Pit River Indians (California) Claim 3,500,000 Acres of Ancestral Land. A photo montage.

Aubrey Grossman, 1095 Market Street, Room 410, San Francisco, Calif. 94102. $2.00.

See also: Klein & Icolari, *Reference Encyclopedia of the American Indian,* pp. 167–68.

Indian Maps and Charts

American Indians: Visual History Wall Map. 1966.
Civic Education Service, 1733 K St., NW, Washington, D.C. 20006. $2.00.
American Indians—Then and Now [1971].
Culture areas in color; shows reservations, pictures of recent Indian happenings.
Scholastic Magazines, Englewood Cliffs, N.J. 07632.
Distribution of Indian Tribes of North America.
Shows location of tribes at the time of the first contact with white settlers. Prepared by A. L. Kroeber. 21" × 38", 35¢.
Southwest Museum, Highland Park, Los Angeles, California 90042.
The Frances Slocum Trail.
Illustrated map, black and white, of region between Peru and Marion, Ind., in Wabash and Mississinewa valley, named for white captive who spent her life among the Indians. Much information on the Miami tribe which inhabited the area. Part of this area is now being flooded by a dam.
By Otho Winger and Ada Louise Duckwall.

Miami County Historical Museum, 11 N. Huntington St., Peru, Ind., 46970.

Guide to Indian Reservation Areas.

Map, shows all federal reservations in red; lists all BIA field and area offices; lists reservations by states, with area, population, attractions, activities, recreation, tourist facilities, and commercial potential.

Washington: Branch of Industrial Development, Bureau of Indian Affairs, Department of the Interior.

Historic Trading Posts and Territories: Hudson's Bay Company.

Color illustrated map showing history of Hudson's Bay Co., and also location of Canadian Indian tribes and earlier place names.

By Stanley Turner.

Hudson's Bay Company, 79 Main St., Winnipeg 1, Manitoba, Canada.

Indian Days in Du Page County [Illinois].

Shows sites of former Indian villages in Du Page Co.; has explanations of some Indian place names; other historic information. Portraits and biographical information on Black Hawk, Waubansee, Shabbona, and Sturgeon's Head, and thumbnail sketches of the Illiniwek and Potawatomi. Border design shows Indian symbols and implements. Brown and white, durable paper. 1966.

Gene Gallo, Winnebago Crafts, Box 365, Elmhurst, Illinois.

Indian Map of the Southwest.

Shows major tribes, languages, culture groups and customs of the Southwest, with all important reservations. Illustrated in color. Butler Art Service, PO Box 88, Orange, Calif. 92669. $1.00.

Indian Trails and Villages of Chicago and of Cook, Du Page, and Will Counties, Ill., 1804, as shown by weapons and implements of the stone age. Cop. 1900 & 1901 by Albert F. Scharf. Black and white. Sold at Chicago Historical Society, 1061 North Clark St., Chicago, Ill. 60614. 25¢.

Indian Tribes in 1650.

Color map, shows locations and activities.

Scholastic Magazines, Englewood Cliffs, N.J. 07632. $1.00.

Indians of the U.S.A.

Illustrated, in color; border design contains names of historic Indians. Shows historic locations of tribes; map shows house types, costumes, crafts and designs; some historic information.

By Louise E. Jefferson. 1944.

Friendship Press, 475 Riverside Drive, New York, N.Y., 10027. $1.25.

Map of the Indian Country in Arizona, New Mexico, Utah, and Colorado.

Color. Shows all reservations in detail, and has enlarged detail map of Hopi villages, plus name index. Designed for motorists. Automobile Club of Southern California (AAA), 2601 Figueroa St., Los Angeles, Calif.

Navajoland, U.S.A.

Picto-map of Navajo reservation in color. Also shows Hopi reservation and illustrations of Navajo scenes, crafts, and activities. Prepared for and published by Navajo Tribal Parks Commission, Window Rock, Ariz.

The North American Indians.

Map prepared under the direction of Sol Tax, professor of anthropology, University of Chicago. Shows 1950 distribution of descendants of the aboriginal population of the United States, Canada, and Alaska. "This map is intended to include all self-identified American Indian communities as of 1950." Also gives population figures for each community. Fifth printing, 1960.

Department of Anthropology, University of Chicago, 1126 E. 59th St., Chicago, Ill. 60637.

Recreational Areas of the United States under Federal or State Administration.

Revised June 1948, and reissued by the U.S. Travel Division, National Park Service, U.S. Dept. of Interior, Washington, D.C.

In eight colors, shows all Indian reservations, including state reservations not always shown on other maps.

Three Maps of Indian Country.

1. Probable location of Indian tribes north of Mexico about A.D. 1500.

2. Culture areas and approximate location of American Indian tribes today.

3. Indian reservations under federal jurisdiction (except Alaska).

All in one folder. Published by Bureau of Indian Affairs, U.S. Dept. of Interior, Washington, D.C.

Order from publications service, Haskell Institute, Lawrence, Kansas.

Maps in Books

John R. Swanton, *The Indian Tribes of North America,* Bulletin 145, Bureau of American Ethnology (Washington: U.S. Government Printing Office, 1953). Contains five maps showing former tribal locations.

F. W. Hodge, ed., *Handbook of American Indians North of Mexico,* Bulletin 30, Bureau of American Ethnology. (2 vols.; Washington: U.S. Government Printing Office, 1907–1910). Vol. I contains color map, "Linguistic Families of American Indians North of Mexico," by J. W. Powell. Reissued in facsimile by Pageant Press, 101 Fifth Ave., New York, N.Y., 10003, and by Rowman and Littlefield, 84 Fifth Ave., New York, N.Y., 10011.

Ruth Underhill, *Red Man's America* (Chicago: University of Chicago Press, 1953) has a simplified linguistic map inside the front cover, and a reservation map inside the back cover.

5   Selected Museums with Significant Collections Relating to American Indians

Arranged alphabetically by states.

A list of this kind can never be made complete or satisfactory to everyone. We have listed nearly all institutions described in the *Museums Directory* (*infra*) as "Anthropology, Ethnology, and Indian Museums," and added many others which are known from other sources, or from personal visits, to possess important Indian collections. Nearly all general museums or natural history and historical museums have some Indian exhibits, and in the larger cities, these collections are more extensive than those in many small museums which specialize in Indian collections.

Many museums issue publications relating to Indians, and this fact is indicated, where known.

MUSEUM LIST

ALABAMA

Mound State Monument   Archaeological Museum
Moundsville

ALASKA

Alaska State Museum
Juneau 99801

Sheldon Jackson Junior College Museum
Sitka 99835

Trail of '98 Museum   Arts and crafts of Chilkat, Tlingit, and
Skagway 99840   Aleut Indians, and Eskimos.

ARIZONA

Amerind Foundation, Inc.
Dragoon

Arizona State Museum
University of Arizona
Tucson 85721

Canyon de Chelly National Monument
Chinle 86503

Heard Museum of Anthropology and
Primitive Art
Phoenix 85004

Montezuma Castle National Monu-   Pueblo ruins.
ment
Camp Verde 96322

Museum of Northern Arizona   "This museum displays ideas, not
PO Box 1389   things." Specializes in archaeology and
Flagstaff 86002   ethnology of local tribes. Publications.

Navajo Tribal Museum   Operated by the Navajo tribe; pub-
PO Box 54   lications.
Window Rock 86515

Pueblo Grande Museum   Library.
4619 E. Washington St.
Phoenix 85034

Smoki Museum
PO Box 123
Prescott 86301

ARKANSAS

Museum of Science and Natural History
MacArthur Park, Little Rock

Exhibits relating to mound builders, and Indians of the Plains and Southwest.

CALIFORNIA

American Indian Historical Society
1451 Masonic Ave.
San Francisco 94117

Museum, art gallery, publications; journal, *The Indian Historian*.

Antelope Valley Indian Research Museum
15701 East Ave.
Lancaster 93534

California State Indian Museum
2618 K St.
Sacramento 95816

Specializes in the culture of California tribes.

Clarke Memorial Museum
Third and E Sts.
Eureka 95501

Monterey State Historical Monument
Holman Exhibit of American Indian Artifacts
210 Olivier St.
Monterey 93940

Robert H. Lowie Museum of Anthropology
University of California
Kroeber Hall, 2620 Bancroft Way
Berkeley 94704

San Diego Museum of Man
Balboa Park
San Diego

Southwest Museum
Highland Park
Los Angeles 90042

Indian art museum, publications, quarterly bulletin, *The Masterkey*.

COLORADO

Denver Art Museum
1300 Logan St.
Denver 80203

Indian art collection, pottery, textiles, woodcarvings, costumes; publications.

Denver Museum of Natural History
City Park
Denver 80206

Koshare Indian Kiva Art Museum
18th and Santa Fe Ave.
La Junta 81050

Mesa Verde National Park Museum
Mesa Verde National Park 81330

Northern San Juan Anasazi culture.
The whole park is a museum, but in-
door exhibits explain the culture which
flourished here.

Ute Indian Museum
Chipeta Springs
Montrose 81401

Dioramas, artifacts, photographs,
maps, costumes, paintings. Maintained
by the State Historical Society of
Colorado.

CONNECTICUT

Peabody Museum, Yale University
New Haven 06511

Tantaquidgeon Indian Museum
Mohegan Hill Place, RFD 4
Uncasville 06382

Highlights history of the Mohegan and
other New England tribes.

DELAWARE

Zwaanendael Museum
Savannah Rd. and Kings Highway
Lewes 19958

Local Indian history.

DISTRICT OF COLUMBIA

National Museum of History and
Technology, Smithsonian Institution
Washington 20560

Some of George Catlin's Indian paintings are here.

U.S. National Museum of Natural
History
Smithsonian Institution
Washington 20560

U.S. Department of Interior Museum
19th and C Sts., N.W.
Washington 20240

FLORIDA

Florida State University Museum
Tallahassee

Southeast Museum of the American
Indian, Crane Foundation
Marathon 33050

GEORGIA

Creek Indian Museum
Indian Springs State Park
Indian Springs 30231

Etowah Indian Mounds Museum
Cartersville 30120

Artifacts and remains from adjacent mounds.

Kolomoki Mounds Museum
Rte. 1, Blakely 31723

New Echota
State Highway 225
Calhoun 30701

Restoration of the old Cherokee capital, offices of the *Cherokee Phoenix,* council house, home of Samuel Worcester, etc. Museum.

Ocmulgee National Monument
PO Box 4186
Macon 31208

One of the largest collections of pre-historic Indian materials.

HAWAII

Bernice P. Bishop Museum
Honolulu

IDAHO

Idaho Historical Society
610 N. Julia Davis Dr.
Boise

History of upper Great Basin tribes; publications.

ILLINOIS

Aurora Historical Museum
304 Oak Ave.
Aurora 60538

Dickson Mounds State Park Museum
Rte. 97
Lewistown

Outstanding example of exposed burials from Mississippi period.

Field Museum of Natural History
Roosevelt Rd. at Lake Shore Dr.
Chicago 60605

Outstanding displays, dioramas, representing all North American culture areas; library, publications.

Hauberg Indian Museum
Black Hawk State Park
Rock Island

Entirely devoted to Black Hawk and the Sauk and Fox tribes; located on the site of Saukenuk, their chief town.

Illinois State Museum
Spring at Edwards
Springfield 62700

Dioramas, publications.

Timke Circle-T Indian Museum
4850 Francisco
Downer's Grove

University of Illinois Museum of Natural History
Green and Mathews Sts.
Urbana 61801

INDIANA   Local Indian history.

Allen County–Fort Wayne Historical Society
1424 W. Jefferson St.
Fort Wayne

Indiana State Museum
Division of State Parks
616 State Office Bldg.
Indianapolis 46209

Indiana University Museum
Bloomington

Miami County Historical Museum   History of the Miami tribe; holds correspondence of Francis Godfroy.
11 N. Huntington St.
Peru 46970

Potawatomi Museum   Distributes books and monographs of other publishers; catalog.
Angola 46703

IOWA

Effigy Mounds National Monument   Exhibits concerning nearby mounds.
Box K
McGregor 52157

Iowa State Museum   Managed by State Dept. of History and Archives, which publishes *Annals of Iowa*.
E. 12th and Grand Ave.
Des Moines 50319

Museum of History and Science
Park Ave. at South St.
Waterloo 50701

KANSAS

El Quartelejo Kiva Indian Museum   Features Cheyenne and Pueblo artifacts.
PO Box 218
Scott City 67871

Wyandotte County Museum
Memorial Bldg.
7th St. and Barnett Ave.
Kansas City 66101

KENTUCKY

Museum of Anthropology
University of Kentucky
Lexington 40506

LOUISIANA

Marksville Prehistoric Indian Park
Action Rd.
Marksville 71351

MAINE

Robert Abbe Museum
Acadia National Park
Bar Harbor

Wilson Museum
Perkins St.
Castine 04421

MARYLAND

Archaeological Society of Maryland
Elkton

The Walters Art Gallery   Watercolors by Alfred Jacob Miller,
Charles and Centre Sts.   nineteenth-century painter of Indians.
Baltimore

MASSACHUSETTS

Fruitlands Museum
Prospect Hill
Harvard 01451

Holyoke Museum   Collections national in scope.
238 Cabot St.
Holyoke 01041

Peabody Museum of Archaeology and   Prehistoric emphasis; has large library.
Ethnology, Harvard University
11 Divinity Ave.
Cambridge 02138

MICHIGAN

Chief Blackbird Home Museum
268 E. Main St.
Harbor Springs 49740

Cranbrook Institute of Science   Features Great Lakes area; publica-
Bloomfield Hills 48013   tions.

Great Lakes Indian Museum
Cross Village 49723

Michigan Historical Commission
Museum
505 N. Washington Ave.
Lansing 48933

Exhibits Museum
University of Michigan
Ann Arbor 48103

Museum of Anthropology
University of Michigan
Ann Arbor 48103

Museum of Anthropology
Wayne State University
Detroit

MINNESOTA

Mille Lacs Indian Museum
Onamia

Minnesota Historical Society Museum
Cedar St. and Central Ave.
St. Paul 55101

Pipestone National Monument
Pipestone

Walker Museum of Natural History
and Indian Arts and Crafts
Conservation Bldg.
Walker 56484

MISSISSIPPI

Old Spanish Fort & Museum
200 Fort St.
Pascagoula 39567

MISSOURI

Kansas City Museum of History and
Science
3218 Gladstone Blvd.
Kansas City 64123

Missouri Historical Society Museum
Jefferson Memorial Bldg.
St. Louis 63112

Missouri State Museum
State Capitol Bldg.
Jefferson City 65101

Museum of Anthropology
University of Missouri
Columbia 65201

St. Joseph Museum
St. Joseph

MONTANA

Custer Battlefield National Monument
and Museum
PO Box 416
Crow Agency 59022

Features exhibits relating to the battle
of the Little Big Horn.

McGill Museum
Montana State University
Bozeman 59715

Montana Historical Society Museum
Roberts at 6th Ave.
Helena 59601

Museum of the Plains Indian
Browning 59417

On the Blackfoot reservation; has
agency records; publications.

NEBRASKA

Museum of the Fur Trade
Box 12
Chadron 69337

Outdoor Indian gardens; restored trading post; crafts.

Nebraska State Historical Society
1500 R St.
Lincoln 68508

Features Indian exhibits of Central
Plains.

Oregon Trail Museum
Scotts Bluff National Monument
Box 427
Gering 69341

Sioux dancing in summer.

NEVADA

Nevada Historical Society
PO Box 1129
Reno 89504

Nevada State Museum
Carson City 89701

NEW HAMPSHIRE

Dartmouth College Museum
East Wheelock St.
Hanover 03755

NEW JERSEY

Newark Museum   Publications.
43–49 Washington St.
Newark 08901

NEW MEXICO

Aztec Ruins National Monument   Pueblo ruins; some restoration.
Rte. 1, Box 101
Aztec 87410

Coronado State Monument
PO Box 95
Bernalillo 87004

Gallup Museum of Indian Arts and
Crafts
103 W. 66th Ave.
Gallup 87301

Museum of Anthropology
University of New Mexico
Albuquerque 87106

Museum of Navajo Ceremonial Art Publications.
PO Box 445
Santa Fe 87501

Museum of New Mexico   Housed in the old governor's palace
PO Box 2087   (1609). Features Southwest tribes;
Santa Fe 87501   Indians sell pottery on the patio.

Museum of New Mexico
Fine Arts Museum
127 S. Palace Ave.
Santa Fe 87501

Roswell Museum and Art Center
Roswell 88201

School of American Research   Southwest, Central, and South
116 Lincoln Ave., Box 1554   America; publications.
Santa Fe 87501

NEW YORK

American Museum of Natural History   One of the largest collections of Indian
79th St. and Central Park West   exhibits in the U.S. Strong in North-
New York 10024   west culture. Library, publications.

Cooperstown Indian Museum
1 Pioneer St.
Cooperstown 13326

Dioramas and exhibits of New York Indians.

Museum of the American Indian
Heye Foundation
Broadway at 155th St.
New York 10032

Exhibits from all culture areas; library, publications.

Museum of Primitive Art
15 W. 54th St.
New York 10019

New York State Museum
31 Washington Ave.
Albany 12210

Iroquois ethnographic material is featured; Morgan, Beauchamp, and Parker collections. Publications.

Rochester Museum of Arts and Sciences
657 East Ave.
Rochester 14607

Emphasis on Iroquois and Algonquian cultures. Library, publications.

Six Nations Indian Museum
Roakdale Rd.
Onchiota 12968

Publications.

NORTH CAROLINA

Museum of the American Indian
Blowing Rock Rd.
PO Box 83B
Boone 28607

Museum of the Cherokee Indian
PO Box 398
Cherokee, 28719

On the Qualla reservation of eastern Cherokees.

Research Laboratories of Anthropology
University of North Carolina
Chapel Hill 27515

NORTH DAKOTA

Fort Lincoln State Park Museum
Mandan 58554

Besides interior exhibits, has re-created Mandan earth dwellings.

Indian Museum
Fort Berthold Reservation
New Town 58763

OHIO

Fort Ancient Museum
7 mi. SE of Lebanon on Rte. 350

Prehistoric earthworks, and artifacts recovered therefrom.

Ohio State Museum
N. High St. and 15th Ave.
Columbus

OKLAHOMA

Anadarko City Museum
Main and First Sts.
Anadarko 73005

Bacone Indian Museum
Bacone College
Muskogee 74401

Cherokee Museum
Northeastern State College
Tahlequah 74464

Creek Indian Council House and   Former Creek capitol.
Museum
Town Square
Okmulgee 74447

East Central State College Museum
Ada 74820

The Five Civilized Tribes Museum   Opened in 1966.
Agency Hill, Honor Heights Drive
Muskogee 74401

Indian City, U.S.A.   Reconstruction of Plains Indian dwell-
PO Box 356   ings on 160-acre tract. Indian dances.
Anadarko 73005

National Hall of Fame for Famous   Bronze busts of distinguished Ameri-
American Indians   can Indians.
PO Box 42
Anadarko 73005

Oklahoma Historical Society Museum   Claims to be the second largest Indian
Lincoln Blvd.   museum in the world.
Norman 73069

Oklahoma Science and Arts Foundation, Inc.
Oklahoma City 73105

Osage Tribal Museum
Osage Agency, Pawhuska

Philbrook Art Center   Distinguished collection of American
2727 S. Rockford Rd.   Indian paintings, costumes, craftwork.
Tulsa 74114

Ponca City Indian Museum
408 S. 7th St.
Ponca City 74601

Southern Plains Indian Museum and
Craft Center
Box 447
Anadarko 73005

Quarterly publication, *Smoke Signals.*
Operated by Indian Arts and Crafts
Board, Dept. of Interior.

Thomas Gilcrease Institute of American History and Art
PO Box 2419
2401 W. Newton St.
Tulsa 74127

Indian crafts, archaeological material,
contemporary American Indian art.

Woolaroc Museum
State Highway 123
Bartlesville 74003

Indian arts and crafts of Oklahoma
and the Southwest.

Oregon

Klamath County Museum
3d and Klamath Sts.
Klamath Falls 97601

Northern Paiute, Klamath, Modoc,
and Shasta Indians.

Oregon Museum of Science and Industry
4015 SW Canyon Rd.
Portland 97221

Features Northwest tribes.

Pennsylvania

American Indian Museum
Rte. 19
Harmony 16037

E. M. Parker Indian Museum
Rte. 1
Brookville 15825

State Museum
Harrisburg 17105

University Museum
University of Pennsylvania
Philadelphia 19104

Rhode Island

Haffenreffer Museum
Brown University
Bristol 02809

Museum of Primitive Culture
Columbia Street and Kingstown Rd.
Peace Dale 02883

Rhode   Island   Historical   Society
Museum
52 Power St.
Providence 02906

Roger Williams Park Museum   Model woodland culture village.
Providence 02905

Tomaquag Indian Memorial Museum   Features southern New England tribes.
Ashaway 02804

SOUTH CAROLINA

The Charleston Museum
125 Rutledge Ave.
Charleston 29401

SOUTH DAKOTA

Pettigrew Museum   Sioux costumes and artifacts; Catlin
131 N. Duluth Ave.   lithographs.
Sioux Falls 57104

Sioux Indian Museum and Crafts Cen- Operated by Indian Arts and Crafts
ter   Board, U.S. Department of Interior.
PO Box 1504
Rapid City 57701

South Dakota State Historical Museum Local prehistory; library.
Soldiers and Sailors Memorial Bldg.
Pierre 57501

TENNESSEE

Chucalissa Indian Village   Museum and rebuilt Indian village.
Fuller State Park
Memphis

TEXAS

Texas Indian Museum
Harwood

Texas Memorial Museum   Focus on Texas tribes.
University of Texas
24th and Trinity
Austin 78705

UTAH

Anthropology Museum
University of Utah
Salt Lake City

VIRGINIA

Jamestown Foundation Museum
Box JF (Jamestown)
Williamsburg 23185

Reconstruction of Powhatan lodge.
Publications.

Valentine Museum
1015 E. Clay St.
Richmond 23219

WASHINGTON

North Central Washington Museum
Chelan and Douglas Sts.
Wenatchee 99801

Sacajawea State Park Museum
Pasco

State Capitol Museum
211 W. 21st Ave.
Olympia 98502

Northwest artifacts, basket collection.

Thomas Burke Memorial Washington
State Museum
University of Washington
Seattle 98105

Focus on Northwest tribes.

Washington State Historical Society
Museum
215 N. Stadium Way
Tacoma 98403

Library, publications.

WISCONSIN

Angus F. Lookaround Memorial
Museum and Studio
Keshena

In a Menominee community.

Logan Museum of Anthropology
Beloit College
Beloit 53512

City of Milwaukee Public Museum
818 W. Wisconsin Ave.
Milwaukee

Superb dioramas and other exhibits;
notable publications.

Historical Museum
Aztalan

Adjoins Aztalan State Park, prehistoric earthworks; northern limit of mound-builder culture.

Neville Public Museum
129 S. Jefferson St.
Green Bay 54301

Plains, Menominee, Chippewa tribes.

State Historical Society of Wisconsin,
Museum
816 State St.
Madison 53706

Notable for its library, which holds the Draper manuscripts, large photograph collection, disk and tape recordings. Publications.

WYOMING

Wyoming State Museum
State Office Bldg.
Cheyenne 82001

Plains tribes.

Whitney Museum of Western Art
Cody

PUERTO RICO

Museum of Anthropology, History and Art
University of Puerto Rico
Rio Piedras

CANADA

Alert Bay Public Library and Museum
Alert Bay, B.C.

Adjacent to the Kwakiutl Indians.

Eskimo Museum
Churchill, Man.

Fort Steele Historic Park Museum
near Cranbrook, B.C.

Kootenai exhibits.

Glenbow Foundation
Calgary, Alta.

Huron Indian Village
Little Lake Park
Midland, Ont.

Authentic restoration, even to game roasting on the fire. Created under auspices of University of Western Ontario.

Luxton Museum
Banff, Alta.

MacBride Museum
Whitehorse, Yukon Terr.

Northern Athapascans.

Museum of Anthropology
University of British Columbia
Vancouver, B.C.

National Museum of Canada
Ottawa, Ont.

Newfoundland Museum
St. John's, N.F.

Northern Handicraft Center and
Museum
Lac LaRonge, Sask.

Pacific National Exhibition
Columbia Bldg.
Vancouver, B.C.

Provincial Museum of Natural History
and Anthropology
Victoria, B.C.

Royal Ontario Museum
Toronto, Ont.

Skeena Treasure House
Hazelton, B.C.

Thunderbird Park
Victoria, B.C.   Outdoor totem poles; also watch them
                                            being carved.

Sources:

Directory, Historical Societies and Agencies in the United States and Canada.
    Nashville: American Association for State and Local History.
Katz, Herbert and Marjorie. *Museums USA.* Garden City, N.Y.: Doubleday,
    1965.
Klein, Bernard, and Icolari, Daniel. *Reference Encyclopedia of the American
    Indian.* New York: B. Klein & Co., 1967, pp. 15–62.
100 Magnificent Museums in Illinois. Chicago: Illinois Bell Telephone Co., n.d.
Museums Directory of the United States and Canada. 2d ed. Washington, D.C.:
    American Association of Museums and the Smithsonian Institution, 1965.

6   Government Agencies Concerned with Indians

United States Federal Agencies

Bureau of Indian Affairs
U.S. Department of the Interior
1951 Constitution Ave. NW
Washington, D.C. 20242

For list of regional and area offices,
see Klein and Icolari, *Encyclopedia of
the American Indian,* pp. 1–14.

Division of Indian Health
Bureau of Health Services
Public Health Service of U.S. Department of Health, Education, and Welfare

7915 Eastern Ave.
Silver Spring, Maryland 20910

Indian Arts and Crafts Board
U.S. Department of Interior Bldg.
Room 4004
Washington, D.C. 20240

Indian Claims Commission
441 G Street, NW
Washington, D.C. 20001

National Council on Indian Opportunity
726 Jackson Pl. NW
Washington, D.C.

Publications Service
Haskell Institute
Lawrence, Kansas 66044

Smithsonian Institution
U.S. National Museum
Washington, D.C. 20560

Volunteers in Service to America
(VISTA)
Washington, D.C. 20506

Canadian Federal Agencies

Department of Indian Affairs and
Northern Development
400 Laurier Ave. West
Ottawa 4, Ontario, Canada

National Indian Advisory Board
Ottawa, Ontario, Canada

United States State Agencies

Arizona Commission on Indian Affairs
Phoenix, Arizona

California State Advisory Commission
on Indian Affairs
Sacramento, California

Governors' Interstate Indian Council
Tulsa, Oklahoma

Twenty-two states participate; each sends two delegates, one Indian, one non-Indian; they represent the views of their governors and states.

Indian Education Division
Department of Education
State of Minnesota
Centennial Building
St. Paul, Minnesota 55101

Interagency Committee on Indian Affairs
c/o Lewis E. Langston
Illinois Department of Businesss and Economic Development
Springfield, Illinois 62706

Maine State Department of Indian Affairs
State House
Augusta, Maine 94330

Created by an act of the 102d Maine legislature to "exercise general supervision over the Indian tribes." Tribes served: Penobscot and Passamaquoddy.

Michigan Indian Commission
Lansing, Michigan

Minnesota Commission on Indian Affairs
Legislative Research Council
State Capitol
St. Paul, Minnesota 55101

New Mexico Commission on Indian Affairs
PO Box 306
Santa Fe, New Mexico 87501

"Directs the presentation and exchange of ideas in respect to Indian affairs of the State by all interested persons."

(New York) State Interdepartmental Committee on Indian Affairs
112 State St.
Albany, New York 12207

"Renders all state services to New York State's eight reservations; education, health, public works, social welfare."

North Dakota Indian Affairs Commission
Bismarck, North Dakota

Official view: "Assimilation must be the dominant goal of all programs and efforts to help Indians."

7   Indian and Indian Interest Organizations and Publications

Persons who want to keep informed on current Indian happenings and problems, or assist Indians, may want to join one of the following organizations, or subscribe to some of the listed publications. A word of caution is in order: some of them have a short life-span, and one should first check to see if the organization or publication is still going, before sending money, except for the older and well-established groups. This list was compiled in July 1970, with some revisions to March 1972. For convenience, it has been divided into several categories.

Some defunct publications are listed, and labeled as such, because they contain information used in the preparation of this book, and may be useful for research purposes if available in libraries.

As we go to press, the Justice Department has issued a *Directory of Organizations Serving Minority Communities,* which lists many Indian organizations and publications. For sale by the Superintendent of Documents, Government Printing Office, Washington, D.C. 20402, for $1.00.

Indian Organizations and Publications

This list includes organizations that are wholly or predominantly Indian, and publications sponsored by them, if any.

ORGANIZATIONS	PUBLICATIONS (or data)
Alberta Native Communication Society Rm. B1, 100 Avenue Bldg. 100th Ave. & 104th St. Edmonton, Alberta, Canada	*The Native People*
American Indian Center 1630 W. Wilson Ave. Chicago, Ill. 60640 (Minimum dues: $5 per year)	*The Warrior* Monthly; $2.50 for 10 issues.
American Indian Center 2201 E. 16th Ave. Denver, Colorado	
American Indian Center 3446 W. First St. Los Angeles, California 90004	*Talking Leaves* Monthly; $2.50 per year.
American Indian Center Phoenix, Arizona	
American Indian Center 1900 Boren Street Seattle, Washington	*Indian Center News*
American Indian Center 114 W. 6th Street Sioux City, Iowa 51103	*City Smoke Signals* Monthly, mimeographed (write for rates).
American Indian Center Wichita, Kansas	
American Indian Development, Inc. (AID) 4820 Guadelupe Trail NW Albuquerque, New Mexico	

ORGANIZATIONS	PUBLICATIONS (or data)
American Indian Development and Education Foundation (AIDE) 205 W. Wacker Drive Chicago, Illinois 60606	"Works to advance small businesses and scholarships in the Indian community."
American Indian and Eskimo Cultural Foundation 919–18th St. NW, Suite 800 Washington, D.C. 20006	*Four Winds,* quarterly, and monthly newsletter. Write for information.
American Indian Historical Society 1451 Masonic Avenue San Francisco, Calif. 94117	*The Indian Historian* Quarterly, $5 per year; single copies, $1.40. Also books and pamphlets.
American Indian Leadership Council	*The Indian* Co-editors: Birgil Kills Straight, Pine Ridge, S.D. 57770, and Frank La-Pointe, Rosebud, S.D. 57570
American Indian Movement (AIM) 1337 S. Franklin Ave. Minneapolis, Minn. 55404 (founded July 28, 1968)	Has a brochure, AIM. Branches reported in Cleveland, Denver, Seattle, Rapid City.
American Indian Press Association News Service Rm. 306, 1346 Connecticut Ave. NW Washington, D.C. 20036	News service.
American Indians Information and Action Group 1414 N. 27th Street Milwaukee, Wisconsin	
AMERIND. (American Indian Movement for Equal Rights in Native-Indian Development) P.O. Box 482 Albuquerque, New Mexico 87103	Incorporated October, 1970. Chapters reported in Phoenix, Gallup, and Brigham City, Utah.
ARROW, Inc. (American Restitution and Righting Old Wrongs) 1346 Connecticut Ave. NW Washington, D.C. 20036	*Arrow,* quarterly. An NCAI affiliate, sponsors and finances welfare projects.
California Indian Education Assn. 708 Mills Ave. Modesto, California 95350	*Early American* bi-monthly $3 annually

ORGANIZATIONS	PUBLICATIONS (or data)
California League for American Indians P.O. Box 389 Sacramento, California 95802	*Indian Affairs in California*
Caughnawaga Historical Society P.O. Box 538 Caughnawaga, Quebec, Canada	*Bulletin* (A Mohawk organization)
Cherokee National Historical Society P.O. Box 515 Tahlequah, Oklahoma 74464	*Cherokee Advocate*
Chicago Indian Village 1354 W. Wilson Ave. Chicago, Illinois 60640	Occasional mimeo bulletins. An action organization, formed in 1970. Dissolved, 1972.
Coalition of American Indian Citizens Box 18421, Capitol Hill Station Denver, Colorado 80218	*Guts and Tripe*
Consolidated Tribes of American Indians of Milwaukee, Inc. 1936 North 35th Street Milwaukee, Wisconsin 53208	Founded 1937.
Denver Native Americans United 2201 East Sixteenth Avenue Denver, Colorado	A coalition of seven organizations, formed in 1970.
Indian Association of Alberta 95 Holmwood Ave. NW Calgary, Alberta, Canada	
Indian Brotherhood Council 8545 Delaware Street Highland, Indiana 46322	Formed in 1971.
Indian Defense League of America Box 305 Niagara Falls, New York	
Indian-Eskimo Association of Canada 277 Victoria Street Toronto 200, Ontario, Canada	
Indian Homemakers Association Box 8544, Station H Vancouver 5, British Columbia, Canada	*The Indian Voice,* monthly 30¢ a copy; $3.00 per year. Focus on Indian women.
Indian League of the Americas, Inc. Brooklyn, New York	

ORGANIZATIONS

PUBLICATIONS (or data)

Indian Press Association
c/o Charles Trimble
Fort Lewis College, College Heights
Durango, Colorado 81301

Organized September 1970.

Indian Rights Committee
3822 Woodlawn Ave. N
Seattle, Washington

Concerned with fishing rights. Not
heard from since 10/68.

Indians for Indians
c/o William Cobe, Chairman
4550 North Clarendon Ave.
Chicago, Illinois 60640

Indians for National Liberation
P.O. Box 18285, Capitol Hill Sta.
Denver, Colorado 80218

Indians of All Tribes
4339 California Street
San Francisco, California 94118

Indians of All Tribes Newsletter
Three issues published in early 1970.
Inquiry regarding current status unan-
swered.

Metis Society
525–24th St. E.
Saskatoon, Saskatchewan, Canada

The New Breed, monthly.
(Metis are French-Indian mixed
bloods.)

National Congress of American Indians
1346 Connecticut Avenue, NW
Washington, D.C. 20036
(Dues: Indians $5; non-Indian as-
sociate membership $10 yr.)

NCAI Sentinel. Promised monthly beginning mid-1970. Subscription $5 an-
nually, or free with membership.
NCAI is composed of both tribal af-
filiates and individual members. It is
the largest Indian organization.

National Indian Youth Council
3102 Central Avenue SE
Albuquerque, New Mexico 87106

Americans Before Columbus.
Frequency unstated; subscription included with membership, $5 annually.

Native Brotherhood of British Columbia
325 Standard Bldg.
510 W. Hastings St.
Vancouver, British Columbia, Canada

The Native Voice

North American Indian Women's
Council
Mrs. James M. Cox, executive director
3201 Shady Brook Drive
Midwest City, Oklahoma 73110

Organized 1970 at Colorado State University, Ft. Collins, Colorado.

ORGANIZATIONS

PUBLICATIONS (or data)

Okmulgee Cultural Foundation
P.O. Box 704
Okmulgee, Oklahoma 74447

A Creek organization.

Original Cherokee Community Organization
Tahlequah, Oklahoma

Organization of fullbloods, formed in 1967.

The Survival of American Indians Association, Inc.
P.O. Box 719
Tacoma, Washington 98402

The Renegade
Apparently issued only thrice, in May 1969 and June 1971 and 1972; data on the fight for Indian fishing rights.

Tribal Indian Land Rights Association
1816 Karen Drive
Del City, Oklahoma

Tribal Indian Land

Union of Ontario Indians
1554 Yonge Street, Room 1
Toronto 7, Ontario, Canada

The Calumet

United Indians of All Tribes
P.O. Box 508
Seattle, Washington 98111

The movement for Indian occupation of Ft. Lawton.

United Native Americans, Inc.
P.O. Box 26149
San Francisco, Calif. 94126

The Warpath
Annual subscription:
$5 for non-Indians
$3 for Indians
Frequency not stated.

United Scholarship Service
1452 Pennsylvania Avenue
Denver, Colorado

Upper Midwest American Indian Center
1718 North Third Street
Minneapolis, Minnesota

Vancouver Indian Center
1200 W. Broadway
Vancouver, British Columbia, Canada

Working Indians Civil Association
Box 537
Pierre, South Dakota

A Sioux organization.

Independent Indian Publications

Akwesasne Notes
c/o Jerry Gambill

"Published monthly except February, August, and November, by Wesleyan

Box 435
Rooseveltown, New York 13693

University, Middletown, Connecticut 06457 (Indian Studies Program)." Send all correspondence to address at left. 50¢ an issue; $5 a year suggested, anything accepted. Tabloid size, 48 pages per issue, mainly reprints from other publications. For nationwide coverage of Indian news, this paper is without a peer.

Chahta Anumpa (The Choctaw Times)
Southeastern Indian Antiquities Survey, Inc.
Box 12392
Nashville, Tennessee 37212

Monthly, 4 pages. Subscription rates for non-Indians, $5 per year; Indian rate not given. Issue seen: Vol. I, No. 7 (December, 1968).

Cherokee Examiner
P.O. Box 687
South Pasadena, California 91030
(defunct)

Published six issues in 1969–70, then merged with *Rainbow People, q.v.*

Dine Ban-Hani [Navajo]
c/o General Delivery
Crownpoint, New Mexico 87313

The Indian Leader
Haskell Institute
Lawrence, Kansas

Indian Views
c/o William Rickard
Rte. 2, Box 140
Sanborn, New York (defunct)

Represented the views of the League of North American Indians and the Indian Defense League of America.

Indian Voices
University of Chicago
1126 E. 59th Street
Chicago, Illinois 60637
(defunct)

Project of Carnegie Cross-Cultural Education Project; published 1963–1968.

League of Nations
1139 Lehman Place
Johnstown, Pennsylvania 15902

Pan-American Indians Newsletter.

Many Smokes
P.O. Box 5895
Reno, Nevada 89503

"National Indian Magazine." One source reports 50¢ a copy; another says $2 a year.

Rainbow People
P.O. Box 164
John Day, Oregon 17845

Frequency unstated, but appears about every two months. Vol. I, No. 4, received March, 1971, has 23 pages. Subscriptions: 12 issues, $3; Institutions, $4. Militant paper.

The Raven Speaks
Box 35733
Dallas, Texas

Frequency not stated; subscriptions $3 per year.

Tundra Times
P.O. Box 1287
Fairbanks, Alaska 99701

"Owned, controlled, and edited by Eskimo, Indian and Aleut Publishing Co., a corporation of Alaska natives." Weekly, regular mail, 1 year, $8; 6 months, $4.50; airmail, 1 year, $19; 6 months, $10.00. Lively and stable paper.

Tribal Publications

The Cherokee One Feather
P.O. Box 501
Cherokee, North Carolina 28719

Weekly, $5 annually; sponsored by the tribal council of the Eastern band of Cherokees.

Fort Apache Scout
P.O. Box 898
White River, Arizona 85941

Monthly; annual sub $1 in Arizona; $1.50 out of state. Official newspaper, White Mountain Apache Tribe.

Jicarilla Chieftain
P.O. Box 147
Dulce, New Mexico 87528

Twice monthly; annual sub $2. Published by the Jicarilla Apache Tribe.

Kainai News
Box 432
Cardston, Alberta, Canada

Monthly, 16 pp. Sub $3.50 annually outside Canada; $3 in Canada for non-members; official paper of the Blood Indian Reserve.

The Native Nevadan
1995 East 2d Street
Reno, Nevada 89502

Monthly; annual sub $2.50.
Official paper, Inter-Tribal Council of Nevada, Inc. (Paiute, Shoshone, Washoe).

The Navajo Times
P.O. Box 428
Window Rock, Arizona 86515

Weekly; subs $4.50 a year; $3.50 for 9 mos.; $3.00 for 6 mos.
Official paper of the Navajo Nation, and a very substantial one.

Rosebud Sioux Herald (*Eyapaha*)
Box 65
Rosebud, South Dakota 57570

Weekly; annual sub $9. Official paper of the Rosebud Sioux.

Southern Ute Drum
Tribal Affairs Bldg.
Ignacio, Colorado 81137

Every two weeks; annual sub $4. Published by the Southern Ute Tribe.

The Ute Bulletin
Community Services Division
Ute Indian Tribe
Ft. Duchesne, Utah

No data.

Educational, Informational, Religious, or Welfare Organizations and Publications on Indian Affairs

ORGANIZATIONS

PUBLICATIONS (or notes)

Ad Hoc Committee on California Indian Education
1349 Crawford Road
Modesto, California 95350

California Indian Education
(report of conference on Indian education 1968; also *Early American,* occasional mimeographed bulletin.)

American Indian Arts Center
(Assn. on American Ind. Affairs)
1051 Third Ave.
New York City

A shop for the sale of authentic Indian arts and crafts.

American Indian Culture Center
3221 Campbell Hall
University of California
Los Angeles, California

American Indian Culture Center Journal, quarterly, $2 per year. Make check payable to the University of California.

American Indian Tradition
PO Box 136
Alton, Illinois (bi-monthly)

Association on American Indian Affairs, Inc.
432 Park Ave. South
New York, New York 10016
(Dues: $10 minimum; student $5)

Indian Affairs (bulletin)
Subscription $3 annually, or free with membership.
Former publication:
The American Indian (quarterly)
1947–1958

The Amerindian
1263 W. Pratt Blvd., #909
Chicago, Illinois, 60626

Bi-monthly news-bulletin $3 a year. Published by Marion Gridley since 1952, has never missed an issue. Focus on Indian achievement.

Bacone College
Bacone, Oklahoma
Bureau of Catholic Indian Missions
2021 H St. NW
Washington, D.C. 20006

Bacone Indian
(student newspaper)

Cook Christian Training School
Tempe, Arizona

Indian Highways

Friends Committee on National Legislation
245 Second St. NE
Washington, D.C. 20002

Monthly newsletter.

Indian Council Fire
737 West Brompton Place
Chicago, Illinois 60657
(Patron dues: $5)

Its only activity is the awarding of an annual achievement award to an outstanding Indian.

Associate Executive Committee of Friends on Indian Affairs
R.R. #2
McLoud, Oklahoma 74851

Indian Progress (bulletin)
$2 per year
Address varies; check first.

Indian Rights Association
1505 Race Street
Philadelphia, Pennsylvania 19102
Dues: $5 a year and up.

Indian Truth
Newsy bulletin, up to 16 pp. Approximately 4 times a year, issued by America's oldest Indian welfare group. Sent to all members and contributors.

Indian Scrapbook
c/o Frederick Goshe
314 College Ave., #1
Palto Alto, Calif. 94306
Quarterly, $1 per issue.

Bureau of Educational Research & Services, College of Education
Arizona State University
Tempe, Arizona 85281

Journal of American Indian Education
Issued 3 times a year; subscription: $3.50.

Labor's Committee for Minnesota Indian Youth
211 Produce Bank Bldg.
7th St. and 1st Ave. North
Minneapolis, Minnesota

National Fellowership of Indian Workers
Home Missions Council
7 Winona St.
Lawrence, Kansas

News Letter

National Indian Education Association
c/o Will Antell, President
Minnesota Department of Education
Centennial Building
St. Paul, Minnesota 55101

Organized 1970.

New Mexico Association on Indian Affairs
PO Box 2195
Santa Fe, New Mexico

Oklahomans for Indian Opportunity
Norman, Oklahoma

Founded by LaDonna Harris

Pow-Wow Trails
Box 268
Somerset, New Jersey
5 times a year, $3; "past and present
American Indian culture."

St. Augustine's American Indian Center
4512 N. Sheridan Rd.
Chicago, Illinois 60640

Bulletin, *The Cross and the Calumet*.
Sponsored by the Episcopal Church.

Government Publications

America Indigena
Inter-American Indian Institute
General Secretariat, Pan-American
Union
17th and Constitution Ave. NW
Washington, D.C. 20036

NOTES
Quarterly, in English, Spanish, and
Portuguese.

Downdraft
Bureau of Indian Affairs
U.S. Department of Interior
1951 Constitution Ave. NW
Washington, D.C.

Indian education.

FIRE (Forwarding Indian Responsibility in Education)
Published for the Bureau of Indian
Affairs by Enki Corporation
PO Box 221
San Fernando, California 91341

Indian Education Newsletter
U.S. Office of Education
400 Maryland Ave. SW
Washington, D.C. 20202

Indian Leader
Haskell Institute
Lawrence, Kansas

The Indian News
Dept. of Indian Affairs and Northern
Development
Ottawa, Ontario, Canada

Quarterly, in French & English (bilingual).
Free to Canadian Indians, price for
others unstated.

Indian Record
Bureau of Indian Affairs
U.S. Department of Interior
1951 Constitution Ave.
Washington, D.C. 20242

Monthly.

Native American Arts
Indian Arts and Crafts Board
Rm. 4004
U.S. Department of Interior
Washington, D.C. 20240

Occasional serial publication, each issue focusing on a special aspect of Indian arts. $1 a copy.

Anthropological, Ethnological, and Historical Organizations and Publications: A Selected List

ORGANIZATION	PUBLICATION
American Anthropological Association 1530 P St. NW Washington, D.C.	*American Anthropologist* Bi-monthly, $15 annually, $2.75 a copy.
American Society for Ethnohistory Secretary-treasurer: Dr. Henry F. Dobyns Center for Anthropological Studies Prescott College PO Box 2299 Prescott, Arizona 86301	*Ethnohistory* Quarterly, since 1954; $5 annually; students $2.50, institutions $8.
Anthropological Association of Canada 1575 Main St. Ottawa 1, Ontario, Canada	*Anthropological Journal of Canada* Quarterly, $4.20 annually, $1.25 a copy.
Oklahoma Historical Society Oklahoma City, Oklahoma 73105	*Chronicles of Oklahoma* Quarterly, $5 annually.
University of Chicago Department of Anthropology 1126 E. 59th St. Chicago, Illinois 60637	*Current Anthropology* Bi-monthly except August; $12 annually, $3 a copy.
Society for Applied Anthropology Lafferty Hall University of Kentucky Lexington, Kentucky 40506	*Human Organization* Quarterly, $8 annually, $2.50 a copy.
Southwest Museum Highland Park Los Angeles, California 90042	*Masterkey* Quarterly, $3.50 annually.

BIBLIOGRAPHY

Bibliography

Note

This bibliography, like the book, is designed not for specialists but for undergraduate college students. It is selective, rather than comprehensive. It is arranged under subject headings, to facilitate easy location of items of special interest, and a table of contents is provided. Faculty could conveniently use this list in making study or research assignments.

Certain subjects of specialized interest are omitted from this bibliography. Among them are linguistics and physical anthropology, as well as certain areas of ethnographic interest. The reasons are that these areas are not likely to concern undergraduate students, and they are outside the historical focus of this work.

A certain order of preference was adopted, with the intent of guiding people to the most readily available materials. Thus, the more recent editions are listed, rather than older editions. Material available in books was favored over that contained in periodicals and similar literature not always easily accessible. Paperback editions are listed before hardcover editions, but the dates of earlier editions are given. In view of the probable audience for this book, it was thought best to omit foreign language and manuscript sources.

No section of the bibliography will be satisfactory, except as an introduction, for persons pursuing advanced study in any aspect of Indian history or culture. For the convenience of these people, a list of specialized bibliographies is provided. Other specialized bibliographies appear under some subject headings.

Contents of Bibliography

1. Pre-Columbian Indians, and Early Post-Contact Indians

Baity, Elizabeth C. *Americans Before Columbus*. New York: Viking Press,
    1951.
Bandelier, Adolph F., and Hewett, Edgar L. *Indians of the Rio Grande Valley*.
    Albuquerque: University of New Mexico Press, 1937.
Baudin, Louis. *A Socialist Empire: The Incas of Peru*. Princeton: D. Van
    Nostrand Co., 1961.

Bluhm, Elaine, ed. *Indian Mounds and Villages in Illinois.* Bulletin no. 2, Illinois Archaeological Survey. Urbana: 1960.

Brundage, Burr C. *Lords of Cuzco.* Norman: University of Oklahoma Press, 1967.

Butcher, Devereux. *Exploring Our Prehistoric Indian Ruins.* Washington: National Parks Association, 1960.

Ceram, C. W. *The First American: A Story of North American Archaeology.* New York: Harcourt, Brace, Jovanovich, 1971.

Coe, Michael D. *Mexico.* London: Thames & Hudson [1962].

————. *The Maya.* London: Thames & Hudson, 1966.

Cole, Fay-Cooper, and Deuel, Thorne. *Rediscovering Illinois.* Chicago: University of Chicago Press, 1937.

Davila, Francisco Gonzalez. *Ancient Cultures of Mexico.* Mexico City: National Museum of Anthropology, 1966.

Deuel, Thorne. *American Indian Ways of Life.* Springfield: Illinois State Museum, 1958.

Flornoy, Bertrand. *The World of the Inca.* Garden City, N.Y.: Doubleday-Anchor, 1958.

Griffin, James B. *Archaeology of the Eastern United States.* Chicago: University of Chicago Press, 1952.

Haury, Emil W. *The Mogollon Culture of Southwestern New Mexico.* Gila Pueblo–Globe Arizona: The Medallion, 1936.

Hibben, Frank C. *Treasure in the Dust: Exploring Ancient North America.* Philadelphia: J. B. Lippincott, 1951.

Howe, Carrol B. *Ancient Tribes of the Klamath Country.* Portland: Binfords & Mort, 1968.

Jennings, Jesse D. *Prehistory of North America.* New York: McGraw-Hill Book Co., 1968.

————, and Norbeck, Edward, eds. *Prehistoric Man in the New World.* Chicago: published for Rice University by the University of Chicago Press, 1964.

León-Portilla, Miguel. *Aztec Thought and Culture.* Norman: University of Oklahoma Press, 1963.

Lewis, Thomas M., and Kneberg, Madeline. *Tribes that Slumber: Indians of the Tennessee Region.* Knoxville: University of Tennessee Press, 1960.

MacGowan, Kenneth, and Hester, Joseph A., Jr. *Early Man in the New World.* Garden City, N.Y.: Doubleday-Anchor, 1962.

Martin, Paul S., Quimby, George I., and Collier, Donald. *Indians Before Columbus.* Chicago: University of Chicago Press, 1947.

Morgan, Lewis H. *Montezuma's Dinner: an Essay on the Tribal Society of the North American Indians,* in *North American Review,* April 1876, reprinted as pamphlet by New York Labor News Co., 1950.

Peithman, Irvin M. *Echoes of the Red Man: an Archaeological and Cultural Survey of the Indians of Southern Illinois.* New York: Exposition Press, 1955.

Quimby, George Irving. *Indian Life in the Upper Great Lakes: 11,000* B.C. *to* A.D. *1800*. Chicago: University of Chicago Press, 1960.

Ritzenthaler, Robert E. *The Prehistoric Indians of Wisconsin*. Milwaukee: Public Museum of the City of Milwaukee, 1953.

Spencer, Robert F., Jennings, Jesse D., *et al. The Native Americans*. New York: Harper & Row, 1965.

Thompson, J. E. S. *The Civilization of the Mayas*. Chicago: Chicago Museum of Natural History, 1953.

————. *The Rise and Fall of Maya Civilization*. Norman: University of Oklahoma Press, 1954.

Towle, Margaret A. *The Ethnobotany of Pre-Columbian Peru*. Chicago: Aldine Publishing Co., 1961.

Vaillant, G. C. *The Aztecs of Mexico*. Harmondsworth, England: Pelican, 1950.

Verrill, A. Hyatt and Ruth. *America's Ancient Civilizations*. New York: Capricorn Books, 1967.

Von Hagen, Victor W. *Realm of the Incas*. New York: Mentor–New American Library, 1957.

————. *The Aztec, Man and Tribe*. New York: Mentor–New American Library, 1958.

————. *World of the Maya*. New York: Mentor–New American Library, 1960.

Watson, Don. *Indians of the Mesa Verde*. Mesa Verde, Colo.: Mesa Verde Museum Association, 1961.

Webb, William S., *et al. Prehistoric Indians of the Ohio Valley*. Columbus: The Ohio Historical Society, 1957.

Willey, Gordon R. *An Introduction to American Archaeology. Vol. I, North and Middle America*. Englewood Cliffs, N.J.: Prentice-Hall, 1966.

————. ed. *Prehistoric Settlement Patterns in the New World*. New York: Wenner-Gren Foundation for Anthropological Research, 1956.

See also Aboriginal Literature.

2. American Indian History and Ethnology, General Treatment

Armstrong, Virginia I. *I Have Spoken: American History through the Voices of Indians*. Chicago: Swallow Press, 1971.

Beals, Carleton. *American Earth: the Biography of a Nation,* Chap. 3. Philadelphia: J. B. Lippincott, 1939.

Benedict, Ruth. *Patterns of Culture*. New York: Pelican Books, 1946.

Brandon, William. "American Indians and American History," *American West,* Spring 1965, pp. 14–25, 91–93.

Collier, John. *The Indians of the Americas*. New York: W. W. Norton & Co., 1947. Paperback ed., abridged, Mentor, 1948 *et seq.*

Debo, Angie. *A History of the Indians of the United States*. Norman: University of Oklahoma Press, 1970.

Drake, Samuel. *The Aboriginal Races of North America*. 15th ed. New York: Hurst & Co., 1880.

Driver, Harold E. *Indians of North America.* Chicago: University of Chicago Press, 1964.

———. *The Americas on the Eve of Discovery.* Englewood Cliffs, N.J.: Prentice-Hall, 1964.

Dunn, Jacob Piatt. *True Indian Stories.* Indianapolis: Sentinel Publishing Co., 1909. Reprint by Lawrence W. Shultz, North Manchester, Ind., 1964,

Eggan, Fred. *Social Anthropology of North American Tribes.* Chicago: University of Chicago Press, 1937.

———. *The American Indian: Perspectives for the Study of Social Change.* Chicago: Aldine Publishing Co., 1966.

Embree, Edwin R. *Indians of the Americas.* Boston: Houghton Mifflin Co., 1939. Reprint, New York: Collier Books, 1970.

Farb, Peter. *Man's Rise to Civilization, as Shown by the Indians of North America from Primeval Times to the Coming of the Industrial State.* New York: E. P. Dutton & Co., 1968.

Farrand, Livingston. *Basis of American History, 1500–1900.* New York: Harper & Bros., 1904. Reissued, Frederick Ungar Publishing Co., n.d.

Forbes, Jack D. *The Indian in America's Past.* Englewood Cliffs, N.J.: Prentice-Hall, 1964.

Garland, Hamlin. *The Book of the American Indian.* New York: Harper & Bros., 1923.

Gladwin, Harold S. *Men Out of Asia.* New York: Whittlesey House, 1947.

Grinnell, George Bird. *The Story of the Indian.* New York: Appleton-Century Co., 1935.

Hagan, William T. *American Indians.* Chicago: University of Chicago Press, 1961.

———. *The Indian in American History.* Publication no. 50, Service Center for Teachers of History, American Historical Association. New York: The Macmillan Co., 1963. Revised 1971.

Haines, Elijah M. *The American Indian.* Chicago: The Massinigan Co., 1888.

Hodge, Frederick Webb, ed. *Handbook of American Indians North of Mexico.* Bulletin 30, Bureau of American Ethnology, 2 vols. Washington: Government Printing Office, 1907–1910. Reissued by Pageant Press and by Rowman and Littlefield, New York (1959).

Huntington, Ellsworth. *Red Man's America.* New Haven: Yale University Press, 1919.

Josephy, Alvin M., Jr. *The Indian Heritage of America.* New York: Alfred A. Knopf, 1968.

———, ed., and Brandon, William, narrator. *The American Heritage Book of Indians.* New York: American Heritage Publishing Co., Inc., 1961. Paperback reissue by Dell Publishing Co., 1964.

Kroeber, A. L. *Cultural and Natural Areas of Native North America.* Berkeley: University of California Press, 1963.

LaFarge, Oliver. *A Pictorial History of the American Indian.* New York: Crown Publishers, 1959.

Linton, Ralph. *Acculturation in Seven American Indian Tribes.* Gloucester, Mass.: Peter Smith, 1963.

McKenney, Thomas L., and Hall, James. *The Indian Tribes of North America.*, ed. by F. W. Hodge and David I. Bushnell, Jr. 3 vols. Edinburgh: John Grant, 1934.

McNickle, D'Arcy. *They Came Here First.* Philadelphia: J. B. Lippincott, 1949.

Marriott, Alice, and Rachlin, Carol. *American Epic: The Story of the American Indian.* New York: G. P. Putnam's Sons, 1969.

Morgan, Lewis H. *Ancient Society.* Chicago: Charles H. Kerr & Co. 1910.

Oswalt, Wendell H. *This Land Was Theirs.* New York: John Wiley & Sons, 1966.

Owen, Roger C.; Deetz, James J.; and Fisher, Anthony D. *The North American Indians: A Sourcebook.* New York: The Macmillan Co., 1967.

Pearce, Roy Harvey. *The Savages of America: A Study of the Indian and the Idea of Civilization.* Rev. ed. Baltimore: Johns Hopkins Press, 1965.

Radin, Paul. *The Story of the American Indian.* New York: Liveright Publishing Corp., 1927.

Schoolcraft, Henry R. *Information Respecting the History, Condition and Prospects of the Indian Tribes of the United States.* 6 vols. Philadelphia: Lippincott, Grambo & Co., 1853. Should be used with Frances S. Nichols, *Index to Schoolcraft's "Indian Tribes of the United States,"* Bulletin 152, Bureau of American Ethnology. Washington: Government Printing Office, 1954.

Spicer, Edward H. *A Short History of the Indians of the United States.* New York: Van Nostrand Reinhold Co., 1969.

Stirling, Matthew W. *Indians of the Americas.* Washington: National Geographic Society, 1955.

Swanton, John R. *The Indian Tribe. ~f North America.* Bulletin 145, Bureau of American Ethnology. Washington: Government Printing Office, 1953.

Tax, Sol, ed. *Indian Tribes of Aboriginal North America.* Selected Papers of the XXIXth International Congress of Americanists. 3 vols. Chicago: University of Chicago Press, 1952.

Underhill, Ruth. *Red Man's America.* Chicago: University of Chicago Press, 1953.

Verrill, Alpheus Hyatt. *Our Indians: The Story of the Indians of the United States.* New York: G. P. Putnam's Sons, 1935.

―――. *The American Indian, North, South and Central America.* New York: New Home Library, 1943.

―――. *The Real Americans.* New York: G. P. Putnam's Sons, 1954.

Vogel, Virgil J. *The Indian in American History.* Chicago: Integrated Education Associates, 1968.

Washburn, Wilcomb E. *The Indian and the White Man.* Garden City, New York: Doubleday-Anchor, 1964.

Wise, Jennings C. *The Red Man in the New World Drama.* Washington: W. F. Roberts Co., 1931.

Wissler, Clark. *Indian Cavalcade*. New York: Sheridan House, 1938. Reissued as *Red Man Reservations*, New York: Collier Books, 1971.

——. *Indians of the United States: Four Centuries of their History and Culture*. Garden City, N.Y.: Doubleday & Co., 1949.

——. *The American Indian*. Gloucester: Peter Smith, 1957.

3. *Indians of Particular Regions, Areas, or States*

American Friends Service Committee. *Indians of California, Past and Present*. San Francisco: AFSC, 1956.

Atkinson, M. Jourdan. *Indians of the Southwest*. San Antonio: Naylor Co., 1963.

Bailey, Paul. *The Thirteen Tribes of Long Island*. Amityville, N.Y.: Long Island Forum, 1956.

Beals, Carleton. *Nomads and Empire Builders: Native Peoples and Cultures of South America*. Philadelphia: Chilton Co., 1961.

Bennett, Wendell C., and Bird, Junius B. *Andean Culture History*. Garden City, N.Y.: Natural History Press, 1968.

Blair, Emma H., ed. *The Indian Tribes of the Upper Mississippi Valley and Region of the Great Lakes*. 2 vols. Cleveland: Arthur H. Clark Co., 1912.

Bureau of Indian Affairs, U.S. Department of the Interior. *Indians of Oklahoma*. Washington: U.S. Government Printing Office, 1965.

(The other pamphlets in this regional series, all by the above publisher, are listed below by title and date only.)

Indians of Arizona. 1966.
Indians of California. 1966.
Indians of the Central Plains. 1966.
Indians of the Dakotas. 1966.
Indians, Eskimos, and Aleuts of Alaska. 1966.
Indians of the Great Lakes Area. 1966.
Indians of the Gulf Coast States. 1966.
Indians of the Lower Plateau. 1966.
Indians of Montana and Wyoming. 1966.
Indians of New Mexico. 1966.
Indians of the Northwest. 1966.
Indians of North Carolina. 1966.
Indians of the Eastern Seaboard. 1967.

Revised editions of some of the above titles have since appeared.

Callender, Charles. *Social Organization of the Central Algonkian Indians*. Milwaukee: Milwaukee Public Museum, 1962.

Canada Geographic Board. *Handbook of Indians of Canada*. Ottawa: 1913. Reprinted from F. W. Hodge, *Handbook of American Indians*, Bulletin 30, Bureau of American Ethnology.

Cotterill, R. S. *The Southern Indians: The Story of the Civilized Tribes Before Removal*. Norman: University of Oklahoma Press, 1954.

Dale, Edward Everett. *The Indians of the Southwest*. Norman: University of Oklahoma Press, 1949.

DeForest, John W. *History of the Indians of Connecticut, from the Earliest Known Period to 1850*. Hamden, Conn.: The Shoestring Press, 1964. (Reprint from 1851.)

Denig, Edwin Thompson. *Five Indian Tribes of the Upper Missouri*, ed. by John C. Ewers. Norman: University of Oklahoma Press, 1961.

Douglas, John M. *The Indians in Wisconsin's History*. Milwaukee: Public Museum of the City of Milwaukee, 1954.

Drucker, Philip. *Indians of the Northwest Coast*. Garden City, N.Y.: Natural History Press, 1963.

Dutton, Bertha P. *New Mexico Indians and their Arizona Neighbors*. Santa Fe: New Mexico Association on Indian Affairs, 1955.

Fay, George E., ed. and publisher. *Journal of the Wisconsin Indians Research Institute*, Wisconsin State University at Oshkosh. Three volumes, containing two numbers each (1965, 1966, 1967), containing papers and documents on Wisconsin tribes. (Removed to Colorado State College, Greeley, Colorado 80631.)

Forbes, Jack D. *Apache, Navaho and Spaniard*. Norman: University of Oklahoma Press, 1950.

————. *Nevada Indians Speak*. Reno: University of Nevada Press, 1967.

Foreman, Grant. *A History of Oklahoma*. Norman: University of Oklahoma Press, 1952.

Freuchen, Peter. *Book of the Eskimos*. Greenwich, Conn.: Fawcett Publications, 1965. (Reprint from World Publishing Co., 1961.)

Greenman, Emerson F. *The Indians of Michigan*. Lansing: Michigan Historical Commission, 1961.

Hafen, LeRoy R. *The Indians of Colorado*. Denver: The State Historical Society of Colorado, 1952.

Heizer, Robert F. *Languages, Territories, and Names of California Indian Tribes*. Berkeley: University of California Press, 1966.

————, and Whipple, M. A. *The California Indians, a Source Book*. Berkeley: University of California Press, 1967.

Hyde, George E. *Indians of the High Plains, from Prehistoric Times to the Coming of Europeans*. Norman: University of Oklahoma Press, 1959.

————. *Indians of the Woodlands, from Prehistoric Times to 1725*. Norman: University of Oklahoma Press, 1962.

"Indians Who Lived in Illinois," title of entire issue of *Illinois History*, XIII, No. 2 (November 1959), and XXIV, No. 2 (November 1970). Published for high school students by Illinois State Historical Society, Springfield.

Jeness, Diamond. *Indians of Canada*. Ottawa: National Museum of Canada, 1932.

Kinietz, W. Vernon. *The Indians of the Western Great Lakes, 1615–1760*. Ann Arbor: University of Michigan Press, 1965.

Kroeber, A. L. *Handbook of the Indians of California.* Berkeley: California Book Co., 1953.

Lowie, R. H. *Indians of the Plains.* New York: McGraw-Hill Book Co., 1954.

McCary, Ben C. *Indians in Seventeenth-Century Virginia.* Williamsburg: The Virginia 350th Anniversary Corporation, 1957.

Newcomb, W. W., Jr. *The Indians of Texas.* Austin: University of Texas Press, 1965.

Rand, James Hall. *The North Carolina Indians.* Chapel Hill: University of North Carolina Press, 1913.

Schulenberg, Raymond F. *Indians of North Dakota.* Bismarck: State Historical Society of North Dakota, 1956.

Smith, Anne M. *New Mexico Indians.* Santa Fe: Museum of New Mexico Press, 1969.

Steward, Julian H., ed. *Handbook of South American Indians.* 7 vols. Bulletin 143, Bureau of American Ethnology. Washington: Government Printing Office, 1946–1959.

Strong, William D. *The Indian Tribes of the Chicago Region.* Chicago: Field Museum of Natural History, 1938.

Swanton, John R. *Indian Tribes of Alaska and Canada.* Seattle: Shorey Publications, 1964.

Temple, Wayne C. *Indian Villages of the Illinois Country: Historic Tribes.* Springfield: Illinois State Museum, 1958.

Underhill, Ruth. *Indians of the Pacific Northwest.* Riverside, Calif.: Sherman Institute Press, for the Bureau of Indian Affairs, 1945.

————. *The Indians of Southern California.* Lawrence, Kansas: Haskell Institute, 1964.

Wallace, Paul A. W. *Indians in Pennsylvania.* Harrisburg, Pa.: Pennsylvania Historical and Museum Commission, 1964.

Wauchope, Robert, general ed. *Handbook of Middle American Indians,* 11 vols. Austin: University of Texas Press, 1964—.

Wilson, Charles B. *Indians of Eastern Oklahoma.* Afton, Okla.: Buffalo Publishing Co., 1956.

Wright, Muriel. *A Guide to the Indian Tribes of Oklahoma.* Norman: University of Oklahoma Press, 1965.

Zorita, Alonso de. *Life and Labor in Ancient Mexico,* trans. by Benjamin Keen. New Brunswick, N.J.: Rutgers University Press, 1963.

4. Indian Tribes

[C] = contemporary problem treatment. [E] = ethnological treatment. [H] = historical treatment.

Anson, Bert. *The Miami Indians.* [H] Norman: University of Oklahoma Press, 1970.

Basso, Keith H. *The Cibecue Apache.* [E] New York: Holt, Rinehart, & Winston, 1970.

Beauchamp, William M. *A History of the New York Iroquois.* [H] Albany: New York State Education Department, 1905.

Belknap, Jeremy, and Morse, Jedidiah. *Report on the Oneida, Stockbridge, and Brotherton Indians, 1796.* [H] New York: Museum of the American Indian, 1955.

Berthrong, Donald J. *The Southern Cheyennes.* [H] Norman: University of Oklahoma Press, 1963.

Brown, Douglas Summers. *The Catawba Indians: The People of the River.* [H] Columbia: University of South Carolina Press, 1966.

Capron, Louis, and Imboden, Otis. "Florida's Emerging Seminoles," *National Geographic Magazine,* November 1969, pp. 716–34. [C]

Caton, J. L. *The Eastern Cherokees.* [H] Knoxville: the author, 1937.

Clark, Elizabeth M. and David W. *Rehabilitation Program on the Cheyenne River Sioux Reservation.* [C] Philadelphia: Indian Rights Association, 1961.

Colden, Cadwallader. *The History of the Five Indian Nations* . . . [H] 2 vols. New York: New Amsterdam Book Co., 1902. Abridged one-volume paperback edition: Ithaca: Cornell University Press, 1964.

Corwin, Hugh D. *Comanche and Kiowa Captives in Oklahoma and Texas.* [H] Lawton, Okla.: the author, 1959.

————. *The Kiowa Indians: Their History and Life Stories.* [H] Lawton, Okla.: the author, 1959.

Debo, Angie. *The Road to Disappearance.* [H] (Creeks) Norman: University of Oklahoma Press, 1941.

————. *The Five Civilized Tribes of Oklahoma: Report on Social and Economic Conditions.* [C] Philadelphia: Indian Rights Association, 1951.

————. *The Rise and Fall of the Choctaw Republic.* [H] Norman: University of Oklahoma Press, 1967.

Emmitt, Robert. *The Last War Trail: The Utes and the Settlement of Colorado.* [H] Norman: University of Oklahoma Press, 1954.

Ewers, John C. *The Story of the Blackfeet.* [H] Lawrence, Kansas: Haskell Institute, 1952.

————. *The Blackfeet: Raiders of the Northwestern Plains.* [H] Norman: University of Oklahoma Press, 1958.

Folsom-Dickerson, W. E. S. *The White Path.* [E] (Alabama-Koasati Indians of Texas). San Antonio: The Naylor Co., 1965.

Gibson, A. M. *The Kickapoos: Lords of the Middle Border.* [H] Norman: University of Oklahoma Press, 1963.

————. *The Chickasaws.* [H] Norman: University of Oklahoma Press, 1971.

Godfroy, Chief Clarence. *Miami Indian Stories.* [H] Winona Lake, Ind.: Light and Life Press, 1961.

Hagan, William T. *The Sac and Fox Indians.* [H] Norman: University of Oklahoma Press, 1958.

Haines, Francis. *The Nez Perces: Tribesmen of the Columbia Plateau.* [H] Norman: University of Oklahoma Press, 1955.

Hickerson, Harold. *The Chippewa and their Neighbors.* [H] New York: Holt, Rinehart, & Winston, 1970.

Howard, James H. *The Ponca Tribe*. Bureau of American Ethnology, Bulletin 195. [E] Washington: Government Printing Office, 1965.

Hyde, George E. *Pawnee Indians*. [H] Denver: University of Denver Press, 1951.

————. *A Sioux Chronicle*. [H] Norman: University of Oklahoma Press, 1956.

Keesing, Felix M. *The Menomini Indians of Wisconsin*. [E] Philadelphia: American Philosophical Society, 1939.

Kluckhohn, Clyde, and Leighton, Dorothea. *The Navaho*. [E] Garden City, N.Y.: Doubleday-Anchor, 1962.

Lancaster, Richard. *Piegan*. [H] Garden City, N.Y.: Doubleday & Co., 1966.

Landes, Ruth. *The Prairie Potawatomi*. [E] Madison: University of Wisconsin Press, 1970.

Lowie, Robert H. *The Crow Indians*. [E] New York: Rinehart & Co., 1958.

McReynolds, Edwin C. *The Seminoles*. [H] Norman: University of Oklahoma Press, 1957.

Madsen, Brigham D. *The Bannock of Idaho*. [H] Caldwell, Idaho: Caxton Printers, 1958.

Malone, Henry T. *Cherokees of the Old South*. [H] Athens: University of Georgia Press, 1956.

Mathews, John J. *Wah'kon-tah: The Osage and the White Man's Road*. [H] Norman: University of Oklahoma Press, 1932.

————. *The Osages: Children of the Middle Waters*. [H] Norman: University of Oklahoma Press, 1961.

Mayhall, Mildred. *The Kiowas*. [H] Norman: University of Oklahoma Press, 1963.

Mead, Margaret. *The Changing Culture of an Indian Tribe*. [E] New York: Capricorn Books, 1966.

Momaday, N. Scott. *The Way to Rainy Mountain*. [H] (Kiowa traditions.) Albuquerque: University of New Mexico Press, 1969.

Morgan, Lewis H. *League of the Ho-De-No-Sau-Nee or Iroquois* [E] 2 vols. New Haven: Human Relations Area Files, 1954.

Nelson, Bruce. *Land of the Dacotahs*. [H] Lincoln: University of Nebraska Press, n.d.

O'Kane, Walter Collins. *The Hopis: Portrait of a Desert People*. [H] Norman: University of Oklahoma Press, 1953.

Peithman, Irwin M. *The Choctaw Indians of Mississippi*. [H] Carbondale: Southern Illinois University Press, 1961.

Pickford, A. E. *Kootenay*. [H] Victoria, B.C.: British Columbia Department of Education, 1952.

Radin, Paul. *The Winnebago Tribe*. [E] Lincoln: University of Nebraska Press, 1971.

Ritzenthaler, R. E. *The Oneida Indians of Wisconsin*. [E-H] Milwaukee: Public Museum of the City of Milwaukee, 1950.

————. *The Potawatomi Indians of Wisconsin*. [E-H] Milwaukee: Public Museum of the City of Milwaukee, 1953.

————. "The Kickapoos Are Still Kicking," [E-H] *Natural History*, April 1965, pp. 200–206, 224.

Robinson, Doane. *A History of the Dakota or Sioux Indians.* [H] Minneapolis: Ross & Haines, 1956. (Reprint from 1904.)

Rohner, Ronald P. *The Kwakiutl.* [E] New York: Holt, Rinehart, & Winston, 1970.

Ruby, Robert H., and Brown, John H. *The Spokane Indians, Children of the Sun.* [H] Norman: University of Oklahoma Press, 1970.

Sandoz, Mari. *Cheyenne Autumn.* [H] New York: McGraw-Hill Book Co., 1953. (Account of the flight of Dull Knife and Little Wolf's band of Cheyennes from Oklahoma in 1878; fictional style, but historically accurate.)

———. *These Were the Sioux.* [H] New York: Dell-Mayflower, 1967.

Sonnichsen, C. L. *The Mescalero Apaches.* [H] Norman: University of Oklahoma Press, 1958, 1966.

Speck, Frank G. *The Iroquois: A Study in Cultural Evolution.* [E-H] Bloomfield Hills, Mich.: Cranbrook Institute of Science, 1955.

Stern, Theodore. *The Klamath Tribe.* [H] Seattle: University of Washington Press, 1965.

Terrell, John U. *The Navajos.* [H] New York: Weybright & Talley, 1970.

Tooker, Elizabeth, *Ethnography of the Huron Indians, 1615–1649.* [E] Bulletin 190, Bureau of American Ethnology. Washington: Government Printing Office, 1964.

Travers, Milton. *The Wampanoag Indian Federation.* [H] Boston: Christopher Publishing House, 1961.

Trenholm, Virginia C. *The Arapahoes, Our People.* [H] Norman: University of Oklahoma Press, 1970.

———, and Carley, Maurine. *The Shoshonis: Sentinels of the Rockies.* [H] Norman: University of Oklahoma Press, 1964.

Trigger, Bruce G. *The Huron.* [E-H] New York: Holt, Rinehart, & Winston, 1969.

Underhill, Ruth. *The Navahos.* [H] Norman: University of Oklahoma Press, 1963.

———. *The Northern Paiute Indians.* [E-H] Lawrence, Kansas: Haskell Institute, 1963.

———. *The Papago Indians of Arizona and their Relatives the Pima.* [E-H] Lawrence, Kansas: Haskell Institute, 1965.

Utley, Robert M. *The Last Days of the Sioux Nation.* [H] New Haven: Yale University Press, 1963.

Van Every, Dale. *Disinherited.* [H] (Cherokee removal). New York: Avon, 1967.

Vogt, Evon. *The Zinacantecos of Mexico: a Modern Maya Way of Life.* [E] New York: Holt, Rinehart, & Winston, 1970.

Wallace, Anthony F. C. *The Death and Rebirth of the Seneca.* [H] New York: Alfred A. Knopf, 1970.

Wallace, Ernest, and Hoebel, E. Adamson. *The Comanches: Lords of the South Plains.* [H] Norman: University of Oklahoma Press, 1952.

Warren, William W. *History of the Ojibway Nation*. [H] Minneapolis: Ross & Haines, 1957. (Reprint from 1885 edition of Minnesota Historical Society.)

Waters, Frank. *Book of the Hopi*. [E] New York: Ballantine Books, 1969. (Reprint from 1963.)

Wilson, Edmund. *Apologies to the Iroquois*. [C] New York: Farrar, Straus, & Cudahy, 1960.

Winger, Otho. *The Potawatomi Indians*. [H] Elgin, Ill.: The Elgin Press, 1939.

Woodward, Grace Steele. *The Cherokees*. [H] Norman: University of Oklahoma Press, 1963.

5. Indian Biography

Anderson, Eva G. *Chief Seattle*. Caldwell, Idaho: Caxton Printers, 1950.

Barrett, S. M., ed. *Geronimo: His Own Story*. New York: Ballantine Books, 1971.

Bass, Althea. *The Arapaho Way: A Memoir of an Indian Boyhood*. [Carl Sweezy]. New York: Clarkson N. Potter, 1967.

Betzinez, Jason, with W. S. Nye. *I Fought with Geronimo*. Harrisburg, Pa.: The Stackpole Co., 1960.

Britt, Albert. *Great Indian Chiefs*. New York: Whittlesey House, 1938.

Brown, Evelyn N. *Kateri Tekakwitha, Mohawk Maid*. New York: Farrar, Straus, & Co., 1963.

Buechner, Cecilia B. *The Pokagons*. Indianapolis: Indiana Historical Society, 1933.

Bureau of Indian Affairs. *Famous Indians: A Collection of Short Biographies*. Washington: Government Printing Office, 1966.

Caughey, John W. *McGillivray of the Creeks*. Norman: University of Oklahoma Press, 1938.

Eastman, Charles A. *Indian Boyhood*. New York: Dover Publications, 1971.

Florida Historical Society. *The Complete Story of Osceola*. Double number of *Florida Historical Quarterly*, Vol. XXXIII (January–April 1955), reprinted by St. Augustine Historical Society.

Foreman, Grant. *Sequoyah*. Norman: University of Oklahoma Press, 1938.

Gridley, Marion E. *Indians of Today*. 3d ed. Chicago: Indian Council Fire, 1960. 4th ed., 1971.

Jackson, Donald, ed. *Autobiography of Black Hawk*. Urbana: University of Illinois Press, 1955. Paperback ed., 1965.

Josephy, Alvin M. *The Patriot Chiefs*. New York: Viking Press, 1961.

Klinck, Carl F. *Tecumseh: Fact and Fiction in Early Records*. Englewood Cliffs, N.J.: Prentice-Hall, 1961.

Kroeber, Theodora. *Ishi in Two Worlds: A Biography of the Last Wild Indian in North America*. Berkeley: University of California Press, 1961.

Lewis, Anna. *Chief Pushmataha, American Patriot*. New York: Exposition Press, 1959.

Linderman, Frank Bird. *American*. [Plenty Coups, Crow Indian]. New York: John Day, 1930.

Lurie, Nancy O. *Mountain Wolf Woman* [Winnebago]. Ann Arbor: University of Michigan Press, 1966.

Nabokov, Peter. *Two Leggings: The Making of a Crow Warrior*. New York: Thomas Y. Crowell, 1967.

Neihardt, John G. *Black Elk Speaks*. Lincoln: University of Nebraska Press, 1961.

Olson, James C. *Red Cloud and the Sioux Problem*. Lincoln: University of Nebraska Press, 1965.

Opler, Morris E. *Apache Odyssey*. New York: Holt, Rinehart, & Winston, 1969.

Parker, Arthur C. *The Life of General Ely S. Parker* [Seneca]. Buffalo: Buffalo Historical Society, 1919.

Peckham, Howard H. *Pontiac and the Indian Uprising*. Chicago: University of Chicago Press, 1961.

Quarles, Marguerite S. *Pocahontas*. Richmond: Association for the Preservation of Virginia Antiquities, 1939.

Radin, Paul. *Autobiography of a Winnebago Indian*. New York: Dover Publications, 1963.

Ritzenthaler, R. E., and Niehoff, Arthur. *Famous American Indians*. Milwaukee: Milwaukee Public Museum, 1958.

Ruby, Robert H., and Brown, John A. *Half-Sun on the Columbia, A Biography of Chief Moses*. Norman: University of Oklahoma Press, 1965.

Sandoz, Mari. *Crazy Horse, the Strange Man of the Oglalas*. New York: Alfred A. Knopf, 1942.

Simmons, Leo W. *Sun Chief: the Autobiography of a Hopi Indian*. New Haven: Yale University Press, 1963.

Tucker, Glenn. *Tecumseh, Vision of Glory*. Indianapolis: Bobbs-Merrill, 1956.

Vestal, Stanley. *Sitting Bull: Champion of the Sioux*. Norman: University of Oklahoma Press, 1957.

Wallace, Anthony F. C. *King of the Delawares: Teedyuscung, 1700–1763*. Freeport, N.Y.: Books for Libraries Press, 1970.

Wharton, Clarence Ray. *Satanta, The Great Chief of the Kiowas and His People*. Dallas: B. Upshaw Co., 1935.

Winger, Otho. *The Last of the Miamis and Little Turtle*. North Manchester, Ind.: L. W. Shultz, 1961.

Wood, Norman B. *Lives of Famous Indian Chiefs*. Aurora, Ill.: American Indian Historical Publishing Co., 1906.

Woodward, Grace Steele. *Pocahontas*. Norman: University of Oklahoma Press, 1969.

6. Accounts of Captives, Explorers, Government Agents, Missionaries, Soldiers, Traders, Travelers, etc.

Adair, James. *The History of the American Indians* . . . London: Edward & Charles Dilly, 1775. Reprint, New York: Johnson Reprint Corp., 1968.

Atwater, Caleb. *The Indians of the Northwest, Their Manners, Customs &c* . . . Columbus: 1850.

Berlandier, Jean Louis. *The Indians of Texas in 1830,* ed. by John C. Ewers. Washington: Smithsonian Institution Press, 1969.

Beverley, Robert. *The History and Present State of Virginia.* Chapel Hill: University of North Carolina Press, 1947.

Blair, Emma H., ed. *The Indian Tribes of the Upper Mississippi Valley and Region of the Great Lakes* . . . 2 vols. Cleveland: Arthur H. Clark Co., 1912.

Bolton, Herbert E., ed. *Spanish Exploration in the Southwest 1542–1706.* New York: Barnes & Noble, 1963.

Bossu, Jean-Bernard. *Travels in the Interior of North America, 1751–1762.* Trans. & ed. by Seymour Feiler. Norman: University of Oklahoma Press, 1962.

Bradbury, John. *Travels in the Interior of America in the Years 1809, 1810, and 1811.* Ann Arbor: University Microfilms, 1966.

Bradford, William. *Of Plymouth Plantation,* ed. by Harvey Wish. New York: Capricorn Books, 1962.

Burrage, Henry S., ed. *Early English and French Voyages, 1524–1608.* New York: Barnes & Noble, 1953.

Carver, Jonathan. *Travels through the Interior Parts of North America in the Years 1766, 1767, and 1768.* Minneapolis: Ross & Haines, 1956.

Catlin, George. *Episodes from Life among the Indians and Last Rambles,* ed. by Marvin C. Ross. Norman: University of Oklahoma Press, 1959.

————. *Letters and Notes on the Manners, Customs, and Conditions of the North American Indians* . . . 2 vols. Minneapolis: Ross & Haines, 1965. Reprint from 1841.

Champlain, Samuel de. *Voyages of Samuel de Champlain, 1604–1618.* New York: Barnes & Noble, 1959. Reprint from 1907.

Charlevoix, Pierre François Xavier de. *Journal of a Voyage to North America.* 2 vols. Chicago: Caxton Club, 1923.

Cieza de Leon, Pedro de. *The Incas.* Trans. by Harriet de Onis and ed. by Victor W. von Hagen. Norman: University of Oklahoma Press, 1969.

Columbus, Christopher. *Columbus Letter of March 14th, 1493.* Chicago: Newberry Library, 1953.

Culbertson, Thaddeus A. *Journal of an Expedition to the Mauvaises Terres and the Upper Missouri in 1850* . . . ed. by John F. McDermott. Bureau of American Ethnology, Bulletin 147. Washington: Government Printing Office, 1952.

Delanglez, Jean, ed. *The Journal of Jean Cavelier.* Chicago: Institute of Jesuit History, 1938.

Denig, Edwin Thompson. *Five Indian Tribes of the Upper Missouri,* ed. by John C. Ewers. Norman: University of Oklahoma Press, 1961.

De Smet, Pierre-Jean. *Life, Letters and Travels of Father Pierre-Jean De Smet, S.J. 1801–1873,* ed. by H. M. Chittenden and A. T. Richardson. New York: Francis P. Harper, 1905.

Diaz del Castillo, Bernal. *The Discovery and Conquest of Mexico.* New York: Grove Press, n.d.

Ferris, Warren Angus. *Life in the Rocky Mountains*, ed. by Paul C. Phillips. Denver: Fred A. Rosenstock, The Old West Publishing Co., 1940.

Filson, John. *The Discovery, Settlement, and Present State of Kentucke* . . . Ann Arbor: University Microfilms, 1966.

Gregg, Josiah. *Commerce on the Prairies*. 2 vols. Ann Arbor: University Microfilms, 1966. One vol. paperback abridgment, University of Nebraska Press, 1967.

Hennepin, Louis. *A New Discovery of a Vast Country in America*. 2 vols. Chicago: A. C. McClurg Co., 1903.

Henry, Alexander. *Travel and Adventures in Canada*. Ann Arbor: University Microfilms, 1966.

Hodge, F. W., and Lewis, T. H., eds. *Spanish Explorers in the Southern United States 1528–1543*. New York: Barnes & Noble, 1959. Reprint from 1907.

Howard, Oliver Otis. *My Life and Experiences Among Hostile Indians*. Hartford: A. D. Worthington, 1907.

Hunter, John D. *Manners and Customs of Several Indian Tribes* . . . Minneapolis: Ross & Haines, 1957. Reprint from 1823.

Irving, Washington. *Astoria, or Anecdotes of an Enterprise Beyond the Rocky Mountains*. 2 vols. Philadelphia: Lea & Blanchard, 1841.

James, Edwin. *Account of an Expedition* . . . *under the Command of Stephen H. Long*. 2 vols. Philadelphia: H. C. Carey & Isaac Lea, 1823.

———, ed. *Narrative of the Captivity and Adventures of John Tanner* . . . Minneapolis: Ross & Haines, 1956. Reprint from 1830.

Jameson, J. Franklin, ed. *Narratives of New Netherland 1609–1664*. New York: Barnes & Noble, 1953. Reprint from 1906.

Jefferson, Thomas. *Notes on the State of Virginia*, ed. by William Peden. Chapel Hill: University of North Carolina Press, 1955.

Kalm, Peter. *Peter Kalm's Travels in North America*. 2 vols. New York: Wilson-Erickson Inc., 1937.

Keating, William H. *Narrative of an Expedition to the Source of St. Peter's River*. Minneapolis: Ross & Haines, 1959. Reprint from 1825.

Kellogg, Louise P., ed. *Early Narratives of the Northwest 1634–1699*. New York: Charles Scribner's Sons, 1917.

Kinzie, Mrs. John H. *Wau-Bun, The Early Day in the Northwest*. Chicago: Rand McNally & Co., 1901.

Krauskopf, Frances, ed. *Ouiatanon Documents*. Indianapolis: Indiana Historical Society, 1955.

Lahontan, Baron de. *New Voyages to North America*, ed. by Reuben G. Thwaites. 2 vols. Chicago: A. C. McClurg Co., 1905.

LaSalle, Cavelier de. *Relation of the Discoveries and Voyages of Cavelier de LaSalle* . . . Chicago: The Caxton Club, 1901.

Lawson, John. *History of North Carolina*. Richmond: Garrett & Massie, 1951.

Lewis, Meriwether, and Clark, William. *The Journals of the Expedition under the Command of Capts. Lewis and Clark* . . . , ed. by Nicholas Biddle. 2 vols. The Heritage Press, 1962.

McKee, Irvin, ed. *The Trail of Death: Letters of Benjamin Marie Petit.* Indianapolis: Indiana Historical Society, 1941.

McLaughlin, James. *My Friend the Indian.* Seattle: Superior Publishing Co., 1969.

Mereness, Newton D., ed. *Travels in the American Colonies.* New York: Antiquarian Press, 1961.

Miles, Nelson. *Personal Recollections and Observations of Gen. Nelson A. Miles.* Chicago: The Werner Co., 1896.

Morgan, Lewis Henry. *The Indian Journals, 1859–62.* Ann Arbor: University of Michigan Press, 1959.

Morris, Thomas. *Journal of Captain Thomas Morris.* Ann Arbor: University Microfilms, 1966.

Morse, Jedidiah. *Report to the Secretary of War on Indian Affairs.* New Haven: S. Converse, 1822.

Myers, A. C., ed. *Narratives of Early Pennsylvania, West New Jersey, and Delaware.* New York: Barnes & Noble, 1953. Reprint from 1912.

Newberry Library. *Narratives of Captivity among the Indians of North America: A List of Books and Manuscripts on this Subject in the Edward E. Ayer Collection . . .* Chicago: Newberry Library, 1961.

————, ed. by Clara A. Smith. *Supplement I,* to above title. Chicago: Newberry Library, 1928.

Palmer, Joel. *Journal of Travels over the Rocky Mountains . . .* Ann Arbor: University Microfilms, 1966.

Pattie, James O. *The Personal Narrative of James O. Pattie of Kentucky.* Ann Arbor: University Microfilms, 1966.

Pease, Theodore, and Werner, Raymond C., eds. *The French Foundations, 1680–1693.* Springfield: Illinois State Historical Library, 1934.

Quaife, Milo M., ed. *The Western Country in the Seventeenth Century.* New York: The Citadel Press, 1962.

Rogers, Robert A. *Concise Account of North America.* London: 1765. Reprint, New York: Johnson Reprint Corp., 1967.

————. *Journals of Major Robert Rogers.* Ann Arbor: University Microfilms, 1966. Also Corinth Books, Citadel Press, 1961.

Romans, Bernard. *A Concise Natural History of East and West Florida.* New Orleans: Pelican Publishing Co., 1962.

Russell, Osborne. *Journal of a Trapper 1834–1843.* Lincoln: University of Nebraska Press, 1967.

Sagard, Gabriel. *The Long Journey to the Country of the Hurons.* Toronto: The Champlain Society, 1939.

Sahagún, Fray Bernardino de. *General History of the Things of New Spain.* Trans. by Charles E. Dibble and Arthur J. O. Anderson. 13 vols. Santa Fe: The School of American Research and the Museum of New Mexico, 1963.

Salley, A. S., ed. *Narratives of Early Carolina 1650–1708.* New York: Barnes & Noble, 1953. Reprint from 1911.

Schultz, J. W. *My Life as an Indian.* Boston: Houghton Mifflin, 1907.

Seger, John H. *Early Days among the Cheyenne and Arapahoe Indians,* ed. by Stanley Vestal. Norman: University of Oklahoma Press, 1933.

Shea, John Gilmary, ed. *Discovery and Exploration of the Mississippi Valley.* 2d ed. New York: Joseph McDonough, 1903.

Tanner, John. *See* James, Edwin, item 2, 1956.

Thwaites, Reuben Gold, ed. *Early Western Travels 1748–1846.* 32 vols. Cleveland: Arthur H. Clark Co., 1904–1906.

Tibbles, Thomas Henry. *Buckskin and Blanket Days.* Lincoln: University of Nebraska Press, 1969.

Tolmie, William F. *The Journals of William Fraser Tolmie, Physician and Fur Trader.* Vancouver, B.C.: Mitchell Press, Ltd. 1963.

Tyler, Lyon G., ed. *Narratives of Early Virginia, 1606–1625.* New York: Barnes & Noble, 1959. Reprint from 1907.

Volney, C. F. *A View of the Soil and Climate of the United States of America.* Philadelphia: J. Conrad & Co., 1804.

[White, Andrew]. *A Relation of Maryland.* Ann Arbor: University Microfilms, 1966.

Winter, George. *The Journals and Indian Paintings of George Winter, 1837–1839.* Indianapolis: Indiana Historical Society, 1948.

Zeisberger, David. "A History of the Indians," ed. by A. B. Hulbert and W. N. Schwarze, *Ohio Archaeological and Historical Quarterly,* XIX, Nos. 1–2 (January and April 1910), pp. 12–153.

See also Missionary Activity; Indian and White Warfare.

7. Indian Arts, Crafts, and Architecture

Boas, Franz. *Primitive Art.* New York: Dover Publications, 1955.

Clifford, Howard, *Much about Totems.* Seattle: Pacific Northern Airlines, n.d.

Covarrubias, Miguel. *The Eagle, the Jaguar, and the Serpent: Indian Art of the Americas.* New York: Alfred A. Knopf, 1954.

Current, William, and Scully, Vincent. *Pueblo Architecture of the Southwest.* Austin: University of Texas Press for the Amon Carter Museum of Western Art, Fort Worth, 1971.

Dockstader, Frederick J. *Indian Art in America: The Arts and Crafts of the North American Indian.* Greenwich, Conn.: The New York Graphic Society, [1960].

———, and Anton, Ferdinand. *Pre-Columbian Art and Later Indian Tribal Arts.* New York: Harry N. Abrams Inc., [1968].

Douglas, F. H. "Indian Vegetable Dyes," *Indian Leaflet Series,* Denver Art Museum, LXIII, 50–52, LXXI, 82–84 (1934–1936).

———, and D'Harnoncourt, Rene. *Indian Art of the United States.* New York: Museum of Modern Art, 1941.

Ewers, John C. *Plains Indian Painting.* Palo Alto: Stanford University Press, 1939.

———. *Blackfeet Crafts.* Washington: U.S. Indian Service, 1945.

Feder, Norman. *Art of the Eastern Plains Indian.* Brooklyn, N.Y.: The Brooklyn Museum, 1964.

Gaines, R. L. *Books on Indian Arts North of Mexico.* New York: Leaflets of the Exposition on Indian Tribal Arts, 1931.

Hodge, F. W. "What the Indian Says in Ornament," *Garden and Home Builder,* XLIV (September 1926), 33, 68, 70.

Indian Arts and Crafts Board. *Native American Arts,* #1. Washington: Government Printing Office, n.d.

Kublen, George. *Art and Architecture of Ancient America.* Baltimore: Penguin Books, 1961.

Lyford, Carrie A. *Ojibway Crafts.* Washington: Bureau of Indian Affairs, 1953.

Miller, Polly, and Gordon, Leon. *Lost Heritage of Alaska.* Cleveland: World Publishing Co., 1967.

Morgan, Lewis Henry. *Houses and House-Life of the American Aborigines.* Chicago: University of Chicago Press, 1965.

Norbeck, Oscar E. *Book of Indian Life Crafts.* New York: Association Press, 1966.

Oglesby, Catherine. *Modern Primitive Arts.* New York: Whittlesey House, 1939.

Parsons, Elsie C. *Isleta Paintings.* Washington, D.C.: Smithsonian Institution, 1962.

Paul, Frances. *Spruce Root Basketry of the Alaska Tlingit.* Lawrence, Kansas: Haskell Institute, 1963.

Peet, Stephen D. "The Architecture of the Civilized Races of America," *American Antiquarian,* XI, No. 4 (July 1889), pp. 206–35.

Peterson, Karen D. *Indians Unchained: Plains Indian Art from Fort Marion.* Norman: University of Oklahoma Press, 1970.

Price, Vincent. "The Lure and Lore of Indian Art." *The American Way,* June, 1971, pp. 12–17.

Ray, Dorothy Jean. *Graphic Arts of the Alaskan Eskimo,* in *Native American Arts,* #2, Indian Arts and Crafts Board. Washington: Government Printing Office, 1969.

Ritzenthaler, R. E. *Indian Cradles.* Milwaukee: Milwaukee Public Museum, n.d.
———. *Masks of the North American Indians.* Milwaukee: Milwaukee Public Museum, n.d.

Robertson, Donald. *Pre-Columbian Architecture.* New York: George Braziller, 1963.

Russell, Charles. "Indian Arts in Tomorrow's World," *The American Indian,* VII, No. 1 (Spring, 1954), 29–36.

Saloman, Julian H. *The Book of Indian Crafts and Indian Lore.* New York: Harper & Bros., 1928.

Spicer, Edward H. "The Sources of American Indian Art," *Journal of American Indian Education,* I, No. 2 (January 1962), 9–12; I, No. 3 (May 1962), 26–31.

Underhill, Ruth. *Pueblo Crafts.* Lawrence, Kansas: Haskell Institute, 1965.

Vaillant, George C. *Indian Arts in North America.* New York: Harper & Bros., 1939.

Wardwell, Allen. *Yakutat South: Indian Art of the Northwest.* Chicago: Art Institute, 1964.

Waterman, T. T. "The Architecture of the American Indian," in A. L. Kroeber and T. T. Waterman, eds., *Sourcebook in Anthropology.* Rev. ed. New York: Harcourt Brace & Co., 1931, pp. 512–24.

Wingert, Paul S. *American Indian Sculpture.* New York: J. J. Augustin, 1949.

————. *Primitive Art: Its Traditions and Styles.* New York: Oxford University Press, 1962.

8. *Education*

A. EDUCATION OF WHITES ABOUT INDIANS

Aden, Robert C. "Stereotyped Teaching in History," *Peabody Journal of Education,* XXXII, No. 3 (November 1954), 160–65.

Association on American Indian Affairs. *A Preliminary Bibliography of Selected Children's Books About American Indians,* ed. by Killian Newman. New York: 1969. (63 books listed; a longer list is in preparation.)

Ballas, Donald J. "Geography and the American Indian," *Journal of Geography,* LXV, No. 4 (April 1966), 156–68.

"Bibliography: American Minority Groups," *Progressive Education,* XII, No. 4 (April 1935), 275–79.

Crawford, Dean A., *et al. Minnesota Chippewa Indians, A Handbook for Teachers.* St. Paul: Upper Midwest Regional Educational Laboratory, 1967.

Dubois, Rachel D. "Our Enemy—the Stereotype," *Progressive Education,* XII, No. 3 (March 1935), 146–50.

Henderson, E. W. "What Shall We Teach about the Indian?" *School and Community,* L (December 1963), 16–17.

Henry, Jeanette. "Our Inaccurate Textbooks," *The Indian Historian,* I, No. 1 (December 1967), 21–24.

————. *Textbooks and the American Indian,* ed. by Rupert Costo. San Francisco: The Indian Historian Press, 1970.

Hoopes, Allan W. "The Need for a History of the American Indian," *Social Studies,* XXIX, No. 1 (January 1938), 26–27.

Locke, Alain. "Minorities and the Social Mind," *Progressive Education,* XII, No. 3 (March 1935), 141–46.

Park, R. R. "Realistic Concepts of Indian Life," *Instructor,* LXXV (November 1965), 110.

Vogel, Virgil J. "The Indian in American History Textbooks," *Integrated Education,* VI, No. 3 (May–June 1968), 16–32.

————. *The Indian in American History.* Chicago: Integrated Education Associates, 1968.

————. "The Indian in American History," *Social Education,* XXXIII, No. 2 (February 1969), 200–203.

B. EDUCATION OF INDIANS

Adams, E. C. *American Indian Education*. New York: Columbia University Press, 1946. (Bibliography.)

Adams, Lucy W. "Indians on the Peace Path," *Journal of Adult Education*, XIII (June 1941), 243–48.

Anderson, Kenneth E., *et al. Educational Achievement of Indian Children*. Lawrence, Kansas: Haskell Institute, 1953.

Aurbach, Herbert A., ed. *Proceedings of the National Research Conference on American Indian Education*. Kalamazoo, Mich.: Society for the Study of Social Problems, 1967.

Banks, James A., and Joyce, William W. *Teaching Social Studies to Culturally Different Children*. Reading, Mass.: Addison Wesley Publishing Co., 1971.

Bayne, Stephen L. "Culture Materials in Schools Programs for Indian Students," *Journal of American Indian Education*, IX, No. 1 (October 1969), 1–6.

Beatty, Willard W., *et al. Education for Action*, selected articles from *Indian Education*, 1936–1943. Chilocco, Okla.: Education Division, U.S. Indian Service, 1944.

————. *Education for Cultural Change*, selected articles from *Indian Education*, 1944–1951. Chilocco, Okla.: Bureau of Indian Affairs, Branch of Education, 1953.

Benham, William J. "A Foundation for Indian Cross-Cultural Education," *Journal of American Indian Education*, VIII, No. 2 (January 1969), 26–37.

Bergt, Laura, and Brenwick, Lucy. "Unequal Schooling in Alaska," *Integrated Education*, VII, No. 5 (September–October 1969), 60–62.

Berry, Brewton. *The Education of American Indians: A Survey of the Literature*. Prepared for the Special Subcommittee on Indian Education, of the Committee on Labor and Public Welfare, U.S. Senate. Washington: Government Printing Office, 1969.

Bryde, John F. "A New Approach to Indian Education?" *Integrated Education*, VI, No. 5 (September–October 1968), 29–36.

Bureau of Indian Affairs, Branch of Education. *Statistics Concerning Indian Education, Fiscal Year 1967*. Lawrence, Kansas: Haskell Press, 1967.

California Indian Education. Report of the first all-Indian statewide conference on California Indian education. Modesto, Calif.: Ad Hoc Committee on California Indian Education, 1968.

Charles, C. M. "A Tutoring-Counseling Program for Indian Students in College," *Journal of American Indian Education*, I, No. 3 (May 1962), 10–12.

Coombs, L. M., *et al. The Indian Child Goes to School*. Lawrence, Kansas: Haskell Institute, n.d.

Dennis, Wayne. *The Hopi Child*. New York: John Wiley, 1965.

Erickson, Donald A., and Schwartz, Henrietta. "What Rough Rock Demonstrates," *Integrated Education*, VIII, No. 2 (March–April 1970), 21–33.

Erikson, Erik H. *Childhood and Society.* 2d ed. rev. New York: W. W. Norton, 1963. (Part II, pp. 109–186.)

First, Jean M. "Cultures in Cross Currents," *Michigan Education Journal,* XXXVII, No. 6 (November 1, 1960), 241+.

Fuchs, Estelle. "Learning to be Navaho-Americans—Innovation at Rough Rock," *Saturday Review,* September 16, 1967, pp. 82 *ff.*

———. "Time to Redeem an Old Promise," *Saturday Review,* January 24, 1970, pp. 54 *ff.*

Gifford, Selene. "Educating the American Indian," *School Life,* XLVII, No. 2 (November 1964), 10–12.

Havighurst, Robert J. *Education.* Boston: Little, Brown, 1968. Chapter on the Hopi.

———, and Neugarten, Bernice. *American Indian and White Children.* Chicago: University of Chicago Press, 1955.

Hohnahni, Dan. "Indian Community Control of Schools," *The Indian Historian,* III, No. 2 (Spring 1970), 57 *ff.*

Horne, Esther B. "Preserve Indian Culture," *School Arts,* XXXV, No. 2 (October 1935), 72, 75.

Hoyt, Elizabeth. "An Approach to the Mind of the Young Indian," *Journal of American Indian Education,* I, No. 1 (June 1961), 17–23.

Jones, Charles F. "Notes on Indian Education," *Journal of Educational Sociology,* XXVII (September 1953), 16–23.

Keeler, W. W. "Challenges in Indian Education," *Journal of American Indian Education,* I, No. 2 (January 1962), 3–8.

Kiva, Lloyd New. "Art and Indian Identity," *Integrated Education,* VII, No. 3 (May–June 1969), 44–50.

Kramer, Max. "An Experiment in Indian Education," *Progressive Education,* XII, No. 3 (March 1935), 155–59.

Ludeman, W. W. "The Indian Student in College," *Journal of Educational Sociology,* XXXIII (March 1960), 333–35.

Malan, Vernon D. "Factors Associated with Prejudice toward Indians," *Journal of American Indian Education,* II, No. 1 (October, 1962), 25–31.

Mekeel, H. Scudder. "An Anthropologist's Observations on Indian Education," *Progressive Education,* XIII, No. 3 (March 1936), 151–59.

Mittelholtz, E. F. "Minnesota's Plan of Indian Education," *Minnesota Journal of Education,* XLIV (December 1963), 9–10.

Nader, Ralph. "Comments on Indian Education," *Integrated Education,* VII, No. 4 (November–December 1969), 3–13.

New, Lloyd H. "Using Cultural Differences as a Basis for Creative Expression," *Journal of American Indian Education,* IV, No. 3 (May 1965), 8–12.

Newsweek. "Indianizing the Red Man: Tribal Ways of Life Stressed in Reservation Schools," Vol. XVII (April 14, 1941), 77.

"Official Horror Story of Federally-Run Chilocco Indian School," *Integrated Education,* VII, No. 4 (July–August 1969), 48–51.

Orata, Pedro T. *Fundamental Education in an Amerindian Community.* Lawrence, Kansas: Haskell Institute, 1953. (For a criticism of this, see Murray and Rosalie Wax, *infra.*)

Powers, Joseph F. *Brotherhood through Education: A Guide for Teachers of American Indians.* Fayette, Iowa: Upper Iowa University, 1965.

Sanchez, Gov. Abel, *et al.* "The History of San Felipe Pueblo People," *Integrated Education,* VI, No. 6 (November–December 1968), 56–60.

Seymour, F. W. "Pedagogues Hunt Indians," *American Mercury,* XXIX, No. 116 (August 1933), 437–45.

Sheps, Efraim. "Indian Youth's Attitude toward Non-Indian Patterns of Life," *Journal of American Indian Education,* IX, No. 2 (January 1970), 19–27.

Thompson, Hildegard. "Education of American Indians," *Education Digest,* XXIX, No. 9 (May 1964), 48–50. (Assimilationist view.)

————, ed. *Education for Cross Cultural Enrichment.* Selected articles from *Indian Education,* 1952–1964; publication of the Office of Education, Bureau of Indian Affairs. Lawrence, Kansas: Haskell Institute, 1964.

U.S. Office of Education Project. "Higher Education of Southwestern Indians with Reference to Success and Failure," *Journal of American Indian Education,* III, No. 2 (January 1965), 5–13.

U.S. Senate. *Indian Education.* "Hearings before the subcommittee on Indian Education of the Committee on Labor and Public Welfare, United States Senate, 90th Congress, 1st and 2d sessions, on the study of the education of Indian children." 4 vols. Washington: Government Printing Office, 1969.

————. *Indian Education: A National Tragedy—A National Challenge.* 1969 Report of above committee. Washington: Government Printing Office, 1969.

(See also Brewton Berry, *supra,* as a part of the foregoing two items.)

Wax, Murray. "American Indian Education as a Cultural Transaction," *Teachers College Record,* LXIV (May 1963), 693–404. (Has bibliography.)

————, and Wax, Rosalie. "Cultural Deprivation as an Educational Ideology," *Journal of American Indian Education,* III, No. 2 (January 1964), 15–18. (A critique of Orata [*supra*]; deplores educators who show contempt for Indian values and customs.)

————, and Dumont, Robert V. *Formal Education in an American Indian Community.* New York: Society for the Study of Social Problems, 1964.

Weinberg, Meyer. *The Education of the Minority Child. A Comprehensive Bibliography of 10,000 Selected Entries.* Chicago: Integrated Education Associates, 1970. (Sec. 6, pp. 207–52, "Indian Americans," has items grouped both by tribe and state or region.)

Wesley, Clarence. "Indian Education," *Journal of American Indian Education,* I, No. 3 (May 1962), 5–9.

Witherspoon, Y. T. "The Measurement of Indian Children's Achievement in Academic Tool Subjects," *Journal of American Indian Education,* I, No. 3 (May 1962), 5–9.

9. *Indian and White Relations, Including Government Relations, the Frontier, Land Tenure, and Indian Removal*

Abel, Annie Heloise. "The History of Events Resulting in Indian Consolidation West of the Mississippi River," in *Annual Report of the American Historical Association for the Year 1906*, Vol. I, 235–450.

———. "Proposals for an Indian State, 1778–1878," in *Annual Report of the American Historical Association for the Year 1907*, Vol. I, 87–104.

Abernethy, Thomas Perkins. *Western Lands and the American Revolution.* New York: Russell & Russell, 1959.

Anson, Bert. "Chief Francis Lafontaine and the Miami Emigration from Indiana," *Indiana Magazine of History*, LX, No. 3 (September 1964), 241–68.

Atkin, Edmond. "Report and Plan of 1755," in Wilbur R. Jacobs, ed., *The Appalachian Indian Frontier*. Lincoln: University of Nebraska Press, 1967. Also in Jacobs, ed., *Indians of the Southern Colonial Frontier*. Columbia: University of South Carolina Press, 1954.

Barrows, William. *The Indian's Side of the Indian Question*. Boston: D. Lothrop Co., 1888.

Berry, Brewton. *Almost White*. New York: The Macmillan Co., 1967. (Indian mixed bloods of lost tribal identity.)

Billington, Ray A. *Westward Expansion, a History of the American Frontier.* New York: The Macmillan Co., 1949.

Boorstin, Daniel. *The Americans: the National Experience*. New York: Random House, 1966. (Scalp bounties, p. 127; questions of Indian land rights, pp. 259–64.)

Buley, R. Carlyle. *The Old Northwest*, 2 vols. Bloomington: University of Indiana Press, 1964.

Bunker, Robert. *Crow Killer*. New York: Signet, n.d.

Carter, Clarence E. *The Territorial Papers of the United States*. U.S. Department of State. Washington: Government Printing Office, 1950——.

Caruso, John A. *The Great Lakes Frontier*. Indianapolis: Bobbs-Merrill Co., 1961.

Cohen, Felix S. *Handbook of Federal Indian Law*. U.S. Department of Interior. Washington: Government Printing Office, 1941.

———. *Handbook of Federal Indian Law, with Reference Tables and Index*. U.S. Department of Interior. Washington: Government Printing Office, 1942.

Coleman, R. V. *The First Frontier*. New York: Charles Scribner's Sons, 1948.

Corkran, David H. *The Creek Frontier, 1540–1783*. Norman: University of Oklahoma Press, 1969.

Debo, Angie. *And Still the Waters Run*. New York: Gordian Press, 1966. (Reprint from 1940; dispossession of Oklahoma Indians.)

DeRosier, Arthur H. *The Removal of the Choctaw Indians*. New York: Harper & Row, 1972.

Dick, Everett. *Vanguards of the Frontier.* New York: D. Appleton-Century, 1941.

Downes, Randolph C. "A Crusade for Indian Reform, 1922–1934," *Mississippi Valley Historical Review,* XXXII (December 1945), 331–54.

Evarts, Jeremiah. *Speeches on the Passage of the Bill for the Removal of the Indians.* Boston: Perkins & Marvin, 1830.

Ewers, John C. *The Role of the Indian in National Expansion.* Washington: National Park Service, 1938.

Federal Indian Law. U.S. Department of Interior. Washington: Government Printing Office, 1958.

Fenton, William N. *American Indian and White Relations to 1830: Needs and Opportunities for Study.* Chapel Hill: University of North Carolina Press, 1957.

Filler, Louis, and Guttman, Allen, eds. *Removal of the Cherokee Nation: Manifest Destiny or National Dishonor?* Boston: D. C. Heath Co., 1962. (Written by participants.)

Foreman, Grant. *Last Trek of the Indians.* Chicago: University of Chicago Press, 1946. (Removal of tribes from the Old Northwest.)

————. *Indian Removal: The Emigration of the Five Civilized Tribes of Indians.* Norman: University of Oklahoma Press, 1953.

Fritz, Henry L. *The Movement for Indian Assimilation, 1860–1890.* Philadelphia: University of Pennsylvania Press, 1963.

Gordon, Leon M. "The Red Man's Retreat from Northern Indiana," *Indiana Magazine of History,* XLVI, No. 1 (March 1950), 39–60.

Guttman, Allen. *States Rights and Indian Removal: The Cherokee Nation vs. the State of Georgia.* Boston: D. C. Heath Co., 1965.

Harmon, George D. *Sixty Years of Indian Affairs, Political, Economic, and Diplomatic, 1789–1850.* Chapel Hill: University of North Carolina Press, 1941.

Heizer, Robert F., and Almquist, Alan F. *The Other Californians.* Berkeley: University of California Press, 1971.

Horsman, Reginald. *Expansion and American Indian Policy.* East Lansing: Michigan State University Press, 1966.

Hough, Emerson. *The Passing of the Frontier.* New Haven: Yale University Press, 1921.

Houghton, Louise S. *Our Debt to the Red Man: The French-Indians in the Development of the United States.* Boston: The Stratford Co., 1918.

Howland, Edward. "Our Indian Brothers," *Harper's New Monthly Magazine,* XVI, No. 335 (April 1878), 768–76.

Institute for Government Research, Brookings Institution. *The Problem of Indian Administration, Report of a Survey.* Lewis Meriam, technical director. Baltimore: Johns Hopkins Press, 1928.

Jackson, Helen Hunt. *A Century of Dishonor.* New York: Harper Torchbooks, 1966.

Jacobs, Wilbur R. *Wilderness Politics and Indian Gifts.* Lincoln: University of Nebraska Press, 1966. (See this author also under Atkin, *supra.*)

James, James Alton. *English Institutions and the American Indian.* Baltimore: Johns Hopkins Press, 1894.

Jensen, Merrill. "The Creation of the National Domain, 1781–84," *Mississippi Valley Historical Review,* XXVI, No. 3 (December 1939), 323–42. (Bobbs-Merrill reprint #H–237.)

Kappler, Charles J., ed. *Indian Affairs, Laws, and Treaties.* 5 vols. Washington: Government Printing Office, 1903–1941.

Kellogg, Louise P. "The Removal of the Winnebago," *Transactions of the Wisconsin Academy of Sciences, Arts and Letters,* XXI. Madison: 1924.

Kroeber, Clifton B., and Wyman, Walker D., eds. *The Frontier in Perspective.* Madison: University of Wisconsin Press, 1965. (See especially Hallowell, p. 229 *ff.*)

Lauber, Almon W. *Indian Slavery in Colonial Times within the Present Limits of the United States.* New York: AMS Press, 1969. Reprint from 1913.

McKenney, Thomas L. *Sketches of Travels among the Northern and Southern Indians . . .* New York: Daniel Burgess & Co., 1854.

MacLeod, William C. *The American Indian Frontier.* New York: Alfred A. Knopf, 1928.

Mardock, Robert Winston. *The Reformers and the American Indian.* Columbia: University of Missouri Press, 1971.

Meriam, Lewis. See Institute for Government Research, *supra.*

Mohr, Walter. *Federal Indian Relations, 1774–1788.* Philadelphia: the author, 1933.

Mörner, Magnus. *Race Mixture in the History of Latin America.* Boston: Little, Brown & Co., 1967.

Nammack, Georgiana C. *Fraud, Politics, and the Dispossession of the Indians.* Norman: University of Oklahoma Press, 1969.

Parkman, Francis. *The Oregon Trail.* Garden City, N.Y.: Doubleday, 1946. Paperback ed., Mentor, 1950.

Pound, Arthur. *Johnson of the Mohawks.* New York: The Macmillan Co., 1930. (Sir William Johnson.)

Priestley, Herbert I. *The Coming of the White Man 1492–1848.* New York: The Macmillan Co., 1930.

Prucha, Francis P. *American Indian Policy in the Formative Years.* Cambridge: Harvard University Press, 1962.

————. *The Indian in American History.* New York: Holt, Rinehart & Winston, 1971.

Royce, Charles C. "Indian Land Cessions in the United States," in *Eighteenth Annual Report of the Bureau of American Ethnology.* Washington: Government Printing Office, 1899.

Service, Elman R. "Indian-European Relations in Colonial Latin America," *American Anthropologist,* LVII (1955), pp. 411–425. Bobbs-Merrill reprint #A–205.

Shaw, Helen Louise. *British Administration of the Southern Indians, 1756–1783.* Lancaster, Pa.: Lancaster Press, 1931.

Stuart, Benjamin F. "The Deportation of Menominee and his Tribe of Pottawattomie Indians," *Indiana Magazine of History*, XVIII, No. 3 (September 1922), 255–65.

The Treaties Between Her Majesty, Queen Victoria, and the Indians of British North America. Regina: Reprinted by the Provincial Committee on Minority Groups in cooperation with the Federation of Saskatchewan Indians, March 1961.

Trelease, Allen W. *Indian Affairs in Colonial New York.* Ithaca: Cornell University Press, 1960.

———. "The Iroquois and the Western Fur Trade: A Problem in Interpretation," *Mississippi Valley Historical Review*, XLIV, No. 1 (June 1962), pp. 32–51. Bobbs-Merrill reprint # H–328.

Turner, Frederick Jackson. *The Frontier in American History.* New York: Henry Holt, 1958.

U.S. Congress, Union Calendar No. 790, 82d Congress, 2d session, House Report No. 2503, *Report with Respect to the House Resolution Authorizing the Committee on Interior and Insular Affairs to Conduct an Investigation of the Bureau of Indian Affairs* . . . Washington: Government Printing Office, 1952. (A valuable handbook of information.)

Van Every, Dale. *Disinherited.* New York: Avon Books, 1967. (Cherokee removal.)

Vaughan, Alden T. *New England Frontier: Puritans and Indians, 1620–1675.* Boston: Little Brown & Co., 1965.

Washburn, Wilcomb E. *Red Man's Land—White Man's Law.* New York: Charles Scribner's Sons, 1971.

Webb, Walter Prescott. *The Great Plains.* New York: Grosset & Dunlap, 1957.

10. Aboriginal Literature

Note

Outside of Mexico, Indians had no written literature in aboriginal times.[1] The following list therefore includes mainly oral literature recorded by whites: Indian oratory, poetry, autobiography, legends, etc., and writings by Indians still living, or recently living, in tribal communities. Some dictated Indian autobiographies are listed in the section on *biography*. Some modern Indian writers are listed under *fiction*. For a list of Indian writers, see: Arlene B. Hirschfelder, *American Indian Authors, A Representative Bibliography.* Association on American Indian Affairs, 432 Park Ave. South, New York, N.Y. 10016. Price $1.

For Indian influence on non-Indian literature, see section 17 of the bibliography on *the American Indian Impact*.

1. In the nineteenth century, however, the Cherokees built a press and literature in their own language, using Sequoyah's alphabet. See Althea Bass, *infra*.

Annals of the Cakchiquels, The, trans. by Adrian Recinos and Delia Goetz. Norman: University of Oklahoma Press, 1953.

Arias-Larreta, Abraham. *Pre-Columbian Literatures: Aztec, Incan, Maya, Quiche.* Book I, History of Indo-American Literature. Los Angeles: New World Library, 1964.

———. *From Columbus to Bolivar.* Book II, History of Indo-American Literature. N.p., 1965.

———. *Pre-Columbian Masterpieces: Popol-Vuh, Apu-Ollontay, Chilam Balam.* Book III, History of Indo-American Literature. Kansas City, Mo.: Indoamerica Library of the New World, 1967.

Astrov, Margot, ed. *The Winged Serpent,* an anthology of Indian prose and poetry. New York: John Day, 1946.

Barnes, Nellie. *American Indian Verse.* Lawrence, Kansas: University of Kansas, 1921.

Bass, Althea. "The Cherokee Press," *Colophon,* IV (March 1933), Pt. 13.

Blackbird, Andrew J. *History of the Ottawa and Chippewa Indians of Michigan . . .* Ypsilanti, Mich.: Ypsilanti Job Printing House, 1887. 2d ed.; Harbor Springs, Mich.: 1897.

Brinton, Daniel G. *The Myths of the New World.* 2d ed. rev. New York: Henry Holt & Co., 1876.

———. *Aboriginal American Authors and their Productions, Especially Those in the Native Languages.* Philadelphia: the author, 1883. Reissued, Chicago: Checagou Reprints, 1970, by John Hobgood, Chicago State College.

———. *The Lenape and Their Legends.* Philadelphia: the author, 1885.

———. *Rig Veda Americanus: Sacred Songs of the Ancient Mexicans.* Philadelphia: the author, 1890.

Carmer, Carl. *Listen for a Lonesome Drum.* New York: Farrar & Rinehart, 1936. (Part III deals with Iroquois lore.)

Clark, Ella E. *Indian Legends of the Pacific Northwest.* Berkeley: University of California Press, 1963.

———. *Indian Legends from the Northern Rockies.* Norman: University of Oklahoma Press, 1966.

Jeremiah Curtin. *Myths of the Modocs.* New York: Benjamin Blom, 1971.

Day, A. Grove. *The Sky Clears: Poetry of the American Indian.* Lincoln: University of Nebraska Press, 1964.

De Angulo, Jaime. *Indian Tales.* New York: Hill & Wang, 1969.

Eastman, Mary. *Dahcotah: Life and Legends of the Sioux.* Minneapolis: Ross & Haines, 1962. Reprint from 1849.

Frederick, Jack, and Kilpatrick, A. G. *Friends of Thunder: Folktales of the Oklahoma Cherokee.* Dallas: Southern Methodist University Press, 1964.

Gheerbrant, Alain, ed. *The Royal Commentaries of the Inca Garcilaso de la Vega, 1539–1616.* New York: Orion Press, 1962.

Goetz, Delia, and Morley, S. G. *Popul Vuh: The Sacred Book of the Ancient Quiche Maya.* Norman: University of Oklahoma Press, 1965.

Gridley, Marion E. *Indian Legends of American Scenes*. Chicago: M. A. Donohue, 1939.

Grinnell, George B. *By Cheyenne Campfires*. New Haven: Yale University Press, 1962.

————. *Blackfoot Lodge Tales*. Lincoln: University of Nebraska Press, 1962.

————. *Pawnee Hero Stories and Folk Tales*. Lincoln: University of Nebraska Press, 1961.

Jacobs, Melville. *The Content and Style of an Oral Literature: Clackamas Chinook Myths and Tales*. Chicago: University of Chicago Press, 1959.

Jones, Louis T. *Aboriginal American Oratory: The Tradition of Eloquence among the Indians of the United States*. Los Angeles: Southwest Museum, 1965.

León Portilla, Miguel. *Pre-Columbian Literatures of Mexico*. Norman: University of Oklahoma Press, 1969.

MacShane, Frank. "American Indian Literature," *Chelsea* magazine, No. 29 (July 1971), pp. 75–91.

Madrano, Don M. *Heap Big Laugh*. Tulsa: the author, 1955. (Indian humor.)

Medwick, Lucille. "The American Indian Poet," *The New York Quarterly*, No. 7 (Summer 1971), pp. 66–86.

Osborne, Harold, and Hamlyn, Paul. *South American Mythology*. n.p., n.d.

Posey, Alexander Lawrence. *Poems of Alexander Lawrence Posey*. Okmulgee, Okla.: Okmulgee Cultural Foundation, 1968. (Creek.)

Radin, Paul. "The Literature of Primitive Peoples," *Diogenes* (Winter 1955), pp. 1–28. Bobbs-Merrill reprint #A-187.

————. *The Trickster: A Study in American Indian Mythology*. New York: Philosophical Library, 1956.

Reade, John. "Aboriginal American Poetry," and "Some Wabanaki Songs," in *Proceedings and Transactions of the Royal Society of Canada for the Year 1887*. Montreal: Dawson Bros., 1888.

Ressler, Theodore W. *Treasury of American Indian Tales*. New York: Association Press, 1957.

Roys, Ralph L. *The Book of Chilam Balam of Chumayel*. Washington: Carnegie Institution of Washington, 1933. New ed., Norman: University of Oklahoma Press, 1967.

Shunatona, Joseph B. *Skookum's Laugh Medicine*. Tulsa: the author, 1957. (Indian humor.)

Thompson, Stith, ed. *Tales of the North American Indians*. Bloomington: Indiana University Press, 1971.

Ullom, Judith C., compiler. *Folklore of North American Indians, an Annotated Bibliography*. Washington: Library of Congress, 1969.

Underwood, T. B., and Sandlin, M. S. *Legends of the Ancient Cherokee*. Asheville, N.C.: Stephens Press, 1956.

Vanderwerth, W. C. *Indian Oratory: A Collection of Famous Speeches by Noted Indian Chieftains*. Norman: University of Oklahoma Press, 1971.

Vaudrin, Bill. *Tanaina Tales from Alaska.* Norman: University of Oklahoma Press, 1969.

Walam Olum, or Red Score, The Migration Legend of the Lenni Lenape or Delaware Indians. Indianapolis: Indiana Historical Soociety, 1954. See also: Brinton, *The Lenape and their Legends (supra)*, and Jacob P. Dunn, *True Indian Stories.* Indianapolis: Sentinel Printing Co., 1909, Chap. X. Reprinted, 1964, Lawrence W. Shultz, North Manchester, Ind.

Walton, I. H. "Navaho Poetry: An Interpretation," *Texas Review,* VII (April 1922), 198–210.

Williams, Mentor L. *Schoolcraft's Indian Legends.* East Lansing: Michigan State University Press, 1957.

Wroth, Lawrence C. "The Indian Treaty as Literature," *Yale Review,* XVII (July 1928), 749–66.

11. Missionary Activity

Bass, Althea. *Cherokee Messenger.* Norman: University of Oklahoma Press, 1968. (Life of Samuel Worcester; reprint from 1936.)

Beauchamp, William M. *Moravian Journals Relating to Central New York, 1745–1766.* Syracuse: Onondaga Historical Association, 1916.

Berkhofer, Robert P., Jr. *Salvation and the Savage: An Analysis of Protestant Missions and American Indian Response, 1787–1862.* Lexington: University of Kentucky Press, 1965.

Bolton, Herbert E. "The Mission as a Frontier Institution in the Spanish-American Colonies," *American Historical Review,* XXIII (1917–1918), 42–61. Bobbs-Merrill reprint #H-28.

Brion, Marcel. *Bartolome de las Casas, Father of the Indians.* New York: E. P. Dutton, 1929.

Charlevoix, Pierre François Xavier de. *Journal of a Voyage to North America.* 2 vols. Chicago: The Caxton Club, 1923.

Cope, Alfred. "Mission to the Menominee: A Quaker's Green Bay Diary," ed. by William C. Haygood, *Wisconsin Magazine of History,* XLIX, No. 4 (Summer 1966), L, No. 1 (Fall 1966), L, No. 2 (Winter 1967), L, No. 3 (Spring 1967).

Cumming, John. "A Puritan among the Chippewas," *Michigan History,* LI, No. 3 (Fall 1967), 213–25. (Abel Bingham, Baptist.)

De Smet, Pierre-Jean, S. J. "Letters & Sketches, with a Narrative of a Year's Residence among the Indian Tribes of the Rocky Mountains," in Reuben G. Thwaites, ed., *Early Western Travels* (q.v., Pt. 6), XXVII.

———. *Life, Letters and Travels of Pierre-Jean DeSmet, S.J. 1801–1873,* ed. by H. M. Chittenden and A. T. Richardson. New York: Francis P. Harper, 1905.

Dougherty, Peter. "Diaries of Peter Dougherty," *Journal of the Presbyterian Historical Society,* XXX (June 1952), 96–114; (September 1952), 175–92; (December 1952), 236–53.

Drury, Clifford. *Presbyterian Panorama—One Hundred and Fifty Years of National Missions History.* Philadelphia: Board of Christian Presbyterian Church in the U.S.A., 1952.

Duratschek, Sister Mary Claudia. *Crusading along Sioux Trails: A History of Catholic Indian Missions of South Dakota.* Yankton, S.D.: Benedictine Convention of the Sacred Heart, 1947.

Faust, Harold S. "The Growth of Presbyterian Missions to the American Indians during the National Period," *Journal of the Presbyterian Historical Society,* XXII (December 1944), 159–61.

Freeman, John F. "The Indian Convert: Theme and Variation," *Ethnohistory,* XII, No. 2 (Spring 1965), 113–28.

Garces, Francisco T. H. *A Record of Travels in Arizona and California, 1775–1776.* San Francisco: John Howell, Books, 1965.

Garritt, J. B. *Historical Sketch of the Missions among the North American Indians.* Philadelphia: Women's Foreign Missionary Society of the Presbyterian Church, 1881.

Gipson, Lawrence Henry, ed. *The Moravian Indian Mission on White River. Diaries and Letters, May 5, 1799, to November 12, 1806.* Indianapolis: Indiana Historical Bureau, 1938.

Gookin, Daniel. "An Historical Account of the Doings and Sufferings of the Christian Indians in New England . . ." in *Transactions and Collections of the American Antiquarian Society* (Cambridge, 1836), II, 424–538.

Gray, Elma E. and Leslie R. *Wilderness Christians: the Moravian Mission to the Delaware Indians.* Ithaca: Cornell University Press, 1956.

Heckewelder, John G. E. *A Narrative of the Mission of the United Brethren among the Delaware and Mohegan Indians . . .* Philadelphia: McCarty & Davis, 1820.

Hickerson, Harold C. "William T. Boutwell of the American Board and the Pillager Chippewa: The History of a Failure," *Ethnohistory,* XII, No. 1 (Winter 1965), 1–29.

Kennedy, J. H. *Jesuit and Savage in New France.* New Haven: Yale University Press, 1950.

Kenton, Edna, ed. *Black Gown and Redskins: Adventures and Travels of the Early Jesuit Missionaries in North America, 1610–1791.* New York: Longmans Green & Co., 1956.

Leger, Sister Mary Celeste. *The Catholic Indian Missions in Maine, 1611–1820.* Washington, D.C.: The Catholic University of America, 1929.

Loskiel, George H. *History of the Mission of the United Brethren among the Indians in North America.* London: Brethren's Society for the Furtherance of the Gospel, 1794.

McCoy, Isaac. *History of Baptist Indian Missions.* Washington: W. H. Morrison, 1840.

McKee, Irving, ed. *The Trail of Death: Letters of Benjamin Marie Petit.* Indianapolis: Indiana Historical Society, 1941.

Palm, Sister Mary Borgias. *The Jesuit Missions of the Illinois Country, 1673–1763.* Cleveland: The Sisters of Notre Dame, 1931.

Pitezel, John H. *Lights and Shades of Missionary Life.* Cincinnati: Walden & Stowe, 1883.

Sagard, Father Gabriel. *The Long Journey to the Country of the Hurons.* Toronto: The Champlain Society, 1939.

Shea, John Gilmary. *History of the Catholic Missions among the Indian Tribes of the United States, 1528–1854.* New York: 1854.

Talbot, Francis. *Saint among Savages: The Life of Isaac Jogues.* New York: Harper & Bros, 1935.

————. *Saint among the Hurons: The Life of Jean de Brebeuf.* New York: Harper, 1949. (Paperback ed., Doubleday, 1956.)

Thompson, Erwin N. *Whitman Mission.* National Park Service Historical Handbook Ser. No. 37. Washington: 1964.

Thwaites, Reuben G., ed. *The Jesuit Relations and Allied Documents.* 75 vols. Cleveland: The Burrows Bros. Co., 1896–1901.

Vogel, Virgil J. "The Missionary as Acculturation Agent: Peter Dougherty and the Indians of Grand Traverse,"*Michigan History*, LI, No. 3 (Fall 1967), 185–201.

Zeisberger, David. *Diary of David Zeisberger, a Moravian Missionary among the Indians of Ohio,* ed. by Eugene F. Bliss. 2 vols. Cincinnati: Robert Clarke & Co., 1885.

12. American Indian Music

Brinton, Daniel G. "Native American Stringed Instruments," *American Antiquarian and Oriental Journal*, XIX (January 1897), 19–21.

Burton, Frederick R. *American Primitive Music.* New York: Moffat, Yard & Co., 1909.

Buttree, Julia M. *The Rhythm of the Redman.* New York: A. S. Barnes & Co., 1930.

Chase, Gilbert. *America's Music, from the Pilgrims to the Present.* New York: McGraw-Hill, 1955. (Chap. XX, Indian Tribal Music, pp. 403–32.)

Cringan, Alexander F. *Iroquois Folk Songs.* Toronto: Toronto Educational Department, 1903.

Curtis [Burlin], Natalie. *The Indians' Book: Songs and Legends of the American Indians.* 2d ed. rev. New York: Dover Publications, 1970. Reprint from 1923.

Densmore, Frances. "Chippewa Music," in *Bureau of American Ethnology Bulletin No. 45.* Washington: Government Printing Office, 1910.

————. "The Rhythm of Sioux and Chippewa Music," *Art and Archaeology*, IX, No. 2 (February 1920), 59–67.

————. *Indian Action Songs.* Boston: C. C. Birchard & Co., 1921.

————. *The American Indians and Their Music.* New York: The Woman's Press, 1926.

————. "The Songs of the Indians," *American Mercury*, VII (January 1926), 65–68.

――――. "The Alabama Indians and their Music," *Publications Texas Folklore Society*, VIII (1937), 270–93.

(The publications of Miss Densmore in Indian music are so numerous that only a small sample can be listed here. Consult library catalogs and bibliographies.)

Fillmore, John C. *The Harmonic Structure of Indian Music*. New York: G. P. Putnam's Sons, 1899.

Fletcher, Alice C. *Indian Story and Song from North America*. Boston: Small, Maynard & Co., 1906.

Howard, John Tasker. *Our American Music*. 3d ed. rev. New York: Thomas Y. Crowell, 1954. (Bibliography, pp. 725–27.)

Jaeger, Ellsworth. *Council Fires*. New York: The Macmillan Co., 1949.

Kilpatrick, Jack F., and Gritts, Anna. *Muskogean Charm Songs Among the Oklahoma Cherokees*. Smithsonian Institution Contributions to Anthropology, II, no. 3. Washington: Government Printing Office, 1967.

Library of Congress. *Folk Music: A Catalog of Folk Songs, Ballads, Dances, Instrumental Pieces, and Folk Tales of the United States and Latin America on Phonograph Records*. Washington: Government Printing Office, 1964.

Lieurance, Thurlow. *Songs of the North American Indians*. Philadephia: Theodore Presser Co., 1920.

Loomis, Harvey W. *Lyrics of the Red Man*. Newton Center, Mass.: The Wa-Wan Press, 1903–4.

McAllester, David P. *Enemy Way Music*. Cambridge: Papers of the Peabody Museum of American Archaeology and Ethnology, XLI, No. 3 (1954). (Navajo music.)

――――. *Indian Music in the Southwest*. Colorado Springs: Taylor Museum, Fine Arts Center, 1961.

Mason, Bernard S. *Dances and Stories of the American Indian*. New York: A. S. Barnes & Co., 1944.

Nettl, Bruno. *North American Indian Musical Styles*. Philadelphia: American Folklore Society, 1954.

Spaeth, Sigmund. *A History of Popular Music in America*. New York: Random House, 1948.

Speck, Frank G., and Sapir, J. D. *Ceremonial Songs of the Creek and Yuchi Indians*. Philadelphia: University of Pennsylvania Anthropological Publications, I, 1911.

Wallaschek, Richard. *Primitive Music*. London: Longmans Green & Co., 1893. (Chap. I, America.)

13. *Aboriginal Religion*

Aberle, David F. *The Peyote Religion Among the Navaho*. Chicago: Aldine Publishing Co., 1966.

Alexander, Hartley Burr. *The World's Rim: Great Mysteries of the North American Indians*. Lincoln: University of Nebraska Press, 1967.

Barnett, H. G. *Indian Shakers: A Messianic Cult of the Pacific Northwest.* Carbondale: Southern Illinois University Press, 1967.

Barrett, S. A. *The Dream Dance of the Chippewa and Menominee Indians of Northern Wisconsin.* Milwaukee: Bulletin of the Public Museum of the City of Milwaukee, I, November 1911.

Brandt, Richard B. *Hopi Ethics: A Theoretical Analysis.* Chicago: University of Chicago Press, 1954.

Brinton, Daniel G. *The Myths of the New World.* 2d ed. rev. New York: Henry Holt & Co., 1876.

Hale, Horatio. *Iroquois Book of Rites.* Toronto: University of Toronto Press, 1963.

Hurdy, John Major. *American Indian Religions.* Los Angeles: Sherbourne Press, 1970.

La Barre, Weston. *The Peyote Cult.* Hamden, Conn., Shoestring Press, 1964. Rev. ed., New York: Schocken Books, 1969.

Landes, Ruth. *Ojibwa Religion and the Midewiwin.* Madison: University of Wisconsin Press, 1968.

————. *The Prairie Potawatomi.* Madison: University of Wisconsin Press, 1968.

Linton, Ralph. *Thunder Ceremony of the Pawnee.* Chicago: Field Museum of Natural History, 1922.

————. *Annual Ceremony of the Pawnee Medicine Men.* Chicago: Field Museum of Natural History, 1923.

————. *Purification of the Sacred Bundles, a Ceremony of the Pawnee.* Chicago: Field Museum of Natural History, 1923.

Maddox, John Lee. *The Medicine Man.* New York: The Macmillan Co., 1923.

Mooney, James. *The Ghost Dance Religion.* Chicago: University of Chicago Press, 1965. (Reprint of *14th Annual Report, BAE,* Pt. 2, 1892–1893.)

Parker, Arthur C. *The Code of Handsome Lake, the Seneca Prophet.* Bulletin No. 530, Education Department, University of the State of New York. Albany: November 1, 1912. (Reprint by Iroqrafts, R.R. #2, Ohsweken, Ontario, n.d.)

Powell, Peter J. *Sweet Medicine. The Continuing Role of the Sacred Arrows, the Sun Dance, and the Sacred Buffalo Hat in Northern Cheyenne History.* 2 vols. Norman: University of Oklahoma Press, 1969.

Radin, Paul. *Primitive Man as Philosopher.* New York: Dover Publications, 1957. Reprint from 1927.

Reichard, Gladys A. *Navaho Religion.* Princeton: Princeton University Press, 1963.

Slotkin, James Sydney. *The Peyote Religion.* Glencoe, Ill.: The Free Press, 1956.

Thompson, J. E. S. *Maya History and Religion.* Norman: University of Oklahoma Press, 1970.

Underhill, Ruth. *Red Man's Religion.* Chicago: University of Chicago Press, 1965.

Waters, Frank. *Book of the Hopi.* New York: Ballantine Books, 1969. Reprint from 1963.

14. Indian and White Warfare

Abel, Annie Heloise. *The American Indian as a Participant in the Civil War.* 2 vols. Cleveland: Arthur ·H. Clarke Co., 1919. Reprint, New York: Johnson Reprint Corp., n.d.

Andrist, Ralph K. *The Long Death—the Last Days of the Plains Indians.* New York: The Macmillan Co., 1964.

Annual Report of the Secretary of War . . . Year Ending June 30, 1877, Vol. I. Washington: Government Printing Office, 1877. (Contains reports of General O. O. Howard, General P. H. Sheridan, Colonel Nelson Miles, and others on the Nez Perce campaign and other activities.)

Beal, Merrill D. *"I Will Fight No More Forever."* Seattle: University of Washington Press, 1963.

Betzinez, Jason, with W. S. Nye. *I Fought with Geronimo.* Harrisburg, Pa.: The Stackpole Co., 1960.

Bourke, John G. *An Apache Campaign in the Sierra Madre.* New York: Charles Scribner's Sons, 1958.

————. *On the Border with Crook.* Columbus: Long's College Book Co., 1950. Reprint from 1891.

Brackenridge, H. H. *Indian Atrocities . . .* Cincinnati: U. P. James, 1867.

Brininstool, E. A. *Fighting Indian Warriors.* Harrisburg, Pa.: The Stackpole Co., 1953.

Brown, Dee. *Bury My Heart at Wounded Knee.* New York: Holt, Rinehart, and Winston, 1971.

Burdick, Usher L., and Hart, Eugene D. *Jacob Horner and the Indian Campaigns of 1876 and 1877.* Baltimore: Wirth Bros., 1942. (Sioux and Nez Perce.)

Cooke, David C. *Fighting Indians of the West.* New York: Dodd Mead Co., 1954. (Paperback ed., Popular Library, 1955.)

Corkran, David H. *The Cherokee Frontier, Conflict and Survival, 1740–62.* Norman: University of Oklahoma Press, 1962.

Crampton, C. Gregory, ed. *The Mariposa Indian War 1850–1851.* Salt Lake City: University of Utah Press, 1957. (California Indians.)

Crook, George. *General George Crook, His Autobiography,* ed. by Martin F. Schmit. Norman: University of Oklahoma Press, 1960.

Cunningham, Frank. *Confederate Indians.* San Antonio: The Naylor Co., 1959. (Oklahoma Indians in the Confederate army.)

Custer, George Armstrong. *My Life on the Plains.* Norman: University of Oklahoma Press, 1962.

Doddridge, Joseph. *Notes on the Settlement and Indian Wars of the Western Parts of Virginia and Pennsylvania.* Albany: Joel Munsell, 1876.

Dodge, Col. Richard I. *Our Wild Indians: Thirty-Three Years' Personal Experience among the Red Men of the Great West.* New York: Archer House, 1959.

Downes, Randolph C. *Council Fires on the Upper Ohio, a Narrative of Indian Affairs in the Upper Ohio Valley until 1795.* Pittsburgh: University of Pittsburgh Press, 1940.

Downey, Fairfax D. *Indian Fighting Army.* New York: Scribner's, 1941. Paperback ed., Bantam, 1957.

————. *Indian Wars of the United States Army, 1776–1865.* New York: Doubleday, 1963.

Dunn, J. P., Jr. *Massacres of the Mountains: A History of the Indian Wars of the Far West, 1815–1875.* New York: Capricorn Books, 1969. Reprint from 1886.

Faulk, Odie B. *The Geronimo Campaign.* New York: Oxford University Press, 1969.

Glassley, Ray H. *Pacific Northwest Indian Wars.* Portland: Binfords & Mort, 1953.

Graham, W. A. *The Custer Myth.* Harrisburg, Pa.: The Stackpole Co., 1954.

Graymont, Barbara. *The Iroquois in the American Revolution.* Syracuse, N.Y.: Syracuse University Press, 1972.

Hagemann, E. R., ed. *Fighting Rebels and Redskins.* Norman: University of Oklahoma Press, 1969.

Heimlich, Herbert H. *Sesquicentennial of the Battle of Tippecanoe.* Lafayette, Ind.: Lafayette Printing Co., 1961.

Hoig, Stan. *The Sand Creek Massacre.* Norman: University of Oklahoma Press, 1961.

Howard, Maj. Gen. Oliver Otis. *My Life and Experiences among Our Hostile Indians.* Hartford: A. D. Worthington & Co., 1907.

————. *Autobiography of Oliver Otis Howard.* 2 vols. New York: The Baker & Taylor Co., 1908.

Howbert, Irving. *The Indians of the Pike's Peak Region, Including an Account of the Battle of Sand Creek . . .* New York: The Knickerbocker Press, 1914.

Hunt, George T. *The Wars of the Iroquois.* Madison: University of Wisconsin Press, 1960.

Josephy, Alvin M., Jr. *The Nez Perce Indians and the Opening of the Northwest.* New Haven: Yale University Press, 1965.

King, Capt. Charles. *Campaigning with Crook.* Norman: University of Oklahoma Press, 1964.

Leach, Douglas Edward. *Flintlock and Tomahawk: New England in King Philip's War.* New York: The Macmillan Co., 1958.

Leckie, William H. *The Military Conquest of the Southern Plains.* Norman: University of Oklahoma Press, 1963.

León-Portilla, Miguel, ed. *The Broken Spears—An Aztec Account of the Conquest of Mexico.* Boston: Beacon Press, 1962.

Lincoln, Charles H., ed. *Narratives of the Indian Wars, 1675–1699*. New York: Barnes & Noble, 1952.

Longstreet, Stephen. *War Cries on Horseback*. Garden City, N.Y.: Doubleday & Co., 1970.

Miles, Nelson A. *Personal Recollections & Observations . . .* Chicago: The Werner Co., 1896.

Mohr, Walter H. *Federal Indian Relations 1774–1788*. Philadelphia: the author, 1933. (Indians in the Revolutionary War.)

Murray, Keith A. *The Modocs and Their War*. Norman: University of Oklahoma Press, 1965.

Newcomb, W. W., Jr. "A Re-examination of the Causes of Plains Warfare," *American Anthropologist* LII (July–September 1950), 317–330. Bobbs-Merrill reprint #A-172.

Nye, W. S. *Carbine and Lance, the Story of Old Fort Sill*. Norman: University of Oklahoma Press, 1938.

Oehler, C. M. *The Great Sioux Uprising*. New York: Oxford University Press, 1959. (Minnesota war, 1862.)

Parkhill, Forbes. *The Last of the Indian Wars*. New York: Collier Books, 1961. (Ute troubles in 1915.)

Parkman, Francis. *The Conspiracy of Pontiac*. 2 vols. Boston: Little, Brown & Co., 1922.

———. *The Battle for North America*, ed. by John Tebbel. Garden City, N.Y.: Doubleday & Co., 1948.

Powers, Mabel. *The Indian as Peacemaker*. New York: Fleming H. Revell, 1932.

Prescott, William H. *History of the Conquest of Mexico* and *History of the Conquest of Peru*. New York: Modern Library, n.d.

Ricket, Don. *War in the West: The Indian Campaigns*. Crow Agency, Mont.: Custer Battlefield Historical & Museum Association, 1956.

Roosevelt, Theodore. *St. Clair's Defeat, 1791*. Fort Wayne, Ind.: Fort Wayne Convention Bureau, 1964.

———. *Anthony Wayne's Expedition into the Northwest*. Fort Wayne, Ind.: Fort Wayne Convention Bureau, 1964.

Sheridan, Philip H. *Personal Memoirs of Philip H. Sheridan, General, United States Army*. 2 vols. New York: D. Appleton Co., 1902.

Shimmel, Lewis S. *Border Warfare in Pennsylvania during the Revolution*. Harrisburg, Pa.: R. L. Myers & Co., 1901.

Sipe, C. Hale. *The Indian Wars of Pennsylvania*. Harrisburg: The Telegraph Press, 1929.

Smith, William. *Expedition against the Ohio Indians* (1765). Ann Arbor: University Microfilms, 1966.

Tebbel, John, and Jennison, Keith. *The American Indian Wars*. New York: Harper & Bros., 1960.

Thwaites, Reuben Gold, and Kellogg, Louise P., eds. *Documentary History of Dunmore's War, 1774*. Madison: State Historical Society of Wisconsin, 1905.

————. *The Revolution on the Upper Ohio, 1775–1777*. Madison: State Historical Society of Wisconsin, 1908.

————. *Frontier Defense on the Upper Ohio, 1777–1778*. Madison: State Historical Society of Wisconsin, 1912.

U.S. Congress, "Massacre of the Cheyenne Indians," in *Report of the Joint Committee on the Conduct of the War*, 2d session, 38th Congress, Vol. III. Washington: Government Printing Office, 1865.

Vestal, Stanley. *New Sources of Indian History, 1850–91*. Norman: University of Oklahoma Press, 1934.

————. *Warpath and Council Fire: The Plains Indians' Struggle for Survival in War and in Diplomacy, 1851–1891*. New York: Random House, 1948.

Wellman, Paul I. *The Indian Wars of the West*. Garden City, N.Y.: Doubleday & Co., 1956.

15. *Modern Indians: Situation and Problems*

American Indians and American Life, special issue of *Annals of the American Academy of Political and Social Science*, Vol. 311 (May 1957), ed. by George E. Simpson and J. Milton Yinger. Philadelphia: 1957.

American Indian Chicago Conference. *Declaration of Indian Purpose*. University of Chicago, June 13–20, 1961.

"The Angry American Indian: Starting Down the Protest Trail," *Time* magazine, February 7, 1970, pp. 14–20.

Armstrong, O. K. "Give the Indians an Even Chance," *Reader's Digest*, November 1966, pp. 101–105.

Backes, Clarus J. "Last Rites for an Indian Nation," *Chicago Tribune* magazine, October 19, 1969, pp. 29–33. (Menominee.)

Baerreis, David A., ed. *The Indian in Modern America*. Madison: State Historical Society of Wisconsin, 1956.

Bahr, Howard; Chadwick, Bruce; and Day, Robert. *Native Americans Today*. New York: Harper & Row, 1971.

Berry, Brewton. *Almost White*. New York: The Macmillan Co., 1967.

Black, Brown and Red. Detroit: News & Letters Committees, 1972.

Bongartz, Roy. " 'Who Am I?' The Indian Sickness," *The Nation*, April 27, 1970, pp. 496–98.

Boyle, Kay. "A Day on Alcatraz with the Indians," *The New Republic*, January 17, 1970, pp. 10–11.

Brand, David. "Red Power," *Wall Street Journal*, April 30, 1969, pp. 26–30.

Brandon, William. "American Indians: The Alien Americans," *The Progressive*, XXXIII, No. 12 (December 1969), pp. 13–17.

————. "The American Indians: The Unamericans," *The Progressive*, XXXIV, No. 1 (January 1970), pp. 35–39.

————. "American Indians: The Real American Revolution," *The Progressive*, XXXIV, No. 2 (February 1970), pp. 26–30.

Bronson, Ruth Muskrat. *Indians Are People Too*. New York: Friendship Press, 1944.

Brophy, Byron. "The American Indian and Government," Chap. XVIII in Francis J. Brown and Joseph S. Roucek, *One America*. New York: Prentice-Hall, 1945, pp. 439–49. (Favors termination and assimilation.)

Brophy, W. A., and Aberle, S. D. *The Indian: America's Unfinished Business*. Norman: University of Oklahoma Press, 1967.

Cahn, Edgar S., ed. *Our Brother's Keeper: the Indian in White America*. New York: World Publishing Co., 1969.

Capron, Louis, and Imboden, Otis. "Florida's Emerging Seminoles," *National Geographic Magazine*, CXXXVI, No. 5 (November 1969), 716–34.

Cash, Joseph H., and Hoover, Herbert T. *To Be an Indian*. N.Y.: Holt, Rinehart and Winston, 1971.

Clark, E. M. and David W. *Rehabilitation Program on the Cheyenne River Sioux Reservation*. Philadelphia: Indian Rights Association, 1961.

Coffey, Ivy. "The Urban Indian," reprint from *Sunday Oklahoman* and *Oklahoma City Times*. Oklahoma City: Oklahoma Publishing Co., 1967.

Collier, John. "Letter to President Eisenhower" (attacks relocation). *The Nation*, January 10, 1953.

———. *On the Gleaming Way*. Denver: Sage Books, 1962. (Southwest Indians today.)

Collier, Peter. "The Red Man's Burden," *Ramparts*, VIII, No. 8 (February 1970), 26–38. (Alcatraz occupation, etc.)

Commission on the Rights, Liberties, and Responsibilities of the American Indian, Fund for the Republic. *A Program for Indian Citizens—A Summary Report*. Albuquerque: January 1961.

Cory, David Munroe. *Within Two Worlds*. New York: Friendship Press, 1955.

Debo, Angie. *The Five Civilized Tribes of Oklahoma: Report on Social and Economic Conditions*. Philadelphia: Indian Rights Association, 1951.

Deloria, Ella. *Speaking of Indians*. New York: Friendship Press, 1944.

Deloria, Vine, *Custer Died for Your Sins*. New York: The Macmillan Co., 1969.

———. *We Talk, You Listen*. New York: The Macmillan Co., 1970.

Economic Research Service, U.S. Department of Agriculture. *Rural Indian Americans in Poverty*. Agricultural Economic Report No. 167. Washington: Government Printing Office, 1969.

Embry, Carlos B. *America's Concentration Camps*. New York: David McKay Co., 1956. (Attack on reservation system.)

Engstrom, George, and Sister Providencia. "City and Reservation Indians," *Social Order*, February 1955.

Farb, Peter. "The American Indian, a Portrait in Limbo," *Saturday Review*, October 16, 1968, pp. 26–29.

Federal Indian Legislation and Policies. Prepared by the 1956 Workshop on American Indian affairs, sponsored by the University of Chicago Department of Anthropology, 1956.

Fey, Harold E., and McNickle, D'Arcy. *Indians and Other Americans*. New York: Harper & Bros., 1959.

First, J. M. "Cultures in Crosscurrents," *Michigan Education Journal*, XXXVIII (November 1960), 241–44+.

Gregory, Dick. *The Shadow that Scares Me,* ed. by James R. McGraw. New York: Pocket Books, 1968. (Washington state fish-in, etc., pp. 145–52.)

Gridley, Marion. Series of four articles on relocation in the *Amerindian,* March-April, May-June, July-August, and September-October, 1956.

Haas, Theodore. *The Indian and the Law,* I & II. Lawrence, Kansas: Haskell Institute, 1949.

Harmer, Ruth. "Uprooting the Indians," *Atlantic* magazine, Vol. 197, No. 3 (March 1956), pp. 54–57.

Hedgepeth, William. "America's Indians," *Look* magazine, XXXIV, No. 11 (June 2, 1970), 23–45.

Hertzberg, Hazel Whitman. *The Search for an American Indian Identity: Modern Pan-Indian Movements.* Syracuse: Syracuse University Press, 1971.

Hodge, William H. *Urban Indian Bibliography: Canada and the United States.* Department of Anthropology, University of Wisconsin at Milwaukee. 17 pp. mimeographed.

Hughes, Everett C. and Helen M. *Where Peoples Meet: Racial and Ethnic Frontiers.* Glencoe: Free Press, 1952. (Chap. 2, "North America: Indians and Immigrants," pp. 18 *ff.*)

Indian American Issues: a Handbook for Discussion. Washington: New Community Press (1970). 12 pp.

Indian Voices: The First Convocation of American Indian Scholars. San Francisco: The Indian Historian Press, 1970.

Isenberg, Barbara. "Red Man's Plight," *Wall Street Journal,* March 9, 1970, pp. 1, 18.

Johnson, President Lyndon B. *The Forgotten American.* Special Indian message to Congress, March 6, 1968, from special issue of *Indian Record,* March 1968. Washington: Government Printing Office, 1968. (Also in *Indian Affairs,* No. 69, January–March 1968.)

Josephy, Alvin M., Jr. *Red Power: The American Indians' Fight for Freedom.* New York: American Heritage Press, 1971.

Kitigawa, Daisuke. "The American Indian," in Arnold M. and Caroline Rose, eds., *Minority Problems.* New York: Harper & Row, 1965. Pp. 26–32.

LaFarge, Oliver. *As Long as the Grass Shall Grow.* New York: Alliance Book Corp., 1940.

———. *The Changing Indian.* Norman: University of Oklahoma Press, 1953.

League of Women Voters. *Indian—And Proud of It!* Washington, D.C.: League of Women Voters, 1971.

Levitan, Sar A., and Hetrick, Barbara. *Big Brother's Indian Program, with Reservations.* New York: McGraw-Hill, 1971.

Lindley, Lawrence F. "Why Indians Need Land," *The Christian Century,* November 6, 1957, pp. 1316–18.

Lindquist, G. E. E. *Indians in Transition.* New York: Division of Home Missions, National Council of Churches of Christ in the U.S.A., 1951.

Lurie, Nancy O., and Levine, Stuart, eds. *The American Indian Today.* Deland,

Florida: Everett Edwards, Inc., 1968. Reissued, Baltimore: Penguin Books, 1970.

McNickle, D'Arcy. "Indian Crisis: A Challenge to Social Science," appendix to *University of Chicago Round Table*, No. 828, February 21, 1954.

———. "It's Almost Never Too Late," *Christian Century*, February 20, 1957, pp. 227–29.

———. *The Indian Tribes of the United States: Ethnic and Cultural Survival*. London: Institute of Race Relations—Oxford University Press, 1962.

Marden, Charles F., and Meyer, Gladys. *Minorities in American Society*. 2d ed. New York: American Book Co., 1962. (Chap. 15, pp. 326–51).

Meyer, William. *Native Americans: The New Indian Resistance*. New York: International Publishers, 1971.

Nader, Ralph. "American Indians: People Without a Future," *Harvard Law Record*, XXII, No. 10 (May 10, 1956).

———. "Lo, the Poor Indian," *The New Republic*, March 30, 1968, pp. 14–15.

National Institute of Mental Health & Indian Health Service. *Suicide among the American Indians*. Washington: Government Printing Office, 1969.

Nelson, Susan. "Indians vs. the City," *Chicago* magazine, VII, No. 2 (April 1970), 26–30.

Philadelphia Yearly Meeting of Friends, Kinzua Project. *The Kinzua Dam Controversy*. Philadelphia [1961].

Provinse, John; Segundo, Thomas; and Tax, Sol. "The American Indian Now," *University of Chicago Round Table*, No. 828, February 21, 1954.

Rabeau, E. S. *To the First Americans*. Third annual report on the Indian health program of the U.S. Public Health Service. Rev. 1969. Washington: U.S. Public Health Service, 1969.

Ridgeway, James. "The Lost Indians" (two articles), *The New Republic*, December 4, 1965, pp. 19–20 (on the Menominee), and December 11, 1965, pp. 19–22 (on the Sioux).

Rietz, Robert. "The American Indian Center," *Illinois Journal of Education*, LXI, No. 4 (April 1970), 63–68. (Chicago Indian Center.)

Roucek, J. S. "Most Oppressed Race in the United States: the Indian," *Educational Forum*, XXIX (May 1965), 477–85.

Schaefer, Jack. "The American Indian," *Holiday*, XIX, No. 2 (February 1956), 26–39+.

Schusky, Ernest. *The Right to Be Indian*. San Francisco: The Indian Historian Press, 1970.

Scholastic Magazine, "The American Indian Today," February 17, 1967, pp. 3–6, 17.

Shotwell, Louisa Rossiter. *This Is the Indian American*. New York: Friendship Press, 1955.

Skillern, Essie Quaid. "A New Era for Indian Americans," *Facts Forum*, V, No. 11 (November 1956), 2–8, 40–46.

Soholt, Sylvia P. "Seattle Squabble: Indians Battle City for Park Area" (Ft. Lawton), *Christian Science Monitor*, May 19, 1970.

Steiner, Stan. *The New Indians.* New York: Harper & Row, 1968. (The rising mood of protest among Indians.)

Terkel, Studs. *Division Street: America.* New York: Avon Books, 1968. (Interview with Benny Bearskin of Chicago, pp. 134–42.)

Underhill, Ruth. "What Do Whites Owe to Indians?" *American Teacher,* XXXIII (February 1949), 11–13.

Van de Mark, Dorothy. "The Raid on the Indian Reservations," *Harper's* magazine, CCXII (March 1956), 46–53.

Vogel, Virgil J. "After 80 Years: The Indians Rise Again," *New Politics,* VIII, No. 2 (Spring 1970), 62–72.

Voget, Fred, ed. "American Indians and Their Economic Development," special issue of *Human Organization,* XX, No. 4 (Winter 1961–1962). (Published by the Society for Applied Anthropology.)

Waddell, Jack O., and Watson, O. Michael. *The American Indian in Urban Society.* Boston: Little, Brown & Co., 1971.

Walker, Deward E., Jr. *The Emergent Native Americans.* Boston: Little, Brown & Co., 1972.

Wax, Murray. *Indian Americans—Unity and Diversity.* Englewood Cliffs, N.J.: Prentice-Hall, 1971.

Welsh, David. "The Royal Screwing of the Passamaquodia," in *A Muckraker's Guide to 1968 and Other Horrors.* San Francisco: *Ramparts* magazine, 1968. Pp. 98–103.

Willhelm, Sidney M. "Red Man, Black Man, and White America: The Constitutional Approach to Genocide," *Catalyst,* No. 4 (Spring 1969), 1–62. (Published at State University of New York at Buffalo.)

Woods, Richard G., and Harkins, Arthur M. *Indian Americans in Chicago.* Minneapolis: Training Center for Community Programs, University of Minnesota, November 1968. (Sociological and statistical study of Indians served by St. Augustine's Center in Chicago.)

See also: Indian and Indian interest publications.

16. *Miscellaneous*

Andrews, Ralph W. *Photographers of the Frontier West.* Seattle: Superior Publishing Co., 1965.

Benedict, Ruth. *Patterns of Culture.* New York: Penguin Books, 1946. (Reprint from Houghton Mifflin, 1934.)

Boas, Franz. *Introduction to Handbook of American Indian Languages,* and Powell, J. Wesley, *Indian Linguistic Families of America North of Mexico.* Lincoln: University of Nebraska Press, 1966. (The second item is a reprint from the *7th Annual Report, Bureau of American Ethnology,* 1885–1886.)

Boy Scouts of America. *Indian Lore Merit Badge Pamphlet.* New Brunswick, N.J.: various editions.

Brown, Mark H., and Felton, W. R. *The Frontier Years: L. A. Huffman, Photographer of the Plains.* New York: Henry Holt & Co., 1954.

Forrest, Earle R. *With a Camera in Navaholand.* Norman: University of Oklahoma Press, 1970.

Gearing, Frederick O. "Why Indians?" *Social Education,* XXXII, No. 2 (February 1968), 128–31, 146.

Gobetz, Gary. "Mexico's Indian Jews," *National Jewish Monthly,* LXXXIV, No. 8 (April 1970), 21–23.

Greenway, John. "Will the Indians Get Whitey?" *National Review,* March 11, 1969, pp. 223–28, 245. (Anthropologist argues that Indians were really worse than they have been portrayed, and heaps much vitriol on their white friends.)

Kelsay, Laura E., compiler. *List of Cartographic Records of the Bureau of Indian Affairs.* Special lists No. 13. Washington: National Archives and Records Service, 1954.

Ladd, Richard S., compiler. *Maps Showing Explorers' Routes, Trails and Early Roads in the United States.* An Annotated List. Washington: Library of Congress, 1962.

Library of Congress. *Image of America: Early Photography 1839–1900. A Catalog* . . . Washington: 1957.

McNitt, Frank. *The Indian Traders.* Norman: University of Oklahoma Press, 1963.

Poe, Charlsie. *Angel to the Papagos.* San Antonio: The Naylor Co., 1964.

Prettyman, W. S. *Indian Territory: A Frontier Photographic Record,* ed. by Robert E. Cunningham. Norman: University of Oklahoma Press, 1958.

Sady, Rachel Reese. "Anthropology and World History Textbooks," *Phi Delta Kappan,* February 1964, pp. 247–51.

Tax, Sol. "What Do Anthropologists Do?" *Social Education,* XXXII, No. 2 (February 1968), 132–34.

Tilden, Freeman. *Following the Frontier.* New York: Alfred A. Knopf, 1964. (Life of frontier photographer F. Jay Haynes.)

Verrill, A. Hyatt. *The Real Americans.* New York: G. P. Putnam's Sons, 1954. (Has biographical sketches of famous Indians.)

Walker, Stanley. "Let the Indian Be the Hero," *New York Times Magazine,* April 24, 1960, pp. 50, 52, 55. (Criticism of TV treatment of Indians.)

Wren, L. L., and Rossman, R. "Mathematics Used by American Indians North of Mexico." *School Science and Mathematics,* XXXIII (April 1933), 363–72.

17. *The American Indian Impact on History and Culture*

A. GENERAL

Alexander, E. P. "Wisconsin Indians: Their Origins and Contributions," *Wisconsin Journal of Education,* LXXIII (January 1943), 235–38.

Beatty, W. W. "Some Indian Contributions to Our Culture," *Childhood Education,* XVIII (April 1942), 353–56.

Brandon, William. "American Indians and American History," *The American West*, II, No. 2 (Spring 1965), 14–25, 91–93.

Brown, Francis J., and Roucek, Joseph L., eds. *One America*. 3d ed. New York: Prentice-Hall, 1952. (Chapter by Robert F. Heizer on "The American Indian: Background and Contributions." 2d ed. has similar chapter by Clark Wissler.)

Carter, E. Russell. *The Gift Is Rich*. New York: Friendship Press, 1968.

Chamberlain, Alexander F. "The Contributions of the American Indian to Civilization," *Proceedings of the American Antiquarian Society*, XVI, new series (October 1903), 91–126.

Cohen, Felix. "Americanizing the White Man," *The American Scholar*, XXI, No. 2 (Spring 1952), 177–91.

Davis, Emily C. *Ancient Americans*. New York: Henry Holt & Co., 1931. (Chap. 18, "We Owe These to the Indians," pp. 272–82.)

Driver, Harold E., ed. *The Americas on the Eve of the Discovery*. Englewood Cliffs, N.J.: Prentice-Hall, 1964. ("The Contributions of the Indians to Modern Life," pp. 165–74.)

———. *Indians of North America*. Chicago: University of Chicago Press, 1965. (Chap. 26, "Achievements and Contributions," pp. 583–612.)

Edwards, Everett E. "American Indian Contributions to Civilization," *Minnesota History*, XV, No. 3 (September 1934), 255–72.

Frachtenberg, Leo J. "Our Indebtedness to the American Indian," *Wisconsin Archaeologist*, XIV, No. 2 (July 1915), 64–69.

Hallowell, A. Irving. "The Impact of the American Indian on American Culture," *American Anthropologist*, new series, LIX, No. 2 (April 1957), 201–207. Bobbs-Merrill reprint #A-102.

———. "The Backwash of the Frontier: The Impact of the Indian on American Culture," in Clifton B. Kroeber and Walker D. Wyman, eds., *The Frontier in Perspective*. Madison: University of Wisconsin Press, 1965. Pp. 229–58.

Hetzel, Theodore B. "We Can Learn from American Indians," *Journal of American Indian Education*, IV, No. 3 (May 1965), 23–26.

James, George Wharton. *What the White Race May Learn from the Indian*. Chicago: Forbes & Co., 1908.

Josephy, Alvin M., Jr. "Indians in History," *Atlantic*, CCXXV, No. 6 (June 1970), 67–72.

Life magazine. "Our Indian Heritage." July 2, 1971.

Locke, Alain, and Stern, Bernhard J. *When Peoples Meet*. New York: Progressive Education Association, 1946. (Chapter by Clark Wissler on "Our Culture Debt to the American Indians.")

Richman, Robin. "Rediscovery of the Red Man," *Life*, December 1, 1967, pp. 52–72.

Rourke, Constance. *The Roots of American Culture*. New York: Harcourt Brace, 1942. (Indian influence on theater, pp. 60–74; Indians as artists' subjects, pp. 286–87; influence of Indian beliefs on Salem witchcraft episode, p. 20.)

Safford, W. E. "Our Heritage from the Indians," *Annual Report Smithsonian Institution . . . June 30, 1926.* Washington: Government Printing Office, 1927.

Skinner, C. L. "Our Children's Indian Heritage," *Parents Magazine,* VIII (October 1933), 16–17+.

Udall, Stewart L. "The Indians: First Americans, First Ecologists," *The American Way,* May 1971, pp. 8–14.

Verrill, A. Hyatt. *The Real Americans.* New York: G. P. Putnam's Sons, 1954. ("What We Owe the Indians," pp. 8–12.)

Vogel, Virgil. *The Indian in American History.* Chicago: Integrated Education Associates, 1968. (Reprint, with bibliography added, of "The Indian in American History Textbooks," *Integrated Education,* VI, No. 3 (May–June 1968), 16–32. Partial reprint in *Social Education,* XXXIII, No. 2 (February 1969), 200–203.

Walker, Edwin F. "America's Indian Background," *Masterkey,* XIX (1945), 7–13, 83–88, 119–25. (Issued separately under same title, as a pamphlet, by the Southwest Museum, Los Angeles, Calif.)

Wissler, Clark. *Indians of the United States: Four Centuries of Their History and Culture.* Garden City. N.Y.: Doubleday, 1949. (Chap. XIX, "When the White Man Went Indian," pp. 251–56; Chap. XXIII, "Did the Indian Live in Vain?," pp. 292–97.)

B. AGRICULTURE AND FOOD

Aller, W. F. "Aboriginal Food Utilization of Vegetables by the Indians of the Great Lakes Region as Recorded in the Jesuit Relations," *West Virginia Archaeologist,* XXXV, No. 3 (1954), 59–73.

Black, Glen A. "Prehistoric American Diet," *Indiana Magazine of History,* XXIX, No. 2 (June 1933), 96–103.

Bourke, John G. "The Folk Foods of the Rio Grande Valley and of Northern Mexico," *Publications Texas Folklore Society,* IX (1931), 85–117.

Carr, Lucien. "The Food of Certain American Indians and Their Methods of Preparing It," *Proceedings American Antiquarian Society,* new series, X (1895), 155–90.

Chamberlain, Lucia Sarah. "Plants Used by the Indians of Eastern North America," *American Naturalist,* XXXV (1901), 1–10.

Chamberlin, Ralph V. "Ethnobotany of the Gosiute Indians of Utah," *Memoirs, American Anthropological Association,* II (1907–15), 331–405.

Chesnut, V. K. "Plants Used by the Indians of Mendocino County, California," *Contributions U.S. National Herbarium,* VII. Washington: Government Printing Office, 1902.

Collins, G. N. "The Origin and Early Distribution of Maize," *American Anthropologist,* new series, XXIII (1921), 503–506.

Coville, Frederick. "Notes on the Plants Used by the Klamath Indians of Oregon," *Contributions U.S. National Herbarium,* V, 87–108. Washington: Government Printing Office, 1897–1901.

De Candolle, Alphonse. *Origin of Cultivated Plants.* New York: D. Appleton & Co., 1902.

Edwards, Everett E., and Rasmussen, Wayne D. *A Bibliography of the Agriculture of the American Indians.* U.S. Department of Agriculture, Misc. Pub. No. 447. Washington: Government Printing Office, 1942.

Gilmore, Melvin R. "Uses of Plants by Indians of the Missouri River Region," in *33d Annual Report, Bureau of American Ethnology* (1911–12), 43–154. Washington: Government Printing Office, 1919.

Havard, Valery. "Drink Plants of the North American Indians," *Bulletin of the Torrey Botanical Club,* XXIII (February, 1896), 33–46.

Holmes, W. H. "Aboriginal Agriculture—the American Indians," in L. H. Bailey, ed., *Cyclopedia of American Agriculture,* 2d ed., New York: The Macmillan Co. (1909–1910), IV, 24–39.

Jenks, Albert Ernest. *The Wild Rice Gatherers of the Upper Great Lakes.* Extract from *19th Annual Report, Bureau of American Ethnology.* Washington: Government Printing Office, 1901.

Kimball, Yeffe, and Anderson, Jean. *The Art of American Indian Cooking.* Garden City, N.Y.: Doubleday, 1965.

Laufer, Berthold. *Introduction of Tobacco into Europe,* Chicago: Field Museum of Natural History, 1924.

———. "The American Plant Migration," *Scientific Monthly,* XXVIII (1929), 239–51.

———. *The American Plant Migration, Part I: The Potato.* Chicago: Field Museum of Natural History, 1938.

Mangelsdorf, Paul C. "The Mystery of Corn," reprint from *Scientific American,* July, 1950.

———, et al. "Domestication of Corn," *Science,* Vol. 143 (February 7, 1964), 538–45. Reprinted by Bobbs-Merrill, No. A-365.

Merrill, E. P. "The Phytogeography of Cultivated Plants in Relation to Assumed Pre-Columbian Eurasian-American Contacts," *American Anthropologist,* new series, XXXIII (July–September, 1931), 357–82.

Newberry, J. S. "Food and Fiber Plants of the North American Indians," *Popular Science Monthly,* XXXII (November, 1887), 31–46.

Paddleford, Clementine. "Have an Indian Thanksgiving," *This Week,* November 5, 1967, pp. 10–11.

Palmer, Edward. "Food Products of the North American Indians," in *Report of the Commissioner of Agriculture, 1870,* pp. 404–28. Washington: Government Printing Office, 1871.

Spinden, H. J. "The Origin and Distribution of Agriculture in America," *Proceedings of the 19th International Congress of Americanists* (1915). Washington: 1917. Reprinted in A. L. Kroeber and T. T. Waterman, eds., *Sourcebook in Anthropology.* New York: Harcourt Brace, 1931, pp. 227–32.

Towle, Margaret. *The Ethnobotany of Pre-Columbian Peru.* Chicago: Aldine Publishing Co., 1961.

Verrill, A. H., in collaboration with Barrett, Otis W. *Foods America Gave the World*. Boston: C. C. Page Co., 1937.

Vogel, Virgil J. "Indian Ways with Farming." *The American Way*, July 1971, pp. 22–28.

Walker, Edwin F. *World Crops Derived from the Indians*. 4th ed. Los Angeles: Southwest Museum, 1967.

Weatherwax, Paul. *Indian Corn in Old America*. New York: The Macmillan Co., 1954.

Will, George F., and Hyde, George E. *Corn Among the Indians of the Upper Missouri*. St. Louis: William Harvey Miner Co., 1917.

Yanovsky, Elias. *Food Plants of the North American Indians*. U.S. Department of Agriculture, Misc. Pub. No. 237, pp. 1–83. Washington: Government Printing Office, 1936.

C. ARTS, ARCHITECTURE, AND SCULPTURE

Painters and Illustrators of Indians

Britzman, Home E., and Adams, Ramon. *Charles M. Russell, The Cowboy Artist*. Pasadena, Calif.: Trails End Publishing Co., 1948.

Bushnell, David I., Jr. "Seth Eastman: The Master Painter of the North American Indian," *Smithsonian Miscellaneous Collections*, Vol. 87, No. 3, Pub. 3136. Washington: Smithsonian Institution, 1932.

De Voto, Bernard. "The First Illustrators of the West," in *Across the Wide Missouri*. Boston: Houghton Mifflin Co., 1947, pp. 391–415.

Donaldson, Thomas. "The George Catlin Indian Gallery in the United States National Museum, with Memoir and Statistics," in *Annual Report of the Board of Regents of the Smithsonian Institution to July, 1885*, Part II. Washington: Government Printing Office, 1886.

Draper, Benjamin. "John Mix Stanley," *Antiques*, XLI (1942), 180–82.

Ewers, John C. *Artists of the Old West*. Garden City, N.Y.: Doubleday & Co., 1965.

Ferguson, C. W. "Americans Nobody Knows: George Catlin," *PTA Magazine*, LX (October 1965), 20–23.

Gridley, Marion E. *America's Indian Statues*. A publication of the Amerindian. Chicago: Towertown Press, 1966.

Haberly, Lloyd. *Pursuit of the Horizon*. (Life of Catlin.) New York: The Macmillan Co., 1948.

Halpin, Marjorie. *Catlin's Indian Gallery*. Washington: Smithsonian Institution, 1965.

Howell, Edgar M. *Herman Stieffel, Soldier Artist of the West*. U.S. National Museum Bulletin No. 225. Washington: Smithsonian Institution, 1960.

Hunter, H. Chadwick. "The American Indian in Painting," *Art and Archaeology*, VIII (1919), 81–97.

Indiana Historical Society. *George Winter: Journals and Indian Paintings, 1837–1839*. Indianapolis: 1948. (Miami Indians of Indiana.)

Kane, Paul. *Wanderings of an Artist among the Indians of North America*. Toronto: The Radisson Society of Canada, 1925.

Kinietz, W. Vernon. *John Mix Stanley and His Indian Paintings*. Ann Arbor: University of Michigan Press, 1942.

McCracken, Harold. *Portrait of the Old West*. New York: McGraw-Hill Book Co., 1952.

———. *George Catlin and the Old Frontier*. New York: McGraw-Hill Book Co., 1959.

———. *Frederic Remington's Own West*. New York: Dial Press, 1960.

McDermott, John Francis. "The J. O. Lewis Port Folio," [*sic*] *Minnesota History*, XXXIII, No. 1 (Spring 1952), 20–21.

———. *Seth Eastman: Pictorial Historian of the Indian*. Norman: University of Oklahoma Press, 1961.

MacLeod, Margaret A. "Peter Rindisbacher, Red River Artist," *The Beaver Magazine* [Winnipeg], December 1945.

Peattie, Louis R. "He Caught the Splendor of the First Americans," *Reader's Digest*, October 1964, pp. 257–62. (George Catlin.)

Quimby, George. *Indians of the Western Frontier*. Chicago: Chicago Museum of Natural History, n.d. (Catlin paintings.)

Rathbone, Perry T. *Charles Wimar, Painter of the Indian Frontier*. St. Louis: City Art Museum of St. Louis, 1946.

Ross, Marvin C. *The West of Alfred Jacob Miller*. Norman: University of Oklahoma Press, 1951.

Taft, Robert. *Artists and Illustrators of the Old West*. New York: Scribner's, 1953.

Indian Arts, Architecture, and Design in White Culture

American Home. Special issue titled "The Southwest," LXXIII, No. 3 (March 1970). (Features Indian architecture in Southwest homes, Indian motifs in home decoration and furnishings, and Indian food used by whites.)

Bossom, Alfred C. "New Styles of American Architecture and What We Might Learn from the Mayas," *World's Work*, LVI (June 1928), 189–95.

Burchard, John, and Bush-Brown, Albert. *The Architecture of America*. Boston: Little, Brown & Co., 1961. (Scattered references; consult index.)

Colton, Amy R. "The Red Man's Contribution to Our Household Art," *Garden and Home Builder*, XLIV (September 1926), 31, 62, 74.

Eastman, Charles. "The Indians' Contribution to the Art of America," *Red Man*, VII (December 1914), 133–40.

Harrington, L. "Revival of Northern Indian Art Forms," *School Arts*, XLVIII (January 1949), 146–49. (Entire issue titled: "North American Handicrafts.")

Hyde, Blanche E. "Indian Art and Its Use in Homes Today," *Practical Home Economics*, XI (December 1933), 355, 369, 372.

Lips, Julius E. *The Savage Hits Back*. New Hyde Park, N.Y.: University Books, 1966.

Lowenstein, Milton D. "Indian Art in Search of Americans," *Journal of American Indian Education*, III, No. 1 (October 1963), 11–13.

American Indian Influence on Costume

Chicago Tribune, October 2, 1967, Sec. 2 ("Feminique"). Indian style clothing, jewelry, furnishings.

———, June 2, 1969, Sec. 2 ("Feminique"). Fringed leather in style.

Good Housekeeping, February 1960. "The Seminoles Started Something," pp. 124, 126.

Ickeringill, Nan. "We're Stealing from the Indians, Again," *New York Times,* July 23, 1968, p. 38.

Kanjer, Judy. "Fashions With Pow . . . Wow!" *Midwest Magazine, Chicago Sunday Sun-Times,* June 15, 1969, pp. 22, 25–26.

Livingstone, Evelyn. "Here's the Real Indian Look," *Chicago Tribune,* March 16, 1969, Sec. 5, p. 3.

———. "Take Me to Your Wigwam," *Chicago Tribune Magazine,* January 11, 1970, pp. 44–47. (Indian styles in women's dress.)

Loosley, Elizabeth W. "Early Canadian Costume," *Canadian Historical Review,* XXIII (1942), 349–62.

Rattner, Joan. "Sophisticated Squaws," *This Week* magazine, *Chicago Daily News,* July 29, 1936. (Southwest Indian styles in women's dresses.)

———. "Indian Winter," *This Week* magazine, *Chicago Daily News,* September 7, 1968, pp. 3–4.

Varro, Barbara. "Indian Powwow in Spring Prints," *Chicago Sunday Sun-Times,* January 5, 1970, p. 42.

Walker, Ray. "Far Out Fashions," *Chicago Tribune,* September 16, 1968, Sec. 2, p. 13. (Indian styles in the hippie set.)

Warwick, Edward, and Pitz, Henry C. *Early American Costume.* New York: Century Co., 1929. (Frontier, Chap. VIII.)

Wilcox, R. Turner. *Five Centuries of American Costume.* New York: Charles Scribner's Sons, 1963.

D. EDUCATION AND CHILD CARE

Buchwald, June, and Smith, Harriet. *Children of Indian America.* Chicago: Chicago Natural History Museum, 1958. (Juvenile.)

Dennis, Wayne. *The Hopi Child.* New York: John Wiley, 1965.

Erikson, Erik H. *Childhood and Society.* 2d ed. rev. New York: W. W. Norton, 1963.

Havighurst, Robert J. *Education.* Boston: Little, Brown & Co., 1968. (Chapter on Hopi Indians.)

———, and Neugarten, Bernice. *American Indian and White Children.* Chicago: University of Chicago Press, 1955.

Pettit, G. A. *Primitive Education in North America.* Berkeley: University of California Press, 1946.

E. GAMES, SPORTS, AND RECREATION

Baldwin, Gordon C. *Games of the American Indian.* New York: W. W. Norton & Co., 1969.

Beauchamp, W. M. "Iroquois Games," *Journal of American Folk-Lore,* IX, No. 35 (October–December 1896), 269–77.

Borhegyi, Stephan F. and Suzanne. *The Rubber Ball Game of Ancient America.* Milwaukee: Milwaukee Public Museum, 1963.

Carter, E. Russell. *The Gift Is Rich.* New York: Friendship Press, 1968. (Chap. 4, "They Taught Us to Play," pp. 29–34.)

Culin, Stewart. "American Indian Games," *American Anthropologist,* new series, V (January–March 1903).

———. "Games of the North American Indians," in *Twenty-Fourth Annual Report, Bureau of American Ethnology, 1902–1908.* Washington: Government Printing Office, 1907.

Fanning, "Indian Games and Toys," *Grade Teacher,* LXXII (September 1954), p. 30.

Folprecht, William. "Spring's Speed Sport," *Scholastic Roto,* XXII, No. 6 (March 1964). (Lacrosse.)

Hallett, L. F. "Indian Games," *Bulletin of the Massachusetts Archaeological Society,* XVI (1955), 25–28.

Hunt, Sarah E., and Cain, Ethel. *Games the World Around.* New York: Ronald Press Co., 1950. (34 North American Indian games, pp. 166–83.)

Lingard, Bil. "Lacrosse, the Fastest Game on Two Feet," reprint from *The Beaver* in *Akwesasne Notes,* II, No. 3 (June 1970), p. 6.

MacFarlan, Allan A. *Book of American Indian Games.* New York: Association Press, 1958.

———. *Living like Indians.* New York: Association Press, 1961. (Campcraft.)

Mason, D. D. "Indian Games," *Instructor,* LXVI (October 1936), pp. 51+.

Menke, Frank G. *The New Encyclopedia of Sports.* New York: S. A. Barnes, 1947.

Saloman, Julian H. *The Book of Indian Crafts and Indian Lore.* New York: Harper & Bros., 1928. (Chap. XII, "Games.")

Winchester, James H. "Roughest Sport of Them All," *Boy's Life,* March 1962, pp. 14–15, 71. (Lacrosse.)

F. Inventions and Industries

Adney, Edwin T., and Chapelle, H. I. *The Bark Canoes and Skin Boats of North America.* Publication of Smithsonian Institution, Museum of History and Technology. Washington: Government Printing Office, 1964.

Appy, E. P. "Ancient Mining in America," *American Antiquarian and Oriental Journal,* XI (January–November 1889), 92–99.

Browne, C. A. "The Chemical Industries of the American Aborigines," *Isis,* XXIII (1935), 406–24.

Griffin, James B., ed. *Lake Superior Copper and the Indians.* Ann Arbor: University of Michigan Press, 1961.

Nordenskjöld, Erland. "The American Indian as an Inventor," *Journal of the Royal Anthropological Institute of Great Britain and Ireland,* LIX (1929), 273–309. Reprinted in A. L. Kroeber and T. T. Waterman, eds., *Sourcebook in Anthropology,* rev. ed. New York: Harcourt Brace & Co., 1931, pp. 489–505. Bobbs-Merrill reprint #A-386.

Stone, Doris, and Balser, Carlos. *Aboriginal Metalwork of Lower Central America*. Chicago: Field Museum of Natural History, 1967.

Wissler, Clark. *The American Indian*. 3d ed. Gloucester, Mass.: Peter Smith, 1957. Reprint from Oxford University Press, 1938. (Chap. VIII, "Special Inventions," pp. 132–40.)

G. Influence on Language

Adams, Ramon. *Western Words: A Dictionary of the American West*. Norman: University of Oklahoma Press, 1968.

Bowen, Robert O. *An Alaskan Dictionary*. Spenard, Alaska: Nooshnik Press, 1965.

Carter, E. Russell. *The Gift Is Rich*. New York: Friendship Press, 1968. (Chap. 5, "Now We Say It This Way," pp. 35–37.)

Chamberlain, Alexander F. "Memorials of the Indian," *Journal of American Folk-Lore*, XV, No. 17 (April–June 1902), 107–16.

———. "Algonkian Words in American English: A Study in the Contact of the White Man and the Indians," *Journal of American Folk-Lore*, XV, No. 19 (October–December 1902), 240–67.

Friederici, Georg. *Amerikanistisches Worterbuch*. Hamburg: Cram, De Gruyter & Co., 1960. (German, Spanish, and English text.)

Laird, Charlton. *The Miracle of Language*. Greenwich, Conn.: Fawcett Publications, 1960, pp. 98–100. Reprint from World Publishing Co., 1960.

Mathews, Mitford. *Dictionary of Americanisms*. 2 vols. Chicago: University of Chicago Press, 1951; one vol. ed., 1956. (Borrowed words, phrases, pp. 866–80, *et passim*.)

Mencken, H. L. *The American Language*. New York: Alfred A. Knopf, 1947, *passim*.

Pei, Mario. *The Story of Language*. Philadelphia: J. B. Lippincott Co., 1949, pp. 388–90.

Skeat, Walter William. "Notes on English Etymology and on Words of Brazilian and Peruvian Origin," *Transactions of the Philological Society* (London), *1885–87*.

———. "The Language of Mexico, and Words of West Indian Origin," *Transactions of the Philological Society* (London), *1888–90*.

———. *Etymological Dictionary of the English Language*. Oxford: Clarendon Press, 1953.

H. Law and Political Theory

Baudin, Louis. *A Socialist Empire, the Incas of Peru*. Princeton, N.J.: D. Van Nostrand Co., 1961.

Cohen, Felix S. *Handbook of Federal Indian Law*. U.S. Department of Interior. Washington: Government Printing Office, 1941.

———. *Handbook of Federal Indian Law, With Reference Tables and Index*. U.S. Department of Interior. Washington: Government Printing Office, 1942.

Engels, Frederick. *The Origin of the Family, Private Property, and the State.* Chicago: Charles H. Kerr & Co., 1902.

Federal Indian Law. U.S. Department of Interior. Washington: Government Printing Office, 1958.

Hargrett, Lester. *A Bibliography of the Constitutions and Laws of the American Indians.* Cambridge: Harvard University Press, 1947.

Hoebel, E. Adamson. "Law and Anthropology," *Virginia Law Review,* XXXII (June 1946), 835–54. Bobbs-Merrill reprint #A-117.

———. *The Law of Primitive Man.* Cambridge: Harvard University Press, 1967.

———, and Llewellyn, Karl N. *The Cheyenne Way: Conflict and Case Law in Primitive Jurisprudence.* Norman: University of Oklahoma Press, 1961.

Jefferson, Thomas. "The Aborigines," in *Notes on the State of Virginia,* ed. by William Peden. Chapel Hill: University of North Carolina Press, 1955.

Kappler, Charles J., ed. *Indian Affairs, Laws, and Treaties.* 5 vols. Washington: Government Printing Office, 1904–1941.

Lowie, Robert H. *Some Aspects of Political Organization among the North American Aborigines.* London: Royal Anthropological Society, 1948.

MacLeod, William C. *The Origin of the State, Reconsidered in the Light of the Data of Aboriginal North America.* Philadelphia: the author, 1928.

Miller, Walter B. "Two Concepts of Authority," *American Anthropologist,* Vol. LVII (April 1955), 271–289. Bobbs-Merrill reprint # A-158.

Morgan, Lewis H. *Ancient Society.* Chicago: Charles H. Kerr & Co., 1910.

———. *Government and Institutions of the Iroquois.* Rochester: Lewis H. Morgan Chapter, New York State Archaeological Association, 1928.

Murra, John V. "On Inca Political Structure," in Vern F. Ray, ed., *Systems of Political Control and Bureaucracy in Human Societies.* Seattle: University of Washington Press, 1958. Bobbs-Merrill reprint # A-169.

Noon, John A. *Laws and Government of the Grand River Iroquois.* New York: Johnson Reprint Corporation, 1964.

Peterson, H. L. "American Indian Political Participation." *Annals of the American Academy of Political and Social Science,* CCCXI (May 1957), 116–26.

Powers, Mabel. *The Indian as Peacemaker.* New York: Fleming H. Revell Co., 1932.

Price, Monroe E. *Native American Law Manual.* Los Angeles: University of California School of Law and California Indian Legal Services, 1970.

Richardson, Jane. *Law and Status among the Kiowa Indians.* Monograph no. 1, American Ethnological Society, 1940. Reissued, Seattle: University of Washington Press, 1966.

Rousseau, Jean Jacques. *The First and Second Discourses,* ed. by Roger D. Masters. New York: St. Martin's Press, 1964.

Waring, Antonio, ed. *Laws of the Creek Nation.* Athens: University of Georgia Press, 1960.

White Roots of Peace. *The Great Law of Peace of the People of the Longhouse.* Rooseveltown, N.Y.: White Roots of Peace, [1970].

Wisconsin Indians Research Institute. *Journal of the Wisconsin Indians Research Institute,* Vols. I–V (1965–69), Constitutions of Wisconsin tribes.

I. AMERICAN INDIAN INFLUENCE ON LITERATURE, INCLUDING DRAMA, FICTION, FOLKLORE, AND POETRY.

Alexander, H. B. "Indian Songs and English Verse," *American Speech,* I, No. 11 (August 1926), 571–74.

Beder, E. F. "Kingston to Newson to Blake; or Bibliographical Adventures among the Indians," *Bulletin New York Public Library,* XLVI (June 1942), 525–30.

Beede, A. McG. *Toward the Sun.* Bismarck, N.D.: Bismarck Tribune Co., 1916. (Poetry.)

Bissell, Benjamin. *The American Indian in English Literature of the Eighteenth Century.* New Haven: Yale University Press, 1925. Reprint, Archon Books, 1968.

Carleton, P. D. "The Indian Captivity," *American Literature,* XV (January 1926), 65–68.

Chaplin, Ralph. *Only the Drums Remembered, a Memento for Leschi.* Tacoma, Wash.: Demmier Printing Co., 1960. (Poem about a Nisqually chief, by the noted IWW poet and songwriter.)

Clark, Barrett H., ed. *Favorite American Plays of the Nineteenth Century.* Princeton: Princeton University Press, 1943.

Coan, Otis W., and Lillard, Richard G. *America in Fiction, an Annotated List of Novels that Interpret Aspects of Life in the United States.* Stanford, Calif.: Stanford University Press, 1949.

Dorson, Richard M., ed. *America Begins: Early American Writing.* New York: Pantheon, 1950.

Eich, L. M. "American Indian Plays," *Quarterly Journal of Speech,* XXX (April 1944), 212–15.

Fairchild, H. N. *The Noble Savage, A Study in Romantic Naturalism.* New York: Columbia University Press, 1928.

Fergusson, Harvey. "The Cult of the Indian," *Scribner's,* LXXXVIII (August 1930), 129–233.

Fiedler, Leslie. *The Return of the Vanishing American.* New York: Stein & Day, 1968.

Field, Rachel. *American Folk and Fairy Tales.* New York: Charles Scribner's, 1943.

Greenway, John. *Folklore of the Great West.* Palo Alto: Great West Publishing Co., 1969.

Hadlock, R. "Indians in Literature," *Instructor,* LXXVI (November 1966), 109–10.

Hartley, Alexander. "For an Indian Theater," *Theatre Arts,* X (March 1926), 191–202.

Keiser, Albert. *The Indian in American Literature.* New York: Oxford University Press, 1933.

La Hood, M. J. "Light in the Forest: History as Fiction," *English Journal,* LV (March 1966), 298–304.

Leary, Lewis. *Articles on American Literature, 1900–1950.* Durham, N.C.: Duke University Press, 1954. (Indian listings: pp. 367–68.)

Life, editors of. *The Life Treasury of American Folklore.* New York: Time Inc., 1961.

Melville, Herman. *The Confidence Man.* New York: Hendricks House, 1954. (Chap. 26, "Concerning the Metaphysics of Indian-hating . . .")

Neihardt, John G. *A Cycle of the West.* Lincoln: University of Nebraska Press, 1967. (Poetry.)

Orians, George H. "The Indian Hater in Early American Fiction," *Journal of American History,* XXVII (1933), 34–44.

———. "The Cult of the Vanishing American: A Century View, 1834–1934," *University of Toledo Studies,* December 1934.

Pearce, Roy Harvey. "The Significance of the Captivity Narrative," *American Literature,* XIX (March 1947), 1–20.

———. "The Metaphysics of Indian Hating," *Ethnohistory,* IV (1957), 27–40.

———. *The Savages of America.* Rev. ed. Baltimore: Johns Hopkins Press, 1965.

Pearce, T. M. "American Traditions and Our Histories of Literature," *American Literature,* XIV (May 1942), 276–84.

Rourke, Constance. *American Humor: A Study of the National Character.* New York: Harcourt Brace & Co., 1931.

———. *The Roots of American Culture and Other Essays.* New York: Harcourt Brace & Co., 1942.

Russell, Jason A. "The Narratives of Indian Captivities," *Education,* LI (October 1930), 84–88.

———. "The Southwest Border Indian in the Writing of William Gilmore Simms," *Education,* LI (November 1930), 144–57.

———. *The Indian in American Literature, 1775–1875.* Ithaca, N.Y.: the author, June 1932. (Summary of dissertation.)

Sarett, Lew. *Slow Smoke.* New York: Henry Holt & Co., 1925. (Poetry.)

———. *The Collected Poems of Lew Sarett.* New York: Henry Holt & Co., 1941.

Seeber, D. D. "Diderot and Chief Logan's Speech," *Modern Language Notes,* LX (March 1945), 176–78.

Skinner, Charles M. *Myths and Legends of Our Own Land.* 2 vols. Philadelphia: J. B. Lippincott, 1896.

Sper, Felix. *From Native Roots: A Panorama of Our Regional Drama.* Caldwell, Idaho: Caxton Printers, 1948.

Untermeyer, Louis, ed. *American Poetry.* New York: Harcourt Brace & Co., 1931. (Two poems by Phillip Freneau; also "Indian Poetry," pp. 687–704.)

Williams, Mentor L. *Schoolcraft's Indian Legends.* East Lansing: Michigan State University Press, 1957.

J. SOME TWENTIETH-CENTURY INDIAN FICTION: A RANDOM SAMPLING

By Indian Authors:

McNickle, D'Arcy (Flathead). *The Surrounded.* New York: Dodd, Mead & Co., 1936. Conflict between tribal traditions and an Indian boy's desire for a wider life.

———. *Runner in the Sun.* New York: Winston, 1954.

Mathews, John Joseph (Osage). *Sundown.* New York: Longmans Green & Co., 1934. The effect of the discovery of oil on Osage life.

Momaday, N. Scott. (Kiowa). *House Made of Dawn.* New York: Harper & Row, 1968. Pulitzer prize novel, 1969. The disintegration of an Indian ex-GI in the city, and his eventual return to the reservation.

Oskison, John Milton (Cherokee). *Brothers Three.* New York: The Macmillan Co., 1935. Novel of an Oklahoma farm family in frontier times. Not an Indian subject, but listed here because of the author's background.

By Non-Indian Authors:

Borland, Hal. *When the Legends Die.* New York: Bantam Books, 1964. (First published by Lippincott, 1963.) "The story of a modern Indian boy who is orphaned in the wilderness and survives in the face of the most incredible odds . . . When he finally escapes he begins a long, tortuous search to find himself that takes him deep into the white world . . ." [Editors]

Capps, Ben. *A Woman of the People.* New York: Duell, Sloan, & Pearce, 1966. White girl captive among the Comanches.

Corle, Edwin. *In Winter Light.* New York: Pennant Books, 1954. (First published by Duell, Sloan, & Pearce, 1949.) Navajo-white conflict.

Ferber, Edna. *Cimarron.* Garden City, N.Y.: Doubleday, 1930. What oil did to the Osages.

Fisher, Vardis. *Pemmican.* New York: Pocket Books, 1957. (First published by Doubleday, 1956.) Indians of the Hudson Bay region.

Forster, Logan A. *Proud Land.* New York: Bantam Books, 1958. (First published by Random House, 1954.) Fictional account of Victorio, Apache war chief.

Gerson, Noel B. *Daughter of Eve.* Garden City, N.Y.: Doubleday, 1958. A novel of Pocahontas.

Holmes, L. P. *Modoc: The Last Sundown.* New York: Bantam Books, 1959. (First published by Dodd Mead, 1957.) The Modoc war.

Jayne, Mitchell F. *Old Fish Hawk.* Philadelphia: Lippincott, 1969. An old Indian's last hunt.

LaFarge, Oliver. *Laughing Boy.* New York: Pocket Books, 1951. (First published by Houghton Mifflin, 1929.) A Pulitzer prize-winning novel of Navajo life.

Laird, Charlton. *Thunder on the River.* Boston: Little, Brown & Co., 1948. A Yankee captive in the Black Hawk war.

McNichols, Charles. *Crazy Weather*. New York: Bantam Books, 1954. (First published by Macmillan, 1943.) Book-of-the-month selection, March 1944. White boy among the Mojaves.

Manfred, Frederick. [Feike Feikema] *Conquering Horse*. New York: McDowell Oblensky, 1959. How a young Sioux came to manhood.

————. *Scarlet Plume*. New York: Trident Press, 1964. Story of a white woman married to a Sioux Indian during the Minnesota uprising of 1862.

Payne, Robert. *The Chieftain*. New York: Pocket Books, 1954. (First published by Prentice-Hall, 1953.) Novel of Chief Joseph and the Nez Perce war.

Richter, Conrad. *The Light in the Forest*. New York: Alfred A. Knopf, 1953. Reprinted seven times by 1965. Filmed by Walt Disney, 1958. Based on a study of Heckewelder and Zeisberger, it is the story of a white boy captured by the Delawares, who learns to prefer the Indian life. ". . . stands as a corrective to the Indian distorted beyond recognition in hundreds of novels, motion pictures, television plays, and articles. Its honest picture of Delaware life restores to the Indian some of the dignity and integrity stolen from him by his detractors. In language and manner the Delaware emerges as a man of faith and honor. And yet the novel does not give the impression that every Indian acted like every other. There is a wide range of behavior. . . ." (M. J. LaHood, *English Journal*, March 1966, p. 304.)

Sandoz, Mari. *Cheyenne Autumn*. New York: McGraw-Hill, 1953. Well-done story of the Cheyenne flight from Oklahoma to Montana in 1878. Filmed in 1964.

Schaefer, Jack. *The Canyon*. Boston: Houghton Mifflin Co. in cooperation with Ballantine Books, 1953. "A story of a young Cheyenne in the days before the white man."

Slaughter, Frank G. *The Warrior*. New York: Permabooks, 1957. (First published by Doubleday, 1956.) A novel of the Seminoles in the time of Osceola.

Tracy, Don. *Cherokee*. New York: Pocket Books, 1958. (First published by Dial Press, 1957.) A novel of the Cherokees during the time of their national destruction.

K. INDIAN MEDICINE, DRUGS, AND PSYCHOLOGY

Ackerknecht, Erwin H. "White Indians: Psychological and Physiological Peculiarities of White Children Abducted and Reared by North American Indians," *Bulletin of the History of Medicine*, XV, No. 1 (January 1944), 15–36.

Adams, William R. "Aboriginal American Medicine and Surgery," *Proceedings Indiana Academy of Science*, LXI (1951), Indianapolis: 1952, 49–53.

Barron, Frank, *et al*. "The Hallucinogenic Drugs," *Scientific American*, CCX, No. 4 (April 1964), 29–37. Reprint: San Francisco: W. H. Freeman Co. (No. 483.)

Bradley, Will T. "Medical Practices of the New England Aborigines," *Journal of the American Pharmaceutical Association*, XXV, No. 2 (February 1936), 138–47.

Brooks, Harlow. "The Medicine of the American Indian," *Journal of Laboratory and Clinical Medicine,* XIX, No. 1 (October 1933), 1–23.

Castaneda, Carlos. *The Teachings of Don Juan: A Yaqui Way of Knowledge.* Berkeley: University of California Press, 1968. Reprint, New York: Ballantine Books, 1969 et seq.

Chesnut, V. K. *Plants Used by the Indians of Mendocino County, California.* U.S. Department of Agriculture, Division of Botany, Contributions of U.S. National Herbarium, VII, No. 3. Washington: Government Printing Office, 1902.

Corlett, William T. *The Medicine Man of the American Indian.* Springfield, Ill.: Charles C Thomas, 1935.

Curtin, L. S. M. *Healing Herbs of the Upper Rio Grande.* Los Angeles: Southwest Museum, 1965.

Fenton, William H. "Contacts Between Iroquois Herbalism and Colonial Medicine," *Annual Report Smithsonian Institution, 1941.* Washington: Government Printing Office, 1942, pp. 503–26.

Holmstedt, Bo, and Kline, Nathan S., eds. *Ethnopharmacologic Search for Psychoactive Drugs, 1967.* U.S. Department of Health, Education, & Welfare. Washington: Public Health Service Publication No. 1645, 1967.

Hrdlička, Aleš. "Disease, Medicine and Surgery among the American Aborigines," *Journal of the American Medical Association,* XCIX, No. 20 (November 12, 1932), 1661–66.

Jung, Carl. *Contributions to Analytical Psychology.* New York: Harcourt Brace & Co., 1928, pp. 136–40.

Krogman, Wilton M. "Medical Practices and Diseases of the Aboriginal American Indians," *Ciba Symposia,* I, No. 1 (April 1939), 11–18.

LaBarre, Weston. "Primitive Psychotherapy in Native American Cultures," *Journal of Abnormal and Social Psychology,* XLII, No. 3 (July 1947), 294–309.

Mahr, August C. "Materia Medica and Therapy among the North American Forest Indians," *Ohio State Archaeological and Historical Quarterly,* LX, No. 4 (1951), 331–54.

Major, Robert C. "Aboriginal American Medicine North of Mexico," *Annals of Medical History,* new series, X, No. 6 (November 1938), 534–49.

Roys, Ralph L. *The Ethno-Botany of the Maya.* New Orleans: Department of Middle American Research, Tulane University, 1931.

Scully, Virginia. *A Treasury of American Indian Herbs.* New York: Crown Publishers, 1970.

Smith, Huron H. "Ethnobotany of the Menomini Indians," *Bulletin of the Public Museum of the City of Milwaukee,* IV, No. 1 (December 10, 1923), 1–174.

———. "Ethnobotany of the Meskwaki Indians," *Bulletin of the Public Museum of the City of Milwaukee,* IV, No. 2 (April 7, 1928), 175–326.

———. "Ethnobotany of the Ojibwe Indians," *Bulletin of the Public Museum of the City of Milwaukee,* IV, No. 3 (May 2, 1932), 327–525.

————. "Ethnobotany of the Forest Potawatomi Indians," *Bulletin of the Public Museum of the City of Milwaukee*, VII, No. 1 (May 9, 1933), 1–230.

Speck, Frank G. "Medical Practices of Northeastern Algonquians," *Proceedings of the Nineteenth International Congress of Americanists, 1915.* Washington: 1917, pp. 303–21.

Stone, Eric. "Medicine among the Iroquois," *Annals of Medical History*, new series, VI, No. 6 (November 1934), 529–39.

————. *Medicine among the American Indians.* New York: Hafner Publishing Co., 1962. Reprint from 1932.

Sturtevant, William C. "Bibliography on American Indian Medicine and Health" (mimeographed). Washington: Smithsonian Institution, Bureau of American Ethnology, March 1962.

Vogel, Virgil J. "American Indian Influence on Medicine and Pharmacology," *The Indian Historian*, I, No. 1 (December 1967), 12–15.

————. *American Indian Medicine.* Norman: University of Oklahoma Press, 1970.

Wallace, Anthony F. C. "Dreams and Wishes of the Soul: A Type of Psychoanalytic Theory among the 17th Century Iroquois," *American Anthropologist*, new series, LX, No. 2 (April 1958), 234–48. Reprinted as "Psychoanalysis among the Iroquois of New York State," in Harold E. Driver, ed., *The Americas on the Eve of the Discovery*, Englewood Cliffs, N.J.: Prentice-Hall, 1964, pp. 69–79. Also Bobbs-Merrill reprint #A–229.

Weaver, Thomas, ed. *Essays in Medical Anthropology.* Southern Anthropology Society Proceedings, No. 1. Athens: University of Georgia Press, 1968.

Williams, John. "Dr. John Williams' Last Legacy, a Useful Family Herbal" (published as "The Indian Doctor"), ed. by Ray Brown and Egil Ramstad, *The Indiana History Bulletin*, XLI, No. 3 (March 1964), 35–56; XLI, No. 4 (April 1964), 59–70. Reprints available in two parts.

Wright, J. S. "Indian Medicine," *School Science and Mathematics*, XLV (April 1945), 329–35.

Youngken, H. W. "Drugs of the North American Indians," *American Journal of Pharmacy*, Pt. I, XCVI (July 1924), 485–502; Pt. II, XCVII (March 1925), 158–85; Pt. III, XCVII (April 1925), 257–71.

L. INDIAN INFLUENCE ON MUSIC

Austin, Mary. "American Indian Dance Drama," *Yale Review*, XIX (June 1930), 732–45.

Chase, Gilbert. *America's Music, from the Pilgrims to the Present.* New York: McGraw-Hill Book Co., 1955, pp. 121, 362–64, 385–401, 519, 523.

Fife, Austin E., and Redden, Francesca. "The Pseudo-Indian Folksongs of the Anglo-Americans and French-Canadians," *Journal of American Folklore*, LXVII (1954), 239–51, 379–94.

Gilbert, Henry F. "Personal Recollections of McDowell," *New Music Review*, II (1912), 132.

Howard, John Tasker. *Our American Music, Three Hundred Years of It.* 3d ed.

rev. New York: Thomas Y. Crowell, 1954, pp. 236–37, 357–59, 381–83, 389–90, 407–11, 590–91, 725–27 (bibliography).

Schuller, Gunther. *Early Jazz.* New York: Oxford University Press, 1968. See also review by Nat Pierce, *Saturday Review,* July 13, 1968, pp. 46–47. (Origin of jazz traced to American Indian influence.)

Simpson, Sally. "Music of Primitive Cultures Core of Today's Rock Groups," *Chicago Tribune,* July 20, 1969, sec. 5, p. 12.

Songs of the Wigwam. Delaware, Ohio: Cooperative Recreation Service, n.d.

Wheelock, Raymond. "Did Swing Come from the Indians?" *Educational Music Magazine,* XXIII (November–December 1943), 20–21, 50.

See also American Indian Music.

M. American Indian Place Names

Beauchamp, William. *Aboriginal Place Names of New York.* Bulletin 108, New York State Museum. Albany: 1907.

Becker, Donald William. *Indian Place Names in New Jersey.* Cedar Grove, N.J.: Phillips-Campbell Publishing Co., 1964.

Douglas-Lithgow, R. S. *Dictionary of American Indian Place and Proper Names in New England.* Salem, Mass.: Salem Press, 1909.

Dunn, Jacob P. *True Indian Stories, with Glossary of Indiana Indian Names.* Indianapolis: Sentinel Printing Co., 1909. Reprint, North Manchester, Ind.: Lawrence W. Shultz, 1964.

Eckstorm, Fannie H. *Indian Place-Names of the Penobscot Valley and the Maine Coast.* Orono, Me.: University Press, 1941.

Federal Writers' Project. *The Seminole Indians in Florida.* Tallahassee: Florida State Department of Agriculture [1940?]. ("Indian Place Names in Florida," pp. 79–81.)

Halbert, H. S. "Choctaw Indian Names in Alabama and Mississippi," *Transactions of the Alabama Historical Society,* III (1898–1899), ed. by T. M. Owen. Tuscaloosa: 1899.

Harrington, John P. *Our State Names.* Washington: Smithsonian Institution, 1955.

Holmer, Nils M. "Indian Place Names in South America and the Antilles," *Names,* VIII, No. 3 (September 1960), 133–149; No. 4 (December 1960), 197–219.

Huden, John C. *Indian Place Names of New England.* New York: Museum of the American Indian, 1962.

Kenny, Hamill. *Indian Place Names of Maryland.* Baltimore: Waverly Press, 1961.

Kroeber, A. L. "California Place Names of Indian Origin," *University of California Publications in American Archaeology and Ethnology,* XII, No. 2 (June 15, 1916), 31–69.

Kuhm, Herbert W. "Indian Place-Names in Wisconsin," *The Wisconsin Archeologist,* new series, XXXIII, Nos. 1–2 (March and June 1952), 1–157.

Mahr, A. C. "Indian River and Place Names in Ohio," *The Ohio Historical Quarterly,* LXVI, No. 2 (April 1957), 137–39.

Martin, Maria Ewing. "Origin of Ohio Place Names," *Ohio Archaeological and Historical Publications*, XIV (Columbus: 1905), 272–290.

Pearce, T. M. *New Mexico Place Names*. Albuquerque: University of New Mexico Press, 1965.

Read, William A. "Louisiana Place Names of Indian Origin," *Bulletin of Louisiana State University*, new series, XIX, No. 2 (Baton Rouge: February 1927).

————. "Indian Place Names in Alabama," *University Studies*, XXIX. Baton Rouge: Louisiana State University Press, 1937.

Ruttenber, E. M. "Footprints of the Red Men: Indian Geographical Names in the Valley of Hudson's River [etc.]," *Proceedings New York State Historical Association*, VI (1906), 4–234.

Rydjord, John. *Indian Place-Names. Their Origin, Evolution, and Meanings, Collected in Kansas . . .* Norman: University of Oklahoma Press, 1968.

Sealock, Richard B., and Seelyn, Pauline A. *Bibliography of Place-Name Literature, United States and Canada*. 2d ed. Chicago: American Library Association, 1967. (See "Indian Names" in subject index; see also *Names* magazine for annual supplements to this work.)

Starr, Frederick. *Aztec Place Names, Their Meaning and Mode of Composition*. Chicago: the author, 1920.

Stewart, George R. *Names on the Land*. New York: Random House, 1945.

Tooker, William Wallace. *The Indian Place-Names on Long Island*. Port Washington, N.Y.: Ira J. Friedman, 1962. Reprint from 1911.

Trumbull, J. Hammond. "The Composition of Indian Geographical Names, Illustrated from the Algonkin Languages," *Collections Connecticut Historical Society*, II (Hartford: 1870), 3–50.

————. *Indian Names of Places [etc.] in and on the Borders of Connecticut*. Hartford: the author, 1881.

Verwyst, Chrysostom. "Geographical Names in Wisconsin, Minnesota, and Michigan Having a Chippewa Origin," *Collections of the State Historical Society of Wisconsin*, XII (Madison: 1892), 390 *ff*.

Vogel, Virgil J. *Indian Place Names in Illinois*. Springfield: Illinois State Historical Society, 1963. Reprint, with slight changes and additions, of four articles from the *Journal of the Illinois State Historical Society*, LV, Nos. 1, 2, 3, 4 (1962).

N. Indian Trails and Portage Paths: Influence on Canals, City Sites, Highways, and Railways

Ayres, Harral. *The Great Trail of New England*. Boston: Houghton Mifflin Co., 1940.

Bolton, Reginald Pelham. "Indian Paths in the Great Metropolis" [New York], *Indian Notes and Monographs*, No. 23. New York: Museum of the American Indian, 1922. Text and maps bound separately.

Dunbar, Seymour. *A History of Travel in America*. New York: Tudor Publishing Co., 1937.

Grover, Frank R. *Some Indian Landmarks on the North Shore.* Chicago: Chicago Historical Society, 1905.

Hulbert, Archer Butler. *Red Men's Roads.* Columbus: Fred J. Herr & Co., 1900.

———. "Indian Thoroughfares of Ohio," *Ohio Archaeological and Historical Quarterly,* VIII (1900), 263–95.

———. *Historic Highways of America.* 16 vols. Cleveland: Arthur H. Clark Co., 1902–1903.

> See especially: Vol. I. *Roads of the Mound Builders*
> Vol. II. *Indian Thoroughfares*
> Vol. VII. *Portage Paths*

Hurlbut, Floy. "Our Highways, An Indian Heritage." *Proceedings Indiana Academy of Science,* LXII (1953), 266–71.

Meyer, William E. "Indian Trails of the Southeast," *Annual Report U.S. Bureau of American Ethnology, 1924–25,* XLII. Washington: Government Printing Office, 1928, pp. 727–857.

Petersen, Clarence. "Indian Trails of Chicagoland," *Chicago Tribune Magazine,* May 27, 1962, Pt. d, pp. 16–21.

Quaife, Milo M. *Chicago's Highways Old and New: from Indian Trail to Motor Road.* Ann Arbor: University Microfilms, 1968. Reprint from 1928.

Rights, Douglas L. "The Trading Path to the Indians," *North Carolina Historical Review,* VIII, No. 4 (October 1931), 403–26.

Scharf, Albert. "Indian Trails and Villages of Chicago," Map, published 1901, showing trails and sites of 1804. Chicago Historical Society.

Spooner, Harry L. "The Other End of the Great Sauk Trail," *Journal of the Illinois State Historical Society,* XXIX, (July 1936), 121–34.

Steward, John F. "The Sac and Fox Trail," *ibid.,* IV, No. 2 (July 1911), 157 *ff.*

Tucker, Sarah Jones. *Indian Villages of the Illinois Country,* Vol. II, Scientific Papers, Pt. I, Atlas. Springfield: Illinois State Museum, 1942. A set of unbound maps, 1600s to 1835, with historical annotation.

Tyler, Poyntz, ed. *American Highways Today.* The Reference Shelf, XXIX, No. 1. New York: H. W. Wilson Co., 1957.

Wallace, Paul A. W. *Indian Paths of Pennsylvania.* Harrisburg: Pennsylvania Historical and Museum Commission, 1965.

Wilcox, Frank. *Ohio Indian Trails.* Kent, Ohio: Kent State University Press, 1970.

18. *List of Bibliographical Resources*

American Anthropologist. General Index, Current Anthropological Literature and Memoirs of the American Anthropological Association, 1888–1928, compiled by A. V. Kidder, *et al.,* 1930.

American Philosophical Society. *List of Papers and Books in the Society's Publications Classified According to Subject.* Philadelphia: The American Philosophical Society, 1940.

Brugge, David M., *et al. Navajo Bibliography.* Window Rock, Ariz.: Navajo Tribal Museum, 1967.

Bureau of Indian Affairs. *Publications Pricelist.* Publications Service, Haskell Institute, Lawrence, Kansas, 66044.

Butler, Ruth L. *A Bibliographical Checklist of North and Middle American Linguistics in the Edward E. Ayer Collections.* Chicago: Newberry Library, 1941.

Dockstader, Frederick J. *The American Indian in Graduate Studies. A Bibliography of Theses and Dissertations.* New York: Museum of the American Indian, Heye Foundation, 1957.

Gallagher, James J. *An Annotated Bibliography of Anthropological Materials for High School Use.* New York: The Macmillan Co., 1967.

Gibson, A. M. "Sources for Research on the American Indian," *Ethnohistory,* VII, No. 2 (Spring 1962), 121–36.

Gibson, G. D. "A Bibliography of Anthropological Bibliographies: The Americas," *Current Anthropology,* I (1960), 61–75.

Hagan, William T. *The Indian in American History.* New York: Published for the American Historical Association by the Macmillan Co., 1963. Rev. 1971.

Hill, Edward E., compiler. *Records of the Bureau of Indian Affairs.* 2 vols. Washington: National Archives and Records Service, 1965.

Hodge, F. W., ed. *Handbook of American Indians North of Mexico.* Bureau of American Ethnology, Bulletin No. 30. 2 vols. Washington: Government Printing Office, 1907–1910, II, 1179–1221. Reissued by Pageant Press and by Rowan and Littlefield, New York, 1959.

Klein, Bernard, and Icolari, Daniel, eds. *Reference Encyclopedia of the American Indian.* New York: B. Klein, 1967, 189–329.

Klyberg, Albert T. *A Critical Bibliography for the March of America Series.* Ann Arbor: University Microfilms, 1966.

Library of Congress. *Guide to the Study of the United States of America.* Washington: 1960.

Martin, John H., compiler. *List of Documents Concerning the Negotiation of Ratified Indian Treaties 1801–1869.* The National Archives, Special List No. 6. Washington: 1949.

Milwaukee Public Museum, Publications List.

Morgan, Edmund S. *The Mirror of the Indian: An Exhibition of Books and Other Source Materials* . . . Providence: Associates of the John Carter Brown Library, 1958. Reviewed, *Mississippi Valley Historical Review,* September 1958, p. 357.

Murdock, George P. *Ethnographic Bibliography of North America.* 3d ed. New Haven: Human Relations Area Files, 1960.

Museum of the American Indian, Heye Foundation. "List of Publications of the Museum of the American Indian," 9th ed., *Indian Notes and Monographs,* No. 49. New York: August 1957.

Pilling, James Constantine. *Bibliographies* of the Eskimo, Siouan, Iroquoian, Mushkhogean, Algonquian, Athapascan, Chinookan, Salishan, and Wakashan Languages, published at Washington by the Bureau of American Ethnology, 1887–1894, BAE Bulletins No. 1, 5, 6, 9, 13, 14, 15, 16, 19.

Rouse, Irving, and Goggin, J. M. *An Anthropological Bibliography of the Eastern Seaboard.* New Haven: Federation of the Yale Peabody Museum, 1947.

Smithsonian Institution. *National Museum and Indians,* Price List 55, September 1967.

Snodgrass, Marjorie P. *Economic Development of American Indians and Eskimos, 1930 through 1967, a Bibliography.* Washington: U.S. Department of Interior, Bureau of Indian Affairs, September 1968.

Southwest Museum Publications. Los Angeles: Southwest Museum.

Thwaites, R. G., ed., *Jesuit Relations and Allied Documents,* Vol. LXXI. Cleveland: Burrows Bros. Co., 1896–1901.

University of Oklahoma Press, current list, including Civilization of the American Indian series, American Exploration and Travel series, and the Western Frontier Library. *The American Indian.* Special list, 25¢ (Norman, Okla. 73069).

Vogel, Virgil J. "Bibliography: A Selected Listing" (The Indian Impact on Our Culture), *The Indian Historian,* I, No. 3 (June 1968), 36–38.

Weimer, David R. *Bibliography of American Culture, 1493–1875.* American Studies Association. Ann Arbor: University Microfilms, 1957.

Whiteford, Andrew Hunter. "North American Indians, 1492–1969," *Choice,* VI, No. 12 (February 1970), 1709–19.

See also: Specialized bibliographies under various subject headings herein.

Index

Rubber, Indian discovery, 10, 292, 296
Russell, Bertrand, 223
Russia, 240, 242, 270

Sacajawea, Shoshoni Indian, 345
Sackett, John, 323
Sahagún, Bernardino de, 15, 35
St. Augustine, Fla., 28
St. Clair, Gen. Arthur, 67; defeated by
  Indians, 74, 76, 287, 339
St. Joseph, Mo., 142
St. Lawrence Seaway, 214
St. Leger, Gen. Barry, 65
St. Louis, Mo., 139
St. Regis reserve, 227
Sainte-Marie, Buffy, 5, 323
Salamanca, N.Y., 153, 215
Samoset, Abnaki Indian, 41
San Francisco, Calif., 226–27; Indian
  Center burned, 229
Sand Creek massacre, 70, 149, 154–59
Santa Fe, N.M., 28
Sarett, Lew, 295
Sassamon, Wampanoag Indian, 32
Satanta, Kiowa chief, 345
Sauganash, Potawatomi Indian, 345
"Savage barrier," 142–44, 287–89
Scalp bounties, 50–52, 288
Scalping, 266
Schlesinger, Arthur M., Jr., 133, 286
Schuyler, Gen. Philip, 64, 75
Sculpture, Indian influence on, 296
Seattle, Indian chief, 346
Secretary of the Interior, 191, 194, 196–
  204; see also Department of Interior
Segundo, Thomas, 332
Self-determination, 151, 153, 172, 196–
  206, 213, 224, 243–45, 273, 276; see
  also Sovereignty; Tribal governments
Sequoya, Cherokee Indian, 289; biog.,
  346
Seven Years War, 32
Shabbona, Potawatomi Indian, 346
Sheridan, Brig. Gen. Michael, 160–62
Sherman, Paschal, 333
Sherman, Gen. William Tecumseh, 162n.
Sigourney, Lydia H., 280–81
Silent Eaters, 181
Silver, mined by Indians, 27, 295

Silverheels, Jay, 299, 323
Simkins, Francis Butler, 286
Simon, Simeon, 333
Sioux treaty of 1868, 227, 344
Sitting Bull, Sioux chief, 150, 180–85,
  292; biog., 346–47
Sixkiller, Jess, 323
Skilton, Charles S., 296
Slavery, of blacks, 27, 70, 92–93, 100,
  136, 142; of Indians, 29, 32, 40, 289
  & n.; by Indians, 93; absent among
  Iroquois, 259
Smallpox, see Diseases
Smith, Jack, 156–59
Smith, Capt. John, of Virginia, 28, 39–40,
  288
Smith, John S., 156–57
Smith, Keely, 232
Smith, William, 260
Snowshoes, 296
Socialism, 19
Socialist Party, 272, 276
Society of Friends, 145; see also Quakers
Sooners, 189
South Carolina, 32; and nullification, 69,
  113, 124, 286
South Dakota, 182–88
Southern Indians, 67; see also Indian
  tribes
Sovereignty, 218; see also Tribal govern-
  ments; Cherokee cases
Spanish, the, 9–20, 27–28, 33–38, 67, 77–
  79, 257–58
Spotted Tail, Sioux chief, 183, 347
Squanto, Wampanoag Indian, 293
Squash, cultivated, 11, 295
Stalker, Jacob, 324
Standing Rock reservation, N.D. and
  S.D., 184–85
Stanley, Samuel, 255
Starr, Kay, 324
Starr, Orange W., 324
Stealing unknown, 85, 87, 140, 282; see
  also Crime; Indian character
Steiner, Stan, 254–55
Stewart, Catherine, 269
Stigler, William G., 333
Story, Justice Joseph, 115, 124
Students, white, aid Indians, 223; Indian,
  occupy Alcatraz, 227